THE ENCYCLOPAEDIA OF ISLAM
ENCYCLOPÉDIE DE L'ISLAM

INDEX OF SUBJECTS/INDEX DES MATIÈRES

THE ENCYCLOPAEDIA OF ISLAM

NEW EDITION

ENCYCLOPÉDIE DE L'ISLAM

NOUVELLE ÉDITION

INDEX OF SUBJECTS
INDEX DES MATIÈRES

to Volumes / des Tomes
I-VIII
and to the Supplement, Fascicules / et du Supplément,
Livraisons
1-6

COMPILED BY/ÉTABLI PAR

P.J. BEARMAN

E.J. BRILL
LEIDEN · NEW YORK · KÖLN
1996

The paper in this book meets the guidelines for permanence and durability of the Committee on Production Guidelines for Book Longevity of the Council on Library Resources.

Library of Congress Cataloging-in-Publication Data

Bearman, P.J.
The Encyclopaedia of Islam, new edition. Index of Subjects = Encyclopédie de l'islam, nouvelle édition. Index des matières / compiled by P.J. Bearman.
p. cm.
English and French.
ISBN 9004097392 (alk. paper)
1. Encyclopaedia of Islam—Indexes. 2. Islam—Indexes. 3. Islamic countries—Indexes. I. Title. II. Title: Encyclopédie de l'islam, nouvelle édition. Index des matières.
DS35.53.E533B4 1992
909'.097671—dc20 92-31738
CIP
Rev.

ISBN 90 04 10594 8

PRINTED IN THE NETHERLANDS

TABLE OF CONTENTS/TABLE DES MATIÈRES

ENGLISH SECTION

Preface vii
List of Entries 1
Index of Subjects 17

SECTION FRANÇAISE

Préface 137
Liste des Entrées 139
Index des Matières 155

PREFACE TO THE THIRD EDITION

This edition of the Index of Subjects includes the addition of a List of Entries which precedes the actual subject index. The List of Entries refers the reader to single articles in the *Encyclopaedia of Islam*. The fact that entries appear in the *Encyclopaedia* under a heading in Arabic (or Persian and Turkish) rather than in English can confound the scholar not conversant with these languages, and an Index of Subjects which follows suit is possibly not as helpful as it could be.

Thus, although there is an article in the *Encyclopaedia* on the reed-pen and reference to this article can be found in the Index of Subjects under the heading WRITING.MATERIALS, a non-Arabist would be hard put to discover it without first looking up all of the references given there. In order to simplify this situation, the List of Entries refers the reader to the article in the *Encyclopaedia* (in this case, for reed-pen, see Ḳalam). For an overview of what the *Encyclopaedia* offers on a larger subject, however, the reader should still consult the Index of Subjects proper. A guide to the use of the Index of Subjects is given on p. 17.

As before, this new edition of the Index of Subjects incorporates references to the latest published volume of the *Encyclopaedia*, Volume VIII, which came out in June 1995.

May 1996 Peri Bearman

LIST OF ENTRIES

References are given either to the main article in the *Encyclopaedia* or to the Index of Subjects proper, which groups all articles concerned with the subject under one heading. An arrow refers the reader to the entry in the Index of Subjects, which follows the List of Entries on p. 17. Countries and names of dynasties or caliphates, which are included *in extenso* in the Index of Subjects, are not given in the following list.

A

Abbreviations [in Suppl.] Abbreviations
Ablution → ABLUTION
Abstinence Istibrāʾ
Academy Madjmaʿ ʿIlmī
Accident ʿAraḍ
Accounting → ACCOUNTING
Acquisition Kasb
Acrobat Djānbāz
Act ʿAmal; Fiʿl
Addax Mahāt
Administration → ADMINISTRATION
Admiral Ḳapudan Pasha
Adoption → ADOPTION
Adultery → ADULTERY
Aesthetics ʿIlm al-Djamāl
Agriculture → AGRICULTURE
Album Muraḳḳaʿ
Alchemy → ALCHEMY
Alfa-grass Ḥalfāʾ
Algebra → MATHEMATICS
Alms → ALMS
Aloe Ṣabr
Alphabet → ALPHABET
Amber Kahrubā
Ambergris ʿAnbar
Americas → NEW WORLD
Analogy Ḳiyās
Anatomy → ANATOMY
Anecdote Nādira
Angel → ANGELOLOGY
Animal → ANIMALS
Ant Naml
Antelope → ANIMALS
Anthropomorphism → ANTHROPOMORPHISM
Antinomianism Ibāḥa (II)
Apostasy → APOSTASY
Appeal Istiʾnāf
Apricot Mishmish
Aqueduct → ARCHITECTURE.MONUMENTS
Arabic → LANGUAGES.AFRO-ASIATIC; LINGUISTICS
Arachnoids → ANIMALS
Arbitrator Ḥakam
Archaeology → ARCHAEOLOGY
Architecture → ARCHITECTURE
Archives → ADMINISTRATION
Arithmetic → MATHEMATICS
Army → MILITARY
Arsenal Dār al-Ṣināʿa
Art → ART
Article Maḳāla
Artisans → PROFESSIONS
Ascensions al-Maṭāliʿ

Asceticism → ASCETICISM
Assignation Ḥawāla
Association Andjuman; Djamʿiyya
Astrolabe Asṭurlāb
Astrology → ASTROLOGY
Astronomy → ASTRONOMY
Atomism Djuzʾ
Avarice Bukhl

B

Bābism → SECTS
Bacchism → WINE.BACCHIC POETRY
Backgammon Nard
Bahais → BAHAIS
Balance al-Mīzān
Banking → BANKING
Barber [in Suppl.] Ḥallāḳ
Barter Muʿāwaḍa
Basques → BASQUES
Bath → ARCHITECTURE.MONUMENTS
Beauty ʿIlm al-Djamāl
Bedding Mafrūshāt; Mifrash
Bedouin → BEDOUINS
Bee Naḥl
Belomancy Istiḳsām
Ben-nut Bān
Berbers → BERBERS
Betrothal Khiṭba
Bible → BIBLE
Bibliography → BIBLIOGRAPHY
Bier Djanāza
Biography → LITERATURE.BIOGRAPHICAL
Bird → ANIMALS
Bitumen Mūmiyāʾ
Blacksmith Ḳayn
Blessing Baraka
Blood [in Suppl.] Dam
Blood-letter [in Suppl.] Faṣṣād
Blood-vengeance Ḳiṣāṣ
Boar, wild Khinzīr
Boat Safīna
Body Djism
Book Kitāb
Bookbinding → WRITING
Booty → MILITARY
Botany → BOTANY
Bow Ḳaws
Bowing → PRAYER
Bread Khubz
Bribery → PAYMENTS
Brick Labin
Bridge → ARCHITECTURE.MONUMENTS
Broadcasting Idhāʿa
Broker Dallāl
Buddhism Budd
Buffalo [in Suppl.] Djāmūs
Building Bināʾ
Butcher [in Suppl.] Djazzār
Butter al-Samn
Byzantines → BYZANTINE EMPIRE

C

Calendar → TIME
Caliph Khalīfa
Caliphate → CALIPHATE
Call to prayer Adhān
Calligraphy → ART
Camel → ANIMALS
Camel-driver [in Suppl.] Djammāl
Camomile [in Suppl.] Bābūnadj

Camphor Kāfūr
Canal Ḳanāt
Capitulations Imtiyāzāt
Caravan → TRANSPORT
Carmathians → SHIITES.BRANCHES
Carpet → ART.TAPESTRY
Cart ʿAdjala; Araba
Cartography → CARTOGRAPHY
Cattle Baḳar
Cause ʿIlla
Cedar-oil Ḳaṭrān
Cemetery Maḳbara
Ceramics → ART.POTTERY
Cession Ḥawāla
Chair Kursī
Chamberlain Ḥādjib
Chameleon Ḥirbāʾ
Chancellery → DOCUMENTS
Charity → ALMS
Charms → CHARMS
Cheetah Fahd
Chest → ANATOMY
Childbirth → CHILD
Childhood → CHILD
Chintz Ḳalamkārī
Chirognomy al-Kaff
Christianity → CHRISTIANITY
Church Kanīsa
Cinema Cinema
Cinnamon [in Suppl.] Dār Ṣīnī
Circumcision → CIRCUMCISION
Cistern Ḥawḍ
Citizen Muwāṭin
Citrus fruits Nārandj
Civilisation Medeniyyet
Clan Āl
Clime Iḳlīm
Cloak Khirḳa
Clock Sāʿa
Clothing → CLOTHING
Clove Ḳaranful
Cock Dīk
Codes → CRYPTOGRAPHY
Coffee Ḳahwa
Coinage → NUMISMATICS
Coitus Bāh
Coitus interruptus ʿAzl
Colour → COLOUR
Column ʿAmūd
Comedians → HUMOUR
Commentary (Koranic) → KORAN
Commerce → COMMERCE
Communications → COMMUNICATIONS
Communism → COMMUNISM
Companions (of the Prophet) → MUḤAMMAD, THE PROPHET
Compass Maghnāṭīs.2
Concubinage → WOMEN
Conference Muʾtamar
Congress Muʾtamar
Conjunction Ḳirān
Constellation → ASTRONOMY
Constitution Dustūr
Consul Consul
Contract → LAW.LAW OF OBLIGATIONS
Cooking → CUISINE
Copper Nuḥās; *and see* Malachite
Copts → CHRISTIANITY.DENOMINATIONS
Coral Mardjān
Cornelian ʿAḳīḳ
Corpse Djanāza
Corpse-washer [in Suppl.] Ghassāl
Cosmetics → COSMETICS
Cosmography → COSMOGRAPHY
Cotton Ḳuṭn
Court (of law) Maḥkama
Court Ceremony → COURT CEREMONY
Courtier Nadīm
Couscous Kuskusū
Creation → CREATION

Creditor Ghārim
Creed ʿAḳīda
Crescent Hilāl
Criticism, literary → LITERATURE
Cross al-Ṣalīb
Crow Ghurāb
Crucifixion Ṣalb
Crusades → CRUSADE(R)S
Cryptography → CRYPTOGRAPHY
Crystal *see* Rock-crystal
Cubit Dhirāʿ
Cuisine → CUISINE
Cumin Kammūn
Cupper [in Suppl.] Faṣṣād
Custody Ḥaḍāna
Custom → CUSTOM
Customary law → LAW

D

Dactylonomy Ḥisāb al-ʿAḳd
Dam → ARCHITECTURE.MONUMENTS
Dance Raḳṣ
Date Nakhl
Day → TIME
Death → DEATH
Debt [in Suppl.] Dayn
Debtor Ghārim
Declension Iʿrāb
Declination al-Mayl
Decoration → ARCHITECTURE; ART.DECORATIVE; MILITARY
Decree, divine al-Ḳadāʾ wa 'l-Ḳadar
Deer Ayyil
Demography [in Suppl.] Demography
Demon Djinn
Dentistry → MEDICINE
Dervish → MYSTICISM
Desert → DESERTS
Devil Iblīs
Dialect → LANGUAGES.AFRO-ASIATIC.ARABIC; LINGUISTICS.PHONETICS
Diamond Almās
Dictionary → DICTIONARY
Diplomacy → DIPLOMACY
Disease → DISEASE
Disputation → THEOLOGY
Dissolution Faskh
Ditch Khandaḳ
Divination → DIVINATION
Divorce → DIVORCE
Documents → DOCUMENTS
Dog Kalb
Donkey Ḥimār
Dove Ḥamām
Dowry → MARRIAGE
Drama → LITERATURE
Drawing → ART
Dreams → DREAMS
Dress → CLOTHING
Dressmaker Khayyāṭ
Drinks → CUISINE
Dromedary → ANIMALS.CAMEL
Drugs → DRUGS
Druggist al-ʿAṭṭār
Drum Darabukka
Druze → DRUZES
Duress [in Suppl.] Ikrāh
Dwelling Bayt; Dār
Dye → DYEING
Dyer → DYEING
Dynasty → DYNASTIES

E

Earthquakes → EARTHQUAKES
Ebony Abanūs
Eclipse Kusūf
Ecliptic Minṭaḳat al-Burūdj
Economics → ECONOMICS
Edict Farmān
Education → EDUCATION
Elegy Marthiya
Elephant Fīl
Elixir al-Iksīr
Eloquence Balāgha; Bayān; Faṣāḥa
Emancipation → EMANCIPATION
Embalming Ḥināṭa
Emigration → EMIGRATION
Encyclopaedia Mawsūʿa
Endive [in Suppl.] Hindibāʾ
Epic Ḥamāsa
Epigraphy → EPIGRAPHY
Epistolography → LITERATURE. EPISTOLARY
Epithet → ONOMASTICS
Equator Istiwāʾ
Equines → ANIMALS
Error Khaṭaʾ
Eschatology → ESCHATOLOGY
Espionage *see* Spy
Estate Ḍayʿa
Eternity Abad; Ḳidam
Ethics → ETHICS
Ethnicity → ETHNICITY
Etiquette → ETIQUETTE
Etymology Ishtiḳāḳ
Eulogy Madīḥ
Eunuch → EUNUCH
Evidence Bayyina
Ewer [in Suppl.] Ibrīḳ
Exception Istithnāʾ
Expedition → MILITARY
Expiation Kaffāra
Eye → ANATOMY; EVIL EYE

F

Faculty Kulliyya
Faïence Kāshī
Faith → FAITH
Falconry → FALCONRY
Family ʿĀʾila
Fan Mirwaḥa
Farming → AGRICULTURE
Fasting → FASTING
Fate → PREDESTINATION
Fauna → ANIMALS
Felines → ANIMALS
Felt Lubūd
Female circumcision Khafḍ
Fennec-fox Fanak
Fennel [in Suppl.] Basbās
Festival → FESTIVAL
Fief Iḳṭāʿ
Film Cinema
Finance → ADMINISTRATION
Fine Djurm
Fire Nār
Fiscal system → TAXATION
Fish → ANIMALS
Fishing Samak.3
Five Khamsa
Flag ʿAlam
Flamingo Nuḥām
Flax Kattān
Flora → FLORA
Flowers → FLORA
Fly Dhubāb
Food → CUISINE

Forest Ghāba
Foreword Muḳaddima
Formulas → ISLAM
Fortress Ḥiṣn
Foundling Laḳīṭ
Fortress → ARCHITECTURE.MONUMENTS.STRONGHOLDS
Fowl Dadjādja
Fox Fanak
Fraction Kasr
Frankincense Lubān
Free Will → PREDESTINATION
Freedom Ḥurriyya; [in Suppl.] Āzādī
Freemasonry [in Suppl.] Farāmūsh-khāna; Farmāsūniyya
Fruit *see* Citrus fruits
Fundamentalism → REFORM.POLITICO-RELIGIOUS.MILITANT
Funeral Djanāza
Fur Farw
Furnishings → FURNISHINGS
Furniture [in Suppl.] Athāth

G

Gain Kasb
Gambling → GAMBLING
Games → RECREATION
Garden → ARCHITECTURE.MONUMENTS.PLEASURE-GARDENS
Gate → ARCHITECTURE.MONUMENTS
Gazehound Salūḳī
Gazelle Ghazāl
Gemstones → JEWELRY
Gender studies → WOMEN
Genealogy → GENEALOGY
Geography → GEOGRAPHY
Geometry → MATHEMATICS
Gesture Ishāra
Gift → GIFTS
Glass → ART
Gloss Hāshiya
Goats [in Suppl.] Ghanam
God Allāh; Ilāh
Gods, pre-Islamic → PRE-ISLAM
Gold Dhahab
Goldsmith Ṣāʾigh
Gospels Indjīl
Government Ḥukūma
Grammar → LINGUISTICS
Greyhound *see* Gazehound
Grocer Baḳḳāl
Guild → GUILDS
Gum resins Ṣamgh
Gunpowder Bārūd
Gynaecology → CHILD
Gypsies → GYPSIES

H

Hagiography → HAGIOGRAPHY
Hair → ANATOMY
Hairdresser {in Suppl.] Ḥallāḳ
Hamito-Semitic Ḥām
Handicrafts → ART
Handkerchief Mandīl
Harbour Mīnāʾ
Hare [in Suppl.] Arnab
Headware → CLOTHING
Health → MEDICINE

Heart Ḳalb
Heaven Samāʾ
Hedgehog Ḳunfu<u>dh</u>
Hell → HELL
Hemerology I<u>kh</u>tiyārāt
Hemp Ḥa<u>sh</u>ī<u>sh</u>
Henbane Ban<u>dj</u>
Henna Ḥinnāʾ
Heraldry → HERALDRY
Hereafter → ESCHATOLOGY
Heresy → HERESY
Hippopotamus [in Suppl.] Faras al-Māʾ
Hire, contract of → LAW
Historiography → LITERATURE.HISTORICAL
Holiness Ḳadāsa
Holy War <u>Dj</u>ihād
Homicide Ḳatl
Homonym Aḍdād
Homosexuality Liwāṭ
Honour ʿIrḍ
Hoopoe Hudhud
Horn Būḳ
Horse Faras
Horseback rider Fāris
Horseback riding Furūsiyya
Horticulture → ARCHITECTURE.MONUMENTS.PLEASURE-GARDENS; FLORA
Hostelry → HOSTELRY
Houris Ḥūr
House *see* Dwelling
Humour → HUMOUR
Hunting → HUNTING
Hydrology → HYDROLOGY
Hydromancy Istinzāl
Hyena [in Suppl.] Ḍabuʿ
Hymn Na<u>sh</u>īd
Hyperbole Mubāla<u>gh</u>a
Hypocrisy Riyāʾ

I

Iconography → ART
Idol → IDOLS
Illness → ILLNESS
Incubation Isti<u>kh</u>āra
Independence Istiḳlāl
Indigo Nīl
Industry → INDUSTRY
Infidel Kāfir
Inflection Imāla
Inheritance → INHERITANCE
Inimitability (of Ḳurʾān) Iʿ<u>dj</u>āz
Ink Midād
Ink-holder [in Suppl.] Dawāt
Innovation Bidʿa
Inscriptions → EPIGRAPHY
Insects → ANIMALS
Insignia → MILITARY.DECORATIONS
Inspection (of troops) Istiʿrāḍ
Instrument Ala
Instrument, musical → MUSIC
Insulting verse Hi<u>dj</u>āʾ
Intellect ʿAḳl
Intercourse, sexual Bāh
Interdiction Ḥa<u>dj</u>r
Interest Ribā
Interrogation Istifhām
Introduction Ibtidāʾ; Muḳaddima
Inventions → INVENTIONS
Invocation Duʿāʾ
Ipseity Huwiyya
Iron al-Ḥadīd
Irrigation → IRRIGATION
Islam → ISLAM
Ivory ʿĀ<u>dj</u>

J

Jackal Ibn Āwā
Javelin Djerīd
Jewelry → JEWELRY
Journalism → PRESS
Judaism → JUDAISM
Judge Ḳāḍī
Jurisconsult → LAW.JURIST
Jurisprudence → LAW
Jurist → LAW
Justice ʿAdl

K

King Malik
Kingdom Mamlaka
Kinship Ḳarāba
Kitchen Maṭbakh
Knowledge ʿIlm; Maʿrifa
Kohl al-Kuḥl
Koran → KORAN
Kurds → KURDS

L

Labour *see* Trade union
Labourers → PROFESSIONS
Lakes → GEOGRAPHY.PHYSICAL GEOGRAPHY.WATERS
Lamentation → LAMENTATION
Land → LAND
Language → LANGUAGES
Law → LAW
Leasing Kirāʾ
Leather Djild
Legend → LEGENDS
Lemon Nārandj
Leprosy [in Suppl.] Djudhām
Letter(s) Ḥarf; Ḥurūf al-Hidjāʾ
Lexicography → LEXICOGRAPHY
Library → EDUCATION.LIBRARIES
Lice Ḳaml
Life Ḥayāt
Light Nūr
Lighthouse → ARCHITECTURE.MONUMENTS
Linen Kattān; Khaysh
Linguistics → LINGUISTICS
Lion al-Asad
Literature → LITERATURE
Lithography → PRINTING
Liver Kabid
Lizard Ḍabb
Locust Djarād
Logic → PHILOSOPHY
Longevity Muʿammar
Louse *see* Lice
Love → LOVE
Lyre Ḳithāra

M

Mace Dūrbāsh
Madman Madjnūn
Magic → MAGIC
Magnet Maghnāṭīs.1

Malachite al-Dahnadj
Malaria Malāryā
Man Insān
Manuscript Nuskha
Map Kharīṭa
Marriage → MARRIAGE
Martyrdom → MARTYRDOM
Marxism Mārk(i)siyya
Masonry Binā᾽
Mathematics → MATHEMATICS
Matter Hayūlā
Mausoleum → ARCHITECTURE.MONUMENTS.TOMBS
Mayor Ra᾽īs
Measurements → WEIGHTS AND MEASUREMENTS
Mechanics → MECHANICS
Medicine → MEDICINE
Melilot [in Suppl.] Iklīl al-Malik
Menstruation Ḥayḍ
Merchants → PROFESSIONS
Messenger Rasūl
Messiah al-Masīḥ
Metallurgy → METALLURGY
Metalware → ART
Metamorphosis → ANIMALS.TRANSFORMATION INTO
Metaphor Isti῾āra
Metaphysics → METAPHYSICS
Meteorology → METEOROLOGY
Metonymy Kināya
Metrics → METRICS
Migration → EMIGRATION
Militancy → REFORM.POLITICO-RELIGIOUS.MILITANT
Military → MILITARY
Milky Way al-Madjarra
Millet [in Suppl.] Djāwars
Minaret Manāra
Mineralogy → MINERALOGY
Miniatures → ART.PAINTING
Mint [in Suppl.] Fūdhandj
Mint (money) Dār al-Ḍarb
Miracle → MIRACLES
Mirror Mir᾽āt
Modernism → REFORM
Modes, musical Maḳām
Molluscs → ANIMALS
Monarchy → MONARCHY
Monastery → CHRISTIANITY
Monasticism Rahbāniyya
Money → NUMISMATICS
Mongols → MONGOLIA
Mongoose Nims
Monk Rāhib
Monkey Ḳird
Months → TIME
Moon Hilāl; al-Ḳamar
Mosaics → ART
Mosque → ARCHITECTURE.MONUMENTS
Mountain → MOUNTAINS
Mountain Goat Ayyil
Mule Baghl
Municipality Baladiyya
Murder Ḳatl
Music → MUSIC
Musk Misk
Mussel Ṣadaf
Myrobalanus [in Suppl.] Halīladj
Myrtle [in Suppl.] Ās
Mystic → MYSTICISM
Mysticism → MYSTICISM
Myths → LEGENDS

N

Name Ism
Narcissus Nardjis

Narcotics → DRUGS
Nationalism → NATIONALISM
Natron [in Suppl.] Bawraḳ
Natural science → NATURAL SCIENCE
Navigation → NAVIGATION
Navy → MILITARY
New World → NEW WORLD
Newspaper Djarīda
Nickname Laḳab
Night Layl and Nahār
Night watch ʿAsas
Nightingale Bulbul
Nilometer Miḳyās
Nomadism → NOMADISM
Noun Ism
Novel Ḳiṣṣa
Nullity Fāsid wa Bāṭil
Number → NUMBER
Numerals → NUMBER
Numismatics → NUMISMATICS

O

Oak ʿAfṣ
Oath Ḳasam
Obelisk → ARCHITECTURE.MONUMENTS
Oboe Ghayṭa
Observatory → ASTRONOMY
Obstetrics → MEDICINE
Ocean → OCEANS AND SEAS
Octagon Muthamman
Oil → OIL
Omen Faʾl
Oneiromancy → DREAMS
Onomastics → ONOMASTICS
Onomatomancy Ḥurūf, ʿIlm al-
Ophthalmology → MEDICINE
Opium Afyūn
Opposites Aḍdād; Ḍidd
Optics → OPTICS
Orange Nārandj
Orchestra Mehter
Order, mystical → MYSTICISM
Organs (body) → ANATOMY
Orientalism Mustashriḳūn
Ornithomancy ʿIyāfa
Oryx Lamṭ; Mahāt
Ostentation Riyāʾ
Ostrich Naʿām
Ottoman Empire → OTTOMAN EMPIRE
Ownership Milk

P

Paediatrics → CHILD
Paganism → PRE-ISLAM
Painting → ART
Palace → ARCHITECTURE. MONUMENTS
Palaeography → EPIGRAPHY; WRITING
Palanquin Maḥmal
Paleography *see* Palaeography
Palm Nakhl
Palmoscopy Ikhtilādj
Panarabism → PANARABISM
Panegyric Madīḥ
Panislamism → PANISLAMISM
Pantheism → RELIGION
Panther Namir
Panturkism → PANTURKISM
Paper Kāghad
Papyrology → PAPYROLOGY

Papyrus Papyrus
Paradise → PARADISE
Parakeet Babbaghā᾽
Parasol Miẓalla
Parchment Raḳḳ
Parliament Madjlis
Paronomasia Muzāwadja
Parrot Babbaghā᾽
Party, political → POLITICS
Past Māḍī
Pastimes → RECREATION
Pasture Marʿā
Patronymic Kunya
Pauper Faḳīr; Miskīn
Pavilion → ARCHITECTURE.MONUMENTS
Pay → PAYMENTS
Pearl al-Durr; Lu᾽lu᾽
Pediatrics *see* Paediatrics
Pen Ḳalam
Penal law → LAW
People Ḳawm
Performers → PROFESSIONS
Perfume → PERFUME
Periodicals → PRESS
Persian → LANGUAGES.INDO-EUROPEAN.IRANIAN; LINGUISTICS
Petroleum → OIL
Pharmacology → PHARMACOLOGY
Philately → PHILATELY
Philology → LINGUISTICS
Philosophy → PHILOSOPHY
Phlebotomist [in Suppl.] Faṣṣād
Phonetics → LINGUISTICS
Physician → MEDICINE
Physiognomancy Ḳiyāfa
Physiognomy → PHYSIOGNOMY
Pig Khinzīr
Pigeon Ḥamām
Pilgrimage → PILGRIMAGE
Pillar Rukn
Piracy → PIRACY
Pirate → PIRACY
Plague → PLAGUE
Planet → ASTRONOMY
Plants → FLORA
Plaster Djiṣṣ
Pleasure-garden → ARCHITECTURE.MONUMENTS
Pledge Rahn
Plough Miḥrāth
Plural Djamʿ
Poem → LITERATURE.GENRES.POETRY
Poetry → LITERATURE
Pole al-Ḳuṭb
Police → MILITARY
Politics → POLITICS
Poll-tax Djizya
Pomegranate blossom [in Suppl.] Djullanār
Porcupine Ḳunfudh
Port Mīnā᾽
Porter Ḥammāl
Postal history → PHILATELY
Postal service → TRANSPORT
Potash al-Ḳily
Pottery → ART
Prayer → PRAYER
Prayer direction Ḳibla
Prayer niche Miḥrāb
Pre-Islam → PRE-ISLAM
Precious stones → JEWELRY
Predestination → PREDESTINATION
Preface Muḳaddima
Pregnancy → CHILD
Press → PRESS
Primary school Kuttāb
Printing Maṭbaʿa
Prisoner → MILITARY
Procedure, legal → LAW
Processions Mawākib
Professions → PROFESSIONS
Profit Kasb
Prologue Ibtidā᾽

Property → PROPERTY
Prophecy → PROPHETHOOD
Prophet → MUḤAMMAD, THE PROPHET; PROPHETHOOD
Prophethood → PROPHETHOOD
Prose → LITERATURE
Prosody → LITERATURE.POETRY; METRICS; RHYME
Prostitution [in Suppl.] Big̲h̲āʾ
Protection Ḥimāya; Id̲j̲āra
Proverb → LITERATURE; PROVERBS
Pulpit Minbar
Punishment → (DIVINE) PUNISHMENT; LAW.PENAL LAW
Pyramid Haram

Q

Qat Ḳāt
Quadrant Rubʿ
Quail Salwā
Quiddity Māhiyya
Qurʾān → KORAN

R

Rabies *see* Dog
Raid → RAIDS
Railway → TRANSPORT
Rain prayer Istisḳāʾ
Rainbow Ḳaws Ḳuzaḥ
Ransoming [in Suppl.] Fidāʾ
Reading (Koranic) → KORAN
Recitation → KORAN.READING
Records → ADMINISTRATION
Recreation → RECREATION
Reed Ḳaṣab
Reed-pen Ḳalam
Reed-pipe G̲h̲ayṭa; Mizmār
Reflection Fikr
Reform → REFORM
Register → ADMINISTRATION.RECORDS
Religion → RELIGION
Reptiles → ANIMALS
Republic D̲j̲umhūriyya
Resurrection Ḳiyāma
Retaliation Ḳiṣāṣ
Retreat K̲h̲alwa
Revelation Ilhām
Rhapsodomancy Ḳurʿa
Rhetoric → RHETORIC
Rhinoceros Karkaddan
Rhyme → RHYME
Rice al-Ruzz
Riddle Lug̲h̲z
Ritual → RITUALS
River → RIVERS
Robe of honour K̲h̲ilʿa
Rock-crystal Billawr
Rod ʿAṣā; Ḳaḍīb
Rodents → ANIMALS
Rooster *see* Cock
Rose Gul
Rug → ART.TAPESTRY

S

Saint → SAINTHOOD
Salamander Samandal
Sale, contract of → LAW
Salt Milḥ
Sand Raml
Sandgrouse Ḳaṭā
Sappan wood Baḳḳam
Satire Hidjā᾽
Scapulomancy Katif
School, primary Kuttāb
Science → SCIENCE
Scorpion ʿAḳrab
Scribe Kātib; [in Suppl.] Dabīr
Sea → OCEANS AND SEAS
Seafaring → NAVIGATION
Seal Khātam; Muhr
Secretary Kātib; [in Suppl.] Dabīr
Semitic languages Sām.2
Sense Ḥiss; Maḥsūsāt
Sermon Khuṭba
Sermoniser Ḳāṣṣ
Servant Khādim
Seven Sabʿ
Seveners → SHIITES.BRANCHES
Sex Djins
Sexuality → SEXUALITY
Shadow play Ḳaragöz; Khayāl al-Ẓill
Sheep [in Suppl.] Ghanam
Shiism → SHIITES
Ship → NAVIGATION
Siege warfare Ḥiṣār
Siegecraft Ḥiṣār; Mandjanīḳ
Silk Ḥarīr
Silver Fiḍḍa
Sin Khaṭī᾽a
Singer → MUSIC
Singing → MUSIC.SONG
Slander Ḳadhf
Slaughterer [in Suppl.] Djazzār
Slave ʿAbd
Slavery → SLAVERY
Snail Ṣadaf
Snake Ḥayya
Snake-charmer Ḥāwī
Soap Ṣābūn
Socialism Ishtirākiyya
Society Djamʿiyya
Soda al-Ḳily; *and see* Natron
Sodium Naṭrūn; *and see* Natron
Sodomy Liwāṭ
Son Ibn
Song → MUSIC
Sorcery → MAGIC
Soul Nafs
Sphere Falak; al-Kura
Spices → CUISINE
Spider ʿAnkabūt
Sport → ANIMALS.SPORT; RECREATION
Springs → GEOGRAPHY.PHYSICAL GEOGRAPHY
Spy Djāsūs
Stable Iṣṭabl
Star → ASTRONOMY
Stone Ḥadjar
Stool Kursı
Story Ḥikāya
Storyteller Ḳāṣṣ; Maddāḥ
Straits → GEOGRAPHY.PHYSICAL GEOGRAPHY.WATERS
Stronghold → ARCHITECTURE.MONUMENTS
Substance Djawhar
Suckling → CHILD
Sufism → MYSTICISM
Sugar-cane Ḳaṣab al-Sukkar
Suicide Intiḥār
Sulphur al-Kibrīt
Sultan-fowl [in Suppl.] Abū Barāḳish.2

Sundial Mizwala
Sunshade Miẓalla
Superstition → SUPERSTITION
Surety-bond Kafāla
Surgeon Djarrāḥ
Swahili → KENYA
Sweeper Kannās
Symbolism Ramz.3

T

Tablet Lawḥ
Tailor Khayyāṭ
Talisman → CHARMS
Tambourine Duff
Tanner [in Suppl.] Dabbāgh
Tapestry → ART
Tar Mūmiyāʾ
Taxation → TAXATION
Tea Čay
Tea-house [in Suppl.] Čāy-khāna
Teak Sādj
Teeth → MEDICINE.DENTISTRY
Tent Khayma
Textiles → ART; CLOTHING.MATERIALS
Theatre → LITERATURE.DRAMA
Theology → THEOLOGY
Theophany Maẓhar
Thief Liṣṣ
Thought Fikr
Tide al-Madd wa 'l-Djazr
Tiles → ART
Tiller Miḥrāth
Time → TIME
Timekeeping → TIME
Tithe → TAXATION
Titulature → ONOMASTICS.TITLES
Tomb → ARCHITECTURE. MONUMENTS
Toothbrush Miswāk
Tooth-pick Miswāk
Tower Burdj
Town Ḳarya; Ḳaṣaba
Toys → RECREATION.GAMES
Trade → COMMERCE; INDUSTRY; NAVIGATION
Trade union Niḳāba
Tradition → LITERATURE.TRADITION-LITERATURE
Translation → LITERATURE
Transport → TRANSPORT
Travel → TRAVEL
Treasury → TREASURY
Treaty → TREATIES
Trees → FLORA
Triangle Muthallath
Tribe → TRIBES
Tribute → TREATIES
Trope Madjāz
Trumpet Būḳ
Turkic languages → LANGUAGES
Turquoise Fīrūzadj
Twelvers → SHIITES.BRANCHES

U

Uncle Khāl
University Djāmiʿa
Urbanism → ARCHITECTURE; GEOGRAPHY
Usurpation Ghaṣb
Usury Ribā

V

Vehicle → TRANSPORT.WHEELED VEHICLES
Veil → CLOTHING.HEADWARE
Ventilation → ARCHITECTURE.URBAN
Verb Fiʿl
Verse Āya
Veterinary science → MEDICINE
Vices → VIRTUES
Vikings al-Madjus
Village Ḳarya
Vine Karm
Viol Rabāb
Viper Afʿā
Volcanoes → GEOGRAPHY.PHYSICAL GEOGRAPHY
Vow Nadhr
Voyage → TRAVEL
Vulture Huma; Nasr

W

Wagon *see* Cart
Walnut [in Suppl.] Djawz
War Ḥarb
Wardrobe → CLOTHING
Washer [in Suppl.] Ghassāl
Washing → ABLUTION
Washing (of the dead) Ghusl
Water Māʾ
Water-carrier Saḳḳāʾ
Waterhouse → ARCHITECTURE.MONUMENTS
Waterways → GEOGRAPHY.PHYSICAL GEOGRAPHY
Waterwheel Nāʿūra
Weapon → MILITARY
Weasel Ibn ʿIrs
Weather → METEOROLOGY
Weaver al-Nassādj; [in Suppl.] Ḥāʾik
Weaver-bird [in Suppl.] Abū Barāḳish.1
Weaving → ART.TEXTILES
Week → TIME
Weights → WEIGHTS AND MEASUREMENTS
Welfare Maṣlaḥa
Well → ARCHITECTURE.MONUMENTS
Werewolf Ḳuṭrub
Wheat Ḳamḥ
Wind → METEOROLOGY
Wine → WINE
Wisdom Ḥikma
Wolf Dhiʾb
Women → WOMEN
Wood Khashab
World ʿĀlam
Wormwood Afsantīn
Wrestling Pahlawān
Writing → WRITING

Y

Young Turks → TURKEY.OTTOMAN PERIOD

Z

INDEX OF SUBJECTS

The Muslim world in the Index of Subjects is the world of today. What once was the greater realm of Persia is given here under Central Asia, Caucasus and Afghanistan, just as part of the region once governed by the Ottoman Empire is covered by individual countries in Eastern Europe and in the Near East. Modern countries, such as Jordan and Lebanon, are given right of place. Countries with a long history of Islam have a subsection 'modern period', where *Encyclopaedia* articles covering the 19th and 20th centuries have been brought together. When a poet is listed as '15th-century', the dating refers to his year of death C.E.

References in regular typeface are to *Encyclopaedia* articles; those printed in boldface type indicate the main article. Entries in capitals and following an arrow refer to lemmata in the Index of Subjects itself. Thus, in the case of

> BEDOUINS **Badw**; Biʾr; Dawār; Ghanīma; Ghazw
> *see also* Liṣṣ; *and* → NOMADISM; SAUDI ARABIA

Badw; Biʾr; Dawār; Ghanīma; Ghazw refer to articles in the *Encyclopaedia* that deal primarily with Bedouins, Badw being the article on Bedouins; Liṣṣ refers to an article in the *Encyclopaedia* that contains information of interest relating to Bedouins; and NOMADISM; SAUDI ARABIA refer the reader to analogous lemmata in the Index of Subjects.

A

ʿABBĀSIDS → CALIPHATE

ABLUTION **Ghusl**; Istindjāʾ; Istinshāḳ; al-Masḥ ʿalā ʾl-Khuffayn
see also Djanāba; Ḥadath; Ḥammām; Ḥawḍ; Ḥayḍ

ABYSSINIA → ETHIOPIA

ACCOUNTING Muḥāsaba.2; Mustawfī
see also Daftar; *and* → ADMINISTRATION.FINANCIAL

ADMINISTRATION Barīd; Bayt al-Māl; Daftar; Diplomatic; **Dīwān**; Djizya; Kātib; [in Suppl.] Demography.I
see also al-Ḳalḳashandī.1
for specific caliphates or dynasties → CALIPHATE; DYNASTIES; OTTOMAN EMPIRE

diplomatic → Diplomacy
financial ʿAṭāʾ; Bayt al-Māl; Daftar; Dār al-Ḍarb; Ḳānūn.ii and iii; Kasb; Khāzin; Khaznadār; Makhzan; Muṣādara.2; Mustawfī; Rūznāma
see also Dhahab; Fiḍḍa; Ḥisba; *and* → Numismatics; Ottoman Empire.administration
fiscal → Taxation
functionaries ʿĀmil; Amīn; Amīr; Amīr al-Ḥādjdj; ʿArīf; Dawādār; Djahbadh; Ḥisba; Īshīk-āḳāsī; Kalāntar; Kātib; Khāzin; Mushīr; Mushrif; Mustakhridj; Mustawfī; Parwānačī; Raʾīs; Ṣāḥib al-Madīna; [in Suppl.] Dabīr
see also Barīd; Consul; Fatwā; Fuyūdj; Kōtwāl; Malik al-Tudjdjār; Mawlā; Muwāḍaʿa.2; *and* → Law.offices; Military.offices; Ottoman Empire
geography → Geography.administrative
legal → Law
military → Military
Ottoman → Ottoman Empire
records **Daftar.I**; Ḳānūn.iii
and → Documents; Ottoman Empire.administration
archives Dār al-Maḥfūẓāt al-ʿUmūmiyya; Geniza
and → Ottoman Empire.administration

Adoption [in Suppl.] ʿĀr
see also ʿĀda.iii

Adultery Ḳadhf; Liʿān
see also al-Marʾa.2
punishment of Ḥadd

Afghanistan Afghān; **Afghānistān**
architecture → Architecture.regions
dynasties Aḥmad Shāh Durrānī; Ghaznawids; Ghūrids; Kart
and → Dynasties.afghanistan and india
language → Languages.indo-iranian.iranian
modern period Djāmiʿa; Dustūr.v; Khaybar; Madjlis.4.B; Maṭbaʿa.5
see also Muhādjir.3
statesmen ʿAbd al-Raḥmān Khān; Ayyūb Khān; Dūst Muḥammad; Ḥabīb Allāh Khān; Muḥammad Dāwūd Khān; [in Suppl.] Amān Allāh
see also [in Suppl.] Faḳīr of Ipi
physical geography Afghānistān.i
mountains Hindū Kush; Kūh-i Bābā; Safīd Kūh
see also Afghānistān.i
waters Dehās; Hāmūn; Harī Rūd; Kābul.1; Ḳunduz.1; Kurram; Murghāb; Pandjhīr; [in Suppl.] Gūmāl

see also Afghānistān.i

population Abdālī; Čahār Aymak; Durrānī; Ghalča; Ghalzay; Moghols; Mohmand; [in Suppl.] Demography.III; Hazāras

see also Afghān.i; Afghānistān.ii; Khaladj; Özbeg.1.d; [in Suppl.] Djirga

toponyms

ancient Būshandj; Bust; Dihistān; Djuwayn.3; Farmūl; Fīrūzkūh.1; Khōst; Khudjistān; Marw al-Rūdh; al-Rukhkhadj

present-day

districts Andarāb.1; Bādghīs; Farwān; Ḳūhistān.3; Lamghānāt

regions Badakhshān; Dardistān; Djūzdjān; Ghardjistān; Ghūr; Kāfiristan; Khost; Nangrahar; [in Suppl.] Hazāradjāt

see also Pandjhīr

towns Andkhūy; Balkh; Bāmiyān; Djām; Farāh; Faryāb.1; Gardīz; Ghazna; Girishk; Harāt; Kābul.2; Ḳandahār; Karūkh; Khulm; Ḳunduz.2; Maymana; Mazār-i Sharīf; Rūdhbār.1; Sabzawār.2; [in Suppl.] Djalālābād

AFRICA Lamlam

Central Africa Cameroons; Congo; Gabon; [in Suppl.] Čad

see also Hausa; Muḥammad Bello; al-Murdjibī; [in Suppl.] Demography.V

for individual countries → CHAD; CONGO; NIGER; NIGERIA; ZAIRE

physical geography

deserts Sāḥil.2

population Kanuri; Kotoko

East Africa Adal; Dawāro; Djibūtī; Eritrea; Ḥabesh; Ḳumr; Madagascar; Mafia

see also Baḥr al-Hind; Baḥr al-Zandj; Emīn Pasha; Kūsh; Mawlid.2; Muṣāḥib; Nawrūz.2; Nikāḥ.II.5; al-Nudjūm; [in Suppl.] Djarīda.viii

for individual countries → ETHIOPIA; KENYA; MADAGASCAR; MALAWI; SOMALIA; SUDAN; TANZANIA; ZANZIBAR

architecture Manāra.3; Masdjid.VI; Mbweni; Minbar.4

literature Miʿrādj.3

see also Kitābāt.6; *and* → KENYA.SWAHILI LITERATURE

physical geography

waters Atbara; Baḥr al-Ghazāl.1

population ʿAbābda; ʿĀmir; Antemuru; Bedja; Beleyn; Bishārīn; Danḳalī; Djaʿaliyyūn; Galla; Māryā; Mazrūʿī; Oromo; [in Suppl.] Demography.V

see also Diglal; Lamlam; al-Manāṣir

North Africa Algeria; Atlas; Ifrīḳiya; Lībiyā; Maghāriba; al-Maghrib (2x); Mashāriḳa

see also al-ʿArab.v; ʿArabiyya.A.iii.3; Badw.II.d; Baladiyya.3; Djamāʿa.ii; Djarīda.B; Djaysh.iii; Ghuzz.ii; Ḥawz; Hilāl; Ḳawmiyya.ii; Kharbga; Kitābāt.4; Lamṭ; Leo Africanus; Libās.ii; Maḥalla; Mānū; Ṣaff.3; [in Suppl.]

ʿĀr; *and* → DYNASTIES.SPAIN AND NORTH AFRICA
for individual countries → ALGERIA; LIBYA; MOROCCO; TUNISIA
architecture → ARCHITECTURE.REGIONS
mysticism → MYSTICISM
physical geography Reg; Rīf; Sabkha; al-Ṣaḥrāʾ
and → *the section Physical Geography under individual countries*
population Ahaggar; Berbers; Dukkāla; Khulṭ; al-Maʿḳil; [in Suppl.] Demography.IV
see also Khumayr; Kūmiya; al-Manāṣir; Mandīl; Moors; *and* → BERBERS
Southern Africa Mozambique
see also [in Suppl.] Djarīda.ix
for individual countries → MOZAMBIQUE
West Africa Côte d'Ivoire; Dahomey; Gambia; Ghana; Guinea; Liberia; Mali; Mūrītāniyā; Niger; Nigeria
see also Fūta Djallon; Kitābāt.5; Ḳunbi Ṣāliḥ; al-Maghīlī; Malam; Mande; Muḥammad b. Abī Bakr; Murīdiyya; Oyo; Samori Ture
for individual countries → BENIN; GUINEA; IVORY COAST; MALI; MAURITANIA; NIGER; NIGERIA; SENEGAL; TOGO
architecture Ḳunbi Ṣāliḥ; Masdjid.VII
physical geography
deserts Sāḥil.2
waters Niger
population Fulbe; Ḥarṭānī; Ifoghas; Kunta; [in Suppl.] Demography.V
see also Lamlam; Mande

AGRICULTURE **Filāḥa**; Marʿā; Raʿiyya
see also Mazraʿa; Mughārasa; Musāḳāt; Muzāraʿa; [in Suppl.] Akkār; *and* → BOTANY; FLORA; IRRIGATION
products Ḳahwa; Ḳamḥ; Karm; Ḳaṣab al-Sukkar; Khamr.2; Ḳuṭn; [in Suppl.] Djāwars; Hindibāʾ
see also Ḥarīr; *and* → CUISINE
terms Āgdāl; Baʿl.2.b; Čiftlik; Ghūṭa; Maṭmūra
tools Miḥrāth
treatises on Abu 'l-Khayr al-Ishbīlī; Ibn Wāfid; Ibn Waḥshiyya

ALBANIA **Arnawutluḳ**; Iskender Beg; Ḳarā Maḥmūd Pasha
see also Muslimūn.1.B.4; Sāmī; *and* → OTTOMAN EMPIRE
toponyms Aḳ Ḥiṣār.4; Awlonya; Delvina; Drač; Elbasan; Ergiri; Korča; Krujë; Lesh

ALCHEMY Dhahab; Fiḍḍa; al-Iksīr; al-Kibrīt; **al-Kīmiyāʾ**
see also Ḳārūn; Maʿdin; al-Nūshādir; *and* → METALLURGY; MINERALOGY

alchemists D̲j̲ābir b. Ḥayyān; Ibn Umayl; Ibn Waḥs̲h̲iyya; al-Rāzī, Abū Bakr; [in Suppl.] Abu 'l-Ḥasan al-Anṣārī; al-D̲j̲ildakī
see also Hirmis; K̲h̲ālid b. Yazīd b. Muʿāwiya; [in Suppl.] al-D̲j̲awbarī, ʿAbd al-Raḥīm; Findiriskī; Ibn Daḳīḳ al-ʿĪd
equipment al-Anbīḳ
terms Rukn.2

ALGERIA **Algeria**
see also ʿArabiyya.A.iii.3; ʿArs̲h̲; Ḥalḳa; *and* → BERBERS; DYNASTIES.SPAIN AND NORTH AFRICA
architecture → ARCHITECTURE.REGIONS.NORTH AFRICA
dynasties ʿAbd al-Wādids; Fāṭimids; Ḥammādids; Rustamids
and → DYNASTIES.SPAIN AND NORTH AFRICA
literature Ḥawfī
modern period D̲j̲āmiʿa; D̲j̲arīda.i.B; Ḥizb.i; Ḥukūma.iv; Maʿārif.2.B; Mad̲j̲lis.4.A.xx
reform Ibn Bādīs; (al-)Ibrāhīmī; Salafiyya.1(b)
see also Fallāḳ
Ottoman period (1518-1830) ʿAbd al-Ḳādir b. Muḥyī al-Dīn; Algeria.ii.(2); ʿArūd̲j̲; Ḥasan Ag̲h̲a; Ḥasan Baba; Ḥasan Pas̲h̲a; al-Ḥusayn; Ḥusayn Pas̲h̲a, Mezzomorto; K̲h̲ayr al-Dīn Pas̲h̲a
physical geography Algeria.i
mountains ʿAmūr; Atlas; Awrās; Bībān; D̲j̲urd̲j̲ura; Kabylia
population Algeria.iii
see also Kabylia; *and* → AFRICA.NORTH AFRICA
religion Algeria.iii
mystical orders ʿAmmāriyya; Raḥmāniyya
see also Darḳāwa; *and* → MYSTICISM
toponyms
ancient Ars̲h̲gūl; As̲h̲īr; al-Manṣūra; Sadrāta; [in Suppl.] Hunayn
present day
oases Biskra; Ḳanṭara.1; al-Ḳulayʿa.2.1; Laghouat; [in Suppl.] Gourara
regions Ḥuḍna; Mzāb; Sāḥil.1.b
towns Adrar.1; al-ʿAnnāba; Ārzāw; ʿAyn Temus̲h̲ent; Bid̲j̲āya; Biskra; Bulayda; Colomb-Béchar; al-D̲j̲azāʾir; Djidjelli; G̲h̲ardāya; Ḳalʿat Banī ʿAbbās; Ḳalʿat Huwwāra; al-Ḳulayʿa.2.2; Ḳusṭanṭīna; Laghouat; al-Madiyya; Masīla; Milyāna; al-Muʿaskar; Mustag̲h̲ānim; Nadrūma; Saʿīda

ALMS K̲h̲ayr; **Ṣadaḳa**

ALPHABET **Abd̲j̲ad**; Ḥarf; Ḥisāb; **Ḥurūf al-Hid̲j̲āʾ**

see also Djafr; Khaṭṭ; [in Suppl.] Budūḥ

for the letters of the Arabic and Persian alphabets, see Ḍād; Dāl; Dhāl; Djīm; Fāʾ; Ghayn; Hāʾ; Ḥāʾ; Hamza; Kāf; Ḳāf; Khāʾ; Lām; Mīm; Nūn; Pāʾ; Rāʾ; Ṣād

secret → CRYPTOGRAPHY

ANATOMY Djism; Katif; [in Suppl.] Aflīmūn

see also Ishāra; Khiḍāb; Ḳiyāfa; [in Suppl.] Dam

chest **Ṣadr**

eye **ʿAyn**; al-Kuḥl; Manāẓir; Ramad

and → MEDICINE.OPHTHALMOLOGISTS; OPTICS

hair ʿAfṣ; Afsantīn; Ḥinnāʾ; Liḥya-yi Sherīf

see also [in Suppl.] Ḥallāḳ

organs Kabid; Ḳalb

teeth → MEDICINE.DENTISTRY

ANDALUSIA **al-Andalus**; Gharb al-Andalus; Moriscos; Mozarab; Mudéjar

see also Kitābāt.3; Libās.ii; Māʾ.7; al-Madjūs; Moors; Muwallad.1; Safīr.2.b; Ṣāʾifa.2; *and* → DYNASTIES.SPAIN AND NORTH AFRICA; SPAIN

administration Dīwān.iii; Ḳūmis; Ṣāḥib al-Madīna

see also Fatā

architecture → ARCHITECTURE.REGIONS

dynasties al-Murābiṭūn.4; al-Muwaḥḥidūn; [in Suppl.] ʿAzafī

see also al-Andalus.vi; (Banū) Ḳasī; *and* → DYNASTIES.SPAIN AND NORTH AFRICA

reyes de taifas period (11th century) ʿAbbādids; Afṭasids; ʿĀmirids; Dhu ʾl-Nūnids; Djahwarids; Ḥammūdids; Hūdids; **Mulūk al-Ṭawāʾif**.2; Razīn, Banū

see also Balansiya; Dāniya; Gharnāṭa; Ibn Ghalbūn; Ibn Rashīḳ, Abū Muḥammad; Ishbīliya; Ḳurṭuba; Mudjāhid, al-Muwaffaḳ; Parias

governors until Umayyad conquest ʿAbd al-Malik b. Ḳaṭan; ʿAbd al-Raḥmān al-Ghāfiḳī; Abu ʾl-Khaṭṭār; al-Ḥurr b. ʿAbd al-Raḥmān al-Thaḳafī; al-Ḥusām b. Ḍirār

see also Kalb b. Wabara; Mūsā b. Nuṣayr

historians of al-Ḍabbī, Abū Djaʿfar; Ibn al-Abbār, Abu ʿAbd Allāh; Ibn ʿAbd al-Malik al-Marrākushī; Ibn Bashkuwāl; Ibn Burd.I; Ibn al-Faraḍī; Ibn Ghālib; Ibn Ḥayyān; Ibn ʿIdhārī; Ibn al-Khaṭīb; Ibn al-Ḳūṭiyya; Ibn Saʿīd al-Maghribī; al-Maḳḳarī; al-Rushāṭī

and → DYNASTIES.SPAIN AND NORTH AFRICA

jurists al-Bādjī; al-Dānī; al-Ḥumaydī; Ibn Abī Zamanayn; Ibn ʿĀṣim; Ibn al-Faradī; Ibn Ḥabīb, Abū Marwān; Ibn Ḥazm, Abū Muḥammad; Ibn Maḍāʾ; Ibn Rushayd; ʿĪsā b. Dīnār; ʿIyāḍ b. Mūsā; al-Ḳalaṣādī; al-Ḳurṭubī, Abū ʿAbd Allāh; al-Ḳurṭubī, Yaḥyā; (al-)Mundhir b. Saʿīd; Ṣāʿid al-Andalusī; [in

Suppl.] Ibn Rushd
see also al-Khushanī; Mālikiyya; [in Suppl.] Ibn al-Rūmiyya

literature Aljamía; ʿArabiyya.B.Appendix; Fahrasa
and → ANDALUSIA.HISTORIANS OF; LITERATURE.POETRY

mysticism → MYSTICISM.MYSTICS

toponyms → SPAIN

ANGELOLOGY **Malāʾika**
see also ʿAdhāb al-Ḳabr; Dīk; Iblīs; Ḳarīn; Rūḥāniyya

angels ʿAzāzīl; Djabrāʾīl; Hārūt wa-Mārūt; Isrāfīl; ʿIzrāʾīl; Mīkāl; Munkar wa-Nakīr; Riḍwān

ANIMALS Dābba; **Ḥayawān**
see also Badw; (Djazīrat) al-ʿArab.v; Farw; Hind.i.l; Khāṣī; Marbaṭ; [in Suppl.] Djazzār; *and* → ZOOLOGY

and art al-Asad; Fahd; Fīl; Ḥayawān.6; Karkaddan; Maʿdin; Namir and Nimr; [in Suppl.] Arnab

and proverbs Ḥayawān.2; Mathal
and see articles on individual animals, in particular Afʿā; Dhiʾb; Fahd; Ghurāb; Ḳaṭā; Khinzīr; Ḳird; Lamṭ; Naml

antelopes Ghazāl; Lamṭ; Mahāt

arachnoids ʿAḳrab; ʿAnkabūt

birds Babbaghāʾ; Dadjādja; Dīk; Ghurāb; Ḥamām; Hudhud; Humā; Ḳaṭā; Naʿām; Nasr; Nuḥām; al-Rukhkh; Salwā; [in Suppl.] Abū Barāḳish
see also Bayzara; Bulbul; ʿIyafa; al-Ramādī

camels **Ibil**
see also (Djazīrat) al-ʿArab.v; Badw.II.c and d; Kārwān; Raḥīl; [in Suppl.] Djammāl; *and* → TRANSPORT.CARAVANS

canines Dhiʾb; Fanak; Ibn Āwā; Kalb; Salūḳī; [in Suppl.] Ḍabuʿ

domesticated Baḳar; Fīl; Ibil; Kalb; Khinzīr; Nims; [in Suppl.] Djāmūs; Ghanam
and → ANIMALS.EQUINES

equines Badw.II; Baghl; **Faras**; Ḥimār; **Khayl**
see also Fāris; Furūsiyya; Ḥazīn; Ibn Hudhayl; Ibn al-Mundhir; Iṣṭabl; Marbaṭ; Maydān; Mīr-Ākhūr

felines ʿAnāḳ; al-Asad; Fahd; Namir and Nimr

fish **Samak**

insects Dhubāb; Djarād; Ḳaml; Naḥl; Naml; Nāmūs.2

molluscs Ṣadaf

reptiles Afʿā; Ḍabb; Ḥayya; Ḥirbāʾ; Samandal
see also Ādam; Almās

rodents [in Suppl.] Faʾr

sport Bayzara; Fahd; Furūsiyya; Ḥamām; Khinzīr; Mahāt; [in Suppl.] Ḍabuʿ

see also Čakïrdjï-bashï; Doghandjï; Kurds.iv.C.5; *and* → HUNTING
transformation into Ḥayawān.3; Ḳird; **Maskh**
wild *in addition to the above, see also* Ayyil; Fanak; Fīl; Ibn ʿIrs; Karkaddan; Ḳird; Ḳunfudh; [in Suppl.] Arnab; Faras al-Māʾ

ANTHROPOMORPHISM Ḥashwiyya; Karrāmiyya
see also Bayān b. Samʿān al-Tamīmī; Djism; Hishām b. al-Ḥakam; Ḥulmāniyya

APOSTASY Mulḥid; Murtadd
see also Ḳatl; *and* → HERESY

ARCHAEOLOGY
and → ARCHITECTURE.REGIONS; EPIGRAPHY; *and the section Toponyms under individual countries*
Turkish archaeologists ʿOthmān Ḥamdī

ARCHITECTURE **Architecture**; Bināʾ
see also Kitābāt; *and* → MILITARY
architects Ḳāsim Agha; Khayr al-Dīn
decoration Fusayfisāʾ; Kāshī; Khaṭṭ; Parčīn-kārī
materials Djiṣṣ; Labin
see also Bināʾ
monuments
aqueducts Ḳanṭara.5 and 6
see also Faḳīr
baths **Ḥammām**; Ḥammām al-Ṣarakh
bridges **Djisr**; Djisr Banāt Yaʿḳūb; Djisr al-Ḥadīd; Djisr al-Shughr
see also Dizfūl; Ḳanṭara
dams **Band**
see also Dizfūl; [in Suppl.] Abū Sinbil; *and* → HYDROLOGY
gates **Bāb**; Bāb-i Humāyūn; Ḥarrān.ii.d
lighthouses **Manār**; al-Nāẓūr
mausolea → ARCHITECTURE.MONUMENTS.TOMBS
monasteries → CHRISTIANITY
mosques Ḥawḍ; Külliyye; Manāra; **Masdjid**; Miḥrāb; Minbar
see also ʿAnaza; Bāb.i; Bahw; Balāṭ; Dikka; Khaṭīb; Muṣallā.2
individual mosques Aya Sofya; al-Azhar; Ḥarrān.ii.(b); Ḥusaynī Dālān; Kaʿba; al-Ḳarawiyyīn; Ḳubbat al-Ṣakhra; Ḳuṭb Mīnār; al-Masdjid al-Aḳṣā; al-Masdjid al-Ḥarām
see also Anḳara; Architecture; Bahmanīs; Dhār.2; Djām; Edirne; Ḥamāt; Ḥimṣ; Kāẓimayn; Ḳazwīn; Maʿarrat al-Nuʿmān; Makka.4
obelisks **Misalla**

palaces Čirāghān; Ḳaṣr al-Ḥayr al-Gharbī; Ḳaṣr al-Ḥayr al-Sharḳī; Kay-ḳubādiyya; Khirbat al-Mafdjar; Khirbat al-Minya; Ḳubādābād; Maḥall; al-Mushattā; [in Suppl.] Djabal Says
see also Gharnāṭa.B; Khirbat al-Bayḍā'; Ḳubbat al-Hawā'; Lashkar-i Bāzār
pavilions Köshk
pleasure-gardens Bustān; Ḥā'ir
see also Bostāndji̊; Gharnāṭa.B; Ḥawḍ; Mā'.12
strongholds Burdj; Ḥiṣār; **Ḥiṣn**; Ḳaṣaba
see also Bāb.ii; al-Ḳalʿa; Ribāṭ
individual strongholds Abū Safyān; Āgra; Alamūt.i.; Alindjaḳ; ʿAmādiya; Anadolu Ḥiṣāri̊; Anamur; Anapa; Asīrgarh; Atak; al-ʿAwāṣim; Bāb al-Abwāb; Bālā Ḥiṣār; Balāṭunus; Barzūya; Baynūn; Bhakkar; Čandērī; Čirmen; al-Dārūm; Djaʿbar; al-Djarbā'; Gaban; Gāwilgaŕh; Ghumdān; Gök Tepe; Golkond́ā; Ḥadjar al-Nasr; Hānsī; Ḥarrān.ii.(a); Ḥiṣn al-Akrād; Ḥiṣn Kayfā; Iṣṭakhr; Kakhtā; Ḳalʿat Nadjm; Ḳalʿat al-Shaḳīf; Ḳalāwdhiya; Ḳalʿe-i Sefīd; Ḳandahār; Kanizsa; al-Karak; Kawkab al-Hawā'; Kharāna; Khartpert; Khērla; Khotin; Khunāṣira; Kilāt-i Nādirī; Ḳoron; Ḳoyul Ḥiṣār; Lanbasar; Lüleburgaz; Mānd́ū; Manōhar; al-Marḳab; Mud́gal; Narnālā; Parendā; al-Rāwandān; Rōhtās; Rūm Ḳalʿesi; Rūmeli Ḥiṣāri̊; Ṣahyūn; [in Suppl.] Bādiya; Bubashtru; al-Dīkdān; Firrīm
see also Ashīr; Bahmanīs; Bīdar; Dawlatābād; Diyār Bakr; Ḥimṣ; Kawkabān.2; Khursābād; Maḥall; Māhūr
tombs **Ḳabr**; **Ḳubba**; **Maḳbara**; Mashhad
see also Muthamman
individual buildings Baḳīʿ al-Gharḳad; Golkond́ā; Ḥarrān.ii.(c); Maklī; Nafīsa; Rādkān; Sahsarām
see also Abarḳūh; Abū Ayyūb al-Anṣārī; Abū Madyan; Āgra; Aḥmad al-Badawī; Aḥmad Yasawī; Bahmanīs; Barīd Shāhīs.II; Djahāngīr; Ghāzī Miyān; Gunbadh-i Ḳābūs; Ḥimṣ; Imāmzāda; Karak Nūḥ; Ḳarbalā'; Ḳazwīn; al-Khalīl; Ḳubbat al-Hawā'; Maʿarrat al-Nuʿmān; al-Madīna
water-houses **Sabīl.2**
see also Ḥawḍ
wells Bā'olī; **Bi'r**; Bi'r Maymūn
regions
Afghanistan and Indian subcontinent Āgra; Bahmanīs; Barīd Shāhīs.II; Bharōč; Bīdar; Bīdjāpūr; Bihār; Čāmpanēr; Dawlatābād; Dihlī.2; Djūnāgaŕh; Ghaznawids; Ghūrids; Golkond́ā; Hampī; Hānsī; Ḥaydarābād; Hind.vii; Ḥusaynī Dālān; Ḳuṭb Mīnār; Lahore; Lakhnaw; Maḥall; Mahisur; Mānd́ū.2; Mughals.7; Multān.2; Nāgawr

see also Burd̲j̲.iii; Bustān.ii; Imām-bārā; Las̲h̲kar-i Bāzār; Māʾ.12; Maḵbara.5; Maklī; Manāra.2; Masd̲j̲id.II; Miḥrāb; Minbar.3; Miẓalla.5; Mut̲h̲amman; Parčīn-kārī; Pīs̲h̲ṭāḵ

Africa → AFRICA; *for North African architecture, see below*

Andalusia   al-Andalus.ix; Burd̲j̲.II; G̲h̲arnāṭa; Is̲h̲bīliya; Ḳurṭuba; Naṣrids.2
    see also al-Nāẓūr

Arabian peninsula   al-Ḥid̲j̲r; Kaʿba; al-Masd̲j̲id al-Ḥarām
    see also Makka.4

Central Asia   Buk̲h̲ārā; Ḥiṣn.iii; Īlk̲h̲āns; Samarḳand.2
    see also Miḥrāb

Egypt   Abu ʾl-Hawl; al-Azhar; Haram; al-Ḳāhira; Mas̲h̲rabiyya.1; Nafīsa
    see also Miḥrāb; Misalla; Miṣr; Saʿīd al-Suʿadāʾ; [in Suppl.] Abū Sinbil

Fertile Crescent   Bag̲h̲dād; Dimas̲h̲ḳ; Ḥarrān.ii; Ḥimṣ; ʿIrāḳ.vii; Ḳubbat al-Ṣak̲h̲ra; al-Ḳuds; Maʿarrat al-Nuʿmān; al-Marḳab.3; al-Masd̲j̲id al-Aḳṣā; al-Raḳḳa; [in Suppl.] Bādiya; Dār al-Ḥadīt̲h̲.I
    see also Ḳaṣr al-Ḥayr al-G̲h̲arbī; Ḳaṣr al-Ḥayr al-S̲h̲arḳī; K̲h̲irbat al-Mafd̲j̲ar; Miḥrāb; al-Rāwandān

Iran   Ḥiṣn.ii; Iṣfahān.2; Iṣṭak̲h̲r; Ḳazwīn; K̲h̲ursābād; Mas̲h̲rabiyya.2; Rādkān; al-Rayy.2; Ṣafawids.V; Salḏj̲ūḳids.VI; Sāmānids.2(b)
    see also Ḳaṣr-i S̲h̲īrīn; Miḥrāb; Ribāṭ-i S̲h̲araf

North Africa   Fās; Fāṭimid Art; Ḥiṣn.i; Ḳalʿat Banī Ḥammād; al-Ḳarawiyyīn
    see also ʿAnaza; Bid̲j̲āya; Miḥrāb

South-east Asia   Ḥiṣn.iv; Indonesia.v; Masd̲j̲id.III-V

Turkey   Adana; Anḳara; Aya Sofya; Diwrīg̲ī; Diyār Bakr; Edirne; Ḥarrān.ii; Ḥiṣn Kayfā; Istanbul; Konya.2; Lāranda; ʿOt̲h̲mānlı̊.V
    see also Ḳaplı̊d̲j̲a; Ḳāsim Ag̲h̲a; K̲h̲ayr al-Dīn; Kös̲h̲k; Miḥrāb; Rūm Ḳalʿesi

terms   ʿAmūd; ʿAnaza; Bahw; Balāṭ; Īwān; Muḳarbaṣ; Muḳarnas; Mut̲h̲amman; Pīs̲h̲ṭāḵ; Riwāḵ

urban   Dār; Funduḳ; Ḥammām; Īwān; Ḳaysāriyya; K̲h̲ān.II; Madrasa.III; Masd̲j̲id; Muṣallā.2; Rabʿ
    see also Kanīsa

ventilation   Mirwaḥa; [in Suppl.] Bādgīr
    see also K̲h̲ays̲h̲

ARMENIA   **Armīniya**; Rewān
    and → CAUCASUS

ART   Arabesque; Fann; Fusayfisāʾ; Kās̲h̲ī; K̲h̲aṭṭ; K̲h̲azaf; Kitābāt; Lawn; Maʿdin.4; Parčīn-kārī; Rasm
    see also Architecture; Billawr; D̲h̲ahab; Fiḍḍa; ʿIlm al-D̲j̲amāl; K̲h̲ātam; Muhr; *and* → ANIMALS.AND ART; ARCHITECTURE

calligraphy **Khaṭṭ**
see also ʿAlī; İnal; Ḳum(m)ī; Muraḳḳaʿ; Nuskha; *and* → Writing
calligraphers ʿAlī Riḍā-i ʿAbbāsī; Ḥamza al-Ḥarrānī; Ibn al-Bawwāb; Ibn Muḳla; Muḥammad Ḥusayn Tabrīzī; Müstaḳīm-zāde
ceramics → Art.pottery
decorative ʿĀdj; al-Asad; Djiṣṣ; Fahd; Ḥayawān.6; Hilāl.ii; Īlkhāns; al-Ḳamar.II; Mashrabiyya; Parčīn-kārī
see also Kāshī; Maʿdin.4
drawing **Rasm**
glass al-Ḳily; ʿOthmānli̊.VII.d; Sāmānids.2(a)
handicrafts Ḳalamkārī; [in Suppl.] Bisāṭ; Dawāt
see also Ḥalfāʾ
metalware Bīdar; Īlkhāns; Maʿdin.4; ʿOthmānli̊.VII.b; Sāmānids.2(a); [in Suppl.] Ibrīḳ
mosaics **Fusayfisāʾ**; Kāshī
painting
miniatures Īlkhāns; Mughals.9; Naḳḳāsh-khāna; ʿOthmānli̊.VIII
see also Fīl; Kalīla wa-Dimna.16; Māndū.3; Miʿrādj.5; al-Mīzān.3; Muraḳḳaʿ; Rustam.2; Sāḳī.3; [in Suppl.] Djawhar; *and* → Animals.and art; Art.drawing
miniaturists Bihzād; Manṣūr; Maṭrāḳči̊; Naḳḳāsh Ḥasan (Pasha); Riḍā ʿAbbāsī; Riḍāʾī
see also ʿAlī; Luḳmān b. Sayyid Ḥusayn
modern painting Djabrān Khalīl Djabrān; ʿOthmān Ḥamdī; [in Suppl.] Dinet; Eyyūboghlu, Bedrī
and → Art.drawing
pottery Anadolu.iii.6; al-Andalus.ix; **Fakhkhār**; Īlkhāns; Iznīḳ; Ḳallala; **Khazaf**; Mināʾī; ʿOthmānli̊.VII.a; Sāmānids.2(a)
regional and period al-Andalus.ix; Berbers.VI; Fāṭimid Art; Ilkhāns; ʿIrāḳ.vii; Mughals.8 and 9; ʿOthmānli̊.VII; Saldjūḳids.VI; Sāmānids.2(a)
silhouette-cutting Fakhrī
tapestry ʿOthmānli̊.VI; Sadjdjāda.2; [in Suppl.] **Bisāṭ**
see also Karkaddan; Mafrūshāt; Mifrash; Mīlās.2
textiles Anadolu.iii.6; al-Andalus.ix; al-Bahnasā; Bursa; Dabīḳ; Ḥarīr; Īlkhāns; Ḳumāsh; Mughals.8; ʿOthmānli̊.VI; al-Rayy.2; Sāmānids.2(a); [in Suppl.] Ḥāʾik
see also Ḳalamkārī; Ḳaṣab; Kattān; Ḳurḳūb; Mandīl; al-Nassādj; *and* → Clothing
tiles **Kāshī**

Asceticism Bakkāʾ; Malāmatiyya
see also Khalwa; Manāḳib; [in Suppl.] Asad b. Mūsā b. Ibrāhīm

for ascetics → MYSTICISM.MYSTICS; SAINTHOOD

ASIA Almalïgh; Baikal
see also Baraba; Mogholistān; *and* → CHINA; MONGOLIA
Central → CENTRAL ASIA
Eurasia → EUROPE
South Burma; Ceylon; Hind; Laccadives; Maldives; Mauritius; Minicoy; Nepal; Nicobars
see also Ruhmī
for individual countries → BANGLADESH; BURMA; INDIA; NEPAL; PAKISTAN; SRI LANKA
South-east Čam; Djāwī; Indochina; Indonesia; Ḳimār; Malay Peninsula; Malaysia; Patani; Philippines; [in Suppl.] Brunei
see also Kitābāt.8; [in Suppl.] Demography.VIII; *and* → ARCHITECTURE; LAW
for individual countries → CHINA; INDONESIA; MALAYSIA: THAILAND

ASSYRIA Khursābād; Nimrūd; Nīnawā.1; [in Suppl.] Athūr

ASTROLOGY Ikhtiyārāt; Ḳaws Ḳuzaḥ; al-Kayd; Ḳirān; Minṭaḳat al-Burūdj; Munadjdjim; **Nudjūm (Aḥkām al-)**
see also Khaṭṭ
astrologers Abū Maʿshar al-Balkhī; al-Bīrūnī; Ibn Abi 'l-Ridjāl, Abu 'l-Ḥasan; Ibn al-Khaṣīb, Abū Bakr; al-Ḳabīṣī; al-Khayyāṭ, Abū ʿAlī; Māshāʾ Allāh
see also Baṭlamiyūs; *and* → ASTRONOMY; DIVINATION
terms al-Djawzahar; Ḥadd; Ḳaṭʿ; Muthallath; Saʿd wa-Naḥs (*and* al-Saʿdāni); al-Sahm.1.b

ASTRONOMY Anwāʾ; Asṭurlāb; Falak; Hayʾa; **ʿIlm al-Hayʾa**; al-Ḳamar.I; al-Kayd; Kusūf; al-Ḳuṭb; al-Madd wa 'l-Djazr; al-Madjarra; al-Manāzil; Minṭaḳat al-Burūdj; al-Nudjūm
see also Djughrāfiyā; Ḳibla.ii; al-Ḳubba; al-Kura; Makka.4; Mīḳāt.2; Mizwala
astronomers ʿAbd al-Raḥmān al-Ṣūfī; Abu 'l-Ṣalt Umayya; ʿAlī al-Ḳūshdjī; al-Badīʿ al-Asṭurlābī; al-Battānī; al-Bīrūnī; al-Biṭrūdjī; Djābir b. Aflaḥ; al-Djaghmīnī; al-Farghānī; Ḥabash al-Ḥāsib al-Marwazī; Ibn Amādjūr; Ibn al-Bannāʾ al-Marrākushī; Ibn ʿIrāḳ; Ibn al-Ṣaffār; Ibn al-Samḥ; Ibn Yūnus; al-Kāshī; al-Khwārazmī, Abū Djaʿfar; al-Khāzin; al-Khazīnī; al-Khudjandī; Kushiyār b. Labān; Ḳuṭb al-Dīn Shīrāzī; al-Madjrīṭī; al-Mārdīnī; al-Marrākushī; Muḥammad b. ʿĪsā al-Māhānī; Muḥammad b. ʿUmar; al-Nayrīzī; [in Suppl.] ʿAbd al-Salām b. Muḥammad
see also Baṭlamiyūs; al-Falakī; Falakī Shirwānī; Ibn al-Haytham; Ḳusṭā b. Lūḳā; [in Suppl.] Ibn al-Adjdābī; *and* → ASTROLOGY

celestial objects **al-Nudjūm**
comets **al-Nudjūm**.III.b
planets al-Ḳamar.I; al-Mirrīkh; al-Mushtarī; **al-Nudjūm**.II
see also Minṭaḳat al-Burūdj; Ruʾyat al-Hilāl; al-Saʿdānⁱ
stars and constellations ʿAḳrab; ʿAnāḳ; al-Asad; Dadjādja; Fard; Kalb; Ḳird; Mahāt; Minṭaḳat al-Burūdj; Muthallath; Naʿām; Nasr; **al-Nudjūm**; Radīf.1; al-Sahm.1.c; Samak.9; [in Suppl.] Arnab; Ghanam
see also al-Kayd; Saʿd wa-Naḥs (*and* al-Saʿdānⁱ); al-Sāḳ
observatory Marṣad
terms al-Djawzahar; Istiḳbāl; al-Maṭāliʿ; al-Maṭlaʿ; al-Mayl; Muḳābala.1; Muḳanṭarāt; Niṣf al-Nahār; Radīf.1; Rubʿ; Ruʾyat al-Hilāl; al-Saḳ; al-Samt

AUSTRIA Beč; **Nemče**
see also Muslimūn.2.ii

B

BĀBISM → SECTS

BAHAIS Bāb; Bābīs; Bahāʾ Allāh; **Bahāʾīs**; Mashriḳ al-Adhkār; Naḳḍ al-Mīthāḳ
see also Lawḥ; Maẓhar; [in Suppl.] Anṣārī

BAHRAIN **al-Baḥrayn**; āl-Khalīfa; Madjlis.4.A.x; Maḥkama.4.ix
see also Ḳarmaṭī
toponyms al-Manāma; al-Muḥarraḳ
see also al-Mushaḳḳar

BALKANS **Balkan**; **Rūmeli**; al-Ṣaḳāliba
and → EUROPE

BANGLADESH **Bangāla**; Madjlis.4.C
see also Bengali; Nadhr al-Islām; [in Suppl.] Djarīda.vii
literature → LITERATURE.IN OTHER LANGUAGES
toponyms Bāḳargandj; Bangāla; Bōgrā; Chittagong; Ḍhākā; Dīnādjpur; Djassawr; Farīdpur
see also Ruhmī

BANKING Muḍāraba; Ribā.5
see also Djahbadh

BASQUES **al-Bashkunish**
see also Ibn Gharsiya

BEDOUINS **Badw**; Biʾr; Dawār; Ghanīma; Ghazw; al-Hidjar
see also Liṣṣ; *and* → NOMADISM; SAUDI ARABIA
writings on Rzewuski

BENIN Kandi; Kotonou; Kouandé

BERBERS **Berbers**; Judaeo-Berber
see also Ḥimāya.ii.II; Imẓad; al-Irdjānī; Ḳallala; Ḳiṣṣa.8; Leff; Libās.ii; Lithām; Mafākhir al-Barbar; Ṣaff.3; *and* → ALGERIA; LANGUAGES.AFRO-ASIATIC
customary law ʿĀda.ii; Ḳānūn.iv
dynasties ʿAbd al-Wādids; ʿAmmār; Marīnids; Midrār; al-Murābiṭūn; al-Muwaḥḥidūn; Razīn, Banū
religion al-Badjalī; Berbers.III; Ḥā-Mīm; Ṣāliḥ b. Ṭarīf
resistance Berbers.I.c; al-Kāhina; Kusayla; Maysara
tribes al-Barānis; Barghawāṭa; Birzāl; al-Butr; Djazūla; Ghāniya; Ghubrīnī; Ghumāra; Glāwā; Gudāla; Ḥāḥā; Hargha; Hawwāra; Hintāta; Ifoghas; Īfran; Iraten; Kutāma; Lamṭa; Lamtūna; Lawāta; Maghīla; Maghrāwa; Malzūza; Maṣmūda; Māssa; Maṭghara; Maṭmāṭa; Mazāta; Midyūna; Misrāta; al-Nafūsa; Nafza; Nafzāwa; [in Suppl.] Awraba

BIBLE **Indjīl**
and → CHRISTIANITY; JUDAISM
biblical personages Ādam; ʿAmālīḳ; Ayyūb; Āzar; ʿAzāzīl; Balʿam; Bilḳīs; Binyāmīn; Bukht-naṣ(ṣ)ar; Dāniyāl; Dāwūd; Djabrāʾīl; Djālūt; Firʿawn; Ḥābīl wa-Ḳābīl; Ḥām; Hāmān; Hārūn b. ʿImrān; Hārūt wa-Mārūt; Ḥawwāʾ; Ḥizḳīl; Ilyās; ʿImrān; Irmiyā; ʿĪsā; Isḥāḳ; Ismāʿīl; Kanʿān; Ḳārūn; Ḳiṭfīr; Kūsh; Lamak; Lazarus; Lūṭ; Maryam; al-Masīḥ; Namrūd; Nūḥ; Rāḥīl; Sām.1; al-Sāmirī
see also Dhu ʾl-Kifl; Djūdī; al-Fayyūm; Hūd; Idrīs
translations
into Arabic Fāris al-Shidyāḳ; Saʿadyā Ben Yōsēf; [in Suppl.] al-Bustānī.2
see also ʿArabiyya.A.ii.1; Judaeo-Arabic.iii.B
into Persian Abu ʾl-Faḍl ʿAllāmī
see also Judaeo-Persian.i.2

BIBLIOGRAPHY **Bibliography**; Fahrasa

BOTANY Adwiya; al-ʿAshshāb; Nabāt
and → AGRICULTURE; FLORA; MEDICINE; PHARMACOLOGY
botanists Abū ʿUbayd al-Bakrī; al-Dīnawarī, Abū Ḥanīfa; Ibn al-Bayṭār; [in Suppl.] al-Ghāfiḳī; Ibn al-Rūmiyya

see also Abu 'l-Khayr al-Ishbīlī; Filāḥa; Nīḳūlā'ūs

BULGARIA **Bulgaria**; Pomaks
see also Küčük Ḳaynardja; Muhādjir.2; Muslimūn.1.B.5
rivers Merič
toponyms Burgas; Deli-Orman; Dobrudja; Filibe; Hezārghrad; Küstendil; Newrokop; Nīkbūlī; ʿOthmān Pazar; Plewna; Rusčuk

BURMA Arakan; **Burma**; Mergui; Rangoon

BYZANTINE EMPIRE Biṭrīḳ; Ḳayṣar; Rūm
see also Anadolu.iii.1 and 2; Hiba.i; Iznīḳ; Ḳalāwdhiya; Ḳubrus; (al-) Ḳusṭanṭīniyya; al-Maṣṣīṣa; Muʾta; Nauplion.1; *and* → PALESTINE; SYRIA; TURKEY
allies Djarādjima; Djarrāḥids; Ghassān; al-Ḥārith b. Djabala; Kinda.1; Salīḥ; [in Suppl.] Djabala b. al-Ḥārith
and → TRIBES
military Alay; Lamas-ṣū; Malāzgird.2; Nafṭ.2; [in Suppl.] Dhāt al-Ṣawārī
see also al-ʿAwāṣim; Cilicia; Ṣāʾifa.1

C

CALIPHATE Ahl al-Ḥall wa 'l-ʿAḳd; Bayʿa; Ḥādjib.i; Ḥarb.ii; Hiba.i; Imāma; Ḳaḍīb; Kātib.i; **Khalīfa**; Libās.i; Madjlis.1; Marāsim.1; Mawākib.1
see also Amīr al-Muʾminīn; Ghulām.i; Khilʿa.ii; Laḳab.2; Māl al-Bayʿa; *and* → COURT CEREMONY
ʿAbbāsids (750-1258) **ʿAbbāsids**; Baghdād; Dīwān.i; Ḥādjib.i; Khalīfa.i.B; Marāsim.1; Mawākib.1; Muṣādara.2; Musawwida; Naḳīb.1; Naḳīb al-Ashrāf.1; Sāmarrāʾ
see also al-Abnāʾ.III; ʿAlī b. ʿAbd Allāh b. al-ʿAbbās; ʿAlids; Architecture.I.3; Ḍarība; Hāshimiyya; al-Hāshimiyya; Laḳab.2; Libās.i.4; Riḍā.2; *and* → DYNASTIES.PERSIA
caliphs Abu 'l-ʿAbbās al-Saffāḥ; al-Amīn; al-Hādī ila 'l-Ḥaḳḳ; Hārūn al-Rashīd; al-Ḳādir bi 'llāh; al-Ḳāhir bi 'llāh; al-Ḳāʾim bi-amr Allāh; al-Mahdī; al-Maʾmūn; al-Manṣūr; al-Muhtadī; al-Muḳtadī; al-Muḳtadir; al-Muḳtafī bi-llāh; al-Muḳtafī li-Amr Allāh; al-Muntaṣir; al-Mustaḍīʾ; al-Mustaʿīn (I); al-Mustaʿīn (II); al-Mustakfī; al-Mustandjid (I); al-Mustandjid (II); al-Mustanṣir (I); al-Mustanṣir (II); al-Mustarshid; al-Mustaʿṣim bi 'llāh; al-Mustaẓhir bi 'llāh; al-Muʿtaḍid bi 'llāh; al-Muʿtamid ʿalā 'llāh; al-Muʿtaṣim bi 'llāh; al-Mutawakkil ʿalā 'llāh; al-Muʿtazz bi 'llāh; al-Muṭīʿ li 'llāh; al-Muttaḳī li 'llāh; al-Nāṣir li-Dīn Allāh, Abu 'l-ʿAbbās; al-Rāḍī bi 'llāh; al-Rāshid

see also ʿAbd Allāh b. ʿAlī; Būrān; al-Khayzurān bint ʿAṭāʾ al-Djurashiyya; Muḥammad b. ʿAlī b. ʿAbd Allāh; al-Muwaffaḳ; al-Ruṣāfa.2

viziers Abū ʿAbd Allāh Yaʿḳūb; Abū Salāma al-Khallāl; Abū ʿUbayd Allāh; ʿAḍud al-Dīn; ʿAlī b. ʿĪsā; al-Barāmika.3; al-Barīdī; al-Djardjarāʾī.1-3; al-Faḍl b. Marwān; al-Faḍl b. al-Rabīʿ; al-Faḍl b. Sahl b. Zadhānfarūkh; al-Fayḍ b. Abī Ṣāliḥ; Ḥamīd; Hibat Allāh b. Muḥammad; Ibn al-Alḳamī; Ibn al-Baladī; Ibn al-Furāt; Ibn Hubayra; Ibn Khāḳan.2 and 3; Ibn Makhlad; Ibn Muḳla; Ibn al-Muslima; Ibn al-Zayyāt; al-Iskāfī, Abu ʾl-Faḍl; al-Iskāfī, Abū Isḥāḳ; Ismāʿīl b. Bulbul; al-Khaṣībī; al-Rabīʿ b. Yūnus; Rabīb al-Dawla; al-Rūdhrāwarī

see also al-Djahshiyārī; Hilāl al-Ṣābiʾ; Khātam

secretaries Aḥmad b. Abī Khālid al-Aḥwal; Aḥmad b. Yūsuf; ʿAmr b. Masʿada; al-Ḥasan b. Sahl; Ibn al-Djarrāḥ; Ibn Khāḳan.1 and 4; Ibn al-Māshiṭa; al-Mūriyānī

historians of al-Djahshiyārī; Ibn Abi ʾl-Dam; Ibn Abī Ṭāhir Ṭayfūr; Ibn al-Djawzī; Ibn al-Naṭṭāḥ; Ibn al-Sāʿī; Ibn al-Ṭiḳṭaḳā; al-Madāʾinī; Ṣābiʾ.(3).4

other personages al-ʿAbbās b. ʿAmr al-Ghanawī; al-ʿAbbās b. al-Maʾmūn; al-ʿAbbās b. Muḥammad; ʿAbd Allāh b. ʿAlī; ʿAbd al-Djabbār b. ʿAbd al-Raḥmān; ʿAbd al-Malik b. Ṣāliḥ; Abū ʿAwn; Abū Muslim; ʿAlī al-Riḍā; Badjkam; Badr al-Kharshanī; Bughā al-Kabīr; Bughā al-Sharābī; Dulafids; al-Fatḥ b. Khāḳān; Harthama b. Aʿyan; al-Ḥasan b. Zayd b. al-Ḥasan; Ḥātim b. Harthama; Ḥumayd b. ʿAbd al-Ḥamīd; Ibn Abi ʾl-Shawārib; Ibn Buhlūl; Ibn al-Djaṣṣāṣ.II; Ibn Ḥamdūn; Ibn Māhān; Ibn al-Mudabbir; Ibn al-Muʿtazz; Ibn Rāʾiḳ; Ibn Thawāba; Ibrāhīm b. ʿAbd Allāh; ʿĪsā b. Mūsā; ʿĪsā b. al-Shaykh; Ḳaḥṭaba; al-Ḳāsim b. ʿĪsā; Maʿn b. Zāʾida; al-Mubarḳaʿ; Muhallabids; Muḥammad b. ʿAbd Allāh (al-Nafs al-Zakiyya); Muḥammad b. Ṭughdj al-Ikhshīd; Muḥammad b. Yāḳūt; Muʾnis al-Faḥl; Muʾnis al-Muẓaffar; al-Muwaffaḳ; Naṣr b. Shabath; al-Nāṭiḳ bi ʾl-Ḥaḳḳ; al-Nūsharī; Rāfiʿ b. Harthama; Rāfiʿ b. al-Layth b. Naṣr b. Sayyār; al-Rāwandiyya; Rawḥ b. Ḥātim; Sādjids; Ṣāliḥ b. ʿAlī; [in Suppl.] Abū Manṣūr b. Yūsuf; Aytākh al-Turkī; Badr al-Muʿtaḍidī; al-Dāmaghānī, Abū ʿAbd Allāh; al-Dāmaghānī, Abu ʾl-Ḥasan; al-Ghiṭrīf b. ʿAṭāʾ; Ibn Dirham

Fāṭimids (909-1171) Dīwān.i and ii.(2); **Fāṭimids**; Ḥādjib.iv; Ḥidjāb.II; al-Ḳāhira; Khalīfa.i.D; Libās.i.5; Marāsim.1; Mawākib.1

see also Laḳab.2; Ṣāḥib al-Bāb

caliphs Abū ʿAbd Allāh al-Shīʿī; al-ʿĀḍid li-Dīn Allāh; al-Āmir; al-ʿAzīz bi ʾllāh; al-Ḥāfiẓ; al-Ḥākim bi-Amr Allāh; al-Ḳāʾim; al-Mahdī ʿUbayd Allāh; al-Manṣūr bi ʾllāh; al-Muʿizz li-Dīn Allāh; al-Mustaʿlī bi ʾllāh; al-Mustanṣir (bi ʾllāh) *viziers* ʿAbbās b. Abi ʾl-Futūḥ; al-ʿĀdil b. al-Salār; al-Afḍal b. Badr al-Djamālī; al-Afḍal (Kutayfāt); Badr al-Djamālī; Bahrām; al-Baṭāʾiḥī; Ḍirghām; Djabr Ibn al-Ḳāsim; al-Djardjarāʾī.4; Ibn Killis; Ibn Maṣāl; Ruzzīk b. Ṭalāʾiʿ; [in Suppl.] Ibn Khalaf.2

secretaries Ibn Mammātī; Ibn al-Ṣayrafī; [in Suppl.] Ibn Khalaf, Abu ʾl-Ḥasan

historians of Ibn al-Ṭuwayr; al-Maḳrīzī; al-Musabbiḥī

see also Djawdhar

other personages Abū Yazīd al-Nukkārī; Bardjawān; Djawdhar; Djawhar al-Ṣiḳillī; Khalaf b. Mulāʿib al-Ashhabī; al-Kirmānī; Nizār b. al-Mustanṣir; al-Nuʿmān

see also al-Farghānī

Rightly-Guided Caliphs (632-661)

caliphs Abū Bakr; ʿAlī b. Abī Ṭālib

see also Ḥarūrāʾ; Ibn Muldjam; Khalīfa.i.A; al-Saḳīfa

other personages Abān b. ʿUthmān; ʿAbd Allāh b. al-ʿAbbās; ʿAbd Allāh b. ʿĀmir; ʿAbd Allāh b. Saʿd; ʿAbd Allāh b. Salām; ʿAbd Allāh b. Wahb; ʿAbd al-Raḥmān b. ʿAwf; ʿAbd al-Raḥmān b. Samura; Abu ʾl-Aswad al-Duʾalī; Abū Ayyūb al-Anṣārī; Abu ʾl-Dunyā; Abū ʿUbayda al-Djarrāḥ; al-Aḥnaf b. Ḳays; al-Aḳraʿ b. Ḥābis; ʿAmr b. al-ʿĀṣ; al-Ashʿarī, Abū Mūsā; al-Ashʿath; al-Ashtar; al-Bāhilī; Ḥabīb b. Maslama; al-Ḳaʿḳāʿ b. ʿAmr; Khālid b. al-Walīd; Muḥammad b. Abī Bakr; al-Muthanna b. Ḥāritha; Saʿīd b. al-ʿĀṣ

and → MUḤAMMAD, THE PROPHET.COMPANIONS OF THE PROPHET *and* FAMILY OF THE PROPHET

Umayyads (661-750) Dimashḳ; Dīwān.i; Ḥādjib.i; Khalīfa.i.A; Mawlā.2.b; [in Suppl.] Bādiya

see also Architecture.I.2; Ḳays ʿAylān; Libās.i.4; Marwānids; *and* → DYNASTIES.SPAIN AND NORTH AFRICA

caliphs ʿAbd al-Malik b. Marwān; Hishām; Marwān I b. al-Ḥakam; Marwān II; Muʿāwiya I; Muʿawiya II

see also Būṣīr; al-Ruṣāfa.3

historians of ʿAwāna b. al-Ḥakam al-Kalbī; al-Azdī

other personages ʿAbbād b. Ziyād; al-ʿAbbās b. al-Walīd; ʿAbd Allāh b. ʿAbd al-Malik; ʿAbd Allāh b. Hammām; ʿAbd Allāh b. Ḥanẓala; ʿAbd Allāh b. Khāzim; ʿAbd Allāh b. Muṭīʿ; ʿAbd Allāh b. al-Zubayr; ʿAbd al-ʿAzīz b. al-Ḥadjdjādj; ʿAbd al-ʿAzīz b. Marwān; ʿAbd al-ʿAzīz b. al-Walīd; ʿAbd al-Raḥmān b. Khālid; ʿAmr b. Saʿīd; Asad b. ʿAbd Allāh; al-Aṣamm.1; Baldj b. Bishr; Bishr b. Marwān; Bishr b. al-Walīd; Bukayr b. Māhān; Bukayr b. Wishāḥ; Busr; al-Ḍaḥḥāḳ b. Ḳays al-Fihrī; al-Djarrāḥ b. ʿAbd Allāh; al-Djunayd b. ʿAbd Allāh; al-Ḥadjdjādj b. Yūsuf; Ḥanẓala b. Ṣafwān; al-Ḥārith b. Suraydj; Ḥassān b. Mālik; Ḥassān b. al-Nuʿmān al-

Ghassānī; al-Ḥurr b. Yazīd; al-Ḥusayn b. Numayr; Ibn al-Ashʿath; Ibn al-Ḥaḍramī; Ibn Hubayra; Khālid b. ʿAbd Allāh al-Ḳasrī; Khālid b. Yazīd b. Muʿāwiya; Kulthūm b. ʿIyāḍ al-Ḳushayrī; Ḳurra b. Sharīk; Ḳutayba b. Muslim; Maʿn b. Zāʾida; Masāmiʿa; Maslama b. ʿAbd al-Malik b. Marwān; Maymūn b. Mihrān; Muʿāwiya b. Hishām; al-Mughīra b. Shuʿba; Muhallabids; Muḥammad b. al-Ḳāsim; Muslim b. ʿUḳba; Naṣr b. Sayyār; al-Nuʿmān b. Bashīr; Rawḥ b. Zinbāʿ; Salm b. Ziyād b. Abīhi; [in Suppl.] ʿAdī b. Arṭāt

see also al-Baṭṭāl; Iyās b. Muʿāwiya

treatises on al-Ḳalḳashandī.1

CARTOGRAPHY Kharīṭa

and → GEOGRAPHY; NAVIGATION

cartographers al-Falakī; Ibn Sarābiyūn; Meḥmed Reʾīs; Pīrī Reʾīs

CAUCASUS Ādharbaydjān.ii; Armīniya; Dāghistān; **al-Ḳabḳ**; al-Kurdj

see also al-Bāhilī; Djarīda.iv; Ḥamza Beg; Ḥizb.iv; Ḳarā Bāgh; Muhādjir.2

physical geography

mountains al-Ḳabḳ

waters Alindjaḳ; Gökče-tengiz; Ḳarā Deniz; Ḳi̊zi̊l-üzen; Ḳuban; Kur; al-Rass; Safīd Rūd

population Abkhāz.2; Alān; Andi; Arči; Avars; Balkar; Čečens; Čerkes; Darghin; Dido; Ingush; Kabards; Ḳapuča; Ḳaračay; Ḳarata; Ḳaytaḳ; Khaputs; Khemshin; Khinalug; Khunzal; Khvarshi̊; Ḳri̊z; Ḳubači; Kwanadi; Laḳ; Laz; Lezgh; Noghay; Ossetians; Rūs; Rutul; [in Suppl.] Demography.VI

see also Ḳumuḳ

toponyms

ancient Alindjaḳ; Arrān; Bādjarwān.1; Balandjar; Dwin

present-day Akhiskha; Bāb al-Abwāb; Bākū; Bardhaʿa; Batumi; Derbend; Gandja; Ḳubba; Lankoran; Makhač-ḳalʿe; Nakhčiwān; [in Suppl.] Djulfā.I

CENTRAL ASIA Badakhshān; Čaghāniyān; Khʷārazm; **Mā warāʾ al-Nahr**; Mogholistān

see also Hayāṭila; Ismāʿīl b. Aḥmad; Ḳarā Khiṭāy; Ḳazaḳ; Nīzak, Ṭarkhān; [in Suppl.] Atali̊ḳ; Djulfā.II; *and* → DYNASTIES.MONGOLS; MONGOLIA; ONOMASTICS

architecture → ARCHITECTURE.REGIONS

belles-lettres → LITERATURE.DRAMA *and* POETRY.TURKISH.IN EASTERN TURKISH

former Soviet Union al-ʿArab.iii.Appendix; Basmačis; Djarīda.iv; Fiṭrat; Ḥizb.v; Khodjaev; Ṣadr al-Dīn ʿAynī; [in Suppl.] Demography.VI

and → *the section Toponyms in this entry*
historians of ʿAbd al-Karīm Bukhārī
see also Ḥaydar b. ʿAlī
mysticism → MYSTICISM; SAINTHOOD
physical geography
deserts Ḳaraḳum; Ḳïzïl-ḳum
mountains Ala Dagh; Altai; Balkhān; Pamirs
see also Čopan-ata
waters Aḳ Ṣu; Amū Daryā; Aral; Atrek; Baḥr al-Khazar; Balkhash; Čaghān-rūd; Ču; Ili; Issïk-kul; Ḳarā-köl; Murghāb
population Balūč; Čāwdors (*and* [in Suppl.] Čawdor); Emreli; Gagauz; Ḳaraḳalpaḳ; Khaladj; Ḳungrāt; Ḳurama; Özbeg; [in Suppl.] Demography.VI
see also Altaians; al-ʿArab.iii.Appendix; Ghalča; Ghuzz; Ḳarluḳ; Ḳazaḳ; Ḳipčaḳ; Ḳïrgïz; Ḳumān; Kumīdjīs; Ḳun; [in Suppl.] Ersarï
toponyms
ancient Abaskūn; Abīward; Akhsīkath; Ardjish; Balāsāghūn; Banākat; Fārāb; Firabr; Gurgandj; Kāth; Ḳayalïḳ; Marw al-Rudh; Marw al-Shāhidjān; Mashhad-i Miṣryān; Nakhshab; Pishpek; [in Suppl.] Dandānḳān; Djand; Īlāḳ
present-day
districts Atek; Ḳaratigin
see also Ākhāl Tekke
regions Farghānā; Khʷārazm; Khuttalān; Labāb; Mangïshlak; [in Suppl.] Dasht-i Ḳïpčaḳ
towns Aḳ Masdjid.2; Alma Ata; Āmul.2; Andidjān; ʿAshḳābād; Awliyā Ata; Bayram ʿAlī; Bukhārā; Čimkent; Djalālābād; Ghudjduwān; Hazarasp; Ḥiṣār; Kash; Khīwa; Khoḳand; Khudjand(a); Kish; Ḳubādhiyān; Marghīnān; Mayhana; Ordūbād; Özkend; Pandjdih; Samarḳand

CHAD Abeshr; Bagirmi; Borkou; Kanem; Kanuri; [in Suppl.] **Čad**

CHARMS Afsūn; Ḥidjāb.IV; Kabid.4; Māshāʾ Allāh; [in Suppl.] Budūḥ
see also Kahrubā; Ḳarwasha; *and* → MAGIC

CHILD **Ṣaghīr**
and → CIRCUMCISION; EDUCATION
childbirth ʿAḳīḳa; Āl; Liʿān; al-Marʾa.2.c; Mawākib.4.2
see also Raḍāʿ
treatises on ʿArīb b. Saʿd al-Kātib al-Ḳurṭubī
childhood Ṣaghīr
see also Ḥaḍāna

pregnancy Rāḳid
suckling Raḍāʿ

CHINA Djarīda.v; Masdjid.V
see also Bahādur; Khoḳand
dynasties Ḳarā Khiṭāy
see also Faghfūr; Gūrkhān
personages
for leaders in uprisings, see below
literary figures Liu Chih; Ma Huan
officials P'u Shou-keng
physical geography
waters Aḳ Ṣu; Ili
population Salar
toponyms
ancient Bishbalïḳ; Khansā
present-day Aḳ Ṣu; Alti Shahr; Kansu; Kāshghar; Khānbalïḳ; Khānfū; Khotan; Ḳuldja; Ning-hsia
treatises on ʿAlī Akbar Khiṭāʾī
uprisings Panthay
leaders Ma Chung-ying; Ma Hua-lung; Ma Ming-hsin; Pai Yen-hu

CHRISTIANITY Ahl al-Kitāb; Dayr; Dayṣāniyya; ʿĪsā; Kanīsa; Maryam; **Naṣārā**; Rāhib; al-Ṣalīb
see also Dhimma; Djizya; Ghiyār; al-Ḥākim bi-Amr Allāh; Ifrandj; Karshūnī; Ḳūmis; Lāhūt and Nāsūt.2; Maʿalthāyā; [in Suppl.] Dāwiyya and Isbitāriyya; Fidāʾ; *and* → BIBLE; CRUSADE(R)S; NUBIA
apologetics Ibn Zurʿa; al-Kindī, ʿAbd al-Masīḥ
communities Anadolu.iii.4; al-Andalus.iv; Istanbul.vii.b; Mozarab
see also Fener
denominations Ḳibṭ; Nasṭūriyyūn
and → JUDAISM.JEWISH SECTS
Catholics Bashīr Shihāb II; Isḥāḳ, Adīb; Ṣābundjī; [in Suppl.] Buṭrus Karāma
Copts Ibn al-ʿAssāl; Ibn Mammātī; Ibn al-Muḳaffaʿ; **Ḳibṭ**; al-Makīn b. al-ʿAmīd; Māriya; al-Mufaḍḍal b. Abi 'l-Faḍāʾil; [in Suppl.] Ibn Kabar; Ibn al-Rāhib
and → EGYPT.TOPONYMS; NUBIA
Greek orthodox Gagauz
see also Paṭrīk
Jacobites Ibn al-ʿIbrī; Ibn Zurʿa
see also al-Kindī, ʿAbd al-Masīḥ; Paṭrīk

Maronites Farḥāt; Isṭifān al-Duwayhī; al-Rayḥānī; Salīm al-Naḳḳāsh; [in Suppl.] Abū Shabaka; al-Bustānī
see also Bsharrā; Durūz.ii; Paṭrīk; *and* → LEBANON
Melkites Abū Ḳurra; al-Antāḳī; Mīkhā'īl al-Ṣabbāgh; al-Muḳawḳis; Sa'īd b. al-Biṭrīḳ; [in Suppl.] Ibn al-Ḳuff
see also Mashāḳa; Paṭrīk
Monophysites al-Akhṭal; al-Ḳuṭāmī
Nestorians Ibn Buṭlān; Ibn al-Ṭayyib; al-Kindī, 'Abd al-Masīḥ; Mattā b. Yūnus; **Nasṭūriyyūn**; Sābūr b. Sahl
Protestants Fāris al-Shidyāḳ; Mashāḳa; [in Suppl.] al-Bustānī.2
see also Nimr
unspecified Baḥdal; Ibn al-Tilmīdh; al-Masīḥī; Petrus Alfonsi; [in Suppl.] Ḥubaysh b. al-Ḥasan al-Dimashḳī; Ibn al-Ṣuḳā'ī
monasteries **Dayr**; Dayr al-Djāthalīḳ; Dayr Ka'b; Dayr Ḳunnā; Dayr Murrān; Dayr Sam'ān
see also Khānḳāh; Rāhib
polemics
anti-Jewish Petrus Alfonsi
pre-Islamic Abraha; 'Adī b. Zayd; 'Amr b. 'Adī; 'Amr b. Hind; Baḥīrā; Bahrām
see also Ghassān; Lakhmids
saints Djirdjīs; Djuraydj
20th-century al-Khūrī; [in Suppl.] Abū Shabaka; Abyaḍ
see also al-Ma'lūf

CIRCUMCISION Khafḍ; **Khitān**
see also 'Abdī; 'Alī; Kurds.iv.A.i; Mawākib.4.11

CLOTHING Banīḳa; Djallāb; Farw; Ḳumāsh; **Libās**
see also Ghiyār; Iḥrām; Khayyāṭ; Khil'a; Kurds.iv.C.1, *and* → MYSTICISM.DRESS
accessories Mandīl; Mirwaḥa
headwear Ḳawuḳlu
veils Ḥidjāb.I; Lithām
materials Farw; Ḥarīr; Kattān; Khaysh; Ḳuṭn
see also Fanak; Ḳalamkārī; Ḳumāsh; Lubūd; Mukhattam

COLOUR **Lawn**; Musawwida
and → DYEING
colours Asfar

COMMERCE Bay'; Imtiyāzāt; Kasb; Ḳirāḍ
see also Inshā'; *and* → INDUSTRY; LAW.LAW OF OBLIGATIONS

commercio-legal terms Mufāwaḍa; Mushāraka
functions Dallāl; Malik al-Tudjdjār
trade Ḳahwa; Kārimī; Ḳuṭn; Lubān
see also Kalah; Kārwān; Ḳaysāriyya; Kirmān; Mīnā'; Ṣafawids.II

COMMONWEALTH OF INDEPENDENT STATES → CAUCASUS; CENTRAL ASIA; COMMUNISM; EUROPE.EASTERN EUROPE

COMMUNICATIONS Barīd; Ḥamām; Manār
see also Anadolu.iii.(5); *and* → TRANSPORT

COMMUNISM Ḥizb.i
see also Lāhūtī

CONGO **Congo**; al-Murdjibī

COSMETICS al-Kuḥl
see also Khiḍāb

COSMOGRAPHY ʿAdjā'ib; ʿĀlam; Falak; Ḳāf; Samā'.1
see also Djughrāfiyā; al-Khaḍir; Kharīṭa; al-Kura; Makka.4; *and* → ASTROLOGY; ASTRONOMY; GEOGRAPHY
treatises on al-Dimashḳī; al-Ḳazwīnī, Zakariyyā'; al-Kharaḳī
see also Kitāb al-Djilwa

COURT CEREMONY **Marāsim**; Mawākib
see also Hiba; Khilʿa; Miẓalla; Naḳḳāra-khāna; Nithār

CREATION **Ibdāʿ**; **Khalḳ**
see also Ḥudūth al-ʿĀlam; Insān

CRETE **Iḳrīṭish**
see also Abū Ḥafṣ ʿUmar al-Ballūṭī
toponyms
towns Ḳandiya

CRUSADE(R)S **Crusades**; [in Suppl.] Dāwiyya and Isbitāriyya
see also al-ʿĀdil.1; al-Afḍal b. Badr al-Djamālī; (Sīrat) ʿAntar; Ayyūbids; Balak; Baybars I; Fāṭimids.5; Ifrandj; Ḳalāwūn; Ḳïlïdj Arslan I; Nūr al-Dīn Maḥmūd b. Zankī; Ṣalāḥ al-Dīn; *and* → *the section Toponyms under* PALESTINE *and* SYRIA
battles al-Manṣūra; Mardj al-Ṣuffar; Nīkbūlī

castles al-Dārūm; Ḥārim; Ḥiṣn al-Akrād; Ḳalʿat al-Shaḳīf; Ṣāfītha
conquests ʿAkkā; Anadolu.iii.1; ʿĀsḳalān; Ayla; Ghazza; Ḥayfā; Ḳayṣariyya; al-Khalīl; Ḳubrus.2; al-Ḳuds.10; Ludd; Maʿarrat al-Nuʿmān
historians of Ibn al-Ḳalānisī
see also al-Nuwayrī, Muḥammad

CRYPTOGRAPHY **Muʿammā**; Ramz.2

CUISINE **Maṭbakh**
drinks Čay; Ḳahwa; Khamr; Kumis; **Mashrūbāt**; Nabīdh
see also Naḥl; [in Suppl.] Čāy-khāna
food **Ghidhāʾ**; Kabid.5; Khubz; Kuskusū; Mishmish; Nārandj; al-Ruzz; al-Samn; [in Suppl.] Basbās; Djawz; Ḥays; Hindibāʾ
see also Baḳḳāl; Filāḥa; Ḳamḥ; Maḍīra; Milḥ; Naḥl; Pist; [in Suppl.] Ibn Shaḳrūn al-Miknāsī
prohibitions Ghidhāʾ.iii and iv.7; Ḳahwa; Khamr; Mashrūbat; Mayta; Nabīdh
see also Dhabīḥa.1; Ḥayawān.4; Nadjis; *and → individual articles under* ANIMALS
spices Kammūn; Ḳaranful; [in Suppl.] **Afāwīh**; Dār Ṣīnī
see also Kārimī; Ḳūṣ; Milḥ

CUSTOM **ʿĀda**; Adab
see also Abd al-Raḥmān al-Fāsī; ʿĀshūrāʾ.II; Hiba; Ḥidjāb.I; Īdjāra; Khilʿa; Mandīl; *and →* LAW.CUSTOMARY LAW
tribal customs ʿAbābda; al-Dhunūb, Dafn; Khāwa; Muwāraba; [in Suppl.] ʿĀr
see also Idjāra

CYPRUS **Ḳubrus**; Madjlis.4.A.xxiv
toponyms
towns Lefḳosha; Maghōsha

(former) CZECHOSLOVAKIA [in Suppl.] **Čeh**

D

DEATH Djanāza; Ḥināṭa; Intiḥār; Ḳabr; Maḳbara; **Mawt**; Niyāḥa; [in Suppl.] Ghassāl
see also Ghāʾib; Ghusl; Ḳatl; Marthiya; *and →* ARCHITECTURE.MONUMENTS.TOMBS; ESCHATOLOGY

DESERTS al-Aḥḳāf; Biyābānak; al-Dahnāʾ; Ḳaraḳum; Ḳizil-ḳum; al-Naḳb; al-

Rubʿ al-Khālī; Sāḥil; al-Ṣaḥrāʾ
see also (Djazīrat) al-ʿArab.ii; Badw.II; Ḥarra; Khabrāʾ; Reg; Samūm

Dictionary **Ḳāmūs**
see also Fāris al-Shidyāḳ; *and* → Lexicography

Diplomacy Imtiyāzāt; Mübādele
see also Amān; Bālyōs; Berātli̊; Daftar; Hiba; Inshāʾ; Kātib; Ḳawwās; Mandates
diplomatic accounts Aḥmad Rasmī; Ibn Faḍlān; Meḥmed Yirmisekiz; [in Suppl.] al-Ghazzāl; Ibn ʿUthmān al-Miknāsī
diplomats Consul; Elči; Safīr.2

Divination **Kihāna**
see also Djafr; Ibn Barradjān; Malāḥim; Nudjūm (Aḥkām al-); *and* → Astrology; Dreams
diviners ʿArrāf; Kāhin
practices Faʾl; Firāsa; Ghurāb; Ḥisāb al-Djummal; Ḥurūf; Ikhtilādj; Istiḳsām; ʿIyāfa; al-Kaff; Katif; Khaṭṭ; Khawāṣṣ al-Ḳurʾān; Ḳiyāfa; Ḳurʿa; Māʾ.1; Riyāfa
see also Būḳalā; Ikhtiyārāt; Mirʾāt
treatises on Fāl-nāma; Ibn al-Bannāʾ al-Marrākushī; Malḥama; [in Suppl.] Ibn ʿAzzūz
see also Djafr; Nudjūm (Aḥkām al-)

(Divine) Punishment **ʿAdhāb**; ʿAdhāb al-Ḳabr; Djazāʾ.ii; Falaḳa; Ḥadd; Maskh; Ṣalb
see also ʿAbd.3.i; ʿĀd; Kaffāra; Ḳiyāma; Munkar wa-Nakīr; Murtadd; *and* → Law

Divorce Barāʾa.I; Faskh
see also ʿAbd.3; ʿĀda; Ghāʾib; Ḥaḍāna; Ibn Suraydj; ʿIdda; ʿIwaḍ; Ḳasam; Liʿān; al-Marʾa.2; Rapak

Documents ʿAlāma; **Diplomatic**; Farmān; Inshāʾ; Kātib; Manshūr; Papyrus; [in Suppl.] Dabīr
see also Barāʾa.I; Ḳaṭʿ; *and* → Administration.records; Writing
Ottoman ʿArḍ Ḥāl; Berāt; **Diplomatic**.iv; Farmān.ii; Irāde; Khaṭṭ-i̊ Humāyūn and Khaṭṭ-i̊ Sherīf
and → Ottoman Empire.administration

Dreams **Ruʾyā**

see also Istikhāra; Nubuwwa; *and individual articles on animals, in particular* Ayyil; Baghl; Ḍabb; Fīl; Ghurāb
treatises on al-Dīnawarī, Abū Saʿīd; Ibn Ghannām; Ibn Shāhīn al-Ẓāhirī; Ibn Sīrīn

DRUGS **Adwiya**; [in Suppl.] Anzarūt
see also Kahrubā; al-Kuḥl; *and* → MEDICINE; PHARMACOLOGY
narcotics Afyūn; Bandj; Ḥashīsh; Ḳāt
see also Filāḥa.iii

DRUZES al-Darazī; **Durūz**; Ḥamza b. ʿAlī; al-Muḳtanā; [in Suppl.] Binn
see also Ḥadd; Maḥkama.4.ii, iii and v; Maʿn; [in Suppl.] Dawr; Ḥinn; *and* → LEBANON
historians of Ṣāliḥ b. Yaḥyā

DYEING ʿAfṣ; Ḥinnāʾ; Ḳalamkārī; Khiḍāb; Nīl
dyer **Ṣabbāgh**

DYNASTIES **Dawla**; Ḥādjib; Mushīr
see also Čāshna-gīr; Khādim al-Ḥaramayn; Laḳab; Libās.i; Malik; Marāsim; Mashwara; Mawākib; Pādishāh; Parda-dār; *and* → ADMINISTRATION; ONOMASTICS.TITLES
Afghanistan and India ʿĀdil-Shāhs; Arghūn; Bahmanīs; Barīd Shāhīs; Dihlī Sultanate; Fārūḳids; Ghaznawids; Ghūrids; Hindū-shāhīs; ʿImād Shāhī; Kart; Khaldjīs; Ḳuṭb Shāhī; Lōdīs; Mughals; Niẓām Shāhīs; [in Suppl.] Bānīdjūrids
see also Afghānistān.v.2 and 3; Awadh; Burhān al-Mulk; Dāwūdpōtrās; Dīwān.v; Hind.iv; Khʷadja-i Djahān; Kōtwāl; Lashkar; Marāsim.5; Mawākib.5; Nithār; Rānā Sāngā; Sammā; [in Suppl.] Fakhr-i Mudabbir; *and* → ARCHITECTURE.REGIONS; MILITARY.INDO-MUSLIM
ʿĀdil-Shāhs (1490-1686) **ʿĀdil-Shāhs**; Bīdjāpūr; Hind.vii.ix
rulers Muḥammad b. Ibrāhīm II
Awadh Nawwābs (1722-1856) **Awadh**
rulers Ghāzi ʾl-Dīn Ḥaydar; Saʿādat ʿAlī Khān; Ṣafdar Djang
viziers Mahdī ʿAlī Khān
Bahmanids (1347-1527) **Bahmanīs**; Hind.vii.vii
see also Bīdar; Gulbargā; Pēshwā
rulers Humāyūn Shāh Bahmanī; Maḥmūd Shihāb al-Dīn; Muḥammad I; Muḥammad II; Muḥammad III
other personages Khalīl Allāh; Maḥmūd Gāwān
Barakzays (1819-1973) **Afghānistān**.v.3.B
kings ʿAbd al-Raḥmān Khān; Ḥabīb Allāh Khān; [in Suppl] Amān Allāh

Bengal Sultans (1336-1576)
sultans Dāwūd Khān Kararānī; Fakhr al-Dīn Mubārakshāh; Ḥusayn Shāh; Maḥmūd; Rādjā Ganesh; Rukn al-Dīn Bārbak Shāh
historians of [in Suppl.] ʿAbbās Sarwānī
Dihlī Sultans (1206-1555) Ḍarība.6.a; **Dihlī Sultanate**; Dīwān.v; Nāʾib.1; Naḳīb.2
see also Burdj.III.2
sultans Fīrūz Shāh Tughluḳ; Ghiyāth al-Dīn Tughluḳ I; Ghiyāth al-Dīn Tughluḳ Shāh II; Iltutmish; Kayḳubād; Khiḍr Khān; Ḳuṭb al-Dīn Aybak; Maḥmūd; Ibrāhīm Lōdī; Mubārak Shāh; Muḥammad b. Tughluḳ; Muḥammad Shāh I Khaldjī; Raḍiyya; [in Suppl.] Balban; Dawlat Khān Lōdī
viziers Kāfūr (*and* Malik Kāfūr); Khān-i Djahān Maḳbūl; Miʾān Bhuʾā
historians of Baranī; al-Djuzdjānī; Niẓāmī (*and* [in Suppl.] Ḥasan Niẓāmī)
other personages Mallū Iḳbāl Khān; [in Suppl.] ʿAbd al-Wahhāb Bukhārī; ʿAyn al-Mulk Multānī; Daryā Khān Noḥānī; Ikhtisān
see also ʿAlī Mardān; Hūlāgū; Khaldjīs; Sammā
Durrānīs (1747-1842)
kings Aḥmad Shāh Durrānī
historians of ʿAbd al-Karīm Munshī
other personages Kāmrān Shāh Durrānī
Fārūḳids (1370-1601)
rulers Mīrān Muḥammad Shāh I
Ghaznawids (977-1186) ʿAmīd; Dīwān.v; **Ghaznawids**
see also Ḥiṣār.iii
rulers Alp Takīn; Bahrām Shāh; Ismāʿīl b. Sebüktigin; Maḥmūd b. Sebüktigin; Masʿūd b. Maḥmūd; Mawdūd b. Masʿūd; Muḥammad b. Maḥmūd b. Sebüktigin
viziers Aḥmad b. Muḥammad; Altūntāsh; al-Faḍl b. Aḥmad al-Isfarāʾinī; Ḥasanak; Maymandī
historians of Bayhaḳī
see also al-Ḳāshānī; [in Suppl.] Fakhr-i Mudabbir
other personages Muḥammad Bakhtiyār Khaldjī
Ghūrids (ca. 1000-1215)
rulers Djahān-sūz; Muḥammad b. Sām
see also Niẓāmī
Gudjarāt Sultans (1391-1583)
sultans Bahādur Shāh Gudjarātī; Maḥmūd
historians of [in Suppl.] Ḥādjdjī al-Dabīr
other personages Malik Ayāz
Kālpī Sultans

sultans Maḥmūd Khān

Kashmīr Sultans (1346-1589)

sultans [in Suppl.] Čaks

see also [in Suppl.] Gul Khātūn

historians of [in Suppl.] Ḥaydar Malik

other personages [in Suppl.] Bayhaḳī Sayyids

Langāh dynasty of Multān

sultans Ḥusayn Shāh Langāh I; Ḥusayn Shāh Langāh II

Madura Sultans

sultans Djalāl al-Dīn Aḥsan

Mālwā Sultans (1401-1531)

sultans Dilāwar Khān; Hūshang Shāh Ghūrī; Maḥmūd

see also Bāz Bahādur

viziers Mēdinī Rāʾī

other personages Malik Mughīth

Mughals (1526-1858) Ḍarība.6.b and c; Dīwān.v; Manṣab; **Mughals**; [in Suppl.] Ilāhī Era

see also Fawdjdār; Kōtwāl; Maṭbakh.4; Nithār; Ṣadr.5; [in Suppl.] Dāgh u taṣḥīḥa; ʿIbādat Khāna

emperors Aḥmad Shāh.I; Akbar; Awrangzīb; Bābur; Bahādur Shāh I; Bahādur Shāh II; Djahāndār Shāh; Djahāngīr; Farrukh-siyar; Humāyūn; Muḥammad Shāh

see also Darshan; Mumtāz Maḥall; Nūr Djahān

viziers Iʿtimād al-Dawla

secretaries Abu ʾl-Faḍl ʿAllāmī; Muḥammad Kāẓim

historians of ʿAbd al-Ḥamīd Lāhawrī; Abu ʾl Faḍl ʿAllāmī; Bakhtāwar Khān; Djawhar; Ghulām Ḥusayn Khān Ṭabaṭabaʾī; ʿInāyat Allāh Khān; Īsar-dās; Khʷāfī Khān; Muḥammad Kāẓim; Muḥammad Sharīf; Mustaʿidd Khān; Muʿtamad Khān; Niʿmat Allāh b. Ḥabīb Allāh Harawī; Nūr al-Ḥaḳḳ al-Dihlawī; [in Suppl.] ʿĀḳil Khān Rāzī

see also Aẓfarī; Badāʾūnī; Maʾathir al-Umarāʾ

other personages ʿAbd al-Raḥīm Khān; ʿAlī Werdī Khān; Āṣaf Khān; Bakhtāwar Khān; Bayram Khān; Burhān al-Mulk; Dāniyāl; Ghulām Ḳādir Rohilla; Hindāl; Iʿtibār Khān; Iʿtiḳād Khān; ʿIwaḍ Wadjīh; Kāmrān; Khān Djahān Lōdī; Khusraw Sulṭān; Mahābat Khān; Makhdūm al-Mulk (*and* [in Suppl.] ʿAbd Allāh Sulṭānpūrī); Mān Singh; Mīr Djumla; Mīrzā ʿAskarī; Mīrzā ʿAzīz "Kōka"; Murād; Murād Bakhsh; Murshid Ḳulī Khān; Niẓām al-Mulk; [in Suppl.] Akbar b. Awrangzīb; ʿĀḳil Khān Rāzī; Ghāzī Khān; Gūran; ʿInāyat Khān (2x)

see also Bāra Sayyids *(and* [in Suppl.] Bārha Sayyids); Marāthās

Niẓām Shāhids (1491-1633) **Niẓām Shāhīs**

rulers Ḥusayn Niẓām Shāh; Malik Aḥmad Baḥrī
other personages Malik ʿAmbar
Sharḳī Sultans of Djawnpūr (1394-1479)
sultans Ḥusayn Shāh; Ibrāhīm Shāh Sharḳī; Maḥmūd Shāh Sharḳī; Malik Sarwar

Africa Fundj; Gwandu
see also Bū Saʿīd; Dār Fūr

Anatolia and the Turks Artuḳids; Aydîn-oghlu; Dānishmendids; Dhu 'l-Ḳadr; Eretna; Germiyān-oghullarî; Ḥamīd Oghullarî; Īnāl; Isfendiyār Oghlu; Ḳarāmān-oghullarî; Ḳarasî; Menteshe-oghullarî; ʿOthmānlî; Saltuḳ Oghullarî
see also Būrids; Derebey; Mangîts; Mengüček; Ramaḍān Oghullarî; *and* → ONOMASTICS.TITLES
Artuḳids (1102-1408)
rulers Īlghāzī; Nūr al-Dīn Muḥammad
Aydîn-oghlu (1308-1425)
amīrs Djunayd
Ottomans (1281-1924) **ʿOthmānlî**
see also ʿOthmān I; *and* → OTTOMAN EMPIRE; TURKEY.OTTOMAN PERIOD
sultans ʿAbd al-ʿAzīz; ʿAbd al-Ḥamīd I; ʿAbd al-Ḥamīd II; ʿAbd al-Madjīd I; ʿAbd al-Madjīd II; Aḥmad I; Aḥmad II; Aḥmad III; Bāyazīd I; Bāyazīd II; Ibrāhīm; Maḥmūd; Meḥemmed I; Meḥemmed II; Meḥemmed III; Meḥemmed IV; Meḥemmed V Reshād; Meḥemmed VI Waḥīd al-Dīn; Murād I; Murād II; Murād III; Murād IV; Murād V; Muṣṭafā I; Muṣṭafā II; Muṣṭafā III; Muṣṭafā IV; Orkhan; ʿOthmān I; ʿOthmān II; ʿOthmān III
see also Bāb-i Humāyūn; Djem; Ertoghrul; Khādim al-Ḥaramayn; Khalīfa.i.E; Khurrem; Kösem Wālide; Mashwara; Muhr.1; Muṣṭafā.1 and 2; Müteferriḳa; Nīlūfer Khātūn; Nūr Bānū; Rikāb; Ṣafiyye Wālide Sulṭān
grand viziers **Ṣadr-ı Aʿẓam**
14th century ʿAlī Pasha Čandārlî-zāde; Djandarlî
15th century Aḥmad Pasha Gedik; Dāwūd Pasha, Kodja; Djandarlî; Khalīl Pasha Djandarlî; Maḥmūd Pasha; Meḥmed Pasha, Ḳaramānī; Meḥmed Pasha, Rūm
16th century Aḥmad Pasha, Ḳara; ʿAlī Pasha Khādim; ʿAlī Pasha Semiz; Ayās Pasha; Čighāla-zāde Sinān Pāshā; Derwīsh Pasha; Ferhād Pasha; Hersek-zāde; Ibrāhīm Pasha; Ibrāhīm Pasha, Dāmād; Khādîm Ḥasan Pasha Ṣoḳollî; Khādîm Süleymān Pasha; Lala Meḥmed Pasha (*and* Meḥmed Pasha, Lālā, Shāhīnoghlu); Luṭfī Pasha; Meḥmed Pasha, Lālā, Melek-Nihād; Mesīḥ Meḥmed Pasha; Mesīḥ Pasha; ʿOthmān Pasha; Pīrī Meḥmed Pasha; Rüstem Pasha

17th century ʿAlī Pasha ʿArabadjï; ʿAlī Pasha Güzeldje; ʿAlī Pasha Sürmeli; Dāwūd Pasha, Ḳara; Derwīsh Meḥmed Pasha; Dilāwar Pasha; Ḥāfiẓ Aḥmed Pasha; Ḥusayn Pasha; Ibrāhīm Pasha, Kara; Ipshir Muṣṭafā Pasha; Ismāʿīl Pasha, Nishāndjï; Ḳarā Muṣṭafā Pasha; Kemānkesh; Khalīl Pasha Ḳayṣariyyeli; Khosrew Pasha, Bosniak; Köprülü.I-III; Meḥmed Pasha, Čerkes; Meḥmed Pasha, Elmās; Meḥmed Pasha, Gürdjü, Khādïm; Meḥmed Pasha, Gürdjü II; Meḥmed Pasha, Öküz; Meḥmed Pasha, Sulṭān-zāde; Meḥmed Pasha, Tabanïyassï; Murād Pasha, Ḳuyudju; Naṣūḥ Pasha; Redjeb Pasha

18th century ʿAbd Allāh Pasha; ʿAlī Pasha Čorlulu; ʿAlī Pasha Dāmād; ʿAlī Pasha Ḥakīm-oghlu; Derwīsh Meḥmed Pasha; Ḥamza Ḥāmid Pasha; Ḥamza Pasha; (Damād) Ḥasan Pasha; (Seyyid) Ḥasan Pasha; (Sherīf) Ḥasan Pasha; Ibrāhīm Pasha, Nevshehirli; Kaḥyā Ḥasan Pasha; Khalīl Pasha Ḥādjdjī Arnawud; Köprülü.V; Meḥmed Pasha, Balṭadjï; Meḥmed Pasha, ʿIwaḍ; Meḥmed Pasha, Melek; Meḥmed Pasha, Muḥsin-zāde; Meḥmed Pasha Rāmī (*and* Rāmī Meḥmed Pasha); Meḥmed Pasha, Tiryāḳī; Meḥmed Pasha, Yegen, Gümrükčü; Meḥmed Pasha, Yegen, Ḥādjdjī; Rāghib Pasha; Saʿīd Efendi

19th century and on Aḥmad Wafīḳ Pasha; ʿAlī Pasha Muḥammad Amīn; Dāmād Ferīd Pasha; Derwīsh Meḥmed Pasha; Djawād Pasha; Fuʾād Pasha; Ḥusayn ʿAwnī Pasha; Ḥusayn Ḥilmī Pasha; Ibrāhīm Edhem Pasha; Ibrāhīm Ḥaḳḳī Pasha; ʿIzzet Pasha; Kečiboynuzu; Khayr al-Dīn Pasha; Khosrew Pasha, Meḥmed; Küčük Saʿīd Pasha; Maḥmūd Nedīm Pasha; Maḥmūd Shewkat Pasha; Meḥmed Saʿīd Ghālib Pasha; Midḥat Pasha; Muṣṭafā Pasha, Bayraḳdār; Reshīd Pasha, Muṣṭafā; [in Suppl.] Esʿad Pasha

see also Bāb-i ʿĀlı; Başvekil; Ḳapï; ʿOthmān-zāde

grand muftis Abu ʾl-Suʿūd; ʿĀrif Ḥikmet Bey; Bahāʾī Meḥmed Efendi; Bostānzāde.2; Čelebi-zāde; Čiwi-zāde; Djamāl al-Dīn Efendi; Dürrīzāde.1-5; Dürrīzāde, ʿAbd Allāh; Esʿad Efendi, Aḥmed; Esʿad Efendi, Meḥmed (3x); Fenārī-zāde; Gūrānī; Ḥasan Fehmī; Ḥayātī-zāde.2; Ḳarā-Čelebi-zāde.4; Kemāl Pasha-zāde; Khōdja Efendi; Khosrew; Meḥmed Ṣāliḥ Efendi; Muṣṭafā Khayrī Efendi; Pīrī-zāde

see also Bāb-i Mashīkhat; Fatwā.ii

high admirals ʿAlī Pasha Güzeldje; Čighāla-zāde Sinān Pasha; Djaʿfar Beg; Djezāʾirli Ghāzī Ḥasan Pasha; Ḥasan Pasha; Ḥusayn Pasha; Kenʿān Pasha; Khalīl Pasha Ḳayṣariyyeli; Khayr al-Dīn Pasha; Piyāle Pasha

see also Raʾīs.3

historians of ʿAbdī; ʿAbdī Efendi; ʿAbdī Pasha; Aḥmad Djewdet Pasha; Aḥmad Rasmī; ʿAlī; ʿAlī Amīrī; ʿĀshïḳ-pasha-zāde; ʿĀṣim; ʿAṭāʾ Bey;

al-Bakrī.1; Bidlīsī; Bihishtī; Čelebi-zāde; Česhmīzāde; Djalālzāde Muṣṭafā Čelebi; Djalālzāde Ṣāliḥ Čelebi; Enwerī; Esʿad Efendi, Meḥmed; Ḥasan Bey-zāde; ʿIzzī; Ḳarā-čelebi-zāde.4; Kātib Čelebi; Kemāl, Meḥmed Nāmiḳ; Kemāl Pasha-zāde; Khayr Allāh Efendi; Luḳmān b. Sayyid Ḥusayn; Luṭfī Efendi; Maṭrāḳči; Meḥmed Ḥākim Efendi; Meḥmed Khalīfe b. Ḥüseyn; Meḥmed Pasha, Ḳaramānī; Meḥmed Zaʿīm; Muḥyi 'l-Dīn Meḥmed; Naʿīmā; ʿOthmān-zāde; Pečewī; Ramaḍān-zāde; Rāshid, Meḥmed; Rūḥī

see also Ḥadīdī

other personages

14th century ʿAlāʾ al-Dīn Beg; Badr al-Dīn b. Ḳāḍī Samāwnā; Ḳāsim.1

15th century Aḥmad Pasha Khāʾin; Ewrenos; Ewrenos Oghullari; Fenārī-zāde; Ḳāsim.2 and 3; Ḳāsim Pasha, Djazarī; Mūsā Čelebi; Muṣṭafā.1 and 2

16th century Bostānzāde; Čiwi-zāde; Derwīsh Pasha; Djaʿfar Čelebi; Djalālzāde Muṣṭafā Čelebi; Ferīdūn Beg; Ḳāsim.4; Ḳāsim Agha; Ḳāsim Pasha; Kemāl Reʾīs; Khosrew Pasha; Ḳorḳud b. Bāyazīd; Maḥmūd Pasha; Maḥmūd Tardjumān; Meḥmed Pasha, Biyiḳli; Muṣṭafā.3; Muṣṭafā Pasha, Ḳara Shāhīn; Muṣṭafā Pasha, Lala; Muṣṭafā Pasha al-Nashshār; Özdemir Pasha; Pertew Pasha.I; Ramaḍān-zāde; Riḍwān Pasha

17th century Ābāza; Ḥaydar-oghlu, Meḥmed; Ḥusayn Pasha; Ḳāsim.5; Ḳāṭirdjī-oghli Meḥmed Pasha; Maʿn-zāda; Meḥmed Khalīfe b. Ḥüseyn; ʿOthmān Pasha, Yegen; [in Suppl.] Aḥmad Pasha Küčük; Čōbān-oghullari

18th century Ābāza; Aḥmad Pasha; Aḥmad Pasha Bonneval; Aḥmad Rasmī; Djānīkli Ḥādjdji ʿAlī Pasha; Meḥmed Ḥākim Efendi; Meḥmed Yirmisekiz; Paswan-oghlu; Patrona Khalīl

19th century and on ʿAbd al-Ḥaḳḳ Ḥāmid; Aḥmad Djewdet Pasha; ʿAlī Pasha Tepedelenli; Ayyūb Ṣabrī Pasha; Bahdjat Muṣṭafā Efendi; Dāwūd Pasha (2x); Djawād Pasha; Djāwīd; Djemāl Pasha; Enwer Pasha; Fāḍil Pasha; Fehīm Pasha; Ḥālet Efendi; Hāmōn; Ḥasan Fehmī; Ḥusayn Pasha; Ibn ʿArabshāh; Ibrāhīm Derwīsh Pasha; ʿIzzet Pasha; Kabakči-oghlu Muṣṭafā; Kāẓim Ḳadrī; Kāẓim Karabekir; Ḳōzān-oghullari; Mukhtār Pasha; Münīf Pasha; Muṣṭafā Pasha, Bushatli; Pertew Pasha.II; Riḍwān Begović; Ṣādiḳ Rifʿat Pasha; [in Suppl.] Camondo

Saldjūḳs of Rūm (1077-1307) **Saldjūḳids**

rulers Kaykāʾūs; Kaykhusraw; Kayḳubād; Ḳilidj Arslan I; Ḳilidj Arslan II; Ḳilidj Arslan III; Ḳilidj Arslan IV; Malik-Shāh.4

historians of Ibn Bībī

other personages Ashraf Oghullarï; Muʿīn al-Dīn Sulaymān Parwāna; Saʿd al-Dīn Köpek

Arabian Peninsula Bū Saʿīd; Hamdānids; Hāshimids (2x); āl-Khalīfa; Mahdids; Nadjāḥids; Rashīd, Āl; Rasūlids; Ṣabāḥ, Āl; [in Suppl.] Djabrids

Āl Saʿūd (1746-)

rulers [in Suppl.] ʿAbd al-ʿAzīz; Fayṣal b. ʿAbd al-ʿAzīz

see also Muḥammad b. Suʿūd

Bū Saʿīd (1741-) **Bū Saʿīd**

sultans Barghash; Saʿīd b. Sulṭān

Carmathians (894-end 11th century)

rulers al-Djannābī, Abū Saʿīd; al-Djannābī, Abū Ṭāhir

Hāshimids (1908-1925)

rulers Ḥusayn (b. ʿAlī)

see also ʿAbd Allāh b. al-Ḥusayn; Fayṣal I; Fayṣal II

Rasūlids (1229-1454) **Rasūlids**

historians of al-Khazradjī

other personages [in Suppl.] Ibn Ḥatim

Ṭāhirids (1454-1517)

rulers ʿĀmir I; ʿĀmir II

Zaydīs (860-) Rassids

imāms Ḥasan al Uṭrūsh; al-Mahdī li-Dīn Allāh Aḥmad; al-Manṣūr bi ʾllāh, ʿAbd Allāh; al-Manṣūr bi ʾllāh, al-Ḳāsim b. ʿAlī; al-Manṣūr bi ʾllāh, al-Ḳāsim b. Muḥammad; al-Muʾayyad bi ʾllāh Muḥammad; Muḥammad al-Murtaḍā li-Dīn Allāh; al-Mutawakkil ʿalā ʾllāh, Ismāʿīl; al-Mutawakkil ʿalā ʾllāh, Sharaf al-Dīn; al-Nāṣir li-Dīn Allah, Aḥmad; al-Rassī; [in Suppl.] al-Ḥādī ila ʾl-Ḥaḳḳ

see also Imāma

other personages al-Muṭahhar; al-Nāṣir li-Dīn Allāh

Zurayʿids (1138-1174)

viziers Bilāl b. Djarīr al-Muḥammadī

Egypt and the Fertile Crescent ʿAbbāsids; ʿAnnazids; Ayyūbids; Bābān; Būrids; Fāṭimids; Ḥamdānids; Ḥasanwayh; Mamlūks; Marwānids; Mazyad; Mirdās

see also ʿAmmār; Begteginids; Djalīlī; Ṣadaḳa, Banū; *and* → EGYPT.MODERN PERIOD.MUḤAMMAD ʿALĪ'S LINE

ʿAbbāsids (749-1258) → CALIPHATE

Ayyūbids (1169-end 15th century) **Ayyūbids**

see also Rank

rulers al-ʿĀdil; al-Afḍal; Bahrām Shāh; al-Kāmil; al-Muʿaẓẓam; al-Nāṣir; Ṣalāḥ al-Dīn; (al-Malik) al-Ṣāliḥ ʿImād al-Dīn; (al-Malik) al-Ṣāliḥ Nadjm al-Dīn Ayyūb

see also Dīwān.ii.(3)

viziers Ibn al-ʿAdīm; Ibn al-Athīr.3; Ibn Maṭrūḥ

secretaries ʿImād al-Dīn; al-Ḳāḍī al-Fāḍil
historians of Abu ʾl-Fidā; Abū Shāma; Ibn Shaddād; ʿImād al-Dīn; al-Maḳrīzī; al-Manṣūr, al-Malik
other personages Abu ʾl-Fidā; Aybak; Ibn al-ʿAssāl; Ḳarāḳūsh, Bahāʾ al-Dīn; Ḳarāḳūsh, Sharaf al-Dīn; al-Muẓaffar, al-Malik
Fāṭimids (909-1171) → CALIPHATE
Ḥamdānids (905-1004)
rulers Nāṣir al-Dawla; [in Suppl.] Abū Taghlib
other personages Ḥusayn b. Ḥamdān; Luʾluʾ
Ikhshīdids (935-969)
rulers Kāfūr
viziers Ibn al-Furāt.5
Mamlūks (1250-1517) Dhu ʾl-Faḳāriyya; Dīwān.ii.(4); Ḥādjib.iv; Hiba.ii; Khādim al-Ḥaramayn; Khaznadār; **Mamlūks**; Mashwara; Nāʾib.1
see also Ḥarfūsh; Ḳumāsh; Mamlūk; Manshūr; Rank; *and* → MILITARY.MAMLUK
sultans Barḳūḳ; Barsbāy; Baybars I; Baybars II; Čaḳmaḳ; Faradj; Ḥasan; Īnāl al-Adjrūd; Ḳāʾit Bāy; Ḳalāwūn; Ḳānṣawh al-Ghawrī; Khalīl; Khushḳadam; Ḳuṭuz; Lādjīn; al-Muʾayyad Shaykh; al-Nāṣir; (al-Malik) al-Ṣāliḥ
administrators Faḍl Allāh; Ibn ʿAbd al-Ẓāhir; Ibn Faḍl al-ʿUmarī; Ibn Ghurāb; Ibn Ḥidjdja; Ibn al-Sadīd (Ibn al-Muzawwiḳ); Ibn al-Sadīd, Karīm al-Dīn; al-Ḳalḳashandī.1 [in Suppl.] Ibn al-Ṣuḳāʿ
historians of Abu ʾl-Maḥāsin b. Taghrībirdī; Baybars al-Manṣūrī; Ibn ʿAbd al-Ẓāhir; Ibn Duḳmāk; Ibn Ḥabīb, Badr al-Dīn; Ibn Iyās; Ibn Shāhīn al-Ẓāhirī; al-Maḳrīzī; al-Mufaḍḍal b. Abi ʾl-Faḍāʾil; al-Nuwayrī, Shihāb al-Dīn; al-Ṣafadī, al-Ḥasan
other personages Abu ʾl-Fidā; al-ʿAynī; Ibn Djamāʿa; Ibn al-Mundhir
Marwānids (983-1085)
rulers Naṣr al-Dawla
Mazyadids (ca. 961-1150) **Mazyad**; Ṣadaḳa, Banū
rulers Ṣadaḳa b. Manṣūr
Mirdāsids (1023-1079) **Mirdās**
see also Asad al-Dawla
Ṭūlūnids (868-905)
rulers Aḥmad b. Ṭūlūn; Khumārawayh
see also Ibn al-Mudabbir.1
historians of al-Balawī; Ibn al-Dāya
other personages [in Suppl.] al-ʿAbbās b. Aḥmad b. Ṭūlūn
ʿUḳaylids (ca. 990-1096)
rulers Muslim b. Ḳuraysh
Mongols Batuʾids; Čaghatay Khānate; Čingizids; Djalāyir; Djānids; Girāy;

Īlkhāns; Ḳarā Khiṭāy; **Mongols**
see also Čūbānids; Ḳāzān; [in Suppl.] Āgahī; Dīwān-begi; Djamāl Ḳarshī; Ordu.2; *and* → ONOMASTICS.TITLES

Batu'ids (1236-1502)
rulers Batu; Berke; Mangū-tīmūr
other personages Mas'ūd Beg

Čaghatayids (1227-1370)
rulers Burāḳ Khān; Čaghatay Khān
historians of Ḥaydar Mīrzā

Djānids (1598-1785)
rulers Nadhr Muḥammad
see also Bukhāra

Girāy Khāns (ca. 1426-1792)
rulers Dawlat Giray; Ghāzī Girāy I; Ghāzī Girāy II; Ghāzī Girāy III; Ḥādjdjī Girāy; Islām Girāy; Ḳaplan Girāy I; Ḳaplan Girāy II; Meḥmed Girāy I; Mengli Girāy I; Ṣāḥib Girāy Khān I
see also Ḳalghay; Meḥmed Baghčesarāyī; Meḥmed Girāy

Great Khāns (1206-1634)
rulers Činghiz Khān; Ḳubilay; Möngke; Ögedey
other personages Ḳaydu; Maḥmūd Yalawač

Ilkhānids (1256-1353)
see also Ṣadr.2
rulers Baydu; Gaykhātū; Ghāzān; Hūlāgū; Öldjeytü
viziers Sa'd al-Dawla
historians of Ḥamd Allāh al-Mustawfī al-Ḳazwīnī; Rashīd al-Dīn Ṭabīb
other personages Djuwaynī, 'Alā' al-Dīn; Ḳutlugh-Shah Noyan

Shaybānids (1500-1598)
rulers 'Abd Allāh b. Iskandar; Abu 'l-Khayr
historians of Abu 'l-Ghāzī Bahādur Khān; [in Suppl.] Ḥāfiẓ Tanīsh

Persia Afrāsiyābids; Aḥmadīlīs; Aḳ Ḳoyunlu; Bādūsbānids; Bāwand; Buwayhids; Dulafids; Faḍlawayh; Farīghūnids; Ḥasanwayh; Hazāraspids; Ildeñizids; Ilek-Khāns; Ilyāsids; Īndjū; Ḳādjār; Kākūyids; Ḳarā-ḳoyunlu; Ḳārinids; Kāwūs; Khwārazm-shāhs; Ḳutlugh-khānids; Lur-i Buzurg; Lur-i Kūčik; Mangīts; Mar'ashīs; Muḥtādjids; Musāfirids; Musha'sha'; Muẓaffarids; Rawwādids; Ṣafawids; Ṣaffārids; Saldjūḳids; Salghurids; Sāmānids
see also Ardalān; Atabak; 'Awfī; Čāshna-gīr; Daylam; Dīwān.iv; Djalāyir; Ghulām.ii; Ḥādjib.iii; Ḥarb.v; al-Ḥasan b. Zayd b. Muḥammad; Hiba.iv; Ḥiṣār.iii; Īlkhāns; Iran. v; Kayānids; Marāsim.3; Mawākib.3

Afshārids (1736-1795)
rulers Nādir Shāh Afshār

historians of   ʿAbd al-Karīm Ka<u>sh</u>mīrī; Mahdī <u>Kh</u>ān Astarābādī
Buwayhids (932-1062)   **Buwayhids**
  rulers   Abū Kālīdjār; ʿAḍud al-Dawla; Ba<u>kh</u>tiyār; <u>Dj</u>alāl al-Dawla;
    Fa<u>kh</u>r al-Dawla; ʿImād al-Dawla; <u>Kh</u>usraw Fīrūz (*and* al-Malik al-
    Raḥīm); Ma<u>dj</u>d al-Dawla; Muʾayyid al-Dawla; Muʿizz al-Dawla;
    Rukn al-Dawla; Ṣamṣām al-Dawla; [in Suppl.] Bahāʾ al-Dawla wa-
    Ḍiyāʾ al-Milla
  viziers   al-ʿAbbās b. al-Ḥusayn; Ibn ʿAbbād; Ibn al-ʿAmīd; Ibn Baḳiyya;
    Ibn Mākūlā.1 and 2; al-Muhallabī, Abū Muḥammad; Sābūr b.
    Arda<u>sh</u>īr; [in Suppl.] ʿAbd al-ʿAzīz b. Yūsuf; Ibn <u>Kh</u>alaf.1; Ibn Saʿdān
  secretaries   Hilāl al-Ṣābiʾ (*and* Ṣābiʾ.(3).9); Ibn Hindū; Ṣābiʾ.(3).7
  historians of   Ṣābiʾ.(3).7
  other personages   al-Basāsīrī; Fasan<u>dj</u>us; Ḥasan b. Ustā<u>dh</u>-hurmuz; Ibn
    Ḥā<u>dj</u>ib al-Nuʿmān; ʿImrān b. <u>Sh</u>āhīn; al-Malik al-ʿAzīz; [in Suppl.]
    Ibrāhīm <u>Sh</u>īrāzī
Dābūyids (660-760)
  rulers   Dābūya
Ildeñizids (1137-1225)
  rulers   Ildeñiz; Özbeg b. Muḥammad Pahlawān; Pahlawān
Ḳā<u>dj</u>ārs (1779-1924)   **Ḳā<u>dj</u>ār**; Mu<u>sh</u>īr al-Dawla
  see also Ḳāʾim-maḳām-i Farāhānī; Ma<u>dj</u>lis al-<u>Sh</u>ūrā; *and* → IRAN.
    MODERN PERIOD
  rulers   Ā<u>gh</u>ā Muḥammad <u>Sh</u>āh; Fatḥ ʿAlī <u>Sh</u>āh; Muḥammad ʿAlī <u>Sh</u>āh
    Ḳā<u>dj</u>ār; Muḥammad <u>Sh</u>āh; Muẓaffar al-Dīn <u>Sh</u>āh Ḳā<u>dj</u>ār; Nāṣir al-Dīn
    <u>Sh</u>āh
  other personages   ʿAbbās Mīrzā; [in Suppl.] Amīr Niẓām; Ḥā<u>dj</u><u>dj</u>ī
    Ibrāhīm <u>Kh</u>ān Kalāntar
<u>Kh</u>anate of <u>Kh</u>īwa
  rulers   Abu ʾl-<u>Gh</u>āzī Bahādur <u>Kh</u>ān
Kh^wārazm-<u>Sh</u>āhs (ca. 995-1231)
  rulers   Atsïz b. Anū<u>sh</u>tigin; <u>Dj</u>alāl al-Dīn <u>Kh</u>^wārazm-<u>sh</u>āh; Maʾmūn b.
    Muḥammad
  historians of   <u>Dj</u>uwaynī; al-Nasawī
  other personages   Burāḳ Ḥā<u>dj</u>ib
Muẓaffarids (1314-1393)
  historians of   Muʿīn al-Dīn Yazdī
Pahlawīs (1926-1979)   **Pahlawī**
  and → IRAN.MODERN PERIOD
  rulers   Muḥammad Riḍā <u>Sh</u>āh Pahlawī; Riḍā <u>Sh</u>āh
Sā<u>dj</u>ids (ca. 856- ca. 930)   **Sā<u>dj</u>ids**
  rulers   Abu ʾl-Sā<u>dj</u>; Muḥammad b. Abi ʾl-Sā<u>dj</u>

Ṣafawids (1501-1732) Bārūd.v; Īs̲h̲īk-āḳāsī; Iʿtimād al-Dawla; Ḳūrčī; Libās.iii; **Ṣafawids**
 see also Ḥaydar; Ḳi̊zi̊l-bās̲h̲; Nuḳṭawiyya; Ṣadr.4; Ṣadr al-Dīn Ardabīlī; Ṣadr al-Dīn Mūsā; Ṣafī al-Dīn Ardabīlī
 rulers ʿAbbās I; Ḥusayn; Ismāʿīl I; Ismāʿīl II
 historians of Ḥasan-i Rūmlū; Iskandar Beg; Ḳummī
  see also [in Suppl.] Ibn al-Bazzāz al-Ardabīlī
 other personages Alḳāṣ Mīrzā; Ḥamza Mīrzā; al-Karakī; Madjlisī
Ṣaffārids (867-ca. 1495) **Ṣaffārids**
 rulers ʿAmr b. al-Lay̲t̲h̲
Saldjuḳs (1038-1194) Amīr Dād; Arslan b. Saldjūḳ; Atabak; **Saldjūḳids**
 and → DYNASTIES.ANATOLIA AND THE TURKS.SALDJŪḲS OF RŪM
 rulers Alp Arslan; Bahrām S̲h̲āh; Barkyārūḳ; Maḥmud b. Muḥammad b. Malik-S̲h̲āh; Malik-S̲h̲āh.1-3; Masʿūd b. Muḥammad b. Malik-S̲h̲āh; Muḥammad b. Maḥmūd b. Muḥammad b. Malik-S̲h̲āh; Muḥammad b. Malik-S̲h̲āh; Riḍwān
  see also Čag̲h̲ri̊-beg
 viziers Anūs̲h̲irwān b. K̲h̲ālid; Djahīr; al-Kundurī; Madjd al-Mulk al-Balāsānī; al-Maybudī.3; Niẓām al-Mulk; Rabīb al-Dawla; [in Suppl.] Ibn Dārust
 historians of al-Bundārī; ʿImād al-Dīn; Nīs̲h̲āpūrī; Rāwandī; [in Suppl.] al-Ḥusaynī
 other personages Āḳ Sunḳur al-Bursuḳī; Arslan-Arg̲h̲ūn; Ayāz; al-Basāsīrī; Būrī-bars; Bursuḳ; Büz-abeh; Ḳāwurd; K̲h̲alaf b. Mulāʿib al-As̲h̲habī; K̲h̲āṣṣ Beg; Kurbuḳa; Niẓāmiyya; [in Suppl.] Ekinči
Salg̲h̲urids (1148-1270) **Salg̲h̲urids**
 rulers Saʿd (I) b. Zangī
Sāmānids (819-1005) **Sāmānids**
 rulers Ismāʿīl b. Aḥmad; Ismāʿīl b. Nūḥ; Manṣūr b. Nūḥ; Naṣr b. Aḥmad b. Ismāʿīl; Nūḥ (I); Nūḥ (II)
 viziers Balʿamī; al-Muṣʿabī; [in Suppl.] al-Djayhānī
 historians of Nars̲h̲ak̲h̲ī
  see also al-Sallāmī
 other personages Arslan b. Saldjūḳ; [in Suppl.] al-Djayhānī
Ṭāhirids (821-873)
 rulers ʿAbd Allāh b. Ṭāhir; Muḥammad b. Ṭāhir
 historians of Ibn al-Daybaʿ
 other personages Muḥammad b. ʿAbd Allāh (b. Ṭāhir)
Tīmūrids (1370-1506)
 see also Ṣadr.3
 rulers Abū Saʿīd b. Tīmūr; Bāyḳarā; Bāysong̲h̲or; Ḥusayn
  see also K̲h̲ān-zāda Bēgum

historians of   Ibn ʿArabs̲h̲āh; K̲h̲wāfī K̲h̲ān
other personages   Mīr ʿAlī S̲h̲īr Nawāʾī; Mīrāns̲h̲āh b. Tīmūr
Zands (1750-1794)
   rulers   Karīm K̲h̲ān Zand; Luṭf ʿAlī K̲h̲ān
     see also Lak
Zangids (1127-1222)
   rulers   Masʿūd b. Mawdūd b. Zangī; Mawdūd b. ʿImād al-Dīn Zankī;
     Nūr al-Dīn Arslān S̲h̲āh; Nūr al-Dīn Maḥmūd b. Zankī
   viziers   al-D̲j̲awād al-Iṣfahānī
     see also Begteginids; Karīm K̲h̲ān Zand; Luʾluʾ, Badr al-Dīn
   historians of   Ibn al-At̲h̲īr.2
Ziyārids (927-ca. 1090)
   rulers   Ḳābūs b. Wus̲h̲magīr b. Ziyār; Kay Kāʾūs b. Iskandar;
     Mardāwīd̲j̲
Spain and North Africa   ʿAbbādids; ʿAbd al-Wādids; Afṭasids; Ag̲h̲labids;
   ʿAlawīs; ʿĀmirids; ʿAmmār; D̲h̲u ʾl-Nūnids; D̲j̲ahwarids; Ḥafṣids;
   Ḥammādids; Ḥammūdids; Hūdids; Ḥusaynids; Idrīsids; (Banū) K̲h̲urāsān;
   Marīnids; Midrār; al-Murābiṭūn; al-Muwaḥḥidūn; Naṣrids; Razīn, Banū;
   Rustamids; Saʿdids
   see also ʿAlāma; Dīwān.iii; Ḥād̲j̲ib.ii and v; Hiba.iii; Ḥiṣār.ii; al-Ḥulal al-
   Maws̲h̲iyya; Ḳaramānlī; K̲h̲alīfa.i.C and D; Laḳab.3; Marāsim.2;
   Mawākib.2; Parias; *and* → CALIPHATE.FĀṬIMIDS
ʿAbbādids (1023-1091)   **ʿAbbādids**; Is̲h̲bīliya
   rulers   al-Muʿtaḍid bi ʾllāh; al-Muʿtamid ibn ʿAbbād
     see also al-Rundī
   viziers   Ibn ʿAmmār, Abū Bakr
ʿAbd al-Wādids (1236-1550)
   rulers   Abū Ḥammū I; Abū Ḥammū II; Abū Tās̲h̲ufīn I; Abū Tās̲h̲ufīn
     II; Abū Zayyān I; Abū Zayyān II; Abū Zayyān III
   historians of   Ibn K̲h̲aldūn, Abū Zakariyyāʾ
Afṭasids (1022-1094)
   rulers   al-Mutawakkil ʿalā ʾllāh, Ibn al-Afṭas
   viziers   Ibn Ḳuzmān.II
   secretaries   Ibn ʿAbdūn; Ibn Ḳabṭūrnu
Ag̲h̲labids (800-909)   al-ʿAbbāsiyya; **Ag̲h̲labids**; Raḳḳāda
   rulers   Ibrāhīm I; Ibrāhīm II
ʿAlawids (1631-   )   **ʿAlawīs**; Ḳāʾid; Mawlāy
   rulers   ʿAbd Allāh b. Ismāʿīl; ʿAbd al-ʿAzīz b. al-Ḥasan; ʿAbd al-
   Raḥmān b. His̲h̲ām; Ḥafīẓ (ʿAbd al-); (Mawlāy) al-Ḥasan; Mawlāy
   Ismāʿīl; Muḥammad III b. ʿAbd Allāh; Muḥammad IV b. ʿAbd al-
   Raḥmān; Muḥammad b. Yūsuf (Muḥammad V); al-Ras̲h̲īd (Mawlāy)
   viziers   Akansūs; Ibn Idrīs (I); [in Suppl.] Bā Ḥmād; Ibn ʿUt̲h̲mān al-
   Miknāsī

historians of Akanṣūs; Ibn Zaydān; al-Kardūdī
other personages Aḥmad al-Nāṣirī al-Salāwī (*and* al-Nāṣir al-Salāwī); Ibn Idrīs (II); Khunātha

Almohads (1130-1269) Hargha; al-ʿIḳāb; Mizwār; **al-Muwaḥḥidūn**
rulers ʿAbd al-Muʾmin; Abū Yaʿḳūb Yūsuf; Abū Yūsuf Yaʿḳūb al-Manṣūr; Ibn Tūmart; al-Maʾmūn; al-Nāṣir
historians of ʿAbd al-Wāḥid al-Marrākushī; al-Baydhaḳ; Ibn Ṣāḥib al-Ṣalāt
see also al-Ḥulal al-Mawshiyya
other personages [in Suppl.] Ibn al-Ḳaṭṭān
see also Abū Ḥafṣ ʿUmar al-Hintātī; Ibn Mardanīsh

Almoravids (1056-1147) Amīr al-Muslimīn; **al-Murābiṭūn**
rulers ʿAlī b. Yūsuf b. Tāshufīn; al-Lamtūnī
secretaries Ibn ʿAbdūn
historians of Ibn al-Ṣayrafī
see also al-Ḥulal al-Mawshiyya
other personages Ibn Bādjdja; Ibn Ḳasī

ʿĀmirids (1021-1096)
rulers ʿAbd al-Malik b. Abī ʿĀmir; al-Muẓaffar
viziers Ibn al-Ḳaṭṭāʿ
other personages ʿAbd al-Raḥmān b. Abī ʿĀmir

Djahwarids (1030-1070)
other personages (al-)Ḥakam ibn ʿUk(k)āsha; Ibn ʿAbdūs

Ḥafṣids (1228-1574)
secretaries Ḥāzim
historians of al-Ḥādjdj Ḥammūda
other personages Ibn ʿArafa

Ḥammādids (972-1152)
rulers Bādīs; al-Manṣūr; al-Nāṣir
see also Ḳalʿat Banī Ḥammād

Ḥammūdids (1010-1057)
viziers Ibn Dhakwān

Hūdids (1039-1142)
rulers al-Muʾtamin

Ḥusaynids (1705-1957)
rulers Aḥmad Bey; al-Ḥusayn (b. ʿAlī); Muḥammad Bey; Muḥammad al-Ṣādiḳ Bey
ministers Khayr al-Dīn Pasha; Muṣṭafā Khaznadār

Idrīsids (789-926)
rulers Idrīs I; Idrīs II

Marīnids (1196-1465)
rulers Abu ʾl-Ḥasan; Abū ʿInān Fāris

Naṣrids (1230-1492) **Naṣrids**
viziers Ibn al-Khaṭīb
other personages [in Suppl.] Ibn al-Sarrādj
Rustamids (777-909) **Rustamids**
historians of Ibn al-Ṣaghīr
Saʿdids (1511-1659) **Saʿdids**
rulers ʿAbd Allāh al-Ghālib; Aḥmad al-Manṣūr; Mawlāy Maḥammad al-Shaykh
see also Mawlāy
viziers Ibn ʿĪsā
historians of ʿAbd al-ʿAzīz b. Muḥammad; al-Ifrānī
other personages [in Suppl.] Abū Maḥallī
Tudjībids (1019-1039)
rulers Maʿn b. Muḥammad; al-Muʿtaṣim
ʿUbaydids
historians of Ibn Ḥamādu
Umayyads (756-1031)
amīrs and caliphs ʿAbd Allāh b. Muḥammad; ʿAbd al-Raḥmān; al-Ḥakam I; al-Ḥakam II; Hishām I; Hishām II; Hishām III; al-Mahdī; al-Mundhir b. Muḥammad
see also Madīnat al-Zahrāʾ; Muʿāwiya b. Hishām; Rabaḍ; al-Ruṣāfa.4; [in Suppl.] Bubashtru
viziers Ibn ʿAlḳama.2; Ibn Shuhayd
secretaries ʿArīb b. Saʿd al-Kātib al-Ḳurṭubī; Ibn Burd.I
other personages ʿAbd al-Raḥmān b. Marwān; Ghālib b. ʿAbd al-Raḥmān; Ḥabīb b. ʿAbd al-Malik; Ḥasdāy b. Shaprūṭ; Ibn ʿAlḳama.1; Ibn Dhakwān; Ibn al-Ḥannāṭ; Ibn Ḳasī; Ibn al-Ḳiṭṭ; al-Manṣūr; Rabīʿ b. Zayd
Zīrids (972-1152)
rulers Buluggīn b. Zīrī; al-Muʿizz b. Bādīs
other personages Ibn Abi ʾl-Ridjāl
see also Ḳurhub
Zīrids of Granada (1012-1090)
rulers ʿAbd Allāh b. Buluggīn

E

EARTHQUAKES *see* Aghri̊ Dagh; Amasya; Anṭākiya; ʿAshḳābād; Čanki̊ri̊; Cilicia; Daybul; Djidjelli; Erzindjan; Ḥarra; Ḥulwān; Istanbul.VI.f; Ḳalhāt; Kāńgŕā; Ḳazwīn; Kilāt; Nīshāpūr; al-Ramla

ECONOMICS Bayʿ; Kasb; Māl
see also Muḍāraba

EDUCATION **Maʿārif**
see also ʿArabiyya.B.IV; Idjāza
educational reform → REFORM
institutions of learning Dār al-Ḥadīth; Djāmiʿa; Köy Enstitüleri; Kuttāb; Madrasa; Maktab; Pesantren
see also Kulliyya; Ṣadr.(c); Samāʿ.2; *and* → EDUCATION.LIBRARIES
individual establishments al-Azhar; Bayt al-Ḥikma; Dār al-Ḥikma; Dār al-ʿUlūm; Ghalaṭa-sarāyi̊; Ḥarbiye; al-Ḳarawiyyīn.ii; al-Khaldūniyya; Makhredj; Mulkiyya; al-Ṣādiḳiyya; [in Suppl.] Institut des hautes études marocaines; Institut des hautes études de Tunis
see also Aligarh; Deoband; Filāḥa.iii; al-Ḳāhira; Lakhnaw; al-Madīna.ii; Makka.3; Muṣṭafā ʿAbd al-Rāziḳ; al-Mustanṣir (I); Nadwat al-ʿUlamāʾ; [in Suppl.] ʿAbd al-Bārī; ʿAbd al-Wahhāb; Farangī Maḥall
learned societies and academies Andjuman; Djamʿiyya; Djemʿiyyet-i ʿIlmiyye-i ʿOthmāniyye; Institut d'Égypte; Khalḳevi; Madjmaʿ ʿIlmī
libraries Dar al-ʿIlm; **Maktaba**
see also ʿAlī Pasha Mubārak; Khāzin; al-Madīna.ii
collections ʿAlī Amīrī (*and* [in Suppl.] ʿAlī Emīrī); Esʿad Efendi, Meḥmed; Khudā Bakhsh; [in Suppl.] ʿAbd al-Wahhāb
see also Geniza
librarians Ibn al-Fuwaṭī; Ibn Ḥadjar al-ʿAsḳalānī; Ibn al-Sāʿī; al-Kattānī
treatises on Ergın, Osman

EGYPT al-Azhar; al-Ḳāhira; Ḳibṭ; **Miṣr**; Nūba; al-Ṣaʿīd
see also al-ʿArab.iv; al-Fusṭāṭ; *and* → DYNASTIES.EGYPT AND THE FERTILE CRESCENT; NUBIA
administration Dār al-Maḥfūẓāt al-ʿUmūmiyya; Dīwān.ii; Ḳabāla; Kharādj.I; Rawk
see also Miṣr.D.1.b; *and* → CALIPHATE.ʿABBĀSIDS *and* FĀṬIMIDS; DYNASTIES.EGYPT AND THE FERTILE CRESCENT.MAMLŪKS; OTTOMAN EMPIRE. ADMINISTRATION
architecture → ARCHITECTURE.REGIONS
before Islam Firʿawn; Manf; Miṣr.D.1; Nūba.2; Saḳḳāra; [in Suppl.] Abū Sinbil
dynasties ʿAbbāsids; Ayyūbids; Fāṭimids; Mamlūks; Muḥammad ʿAlī Pasha *and* → DYNASTIES.EGYPT AND THE FERTILE CRESCENT
historians of Abu 'l-Maḥāsin b. Taghrābirdī; ʿAlī Pasha Mubārak; al-Bakrī.2; al-Balawī; al-Damurdāshī; al-Djabartī; Ibn ʿAbd al-Ḥakam.4; Ibn Duḳmāk; Ibn Iyās; Ibn Muyassar; al-Kindī, Abū ʿUmar Muḥammad; al-Maḳrīzī; al-

Nuwayrī, Muḥammad; Rifāʿa Bey al-Ṭahṭāwī; al-Ṣafadī, al-Ḥasan; Salīm al-Naḳḳās͟h

and → DYNASTIES.EGYPT AND THE FERTILE CRESCENT

modern period Ḍarība.4; D͟jarīda.i.A; D͟jāmiʿa; Dustūr.iii; Ḥizb.i; Ḥukūma.iii; al-Ik͟hwān al-Muslimūn; Iltizām; Imtiyāzāt.iv; Institut d'Égypte; Maʿārif.1.ii; Mad͟jlis.4.A.xvi; Mad͟jmaʿ ʿIlmī.i.2.b; Maḥkama.4.i; Miṣr.D.7; Salafiyya.2(a)

see also Baladiyya.2; al-Bannāʾ; Mad͟jlis al-S͟hūrā

influential persons D͟jamāl al-Dīn al-Afg͟hānī; al-Marṣafī; Muḥammad ʿAbduh; Muṣṭafā Kāmil Pas͟ha; al-Muwayliḥī.1; Rifāʿa Bey al-Ṭahṭāwī; Salāma Mūsā; [in Suppl.] Abu 'l-ʿAzāʾim; al-ʿAdawī; al-Bakrī; al-Biblāwī; D͟jawharī, Ṭanṭāwī; al-ʿIdwī al-Ḥamzāwī; ʿIllays͟h

Muḥammad ʿAlī's line ʿAbbās Ḥilmī I; ʿAbbās Ḥilmī II; Fuʾād al-Awwal; Ḥusayn Kāmil; Ibrāhīm Pas͟ha; Ismāʿīl Pas͟ha; Muḥammad ʿAlī Pas͟ha; Saʿīd Pas͟ha; [in Suppl.] Bak͟hīt al-Muṭīʿī al-Ḥanafī; Fārūḳ

see also ʿAzīz Miṣr; K͟hidīw; [in Suppl.] Dāʾira Saniyya; Ibʿādiyya

statesmen ʿAlī Pas͟ha Mubārak; al-Bārūdī; Fikrī; Ismāʿīl Ṣidḳī; Luṭfī al-Sayyid; Muḥammad Farīd Bey; Muḥammad Nad͟jīb; al-Naḥḥās; Nūbār Pas͟ha; Saʿd Zag͟hlūl; al-Sādāt; [in Suppl.] ʿAbd al-Nāṣir

see also Muṣṭafā Kāmil Pas͟ha

Ottoman period (1517-1798) D͟hu 'l-Faḳāriyya; Ḳāsimiyya; Ḳāzdug͟hliyya; Miṣr.D.6; Muḥammad ʿAlī Pas͟ha

see also Ḥurriyya.ii

beys ʿAlī Bey; Muḥammad Abu 'l-D͟hahab (*and* [in Suppl.] Abu 'l-D͟hahab)

physical geography

waters Burullus; al-Nīl

see also Miḳyās; Rawḍa

population ʿAbābda; Ḳibṭ

see also [in Suppl.] Demography.IV; *and* → CHRISTIANITY.DENOMINATIONS.COPTS

toponyms

ancient Adfū; Bābalyūn; al-Bahnasā; Burullus; Dabīḳ; al-Ḳulzum; Manf

present-day

regions Buḥayra; al-Fayyūm; al-G͟harbiyya; Girgā

see also al-Ṣaʿīd

towns ʿAbbāsa; Abūḳīr; Ak͟hmīm; al-ʿAllāḳī; al-ʿArīs͟h; Asyūṭ; Aṭfīḥ; ʿAyn S͟hams; Banhā; Banī Suwayf; Bilbays; Būlāḳ; Būṣīr; Dahs͟hūr; Daḳahliyya; Damanhūr; Dimyāṭ; al-Farāfra; al-Fusṭāṭ; Girgā; Ḥulwān; al-Iskandariyya; Ismāʿīliyya; Isna; al-Ḳāhira; Ḳalyūb; Ḳanṭara.3; Ḳifṭ; Ḳunā; Ḳūṣ; Ḳuṣayr; al-Maḥalla al-Kubrā; al-Manṣūra; Manūf; Port Saʿīd; Rafaḥ; Ras͟hīd; Saḳḳāra; Samannūd; [in Suppl.] Abū Zaʿbal *see also* al-Muḳaṭṭam; Rawḍa

EMANCIPATION Ḥurriyya
for manumission, see ʿAbd; *and for women* → WOMEN

EMIGRATION Djāliya; **Hidjra**
see also al-Mahdjar; Muhādjir; al-Muhādjirūn; Pārsīs; *and* → NEW WORLD

EPIGRAPHY **Kitābāt**
see also Eldem, Khalīl Edhem; Ḥisāb al-Djummal; Khaṭṭ; Musnad.1
sites of inscriptions Lībiyā.2; Liḥyān; Orkhon
see also Ḥaḍramawt; Sabaʾ; Ṣafaitic

ESCHATOLOGY ʿAdhāb al-Ḳabr; Ākhira; al-Aʿrāf; Barzakh; Baʿth; Djahannam; Djanna; Djazāʾ; Dunyā; Ḥawḍ; Ḥisāb; Isrāfīl; ʿIzrāʾīl; Ḳiyāma; Maʿād; al-Mahdī; Mawḳif.2; Munkar wa-Nakīr; Sāʿa.3
see also Ḳayyim; *and* → DEATH; PARADISE
hereafter Adjr.1; **Ākhira**
see also Dunyā
signs ʿAṣā; Dābba; al-Dadjdjāl
see also Baʿth

ETERNITY **Abad**; Ḳidam

ETHICS Adab; **Akhlāḳ**; Ḥisba
see also Ḥurriyya; al-Maḥāsin wa ʾl-Masāwī; Miskawayh; *and* → VIRTUES

ETHIOPIA Adal; Aḥmad Grāñ; Awfāt; Bāli; Djabart; Djimmā; **Ḥabash**; Ḥabashat; al-Nadjāshī
see also Ḥabesh; Kūsh; *and* → LANGUAGES.AFRO-ASIATIC
historians of ʿArabfaḳih
population ʿĀmir; Diglal; Djabart; Galla; Māryā; Oromo; Rashāʾida
toponyms Assab; Dahlak; Dire Dawa; Eritrea; Harar; Maṣawwaʿ; Ogādēn

ETHNICITY Maghāriba; Mashāriḳa
see also Fatā; Ibn Gharsiya; Ismāʿīl b. Yasār; Mawlā

ETIQUETTE **Adab**
see also Āʾīn; Hiba; *and* → LITERATURE

EUNUCH **Khāṣī**
see also Khādim; Mamlūk.3

Europe
Eastern Europe   Arnawutluḳ; Balkan; Bulgaria; Itil; Leh; [in Suppl.] Čeh
     see also Bulg̲h̲ār; Ḥizb.v; Ibrāhīm b. Yaʿḳūb; Muhād̲j̲ir.2; Muslimūn.1;
     Rūmeli; al-Ṣaḳāliba
     for individual countries → Albania; Bulgaria; (former) Czechoslova-
     kia; Hungary; Poland; (former) Yugoslavia
   former Soviet Union   Ḳi̊ri̊m
     see also Bulg̲h̲ār; D̲j̲adīd; Ḥizb.v; Ḳayyūm Nāṣirī
     dynasties   Girāy
     population   Bas̲h̲d̲j̲irt; Besermyans; Beskesek-abaza; Buk̲h̲ārli̊k;
       Burṭās; Čeremiss; Čuli̊m; Čuwas̲h̲; Gagauz; Ḳarapapak̲h̲; Lipḳa; Rūs
       see also Ḳang̲h̲li; K̲h̲azar; Kimäk; Pečenegs; al-Ṣaḳāliba
     toponyms
       ancient   Atil; Saḳsīn
       present-day   Aḳ Kirmān; Aḳ Masd̲j̲id.1; Astrak̲h̲ān; Azaḳ; Bāg̲h̲če
       Sarāy; Ismāʿīl; Ḳamāniča; Ḳaraṣū-bāzār; Ḳāsimov; Ḳāzān; Kefe;
       Kerč; K̲h̲otin; Ḳi̊lburun
Western Europe   al-Bas̲h̲kunis̲h̲; Ifrand̲j̲; Iḳrīṭis̲h̲; Īṭaliya; Ḳubrus; Malta; Nemče
     see also Ibn Idrīs (II); Ibrāhīm b. Yaʿḳūb; al-Mad̲j̲ūs; Muslimūn.2
     for individual countries → Austria; Crete; Cyprus; France; Greece;
     Italy; Portugal; Spain

Evil Eye   ʿAyn
     see also Karkaddan; *and* → Charms; Islam.popular beliefs

F

Faith   ʿAḳīda; Īmān
     and → Islam; Religion

Falconry   Bayzara; Čaḳi̊rd̲j̲i̊-bas̲h̲i̊; Dog̲h̲and̲j̲i̊

Fasting   ʿĀs̲h̲ūrāʾ; Ramaḍān
     see also ʿĪd al-Fiṭr

Fatimids   → Caliphate

Festival   ʿĪd; Kandūrī; Mawlid; Mawsim
     see also Maṭbak̲h̲.2
festivals   ʿAnṣāra; ʿĀs̲h̲ūrāʾ.II; Bārā Wafāt; ʿĪd al-Aḍḥā; ʿĪd al-Fiṭr; K̲h̲iḍr-ilyās;
     Mihragān; Nawrūz

see also G͟hadīr K͟humm; Kurds.iv.C.3; Lālis͟h; Lĕbaran; Ra'ʾs al-ʿĀm

FLORA (D̲jazīrat) al-ʿArab.v; Būstān; Filāḥa; Hind.i.k
and → BOTANY
flowers Nard̲jis; [in Suppl.] Bābūnad̲j; D̲jullanār
see also Filāḥa.iv; Lāle Devri; Lālezarī; Nawriyya; *and* → ARCHITECTURE.MONUMENTS.PLEASURE-GARDENS
plants Ad̲h̲argūn; Afsantīn; Afyūn; Ḥalfāʾ; Ḥinnāʾ; Kammūn; Ḳaranful; Karm; Ḳaṣab; Naʿam; **Nabāt**; Namir and Nimr; Nasr; Ṣabr; [in Suppl.] Aḳūnīṭun; Ās; Bābūnadj; Djāwars; Fūd̲h̲and̲j; Hindibāʾ; Iklīl al-Malik
see also Maryam; Naḥl; Ṣamg͟h; *and* → DRUGS.NARCOTICS
trees Abanūs; ʿAfṣ ; Argan; Baḳḳam; Bān; K͟has͟hab; Nak͟hl; Sād̲j; [in Suppl.] D̲jawz; D̲jullanār
see also ʿAyn S͟hams; G͟hāba; Kāfūr; Kahrubā; Ḳaṭrān; Lubān; Ṣamg͟h; [in Suppl.] Halīlad̲j

FRANCE Arbūna; Fraxinetum
see also Balāṭ al-S͟huhadāʾ; Muslimūn.2; Rifāʿa Bey al-Ṭahṭāwī

FRANKS **Ifrand̲j**
and → CRUSADE(R)S

FURNISHINGS Mafrūs͟hāt; [in Suppl.] **At͟hāt͟h**

G

GAMBLING **Ḳimār**; al-Maysir
and → ANIMALS.SPORT; RECREATION.GAMES

GENEALOGY **Ḥasab wa-Nasab**; **Nasab**
see also ʿIrḳ; Naḳīb al-As͟hrāf; *and* → LITERATURE.GENEALOGICAL; ONOMASTICS

GEOGRAPHY **D̲jug͟hrāfiyā**; Iḳlīm; Istiwāʾ; K͟harīṭa; al-Ḳubba
see also Mag͟hrib; Makka.4; Mas͟hriḳ
for the detailed geography of areas, see Adamawa; Ād̲h̲arbayd̲jān.i; Afg͟hānistān.i; Aḳ Ṣu; Algeria.i; Anadolu.ii; al-Andalus.ii and iii.2; (D̲jazīrat) al-ʿArab.ii; Armīniya; Arnawutluḳ.3; ʿAsīr; Baḥr; D̲jazīra; Filāḥa; Ḥammāda; Indonesia; ʿIrāḳ; Iran; Lībiyā; al-Mag͟hrib
administrative Kūra; Mamlaka; Mik͟hlāf; Rustāḳ.1
see also D̲jund; Iḳlīm

- *geographers* Abu 'l-Fidā; Abū ʿUbayd al-Bakrī; ʿĀshîķ; al-Balkhī, Abū Zayd; al-Dimashķī; Ibn ʿAbd al-Munʿim al-Ḥimyarī; Ibn al-Faķīh; Ibn Ghālib; Ibn Ḥawķal; Ibn Khurradādhbih; Ibn Mādjid; Ibn Rusta; Ibn Sarābiyūn; al-Idrīsī; al-Iṣṭakhrī; al-Ķazwīnī; al-Masʿūdī; al-Muhallabī, Abu 'l-Ḥusayn; al-Muķaddasī
  - *see also* Baṭlamiyūs; Istibṣār; Ķāsim b. Aṣbagh; al-Masālik wa 'l-Mamālik; [in Suppl.] al-Djayhānī; Ḥudūd al-ʿĀlam
- *literature* Djughrāfiyā.IV.c and V
  - *and* → LITERATURE.TRAVEL-LITERATURE
- *physical geography*
  - *deserts* → DESERTS
  - *mountains* → MOUNTAINS
  - *salt flats* **Sabkha**
  - *springs* ʿAyn Dilfa; ʿAyn Mūsā; al-Ḥamma; Ḥasan Abdāl
    - *see also* Ķaplîdja
  - *volcanoes* *see* ʿAdan; Aghrî Dagh; Damāwand; Ḥarra; Ladjāʾ; al-Ṣafā.2; [in Suppl.] Djabal Says
  - *waters*
    - *lakes* Baikal; Bakhtigān; Balkhash; Burullus; Gökče-tengiz; Hāmūn; al-Ḥūla; İssîk-kul; Ķarā-köl
      - *see also* Buḥayra; al-Ķulzum; *and* → OCEANS AND SEAS
    - *rivers* → RIVERS
    - *straits* Bāb al-Mandab; Boghaz-iči; Čanaķ-ķalʿe Boghazî
- *terms* Ḥarra; Khabrāʾ; Nahr; Reg; Rīf; Sabkha
- *urban* Ķarya; Ķaṣaba; Khiṭṭa; Maḥalle; Medina; Rabaḍ
  - *see also* Fener; Ḥayy; Khiṭaṭ; Mallāḥ; *and* → ARCHITECTURE.URBAN

GIFTS **Hiba**

- *see also* Bakhshīsh; Nithār; Pīshkash; Rashwa

GREECE

- *see also* Muhādjir.2; Muslimūn.1.B.3; Pomaks
- *toponyms*
  - *districts* Karlî-īli
  - *islands* Čoka Adasî; Eğriboz; Körfüz; Levkas; Limni; Midilli; Naķshe; On Iki Ada; Para; Rodos; Ṣaķîz
    - *see also* Djazāʾir-i Baḥr-i Safīd
  - *regions* Mora
  - *towns* Atīna; Aynabakhtî; Baliabadra; Dede Aghač; Dimetoķa; Karaferye; Ķawāla; Kerbenesh; Kesriye; Ķordos; Ķoron; Livadya; Menekshe; Modon; Nauplion; Navarino; Olendirek; Preveze
    - *see also* [in Suppl.] Gümüldjine

GUILDS
Arabic Amīn; ʿArīf; Futuwwa.ii and iii; Ḥammāl; Ḥarfūsh; Khātam; Khayyāṭ
Turkish Akhī; Akhī Baba; Anadolu.iii.6; Ḥarīr.ii; Ketkhudā.ii; [in Suppl.] Ikhtiyāriyya; Inḥiṣār
see also Akhī Ewrān; ʿĀlima; Čāʾūsh; Kannās; Mawākib.4.4; Muhr.1

GUINEA Fūta Djallon; **Guinea**; Konakry

GYPSIES **Čingāne**; **Lūlı**; Nūrı

H

HADITH → LITERATURE.TRADITION-LITERATURE

HAGIOGRAPHY **Manāḳib**
and → SAINTHOOD
hagiographers Aflākī; ʿAṭāʾī; al-Bādisī.2; "Djamālī"; Ḥasan Dihlawī; Ibn ʿAskar; Ibn Maryam; al-Ifrānī; al-Ḳādirī al-Ḥasanī, Abū ʿAbd Allāh
see also Aḥmad Bābā; Bāḳīkhānlī; al-Kattānī

HELL Aṣḥāb al-Ukhdūd; **Djahannam**; Saʿīr; Saḳar
see also al-Aʿrāf

HEPHTHALITES Hayāṭila; Nīzak, Ṭarkhān

HERALDRY al-Asad; Rank

HERESY Bidʿa; Dahriyya; Dīn-i Ilāhī; Ghulāt; Ḳābiḍ; Kāfir; Khūbmesīḥīs; Mulḥid
see also al-Ṣalīb
heretics Abū ʿĪsā al-Warrāḳ; Abu 'l-Khaṭṭāb al-Asadī; Bashshār b. Burd; Bishr b. Ghiyāth al-Marīsī; Ibn Dirham; Ibn al-Rawandī; Mollā Ḳābiḍ; Muḥammad b. ʿAlī al-Shalmaghānī
and → SECTS
refutations of Ibn al-Djawzī, ʿAbd al-Raḥmān; [in Suppl.] Afḍal al-Dīn Turka

HOSTELRY **Funduḳ**; **Khān**; Manzil
see also Ribāṭ.1.b

HUMOUR al-Djidd wa 'l-Hazl; Nādira
see also Hidjāʾ.ii; Mudjūn

comic figures Djuhā; Ibn al-Djaṣṣāṣ.II; Naṣr al-Dīn Khodja
humourists Ashʿab; al-Ghāḍirī; Ibn Abī ʿAtīḳ; Ibn Dāniyāl; Ḳaṣāb, Teodor; [in Suppl.] Abu ʾl-ʿAnbas al-Ṣaymarī

HUNGARY Budīn; Eğri; Esztergom; Istolnī (Istōnī) Belghrād; **Madjar**; Mohács; Pécs; Pest
see also Bashdjirt; Kanizsa; Maḥmūd Tardjumān; Mezőkeresztes; Muslimūn.1.B.1; Ofen

HUNTING Bayzara; Fahd; Khinzīr; Mahāt; Naʿām; Namir and Nimr; Salūḳī; [in Suppl.] Ḍabuʿ
see also Kurds.iv.C.5
treatises on Kushādjim; [in Suppl.] Ibn Manglī

HYDROLOGY Biʾr; Ḳanāt; Māʾ; Maʾṣir
see also Filāḥa; Ḳanṭara.5 and 6; Madjrīṭ; al-Mīzān.2; Sāʿa.1; *and* → GEOGRAPHY.WATERS

I

IDOLS Nuṣub
and → PRE-ISLAM.IN ARABIAN PENINSULA

ILLNESS Madjnūn; Malāryā; Ramad; [in Suppl.] Djudhām
see also Kalb; Ḳuṭrub
treatises on Ḥayātī-zāde; Ibn Buṭlān; Ibn Djazla
and → MEDICINE

INDIA **Hind**; Hindī
see also ʿĀda.iii; Balharā; Imām-bārā; Maṭbaʿa.4; *and* → LITERATURE; MILITARY; MUSIC
administration Baladiyya.5; Ḍarība.6; Dīwān.v; Djizya.iii; Ḥisba.iv; Kātib.iii; Kharādj.IV; Pargana; Safīr.3
see also Kitābāt.10; Māʾ.9; *and* → MILITARY.INDO-MUSLIM
agriculture Filāḥa.v
architecture → ARCHITECTURE.REGIONS
belles-lettres → LITERATURE.IN OTHER LANGUAGES.HINDI WRITERS *and* POETRY.INDO-PERSIAN
dynasties ʿĀdil-Shāhs; Bahmanīs; Barīd Shāhīs; Dihlī Sultanate; Farūḳids; Ghaznavids; Ghūrids; Hindū-Shāhīs; ʿImād Shāhī; Khaldjīs; Ḳuṭb Shāhīs; Lodīs; Mughals; Niẓām Shāhīs

see also Awadh; Dār al-Ḍarb; Rānā Sāngā; *and* → DYNASTIES.AFGHANISTAN AND INDIA

education Dār al-ʿUlūm.c and d; Djāmiʿa; Madjmaʿ ʿIlmī.iv; Madrasa.II; Nadwat al-ʿUlamāʾ; [in Suppl.] Farangī Maḥall
see also Aḥmad Khān; Deoband; Maḥmūdābād Family

historians of Ghulām Ḥusayn Khān Ṭabāṭabāʾī; Niẓām al-Dīn Aḥmad b. al-Harawī
see also Djaʿfar Sharīf; al-Maʿbarī; Mīr Muḥammad Maʿṣūm; *and* → DYNASTIES.AFGHANISTAN AND INDIA; LITERATURE.HISTORICAL

languages Gudjarātī; Hindī; Hindustānī.i and ii; Lahndā; Marāṭhī; Pandjābī.1
see also Kitābāt.10; *and* → LANGUAGES.INDO-IRANIAN

modern period Djamʿiyya.v; Hindustānī.iii; Ḥizb. vi; Indian National Congress; Iṣlāḥ.iv; Kashmīr.ii; Ḳawmiyya.vi; Khāksār; Khilāfa; Madjlis.4.C; al-Marʾa.5; Nikāḥ.II.3; [in Suppl.] Djarīda.vii
see also Mahsūd; Mappila; [in Suppl.] Faḳīr of Ipi; *and* → INDIA.EDUCATION

Indian Mutiny Aẓīm Allāh Khān; Bakht Khān; Imdād Allāh; Kānpur

Khilāfat movement **Khilāfa**; Muḥammad ʿAlī; Mushīr Ḥusayn Ḳidwāʾī; [in Suppl.] ʿAbd al-Bārī; Ḥasrat Mohānī
see also Amīr ʿAlī

statesmen Nawwāb Sayyid Ṣiddīḳ Ḥasan Khān; Sālār Djang; [in Suppl.] Āzād, Abu ʾl-Kalām
see also Maḥmūdābād Family

mysticism → MYSTICISM.MYSTICS; SAINTHOOD

physical geography

waters Djamnā; Gangā
see also Nahr.2

population Bhaṭṭi; Bohorās; Dāwūdpōtras; Djāṭ; Gakkhaṛ; Gandāpur; Gūdjar; Ḥabshī; Hind.ii; Khaṭak; Khokars; Lambadis; Mappila; Mēd; Memon; Mēʾō; Naitias; Pārsīs; Rādjpūts; Rohillas; [in Suppl.] Demography.VII
see also Khōdja; Marāṭhās

Tamils Ceylon; Labbai; Marakkayar; Rawther

religion Ahl-i Ḥadīth; Barāhima; Djayn; Hindū; Ibāḥatiya; Mahdawīs; Pandj Pīr
see also Khwādja Khiḍr; Pārsīs; [in Suppl.] Andjuman-i Khuddām-i Kaʿba; *and* → MYSTICISM; SAINTHOOD; THEOLOGY

reform Aḥmad Brēlwī; al-Dihlawī, Shāh Walī Allāh; Ismāʿīl Shahīd; Karāmat ʿAlī; Nānak

toponyms

ancient Arūr; Čāmpānēr; Čhat; Djāba; Djandjīra; Fatḥpūr-sikrī; Hampī; Ḥusaynābād; Kūlam; Lakhnawtī; al-Manṣūra; Mēwāṛ; Nandurbār; Nārnawl; Pāndʾuʾā

present-day

regions Assam; Bihār; Bombay State; Dakhan; Djaypur; Doʾāb;

Gudjarāt; Hariyānā; Ḥaydarābād.b; Kāmrūp; Kashmīr; Khāndēsh; Ḳūhistān.4; Ladākh; Lūdhiāna; Maʿbar; Mahisur; Malabar; Mēwāt; Muẓaffarpur; Nāgpur; Palamāw; Pālānpur; Pandjāb; Rādhanpūr; Rāmpur; Rohilkhand; [in Suppl.] Djammū
see also Alwār; Banganapalle; Bāonī; Berār; Djōdhpur; Hunza and Nagir

towns Adjmēr; Āgra; Aḥmadābād; Aḥmadnagar; Aligarh; Allāhābād; Ambāla; Amritsar; Anhalwāra; Arcot; Awadh; Awrangābād; Awrangābād Sayyid; Aʿẓamgarh; Badāʾūn; Bālā-ghāt; Bāndā; Bānkīpūr; Banūr; Bareilly; Barōda; Benares; Bharatpūr; Bharoč; Bhattinda; Bhōpāl; Bīdar; Bīdjāpūr; Bidjnawr; Bilgrām; Bombay City; Bulandshahr; Burhānpūr; Buxar; Calcutta; Čandērī; Dawlatābād; Deoband; Dhār; Dhārwār; Dihlī; Diū; Djālor; Djawnpur; Djūnāgaŕh; Djunnar; Dwārkā; Farīdkōť; Farrukhābād; Fayḍābād; Fīrūzpūr; Gulbargā; Gwāliyār; Hānsī; Ḥaydarābād.a; Ḥiṣār Fīrūza; Īdar; Islāmābād; Iťāwā; Kalpī; Kalyāni; Kanawdj; Kāńgŕā; Kannanūr; Kānpur; Karnāl; Karnāťak; Katahr; Khambāyat; Khayrābād; Khuldābād; Kōŕā; Koyl; Lakhnaw; Lalitpur; Lūdhiāna; Madras; Mahīm; Māhīm; Māhūr; Mālda; Mālwā; Mānḋū; Manēr; Mangrōl; Mathurā; Mīraťh; Mīrzāpur; Multān; Mungīr; Murādābad; Murshidābād; Muẓaffarpur; Nadjībābād; Nagar; Nāgawr; Nāgpur; Naldrug; Nāndeŕ; Pānīpat; Parendā; Pāťan; Paťnā; Pūna; Rādjmahāl; Rāyčūr; Sahāranpūr; Sahsarām; [in Suppl.] Amrōhā; Eličpur; Ghāzīpur
and → ASIA.SOUTH

INDONESIA Baladiyya.7; Djāmiʿa; Dustūr.xi; Ḥizb.vii; Ḥukūma.vi; **Indonesia**; Maḥkama.6; Malays; Masjumi; [in Suppl.] Ḍarība.7; Hoesein Djajadiningrat
see also ʿĀda.iv; Nikāḥ.II.4; Pasisir; Prang Sabīl
architecture → ARCHITECTURE.REGIONS
education Pesantren
literature Indonesia.vi; Ḳiṣṣa.6; Miʿrādj.4
see also Kitābāt.8; Malays; *and* → LITERATURE.POETRY.MYSTICAL
population Malays; Minangkabau; [in Suppl.] Demography.VIII
religion → MYSTICISM.MYSTICS
festivals Kandūrī; Lĕbaran
revivalist movement Padri
toponyms Ambon; Atjèh; Banda Islands; Bandjarmasin; Bangka; Batjan; Billiton; Borneo (*and* [in Suppl.]); Celebes; Djakarta; Kubu; Kutai; Lombok; Madura; Makassar; Palembang; Pasè; Pasir; Pontianak; Riau; Sambas

INDUSTRY Ḥarīr; Kattān; Ḳuṭn; Lubūd; Milḥ
see also Bursa; al-Iskandariyya; Ḳayṣariyya

INHERITANCE ʿĀda.iii; Akdariyya; ʿAwl; **Farāʾiḍ**; **Mīrāth**; al-Sahm.2
see also Ḳassām; Khāl; Makhredj; Mukhallefāt
works on al-Sadjāwandī, Sirādj al-Dīn

INVENTIONS ʿAbbās b. Firnās; Ibn Mādjid; Mūsā (Banū); Sāʿa.1

IRAN al-Furs; **Iran**; Kurds; Lur
see also al-ʿArab.iii; Ḥarb.v; Kitābāt.9; Libās.iii; *and* → DYNASTIES.PERSIA; SHIITES; ZOROASTRIANS
administration Ḍarība.5; Diplomatic.iii; Dīwān.iv; Ghulām.ii; Imtiyāzāt.iii; Kātib.ii; Khāliṣa; Kharādj.II; Maḥkama.3; Parwānačī
see also Kalāntar; *and* → IRAN.MODERN PERIOD
agriculture Filāḥa.iii
architecture → ARCHITECTURE.REGIONS
before Islam Anūsharwān; Ardashīr; Bahrām; Dārā; Dārābdjird; Dihḳan; Djamshīd; Farīdūn; al-Ḥaḍr; Hayāṭila; Hurmuz; al-Hurmuzān; Ḳārinids; Kayānids; Kay Kāʾūs; Kay Khusraw; Khurshīd; Kisrā; Marzpān; Mazdak; Mulūk al-Ṭawāʾif.1; Parwīz, Khusraw (II); Pīshdādids; [in Suppl.] Farrukhān
see also Afrāsiyāb; Buzurgmihr; Hamadhān; Ikhshīd; Iran.iv; Ispahbadh; Ḳaṣr-i Shīrīn; Ḳūmis; al-Madāʾin; al-Rayy; Rustam b. Farrukh Hurmuzd; [in Suppl.] Dabīr; *and* → ZOROASTRIANS
historians of Ḥamza al-Iṣfahānī; Ibn Manda; al-Māfarrūkhī; al-Rāfiʿī
and → DYNASTIES.PERSIA
language → LANGUAGES.INDO-IRANIAN
literature → LITERATURE
modern period Baladiyya.4; Djāmiʿa; Djamʿiyya.iii; Djarīda.ii; Dustūr.iv; Ḥizb.iii; Ḥukūma.ii; Iran.v.b; Iṣlāḥ.ii; Ḳawmiyya.iii; Maʿārif.3; Madjlis.4.A.iii; Madjmaʿ ʿIlmī.ii; al-Marʾa.3; [in Suppl.] Demography.III
see also Khazʿal Khān; Madjlis al-Shūrā; Maḥkama.3; [in Suppl.] Amīr Niẓām; *and* → DYNASTIES.PERSIA.ḲĀDJĀRS *and* PAHLAWĪS; SHIITES
activists Fidāʾiyyān-i Islām; Kāshānī, Āyātullāh; Kasrawī Tabrīzī; Khʷānsārī, Sayyid Muḥammad; Khiyābānī, Shaykh Muḥammad; Khurāsānī; Kūčak Khān Djangalī; Lāhūtī; Maḥallātī; Malkom Khān; Muṣaddiḳ; Muṭahharī; Nāʾīnī; Nūrī, Shaykh Faḍl Allāh; Ṣamṣām al-Salṭana; [in Suppl.] Āḳā Khān Kirmānī; Āḳā Nadjafī; Amīr Kabīr; Ḥaydar Khān ʿAmū Ughlī
see also Djangalī; Kurds.iii. C; [in Suppl.] Azādī; Farāmūsh-khāna

physical geography

deserts Biyābānak

mountains Ala Dagh; Alburz; Alwand Kūh; Bīsutūn; Damāwand; Hamrīn; Hawrāmān

waters Bakhtigān, Hāmūn; Karkha; Kārūn; Mānd;Ruknābād; Safīd Rūd

see also Baḥr Fāris

population Bakhtiyārī; Bāzūkiyyūn; Bilbās; Djāf; Eymir.3; Göklān; Gūrān; (Banū) Kaʿb; Ḳarā Gözlu; Ḳāshḳāy; Kurds; Lām; Lur

see also Daylam; Dulafids; Eymir.2; Fīrūzānids; Iran.ii; Ḳufṣ; [in Suppl.] Demography.III

religion Iran.vi; Ṣafawids.IV

and → Mysticism.mystics; Sainthood

toponyms

ancient Abarshahr; Ardalān; Arradjān; ʿAskar Mukram; Bādj; Bākusāyā; Bayhaḳ; Dārābdjird; Daskara; Dawraḳ; Dihistān; Dīnawar; al-Djazīra; Djibāl; Djīruft; Gurgān; Ḥafrak; Ḥulwān; Īdhadj; Iṣṭakhr; (al-)Karadj; Khargird.2; Ḳūmis; Ḳurḳūb; Mihragān.iv.1; Narmāshīr; Nasā; Nawbandadjān; al-Rayy; Rūdhbār.2; Rūdhrāwar; [in Suppl.] Arghiyān; Ghubayrā

present-day

islands al-Fārisiyya

provinces Ādharbaydjān; Balūčistān; Fārs; Gīlān; Hamadhān; Iṣfahān; Khurāsān; Khūzistān; Kirmān; Kirmānshāh; Kurdistān; Māzandarān

see also Astarābādh.2; Rūyān

regions Bākharz; Hawrāmān; Ḳūhistān.1; Makrān; [in Suppl.] Bashkard

see also Gulistān

towns Ābādah; Abarḳūh; ʿAbbādān; ʿAbbāsābād; Abhar; al-Ahwāz; Āmul.1; Ardakān; Ardistān; Asadābādh; Ashraf; Astarābādh.1; Āwa; Bam; Bampūr; Bandar ʿAbbās; Bandar Pahlawī; Bārfurūsh; Barūdjird; Barzand; Bīrdjand; Bisṭām; Būshahr; Dāmghān; Dizfūl; Djannāba; Djuwayn.1 and 2; Faraḥābād; Faryāb; Fasā; Fīrūzābād; Fūman; Gulpāyagān; Gunbadh-i Ḳābūs; Hurmuz; Iṣfahān; Isfarāyīn; Kāshān; Ḳaṣr-i Shīrīn; Kāzarūn; Ḳazwīn; Khʷāf; Khalkhāl; Khʷār; Khārag; Khargird.1; Khōī; Khurramābād; Khurramshahr; Kinkiwar; Ḳishm; Ḳūčān; Ḳūhistān.2; Ḳuhrūd; Ḳum; Lāhīdjān; Lār (2x); Linga; Luristān; Mahābād; Mākū; Marāgha; Marand; Mashhad; Miyāna; Narāḳ; Naṭanz; Nayrīz; Nihāwand; Nīshāpūr; Rafsandjān; Rāmhurmuz; Rasht; Rūdhbār.3; Sabzawār.1; Ṣaḥna; Ṣāʾīn Ḳalʿa; Saḳḳiz; Salmās; [in Suppl.] Bashkard; Biyār; Djārdjarm; Djulfa.II; Hawsam

and → Kurds.toponyms

IRAQ **ʿIrāḳ**; Kurds
see also al-ʿArabiyya; Djalīlī; Lakhmids; *and* → CALIPHATE.ʿABBĀSIDS; DYNASTIES.EGYPT AND THE FERTILE CRESCENT
architecture → ARCHITECTURE.REGIONS
before Islam → PRE-ISLAM.IN FERTILE CRESCENT
historians of al-Azdī; Baḥshal; Ibn Abī Ṭāhir Ṭayfūr; Ibn al-Bannāʾ; Ibn al-Dubaythī; al-Khaṭīb al-Baghdādī
see also Ibn al-Nadjdjār; *and* → CALIPHATE.ʿABBĀSIDS; DYNASTIES.EGYPT AND THE FERTILE CRESCENT
modern period Djarīda.i.A; Djāmiʿa; Dustūr.vi; Ḥizb.i; Ḥukūma.iii; Kurds. iii.C; Madjlis.4.A.iv; Madjmaʿ ʿIlmī.i.2.c; Maḥkama.4.iv; Mandates
see also Bābān; Kūt al-ʿAmāra; al-Mawṣil.2
monarchy Fayṣal I; Fayṣal II; Ghazī
see also Hāshimids
opposition leaders Ḳāsim ʿAbd al-Karīm; Muṣṭafā Barzānī
prime ministers Nūrī al-Saʿīd; Rashīd ʿAlī al-Gaylānī
physical geography
waters Abu ʾl-Khaṣīb; al-ʿAḍaym; Didjla; Diyālā; al-Furāt; Khābūr; al-Khāzir
population Bādjalān; Bilbās; Djubūr; Dulaym; Lām; al-Manāṣir
see also [in Suppl.] Demography.III; *and* → KURDS
toponyms
ancient Abarḳubādh; ʿAḳarḳūf; ʿAlth; al-Anbār; Bābil; Badjimzā; Bādjisrā; Bādūrayā; Bākhamrā; Baradān; Barāthā; Bawāzīdj; Bihḳubādh; Birs; Dayr ʿAbd al-Raḥmān; Dayr al-ʿĀḳūl; Dayr al-Aʿwar; Dayr al-Djamādjim; Diyār Rabīʿa; Djabbul; al-Djazīra; Fallūdja; Ḥadītha.I; Ḥarbāʾ; Ḥarūrāʾ; Ḥawīza; al-Ḳādisiyya; Kalwādhā; Kaskar; Ḳaṣr ibn Hubayra; Khāniḳīn; al-Khawarnaḳ; Kūthā; Ḳuṭrabbul; al-Madāʾin; Niffar; Nimrūd; Nīnawā; al-Nukhayla; al-Ruṣāfa.1; Sāmarrāʾ
see also al-Karkh; Nuṣratābād
present-day
regions Bahdīnān; al-Baṭīḥa; Maysān
see also Lālish
towns Altın Köprü; ʿAmādiya; ʿAmāra; ʿĀna; ʿAyn al-Tamr; Badra; Baghdād; Baʿḳūba; Balāwāt; Bārzān; al-Baṣra; Daḳūḳāʾ; Daltāwa; Dīwāniyya; al-Fallūdja; Ḥadītha.II; al-Ḥilla; Hīt; Irbil; Karbalāʾ; Kāẓimayn; Kirkūk; al-Kūfa; Kūt al-ʿAmāra; Maʿalthāyā; al-Mawṣil; al-Nadjaf; al-Nāṣiriyya; Nuṣratābād; Rawāndiz; Sāmarrāʾ; al-Samāwa.2; [in Suppl.] Athūr
see also Djalūlāʾ; *and* → KURDS.TOPONYMS

IRRIGATION Band; Ḳanāt; Māʾ; Nāʿūra

see also Filāḥa; Kārūn; al-Nahrawān; *and* → Rivers

water **Māʾ**

see also Ḥawḍ; Sabīl.2; Saḳḳāʾ; *and* → Architecture.monuments; Navigation; Oceans and Seas; Rivers

Islam ʿAḳīda; Dīn; Djamāʿa; **Islām**; Masdjid; Muḥammad; Murtadd; Muslim; Rukn.1; Ṣadaḳa

see also Iṣlāḥ; Iʿtikāf; Nubuwwa; Rahbāniyya; *and* → Alms; Fasting; Koran; Pilgrimage; Prayer

conversion to Islām.ii

European converts Pickthall

five pillars of Islam Ḥadjdj; Ṣalāt

see also al-Ḳurṭubī, Yaḥyā; Rukn.1

formulas Allāhumma; Basmala; Ḥamdala; In Shāʾ Allāh; Māshāʾ Allāh; Salām

see also [in Suppl.] Abbreviations

popular beliefs ʿAyn; Dīw; Djinn; Ghūl; Muḥammad.2; [in Suppl.] ʿĀʾisha Ḳandīsha; Ḥinn

see also ʿAnḳāʾ; *and* → Law.customary law

Israel → Palestine

Italy **Īṭaliya**; Ḳawṣara; Ḳillawriya; Rūmiya

and → Sicily

Ivory Coast **Côte d'Ivoire**; Kong

J

Jacobites → Christianity.denominations

Jewelry [in Suppl.] **Djawhar**

see also Khātam

pearls and precious stones ʿAḳīḳ; al-Durr; Kūh-i Nūr; Luʾluʾ; Mardjān

see also Dhahab; Fiḍḍa; Ḥadjar; Kahrubā; Maʿdin.2.3

Jordan Dustūr.x; Ḥukūma.iii; Madjlis.4.A.vii; Maḥkama.4.vi; Mandates

physical geography

mountains al-Djibāl

population al-Ḥuwayṭāt; al-Manāṣir

see also [in Suppl.] Demography.III

statesmen ʿAbd Allāh b. al-Ḥusayn

see also Hāshimids

toponyms
ancient Adhrūḥ; Ayla; al-Balḳāʾ; Djarash; al-Djarbāʾ; al-Djibāl; Faḥl; al-Ḥumayma; al-Muwaḳḳar
present-day ʿAdjlūn; al-ʿAḳaba; ʿAmmān; Bayt Rās; al-Ghawr.1; Irbid.I; Maʿān; al-Salṭ

JUDAISM Ahl al-Kitāb; Banū Isrāʾīl
see also Filasṭīn; Hūd; Nasīʾ; al-Sāmira; *and* → BIBLE; PALESTINE
communities al-Andalus.iv; al-Fāsiyyūn; Iran.ii and vi; Iṣfahān.1; al-Iskandariyya; Istanbul.vii.b; al-Ḳuds; Lār.2; Mallāḥ; Marrākush
influences in Islam ʿĀshūrāʾ.I
see also Ḳibla; Muḥammad.i.I.C.2
Jewish personages in Islam ʿAbd Allāh b. Salam; Abū ʿĪsā al-Iṣfahānī; Abū Naḍḍāra; Dhū Nuwās; Hāmōn; Ḥasdāy b. Shaprūṭ; Ibn Abi ʾl-Bayān; Ibn Djāmiʿ; Ibn Djanāḥ; Ibn Gabirol; Ibn Kammūna; Ibn Maymūn; Ibn Yaʿīsh; Ibrāhīm b. Yaʿḳub; Isḥaḳ b. Sulaymān al-Isrāʾīlī; Kaʿb b. al-Ashraf; al-Kōhēn al-ʿAṭṭār; Māsardjawayh; Māshāʾ Allāh; Mūsā b. ʿAzra; al-Rādhāniyya; Saʿadyā Ben Yōsēf; Saʿd al-Dawla; al-Samawʾal b. ʿĀdiyā; [in Suppl.] Ibn Biklārish
see also Abu ʾl-Barakāt; Kaʿb al-Aḥbār; Ḳaynuḳāʿ; Ḳurayẓa
Jewish sects ʿĀnāniyya; al-ʿĪsāwiyya; Karaites
Judaeo-Christian sects Ṣābiʾa.1
see also Naṣārā
Jewish-Muslim relations
persecution Dhimma; Djizya; Ghiyār; al-Ḥākim bi-Amr Allāh; al-Maghīlī
polemics Abū Isḥāḳ al-Ilbīrī; Ibn Ḥazm, Abū Muḥammad
see also Ahl al-Kitāb
with Muḥammad Fadak; Ḳaynuḳāʿ; Khaybar; Ḳurayẓa; al-Madīna.i.1; Naḍīr
see also Muḥammad.1.I.C
language and literature Judaeo-Arabic; Judaeo-Berber; Judaeo-Persian; Ḳiṣṣa.8; Risāla.1.VII
see also Geniza; Musammaṭ; Muwashshaḥ; *and* → LEXICOGRAPHY; LITERATURE.IN OTHER LANGUAGES

K

KENYA Gede; **Kenya**; Kilifi; Lamu; Malindi; Manda; Mazrūʿī; Mombasa; Pate
see also Nabhān; [in Suppl.] Djarīda.viii
Swahili literature Ḳiṣṣa.7; Madīḥ.5; Marthiya.5; Mathal.5; [in Suppl.] Ḥamāsa.vi
see also Miʿrādj.3

KORAN Allāh.i; Āya; Fāṣila; Iʿdjāz; Ḳirāʾa; **al-Ḳurʾān**; Muḳaṭṭaʿāt; Muṣḥaf; Naskh
see also ʿArabiyya.A.ii; Basmala; Faḍīla; Hamza; Indjīl; Iṣlāḥ.i.B.1; Khalḳ.II; Khawāṣṣ al-Ḳurʾān
commentaries
in Arabic ʿAbd al-Razzāḳ al-Ḳāshānī; Abu 'l-Faḍl ʿAllāmī; Abū Ḥayyān al-Gharnāṭī; Abu 'l-Layth al-Samarḳandī; Abu 'l-Suʿūd; Abū ʿUbayda; al-ʿAskarī.ii; al-Baghawī; Baḳī b. Makhlad; al-Bayḍāwī; al-Bulḳīnī.4; al-Dāmād; al-Dārimī; Djīwan; Fakhr al-Dīn al-Rāzī; Fayḍī; Ghulām Ḥusayn Khān Ṭabāṭabāʾī; Gīsū Darāz; Gūrānī; Ibn Abi 'l-Ridjāl; Ibn ʿAdjība; Ibn Barradjān; Ibn Kathīr, ʿImād al-Dīn; Ismāʿīl Ḥaḳḳi; al-Kalbī.I; Kalīm Allāh al-Djahānābādī; Kemāl Pasha-zāde; al-Ḳurṭubī, Abū ʿAbd Allāh; al-Ḳushayrī.1; al-Maḥallī; al-Māturīdī; Mudjāhid b. Djabr al-Makkī; Mudjīr al-Dīn al-ʿUlaymī; Muḥsin-i Fayḍ-i Kāshānī; Muḳātil b. Sulaymān; al-Nīsābūrī; al-Rāghib al-Iṣfahānī; al-Rummānī; Sahl al-Tustarī; [in Suppl.] ʿAbd al-Wahhāb Bukhārī; Abu 'l-Fatḥ al-Daylamī; al-Aṣamm
see also ʿAbd Allāh b. al-ʿAbbās; Abū Nuʿaym al-Mulāʾī; Aḥmadiyya; al-ʿAlamī; al-Dihlawī, Shāh Walī Allāh; Djafr; Djilwatiyya; Ḥādjdjī Pasha; Hind.v.e; Ibn Masʿūd; Ḳuṭb al-Dīn Shīrāzī; al-Manār
late 19th and 20th centuries al-Ālūsī.2; Aṭfiyāsh; Mawdūdī; Muḥammad b. Aḥmad al-Iskandarānī; Muḥammad Abū Zayd; Muḥammad Farīd Wadjdī; [in Suppl.] Djawharī, Ṭanṭāwī
in Persian Abu 'l-Futūḥ al-Rāzī; al-Dawlatābādī; Djāmī; Kāshifī; al-Maybudī.1; Muṣannifak
in Turkish Aḳ Ḥiṣārī.b
in Urdu Ashraf ʿAlī
createdness of Miḥna
see also Djahmiyya
readers ʿAbd Allāh b. Abī Isḥāḳ; Abū ʿAmr b. al-ʿAlāʾ; al-Aʿmash; ʿĀṣim; al-Dānī; Ḥamza b. Ḥabīb; Ibn ʿĀmir; ʿĪsā b. ʿUmar; al-Kisāʾī; Nāfiʿ al-Laythī; al-Sadjāwandī, Abū ʿAbd Allāh
see also Abu 'l-ʿĀliya al-Riyāḥī; al-Dāraḳuṭnī; Ḥafṣ b. Sulaymān; Ibn al-Djazarī; Ibn al-Faḥḥām; Ibn Mudjāhid; Ibn Shanabūdh; al-Ḳasṭallānī; Makkī; al-Malaṭī; Mudjāhid b. Djabr al-Makkī; [in Suppl.] Ibn Miḳsam
reading Adāʾ; Ḥarf; Ḳaṭʿ; Khatma; **Ḳirāʾa**
recensions ʿAbd Allāh b. al-Zubayr; ʿAbd al-Malik b. Marwān; Abu 'l-Dardāʾ; ʿĀʾisha bint Abī Bakr; ʿĀṣim; al-Dimyāṭī; al-Ḥadjdjādj b. Yūsuf; Ibn Masʿūd; Nāfiʿ al-Laythī
see also Abu 'l-Aswad al-Duʾalī; ʿArabiyya.ii.1 and 2; al-Ḥuṣrī.II
stories ʿĀd; Ādam; Aṣḥāb al-Kahf; Ayyūb; Bilḳīs; Dāwūd; Djālūt; Firʿawn; Ḥābīl wa Ḳābīl; Ḥawwāʾ; Ibrāhīm; ʿĪsā; al-Iskandar; al-Khaḍir; Lūṭ; Maryam; Mūsā; Nūḥ

see also Ḳiṣaṣ al-Anbiyāʾ; *and* → BIBLE.BIBLICAL PERSONAGES
suras al-Aḥḳāf; Aṣḥāb al-Kahf; Fātiḥa; al-Fīl; Ghāshiya; Kawthar; Luḳmān; al-Muʿawwidhatānⁱ; al-Muddaththir and al-Muzzammil; al-Musabbiḥāt; Sadjda; al-Ṣāffāt
see also Ḥayawān.3
terms Aḥkām; ʿĀlam; Amr; al-Aʿrāf; ʿAṣā; Aṣḥāb al-Kahf; Aṣḥāb al-Rass; Aṣḥāb al-Ukhdūd; Āya; Baḥīra; al-Baḥrayn; Baʿl; Barāʾa; Baraka; Barzakh; Birr; Dābba; Daʿwa; Dharra; Dīn; Djahannam; Djāhiliyya; Djanna; Djinn; Dunyā; Faḳīr; Farāʾiḍ; Fitna; Fiṭra; Furḳān; al-Ghayb; Ḥadd; Ḥaḳḳ; Ḥanīf; Hātif; Ḥawārī; Ḥayāt; Ḥidjāb; Ḥisāb; Ḥizb; Ḥudjdja; Ḥūr; Iblīs; Īlāf; Ilhām; ʿIlliyyūn; Kaffāra; Kāfir; Kalima; Ḳarīn; Ḳarya; Ḳawm; Ḳayyim; Khalḳ, Khaṭīʾa; Ḳiyāma; Kursī; Ḳuwwa.2; Lawḥ; Madjnūn; Maḳām Ibrāhīm; Milla; Millet; Miskīn; Mīthāḳ; al-Munāfiḳūn.1; Nadhīr; Nafs.I; Nār; Raḥma; Rizḳ; Rudjūʿ; Rukn; Ṣabr; Ṣadr; al-Ṣāffāt; Ṣaḥīfa; Sakīna; Salām; al-Ṣāliḥūn; [in Suppl.] Asāṭīr al-Awwalīn
see also Ḥikāya.I; Sabab.1; Samāʾ.1
translations Ḳurʾān.9
see also Aljamía
into English Aḥmadiyya; Pickthall
into Malay ʿAbd al-Raʾūf al-Sinkilī
into Persian al-Dihlawī, Shāh Walī Allāh
see also Khaṭṭ.ii
into Swahili Kenya (891a)
into Urdu ʿAbd al-Ḳādir Dihlawī; Djawān; Rafīʿ al-Dīn

KURDS **Kurds**
see also Kitab al-Djilwa; *and* → IRAN; IRAQ; TURKEY
dynasties ʿAnnāzids; Bābān; Faḍlawayh; Ḥasanwayh; Marwānids; Rawwādids
see also Kurds.iii.B
Kurdish national movement Badrkhānī; Ḳāḍī Muḥammad; Kurds.iii.C; Muṣṭafā Barzānī
see also Bārzān; Mahābād
toponyms Ardalān; Bahdīnān; Barādūst; Bārzān; Djawānrūd; Hakkārī.2; Rawāndiz; Saḳḳiz
see also Kirkūk; Kurds.ii; Orāmār
tribes Djāf; Hakkārī.1; Hamawand; Kurds.iii.B and iv.A.2; Lak.1

KUWAIT Djarīda.i.A; Dustūr.xvi; **al-Kuwayt**; Madjlis.4.A.ix; Maḥkama.4.ix; Ṣabāḥ, Āl
see also (Djazīrat) al-ʿArab; al-ʿArabiyya; Djāmiʿa
toponyms al-Dibdiba; [in Suppl.] Aḥmadī
see also Ḳarya al-ʿUlyā

L

LAMENTATION   Bakkā'; **Niyāḥa**; Rawḍa-ḵʰānī

LAND   → TAXATION
in the sense of agriculture, see Filāḥa
in the sense of surveying, see Misāḥa; Rawk

LANGUAGES   **Lug̲h̲a**
and → LINGUISTICS
Afro-Asiatic   Ḥām; Sām.2
    see also Kars̲h̲ūnī; Maʿlūlā.2
    Arabic   Algeria.v; Aljamía; al-Andalus.x; **Arabiyya**.A; ʿIrāḳ.iv.a; Judaeo-
        Arabic.i and ii; Lībiyā.2; al-Mag̲h̲rib.VII; Malta.2; Mūrītāniyā.6
        see also Ibn Makkī; Ḳarwas̲h̲a; K̲h̲aṭṭ; Mad̲j̲maʿ ʿIlmī.i; [in Suppl.]
        Ḥaḍramawt.iii
        dialects   Arabiyya.A.iii; al-Ṣaʿīd.2
            and → LINGUISTICS.PHONETICS; LITERATURE.POETRY.VERNACULAR
    Berber   **Berbers**.V; Judaeo-Berber; Mūrītāniyā.6
        see also Mzāb
        Berber words in Arabic   Āfrāg; Agadir; Āgdāl; Aménokal; Amg̲h̲ar;
        Argan; Ayt; Imẓad
            see also Ḳallala; Rīf.I.2(a)
    Chadic   Hausa.ii
    Ethiopian   Eritrea.iv; Ḥabas̲h̲.iv; Kūs̲h̲
    Hebrew   Ibn D̲j̲anāḥ
    (Niger-)Kordofanian   Nūba.3
    Nilo-Saharan   Nūba.3
    North Arabian   Ṣafaitic
        see also Liḥyān; *and* → EPIGRAPHY
    South Arabian   Sabaʾ
        see also Ḥaḍramawt (*and* [in Suppl.] Ḥaḍramawt.iii); al-Ḥarāsīs; *and* →
        EPIGRAPHY
        Modern South Arabian   Mahrī
            see also al-Ḥarāsīs; [in Suppl.] Ḥaḍramawt.iii
    Teda-Daza   Kanuri
Austronesian   Atjèh; Indonesia.iii; Malays
Ibero-Caucasian   Andi; Beskesek-abaza; Čerkes; Dāg̲h̲istān; Darg̲h̲in; al-Ḳabḳ;
    Ḳayyūm Nāṣirī
Indo-European   Arnawutluḳ.1
    see also al-Ḳabḳ

Indo-Iranian
   Indian   Afghānistān.iii; Bengali.i; Ceylon; Chitral.II; Dardic and Kāfir
      Languages; Gudjarātī; Hind.iii; Hindī; Hindustānī; Kashmīrī; Lahndā;
      Maldives.2; Marāt̲h̲ī; Pandjābī.1
      see also Madjmaʿ ʿIlmī.iv; [in Suppl.] Burus̲h̲aski
   Iranian   Afg̲h̲ān.ii; Afg̲h̲ānistān.iii; Balūčistān.B; Darī; Gūrān; Hind.
      iii; ʿIrāḳ.iv.b; Judaeo-Persian.ii; Kurds.v; Lur
      see also Dāg̲h̲istān; al-Ḳabḳ; K̲h̲ʷārazm; Madjmaʿ ʿIlmī.ii; Ossetians
Turkic   Ād̲h̲arī; Balkar; Bulg̲h̲ār; Gagauz; K̲h̲aladj.2
      see also Afg̲h̲ānistān.iii; Dāg̲h̲istān; al-Ḳabḳ; K̲h̲azar; Madjmaʿ ʿIlmī.iii

LAW   ʿĀda; Dustūr; **Fiḳh**; Idjmāʿ; **Ḳānūn**.i and iii; Ḳiyas; Maḥkama
   see also Aṣḥāb al-Raʾy; Ḥuḳūḳ; *and* → INHERITANCE
   for questions of law, see ʿAbd.3; Djāsūs; Filāḥa.i.4; Ḥarb.i; Ḥarīr; In S̲h̲āʾ Allāh;
      Intiḥār; Ḳabr; Kāfir; K̲h̲āliṣa; K̲h̲iṭba; Māʾ; al-Marʾa; Murtadd; Raḍāʿ; Raḳid;
      Ras̲h̲wa; Safar.1
Anglo-Mohammedan law   ʿĀda.iii; Amīr ʿAlī; Munṣif
      see also Ḥanafiyya
customary law   **ʿĀda**; Dak̲h̲īl; Ḳānūn.iv; [in Suppl.] Djirga
      see also Baranta; Berbers.IV; al-Māmī; al-Marʾa.2; Mus̲h̲āʿ
early religious law   Abū Ḥanīfa; Abū Yūsuf; al-As̲h̲ʿarī, Abū Burda; ʿAṭāʾ b. Abī
      Rabāḥ; al-Awzāʿī; Ibn Abī Laylā.II; Ibn S̲h̲ubruma; al-Layt̲h̲ b. Saʿd; Mālik
      b. Anas; Maymūn b. Mihrān; al-Nak̲h̲aʿī, Ibrāhīm; [in Suppl.] Fuḳahāʾ al-
      Madīna al-Sabʿa; Ibn Abi ʾl-Zinād
Ibāḍī law   ʿAbd al ʿAzīz b. al-Ḥādjdj Ibrāhīm; Abū G̲h̲ānim al-K̲h̲urāsānī; Abū
      Muḥammad b. Baraka (*and* Ibn Baraka); Abū Zakariyyāʾ al-Djanāwunī; Ibn
      Djaʿfar
      see also al-Djayṭālī; Maḥkama.4.ix (Oman)
in South-east Asia   Penghulu; Rapak
jurisprudence   Fatwā; **Fiḳh**; Īdjāb; Idjmāʿ; Idjtihād; Ik̲h̲tilāf; Istiḥsān; Ḳiyās;
      Maṣlaḥa; Nāzila
      see also Sadd al-D̲h̲arāʾiʿ
jurist   **Faḳih**; Mardjaʿ-i Taḳlīd; Mudjtahid
   Ḥanafī   Abū Ḥanīfa al-Nuʿmān; Abu ʾl-Layt̲h̲ al-Samarḳandī; Abu ʾl-Suʿūd;
      al-ʿAmīdī; al-Bihārī; al-Djaṣṣāṣ; al-Ḥalabī; Ḥamza al-Ḥarrānī; Ibn
      ʿĀbidīn; Ibn Buhlūl; Ibn G̲h̲ānim; Ibn Ḳuṭlūbug̲h̲ā; Ibn Nudjaym; Ibn al-
      Shiḥna; Ḳāḍī K̲h̲ān; al-Kāsānī; Ḳasṭallānī; al-Ḳudūrī, Abu ʾl-Ḥusayn
      Aḥmad; al-Marg̲h̲īnānī; al-Nasafī.4; al-Sadjāwandī, Sirādj al-Dīn; [in
      Suppl.] Abū ʿAbd Allāh al-Baṣrī; Abu ʾl-Barakāt; al-Dāmag̲h̲ānī, Abū
      ʿAbd Allāh Muḥammad b. ʿAlī; al-Dāmag̲h̲ānī, Abu ʾl-Ḥasan ʿAlī b.
      Muḥammad

see also ʿAbd al-Ḳādir al-Ḳurashī; al-Fatāwā al-ʿĀlamgīriyya; Ibn Duḳmāḳ

Ḥanbalī Aḥmad b. Ḥanbal; al-Bahūtī; al-Barbahārī; Ghulām al-Khallāl; Ibn ʿAḳīl; Ibn al-Bannāʾ; Ibn Baṭṭa al-ʿUkbarī; Ibn al-Djawzī; Ibn al-Farrāʾ; Ibn Ḥāmid; Ibn Ḳayyim al-Djawziyya; Ibn Ḳudāma al-Maḳdisī; Ibn Mufliḥ; Ibn Radjab; Ibn Taymiyya; al-Kalwadhānī; al-Khallāl; al-Khiraḳī; al-Marwazī
and → THEOLOGY

Mālikī Aḥmad Bābā; Asad b. al-Furāt; al-Bādjī; al-Bāḳillānī; Bannānī; al-Burzulī; al-Dānī; al-Fāsī; Ibn ʿAbd al-Ḥakam; Ibn Abī Zamanayn; Ibn Abī Zayd al-Ḳayrawānī; Ibn ʿAmmār, Abu ʾl-ʿAbbās; Ibn ʿArafa; Ibn ʿĀṣim; Ibn al-Faraḍī; Ibn Farḥūn; Ibn Ḥabīb, Abū Marwān; Ibn al-Ḥādjdj; Ibn al-Ḥādjib; Ibn al-Ḳāsim; Ibn Maḍāʾ; Ibn Rushayd; Ibn Sūda; al-Ibshīhī(1); ʿĪsā b. Dīnār; ʿIyāḍ b. Mūsā; al-Ḳābisī; al-Ḳalaṣādī; al-Kardūdī; Ḳaṣṣāra; Khalīl b. Isḥāḳ; al-Khushanī; al-Ḳurṭubī, Abū ʿAbd Allāh; al-Ḳurṭubī, Yaḥyā; Mālik b. Anas; al-Manūfī.4 and 5; al-Māzarī; Muḥammad b. Saḥnūn; Saḥnūn; Sālim b. Muḥammad; [in Suppl.] Abū ʿImrān al-Fāsī; al-Azdī; Ibn Daḳīḳ al-ʿĪd; Ibn Dirham; Ibn Rushd
see also Ibn ʿAbd al-Barr; al-Ḳaṣṣār; Laḳīṭ

Shāfiʿī al-ʿAbbādī; Abū Shudjāʿ; Bādjūrī; al-Baghawī; al-Bulḳīnī; Daḥlān; al-Djanadī; al-Djīzī; al-Djuwaynī; Ibn Abī ʿAṣrūn; Ibn Abi ʾl-Dam; Ibn ʿAḳīl; Ibn ʿAsākir; Ibn Djamāʿa; Ibn Ḥabīb, Badr al-Dīn; Ibn Ḥadjar al-Haytamī; Ibn Ḳāḍī Shuhba.1; Ibn Ḳāsim al-Ghazzī; Ibn al-Ṣalāḥ; Ibn Suraydj; al-Ḳalḳashandī; al-Ḳalyūbī; al-Ḳazwīnī, Abū Ḥātim; al-Ḳazwīnī, Djalāl al-Dīn; al-Ḳazwīnī, Nadjm al-Dīn; al-Kiyā al-Harrāsī; Makhrama; al-Māwardī; al-Mutawallī; al-Muzanī; al-Nawawī; al-Rāfiʿī; al-Ramlī; [in Suppl.] Abū Zurʿa; Ibn Daḳīḳ al-ʿĪd
see also Abū Thawr; Dāwūd b. Khalaf; al-Isfarāyīnī

Shiite → SHIITES

Ẓāhirī Dāwūd b. Khalaf; al-Ḥumaydī; Ibn Dāwūd; Ibn Ḥazm, Abū Muḥammad; (al-)Mundhir b. Saʿīd
see also [in Suppl.] Ibn al-Rūmiyya

law of obligations ʿAḳd; ʿĀriyya; Bayʿ; Ḍamān; Dhimma; Fāsid wa Bāṭil; Faskh; Hiba; Īdjāb; Īdjār; Iḳrār; Inkār; ʿIwaḍ; Kafāla; Khiyār; Ḳirāḍ; Muʿāmalāt; Muʿāwaḍa.3; Muḍāraba; Mufāwaḍa; Mughārasa; Mushāraka; Rahn; [in Suppl.] Dayn; Ghārūḳa
see also ʿAmal.4; Djāʾiz; Ghasb; Ḳabḍ.i; Ḳasam; Maḍmūn; [in Suppl.] Ikrāh

contract of hire and lease Adjr; **Īdjār**; Kirāʾ; Musāḳāt; Muzāraʿa; [in Suppl.] Ḥikr; Inzāl

contract of sale Barāʾa.I; **Bayʿ**; Iḳāla; ʿIwaḍ; Muʿāwaḍa.1; Muwāḍaʿa.1; Salam; [in Suppl.] Darak

see also Ḍarūra; Ildjāʾ; Mukhāṭara; Ṣafḳa; Salaf
law of procedure ʿAdl; Amīn; Bayyina; Daʿwā; Ghāʾib; Ḥakam; Ḳaḍāʾ; Maẓālim
offices Faḳīh; Ḥakam; Ḳāḍī; Ḳāḍī ʿAskar; Ḳassām; Mardjaʿ-i Taḳlīd; Nāʾib.1
see also Amīn; Fatwā; Khalīfa.ii; Maḥkama
Ottoman Bāb-i Mashīkhat; Djazāʾ.ii; Djurm; Fatwā.ii; ʿIlmiyye; Ḳānūn.iii; Ḳānūnnāme; Ḳassām; Maḥkama.2; Makhredj; Medjelle; Medjlis-i Wālā; Mewlewiyyet; Narkh
see also Ḥanafiyya; al-Ḥaramayn; *and* → Dynasties.Anatolia and the Turks.Ottomans.Grand Muftis
penal law ʿĀḳila; Diya; Ḥadd; Ḳadhf; Ḳatl; Khaṭaʾ; Ḳiṣāṣ.5; Ṣalb
see also Muḥṣan; al-Ṣalīb; [in Suppl.] Ikrāh
reform → Reform
schools Ḥanābila; Ḥanafiyya; Mālikiyya
see also Ibn Abī Laylā
terms Adāʾ; Adjr.2; ʿAdl; Aḥkām; Ahl al-Ḥall wa ʾl-ʿAḳd; ʿAḳd; Akdariyya; ʿAḳīḳa; ʿĀḳila; ʿAmal.3 and 4; Amān; ʿĀmil; Amīn; ʿĀriyya; ʿArsh; ʿAwl; ʿAzīma.1; Baʿl.2.b; Bāligh; Barāʾa.I; Bayʿ; Bayʿa; Bayyina; Burhān; Ḍamān; Dār al-ʿAhd; Dār al-Ḥarb; Dār al-Islām; Dār al-Ṣulḥ; Ḍarūra; Daʿwā; Dhabīḥa; Dhimma; Diya; Djāʾiz; Djanāba; Djazāʾ.ii; Djihād; Djizya; Djurm; Faḳīh; Farāʾiḍ; Farḍ; Fāsid wa-Bāṭil; Fāsiḳ; Faskh; Fatwā; Fayʾ; Fiḳh; Ghāʾib; Ghanīma; Ghārim; Ghaṣb; Ghusl; Ḥaḍāna; Ḥadath; Ḥadd; Ḥadjr; Hady; Ḥakam; Ḥaḳḳ; Ḥawāla; Ḥayḍ; Hiba; Ḥiyal.4; Ḥuḳūḳ; Ḥulūl; ʿIbādāt; Ibāḥa.I; ʿIdda; Idhn; Īdjāb; Īdjār; Idjmāʿ; Idjtihād; Iḥrām; Iḥyāʾ; Iḳāla; Ikhtilāf; Iḳrār; Ildjāʾ; Inkār; Inṣāf; Istibrāʾ; Istiḥsān; Istiʾnāf; Istiṣḥāb; ʿIwaḍ; Ḳabāla; Ḳabḍ.i; Ḳaḍāʾ; Ḳadhf; Kafāʾa; Kafāla; Ḳānūn; Ḳānūnnāme; Ḳasam; Ḳatl; Khaṭaʾ; Khiyār; Kirāʾ; Ḳirāḍ; Ḳiṣāṣ; Ḳiyās; Liʿān; Liṣṣ; Luḳaṭa; Maḍmūn; Mafṣūl; Mahr; Maṣlaḥa; Mawāt; Mawlā.5; Maẓālim; Milk; Muʿāmalāt; Muʿāwaḍa; Muḍāraba; Mudjtahid; Mufāwaḍa; Mughārasa; Muḥṣan; Mukhāṭara; Munāṣafa; Musāḳāt; Mushāraka; Mutʿa; Muṭlaḳ; Muwāḍaʿa.1; Muzāraʿa; Nadjis; Nāfila; Naṣṣ; Nāzila; Niyya; Rahn; Ribā; Rukhṣa.1; Sabab.2; Ṣadaḳa; Sadd al-Dharāʾiʿ; Ṣafḳa; Ṣaḥīḥ.2; al-Sahm.2; Salaf; Salam; [in Suppl.] ʿAḳār; Darak; Dayn; Djabr; Ghārūḳa; Ḥikr; Ikrāh; Inzāl
see also Bayt al-Māl; Hudna; Ṣaghīr

Lebanon Djarīda.i.A; Djāmiʿa; Dustūr.ix; Ḥizb.i; Ḥukūma.iii; **Lubnān**; Madjlis.4.A.vi; Maḥkama.4.iii; Mandates; Mutawālī
see also Baladiyya.2; Djāliya; Ḳays ʿAylān; al-Maʿlūf; [in Suppl.] Aḥmad Pasha Küčük; al-Bustānī; Demography.III
governors Bashīr Shihāb II; Dāwūd Pasha; Djānbulāt; Fakhr al-Dīn; Ḥarfūsh
see also Maʿn; Maʿn-zāda

historians of Iskandar Agha
toponyms
ancient ʿAyn al-Djarr
present-day
regions al-Biḳāʿ
towns Baʿlabakk; Batrūn; Bayrūt; Bsharrā; Bteddīn; Djubayl; Karak Nūḥ

LEGENDS Ḥikāya
and → BIBLE.BIBLICAL PERSONAGES; ESCHATOLOGY; KORAN.STORIES
legendary beings ʿAnḳāʾ; al-Burāḳ; Dīw; al-Djassāsa; Djinn; Ghūl; Hātif; ʿIfrīt; Ḳuṭrub; Parī
see also al-Rukhkh
legendary locations Damāwand; Djūdī; Ergenekon; Ḥūsh; Ḳi̊zi̊l-elma
legendary people Abū Righāl; Abū Safyān; Abū Zayd; ʿAdnān; Afrāsiyāb; Ahl al-Ṣuffa; Amīna; Āṣāf b. Barakhyā; Asḥāb al-Kahf; Barṣīṣā; al-Basūs; Bilḳīs; al-Dadjdjāl; Djamshīd; Ḥabīb al-Nadjdjār; Ḥanẓala b. Ṣafwān; Hind bint al-Khuss; Hirmis; Hūshang; Ibn Buḳayla; al-Kāhina; Ḳaḥṭān; Kāwah; al-Khaḍir; Luḳmān; Masʿūd; Naṣr al-Dīn Khodja; Sām
see also Akhī Ewrān; ʿAmr b. ʿAdī; ʿAmr b. Luḥayy; Aṣḥāb al-Rass; Ḳuss b. Sāʿida; Muʿammar; *and* → KORAN.STORIES
legendary stories ʿAbd Allāh b. Djudʿān; Aktham b. Ṣayfī; Almās; al-Baṭṭāl; Buhlūl; Damāwand; Djirdjīs; Djūdī; al-Durr; Fāṭima; al-Ghazāl; al-Ḥaḍr; Ḥāʾiṭ al-ʿAdjūz; Haram; Hārūt wa-Mārūt; Hudhud; Isrāʾīliyyāt; Khālid b. Yazīd b. Muʿāwiya; Ḳiṣaṣ al-Anbiyāʾ; Nūḥ

LEXICOGRAPHY **Ḳāmūs**; Laḥn al-ʿĀmma
and → LINGUISTICS
lexicographers
Arabic Abū Zayd al-Anṣārī; al-Azharī; al-Djawālīḳī; al-Djawharī; Farḥāt; al-Fīrūzābādī; Ibn al-Birr; Ibn Durayd; Ibn Fāris; Ibn Makkī; Ibn Manẓūr; Ibn Sīda; Ibn al-Sikkīt; al-Ḳazzāz; al-Khalīl b. Aḥmad; Muḥammad Murtaḍā; Nashwān b. Saʿīd; al-Ṣaghānī, Raḍiyy al-Dīn; [in Suppl.] Abū ʿAmr al-Shaybānī; Abū Isḥāḳ al-Fārisī; al-Bustānī.1 and 2; al-Fārābī
see also Abū Ḥātim al-Rāzī; Akhtarī; al-Rāghib al-Iṣfahānī; [in Suppl.] Ibn Kabar
Hebrew Ibn Djanāḥ
see also Judaeo-Arabic.iii.B
Persian ʿAbd al-Rashīd al-Tattawī; Aḥmad Wafīḳ Pasha; Burhān; [in Suppl.] Dehkhudā
see also Ārzū Khān; Mahdī Khān Astarābādī; Riḍā Ḳulī Khān
Turkish Akhtarī; al-Kāshgharī; Kāẓi̊m Ḳadrī; Niʿmat Allāh b. Aḥmad; Sāmī

see also Esʿad Efendi, Meḥmed; Luṭfī Efendi; Riyāḍī
terms Fard

LIBYA Djāmiʿa; Djarīda.i.B; Dustūr.xii; **Lībiyā**; Madjlis.4.A.xviii
see also ʿArabiyya.A.iii.3; al-Bārūnī; Ḳaramānlī; Khalīfa b. ʿAskar; *and* → DYNASTIES.SPAIN AND NORTH AFRICA
population → AFRICA.NORTH AFRICA; BERBERS
toponyms
ancient Ṣabra
present-day
oases Awdjila; Baḥriyya; al-Djaghbūb; Djawf Kufra; al-Djufra; Ghadamès; Kufra
regions Barḳa; al-Djufra; Fazzān
see also Nafūsa
towns Adjdābiya; Benghāzī; Darna; Djādū; Murzuḳ
see also Ghāt

LINGUISTICS **Lugha**; Naḥw
see also Balāgha; Bayān; Laḥn al-ʿĀmma; *and* → LANGUAGES; LEXICOGRAPHY
grammarians
8th-9th centuries ʿAbd Allāh b. Abī Isḥāḳ; Abū ʿAmr al-ʿAlāʾ; Abū Ḥātim al-Sidjistānī; Abū ʿUbayd al-Ḳāsim b. Sallām; Abū ʿUbayda; Abū Zayd al-Anṣārī; al-Akhfash.I and II; al-Aṣmaʿī; al-Bāhilī; Djūdī al-Mawrūrī; al-Farrāʾ; Ibn al-Aʿrābī; Ibn Sallām al-Djumaḥī; Ibn al-Sikkīt; ʿĪsā b. ʿUmar; al-Khalīl b. Aḥmad; al-Kisāʾī; Ḳuṭrub; al-Layth b. al-Muẓaffar; al-Māzinī; al-Mubarrad; al-Mufaḍḍal al-Ḍabbī; Muḥammad b. Ḥabīb; al-Ruʾāsī; [in Suppl.] Abu ʾl-ʿAmaythal; Abū ʿAmr al-Shaybānī
see also [in Suppl.] Abu ʾl-Bayḍāʾ al-Riyāḥī
10th-11th centuries Abū ʿUbayd al-Bakrī; al-Adjdābī; al-Akhfash.III; al-Anbārī, Abū Bakr; al-Anbārī, Abū Muḥammad; al-ʿAskarī; Djaḥẓa; al-Fārisī; Ghulām Thaʿlab; Ḥamza al-Iṣfahānī; Ibn al-ʿArīf; Ibn al-Birr; Ibn Djinnī; Ibn Durayd; Ibn Durustawayh; Ibn Fāris; Ibn al-Ḥādjdj; Ibn al-Iflīlī; Ibn Kaysān; Ibn Khālawayh; Ibn al-Khayyāṭ; Ibn al-Ḳūṭiyya; Ibn Makkī; Ibn al-Naḥḥās; Ibn al-Sarrādj; Ibn Sīda; al-Ḳālī; al-Ḳazzāz; Ḳudāma; al-Marzūḳī; Nifṭawayh; al-Rabaḥī; al-Rabaʿī; al-Rummānī; [in Suppl.] Abū Isḥāḳ al-Fārisī; Abū Riyāsh al-Ḳaysī; Abu ʾl-Ṭayyib al-Lughawī; Abū Usāma al-Harawī; al-Djurdjānī; al-Ḥātimī; Ibn Kaysān; Ibn Miḳsam
12th-18th centuries ʿAbd al-Ḳādir al-Baghdādī; Abū Ḥayyān al-Gharnāṭī; al-Anbārī, Abu ʾl-Barakāt; al-Astarābādhī; al-Azharī; al-Baṭalyawsī; al-Djawālīḳī; al-Djazūlī; Fakhrī; Farḥāt; al-Ḥarīrī; Ibn al-Adjdābī; Ibn Ādjurrūm; Ibn ʿAḳīl; Ibn ʿĀṣim; Ibn al-Athīr.1; Ibn Barrī, Abu ʾl-Ḥasan;

Ibn Barrī, Abū Muḥammad; Ibn al-Ḥādjdj; Ibn al-Ḥādjib; Ibn Hishām; Ibn Khātima; Ibn Maḍā'; Ibn Mālik; Ibn Mu'ṭī; Ibn al-Ṣā'igh; Ibn al-Shadjarī al-Baghdādī; al-Maydānī; al-Muṭarrizī; [in Suppl.] Abu 'l-Barakāt; al-Balaṭī, Abu 'l-Fatḥ 'Uthmān; Ibn al-Adjdābī; Ibn Hishām al-Lakhmī

19th-20th centuries Fāris al-Shidyāḳ; Ibn al-Ḥādjdj; al-Nabarāwī; [in Suppl.] Arat

see also Fu'ād Pasha

phonetics Ḥurūf al-Hidjā'.II; Makhāridj al-Ḥurūf; Mushtarik

see also Ḍād; Dāl; Dhāl; Djīm; Fā'; Ghayn; Hā'; Ḥā'; Hamza; Hāwī; Ḥurūf al-Hidjā'; Imāla; Kāf; Ḳāf; Khā'; Lām; Mīm; Nūn; Pā'; Rā'; Ṣād

for Arabic dialects, see Algeria.v; Andalus.x; 'Irāḳ.iv; Lībīya.2; al-Maghrib.VII; Mahrī; Malta.2

terms Aḍdād; Āla.i.; 'Āmil; 'Aṭf; Dakhīl; Djām'; Fard; Fi'l; Gharīb; Ḥaraka wa-Sukūn.ii; Ḥarf; Hāwī; Ḥikāya.I; Ḥukm.II; Ḥulūl; Ibdāl; Iḍāfa; Idghām; Iḍmār; 'Illa.i; Imāla; I'rāb; Ishtiḳāḳ; Ism; Istifhām; Istithnā'; Kasra; Ḳaṭ'; Khabar; Ḳiyās.2; Māḍī; Ma'nā.1; Mu'arrab; Mubālagha.a; Mubtada'.1; Muḍāri'; Mudhakkar; Muḍmar; Musnad.2; Muṭlaḳ; Muwallad.2; Muzdawidj; Nafy; Naṣb; Na't; Nisba.1; Raf'.1; Sabab.4; Ṣaḥīḥ.3; Sālim.2; [in Suppl.] Ḥāl

see also Basīṭ wa-Murakkab; Ghalaṭāt-i Meshhūre; Ḥurūf al-Hidjā'

LITERATURE **Adab**; 'Arabiyya.B; 'Irāḳ.v; Iran.vii; 'Othmānli.III

autobiographical Nu'ayma, Mīkhā'īl; Sālim

biographical Faḍīla; **Manāḳib**; Mathālib

see also 'Ilm al-Ridjāl; Ma'āthir al-Umarā'; Mughals.10; *and* → HAGIOGRAPHY; LITERATURE.HISTORICAL *and* POETRY; MEDICINE.PHYSICIANS.BIOGRAPHIES OF; MUḤAMMAD, THE PROPHET

criticism Ibn al-Athīr.3; Ibn Rashīḳ; Ḳudāma; [in Suppl.] al-Djurdjānī; al-Ḥātimī

modern Kemāl, Meḥmed Nāmiḳ; Köprülü; Kurd 'Alī; al-Māzinī; Olghun, Meḥmed Ṭāhir; [in Suppl.] Alangu; Atač

terms Mubālagha.b

drama **Masraḥ**

Arabic Khayāl al-Ẓill; Masraḥ.1 and 2

see also 'Arabiyya.B.V

playwrights Abū Naḍḍāra; Faraḥ Anṭūn; Ibn Dāniyāl; al-Ḳusanṭīnī; al-Ma'lūf; Nadjīb al-Ḥaddād; Nadjīb Muḥammad Surūr; al-Naḳḳāsh; Ṣalāḥ 'Abd al-Ṣabūr; Salīm al-Naḳḳāsh; [in Suppl.] al-Bustānī.1

see also Isḥāḳ, Adīb; Ismā'īl Ṣabrī; Khalīl Muṭrān

Central Asian Masraḥ.5

Persian Masraḥ.4

playwrights Muḥammad Dja'far Ḳaradja-dāghī; [in Suppl.] Amīrī

Turkish Ḳaragöz; Ḳawuḳlu; Masraḥ.3; Orta Oyunu

playwrights ʿAbd al-Ḥaḳḳ Ḥāmid; Aḥmad Wafīḳ Pasha; Ākhund-zāda; Djewdet; Karay, Refīḳ Khālid; Ḳaṣāb, Teodor; Kemāl, Meḥmed Nāmiḳ; Khayr Allāh Efendi; Manāṣtirli Meḥmed Rifʿat; Meḥmed Raʾūf; Mīzāndji Meḥmed Murād; Muḥibb Aḥmed "Diranas"; Muṣāḥib-zāde Djelāl; Oktay Rifat; [in Suppl.] Alus; Bashḳut; Čamlibel; Ḥasan Bedr al-Dīn

see also Djanāb Shihāb al-Dīn; Ebüzziya Tevfik; Ekrem Bey; Kaygili, ʿOthmān Djemāl; Khālide Edīb; Muʿallim Nādjī

Urdu Masraḥ.6

playwrights Amānat; [in Suppl.] Āgha Ḥashar Kashmīrī

epistolary **Inshāʾ**; Kātib; **Risāla**

see also Ṣadr.(b)

letter-writers ʿAbd al-Ḥamīd; Aḥmad Sirhindī; ʿAmr b. Masʿada; al-Babbaghāʾ; Ghālib; Ḥāletī; al-Hamadhānī; Harkarn; Ibn ʿAmīra; Ibn al-Athīr.3; Ibn Idrīs.I; Ibn Ḳalāḳis; Ibn al-Khaṣīb; Ibn al-Ṣayrafī; al-Ḳabtawrī; Kānī; Khalīfa Shāh Muḥammad; Khʷāndamīr; al-Khʷārazmī; al-Maʿarrī; Makhdūm al-Mulk Manīrī; Meḥmed Pasha Rāmī (*and* Rāmī Meḥmed Pasha); Muḥammad b. Hindū-Shāh; Oḳču-zāde; Rashīd al-Dīn (Waṭwāṭ); Saʿīd b. Ḥumayd; [in Suppl.] ʿAbd al-ʿAzīz b. Yūsuf; Amīr Niẓām; Ibn Khalaf

see also Aljamía; al-Djunayd; Ibn al-ʿAmīd.1; Ibn al-Khaṭīb; Mughals.10

etiquette-literature **Adab**; al-Maḥāsin wa 'l-Masāwī

see also al-Djidd wa 'l-Hazl; Djins; Ḥiyal; Iyās b. Muʿāwiya; Kalīla wa-Dimna; Kātib; Marzban-nāma; Nadīm

authors Abū Ḥayyān al-Tawḥīdī; al-Bayhaḳī; Djāḥiẓ; al-Ghuzūlī; Hilāl al-Ṣābiʾ; al-Ḥuṣrī.I; Ibn ʿAbd Rabbih; Ibn Abi 'l-Dunyā; Ibn al-Muḳaffaʿ; al-Ḳalyūbī; al-Ḳāshānī; al-Kisrawī; al-Marzubānī; Merdjümek; al-Nīsābūrī; al-Rāghib al-Iṣfahānī

see also al-Djahshiyārī; al-Ḳalḳashandī.1

genealogical Mathālib

genealogists al-Abīwardī; al-Djawwānī; al-Hamdānī; al-Kalbī.II; al-Ḳalḳashandī.1; Ḳāsim b. Aṣbagh; al-Marwazī; Muṣʿab; al-Rushāṭī; [in Suppl.] Fakhr-i Mudabbir

see also Ibn Daʾb; al-Ḳādirī al-Ḥasanī; al-Khʷārazmī; Mihmindār

genres

poetry Ghazal; Hidjāʾ; Ḳaṣīda; Khamriyya; Madīḥ; Marthiya; Mathnawī; Mufākhara; Munṣifa; Musammaṭ; Muwashshaḥ; Nawriyya

see also ʿArabiyya.B; Iran.vii; Rabīʿiyyāt; Sāḳī.2

prose Adab; Adjāʾib; Awāʾil; Badīʿ; Bilmedje; Djafr; Faḍīla; Fahrasa; Ḥikāya; Ilāhī; Inshāʾ; Isrāʾīliyyāt; Kān wa-Kān; Khiṭaṭ; Ḳiṣṣa; al-Ḳūmā;

Laḥn al-ʿĀmma; Lug̲h̲z; al-Mag̲h̲āzī; al-Maḥāsin wa ʾl-Masāwī; Maḳāla; Maḳāma; Malḥūn; Manāḳib; Masāʾil wa-Ad̲j̲wiba; al-Masālik wa ʾl-Mamālik; Mat̲h̲ālib; Mawsūʿa; Muḳaddima; Muk̲h̲taṣar; Munāẓara; Nādira; Naḳāʾiḍ; Naṣīḥat al-Mulūk; Risāla; [in Suppl.] Arbaʿūn Ḥadīt̲h̲; Ḥabsiyya

see also Alf Layla wa-Layla (363b); ʿArabiyya.B; Bibliography; D̲j̲ug̲h̲rāfiyā; Fatḥnāme; Ḥayawān; Ḥiyal; Iran.vii; Malāḥim; Mat̲h̲al

historical   Isrāʾīliyyāt; al-Mag̲h̲āzī

     see also Fatḥnāme; Ṣaḥāba; *and* → *the sections* BIOGRAPHICAL, MAG̲H̲ĀZĪ-LITERATURE, *and* TRADITION-LITERATURE *under this entry*

Arabic

     on countries/cities   → *individual countries*

     on dynasties/caliphs   → *individual dynasties under* DYNASTIES

     universal histories   Abu ʾl-Fidā; Abū Mik̲h̲naf; Akansūs; al-Antākī; ʿArīb b. Saʿd al-Kātib al-Ḳurṭubī; al-ʿAynī; al-Bakrī.1 and 2; al-Balād̲h̲urī; Baybars al-Manṣūrī; al-Birzālī; Daḥlān; al-D̲h̲ahabī; al-Diyārbakrī; al-D̲j̲annābī; al-D̲j̲azarī; al-Farg̲h̲ānī; Ḥamza al-Iṣfahānī; Ḥasan-i Rūmlū; al-Hayt̲h̲am b. ʿAdī; Ibn Abī S̲h̲ayba; Ibn Abī Ṭayyiʾ; Ibn Aʿt̲h̲am al-Kūfī; Ibn al-At̲h̲īr.2; Ibn al-Dawādārī; Ibn al-D̲j̲awzī (Sibṭ); Ibn al-Furāt; Ibn Kat̲h̲īr; Ibn K̲h̲aldūn; Ibn K̲h̲ayyāṭ al-ʿUṣfurī; Ibn al-Sāʿī; al-Kalbī.II; Kātib Čelebi; al-Kutubī; al-Makīn b. al-ʿAmīd; al-Masʿūdī; Miskawayh; Münedjdjim Bas̲h̲ī; al-Muṭahhar b. Ṭāhir al-Maḳdisī; al-Nuwayrī, S̲h̲ihāb al-Dīn; Saʿīd b. al-Biṭrīḳ

     see also Ak̲h̲bār Mad̲j̲mūʿa

     8th-century authors   Abū Mik̲h̲naf; ʿAwāna b. al-Ḥakam al-Kalbī

     9th-century authors   al-Balād̲h̲urī; al-Fāḳihī; al-Farg̲h̲ānī; al-Hayt̲h̲am b. ʿAdī; Ibn ʿAbd al-Ḥakam.4; Ibn Abī S̲h̲ayba; Ibn Abī Ṭāhir Ṭayfūr; Ibn Aʿt̲h̲am al-Kūfī; Ibn K̲h̲ayyāṭ al-ʿUṣfurī; Ibn al-Naṭṭāḥ; al-Kalbī.II; al-Madāʾinī; Naṣr b. Muzāḥim

     10th-century authors   ʿArīb b. Saʿd al-Kātib al-Ḳurṭubī; al-Azdī; Baḥs̲h̲al; al-Balawī; al-D̲j̲ahs̲h̲iyārī; Ḥamza al-Iṣfahānī; Ibn al-Dāya; Ibn al-Ḳūṭiyya; Ibn Manda; Ibn al-Ṣag̲h̲īr; al-Kindī, Abū ʿUmar Muḥammad; al-Masʿūdī

     11th-century authors   al-Antākī, Abu ʾl-Farad̲j̲; Ibn al-Bannāʾ; Ibn Burd.I; Ibn Ḥayyān; Ibn al-Raḳīḳ; al-Māfarrūk̲h̲ī

     12th-century authors   al-ʿAẓīmī; Ibn al-D̲j̲awzī; Ibn G̲h̲ālib; Ibn al-Kalānisī; Ibn Ṣāḥib al-Ṣalāt; Ibn al-Ṣayrafī, Abū Bakr; Ibn S̲h̲addād, Abū Muḥammad; ʿImād al-Dīn

     see also al-Bayd̲h̲aḳ; Ibn Manda

     13th-century authors   ʿAbd al-Wāḥid al-Marrākus̲h̲ī; Abū S̲h̲āma; al-Bundārī; al-D̲j̲anadī; Ibn Abi ʾl-Dam; Ibn Abī Ṭayyiʾ; Ibn al-ʿAdīm; Ibn al-At̲h̲īr.2; Ibn al-D̲j̲awzī (Sibṭ); Ibn Ḥamādu; Ibn al-Mud̲j̲āwir;

Ibn Muyassar; Ibn al-Nadjdjār; Ibn al-Sāʿī; Ibn Saʿīd al-Maghribī; Ibn Shaddād, ʿIzz al-Dīn; Ibn Shaddād, Bahāʾ al-Dīn; Ibn al-Ṭuwayr; al-Makīn b. al-ʿAmīd; al-Manṣūr, al-Malik; al-Rāfiʿī; [in Suppl.] Ibn ʿAskar; Ibn Ḥātim

14th-century authors Abu ʾl-Fidā; Baybars al-Manṣūrī; al-Birzālī; al-Dhahabī; al-Djazarī; Ibn Abī Zarʿ; Ibn al-Dawādārī; Ibn Duḳmāḳ; Ibn al-Furāt, Nāṣir al-Dīn; Ibn Ḥabīb, Badr al-Dīn; Ibn ʿIdhārī; Ibn Kathīr, ʿImād al-Dīn; Ibn Khaldūn; Ibn al-Khaṭīb; Ibn al-Ṭiḳṭaḳā; al-Khazradjī, Muwaffaḳ al-Dīn; al-Kutubī; al-Mufaḍḍal b. Abi ʾl-Faḍāʾil; al-Ṣafadī, Ṣalāḥ al-Dīn

15th-century authors Abu ʾl-Maḥāsin b. Taghrībirdī; ʿArabfaḳīh; al-ʿAynī; al-Fāsī; Ibn ʿArabshāh; Ibn Shāhīn al-Ẓāhirī; al-Maḳrīzī; al-Sakhāwī

16th-century authors al-Diyārbakrī; al-Djannābī, Abū Muḥammad; Ḥasan-i Rūmlū; Ibn al-Daybaʿ; Ibn Iyās; Mudjīr al-Dīn al-ʿUlaymī

17th-century authors ʿAbd al-ʿAzīz b. Muḥammad; al-Bakrī (b. Abi ʾl-Surūr); Ibn Abī Dīnār; Kātib Čelebi; al-Maḳḳarī; al-Mawzaʿī

18th-century authors al-Damurdāshī; al-Ḥādjdj Ḥammūda; al-Ifrānī; Münedjdjim Bashi̊

19th-century authors Aḥmad al-Nāṣirī al-Salāwī (*and* al-Nāṣir al-Salāwī); Akanṣūs; ʿAlī Pasha Mubārak; Daḥlān; al-Djabartī; Ghulām Ḥusayn Khān Ṭabāṭabāʾī; Ibn Abi ʾl-Ḍiyāf

see also al-Kardūdī

20th-century authors Ibn Zaydān; Kurd ʿAlī

Indo-Persian Mughals.10

13th and 14th-century authors Baranī; al-Djuzdjānī

15th and 16th-century authors Abu ʾl-Faḍl ʿAllāmī; Djawhar; Gulbadan Bēgam; Niẓām al-Dīn Aḥmad b. al-Harawī; [in Suppl.] ʿAbbās Sarwānī

17th and 18th-century authors ʿAbd al-Ḥamīd Lāhawrī; ʿAbd al-Karīm Kashmīrī; Bakhtāwar Khān; Firishta; Ghulām Ḥusayn Khān Ṭabāṭabāʾī; Ghulām Ḥusayn "Salīm"; ʿInāyat Allāh Khān; Ḳāniʿ; Khʷāfī Khān; Mīr Muḥammad Maʿṣūm; Niʿmat Allāh b. Ḥabīb Allāh Harawī; Niʿmat Khān; Nūr al-Ḥaḳḳ al-Dihlawī; [in Suppl.] ʿĀḳil Khān Rāzī; Ḥādjdjī al-Dabīr; Ḥaydar Malik

see also Badāʾūnī

19th-century authors ʿAbd al-Karīm Munshī

see also Aẓfarī

Persian [in Suppl.] Čač-nāma

universal histories Mīrkhʷānd; Niẓām-shāhī

10th-century authors Balʿamī.2

11th and 12th-century authors Anūshirwān b. Khālid; Bayhaḳī; al-Bayhaḳī, Ẓahīr al-Dīn; Gardīzī; [in Suppl.] Ibn al-Balkhī

13th and 14th-century authors Banākitī; Djuwaynī; Ḥamd Allāh al-Mustawfī al-Ḳazwīnī; Ibn Bībī; Ibn-i Isfandiyār; [in Suppl.] al-Aḳsarāyī; Ḥasan Niẓāmī; al-Ḥusaynī

15th and 16th-century authors ʿAbd al-Razzāḳ al-Samarḳandī; Bidlīsī; Djamāl al-Ḥusaynī; Ghaffārī; Ḥāfiẓ-i Abrū; Ḥaydar Mīrzā; Khʷāndamīr; Ḳum(m)ī; al-Lārī; Rāzī, Amīn Aḥmad; [in Suppl.] Ḥāfiẓ Tanïsh

17th and 18th-century authors ʿAbd al-Fattāh Fūmanī; Ḥaydar b. ʿAlī; Iskandar Beg; Mahdī Khān Astarābādī

see also Īsar-dās

19th and 20th-century authors ʿAbd al-Karīm Bukhārī; [in Suppl.] Fasāʾī

see also ʿAlī b. Shams al-Dīn

Turkish

and → DYNASTIES.ANATOLIA AND THE TURKS.OTTOMANS.HISTORIANS OF

universal histories

see also Neshrī

15th and 16th-century authors ʿAlī; ʿĀshïḳ-pasha-zāde; Bihishtī; Djalālzāde Muṣṭafā Čelebi; Djalālzāde Ṣāliḥ Čelebi; Kemāl Pasha-zāde; Luḳmān b. Sayyid Ḥusayn; Maṭrāḳčï; Meḥmed Pasha, Ḳaramānī; Meḥmed Zaʿīm; Neshrī; Riḍā

see also Ḥadīdī; Medjdī

17th and 18th-century authors ʿAbdī; ʿAbdī Efendi; ʿAbdī Pasha; Aḥmad Rasmī; Čelebi-zāde; Česhmīzāde; Enwerī; Ḥasan Bey-zāde; Ḥibrī; ʿIzzī; Ḳarā-čelebi-zāde.4; Kātib Čelebi; Kemāl, Meḥmed Nāmïḳ; Meḥmed Khalīfe b. Hüseyn; Münedjdjim Bashï; ʿOthmān-zāde

19th and 20th-century authors Aḥmad Djewdet Pasha; Aḥmad Rafīḳ; ʿAlī Amīrī; ʿĀṣim; ʿAṭāʾ Bey, Ṭayyārzāda; (Meḥmed) ʿAṭāʾ Beg; Esʿad Efendi, Meḥmed; Khayr Allāh Efendi; Luṭfī Efendi; Mīzāndjï Meḥmed Murād

see also Ḥilmī

in Eastern Turkish Abu ʾl-Ghāzī Bahādur Khān; Bāḳïkhānlï; Muʾnis

in other languages Afghān.iii; Aljamía; Bengali.ii; Berbers.VI; Beskesek-abaza; Bosna.3; Hausa.iii; Hindī; Indonesia.vi; Judaeo-Arabic.iii; Judaeo-Persian.i; Kano; Ḳiṣṣa.8; Lahndā.2; Laḳ; Masraḥ.6; Pandjābī.2

for Swahili → KENYA; *for Malaysian* → MALAYSIA; *and* → LITERATURE. POETRY.MYSTICAL

Bengali authors Nadhr al-Islām; Nūr Ḳuṭb al-ʿĀlam

Hindi authors Malik Muḥammad Djāyasī; Nihāl Čand Lāhawrī; Prēm Čand

see also ʿAbd al-Raḥīm Khān; Inshāʾ; Lallūdjī Lāl
Judaeo-Arabic authors Mūsā b. ʿAzra; al-Samawʾal b. ʿĀdiyā
and → JUDAISM.LANGUAGE AND LITERATURE
Pashto authors Khushḥāl Khān Khaṭak
Tatar authors Ghafūrī, Medjīd
maghāzī-literature Abū Maʿshar al-Sindī; Ibn ʿĀʾidh; al-Kalāʿī; **al-Maghāzī**; Mūsā b. ʿUḳba
see also al-Baṭṭāl
personages in literature Abū Ḍamḍam; Abu ʾl-Ḳāsim; Abū Zayd; Ali Baba; Ayāz; Aywaz.2; al-Basūs; al-Baṭṭāl; Bekrī Muṣṭafā Agha; Buzurgmihr; Dhu ʾl-Himma; Djamshīd; Djuḥā; al-Ghāḍirī; Ḥamza b. ʿAbd al-Muṭṭalib; Ḥātim al-Ṭāʾī; Ḥayy b. Yaḳẓān; Köroghlu; Manas; Naṣr al-Dīn Khodja; Rustam; Sām
picaresque Maḳāma; Mukaddī
poetry ʿArūḍ; Ghazal; Ḥamāsa; Hidjāʾ; Ḳāfiya; Ḳaṣīda; Khamriyya; Lughz; Madīḥ; Maʿnā.3; Marthiya; Mufākhara; Mukhtārāt; Munṣifa; Musammaṭ; Muwashshaḥ; Muzdawidj; Nawriyya
see also Rāwī; *and* → METRICS
Andalusian ʿArabiyya.B.Appendix; Khamriyya.vi; Muwashshaḥ; Nawriyya
anthologies al-Fatḥ b. Khāḳān; al-Fihrī; Ibn Bassām; Ibn Diḥya; Ibn Faradj al-Djayyānī
8th-century poets Ghirbīb b. ʿAbd Allāh
9th-century poets ʿAbbās b. Firnās; ʿAbbās b. Nāṣiḥ; al-Ghazāl
see also Ibn ʿAlḳama.2
10th-century poets Ibn ʿAbd Rabbih; Ibn Abī Zamanayn; Ibn Faradj al-Djayyānī; Ibn Ḳuzmān.I; Muḳaddam b. Muʿāfā; al-Ramādī
11th century poets Abū Isḥāḳ al-Ilbīrī; Ibn al-Abbār; Ibn ʿAbd al-Ṣamad; Ibn ʿAmmar; Ibn Burd.II; Ibn Darrādj al Ḳasṭallī; Ibn Gharsiya; Ibn al-Ḥaddād; Ibn al-Ḥannāṭ; Ibn al-Labbāna; Ibn Māʾ al-Samāʾ; Ibn al-Shahīd; Ibn Shuhayd; Ibn Zaydūn; al-Muʿtamid ibn ʿAbbād
see also Ṣāʿid al-Baghdādī
12th-century poets al-Aʿmā al-Tuṭīlī; Ḥafṣa bint al-Ḥādjdj; Ibn ʿAbdūn; Ibn Baḳī; Ibn Ḳabṭūrnu; Ibn Khafādja; Ibn Ḳuzmān.II and V; Ibn al-Ṣayrafī; al-Ḳurṭubī; al-Ruṣāfī; Ṣafwān b. Idrīs
see also Mūsā b. ʿAzra
13th-century poets Ḥāzim; Ibn al-Abbār; Ibn ʿAmīra; Ibn Sahl; Ibn Saʿīd al-Maghribī; al-Ḳabtawrī
14th-century poets Ibn al-Ḥādjdj; Ibn Khātima; Ibn Luyūn; Ibn al-Murābiʿ
Arabic ʿAtāba; Ghazal.i; Ḥamāsa.i; Hidjāʾ; Kān wa-Kān; Ḳaṣīda.1; al-Ḳūmā; Madīḥ.1; Maḳṣūra; Malḥūn; Marthiya.1; Mawāliyā; Mawlidiyya;

Mukhtārāt.1; Musammaṭ.1; Muwashshaḥ; Naḳāʾiḍ; Nasīb; Rubāʿī.3
see also ʿAntar; ʿArabiyya.B.II; Bānat Suʿād; Burda.2; ʿIlm al-Djamāl; Ḳalb.II; Kalīla wa-Dimna; Madjnūn Laylā.1; Mawlid; al-Muʿallaḳāt; Muwallad.2; *and* → LITERATURE.POETRY.ANDALUSIAN *and* POETRY. MYSTICAL

anthologies al-Muʿallaḳāt; al-Mufaḍḍaliyyāt; **Mukhtārāt**.1

anthologists Abu ʾl-Faradj al-Iṣbahānī; Abū Tammām; al-ʿAlamī; al-Bākharzī; al-Buḥturī; Diʿbil; al-Hamdānī; Ḥammād al-Rāwiya; Ibn Abī Ṭāhir Ṭayfūr; Ibn Dāwūd; Ibn al-Ḳutayba; Ibn al-Muʿtazz; Ibn al-Ṣayrafī; ʿImād al-Dīn; al-Nawādjī; [in Suppl.] Abū Zayd al-Ḳurashī; al-Bustānī.3

pre-Islamic poets ʿAbīd b. al-Abraṣ; Abū Dhuʾayb al-Hudhalī; Abū Duʾād al-Iyādī; Abū Kabīr al-Hudhalī; ʿAdī b. Zayd; al-Afwah al-Awdī; al-Aghlab al-ʿIdjlī; ʿAlḳama; ʿĀmir b. al-Ṭufayl; ʿAmr b. al-Ahtam; ʿAmr b. Ḳamīʾa; ʿAmr b. Kulthūm; ʿAntara; al-Aʿshā; al-Aswad b. Yaʿfur; Aws b. Ḥadjar; Bishr b. Abī Khāzim; Bisṭām b. Ḳays; Durayd b. al-Ṣimma; al-Ḥādira; al-Ḥārith b. Ḥilliza; Ḥassān b. Thābit; Ḥātim al-Ṭāʾī; Ibn al-Iṭnāba al-Khazradjī; Imruʾ al-Ḳays b. Ḥudjr; Ḳays b. al-Khaṭīm; al-Khansāʾ; Laḳīṭ al-Iyādī; Laḳīṭ b. Zurāra; al-Munakhkhal al-Yashkurī; Muraḳḳish; al-Mutalammis; al-Nābigha al-Dhubyānī; Salāma b. Djandal; al-Samawʾal b. ʿĀdiyā
see also ʿArabiyya.B.I; Ghazal; Hudhayl; al-Muʿallaḳāt; al-Mufaḍḍaliyyāt; Mufākhara.2; Nasīb.2.a

mukhaḍramūn poets (6th-7th centuries) al-ʿAbbās b. Mirdās; ʿAbd Allāh b. Rawāḥa; Abū Khirāsh; Abū Miḥdjān; ʿAmr b. Maʿdīkarib; Ḍirār b. al-Khaṭṭāb; Ḥassān b. Thābit; al-Ḥuṭayʾa; Ibn (al-)Aḥmar; Kaʿb b. Mālik; Kaʿb b. Zuhayr; Khidāsh b. Zuhayr al-Aṣghar; Labīd b. Rabīʿa; Maʿn b. Aws al-Muzanī; **Mukhaḍram**; Mutammim b. Nuwayra; al-Nābigha al-Djaʿdī; al-Namir b. Tawlab al-ʿUklī; [in Suppl.] Abu ʾl-Ṭamaḥān al-Ḳaynī; Ibn Muḳbil
see also Hudhayl; Nasīb.2.b

7th and 8th-century poets al-ʿAbbās b. al-Aḥnaf; ʿAbd Allāh b. Hammān; Abū ʿAṭāʾ al-Sindī; Abū Dahbal al-Djumaḥī; Abū Dulāma; Abu ʾl-Nadjm al-ʿIdjlī; Abū Ṣakhr al-Hudhalī; Abu ʾl-Shamaḳmaḳ; Adī b. al-Riḳāʿ; al-ʿAdjdjādj; al-Aḥwaṣ; al-Akhṭal; al-ʿArdjī; Aʿshā Hamdān; al-Ashdjaʿ b. ʿAmr al-Sulamī; Ayman b. Khuraym; al-Baʿīth; Bashshār b. Burd; Dhu ʾl-Rumma; Djamīl; Djarīr; Dukayn al-Rādjiz; al-Farazdaḳ; al-Ḥakam b. ʿAbdal; al-Ḥakam b. Ḳanbar; Ḥammād ʿAdjrad; Ḥamza b. Bīḍ; Ḥāritha b. Badr al-Ghudānī; al-Ḥuḍayn; Ḥumayd b. Thawr; Ḥumayd al-Arḳaṭ; Ibn Abī ʿUyayna; Ibn al-Dumayna; Ibn Harma; Ibn Ḳays al-Ruḳayyāt; Ibn Ladjaʾ; Ibn al-Mawlā; Ibn Mayyāda; Ibn Mufarrigh; Ibn Muṭayr; Ibn Sayḥān; ʿImrān

b. Ḥiṭṭān; ʿInān; Ismāʿīl b. Yasār; Kaʿb b. Djuʿayl al-Taghlabī; Ḳaṭarī b. al-Fudjāʾa; al-Kumayt b. Zayd al-Asadī; al-Ḳuṭāmī; Kuthayyir b. ʿAbd al-Raḥmān; Laylā al-Akhyaliyya; Manṣūr al-Namarī; Marwān b. Abī Ḥafṣa and Marwān b. Abi ʾl-Djanūb; Miskīn al-Dārimī; Mūsā Shahawātin; Musāwir al-Warrāḳ; Muṭīʿ b. Iyās; Nubāta b. ʿAbd Allāh; Nuṣayb; Nuṣayb b. Rabāḥ; al-Rāʿī; Ruʾba b. al-ʿAdjdjādj; Ṣafī al-Dīn al-Ḥillī; Ṣafwān al-Anṣārī; SaḥbānWāʾil; Ṣāliḥ b. ʿAbd al-Ḳuddūs; Salm al-Khāsir; [in Suppl.] ʿAbd al-Raḥmān b. Ḥassān; Abū ʿAmr al-Shaybānī; Abū Ḥayyā al-Numayrī; Abū Ḥuzāba; Abū Nukhayla; Bakr b. al-Naṭṭāḥ

see also Nasīb.2.c and d

9th and 10th-century poets Abān b. ʿAbd al-Ḥamīd; ʿAbd Allāh b. Ṭāhir; Abu ʾl-ʿAtāhiya; Abu ʾl-ʿAynāʾ; Abū Dulaf; Abu ʾl-Faradj al-Iṣbahānī; Abū Firās; Abū Nuwās; Abu ʾl-Shīṣ; Abū Tammām; Abū Yaʿḳūb al-Khuraymī; al-ʿAkawwak; ʿAlī b. al-Djahm; al-ʿAttābī; al-Babbaghāʾ; al-Baṣīr; al-Buḥturī; al-Bustī; Diʿbil; Dīk al-Djinn al-Ḥimṣī; al-Djammāz; al-Hamdānī; (al-)Ḥusayn b. al-Ḍaḥḥāk; Ibn al-ʿAllāf; Ibn Bassām; Ibn al-Ḥadjdjādj; Ibn Kunāsa; Ibn Lankak; Ibn al-Muʿadhdhal; Ibn Munādhir; Ibn al-Muʿtazz; Ibn al-Rūmī; al-Ḳāsim b. ʿĪsā; Khālid b. Yazīd al-Kātib al-Tamīmī; al-Khālidiyyāni; al-Khaṭṭābī; al-Khubzaʾaruzzī; al-Kisrawī; Kushādjim; al-Maʾmūnī; Muḥammad b. ʿAbd al-Raḥmān al-ʿAṭawī; Muḥammad b. Ḥāzim al-Bāhilī; Muḥammad b. Umayya; Muḥammad b. Yasīr al-Riyāshī; al-Muṣʿabī; Muslim b. al-Walīd; al-Mutanabbī; Naṣr b. Nuṣayr; Sahl b. Hārūn b. Rāhawayh; Saʿīd b. Ḥumayd; [in Suppl.] Abu ʾl-ʿAmaythal; Abu ʾl-Asad al-Ḥimmānī; Abu ʾl-Ḥasan al-Maghribī; Abū Hiffān; Abu ʾl-ʿIbar; Abū Riyāsh al-Ḳaysī; Abū Saʿd al-Makhzūmī; Abū Shurāʿa; ʿAlī b. Muḥammad al-Tūnisī al-Iyādī; Faḍl al-Shāʿira; al-Fazārī; al-Ḥamdawī

see also al-Hamadhānī; Ibn Abī Zamanayn; Nasīb.2.d

11th-13th-century poets al-Abīwardī; ʿAmīd al-Dīn al-Abzārī; al-Arradjānī; al-Badīʿ al-Asṭurlābī; Bahāʾ al-Dīn Zuhayr; al-Bākharzī; Ḥayṣa Bayṣa; al-Ḥuṣrī.II; Ibn Abi ʾl-Ḥadīd; Ibn Abī Ḥaṣīna; Ibn al-ʿAfīf al-Tilimsānī; Ibn al-Habbāriyya; Ibn Ḥamdīs; Ibn Ḥayyūs; Ibn Hindū; Ibn al-Ḳaṭṭān; Ibn al-Ḳaysarānī.2; Ibn Khamīs; Ibn Maṭrūḥ; Ibn al-Nabīh; Ibn Rashīḳ; Ibn Sanāʾ al-Mulk; Ibn al-Shadjarī al-Baghdādī; Ibn Sharaf al-Ḳayrawānī; Ibn Shibl; Ibn al-Taʿāwīdhī; al-Kammūnī; Ḳurhub; al-Maʿarrī; al-Marwazī; Mihyār; Muḥammad b. ʿAlī b. ʿUmar; al-Rūdhrāwarī; al-Ṣaghānī, ʿAbd al-Muʾmin; Ṣāʿid al-Baghdādī; [in Suppl.] Abu ʾl-Ḥasan al-Anṣārī; al-Balaṭī, Abu ʾl-Fatḥ ʿUthmān; al-Būṣīrī; al-Ghazzī

see also al-Khazradjī; Nasīb.2.d

14th-18th-century poets ʿAbd al-ʿAzīz b. Muḥammad; ʿAbd al-Ghanī; al-Bakrī; al-Būrīnī; Farḥāt; Ibn Abī Ḥadjala; Ibn ʿAmmār; Ibn Ḥidjdja; Ibn Nubāta; Ibn al-Ṣāʾigh; Ibn al-Wannān

see also Khiḍr Beg

19th and 20th-century poets al-Akhras; al-Bārūdī; Fāris al-Shidyāḳ; al-Fārūḳī; Fikrī; Ḥāfiẓ Ibrāhīm; Ibn Idrīs (I); Ismāʿīl Ṣabrī; Ismāʿīl Ṣabrī Pasha; Ḳaddūr al-ʿAlamī; al-Kāẓimī, ʿAbd al-Muḥsin; Khalīl Muṭrān; al-Khūrī; al-Maʿlūf; al-Manfalūṭī; Mardam.2; Maʿrūf al-Ruṣāfī; al-Māzinī; Nādjī; Nadjīb al-Ḥaddād; Nadjīb Muḥammad Surūr; Saʿīd Abū Bakr; Ṣalāḥ ʿAbd al-Ṣabūr; [in Suppl.] Abū Māḍī; Abū Shādī; al-ʿAḳḳād; al-Bustānī; Buṭrus Karāma; Ibn ʿAmr al-Ribāṭī; Ibn al-Ḥādjdj

transmission of **Rāwī**

transmitters Ḥammād al-Rāwiya; Ibn Daʾb; Ibn Kunāsa; Khalaf b. Ḥayyān al-Aḥmar; Khālid b. Ṣafwān b. al-Ahtam; al-Kisrawī; al-Mufaḍḍal al-Ḍabbī; Muḥammad b. al-Ḥasan b. Dīnār; [in Suppl.] Abū ʿAmr al-Shaybānī

and → LINGUISTICS.GRAMMARIANS.8TH-9TH CENTURIES

Indo-Persian Mughals.10; Sabk-i Hindī

see also Pandjābī.2; *and* → LITERATURE.POETRY.MYSTICAL

11th-century poets Masʿūd-i Saʿd-i Salmān; [in Suppl.] Abu ʾl-Faradj b. Masʿūd Rūnī

14th-century poets Amīr Khusraw; Ḥasan Dihlawī; [in Suppl.] Ḥamīd Ḳalandar

16th-century poets Fayḍī

see also ʿAbd al-Raḥīm Khān

17th and 18th-century poets Ārzū Khān; Ashraf ʿAlī Khān; Bīdil; Dard; Ghanī; Ghanīmat; Ḥazīn; Idrākī Bēglārī; Ḳāniʿ; Ḳudsī, Muḥammad Djān; Makhfī; Malik Ḳummi; Munīr Lāhawrī; Nāṣir ʿAlī Sirhindī; Naẓīrī; Salīm, Muḥammad Ḳulī; [in Suppl.] Ghanīmat Kundjāhī

19th-century poets Aẓfarī; Ghālib; Rangīn; [in Suppl.] Adīb Pīshāwarī

see also Afsūs

love **Ghazal**; **Nasīb**; Raḳīb

see also Ibn Sahl; al-Marzubānī; *and* → LOVE.PLATONIC LOVE

mystical

Arabic ʿAbd al-Ghanī; al-Bakrī, Muḥammad; al-Bakrī, Muṣṭafā; al-Dimyāṭī; al-Ḥallādj; Ibn ʿAdjība; Ibn ʿAlīwa; Ibn al-ʿArabī; al-Madjdhūb; Makhrama.3

see also ʿAbd al-Ḳādir al-Djīlānī; Abū Madyan; al-Ḳādirī al-Ḥasanī; [in Suppl.] al-Hilālī

Central Asian Aḥmad Yasawī

Indian Bāḳī bi ʾllāh; Bīdil; Dard; "Djamālī"; Hānsawī; Ḥusaynī Sādāt Amīr; Imdād Allāh; Malik Muḥammad Djāyasī; [in Suppl.] Ḥamīd Ḳalandar *see also* Bhitāʾī; Pandjābī.2

Indonesian Ḥamza Fanṣūrī

Persian Aḥmad-i Djām; ʿAṭṭār; Bābā-Ṭāhir; Djalāl al-Dīn Rūmī; Faḍl Allāh Ḥurūfī; Ghudjduwānī; Humām al-Dīn b. ʿAlāʾ Tabrīzī; ʿIrāḳī; Kamāl Khudjandī; Ḳāsim-i Anwār; Kirmānī; Lāhidjī; Maḥmūd Shabistarī; [in Suppl.] ʿĀrif Čelebī; ʿImād al-Dīn ʿAlī, Faḳīh-i Kirmānī

see also Abū Saʿīd b. Abi ʾl-Khayr; Kharaḳānī; [in Suppl.] Aḥmad-i Rūmī

Turkish ʿĀshiḳ Pasha; Faṣīḥ Dede; Gulshanī; Gülshehrī; Hüdāʾī; Münedjdjim Bashî; Nefes; Nesīmī; Refīʿī; [in Suppl.] Eshrefoghlu; Esrār Dede

see also Ḥusām al-Dīn Čelebi; Ismāʿīl al-Anḳarawī; Ismāʿīl Ḥaḳḳī; Ḳayghusuz Abdāl; Khalīlī

Persian Ghazal.ii; Ḥamāsa.ii; Hidjāʾ.ii; Ḳaṣīda.2; Khamsa; Madīḥ.2; Malik al-Shuʿarāʾ; Marthiya.2; Mathnawī.2; Mukhtārāt.2; Musammaṭ; Mustazād; Rubāʿī.1; [in Suppl.] Ḥabsiyya

see also Barzū-nāma; Farhād wa-Shirīn; Iskandar Nāma.ii; Kalīla wa-Dimna; Madjnūn Laylā.2; Radīf.2; Ṣafawids.III; Sāḳī.2; *and* → LITERATURE.POETRY.INDO-PERSIAN *and* POETRY.MYSTICAL

anthologies **Mukhtārāt**.2

anthologists ʿAwfī; Dawlat-Shāh; Luṭf ʿAlī Beg; [in Suppl.] Djādjarmī.2

biographies Sām Mīrzā

9th-century poets Muḥammad b. Waṣīf

see also Sahl b. Hārūn b. Rāhawayh

10th-century poets Bābā-Ṭāhir; Daḳīḳī; Kisāʾī; al-Muṣʿabī; Rūdakī; [in Suppl.] Abū Shakūr Balkhī

11th-13th-century poets ʿAbd al-Wāsiʿ Djabalī; Anwarī; Asadī; ʿAṭṭār; Azraḳī; Bābā Afḍal; Djalāl al-Dīn Rūmī; Falakī Shirwānī; Farrukhī; Firdawsī; Gurgānī; Humām al-Dīn b. ʿAlāʾ Tabrīzī; ʿImādī (*and* [in Suppl.]); ʿIrāḳī; Kamāl al-Dīn Ismāʿīl; Ḳaṭrān; Khʷādjū; Khāḳānī; Labībī; Lāmiʿī; Mahsatī; Manūčihrī; Muʿizzī; Mukhtārī; Niẓāmī Gandjawī; Pūr-i Bahāʾ; Ṣābir; Saʿdī; [in Suppl.] ʿAmʿaḳ; Djādjarmī; Djamāl al-Dīn Iṣfahānī

14th and 15th-century poets ʿAṣṣār; Awḥadī; Banākitī; Busḥāḳ; Djāmī; Faḍl Allāh Ḥurūfī; Fattāḥī; Ḥāfiẓ; Ḥāmidī; Ibn-i Yamīn; ʿIṣāmī; Kātibī; Nizārī Ḳuhistānī; Rāmī Tabrīzī; Salmān-i Sāwadjī; [in Suppl.] ʿĀrifī; Badr-i Čāčī; ʿImād al-Dīn ʿAlī, Faḳīh-i Kirmānī

see also Djem; Ḥamd Allāh al-Mustawfī al-Ḳazwīnī

16th-century poets Bannāʾī; Baṣīrī; Fighānī; Hātifī; Hilālī; Muḥtasham-i Kāshānī; Mushfiḳī; Nawʿī; Saḥābī Astarābādī; Sām Mīrzā *see also* Luḳmān b. Sayyid Ḥusayn

17th-century poets Asīr; al-Dāmād; Ḳadrī; Ḳalīm Abū Ṭālib; Kāshif; Lāhīdjī.2; Nāẓim Farrukh Ḥusayn; Ṣāʾib; Saʿīdā Gīlānī

see also al-ʿĀmilī; Ghanīmat; Khushḥāl Khān Khaṭak; [in Suppl.] Findiriskī; *and* → LITERATURE.POETRY.INDO-PERSIAN

18th-century poets Hātif; Ḥazīn; Luṭf ʿAlī Beg; Nadjāt

see also Āzād Bilgrāmī

19th and 20th-century poets Bahār; Furūgh; Furūghī; Ḳāʾānī; Ḳurrat al-ʿAyn; Lāhūtī; Nafīsī, Saʿīd; Nashāṭ; Nīmā Yūshīdj; Parwīn Iʿtiṣāmī; Pūr-i Dāwūd; Rashīd Yāsimī; Riḍā Ḳulī Khān; Ṣabā; Sabzawārī; [in Suppl.] ʿĀrif, Mīrzā; Ashraf al-Dīn Gīlānī; Dehkhudā

see also Ghālib; Iḳbāl; Ḳāʾim-maḳām-i Farāhānī

Turkish Ḥamāsa.iii; Hidjāʾ.iii; Ḳaṣīda.3; Khamsa; Ḳoshma; Madīḥ.3; Māni; Marthiya.3; Mathnawī.3; Mukhtārāt.3; Musammaṭ.1; Rabīʿiyyāt; Rubāʿī.2; [in Suppl.] Ghazal.iii

see also Alpamı̊sh; ʿĀshiḳ; Farhād wa-Shirīn; Ilāhī; Iskandar Nāma.iii; Karadja Oghlan; Madjnūn Laylā.3; Ozan; *and* → LITERATURE.POETRY.MYSTICAL

anthologies **Mukhtārāt**.3

biographies Riḍā; Riyāḍī; Sālim

11th and 12th-century poets Aḥmad Yuknakī; Ḥakīm Ata; Ḳutadghu Bilig

13th and 14th-century poets Aḥmadī; ʿĀshı̊ḳ Pasha; Burhān al-Dīn; Dehhānī; Gülshehrī

15th-century poets Āhī; Aḥmad Pasha Bursalı̊; Dāʿī; Firdewsī; Gulshanī; Ḥamdī, Ḥamd Allāh; Ḳāsim Pasha; Ḳayghusuz Abdāl; Khalīlī; Khiḍr Beg

see also Djem; Ḥāmidī

16th-century poets Āgehī; ʿAzīzī; Bāḳī; Baṣīrī; Bihishtī; Dhātī; Djaʿfar Čelebi; Djalāl Ḥusayn Čelebi; Djalālzāde Muṣṭafā Čelebi; Djalālzāde Ṣāliḥ Čelebi; Faḍlī; Faḳīrī; Fawrī; Ferdī; Fighānī; Fuḍūlī; Ghazālī; Gulshanī; Ḥadīdī; Ḳarā-čelebi-zāde; Kemāl Pasha-zāde; Khāḳānī; Khayālī; Ḳorḳud b. Bāyazīd; Lāmiʿī; Laṭīfī; Luḳmān b. Sayyid Ḥusayn; Meʾalī; Medjdī; Mesīḥī; Mihrī Khātūn; Naẓmī, Edirneli; Nedjātī Bey; Newʿī; Rewānī

17th-century poets ʿAṭāʾī; ʿAzmī-zāde; Bahāʾī Meḥmed Efendi; Faṣīḥ Dede; Fehīm, Undjuzāde Muṣṭafā; Ḥāletī; Ḳarā-čelebi-zāde; Ḳul Muṣṭafā; Ḳuloghlu; Nāʾilī; Nāẓı̊m, Muṣṭafā; Naẓmī, Sheykh Meḥmed; Nefʿī; Niyāzī; ʿÖmer ʿĀshı̊ḳ; Riyāḍī

18th-century poets Belīgh, Ismāʿīl; Belīgh, Meḥmed Emīn; Čelebi-zāde; Česhmīzāde; Fiṭnat; Gevherī; Ghālib; Ḥāmī-i Āmidī; Ḥashmet; Kānī; Meḥmed Pasha Rāmī (*and* Rāmī Meḥmed Pasha); Nābī; Naḥīfī;

Naẓīm; Nedīm; Nes͟h'et; Newres.1; 'Ot͟hmān-zāde; Rāg͟hib Pas͟ha

19th-century poets 'Ārif Hikmet Bey; 'Aynī; Dadalog͟hlu; Derdli; D͟hihnī; Fāḍil Bey; Faṭīn; Fehīm, Süleymān; Ismā'īl Ṣafā; 'Izzet Molla; Kemāl, Meḥmed Nāmîḳ; Laylā K͟hānîm; Menemenli-zāde Meḥmed Ṭāhir; Mu'allim Nādjī; Newres.2; Pertew Pas͟ha.II; Redjā'ī-zāde

20th-century poets 'Abd al-Ḥāḳḳ Ḥāmid; Djanāb S͟hihāb al-Dīn; Djewdet; Ekrem Bey; Hās͟him; Kanık; Köprülü (Meḥmed Fuad); Ḳoryürek; Laylā K͟hānîm; Meḥmed 'Ākif; Meḥmed Emīn; Muḥibb Aḥmed "Diranas"; Nāẓim Ḥikmet; Oktay Rifat; Ork͟han Seyfī; Ortač, Yūsuf Ḍiyā; Sāhir, Ḍjelal; [in Suppl.] 'Ās͟hîk Weysel; Bülükbas͟hî; Čamlîbel; Es͟href; Eyyuboghlu; Gövsa

see also [in Suppl.] Ergun; Fîndîḳoghlu

in Eastern Turkish Ād͟harī.ii; Bābur; Bāḳîk͟hānlî; D͟hākir; Djambul Djabaev; G͟hāzī Girāy II; Ḥamāsa.iv; Hidja'.iii; Iskandar Nāma.iii; Ismā'īl I; Ḳayyūm Nāṣirī; Ḳutadg͟hu Bilig; Luṭfī; Mīr 'Alī S͟hīr Nawā'ī; Mu'nis; Sakkākī

translations from Western langs. Ismā'īl Ḥaḳḳī 'Ālīs͟hān; Kanık

Urdu G͟hazal.iv; Ḥamāsa.v; Hidja'.iv; Ḳaṣīda.4; Madīḥ.4; Madjnūn Layla.4; Mart͟hiya.4; Mat͟hnawī.4; Muk͟htārāt.4; Musammaṭ.2; Mus͟hā'ara

17th-century poets Nuṣratī

18th-century poets As͟hraf 'Alī K͟hān; Dard; Djur'at; Maẓhar; [in Suppl.] Ḥasan, Mīr G͟hulām

see also Ārzū K͟hān

19th-century poets Amānat; Anīs; Aẓfarī; Dabīr, Salāmat 'Alī; Dāg͟h; D͟hawḳ; G͟hālib; Faḳīr Muḥammad K͟hān; Ḥālī; Ilāhī Bak͟hs͟h "Ma'rūf"; Ins͟hā'; Mīr Muḥammad Taḳī; Muḥsin 'Alī Muḥsin; Mu'min; Mus͟hafī; Nāsik͟h; Nasīm; Rangīn; [in Suppl.] Ātis͟h

see also [in Suppl.] Āzād

20th-century poets Akbar, Ḥusayn Allāhābādī; Āzād; Djawān; Iḳbāl; Muḥammad 'Alī; Rās͟hid, N.M.; Ruswā; [in Suppl.] Ḥasrat Mohānī

see also Āzurda

vernacular Nabaṭī

prose Adab; Ḥikāya; Ḳiṣṣa; Maḳāma; Muḳaddima; Naṣīḥat al-Mulūk; Risāla

and → LITERATURE.ETIQUETTE-LITERATURE *and* HISTORICAL; PRESS

Arabic 'Arabiyya.B.V; Ḥikāya.i; Ḳiṣṣa.2; Maḳāla.1; Maḳāma; Nahḍa; Naṣīḥat al-Mulūk.1; Risāla.1; Sadj'.3

and → LITERATURE.DRAMA; PRESS

works Alf Layla wa-Layla; Baybars; Bilawhar wa-Yūdāsaf; D͟hu 'l-Himma; Kalīla wa-Dimna; Luḳmān.3

9th and 10th-century authors al-Djāḥiẓ; al-Hamad͟hānī; Ibn al-Muḳaffa'; [in Suppl.] Abu 'l-'Anbas al-Ṣaymarī

11th-13th-century authors al-Ḥarīrī; Ibn Nāḳiyā; [in Suppl.] Abu 'l-Muṭahhar al-Azdī; al-Djazarī
14th-18th-century authors Ibn Abī Ḥadjala
see also al-Ibshīhī
19th and 20th-century authors Aḥmad Amīn; Faraḥ Anṭūn; Ḥāfiẓ Ibrāhīm; Maḥmūd Taymūr; al-Maʿlūf; al-Manfalūṭī; Mayy Ziyāda; al-Māzinī; Muḥammad Ḥusayn Haykal; al-Muwayliḥī.2; Nuʿayma, Mīkhāʾīl; al-Rayḥānī; Salāma Mūsā; [in Suppl.] Abū Shādī; al-ʿAḳḳād; al-Bustānī.6
see also Djamīl al-Mudawwar; al-Khālidī; Kurd ʿAlī

Persian Ḥikāya.ii; Iran.vii; Ḳiṣṣa.4; Maḳāla.2; Naṣīḥat al-Mulūk.2; Risāla.2
see also Ṣafawids.III; *and* → LITERATURE.DRAMA; PRESS
works Bakhtiyār-nāma; Dabistān al-Madhāhib; Ḳahramān-nāma; Kalīla wa-Dimna; Madjnūn Laylā.2; Marzbān-nāma
see also Niẓām al-Mulk; Niẓāmī ʿArūḍī Samarḳandī
11th and 12th-century authors Ḥamīdī; al-Ḳāshānī; Kay Kāʾūs b. Iskandar; Nāṣir-i Khusraw; Naṣr Allāh b. Muḥammad; Niẓāmī ʿArūḍī Samarḳandī; Rashīd al-Dīn (Waṭwāṭ); al-Samʿānī, Abu 'l-Ḳāsim
13th-century authors Saʿdī
14th-century authors Nakhshabī
15th-century authors Kāshifī
17th and 18th-century authors ʿInāyat Allāh Kańbū; Mumtāz
19th and 20th-century authors Bahār; Hidāyat, Ṣādiḳ; Nafīsī, Saʿīd; [in Suppl.] Āl-i Aḥmad; Bihrangī; Dehkhudā
see also Furūgh.2

Turkish Ḥikāya.iii; Ḳiṣṣa.3; Maddāḥ; Maḳāla.3; Risāla.3
see also Bilmedje; *and* → LITERATURE.DRAMA; PRESS
works Alpamïsh; Billur Köshk; Dede Ḳorḳut; Ḳahramān-nāma; Oghuz-nāma
see also Merdjümek
17th-century authors Nergisī
18th-century authors ʿAlī ʿAzīz, Giridli; Nābī
19th and 20th-century authors Aḥmad Ḥikmet; Aḥmad Midḥat; Aḥmad Rāsim; Djanāb Shihāb al-Dīn; Ebüzziya Tevfik; Ekrem Bey; Fiṭrat; Hïsar; Ḥusayn Djāhid; Ḥusayn Raḥmī; Karay, Refīḳ Khālid; Ḳaṣāb, Teodor; Kaygïlï, ʿOthmān Djemāl; Kemāl; Kemāl, Meḥmed Nāmïḳ; Kemal Tahir; Khālid Ḍiyāʾ; Khālide Edīb; Laylā Khānïm; Meḥmed Raʾūf; Oktay Rifat; ʿÖmer Seyf ül-Dīn; Orkhan Kemāl; Reshād Nūrī; Sabahattin Ali; Sāmī; [in Suppl.] Atač; Atay; Čaylaḳ Tewfīḳ; Esendal; Haliḳarnas Balïḳčïsï
see also Aḥmad Iḥsān; Ileri, Djelāl Nūrī; İnal; Ismāʿīl Ḥaḳḳi ʿĀlīshān;

Ḳiṣṣa.3(b); [in Suppl.] Eyyūboghlu
in Eastern Turkish Rabghūzī
Urdu Ḥikāya.iv; Ḳiṣṣa.5
and → LITERATURE.DRAMA; PRESS
19th and 20th-century authors Amān, Mīr; Djawān; Faḳīr Muḥammad Khān; Iḳbāl; Nadhīr Aḥmad Dihlawī; Prēm Čand; Ruswā; [in Suppl.] Āzād
proverbs in Mathal.4
see also Ḥamza al-Iṣfahānī; Rashīd al-Dīn (Waṭwāṭ)
terms ʿArūḍ; ʿAtāba; Badīʿ; Balāgha; Bayān; Dakhīl; Fard; Faṣāḥa; Fāṣila; Ibtidaʾ; Idjaza; Iḍmar; Iḳtibas; Intihaʾ; Irtidjāl; Istiʿara; Ḳabḍ.iii; Ḳafiya; Ḳaṭʿ; Kināya; Luzūm mā lā yalzam; al-Maʿānī wa ʾl-Bayān; Madjāz; Maʿnā.3; Muʿāraḍa; Muzāwadja; Radīf.2; Radjaz.4
and → LITERATURE.GENRES; METRICS
topoi Bukhl; Bulbul; Ghurāb; Gul; Ḥamām; Ḥayawān.5; Inṣāf; al-Ḳamar.II; Ḳaṭā; Nardjis; Raḥīl; Sāḳī
see also Ghazal.ii; ʿIshḳ; Khamriyya; Rabīʿiyyāt
tradition-literature Athar; **Ḥadīth**; Ḥadīth Ḳudsī; Hind.v.e; [in Suppl.] Arbaʿūn Ḥadīth
see also Ahl al-Ḥadīth; Ḥashwiyya; Khabar; Mustamlī; Naskh; Riwāya
authoritative collections Abū Dāʾūd al-Sidjistānī; Aḥmad b. Ḥanbal; Anas b. Mālik; al-Bayhaḳī; al-Bukhārī, Muḥammad b. Ismāʿīl; al-Dāraḳuṭnī; al-Dārimī; Ibn Ḥibbān; Ibn Mādja; Muslim b. al-Ḥadjdjādj; al-Nasāʾī
see also al-ʿAynī; Ibn Hubayra
terms al-Djarḥ wa ʾl-Taʿdīl; Fard; Gharīb; Ḥikāya.I; Idjāza; Isnād; Khabar al-Wāḥid; Mashhūr; Matn; Muʿanʿan; Munkar; Mursal; Muṣannaf; Musnad.3; Mustamlī; Mutawātir.(a); Rafʿ.2; Ridjāl; Ṣaḥīḥ.1; Ṣāliḥ
see also Ḥadīth
traditionists Rāwī; Ridjāl
see also al-Rāmahurmuzī
7th century ʿAbd Allāh b. ʿUmar b. al-Khaṭṭāb; Abū Bakra; Abū Hurayra; al-Aʿmash; Ibn Abī Laylā.I; Ibn Masʿūd; Kaʿb al-Aḥbār; al-Khawlānī, Abū Idrīs; al-Khawlānī, Abū Muslim; [in Suppl.] Djābir b. ʿAbd Allāh
8th century Abu ʾl-ʿĀliya al-Riyāḥī; Abū Mikhnaf; al-Ashʿarī, Abū Burda; Djābir b. Zayd; al-Fuḍayl b. ʿIyāḍ; Ghundjār; al-Ḥasan b. Ṣāliḥ b. Ḥayy al-Kūfī; al-Ḥasan al-Baṣrī; Ibn Abī Laylā.II; Ibn Daʾb; Ibn Isḥāḳ; Ibn al-Naṭṭāḥ; Ibn Shubruma; Ibn Sīrīn; ʿIkrima; al-Layth b. Saʿd; Maymūn b. Mihrān; Muḳātil b. Sulaymān; Nāfiʿ; al-Nakhaʿī, Ibrāhīm; Saʿīd b. Abī Arūba; [in Suppl.] Abū ʿAmr al-Shaybānī; Ibn Djuraydj

9th century Abū Nuʿaym al-Mulāʾī; Baḳī b. Makhlad; Ibn Abī Khaythama; Ibn Abi 'l-Shawārib; Ibn Abī Shayba; Ibn ʿĀʾisha.IV; Ibn Rāhwayh; Ibn Saʿd; Ibn Sallām al-Djumaḥī; Ibrāhīm al-Ḥarbī; al-Karābīsī.2; al-Marwazī; Muslim b. al-Ḥadjdjādj; Nuʿaym b. Ḥammād; [in Suppl.] Abū ʿĀṣim al-Nabīl; Asad b. Mūsā b. Ibrāhīm
see also Ibn Khayyāṭ al-ʿUṣfurī; Ibn Ḳuṭlūbughā

10th century Abū ʿArūba; al-Anbārī, Abū Bakr; al-Anbārī, Abū Muḥammad; Ghulām Thaʿlab; Ibn al-ʿAllāf; Ḳāsim b. Aṣbagh; al-Khaṭṭābī; [in Suppl.] Ibn ʿUḳda

11th century al-Ḥākim al-Naysābūrī; Ibn ʿAbd al-Barr; Ibn al-Bannāʾ; Ibn Fūrak; Ibn Mākūlā.3; al-Ḳābisī; al-Khaṭīb al-Baghdādī; al-Sahmī

12th century al-Baghawī; Ibn al-ʿArabī; Ibn ʿAsākir; Ibn Ḥubaysh; Ibn al-Ḳaysarānī.1; Ibn al-Nadjdjār; al-Lawātī; Razīn b. Muʿāwiya; al-Rushāṭī; al-Ṣadafī
see also al-Samʿānī, Abū Saʿd

13th century al-Dimyāṭī al-Shāfiʿī; Ibn al-Athīr.1; Ibn Diḥya; Ibn Faraḥ al-Ishbīlī; al-Ṣaghānī, Raḍiyy al-Dīn; [in Suppl.] Ibn Daḳīḳ al-ʿĪd

14th century al-Dhahabī; Ibn Kathīr; al-Mizzī

15th century Ibn Ḥadjar al-ʿAsḳalānī; al-Ibshīhī.2; al-Ḳasṭallānī; Muʿīn al-Miskīn
see also Ibn Ḳuṭlūbughā

Shiite ʿAbd Allāh b. Maymūn; Dindān; Djaʿfar al-Ṣādiḳ; Ibn Bābawayh(i); al-Kashshī; al-Kāẓimī, ʿAbd al-Nabī; al-Kulaynī, Abū Djaʿfar Muḥammad; Madjlisī; Muḥammad b. Makkī; [in Suppl.] Akhbāriyya; al-Barḳī; Djābir al-Djuʿfī
see also Asmāʾ

translations from Western languages

into Arabic Muḥammad Bey ʿUthmān Djalāl

into Persian Muḥammad Ḥasan Khān; Nafīsī, Saʿīd

into Turkish Ismāʿīl Ḥaḳḳi ʿĀlīshān; Kanık

travel-literature Djughrāfiyā.(d); **Riḥla**

authors ʿAbd al-Ghanī; al-ʿAbdarī; Abū Dulaf; Abū Ṭālib Khān; Aḥmad Iḥsān; ʿAlī Bey al-ʿAbbāsī; ʿAlī Khān; al-ʿAyyāshī; Ewliyā Čelebi; Fāris al-Shidyāḳ; al-Ghassānī; Ghiyāth al-Dīn Naḳḳāsh; Ibn Baṭṭūṭa; Ibn Djubayr; Ibn Idrīs(II); Kurd ʿAlī; Ma Huan; Meḥmed Yirmisekiz; Nāṣir-i Khusraw; [in Suppl.] al-Ghazzāl; Ibn Nāṣir.3
see also Hārūn b. Yaḥyā; Ibn Djuzayy; Ibn Rushayd; Ibn Saʿīd al-Maghribī; Ibrāhīm b. Yaʿḳūb; Khayr Allāh Efendi; Leo Africanus

narratives [in Suppl.] Akhbār al-Ṣīn wa 'l-Hind

wisdom-literature al-Aḥnaf b. Ḳays; ʿAlī b. Abī Ṭālib; Buzurgmihr; Hūshang; Luḳmān; Sahl b. Hārūn b. Rāhawayh; [in Suppl.] Djāwīdhān Khirad
see also Aktham b. Ṣayfī; Buhlūl; al-Ibshīhī

wondrous literature Abū Ḥāmid al-Gharnāṭī; ʿ**Adjāʾib**; Buzurg b. Shahriyār; al-Ḳazwīnī
see also Ibn Sarābiyūn; Ḳiṣaṣ al-Anbiyāʾ

LOVE ʿ**Ishḳ**
see also Ishāra; Ḳalb.II; *and* → LITERATURE.POETRY.LOVE
mystical love ʿĀshiḳ; ʿIshḳ
and → LITERATURE.POETRY.MYSTICAL; MYSTICISM
platonic love Djamīl al-ʿUdhrī; Ghazal.i.3; Ibn Dāwūd; Kuthayyir b. ʿAbd al-Raḥmān; Laylā al-Akhyaliyya; Nuṣayb b. Rabāḥ; al-Ramādī
and → LITERATURE.POETRY.LOVE
treatises on al-Antāḳī, Dāʾūd; Ibn Ḥazm, Abū Muḥammad; Rafīʿ al-Dīn
see also Bukhtīshūʿ

M

MADAGASCAR **Madagascar**; Massalajem

MAGIC ʿAzīma.2; Djadwal; Istinzāl; Khāṣṣa; Nīrandj; Ruḳya; [in Suppl.] Budūḥ
see also ʿAbd Allāh b. Hilāl; Antemuru; Djinn; Ḥadjar; Ḥurūf; Istikhāra; Istiḳsām; Istisḳāʾ; Kabid.4; al-Ḳamar.II; Ḳatl.ii.2; Khawāṣṣ al-Ḳurʾān; Kihāna; Kitābāt.5; Rūḥāniyya
treatises on al-Maḳḳarī; [in Suppl.] Ibn ʿAzzūz; al-Būnī

MALAWI Kota Kota

MALAYSIA Malacca; **Malay Peninsula**; Malays; **Malaysia**
see also Baladiyya.6; Djāmiʿa; Indonesia; Kandūrī; Kitābāt.8; Partai Islam se Malaysia (Pas); Rembau
architecture → ARCHITECTURE.REGIONS
belles-lettres ʿAbd Allāh b. ʿAbd al-Ḳādir; Dāwūd al-Faṭānī; Ḥikāya.v; Ḳiṣṣa.6; Malays
see also Indonesia.vi
states Penang; Perak; Sabah

MALI Adrar.2; Aḥmad al-Shaykh; Aḥmadu Lobbo; Ḥamāliyya; Kaʿti; **Mali**; Mansa Mūsā
see also Mande
historians of al-Saʿdī
toponyms
regions Kaarta
towns Bamako; Dienné; Gao

MAMLUKS **Mamlūks**
see also Ḥarfūsh; Manshūr; Mihmindār; Rank; *and* → DYNASTIES.EGYPT AND THE FERTILE CRESCENT; MILITARY.MAMLUK

MARONITES → CHRISTIANITY.DENOMINATIONS; LEBANON

MARRIAGE Djilwa; Khiṭba; Mutʿa; **Nikāḥ**; [in Suppl.] Djabr
see also ʿAbd.3.e; ʿĀda.iii and iv.4; ʿArūs Resmi; Fāsid wa-Bāṭil.III; Ghāʾib; Ḥaḍāna; Kafāʾa; Kurds.iv.A.1; al-Marʾa.2; Mawākib.4.3 and 5; Raḍāʿ
dowry **Mahr**; Ṣadāḳ

MARTYRDOM Fidāʾī; Maẓlūm
see also Ḥabīb al-Nadjdjār; (al-)Ḥusayn b. ʿAlī b. Abī Ṭālib; Khubayb; Madjlis.3; Mashhad; Masʿūd; [in Suppl.] ʿAbd Allāh b. Abī Bakr al-Miyānadjī

MATHEMATICS Algorithmus; al-Djabr wa ʾl-Muḳābala; Fard; Ḥisāb al-ʿAḳd; Ḥisāb al-Ghubār; **ʿIlm al-Ḥisāb**; Kasr; Ḳaṭʿ; Ḳuṭr; Māl; Manshūr; Misāḥa; Muḳaddam; Muṣādara.1; Muthallath; **al-Riyāḍiyyāt**; al-Sahm.1.a; [in Suppl.] ʿIlm al-Handasa
see also al-Mīzān; [in Suppl.] Halīladj
algebra **al-Djabr wa ʾl-Muḳābala**
geometry **Misāḥa**; [in Suppl.] **ʿIlm al-Handasa**
mathematicians Abū Kāmil Shudjāʿ; Abu ʾl-Wafāʾ al-Būzadjānī; ʿAlī al-Ḳūshdjī; al-Bīrūnī; Ibn al-Bannāʾ al-Marrākushī; Ibn al-Haytham; Ibn ʿIrāḳ; Isḥāḳ Efendi; al-Ḳalaṣādī; al-Karābīsī.1; al-Karadjī; al-Kāshī; al-Khʷārazmī; al-Khāzin; al-Khudjandī; Kushiyār b. Labān; al-Madjrīṭī; al-Mārdīnī; Muḥammad b. ʿĪsā al-Māhānī; Muḥammad b. ʿUmar
see also Balīnūs; Ḳusṭā b. Lūḳā

MAURITANIA Adrar.3; Atar; Ḥawḍ; Māʾ al-ʿAynayn al-Ḳalḳamī; Madjlis.4.A.xxii; **Mūritāniyā**
see also Dustūr.xv; Lamtūna; al-Māmī
toponyms
ancient Awdaghost; Ghāna; Ḳunbi Ṣāliḥ
present-day Nouakchott

MECHANICS Ḥiyal.2; al-Ḳarasṭūn; [in Suppl.] al-Djazarī; **Ḥiyal**
see also Ibn al-Sāʿātī; *and* → HYDROLOGY

MEDICINE
and → ANATOMY; DRUGS; ILLNESS; PHARMACOLOGY
centres of Bīmāristān; Gondēshāpūr; Ḳalāwūn; [in Suppl.] Abū Zaʿbal

see also Baghdād; Dimashḳ; al-Madīna
dentistry
dental care Miswāk
see also ʿAḳīḳ; Mardjān
treatises on Hāmōn
see also Ibn Abi ʾl-Bayān
medical handbooks/encyclopaedias ʿAlī b. al-ʿAbbās; al-Djurdjānī, Ismāʿīl b. al-Ḥusayn; Ibn al-Nafīs; Ibn Sīnā; al-Masīḥī
medicines Abanūs; Adhargūn; ʿAfṣ; Afsantīn; Almās; ʿAnbar; Baḳḳam; Bān; al-Dahnadj; Dhahab; al-Durr; Fiḍḍa; Ḥinnāʾ; Kāfūr; Ḳaranful; Ḳaṭrān; al-Ḳily; al-Kuḥl; Lubān; Maghnaṭıs.1; Mardjān; Millı.2, Misk; Mūmiyāʾ; Ṣabr; Ṣābūn; Sādj; Ṣamgh; [in Suppl.] Ās; Bawraḳ; Djawz; Halīladj; Hindibāʾ; Iklīl al-Malik
see also Bāzahr; al-Iksīr; Kabid.3; [in Suppl.] Afāwīh; Dam; *for medicinal use of animal parts, see articles on specific animals*
obstetrics ʿArīb b. Saʿd al-Kātib al-Ḳurṭubī
and → CHILD.CHILDBIRTH
ophthalmologists ʿAlī b. ʿĪsā; ʿAmmār al-Mawṣilī; al-Ghāfiḳī; Ibn Dāniyāl; Khalīfa b. Abi ʾl-Maḥāsin
see also ʿAyn; Ḥunayn b. Isḥāḳ al-ʿIbādī; Ibn al-Nafīs; Ibn Zuhr.V; *and* → ANATOMY.EYE
physicians Djarrāḥ; Ḥāwī; [in Suppl.] Faṣṣād
see also ʿAyn; Constantinus Africanus; Ḥikma; Kabid.3; Masāʾil wa-Adjwiba; *and* → MEDICINE.OPHTHALMOLOGISTS; PHARMACOLOGY
biographies of Ibn Abī Uṣaybiʿa; Ibn Djuldjul; Ibn al-Ḳāḍī; Isḥāḳ b. Ḥunayn
see also Ibn al-Ḳifṭī
7th century [in Suppl.] al-Ḥārith b. Kalada
9th century Bukhtīshūʿ; Ḥunayn b. Isḥāḳ al-ʿIbādī; Ibn Māsawayh; Sābūr b. Sahl
see also Māsardjawayh
10th century ʿAlī b. al-ʿAbbās; ʿArīb b. Saʿd al-Kātib al-Ḳurṭubī; Ibn Djuldjul; Isḥāḳ b. Ḥunayn; Isḥāḳ b. Sulaymān al-Isrāʾīlī; Ḳusṭā b. Lūḳā; al-Rāzī, Abū Bakr; Ṣābiʾ.(3); Saʿīd al-Dimashḳī; [in Suppl.] Ibn Abi ʾl-Ashʿath
11th century al-Anṭākī, Abu ʾl-Faradj; Ibn Buṭlān; Ibn Djanāḥ; Ibn Djazla; Ibn al-Djazzār; Ibn Riḍwān; Ibn Sīnā; Ibn al-Ṭayyib; Ibn Wāfid; Ibn Zuhr.II; al-Masīḥī
12th century Abu ʾl-Barakāt; al-Djurdjānī, Ismāʿīl b. al-Ḥusayn; Ibn Djāmiʿ; Ibn al-Tilmīdh; Ibn Zuhr.III and IV; al-Marwazī, Sharaf al-Zamān; [in Suppl.] Ibn Biklārish
see also Ibn Rushd
13th century Ibn Abi ʾl-Bayān; Ibn Abī Uṣaybiʿa; Ibn Hubal; Ibn al-Nafīs; Ibn Ṭumlūs; Saʿd al-Dawla; [in Suppl.] Ibn al-Ḳuff

14th century Ḥādjdjī Pasha; Ibn al-Khaṭīb; Isḥāḳ b. Murād; Ḳuṭb al-Dīn Shīrāzī
15th century Bashīr Čelebi
16th century al-Anṭākī, Dāʾūd; Hāmōn
17th century Ḥayātī-zāde
18th century [in Suppl.] Ādarrāḳ; Ibn Shaḳrūn al-Miknāsī
19th century and on Bahdjat Muṣṭafā Efendi; Muḥammad b. Aḥmad al-Iskandarānī; [in Suppl.] ʿAbd al-Salām b. Muḥammad
Greek Diyusḳuridīs; Djālīnūs; Rūfus al-Afsīsī; [in Suppl.] Ahrun; Buḳrāṭ
see also Ḥunayn b. Isḥāḳ al-ʿIbādī; Ibn Riḍwān; Ibn al-Ṭayyib; Isḥāḳ b. Ḥunayn; Iṣṭifān b. Basīl; [in Suppl.] Ḥubaysh b. al-Ḥasan al-Dimashḳī; Ibn Abi ʾl-Ashʿath
Jewish Hāmōn; Ibn Abi ʾl-Bayān; Ibn Djāmiʿ; Ibn Djanāḥ; Isḥāḳ b. Sulaymān al-Isrāʾīlī; Māsardjawayh; Saʿd al-Dawla; [in Suppl.] Ibn Biklārish
see also Abu ʾl-Barakāt; Ḥayātī-zāde.1
Ottoman Bahdjat Muṣṭafā Efendi; Bashīr Čelebi; Ḥādjdjī Pasha; Hāmōn; Ḥayātī-zāde; Isḥāḳ b. Murād
see also Ḥekīm-bashi̊
terms Bīmāristān; Djarrāḥ; Ḥidjāb; Ḳuwwa.5; Sabab.1
see also Ḥāl
veterinary Bayṭār; Ibn Hudhayl; Ibn al-Mundhir

MELKITES → CHRISTIANITY.DENOMINATIONS

MESOPOTAMIA → IRAQ

METALLURGY Ḳalʿī; Khārṣīnī; **Maʿdin**
see also Kalah; al-Mīzān.1; *and* → MINERALOGY.MINES
metals Dhahab; Fiḍḍa; al-Ḥadīd; Nuḥās
and → MINERALOGY.MINERALS; PROFESSIONS.ARTISANS

METAPHYSICS **Mā baʿd al-Ṭabīʿa**
see also ʿAbd al-Laṭīf al-Baghdādī; Māhiyya; Muṭlaḳ

METEOROLOGY al-Āthār al-ʿUlwiyya
see also Anwāʾ; Sadjʿ.2; [in Suppl.] Ibn al-Adjdābī
winds **Rīḥ**; Samūm

METRICS **ʿArūḍ**
see also al-Djawharī; al-Khalīl b. Aḥmad; al-Khazradjī; *and* → LITERATURE.POETRY
metres Mudjtathth; Mutadārik; Mutaḳārib; Mutawātir.(b); Radjaz; Ramal.1

terms Dakhīl; Fard; Kaṭʿ; Sabab.3; Ṣadr.(a); Sālim.3

MILITARY Baḥriyya; Djaysh; **Ḥarb**; [in Suppl.] Baḥriyya
see also Dār al-Ḥarb; Djihād; Fatḥnāme; Ghazw; Naḳḳāra-khāna
architecture Ribāṭ
and → ARCHITECTURE.MONUMENTS.STRONGHOLDS
army **Djaysh**; Istiʿrāḍ (ʿArḍ); **Lashkar**; Radīf.3
see also Djāsūs; Ṣaff.2; *and* → MILITARY.MAMLUK *and* OTTOMAN
contingents Bāzinḳir; Djāndār; Djaysh.iii.2; Djund; Ghulām; Gūm; Ḳūrčī; Maḥalla; Mamlūk; Mutaṭawwiʿa
see also Almogávares; Fāris
battles
and → MILITARY.EXPEDITIONS
before 622 Buʿāth; Dhū Ḳār; Djabala; Fidjār; Ḥalīma; [in Suppl.] Dāḥis
see also Ayyām al-ʿArab; Ḥanẓala b. Mālik
622-632 Badr; Biʾr Maʿūna; Buzākha; Ḥunayn; Khandaḳ; Khaybar; Muʾta
see also Mālik b. ʿAwf
633-660 Adjnādayn; ʿAḳrabāʾ; al-Djamal; Djisr; Faḥl; Ḥarūrāʾ; al-Ḳādisiyya.2; Mardj al-Ṣuffar; [in Suppl.] Dhāt al-Ṣawārī
see also ʿAbd Allāh b. Saʿd; ʿĀʾisha bint Abī Bakr; ʿAlī b. Abī Ṭālib; al-Hurmuzān; al-Nahrawān; Rustam b. Farrukh Hurmuzd
661-750 ʿAyn al-Warda; Balāṭ al-Shuhadāʾ; Baldj b. Bishr; al-Bishr; Dayr al-Djamādjim; Dayr al-Djāthalīḳ; al-Ḥarra; al-Khāzir; Mardj Rāhiṭ
see also (al-)Ḥusayn b. ʿAlī b. Abī Ṭālib; Kulthūm b. ʿIyāḍ al-Ḳushayrī; (al-)Ḳusṭanṭīniyya
751-1258 al-Arak; Bakhamra; Dayr al-ʿĀḳūl; Fakhkh; Ḥaydarān; Hazārasp; al-ʿIḳāb; Köse Dāgh; Malāzgird.2; [in Suppl.] Dandānḳān
see also Ḥadjar al-Nasr; al-Madjūs; al-Manṣūr bi ʾllāh, Ismāʿīl; Mardj Dābiḳ
1258-18th century ʿAyn Djālūt; Čāldirān; Dābiḳ; Djarba; Ḥimṣ; Ḳoṣowa; Mardj Dābiḳ; Mardj Rāhiṭ; Mardj al-Ṣuffar; Mezőkeresztes; Mohács.a and b; Nīkbūlī; Pānīpat
see also Baḥriyya.iii; Fatḥnāme; Ḥarb; Nahr Abī Fuṭrus; ʿOthmān Pasha
after 18th century Abuklea; Atjèh; Česhme; Farwān; Gök Tepe; Isly; Kūt al-ʿAmāra; Maysalūn; Nizıb; Rīf.II
see also al-ʿAḳaba; Gulistān
bodies ʿAyyār; Dawāʾir; Djaysh.iii.1; Futuwwa; Ghāzī
see also ʿAlī b. Muḥammad al-Zandjī; al-Ikhwān; Khashabiyya
booty Fayʾ; **Ghanīma**
see also Baranta; Ghazw; Khāliṣa; Pendjik; *and* → MILITARY.PRISONERS
decorations **Nishān**

expeditions Ghāzī; **Ṣā'ifa**
see also Ghazw
Indo-Muslim Bārūd.vi; Ghulām.iii; Ḥarb.vi; Ḥiṣār.vi; Lashkar
see also Isti'rāḍ (Arḍ)
Mamluk al-Baḥriyya; Baḥriyya.II; Bārūd.iii; Burdjiyya; Ḥalḳa; Ḥarb.iii; Ḥiṣār.iv; **Mamlūk**
see also Amīr Ākhūr; al-Amīr al-Kabīr; Atābak al-'Asākir; 'Ayn Djālūt; Čerkes.ii; Ḥimṣ; 'Īsā b. Muhannā; Khāṣṣakiyya; Ḳumāsh; Rikābdār
navy **Baḥriyya**; Dār al-Ṣinā'a; Daryā-begi; Ḳapudan Pasha; Lewend.1; Nassads; Ra'īs.3; Riyāla; [in Suppl.] **Baḥriyya**
see also 'Azab; Gelibolu; Kātib Čelebi; [in Suppl.] Dhāt al-Ṣawārī; *and* → DYNASTIES.ANATOLIA AND THE TURKS.OTTOMANS.HIGH ADMIRALS; NAVIGATION.SHIPS; PIRACY
offices Amīr; 'Arīf; Atābak al-'Asākir; Fawdjdār; Ispahbadh; Ispahsālār; Isti'rāḍ ('Arḍ); Ḳā'id; Manṣab; Sālār
see also Amīr al-Umarā'; Dārūgha; Ḳāḍī 'Askar; Ḳūrčī; *and* → MILITARY.OTTOMAN
Ottoman Bāb-i Ser'askeri; Baḥriyya.iii; Balyemez; Bārūd.iv; Devshirme; Djebeli; Ghulām.iv; Ḥarb.iv; Ḥarbiye; Ḥiṣār.v; Müsellem; Radīf.3; [in Suppl.] Djebedji
see also 'Askarī; Ḍabṭiyya; Gelibolu; Gūm; Ḥareket Ordusu; Isti'rāḍ (Arḍ); Ḳapïdji; Karakol; Martolos; Mensūkhāt; Mondros; Nefīr; Ordu; Pendjik; *and* → MILITARY.NAVY
army contingents al-Abnā'.V; 'Adjamī Oghlān; Akïndjï; Alay; 'Azab; Bashï-bozuḳ; Bölük; Deli; Devedji; Djānbāzān; Eshkindji; Ghurabā'; Gönüllü; Khāṣṣekī; Khumbaradjï; Lewend; Niẓām-ï Djedīd; Odjaḳ; Orta; [in Suppl.] Djebedji
see also Akhī; Nefīr
officers Bayraḳdār; Biñbashï; Bölük-bashï; Čā'ūsh; Čorbadjï.1; Ḍābiṭ; Daryā-begi; Ḳapudan Pasha; Mushīr; Rikābdār; Riyāla
pay 'Aṭā'; In'ām; Māl al-Bay'a; Rizḳ.3
police Aḥdāth; 'Asas; Ḍabṭiyya; Karakol
see also Dawā'ir; Futuwwa; Kōtwāl; Martolos; Naḳīb.2
prisoners Lamas-ṣū; Mübādele.ii; [in Suppl.] Fidā'
and → MILITARY.BOOTY
reform → REFORM.MILITARY
tactics Ḥarb; Ḥiṣār; Ḥiyal.1
see also Fīl; *and* → ARCHITECTURE.MONUMENTS.STRONGHOLDS
treatises on Ibn Hudhayl; [in Suppl.] Fakhr-i Mudabbir
see also Ḥarb.ii; Ḥiyal.1
weapons 'Anaza; 'Arrāda; Balyemez; Bārūd; Dūrbāsh; Ḳaws; Mandjanīḳ; Nafṭ.2
see also 'Alam; Asad Allāh Iṣfahānī; Hilāl.ii; Ḥiṣār; Ḳal'ī; Lamṭ; Marātib

MINERALOGY **Maʿdin**
see also al-Mīzān.1
minerals Abū Ḳalamūn; ʿAḳīḳ; Almās; Bārūd; Billawr; al-Dahnadj; Fīrūzadj; al-Kibrīt; al-Kuḥl; Maghnāṭīs.1; Milḥ; Mūmiyāʾ; Naṭrūn; [in Suppl.] Bawraḳ
see also al-Andalus.v; Damāwand; Golkonḍā; Ḥadjar; Kirmān; Maʿdin; Malindi; *and* → JEWELRY; METALLURGY
mines al-ʿAllāḳī; Anadolu.iii.6; al-Andalus.v.2; ʿAraba; Armīniya.III; Azalay; Badakhshān; Billiton; Bilma; Čankiri; al-Djabbūl; Djayzān; al-Durūʿ; Farghānā; Firrīsh; Gümüsh-khāne; Kalah; Ḳarā Ḥiṣār.2 and 3; Ḳayṣariyya; al-Ḳily; Ḳishm; Maʿdin.2; al-Maʿdin
see also Fāzūghlī; Filasṭīn; Milḥ

MIRACLES **Karāma; Muʿdjiza**
see also Āya; Dawsa; Māʾ al-ʿAynayn al-Ḳalḳamī; Miʿrādj; *and* → SAINTHOOD

MONARCHY Malik; Mamlaka
see also Darshan

MONASTICISM **Rahbāniyya**
and → CHRISTIANITY.MONASTERIES

MONGOLIA Ḳaraḳorum; Khalkha; **Mongolia**; Mongols
Mongols Batuʾids; Čaghatay Khānate; Čūbānids; Djalāyir; Djānids; Giray; Hayāṭila; Ilkhāns; Kalmuk; Ḳarā Khiṭāy; Ḳūrīltāy; Mangit; **Mongols**
see also ʿAyn Djālūt; Dūghlāt; Ergenekon; Ḥimṣ; Khānbaliḳ; Ḳūbčūr; Ḳungrāt; Libās.iii; Ötüken; *and* → DYNASTIES.MONGOLS
historians of Rashīd al-Dīn Ṭabīb
and → DYNASTIES.MONGOLS *and the section Historians of under individual dynasties*
physical geography
waters Orkhon

MONOPHYSITES → CHRISTIANITY.DENOMINATIONS

MOROCCO **al-Maghrib**
see also ʿArabiyya.A.iii.3; Ḥimāya.ii; Mallāḥ; Rīf.II
architecture → ARCHITECTURE.REGIONS.NORTH AFRICA
dynasties ʿAlawīs; Idrīsids; Marīnids; Saʿdids
see also Bū Ḥmāra; Ḥasanī; [in Suppl.] Aḥmad al-Hība; *and* → DYNASTIES.SPAIN AND NORTH AFRICA
historians of Aḥmad al-Nāṣirī al-Salāwī (*and* al-Nāṣir al-Salāwī); Akanṣūs; Ibn Abī Zarʿ; Ibn al-Ḳāḍī

see also Ibn al-Raḳīḳ; al-Kattānī; [in Suppl.] ʿAllāl al-Fāsī; *and* → DYNASTIES.SPAIN AND NORTH AFRICA

modern period Baladiyya.3; Djāmiʿa; Djarīda.i.B; Djaysh.iii.2; Dustūr.xvii; Ḥizb.i; Ḥukūma.iv; Maʿārif.2.C; Madjlis.4.A.xxi; Madjmaʿ ʿIlmī.i.2.d; Maḥkama.4.x; Makhzan; [in Suppl.] Institut des hautes études marocaines

reform Salafiyya.1(c)

statesmen [in Suppl.] ʿAllāl al-Fāsī

population Glāwā; Dukkāla; Ḥarṭānī; Khulṭ; [in Suppl.] Awraba

see also al-Fāsiyyūn; *and* → BERBERS

religion al-Maghrib.VI

mystical orders Darḳāwa; Hansaliyya; Hazmīriyyūn; ʿIsāwā; al-Nāṣiriyya; [in Suppl.] Ḥamādisha

for Djazūliyya, *see* al-Djazūlī, Abū ʿAbd Allāh

see also [in Suppl.] ʿĀʾisha Ḳandīsha; *and* → MYSTICISM; SAINTHOOD

toponyms

ancient Anfā; Bādis; al-Baṣra; Fāzāz; al-Ḳaṣr al-Ṣaghīr; Nakūr

present-day

islands [in Suppl.] al-Ḥusayma

regions Darʿa; Figuig; Gharb; Ḥawz; Ifni; Rīf.I.2

towns Agadir-ighir; Āghmāt; al-ʿArāʾish; Aṣfī; Aṣīla; Azammūr; Damnāt; (al-)Dār al-Bayḍāʾ; al-Djadīda; Dubdū; Faḍāla; Fās; Garsīf; al-Ḳaṣr al-Kabīr; al-Mahdiyya; Marrākush; Mawlāy Idrīs; Melilla; Miknās; Ribāṭ al-Fatḥ; Sabta; Salā; [in Suppl.] Azrū; Benī Mellāl

see also al-Ḥamrāʾ

MOUNTAINS Adjaʾ and Salmā; Adrar.2; Aghri̊ Dagh; Aïr; Ala Dagh; Aladja Dagh; Alburz; Altai; Alwand Kūh; ʿAmūr; Atlas; Awrās; Balkhān; Beshparmaḳ; Bībān; Bingöl Dagh; Bīsutūn; Čopan-ata; Damāwand; Deve Boynu; Djabala; al-Djibāl; Djūdī; Djurdjura; Elma Daghi̊; Erdjiyas Daghi̊; Fūta Djallon; Gāwur Daghlari̊; Ḥaḍūr; Ḥamrīn; Ḥarāz; Hawrāmān; Hindū Kush; Ḥiṣn al-Ghurāb; Ḥufāsh; al-Ḳabḳ; Kabylia; Ḳaraḳorum; Ḳāsiyūn; Khumayr; Kūh-i Bābā; al-Lukkām; Nafūsa; Pamirs; Safīd Kūh

see also Hind.i.i; Ḳarā Bāgh; *and* → *the section Physical Geography under individual countries*

MOZAMBIQUE Kerimba; Makua; **Mozambique**; Pemba

MUḤAMMAD, THE PROPHET Hidjra; Ḥirāʾ; al-Ḥudaybiya; Khaybar; Khuzāʿa; Ḳudāʿa; Ḳuraysh; al-Madīna.i.2; Mawlid; Miʿrādj; **Muḥammad**; Ṣaḥāba

see also al-Ḳurʾān; Muʾākhāt; al-Muʾallafa Ḳulūbuhum; Nubuwwa; Nūr Muḥammadī; [in Suppl.] Bayʿat al-Riḍwān

belongings of Athar; al-Burāḳ; Burda.1; Dhu ʾl-Faḳār; Duldul; Emānet-i

Muḳaddese; Ḳadam Sharīf; Khirḳa-yi Sherīf; Liḥya-yi Sherīf
biographies of ʿAbd al-Ḥaḳḳ b. Sayf al-Dīn; al-Bakrī, Abu ʾl-Ḥasan; Daḥlān; al-Diyārbakrī; al-Djawwānī; al-Ḥalabī, Nūr al-Dīn; Ibn Hishām; Ibn Isḥāḳ; Ibn Sayyid al-Nās; ʿIyāḍ b. Mūsā; Ḳarā-čelebi-zāde.4; al-Ḳasṭallānī; Liu Chih; al-Maghāzī; Mughulṭāy; Muḥammad Ḥusayn Haykal; Muʿīn al-Miskīn
see also Hind.v.e; Ibn Saʿd; al-Khargūshī; [in Suppl.] Dinet
companions of Abū Ayyūb al-Anṣārī; Abū Bakra; Abu ʾl-Dardāʾ; Abū Dharr; Abū Hurayra; ʿAdī b. Ḥātim; ʿAmmār b. Yāsir; Anas b. Mālik; al-Arḳam; al-Ashʿarī, Abū Mūsā; ʿAttāb; al-Barāʾ (b. ʿĀzib); al-Barāʾ (b. Maʿrūr); Bashīr b. Saʿd; Bilāl b. Rabāḥ; Bishr b. al-Barāʾ; Burayda b. al-Ḥuṣayb; Diḥya; Djāriya b. Ḳudāma; Ghasīl al-Malāʾika; Hāshim b. ʿUtba; Ḥurḳuṣ b. Zuhayr al-Saʿdī; Ibn Masʿūd; Kaʿb b. Mālik; Khabbāb b. al-Aratt; Khālid b. Saʿīd; Ḳutham b. al-ʿAbbās; Maslama b. Mukhallad; al-Miḳdād b. ʿAmr; Muʿāwiya b. Ḥudaydj; al-Mughīra b. Shuʿba; Muḥammad b. Abī Ḥudhayfa; Muṣʿab b. ʿUmayr; al-Nābigha al-Djaʿdī; al-Nuʿmān b. Bashīr; Saʿd b. Abī Waḳḳāṣ; Ṣafwān b. al-Muʿaṭṭal; Saʿīd b. Zayd; [in Suppl.] Djābir b. ʿAbd Allāh; Ibn Mītham
see also Ahl al-Ṣuffa; al-Ḳaʿḳāʿ; Khawlān.2; Ḳuss b. Sāʿida; Rawḥ b. Zinbāʿ; al-Salaf wa ʾl-Khalaf
family of al-ʿAbbās b. ʿAbd al-Muṭṭalib; ʿAbd Allāh b. ʿAbd al-Muṭṭalib; ʿAbd al-Muṭṭalib b. Hāshim; Abū Lahab; Abū Ṭālib; ʿAḳīl b. Abī Ṭālib; ʿAlī b. Abī Ṭālib; Āmina; Djaʿfar b. Abī Ṭālib; Fāṭima; Ḥalīma bint Abī Dhuʾayb; Ḥamza b. ʿAbd al-Muṭṭalib; (al-)Ḥasan b. ʿAlī b. Abī Ṭālib; al-Ḥasan b. Zayd b. al-Ḥasan; Hāshim b. ʿAbd Manāf; (al-)Ḥusayn b. ʿAlī b. Abī Ṭālib; Ruḳayya
see also Ahl al-Bayt
wives of ʿĀʾisha bint Abī Bakr; Ḥafṣa; Khadīdja; Māriya; Maymūna bint al-Ḥārith; Ṣafiyya

MUSIC Ghināʾ; Ḳayna; Maḳām; Malāhī; **Mūsīḳī**; Ramal.2; [in Suppl.] Īḳāʿ
see also Kurds.iv.C.4; Lamak; Naḳḳāra-khāna; al-Rashīdiyya; Samāʿ.1
Andalusian al-Ḥāʾik
composers Ibrāhīm al-Mawṣilī; Ismāʿīl Ḥaḳḳi; al-Ḳusanṭīnī; Lāhūtī; Laylā Khānîm; Maʿbad b. Wahb; Ṣafī al-Dīn al-Urmawī; [in Suppl.] ʿAllawayh al-Aʿsar; al-Dalāl; Ḥabba Khātūn
Indian **Hind.viii**; Khayāl
see also Bāyazīd Anṣārī; [in Suppl.] Ḥabba Khātūn
instruments Būḳ; Darabukka; Duff; Ghayṭa; Imẓad; Ḳithāra; Miʿzaf; Mizmār; Nefīr; Rabāb
see also Mehter; Mūrisṭus; Naḳḳāra-khāna
musicians ʿAzza al-Maylāʾ; Djaḥẓa; Ibn Djāmiʿ; Ibn Muḥriz; Ibrāhīm al-Mawṣilī; Isḥāḳ b. Ibrāhīm al-Mawṣilī; Ṣafī al-Dīn al-Urmawī; [in Suppl.]

ʿAllawayh al-Aʿsar; Barṣawmā al-Zāmir; al-Dalāl; Faḍl al-Shāʿira
see also al-Ḳāsim b. ʿĪsā
Persian Mihragān.iv.3
see also Lāhūtī; Naḳḳāra-khāna
song **Ghināʾ**; Ḳayna; Khayāl; Nashīd; Nawba
see also Abu ʾl-Faradj al-Iṣbahānī; Ḥawfī; Ilāhī; Mawāliyā.3
singers ʿĀlima; ʿAzza al-Maylāʾ; Djamīla; al-Gharīḍ; Ḥabāba; Ibn ʿĀʾisha.I; Ibn Bāna; Ibn Djāmiʿ; Ibn Misdjaḥ; Ibn Muḥriz; Ibn Suraydj; Ibrāhīm al-Mawṣilī; Ḳayna; Maʿbad b. Wahb; Mālik b. Abi ʾl-Samḥ; Mukhāriḳ; Nashīṭ; Rāʾiḳa; Sāʾib Khāthir; Sallāma al-Zarḳāʾ; [in Suppl.] Badhl al-Kubrā; al-Dalāl; al-Djarādatāni; Faḍl al-Shāʿira; Ḥabba Khātūn
see also ʿĀshiḳ; al-Barāmika.5
treatises on ʿAbd al-Ḳādir b. Ghaybī; Abu ʾl-Faradj al-Iṣbahānī; al-Ḥāʾik; Ibn Bāna; Ibn Khurradādhbih; Mashāḳa; (Banu ʾl-) Munadjdjim.4; Mūrisṭus; Mushāḳa; Ṣafī al-Dīn al-Urmawī
see also Abu ʾl-Maḥāsin b. Taghrībirdī; İnal; Malāhī
Turkish Ilāhī; Ḳoshma; Mehter
see also Laylā Khānïm; Māni; Nefīr

MYSTICISM Allāh.III.4; Darwīsh; Dhikr; Ibāḥa.II; Karāma; Murīd; Murshid; Pīr; Samāʿ.1
see also Sadjdjāda.3; Saʿīd al-Suʿadāʾ; *and* → DYNASTIES.PERSIA.ṢAFAWIDS
concepts Baḳāʾ wa-Fanāʾ; al-Insān al-Kāmil; Ishrāḳ; Lāhūt and Nāsūt
see also Allāh.III.4; al-Ḥallādj.IV; Ibn al-ʿArabī; al-Niffarī
dervishes **Darwīsh**; Raḳṣ
see also [in Suppl.] Buḳʿa; *and* → MYSTICISM.ORDERS
dress Khirḳa; Pālāhang
early ascetics ʿĀmir b. ʿAbd al-Ḳays al-ʿAnbarī; al-Ḥasan al-Baṣrī; al-Fuḍayl b. ʿIyāḍ; Ibrāhīm b. Adham
see also Bakkāʾ
mystical poetry → LITERATURE.POETRY
mystics Darwīsh
see also Pist; *and* → HAGIOGRAPHY
African (excluding North Africa) [in Suppl.] al-Duwayḥī
see also Ṣāliḥiyya
Andalusian Abū Madyan; Ibn al-ʿArabī; Ibn al-ʿArīf, Abu ʾl-ʿAbbās; Ibn ʿĀshir; Ibn Barradjān; Ibn Ḳasī; Ibn Masarra
Arabic (excluding Andalusian and North African) ʿAbd al-Ghanī; ʿAbd al-Ḳādir al-Djīlānī; ʿAbd al-Karīm al-Djīlī; ʿAdī b. Musāfir; Aḥmad al-Badawī; ʿAydarūs; al-Bakrī, Muḥammad; al-Bakrī, Muṣṭafā; Bishr al-Ḥāfī; al-Bisṭāmī, ʿAbd al-Raḥmān; al-Damīrī; al-Dasūḳī, Ibrāhīm b. ʿAbd al-ʿAzīz; al-Dasūḳī, Ibrāhīm b. Muḥammad; Dhu ʾl-Nūn, Abu ʾl-Fayḍ;

al-Dimyāṭī, al-Bannā'; al-Dimyāṭī, Nūr al-Dīn; al-Djunayd; al-Ghazālī, Abū Ḥāmid; al-Ghazālī, Aḥmad; al-Ḥallādj; al-Harawī al-Mawṣilī; Ibn ʿAṭā' Allāh; al-Ḳazwīnī, Nadjm al-Dīn; al-Kharrāz; al-Kurdī; al-Ḳushashī; Makhrama; al-Manūfī; al-Muḥāsibī; al-Munāwī; al-Niffarī; al-Nūrī; Rābiʿa al-ʿAdawiyya al-Ḳaysiyya; al-Rifāʿī; Sahl al-Tustarī; [in Suppl.] Abu 'l-ʿAzā'im; al-ʿAdawī; al-ʿAfīfī; al-Ḥiṣāfī

see also Abū Nuʿaym al-Iṣfahānī; Abū Ṭālib al-Makkī; Bā ʿAlawī; Baḥraḳ; Bakriyya; Bayyūmiyya; Faḍl, Bā; Faḳīh, Bā; Faḳīh, Bal; Hurmuz, Bā; Ḳādiriyya; Marwāniyya; Saʿdiyya; [in Suppl.] al-Bakrī; Demirdāshiyya

Central Asian Aḥmad Yasawī; Ḥakīm Ata; Naḳshband; [in Suppl.] Aḥrār

see also Ḳalandariyya; Pārsā'iyya

Indian Abū ʿAlī Ḳalandar; Aḥmad Sirhindī; Ashraf ʿAlī; Bahā' al-Dīn Zakariyyā; Bāḳī bi 'llāh (*and* [in Suppl.]); al-Banūrī; Budhan; Burhān al-Dīn Gharīb; Burhān al-Dīn Ḳuṭb-i ʿĀlam; Čirāgh-i Dihlī; Čishtī; Djahanārā Bēgam; Djalāl al-Dīn Ḥusayn al-Bukhārī; "Djamālī"; Farīd al-Dīn Masʿūd "Gandj-i-Shakar"; Gīsū Darāz; Hānsawī; Ḥusaynī Sādāt Amīr; Imdād Allāh; Kalīm Allāh al-Djahānābādī; Ḳuṭb al-Dīn Bakhtiyār Kākī; Malik Muḥammad Djāyasī; Miyān Mīr, Miyādjī; Mubārak Ghāzī; Muḥammad Ghawth Gwāliyārī; al-Muttaḳī al-Hindī; Muẓaffar Shams Balkhī; Niẓām al-Dīn Awliyā'; Niẓām al-Dīn, Mullā Muḥammad; Nūr Ḳuṭb al-ʿĀlam; [in Suppl.] ʿAbd al-Bārī; ʿAbd al-Wahhāb Bukhārī; Bulbul Shāh; Farangī Maḥall; Gadā'ī Kambō; Ḥamīd Ḳalandar; Ḥamīd al-Dīn Ḳāḍī Nāgawrī; Ḥamīd al-Dīn Ṣūfī Nāgawrī Siwālī; Ḥamza Makhdūm

see also ʿAydarūs; Čishtiyya; Dārā Shukōh; Dard; Djīwan; Hind.v; Khalīl Allāh (*and* Khalīl Allāh But-shikan); Malang; Mughals.6; Naḳshbandiyya.3

Indonesian ʿAbd al-Ra'ūf al-Sinkilī; ʿAbd al-Ṣamad al-Palimbānī; Ḥamza Fanṣūrī

North African ʿAbd al-Ḳādir al-Fāsī; ʿAbd al-Salām b. Mashīsh; Abu 'l-Maḥāsin al-Fāsī; Abū Muḥammad Ṣāliḥ; Aḥmad b. Idrīs; ʿAlī b. Maymūn; al-ʿAyyāshī; al-Daḳḳāḳ; al-Djazūlī; al-Hāshimī; Ḥmād u-Mūsā; Ibn ʿAbbād; Ibn ʿAdjība; Ibn ʿAlīwa; Ibn ʿArūs; Ibn Ḥirzihim; al-Ḳādirī al-Ḥasanī; al-Kūhin; al-Lamaṭī; Mā' al-ʿAynayn al-Ḳalḳamī; al-Madjdhūb; [in Suppl.] al-Asmar; al-Dilā'; al-Fāsī; Ibn ʿAzzūz

see also ʿAmmāriyya; ʿArūsiyya; Darḳāwa; Hansaliyya; Hazmīriyyūn; al-Ifrānī; ʿĪsāwā; Madaniyya; al-Nāṣiriyya; Raḥmāniyya; [in Suppl.] Ḥamādisha

Persian ʿAbd al-Razzāḳ al-Ḳāshānī; Abū Saʿīd b. Abi 'l-Khayr; Abū Yazīd al-Bisṭāmī; Aḥmad-i Djām; ʿAlā' al-Dawla al-Simnānī; ʿAlī al-Hamadānī; al-Anṣārī al-Harawī; Ashraf Djahāngīr; Bābā-Ṭāhir; Djalāl al-Dīn Rūmī; Faḍl Allāh Ḥurūfī; Ghudjduwānī; Ḥamdūn al-Ḳaṣṣār; Hudjwīrī; Ibn Khafīf; ʿIrāḳī; al-Kalābādhī; Kamāl Khudjandī; Ḳāsim-i Anwār; Kāzarūnī; Khalīl Allāh (*and* Khalīl Allāh But-shikan); Kharaḳānī; al-Khargūshī; Kirmānī; Kubrā; al-Ḳushayrī.1; Lāhīdjī.1; Maḥmūd Shabistarī; Nadjm al-Dīn Rāzī Dāya; Naḳshband; Rūzbihān; Saʿd al-Dīn al-Ḥammūʾī; Saʿd al-Dīn Kāshgharī; Ṣadr al-Dīn Ardabīlī; Ṣadr al-Dīn Mūsā; Ṣafī; Saʿīd al-Dīn Farghānī; [in Suppl.] ʿAbd Allāh b. Abī Bakr al-Miyānadjī; Abū ʿAlī; Aḥmad-i Rūmī; ʿAyn al-Ḳuḍāt al-Hamadhānī; Ibn al-Bazzāz al-Ardabīlī

see also Djāmī; Madjlisī-yi Awwal; Naḳshbandiyya.1; Niʿmat-Allāhiyya; Ṣafawids.I.ii

Turkish Aḳ Shams al-Dīn; Altï Parmak; ʿĀshïḳ Pasha; Badr al-Dīn b. Ḳāḍī Samāwnā; Baraḳ Baba; Bīdjān; Emīr Sulṭān; Faṣīḥ Dede; Fehmī; Gulshanī; Gülshehrī; Ḥādjdjī Bayrām Walī; Hüdāʾī; Ḥusām al-Dīn Čelebi; Ismāʿīl al-Anḳarawī; Ismāʿīl Ḥaḳḳi; Ḳayghusuz Abdāl; Khalīlī; Ḳuṭb al-Dīn-zāde; Merkez; Niyāzī; [in Suppl.] ʿĀrif Čelebī; Eshrefoghlu; Esrār Dede

see also Ashrafiyya; Bakriyya; Bayrāmiyya; Bektāshiyya; Djilwatiyya; Gülbaba; Ilāhī; Khalwatiyya; Mawlawiyya; Naḳshbandiyya.2

orders ʿAmmāriyya; ʿArūsiyya; Ashrafiyya; Bakriyya; Bayrāmiyya; Bayyūmiyya; Bektāshiyya; Čishtiyya; Darḳāwa; Djilwatiyya; Hansaliyya; Hazmīriyyūn; ʿĪsāwā; Ḳādiriyya; Ḳalandariyya; Khalwatiyya; Madaniyya; Marwāniyya; Mawlawiyya; Mīrghaniyya; Murīdiyya; Naḳshbandiyya; al-Nāṣiriyya; Niʿmat-Allāhiyya; Pārsāʾiyya; Raḥmāniyya; Rifāʿiyya; Saʿdiyya; Ṣāliḥiyya; [in Suppl.] Demirdāshiyya; Ḥamādisha

for ʿAdawiyya, *see* ʿAdī b. Musāfir; *for* ʿAfīfiyya, *see* [in Suppl.] al-ʿAfīfī; *for* Dasūḳiyya (Burhāmiyya), *see* al-Dasūḳī, Ibrāhīm b. ʿAbd al-ʿAzīz; *for* al-Djazūliyya, *see* al-Djazūlī; *for* Gulshaniyya, *see* Gulshanī; for Idrīsiyya, *see* Aḥmad b. Idrīs; *for* Kāzarūniyya (Murshidiyya, Isḥāḳiyya), *see* Kāzarūnī; *for* Kubrawiyya, *see* Kubrā; *for* Suhrawardiyya, *see* Bahāʾ al-Dīn Zakariyyā

see also Nūrbakhshiyya; Ṣafawids.I.ii

terms Abdāl; ʿĀshiḳ; Awtād; Baḳāʾ wa-Fanāʾ; Basṭ; Bīsharʿ; Čāʾūsh; Darwīsh; Dawsa; Dede; Dhawḳ; Dhikr; Djilwa; Faḳīr; Fikr; al-Ghayb; Ghayba; Ghufrān; Ḥaḍra; Ḥaḳīḳa.3; Ḥaḳḳ; Ḥāl; Ḥidjāb.III; Ḥuḳūḳ; Ḥulūl; Ḥurriyya; Huwa huwa; Ikhlāṣ; Ilhām; ʿInāya; al-Insān al-Kāmil; Ishān; Ishāra; ʿIshḳ; Ishrāḳ; Ithbāt; Ittiḥād; Ḳabḍ.ii; Kāfir; Ḳalb.I; Kalima; Karāma; Kashf; Khalīfa.iii; Khalwa; Khānḳāh; Khirḳa; al-Ḳuṭb; Lāhūt and Nāsūt; Madjdhūb; Manzil; Maʿrifa; Muḥāsaba.1; Munādjāt; Murīd; Murshid; Nafs; Odjaḳ; Pālāhang; Pīr; Pūst; Pūst-neshīn; Rābiṭa; Ramz.3; Rātib; Ribāṭ; Riḍā.1; Rind; Rūḥāniyya; Rukhṣa.2; Ṣabr; Ṣadr; [in Suppl.] Buḳʿa; Ghawth

see also Čelebī; Futuwwa; Gülbaba; Lawḥ; Lawn

N

NATIONALISM Istiḳlāl; **Ḳawmiyya**
see also Djangalī; Khilāfa; Pāshtūnistān; *and* → POLITICS.MOVEMENTS

NATURAL SCIENCE **al-Āthār al-ʿUlwiyya**; **Ḥikma**; Masāʾil wa-Adjwiba
see also Nūr.1
natural scientists al-Bīrūnī; al-Dimashḳī; Ibn Bādjdja; Ibn al-Haytham; Ibn Rushd; Ibn Sīnā; Ikhwān al-Ṣafāʾ; al-Ḳazwīnī; al-Marwazī, Sharaf al-Zamān
and → ALCHEMY; ASTRONOMY; BOTANY; METAPHYSICS; ZOOLOGY

NAVIGATION Djughrāfiya; Ibn Mādjid; Iṣbaʿ; Kharīṭa; Maghnāṭīs.2; Manār; Meḥmed Reʾīs; **Milāḥa**; Mīnāʾ
see also al-Khashabāt; Rīḥ
ships Milāḥa (esp. 4); Nassads; **Safīna**
see also Baḥriyya.2; Kelek; *and* → MILITARY.NAVY
shipyards Dār al-Ṣināʿa

NEPAL **Nepal**

NESTORIANS → CHRISTIANITY.DENOMINATIONS

NEW WORLD Djāliya; Djarīda.i.C.; **al-Mahdjar**
emigrants Djabrān Khalīl Djabrān; al-Maʿlūf; Nuʿayma, Mīkhāʾīl; al-Rayḥānī; [in Suppl.] Abū Māḍī; Abū Shādī
see also Pārsīs

NIGER **Niger**
toponyms Bilma; Djādū; Kawār

NIGERIA Hausa; **Nigeria**
see also Djarīda.vi; Fulbe; al-Kānemī; Kanuri; Nikāḥ.II.6
leaders Muḥammad Bello
see also Gwandu
toponyms
provinces Adamawa; Bornū
towns Ibadan; Kano; Katsina; Kūkawa

NOMADISM **Badw**; Horde; Īlāt; Khāwa; Khayma; Marʿā
see also Baḳḳāra; Baranta; Dakhīl; Dawar; Ḥayy; Ḳayn; *and* → BEDOUINS; GYPSIES; TRIBES

nomadic possessions Khayma; Mifrash
see also Khayl

Nubia ʿAlwa; Barābra; Dongola; al-Marīs; **Nūba**
see also Baḳṭ; Dār al-Ṣulḥ; Ibn Sulaym al-Aswānī; al-Muḳurra; *and* → Egypt.toponyms; Sudan.toponyms
languages Nūba.3
peoples Nūba.4

Number Abdjad; Ḥisāb al-ʿAḳd; Ḥisāb al-Djummal; Ḥurūf; ʿIlm al-Ḥisāb
and → Mathematics
numbers Khamsa; Sabʿ

Numismatics Dār al-Ḍarb
see also ʿAlī Pasha Mubārak; Andarāb.1; Ismāʿīl Ghālib; Makāyil; Mawlāy Idrīs; Nithār
coinage Aḳče; Bālish; Čao; Čeyrek; Dīnār; Dirham.2; Fals; Ḥasanī; Larin; Mohur; Pāʾī; Pāra; Pawlā; Paysā; Riyāl; Rūpiyya; Ṣadīḳī
see also Abarshahr; al-Abbāsiyya; ʿAbd al-Malik b. Marwān; al-Afḍal (Kutayfāt); ʿAlī Bey; Ānī; Bāghče Sarāy; Dhahab; Fidda; Filori; Ghāzi ʾl-Dīn Ḥaydar; Hilāl.ii; Islāmābād; Iṣṭakhr; Ḳaṭarī b. al-Fudjāʾa; Khurshīd; al-Kurdj; Māh al-Baṣra; al-Manṣūr, al-Malik Muḥammad; Māzandarān.7; Muṣṭafā.1; Ṣāḥib Ḳirān; [in Suppl.] Biyār; Farrukhān.2; Firrīm; al-Ghiṭrīf b. ʿAṭāʾ; *and* → Dynasties
for coinage under dynasties, see in particular Artuḳids; Barīd Shāhīs; Khʷārazm-shāhs; Lōdīs.5; Mughals.10; al-Muwaḥḥidūn; ʿOthmānli̊.IX; Rasūlids.2; Ṣafawids.VI; Saldjūḳids.VIII
terms ʿAdl.2; Salām (*and* Sālim.1)

O

Oceans and Seas **Baḥr**; al-Madd wa ʾl-Djazr
see also Kharīṭa; *and* → Cartography; Navigation
waters Aral; Baḥr Adriyās; Baḥr Bunṭus; Baḥr Fāris; Baḥr al-Hind; Baḥr al-Khazar; Baḥr al-Ḳulzum; Baḥr Lūṭ; Baḥr Māyuṭis; al-Baḥr al-Muḥīṭ; Baḥr al-Rūm; Baḥr al-Zandj; Marmara Deñizi

Oil **Nafṭ**.3
oilfields ʿAbbādān; Abḳayḳ; Alti̊n Köprü; al-Baḥrayn; al-Dahnāʾ; al-Ghawār; al-Ḥasā; al-Ḳaṭīf; Khārag; Khūzistān; Kirkūk; Kirmānshāh; al-Kuwayt; Lībiyā; Nadjd.3; Rām-hurmuz; Raʾs (al-)Tannūra; [in Suppl.] Aḥmadī

see also Djannāba; Fārs; al-Khubar

OMAN Bū Saʿīd; Madjlis.4.A.xiii; Maḥkama.4.ix; Nabhān
see also [in Suppl.] al-Ḥārithī
population ʿAwāmir; al-Baṭāḥira; al-Djanaba; al-Durūʿ; Hināʾ; al-Ḥubūs; al-ʿIfār; (Banū) Kharūṣ; Mahra; Mazrūʿī; Nabhān
and → TRIBES.ARABIAN PENINSULA
toponyms
islands Khūryān-mūryān; Maṣīra
regions al-Bāṭina; Raʾs Musandam; al-Rustāḳ
towns al-Buraymī; Ḥāsik; ʿIbrī; Ḳalhāt; Masḳaṭ, Maṭraḥ; al-Mirbāṭ; Nizwa; al-Rustāḳ; Ṣalāla
see also (Djazīrat) al-ʿArab; [in Suppl.] Gwādar

ONOMASTICS Bā; Ibn; Ism; Kisrā; Kunya; Laḳab; Nisba.2
see also al-Asmāʾ al-Ḥusnā; Oghul
epithets Ata; Baba; Ghufrān; Humāyūn
in form of address Agha; Ākhūnd; Beg; Begum; Čelebī; Efendi; Khʷādja; Khātūn; Khudāwand
see also Akhī
proper names Aḥmad; Dhu 'l-Faḳār; Humā; Marzpān; Meḥemmed; Mihragān.iv.2
see also al-Asad; Payghū
titles
African Diglal
Arabic ʿAmīd; Amīr al-Muʾminīn; Amīr al-Muslimīn; Asad al-Dawla; ʿAzīz Miṣr; ʿIzz al-Dawla; ʿIzz al-Dīn; Khādim al-Ḥaramayn; Khidīw; Malik; Mihmindār; Mushīr
see also Dawla.2
Central Asian Afshīn; Ikhshīd; Ḳosh-begi; [in Suppl.] Atalïḳ; Dīwān-begi; İnaḳ
Indo-Muslim Āṣāf-Djāh; Khʷādja-i Djahān; Khān Khānān; Nawwab; Niẓām; Pēshwā; Ṣāḥib Ḳirān
Mongolian Noyan; Ṣāḥib Ḳirān
Persian Agha Khān; Ispahbadh; Ispahsālār; Iʿtimād al-Dawla; Khʷādja; Marzpān; Mīr; Mīrzā; Mollā; Pādishāh; Ṣadr; Sālār
South-east Asian Penghulu
Turkish Alp; Beglerbegi; Dāmād; Daryā-begi; Dayï; Gülbaba; Khʷādjegān-i Dīwān-i Humāyūn; Khāḳān; Khān; Khudāwendigār; Mīr-i Mīrān; Mushīr; Pasha; Payghū; Ṣadr-i Aʿẓam
see also Čorbadjï

OPTICS Ḳaws Ḳuzaḥ; Manāẓir
see also Mirʾāt
works on Ibn al-Haytham; Kamāl al-Dīn al-Fārisī
see also Ḳuṭb al-Dīn Shīrāzī

OTTOMAN EMPIRE Anadolu.iii.2 and 3; Ertoghrul.1; Istanbul; Lāle Devri; **ʿOthmānli**
see also Bāb-i ʿĀlī; Ḥidjāz Railway; Maṭbakh.2; Pasha Ḳapusu; *and* → DYNASTIES.ANATOLIA AND THE TURKS; EUROPE.EASTERN; LAW.OTTOMAN; MILITARY.OTTOMAN; *and the section Ottoman Period under individual countries*
administration Berātli; Ḍabṭiyya; Dīwān-i Humāyūn; Eyālet; Imtiyāzāt.ii; Khāṣṣ; Khazīne; Mashwara; Millet.3; Mukhtār; Mülāzemet; Mulāzim; Mulkiyya; Nāḥiye; Nishāndji; Reʾīs ül-Küttāb; [in Suppl.] Dāʾira Saniyya
see also Ḳaḍāʾ; Maʾmūr; Odjaḳ; *and* → DOCUMENTS.OTTOMAN; LAW.OTTOMAN; MILITARY.OTTOMAN
archives and registers Başvekalet Arşivi; Daftar-i Khāḳānī; Ḳānūn.iii; Maṣraf Defteri; Mühimme Defterleri; Sāl-nāme
see also Daftar.III; Ferīdūn Beg; Maḥlūl
financial Arpaliḳ; Ashām; Bayt al-Māl.II; Daftardār; Dār al-Ḍarb; Dirlik; Djayb-i Humāyūn; Duyūn-i ʿUmūmiyye; Irsāliyye; Ḳāʾime; Khazīne; Māliyye; Muḥāsaba.2; Mukhallefāt; Muṣādara.3; Rūznāmedji; Sāliyāne
see also Bakhshīsh
fiscal Ḍarība.3; Djizya.ii; Ḥisba.ii; Kharādj.III; Muḥaṣṣil; Mültezim; ʿOthmānli.II; Resm
see also Mutaṣarrif
agriculture Filāḥa.iv; Māʾ.8; Raʿiyya.2
and → AGRICULTURE
court ceremony Čāʾūsh; Khirḳa-yi Sherīf; Marāsim.4; Mawākib.4; Mehter
diplomacy Bālyōs; Consul; Elči; Hiba.v; Penče
see also Berātli; Imtiyāzāt.ii; Ḳawwās; *and* → DIPLOMACY
education Ghalaṭa-sarāyi; Külliyye; Maʿārif.I.i; Makhredj; Mulkiyya; Ṣaḥn-i Thamān
see also Ḥarbiye; *and* → EDUCATION; REFORM.EDUCATIONAL
functionaries Āmeddji; Aʿyān; Bazirgan; Bostāndji; Bostāndji-bashi; Čakirdji-bashi; Čāshnagīr-bashi; Ḍābiṭ; Ḍabṭiyya; Daftardār; Dilsiz; Doghandji; Elči; Emīn; Ghulām.iv; Ḥekīm-bashi; Ič-oghlani; ʿIlmiyye; Ḳāʾim-maḳām; Ḳapu Aghasi; Ḳawwās; Ketkhudā.1; Khaznadār; Khʷādjegān-i Dīwān-i Humāyūn; Maʾmūr; Mewḳūfātči; Mīr-Ākhūr; Mushīr; Mustashār; Mutaṣarrif; Nishāndji; Reʾīs ül-Küttāb; Rūznāmedji; Ṣadr-ı Aʿẓam
see also ʿAdjamī oghlān; ʿAsas; Bālā; Balṭadji; Bālyōs; Bīrūn; Enderūn; al-Ḥaramayn; Khāṣī.III; Khāṣṣ Oda; Khāṣṣekī; Mābeyn; *and* → LAW.OTTOMAN; MILITARY.OTTOMAN

history ʿOthmānli̊.I
and → DYNASTIES.ANATOLIA AND THE TURKS; LITERATURE.HISTORICAL.TURKISH; TURKEY.OTTOMAN PERIOD
industry and trade Ḥarīr.ii; Kārwān; Ḳuṭn.2; Milḥ.3; ʿOthmānli̊.II
see also Maʿdin.3
literature → LITERATURE
modernisation of Baladiyya.1; Ḥukūma.i; Ḥurriyya.ii; Iṣlāḥ.iii; Ittiḥād we Teraḳḳī Djemʿiyyeti; Madjlis.4.A.i; Madjlis al-Shūrā
and → TURKEY.OTTOMAN PERIOD

P

PAKISTAN Djināḥ; Dustūr.xiv; Ḥizb.vi; Ḥukūma.v; Madjlis.4.C; al-Marʾa.5; **Pākistān**; [in Suppl.] Djarīda.vii
see also Ahl-i Ḥadīth; Dār al-ʿUlūm.c; Djamʿiyya.v; Djūnāgaṛh; Hind.ii and iv; Kashmīr.ii; Ḳawmiyya.vi; Khaybar; Muhādjir.3; Pashtūnistān; *and* → INDIA
architecture → ARCHITECTURE.REGIONS
education Djāmiʿa
physical geography
waters Kurram; Mihrān
population Afrīdī; Dāwūdpōtrās; Mahsūd; Mohmand; Mullagorī; [in Suppl.] Demography.VII; Gurčānī
see also Djirga
statesmen Djināḥ; Liyaḳat ʿAlī Khān
see also Mawdūdī
toponyms
ancient Čīnīōt; Daybul; Ḳandābīl; Khayrābād.ii
present-day
districts Chitral; Ḥāfiẓābād; Hazāra; Khārān; Khayrpūr; Kilāt.2; Kōhāt; Kwaṫṫa; Mastūdj
regions Balūčistān; Dardistān; Dēradjāt; Dīr; Djahlāwān; Kaččhī; Las Bēla; Makrān; Pandjāb
towns Amarkot; Bādjawr; Bahāwalpūr; Bakkār; Bannū; Bhakkar; Gūdjrāṅwāla; Gudjrāt; Ḥasan Abdāl; Ḥaydarābād; Islāmābād; Karāčī; Kilāt.1; Ḳuṣdār; Kwaṫṫa; Lāhawr; Mastūdj; Peshāwar; Rawalpindi; [in Suppl.] Gilgit; Gwādar

PALESTINE Djarīda.i.A; **Filasṭīn**; Ḥizb.i; Madjlis.4.A.xxiii; Maḥkama.4.v; Mandates
see also Djarrāḥids; Ḳays ʿAylān; al-Khālidī; al-Sāmira; [in Suppl.] Demography.III; *and* → CRUSADE(R)S

architecture Ḳubbat al-Ṣakhra; al-Ḳuds; al-Masdjid al-Aḳṣā
see also Kawkab al-Hawāʾ
historians of Mudjīr al-Dīn al-ʿUlaymī
physical geography
waters Baḥr Lūṭ; al-Ḥūla; Nahr Abī Fuṭrus
toponyms
ancient Arsūf; ʿAthlīth; ʿAyn Djālūt; Bayt Djibrīn; al-Dārūm; Irbid.II; Sabasṭiyya.1
present-day
regions al-Ghawr.1; Mardj Banī ʿĀmir; al-Naḳb
towns ʿAkkā; ʿAmwās; ʿĀsḳalān; Baysān; Bayt Laḥm; Bīr al-Sabʿ; Ghazza; Ḥayfā; Ḥiṭṭīn; al-Khalīl; al-Ḳuds; Ladjdjūn; Ludd; Nābulus; al-Nāṣira; Rafaḥ; al-Ramla; Rīḥā.1; Ṣafad
see also Ḳayṣariyya
under British mandate Filasṭīn.2; Muḥammad ʿIzzat Darwaza; [in Suppl.] Amīn al-Ḥusaynī
see also Mandates

PANARABISM Ḳawmiyya; **Pan-Arabism**; [in Suppl.] al-Djāmiʿa al-ʿArabiyya
partisans of al-Kawākibī; Nūrī al-Saʿīd; Rashīd Riḍā; [in Suppl.] ʿAbd al-Nāṣir
see also al-Kāẓimī, ʿAbd al-Muḥsin

PANISLAMISM Ḳawmiyya; **Pan-Islamism**; **al-Rābiṭa al-Islāmiyya**
see also Dustūr.xviii; Iṣlāḥ.ii; Khilāfa; Muʾtamar
partisans of ʿAbd al-Ḥamīd II; Djamāl al-Dīn al-Afghānī; Fiṭrat; Gasprali (Gasprinski), Ismāʿīl; Ḥālī; Küčak Khān Djangalī; Māʾ al-ʿAynayn al-Ḳalḳamī; Meḥmed ʿĀkif; Rashīd Riḍā; Ṣafar; [in Suppl.] Andjuman-i Khuddām-i Kaʿba; al-Bakrī
see also Djadīd

PANTURKISM Ḳawmiyya.iv; **Pan-Turkism**
partisans of Gasprali (Gasprinski), Ismāʿīl; Gökalp, Ziya; Riḍā Nūr

PAPYROLOGY Ḳirṭās; Papyrus
see also Diplomatic.i.15; *and* → DOCUMENTS

PARADISE al-ʿAshara al-Mubashshara; Dār al-Salām; **Djanna**; Ḥūr; Kawthar; Riḍwān; Salsabīl
see also al-Aʿrāf

PAYMENTS ʿAṭāʾ; Djāmakiyya; Ḥawāla; Inʿām; Māl al-Bayʿa; Maʿūna
bribery Marāfiḳ; **Rashwa**

PERFUME Bān; Ḥinnāʾ; Kāfūr; Misk
see also al-ʿAṭṭār; Maʿdin.4

PERSIA → IRAN

PHARMACOLOGY Adwiya; Aḳrābādhīn
see also Diyusḳuridīs; Djālīnūs; Nabāt; *and* → BOTANY; DRUGS; MEDICINE
pharmacologists Ibn al-Bayṭār; Ibn Samadjūn; Ibn al-Tilmīdh; Ibn Wāfid; al-Kōhēn al-ʿAṭṭār; Sābūr b. Sahl; [in Suppl.] al-Ghāfiḳī; Ibn Biklārish; Ibn al-Rūmiyya
see also al-ʿAshshāb; al-ʿAṭṭār

PHILATELY **Posta**
and → TRANSPORT.POSTAL SERVICE

PHILOSOPHY Falāsifa; **Falsafa**; Ḥikma; Mā baʿd al-Ṭabīʿa; Manṭiḳ; Naẓar
see also ʿĀlam.1; Allāh.iii.2; al-Maḳūlāt
logic **Manṭiḳ**
terms Āla.iii; ʿAraḍ; Dalīl; Faṣl; Fiʿl; Ḥadd; Ḥaḳīḳa.2; Ḥudjdja; Ḥukm.I; Huwa huwa.A; Muḳaddam; Natīdja
see also Ḳaṭʿ
philosophers **Falāsifa**
Christian Ibn al-Ṭayyib; Ibn Zurʿa; Mattā b. Yūnus
Greek Aflāṭūn; Anbaduḳlis; Arisṭūṭālīs; Balīnūs; Baṭlamiyūs; Buruḳlus; Djālīnus; Fīthāghūras; Furfūriyūs; al-Iskandar al-Afrūdīsī
see also Ḥunayn b. Isḥāḳ al-ʿIbādī; Īsāghūdjī; Isḥāḳ b. Ḥunayn; Lawn; al-Maḳūlāt; Mattā b. Yūnus; Nīḳūlāʾūs
Islamic
9th century Abu ʾl-Hudhayl al-ʿAllāf; al-Kindī, Abū Yūsuf
see also Dahriyya; Falāsifa; Lawn
10th century Abū Sulaymān al-Manṭiḳī; al-Fārābī; Ibn Masarrā; al-Mawṣilī; al-Rāzī, Abū Bakr; [in Suppl.] al-ʿĀmirī
11th century Abū Ḥayyān al-Tawḥīdī; Bahmanyār; Ibn Ḥazm; Ibn Sīnā; Miskawayh
12th century Abu ʾl-Barakāt; al-Baṭalyawsī; Ibn Bādjdja; Ibn Rushd; Ibn Ṭufayl
see also al-Ghazālī; Ḥayy b. Yaḳẓān; Ishrāḳiyyūn
13th century al-Abharī; Ibn Sabʿīn; al-Kātibī;; Ṣadr al-Dīn al-Ḳūnawī
see also Fakhr al-Dīn al-Rāzī
14th century Djamāl al-Dīn Aḳsarayī
16th century al-Maybudī.2
17th century al-Dāmād; Lāhīdjī.2; [in Suppl.] Findiriskī

19th century al-Fārūḳī; Sabzawārī; [in Suppl.] Abu 'l-Ḥasan Djilwa
Jewish Ibn Gabirol; Ibn Kammūna; Isḥāḳ b. Sulaymān al-Isrāʾīlī; Judaeo-Arabic.iii; Saʿadyā Ben Yōsēf
see also Abu 'l-Barakāt
terms Abad; ʿAdam; ʿAḳl; ʿAmal.1 and 2; Anniyya; Awwal; Basīṭ wa-Murakkab; Dhāt; Dhawḳ; Ḍidd; Djawhar; Djins; Djism; Djuzʾ; Fard; Ḥadd; Ḥaraka wa-Sukūn.I.1; Hayʾa; Ḥayāt; Hayūlā; Ḥiss; Ḥudūth al-ʿĀlam; Ḥulūl; Huwiyya; Ibdāʿ; Idrāk; Iḥdāth; Ikhtiyār; ʿIlla.ii; ʿInāya; Inṣāf; ʿIshḳ; Ishrāḳ; al-Ḳaḍāʾ wa 'l-Ḳadar.A.3; Kawn wa-Fasād; Ḳidam; Ḳuwwa.4, 6 and 7; Maʿād; Māhiyya; Maḥsūsāt; Malaka; Maʿnā.2; Nafs; Nihāya; Nūr.2; Saʿāda; Sabab.1
see also Athar.3; ʿAyn; Dahriyya; Insān; Ḳaṭʿ; Ḳiyāma

PHYSIOGNOMY Firāsa; Ḳiyāfa; [in Suppl.] Aflīmūn
and → ANATOMY

PILGRIMAGE ʿArafa; al-Djamra; **Ḥadjdj**; Hady; Iḥrām; Kaʿba; Minā; Muṭawwif; al-Muzdalifa; Radjm; al-Ṣafā.1
see also Amīr al-Ḥādjdj; Ḥidjāz Railway; Kārwān; Kāẓimayn; Makka; [in Suppl.] ʿAtabāt; Darb Zubayda; Fayd; *and* → ISLAM

PIRACY **Ḳurṣān**
see also al-ʿAnnāba; ʿArūdj; Ḥasan Baba; Ḥusayn Pasha, Mezzomorto; Kemāl Reʾīs; Khayr al-Dīn Pasha; Lewend

PLAGUE ʿAmwās
see also Ibn Khaldūn, Walī al-Dīn
treatises on Ibn Khātima; Ibn Riḍwān; al-Masīḥī

POLAND **Leh**
see also Islām Girāy; Ḳamāniča; Köprülü; Lipḳa; Muslimūn.1.A.1; *and* → OTTOMAN EMPIRE

POLITICS Baladiyya; Dawla; Djumhūriyya; Dustūr; Ḥimāya.2; Ḥizb; Ḥukūma; Ḥurriyya.ii; Istiḳlāl; Ḳawmiyya; Madjlis; Makhzan; Mandates; Mashyakha; Medeniyyet; Musāwāt; Muwāṭin; Nāʾib.2; [in Suppl.] Āzādī; al-Djāmiʿa al-ʿArabiyya
see also Ahl al-Ḥall wa 'l-ʿAḳd; Imtiyāzāt; Mashwara; Salṭana; *and* → ADMINISTRATION; DIPLOMACY; OTTOMAN EMPIRE
doctrines Ḥizb.i; Ishtirākiyya; Mārk(i)siyya; [in Suppl.] Hidjra
see also Musāwāt; Muslimūn.4; Radjʿiyya; *and* → PANARABISM; PANISLAMISM; PANTURKISM
movements Djadīd; Djangalī; Istiḳlāl; Ittiḥād we Teraḳḳī Djemʿiyyeti; Khāksār;

Khilāfa; al-Rābiṭa al-Islāmiyya
see also Fiṭrat; Ḥamza Beg; Ḥizb; Ḥurriyya.ii; Kūčak Khān Djangalī; [in Suppl.] ʿAbd al-Bārī; *and* → PANARABISM; PANISLAMISM; PANTURKISM

parties Demokrat Parti; **Ḥizb**; Ḥürriyet we I'tilāf Fi̊rḳasi̊; Partai Islam se Malaysia (Pas)
see also Andjuman; Djamʿiyya; (Tunali̊) Ḥilmī; Ḥizb.i; Ishtirākiyya; Khīyābānī, Shaykh Muḥammad; Leff; Luṭfī al-Sayyid; Mārk(i)siyya; Muṣṭafā Kāmil Pasha; [in Suppl.] ʿAbd al-Nāṣir; *and* → REFORM

reform → REFORM

PORTUGAL **Burtuḳāl**; Gharb al-Andalus
see also Ḥabesh; *and* → SPAIN

toponyms Bādja; Ḳulumriya; al-Maʿdin; Mīrtula

PRAYER Adhān; Dhikr; Djumʿa; **Duʿā'**; Fātiḥa; Iḳama; Khaṭīb; Khuṭba; Ḳibla; Ḳunūt; Ḳuʿūd; Maḥyā; Masdjid; Miḥrāb; Mīḳāt; Muṣallā; Rakʿa; Rātib; **Ṣalāt**; Ṣalāt al-Khawf
see also Amīn; Dikka; Ghā'ib; Gulbāng; Isti'nāf; Maḳām Ibrāhīm; al-Masḥ ʿalā 'l-Khuffayn; Namāzgāh; *and* → ABLUTION; ARCHITECTURE.MOSQUES; ISLAM

bowing Sadjda

carpet Sadjdjāda

of petition Istisḳā'; Munāshada

PRE-ISLAM al-ʿArab.i; (Djazīrat) al-ʿArab.vii; Armīniya.II.1; Badw.III; Djāhiliyya; Ghassān; Kinda.1 and Appendix; Lakhmids; Liḥyān; Maʿin; Makka.1; Nabaṭ; Rūm
see also Ḥayawān.2; Ilāh; al-Kalbī.II; Lībiyā.2; *and* → ASSYRIA; BYZANTINE EMPIRE; MILITARY.BATTLES; ZOROASTRIANS

customs/institutions ʿAtīra; Baliyya; Ghidhā'.1 and ii; Ḥadjdj.i, Ḥilf, Ḥimā; Ḥimāya; Istisḳā'; Kāhin; Khafāra; Mawlā; Nuṣub; Raḍāʿ.2; Sādin
see also Fay'; Ghanīma; Īlāf; Karkūr; Nār; Ṣadā

gods Dhu 'l-Khalaṣa; Hubal; Isāf wa-Nā'ila; Ḳaws Ḳuzaḥ; al-Lāt; Manāf; Manāt; Nasr
see also ʿAmr b. Luḥayy; Djāhiliyya; Ilāh; Kaʿba.V; al-Ḳamar.II; Mawḳif.3; Rabb

in Arabian peninsula Abraha; (Djazīrat) al-ʿArab.i and vi; Bakr b. Wā'il; Djadhīma al-Abrash; Ghumdān; Ḥabashat; Ḥādjib b. Zurāra; Ḥaḍramawt; Hāshim b. ʿAbd Manāf; Hind bint al-Khuss; Ḥums; Ḳatabān; Ḳayl; Ḳuṣayy; Ḳuss b. Sāʿida; Mārib; Nuṣub; Saba'; Sadjʿ.1; Salḥīn; [in Suppl.] Ḥaḍramawt.i
see also Badw.III; Dār al-Nadwa; Ḥanīf.4; Kinda.Appendix; *and* → LITERATURE.POETRY.ARABIC; OMAN.TOPONYMS; SAUDIA ARABIA.TOPONYMS; TRIBES.ARABIAN PENINSULA; YEMEN.TOPONYMS

in Egypt → EGYPT.BEFORE ISLAM

in Fertile Crescent Khursābād; Manbidj; Maysān; Nabaṭ; [in Suppl.] Athūr

see also Biṭrīḳ.I; Ḥarrān

Ghassānids Djabala b. al-Ayham; Djilliḳ; **Ghassān**; al-Ḥārith b. Djabala; [in Suppl.] Djabala b. al-Ḥārith

Lakhmids ʿAmr b. ʿAdī; ʿAmr b. Hind; al-Ḥīra; **Lakhmids**; al-Mundhir IV; al-Nuʿmān (III) b. al-Mundhir

in Iran → IRAN.BEFORE ISLAM

PREDESTINATION Adjal; Allāh.II.B; Iḍṭirār; Ikhtiyār; Istiṭāʿa; **al-Ḳaḍāʾ wa ʾl-Ḳadar**; Ḳadariyya; Kasb; Ḳisma

see also ʿAbd al-Razzāḳ al-Ḳāshānī; Badāʾ; Dahr; Duʿāʾ.II.b; Ḳaḍāʾ

advocates of Djabriyya; Djahmiyya; al-Karābīsī.2

opponents of Ghaylān b. Muslim; **Ḳadariyya**; Ḳatāda b. Diʿāma; Maʿbad al-Djuhanī

PRESS **Djarīda**; Maḳāla; **Maṭbaʿa**

Arabic ʿArabiyya.B.V.a; Baghdād (906b); Būlāḳ; **Djarīda**.i; Ḳiṣṣa.2; Maḳāla.1; al-Manār; **Maṭbaʿa**.1; al-Rāʾid al-Tūnusī

see also Nahḍa

journalism Abū Naḍḍāra; al-Bārūnī; Djabrān Khalīl Djabrān; Djamāl al-Dīn al-Afghānī; Djamīl; Fāris al-Shidyāḳ; Ibn Bādīs; Isḥāḳ, Adīb; al-Kawākibī; al-Khaḍir; Khalīl Ghānim; Khalīl Muṭrān; Kurd ʿAlī; Luṭfī al-Sayyid; al-Maʿlūf; Mandūr; al-Manūfī.7; al-Māzinī; Muṣṭafā ʿAbd al-Rāziḳ; al-Muwayliḥī; al-Nadīm, ʿAbd Allāh; Nadjīb al-Ḥaddād; Nimr; Rashīd Riḍā; Ṣafar; Saʿīd Abū Bakr; Salāma Mūsā; Salīm al-Naḳḳāsh; [in Suppl.] Abū Shādī; al-Bustānī

see also al-Mahdjar

Indian **Maṭbaʿa**.4; [in Suppl.] **Djarīda**.vii

journalism Muḥammad ʿAlī; Ruswā; [in Suppl.] Āzād; Ḥasrat Mohānī

see also Nadwat al-ʿUlamāʾ

Persian **Djarīda**.ii; Maḳāla; **Maṭbaʿa**.3

journalism Furūghī.3; Lāhūtī; Malkom Khān; Rashīd Yāsimī; [in Suppl.] Amīrī

Turkish **Djarīda**.iii; Djemʿiyyet-i ʿIlmiyye-i ʿOthmāniyye; Ibrāhīm Müteferriḳa; Maḳāla; **Maṭbaʿa**.2; Meshʿale; Mīzān

see also Ādharī.ii

journalism Aḥmad Iḥsān; Aḥmad Midḥat; Djewdet; Ebüzziya Tevfik; Gasprali (Gasprinski), Ismāʿīl; Ḥasan Fehmī; (Aḥmed) Ḥilmī; Hi̊sar; Ḥusayn Djāhid; Ileri, Djelāl Nūrī; İnal; Ḳaṣāb, Teodor; al-Kāẓimī, Meḥmed Sālim; Kemāl; Kemāl, Meḥmed Nāmi̊ḳ; Khālid Ḍiyāʾ; Köprülü

(Meḥmed Fuad); Manāṣtîrlî Meḥmed Rifʿat; Meḥmed ʿĀkif; Mīzāndjî Meḥmed Murād; Örik, Nahīd Ṣîrrī; Orkhan Seyfī; Ortač, Yūsuf Ḍiyā; Rîḍā Nūr; Sāhir, Djelāl; Sāmī; [in Suppl.] Aghaoghlu; Atay; Čaylaḳ Tewfīḳ; Eshref
see also Badrkhānī; Fedjr-i Ātī; Khalīl Ghānim; Saʿīd Efendi

PROFESSIONS al-ʿAṭṭār; Baḳḳāl; Bayṭār; Dallāl; Djānbāz; Djarrāḥ; Ḥammāl; Kannās; Kātib; Ḳayn; Ḳayna; Khayyāṭ; Mukārī; Munādī; Munadjdjim; al-Nassādj; Ṣabbāgh; Ṣāʾigh; Saḳḳāʾ; [in Suppl.] Dabbāgh; Djammāl; Djazzār; Faṣṣād; Ghassāl; Ḥāʾik; Ḥallāḳ
see also Asad Allāh Iṣfahānī; Aywaz.1; Khādim; *and* → LAW.OFFICES; MILITARY.OFFICES
artisans Ṣabbāgh; Ṣāʾigh; [in Suppl.] Ḥaʾik
labourers Ḥammāl; Kannās; Ḳayn; Khayyāṭ; [in Suppl.] Dabbāgh; Djazzār; Ghassāl; Ḥallāḳ
merchants al-ʿAṭṭār; Baḳḳāl; Mukārī; [in Suppl.] Djammāl
performers Djānbāz; Ḳayna

PROPERTY **Māl**; Milk; [in Suppl.] ʿAḳār
see also Munāṣafa; *and* → TAXATION.TAXES

PROPHETHOOD **Nubuwwa**; Rasūl
and → MUḤAMMAD, THE PROPHET
prophets Ādam; Alīsaʿ; Ḥā-Mīm; Hārūn b. ʿImrān; Hūd; Ibrāhīm; Idrīs; Lūṭ; Muḥammad; Mūsā; Nūḥ; Sadjāḥ; Ṣāliḥ
see also Fatra; ʿIṣma; Khālid b. Sinān; al-Kisāʾī, Ṣāḥib Ḳiṣaṣ al-Anbiyāʾ; Ḳiṣaṣ al-Anbiyāʾ; Luḳmān; *and* → MUḤAMMAD, THE PROPHET

PROVERBS **Mathal**; al-Maydānī
see also Iyās b. Muʿāwiya; Nār; *and* → ANIMALS.AND PROVERBS; LITERATURE

Q

QATAR al-Dawḥa; Hādjir; **Ḳaṭar**; Madjlis.4.A.xi; Maḥkama.4.ix

R

RAIDS Baranta; Ghanīma; **Ghazw**
and → BEDOUINS; MILITARY.EXPEDITIONS

RECREATION Cinema; Ḳaragöz; Khayāl al-Ẓill; Masraḥ; Orta Oyunu
games Djerīd; Kharbga; Ḳimār; **Laʿib**; al-Maysir; Mukhāradja; Nard
see also Ishāra; Kurds.iv.C.5; Maydān; *and* → ANIMALS.SPORT
sports Čawgān; Pahlawān

REFORM Djamʿiyya; **Iṣlāḥ**
see also Baladiyya; Ḥukūma; al-Manār; *and* → WOMEN.EMANCIPATION
educational Aḥmad Djewdet Pasha; Aḥmad Khān; al-Azhar.IV; Ḥabīb Allāh Khān; Maʿārif; Münīf Pasha; Nadwat al-ʿUlamāʾ; [in Suppl.] al-ʿAdawī
see also al-Marṣafī
financial Muḥaṣṣil
legal Abu ʾl-Suʿūd; Aḥmad Djewdet Pasha; Küčük Saʿīd Pasha; Medjelle; Mīrāth.2; Nikāḥ.II
see also Djazāʾ.ii; Ileri, Djelāl Nūrī; Imtiyāzāt.iv; Khayr al-Dīn Pasha; Maḥkama
military Niẓām-i̊ Djedīd
politico-religious Atatürk; Djamāl al-Dīn al-Afghānī; Ileri, Djelāl Nūrī; Ibn Bādīs; (al-)Ibrāhīmī; Ismāʿīl Ṣidḳī; Ḳāsim Amīn; Khayr al-Dīn Pasha; Midḥat Pasha; Muḥammad ʿAbduh; Muḥammad Bayram al-Khāmis; Nurculuk; Padri; Rashīd Riḍā; [in Suppl.] ʿAbd al-Nāṣir
see also Baladiyya; Bast; Djamʿiyya; Dustūr; Ḥarbiye; Ibrāhīm Müteferriḳa; al-Ikhwān al-Muslimūn; Iṣlāḥ; Mappila.5.ii; Salafiyya; [in Suppl.] Abu ʾl-ʿAzāʾim; *and* → POLITICS
militant al-Bannāʾ; Fidāʾiyyān-i Islām; Ḥamāliyya; Ibn Bādīs; al-Ikhwān al-Muslimūn; Mawdūdī
see also Ibn al-Muwaḳḳit; Mudjāhid; [in Suppl.] al-Djanbīhī

RELIGION ʿAḳīda; **Dīn**; al-Milal waʾl-Niḥal; Milla; Millet.1
see also Ḥanīf; *and* → CHRISTIANITY; ISLAM; JUDAISM
other than the major three Bābīs; Bahāʾīs; Barāhima; Budd; Dhu ʾl-Sharā; Djayn; Gabr; Hindū; Ibāḥatiya; Ṣābiʾ; Ṣābiʾa; al-Sāmira
see also Aghāthūdhīmūn; Bakhshī; al-Barāmika.1; Hirmis; Hurmuz; Khʷādja Khiḍr; Kitāb al-Djilwa; Mānī; al-Milal waʾl-Niḥal; Millet; Nānak; *and* → BAHAIS; DRUZES; ZOROASTRIANS
pantheism ʿAmr b. Luḥayy; Djāhiliyya; Kaʿba.V
see also Ḥarīriyya; Ḥadjdj.i; Ibn al-ʿArabī; Ibn al-ʿArīf; Kāfiristān; Kamāl Khudjandī; *and* → PRE-ISLAM.GODS
popular → ISLAM.POPULAR BELIEFS

RHETORIC Badīʿ; Balāgha; Bayān; Faṣāḥa; Ḥaḳīḳa.1; Ibtidāʾ; Idjāza; Iḳtibās; Intihāʾ; Istiʿāra; Kināya; al-Maʿānī wa ʾl-Bayān; Madjāz; Mubālagha; Muḳābala.3; Muwāraba; Muzāwadja; Muzdawidj; Ramz.1
see also Ishāra

treatises on al-ʿAskarī.ii; Ḥāzim; Ibn al-Muʿtazz; al-Ḳazwīnī (Khaṭīb Dimashḳ); al-Rādūyānī; al-Sakkākī; [in Suppl.] al-Djurdjānī; Ibn Wahb

Rhyme **Ḳāfiya**; Luzūm mā lā yalzam
and → Literature.poetry; Metrics

Rituals ʿAḳīḳa; ʿAnṣāra; ʿĀshūrāʾ; Khitān; Rawḍa-khwānī
see also Bakkāʾ; Ḥammām; ʿIbādāt; al-Maghrib.VI; [in Suppl.] Dam; *and* → Customs

Rivers **Nahr**
see also Maʾṣir; *and* → Navigation
waters al-ʿAḍaym; ʿAfrīn; Alindjaḳ; al-ʿAlḳamī; Amū Daryā; al-ʿĀṣī; Atbara; Atrek; Baḥr al-Ghazāl.1; Baradā; Čaghān-rūd; Congo; Čoruh; Ču; Darʿa; Dawʿan; Dehās; Didjla; Diyālā; Djamna; Djayḥān; al-Furāt; Gangā; Gediz Čayi̊; Göksu; al-Ḥamma; Harī Rūd; Ibruh; Ili; Isly; Itil; Kābul.1; Karkha; Kārūn; Khābūr; Khalkha; al-Khāzir; Ḳi̊zi̊l-irmāḳ; Ḳi̊zi̊l-üzen; Ḳuban; Ḳunduz; Kur; Kurram; Lamas-ṣū; Mānd; Menderes; Merič; Mihrān; al-Mudawwar; Nahr Abī Fuṭrus; Niger; al-Nīl; Ob; Orkhon; Özi; al-Rass; Safīd Rūd; Sakarya; [in Suppl.] Gūmāl
see also Hind.i.j; ʿĪsā, Nahr; *and* → *the section Physical Geography under individual countries*

Romania Ada Ḳalʿe; Babadaghi̊; Bender; Boghdān; Budjāḳ; Bükresh; Deli-Orman; Dobrudja; Eflāḳ; Erdel; Ibrail; Isakča; Köstendje; Medjīdiyye; Nagyvárad
see also Muslimūn.1.B.2

Russia → Commonwealth of Independent States

S

Sacred Places Abū Ḳubays; al-Ḥaram al-Sharīf; Ḥudjra; Kaʿba; Karbalāʾ; Kāẓimayn; al-Khalīl; al-Ḳuds.II; al-Madīna; Makka; al-Muḳaṭṭam; al-Nadjaf
see also Ḥawṭa; Ḥimā; Ḳāsiyūn; Mawlāy Idrīs; Mudjāwir; *and* → Architecture.monuments; Sainthood

Sacrifices ʿAḳīḳa; ʿAtīra; Baliyya; Dhabīḥa; Fidya; Hady; Ḳurbān
see also Ibil; ʿĪd al-Aḍḥā; Kaffāra; Nadhr; [in Suppl.] Dam

Sainthood Mawlid
see also ʿAbābda; Mawlā.I; *and* → Christianity; Hagiography; Mysticism

saints

- *Arabic* Aḥmad b. ʿĪsā; Aḥmad al-Badawī; Nafīsa
  - *see also* Ḳunā; *and* → Mysticism
  - *North African* Abū Muḥammad Ṣāliḥ; Abū Yaʿazzā; ʿĀʾisha al-Mannūbiyya; al-Bādisī.1; al-Daḳḳāḳ; al-Djazūlī, Abū ʿAbd Allāh; Ḥmād u-Mūsā; Ibn ʿArūs; al-Ḳabbāb; Ḳaddūr al-ʿAlamī; al-Khaṣāṣī; Muḥriz b. Khalaf; al-Sabtī; [in Suppl.] Ḥamādisha
    - *see also* al-Maghrib.VI; Sabʿatu Ridjāl; *and* → Mysticism
- *Central Asian* Aḥmad Yasawī
- *Indian* Abū ʿAlī Ḳalandar; Ashraf Djahāngīr; Badīʿ al-Dīn; Badr; Bahāʾ al-Dīn Zakariyyā; Čishtī; Farīd al-Dīn Masʿūd "Gandj-i Shakar"; Ghāzī Miyān; Gīsū Darāz; Imām Shāh; Khʷādja Khiḍr; Maghribī; Makhdūm al-Mulk Manīrī; Masʿūd; Niẓām al-Dīn Awliyāʾ; Nūr Ḳuṭb al-ʿĀlam; Ratan; [in Suppl.] Bābā Nūr al-Dīn Rishī; Gadāʾī Kambō; Gangōhī; Ḥamīd al-Dīn Ḳāḍī Nāgawrī; Ḥamīd al-Dīn Ṣūfī Nāgawrī Siwālī
  - *see also* Ḥasan Abdāl; Pāk Pātan
- *Persian* ʿAlī al-Hamadānī; Bābā-Ṭāhir
- *Turkish* Akhī Ewrān; Emīr Sulṭān; Ḥādjdjī Bayrām Walī; Ḥakīm Ata; Ḳoyun Baba; Merkez

terms Abdāl; Ilhām

Saudi Arabia (Djazīrat) al-ʿArab; Djarīda.i.A; Djāmiʿa; Dustūr.vii; al-Hidjar; al-Ikhwān; Madjlis.4.A.viii; Maḥkama.4.vii
- *see also* Bā ʿAlawī; Badw; Baladiyya.2; Barakāt; Makka; [in Suppl.] Demography.III; *and* → Pre-islam.in arabian peninsula; Tribes.arabian peninsula

before Islam → Pre-Islam.in arabian peninsula

dynasties Hāshimids (2x); Rashīd, Āl
- *see also* Muḥammad b. Suʿūd; [in Suppl.] ʿAbd al-ʿAzīz; Fayṣal b. ʿAbd al-ʿAzīz; *and* → Dynasties.arabian peninsula

historians of al-Azraḳī; Daḥlān; al-Fāḳihī; al-Fāsī; Ibn Fahd; Ibn Manda; Ibn al-Mudjāwir; Ibn al-Nadjdjār; al-Samhūdī
- *see also* al-Diyārbakrī

physical geography

- *deserts* al-Aḥḳāf; al-Dahnāʾ; Nafūd; al-Rubʿ al-Khālī
  - *see also* Badw.II; Ḥarra
- *mountains* Djabala; Ḥufāsh; Raḍwā
  - *see also* Adjaʾ and Salmā
- *plains* ʿArafa; al-Dibdiba; al-Ṣammān
- *wadis* al-ʿAtk; al-Bāṭin; Bayḥān; Bayḥān al-Ḳaṣāb; Djayzān; Fāʾw; Ḥamḍ, Wādī al-; al-Rumma; al-Sahbāʾ
- *waters* Dawʿan

population → TRIBES.ARABIAN PENINSULA
toponyms
ancient Badr; al-Djār; Fadak; al-Ḥidjr; al-Ḥudaybiya; Ḳurḥ; Madyan Shuʿayb; al-Rabadha
see also Fāʾw
present-day
districts al-Aflādj; al-Djawf; al-Ḳaṣīm; al-Khardj
islands Farasān
oases al-Dirʿiyya; Dūmat al-Djandal; al-Ḥasā; al-Khurma
regions ʿAsīr; ʿAwlaḳī; Bayḥān; al-Ḥāḍina; Ḥaly; al-Ḥawṭa; al-Ḥidjāz; Ḳurayyāt al Milḥ; Nadjd; Nafūd; Raʾs (al-)Tannūra; al-Rubʿ al-Khālī
towns Abhā; Abḳayḳ; Abū ʿArīsh; Burayda; al-Dammām; al-Djawf; Djayzān; al-Djubayl; al-Djubayla; Djudda; Fakhkh; Ghāmid; Ḥāyil; al-Hufūf; Ḥuraymilā; Ḳarya al-Suflā; Ḳarya al-ʿUlyā; al-Ḳaṣāb; al-Ḳaṭīf; Khamīs Mushayṭ; Khaybar; al-Khubar; al-Ḳunfudha; al-Madīna; Makka; Minā; al-Mubarraz; Nadjrān; Rābigh; al-Riyāḍ; [in Suppl.] Fayd
see also (Djazīrat) al-ʿArab; al-ʿĀriḍ; Bīsha; Ḍariyya

SCIENCE **ʿIlm**; Mawṣūʿa
see also Ibn Abī Uṣaybiʿa; [in Suppl.] al-Bustānī; Ibn al-Akfānī.3; Ibn Farīghūn; *and* → ALCHEMY; ASTROLOGY; ASTRONOMY; BOTANY; MATHEMATICS; MECHANICS; MEDICINE; OPTICS; PHARMACOLOGY; ZOOLOGY

SECTS ʿAdjārida; Ahl-i Ḥadīth; Ahl-i Ḥaḳḳ; Aḥmadiyya; ʿAlids; Azāriḳa; al-Badjalī; Baḳliyya; Bihʾafrıd b. Farwardīn; Bohorās; Burghūthiyya; Djabriyya; Djahmiyya; al-Djanāḥiyya; Durūz; Farāʾiḍiyya; Ghurābiyya; Ḥarīriyya; Ḥashīshiyya; Ḥulmāniyya; Ḥurūfiyya; al-Ibāḍiyya; Ḳarmaṭī; Karrāmiyya; Kaysāniyya; al-Khalafiyya; Khāridjites; Khashabiyya; Khaṭṭābiyya; Khōdja; Khūbmesīḥīs; Khurramiyya; Kuraybiyya; Mahdawīs; Manṣūriyya; al-Mughīriyya; Muḥammadiyya; Mukhammisa; Muṭarrifiyya; al-Muʿtazila; Nadjadāt; Nāwūsiyya; al-Nukkār; Nuḳṭawiyya; Nūrbakhshiyya; Nuṣayriyya; Rawshaniyya; [in Suppl.] Dhikrīs
see also Abu ʾl-Maʿālī; ʿAlī Ilāhī; Bābāʾī; Bābīs; Bāyazīd Anṣārī; Bīsharʿ; Dahriyya; al-Dhammiyya; Dīn-i Ilāhī; Ghassāniyya; Ghulāt; Ḥā-Mīm; Imām Shāh; ʿIrāḳ.vi; Kasrawī Tabrīzī; al-Kayyāl; Kāẓim Rashtī; Ḳïzïl-bāsh; al-Malaṭī; Mazdak; Mudjtahid.III; Sālimiyya; *and* → MYSTICISM.ORDERS
Alids ʿAbd Allāh b. Muʿāwiya; Abū ʿAbd Allāh Yaʿḳūb; Abu ʾl-Aswad al-Duʾalī; Abū Hāshim; Abū Nuʿaym al-Mulāʾī; Abū Salāma al-Khallāl; Abu ʾl-Sarāyā al-Shaybānī; ʿAlī b. Muḥammad al-Zandjī; **ʿAlids**; al-Djawwānī; Hāniʾ b. ʿUrwa al-Murādī; al-Ḥasan b. Zayd b. Muḥammad; Ḥasan al-Uṭrūsh; Ḥudjr; al-Ḥusayn b. ʿAlī, Ṣāḥib Fakhkh; Ibrāhīm b. al-Ashtar; Khidāsh; Muḥam-

mad b. ʿAbd Allāh (al-Nafs al-Zakiyya); al-Mukhtār b. Abī ʿUbayd; Muslim b. ʿAḳīl b. Abī Ṭālib
see also Dhu ʾl-Faḳār; al-Djanāḥiyya; al-Djārūdiyya; Ghadīr Khumm; al-Maʾmūn; *and* → SHIITES

Bābism Bāb; **Bābīs**; Kāshānī; Ḳurrat al-ʿAyn; Maẓhar; Muḥammad ʿAlī Bārfurūshī; Muḥammad ʿAlī Zandjānī; Muḥammad Ḥusayn Bushrūʾī
see also al-Aḥsāʾī; Mudjtahid.III; Nuḳṭat al-Kāf; al-Sābiḳūn

Druzes → DRUZES

Ibāḍīs ʿAbd al-ʿAzīz b. al-Ḥādjdj Ibrāhīm; Abū Ghānim al-Khurāsānī; Abū Ḥafṣ ʿUmar b. Djamīʿ; Abū Ḥātim al-Malzūzī (*and* al-Malzūzī); Abu ʾl-Khaṭṭāb al-Maʿāfirī; Abū Muḥammad b. Baraka; Abu ʾl-Muʾthir al-Bahlawī; Abū Zakariyyāʾ al-Djanāwunī; Abū Zakariyyāʾ al-Wardjlānī; Aṭfiyāsh; al-Barrādī; al-Bughṭūrī; al-Dardjīnī; Djābir b. Zayd; al-Djayṭālī; al-Djulandā; **al-Ibāḍiyya**; Ibn Baraka; Ibn Djaʿfar; al-Irdjānī; al-Lawātī; Maḥbūb b. al-Raḥīl al-ʿAbdī; al-Mazātī; al-Nafūsī; [in Suppl.] Abū ʿAmmār; al-Ḥārithī
see also ʿAwāmir; Azd; Ḥalḳa; al-Khalafiyya; (Banū) Kharūṣ; *and* → DYNASTIES.SPAIN AND NORTH AFRICA.RUSTAMIDS; LAW; SECTS.KHARIDJITES

historians of Abu ʾl-Muʾthir al-Bahlawī; Abū Zakariyyāʾ al-Wardjlānī; al-Barrādī; al-Bughṭūrī; al-Dardjīnī; Ibn al-Ṣaghīr; Ibn Salām; al-Lawātī; Maḥbūb b. al-Raḥīl al-ʿAbdī; al-Mazātī; al-Sālimī
see also al-Nafūsī

Jewish → JUDAISM

Kharidjites Abū Bayhas; Abū Fudayk; Abū Yazīd al-Nukkārī; al-Ḍaḥḥāḳ b. Ḳays al-Shaybānī; Ḥurḳūṣ b. Zuhayr al-Saʿdī; ʿImrān b. Ḥiṭṭān; Ḳaṭarī b. al-Fudjāʾa; **Khāridjites**; Ḳurrāʾ; Ḳuʿūd; Mirdās b. Udayya; Nāfiʿ b. al-Azraḳ; al-Nukkār
see also ʿAdjārida; Azāriḳa; Ḥarūrāʾ; al-Ibāḍiyya; Ibn Muldjam; Imāma; Istiʿrāḍ; al-Manṣūr bi ʾllāh; Nadjadāt

Shiite → SHIITES

Uṣūlīs Mudjtahid.III

SENEGAL Djolof; [in Suppl.] Dakar
see also Murīdiyya

SEXUALITY ʿAzl; Bāh; Djins; Khitān; Liwāṭ; [in Suppl.] Bighāʾ
see also Djanāba; Khāṣī

SHIITES ʿAbd Allāh b. Sabaʾ; ʿAlids; Ghulāt; Imāma; Ismāʿīliyya; Ithnā ʿAshariyya; Sabʿiyya
see also Abu ʾl-Sarāyā al-Shaybānī; ʿAlī b. Abī Ṭālib; ʿAlī Mardān; Madjlis.3; [in Suppl.] Batriyya; *and* → SHIITES.SECTS

branches Ismāʿīliyya; Ithnā ʿAshariyya; Ḳarmaṭī
see also Hind.v.d; *and* → SHIITES.SECTS
Carmathians (Djazīrat) al-ʿArab.vii.2; al-Djannābī, Abū Saʿīd; al-Djannābī, Abū Ṭāhir; Ḥamdān Ḳarmaṭ; al-Ḥasan al-Aʿṣam; **Ḳarmaṭī**
see also ʿAbdān; al-Baḥrayn; Baḳliyya; Daʿwa
Ismāʿīliyya ʿAbd Allāh b. Maymūn; Abū ʿAbd Allāh al-Shīʿī; Abu ʾl-Khattāb al-Asadī; Allāh.iii.1; (Djazīrat) al-ʿArab.vii.2; Bāb; Bāṭiniyya; Bohorās; Dāʿī; Daʿwa; Fāṭimids; Ḥaḳāʾiḳ; Hind.v.d; Ibn ʿAttāsh; Ikhwān al-Ṣafāʾ; Imāma; **Ismāʿīliyya**; Lanbasar; Madjlis.2; al-Mahdī ʿUbayd Allāh; Malāʾika.2; Manṣūr al-Yaman; Maymūn-diz; Sabʿiyya; [in Suppl.] Dawr
see also Ḥawwāʾ; Ikhlāṣ; Maṣyād; Sabʿ; Salamiyya; *and* → CALIPHATE.FĀṬIMIDS; SHIITES.IMAMS
authors Abū Ḥātim al-Rāzī; Abū Yaʿḳūb al-Sidjzī; al-Kirmānī; al-Muʾayyad fi ʾl-Dīn; al-Nasafī.1; Nāṣir-i Khusraw; [in Suppl.] Djaʿfar b. Manṣūr al-Yaman; Idrīs b. al-Ḥasan
and → SHIITES.BRANCHES.ṬAYYIBĪS
Nizārīs Agha Khān; Alamūt.ii; Buzurg-ummīd; Fidāʾī; Ḥasan-i Ṣabbāḥ; Ḥashīshiyya; Khōdja; Maḥallātī; Nizār b. al-Mustanṣir; **Nizāriyya**; Nūr al-Dīn Muḥammad II; Pīr Ṣadr al-Dīn; Pīr Shams; Rāshid al-Dīn Sinān; Rukn al-Dīn Khurshāh; Sabz ʿAlī
Sevener Sabʿiyya
see also Sabʿ
Ṭayyibīs al-Ḥāmidī; Luḳmāndjī; al-Makramī; Makramids; Muḥammad b. Ṭāhir al-Ḥārithī; [in Suppl.] ʿAlī b. Ḥanzala b. Abī Sālim; ʿAlī b. Muḥammad b. Djaʿfar; Amīndjī b. Djalāl b. Ḥasan
Twelver Imāma; **Ithnā ʿAshariyya**; Mudjtahid.II; Mutawālī; al-Rāfiḍa
and → SHIITES.IMAMS
Zaydīs al-Ḥasan b. Ṣāliḥ b. Ḥayy al-Kūfī; Ibn Abi ʾl-Ridjāl; al-Mahdī li-Dīn Allāh Aḥmad; Muḥammad b. Zayd; al-Nāṣir li-Dīn Allāh; al-Rassī; [in Suppl.] Abu ʾl-Barakāt; Abu ʾl-Fatḥ al-Daylamī; Aḥmad b. ʿĪsā; Djaʿfar b. Abī Yaḥyā; al-Ḥākim al-Djushamī
see also Imāma; Muṭarrifiyya; Rassids; *and* → DYNASTIES.ARABIAN PENINSULA

doctrines and institutions Bāṭiniyya; Djafr; Ḳāʾim Āl Muḥammad; Khalḳ.VII; Madjlis.2 and 3; al-Mahdī; Malāʾika.2; Mardjaʿ-i Taḳlīd; Maẓhar; Maẓlūm; Mudjtahid.II; Mutʿa.V; Radjʿa; Safīr.1; [in Suppl.] Āyatullāh
see also Adhān; Ahl al-Bayt; ʿAḳīda; Bāb; Ghayba; Ḥudjdja; Imāma; ʿIlm al-Ridjāl; Imām-bārā; Imāmzāda; Mollā; *and* → THEOLOGY.TERMS.SHIITE

dynasties Buwayhids; Fāṭimids; Ṣafawids
see also Mushaʿshaʿ

imams ʿAlī b. Abī Ṭālib; ʿAlī al-Riḍā; al-ʿAskarī; Djaʿfar al-Ṣādiḳ; (al-)Ḥasan b. ʿAlī b. Abī Ṭālib; (al-)Ḥusayn b. ʿAlī b. Abī Ṭālib; Muḥammad b. ʿAlī al-

Riḍā; Muḥammad b. ʿAlī (al-Bāḳir); Muḥammad al-Ḳāʾim; Mūsā al-Kāẓim
  see also Bāb; G̲h̲ayba; Imāmzāda; Malāʾika.2; Maẓlūm; Riḍā.2; Safīr.1
jurists   al-ʿĀmilī; al-Ḥillī.2; al-Māmaḳānī; al-Mufīd; Muḥammad b. Makkī; [in
  Suppl.] Anṣārī; Bihbihānī
  see also ʿĀḳila; Mad̲j̲lisī; Mad̲j̲lisī-yi Awwal; Mard̲j̲aʿ-i Taḳlīd;
  Mud̲j̲tahid.II; Mutʿa.V
places of pilgrimage   Karbalāʾ; Kāẓimayn; al-Nad̲j̲af; [in Suppl.] ʿAtabāt
rituals   Rawḍa-k̲h̲ʷānī
sects   Ahl-i Ḥaḳḳ; ʿAlids; Baḳliyya; Bohorās; D̲j̲ābir b. Ḥayyān; al-D̲j̲anāḥiyya;
  al-D̲j̲ārūdiyya; G̲h̲urābiyya; Ḥurūfiyya; Ibāḥa.II; Kaysāniyya; K̲h̲as̲h̲a-
  biyya; K̲h̲aṭṭābiyya; K̲h̲ōd̲j̲a; K̲h̲urramiyya; Kuraybiyya; Manṣūriyya; al-
  Mug̲h̲īriyya; Muḥammadiyya; Muk̲h̲ammisa; Muṭarrifiyya; al-Muʿtazila;
  Nāwūsiyya; Nūrbak̲h̲s̲h̲iyya; Nuṣayriyya; al-Rāwandiyya; Salmāniyya
  see also ʿAbd Allāh b. Sabaʾ; Bāṭiniyya; Bayān b. Samʿān al-Tamīmī;
  Bektās̲h̲iyya; G̲h̲ulāt; Hind.v.d; Imām S̲h̲āh; Ḳaṭʿ; al-Kayyāl; Kāẓim Ras̲h̲tī;
  Ḳ̣izil-bās̲h̲; Mus̲h̲aʿs̲h̲aʿ; [in Suppl.] Ibn Warsand; *and* → DRUZES;
  SECTS.ʿALIDS
  Kaysāniyya   Abū Hās̲h̲im; Kaysān; **Kaysāniyya**
  K̲h̲aṭṭābiyya   Abu ʾl-K̲h̲aṭṭāb al-Asadī; Bas̲h̲s̲h̲ār al-S̲h̲aʿīrī; Bazīg̲h̲ b. Mūsā;
    K̲h̲aṭṭābiyya
    see also Muk̲h̲ammisa; al-Ṣāmit
  K̲h̲urramiyya   Bābak; [in Suppl.] Bād̲h̲ām
  Muk̲h̲ammisa   **Muk̲h̲ammisa**
    see also al-Muḥassin b. ʿAlī
  S̲h̲ayk̲h̲ism   al-Aḥsāʾī; Ras̲h̲tī, Sayyid Kāẓim
terms   → THEOLOGY.TERMS.SHIITE
theologians   al-Dāmād; al-Ḥillī.1; His̲h̲ām b. al-Ḥakam; al-Ḥurr al-ʿĀmilī; Ibn
  Bābawayh(i); Ibn S̲h̲ahrās̲h̲ūb; al-Karakī; Kās̲h̲if al-G̲h̲iṭāʾ; K̲h̲ʷānsārī,
  Sayyid Mīrzā; al-Kulaynī, Abū D̲j̲aʿfar Muḥammad; Lāhīd̲j̲ī.2; Mīr Lawḥī;
  al-Mufīd; Mullā Ṣadrā S̲h̲īrāzī; al-Nasafī.1; [in Suppl.] Ak̲h̲bāriyya; Anṣārī;
  Fayḍ-i Kās̲h̲ānī; Ibn Abī D̲j̲umhūr al-Aḥsāʾī; Ibn Mītham
  see also al-ʿAyyās̲h̲ī; Ḥud̲j̲d̲j̲a; Imāma; K̲h̲alḳ.VII; Mollā
  20th-century   Kās̲h̲ānī; K̲h̲ʷānsārī, Sayyid Muḥammad; K̲h̲iyābānī, S̲h̲ayk̲h̲
    Muḥammad; K̲h̲urāsānī; Muṭahharī; Nāʾīnī; [in Suppl.] Āḳā Nad̲j̲afī;
    Burūd̲j̲irdī; Ḥāʾirī

SIBERIA
physical geography
  waters Ob
population Buk̲h̲ārlǐk

SICILY Benavert; Ibn al-Ḥawwās; Ibn al-Khayyāṭ; Ibn al-Thumna; Kalbids
see also Aghlabids.iii; Asad b. al-Furāt; Fāṭimids; Ibn Ḥamdīs; Ibn al-Ḳaṭṭāʿ; Ibn Makkī
toponyms Balarm; Benavent; Djirdjent; Ḳaṣryānnih
see also al-Khāliṣa

SLAVERY **ʿAbd**; Ghulām; ʿItḳnāme; Ḳayna; Khāṣī; Mamlūk; Mawlā; al-Ṣaḳāliba
see also Ḥabash.i; Ḥabshī; Hausa; ʿIdda.5; Istibrāʾ; Khādim; Ḳul; Maṭmūra; *and* → MUSIC.SONG.SINGERS

SOMALIA
see also Ḥabesh; Muḥammad b. ʿAbd Allāh Ḥassān; Ogādēn
religious orders Ṣāliḥiyya
toponyms
regions Guardafui
see also Ogaden
towns Barawa; Berberā; Hargeisa; Maḳdishū; Merka

SOUTH(-EAST) ASIA → ASIA

SOVIET UNION → CAUCASUS; CENTRAL ASIA.FORMER SOVIET UNION; COMMUNISM; EUROPE.EASTERN EUROPE; SIBERIA

SPAIN Aljamía; Almogávares; al-Burt; al-Bushārrāt; Moriscos
see also Ibn al-Ḳiṭṭ; Ifnī; al-ʿIḳāb, *and* → ANDALUSIA; DYNASTIES.SPAIN AND NORTH AFRICA
physical geography
waters al-Ḥamma; Ibruh; al-Mudawwar; [in Suppl.] Araghūn
toponyms
ancient Barbashturu; Bulāy; Ḳasṭīliya.1; Labla; al-Madīna al-Zāhira; [in Suppl.] Āfrāg; Balyūnash
see also Rayya
present-day
islands al-Djazāʾir al-Khālida; Mayūrḳa; Minūrḳa
regions Ālaba wa ʾl-Ḳilāʿ; Djillīḳiyya; Faḥṣ al-Ballūṭ; Firrīsh; Ḳanbāniya; Ḳashtāla; Navarra; [in Suppl.] Araghūn
towns Alsh; Arkush; Arnīṭ; Badjdjāna; Balansiya; Bālish; Banbalūna; Barshalūna; al-Basīt; Basta; Baṭalyaws; Bayyāna; Bayyāsa; Biṭrawsh; al-Bunt; Burghush; Dāniya; Djarunda; Djayyān; al-Djazīra al-Khaḍrāʾ; Djazīrat Shuḳr; Finyāna; Gharnāṭa; Ifrāgha; Ilbīra; Ishbīliya; Istidja; Ḳabra; Ḳādis; Ḳalʿat Ayyūb; Ḳalʿat Rabāḥ;

Ḳanṭara.2; Ḳarmūna; Ḳarṭādjanna; al-Ḳulayʿa; Ḳūnka; Ḳūriya; Ḳurṭuba; Laḳant; Lārida; Lawsha; Liyūn; Lūrḳa; al-Maʿdin; Madīnat Sālim; Madīnat al-Zahrāʾ; Madjrīṭ; Mālaḳa; Mārida; al-Mariyya; Mawrūr; al-Munakkab; Mursiya; Runda; [in Suppl.] Ashturḳa
see also al-Andalus.iii.3; Balāṭ; Djabal Ṭāriḳ; al-Ḳalʿa; *and* → PORTUGAL

SRI LANKA **Ceylon**

SUDAN Dār Fūr; Dustūr.xiii; Ḥizb.i; Madjlis.4.A.xvii; al-Mahdiyya
see also Baladiyya.2; Fundj; Ḥabesh; Nūba
Mahdist period ʿAbd Allāh b. Muḥammad al-Taʿāʾishī; Khalīfa.iv; **al-Mahdiyya**
see also Awlād al-Balad; Dār Fūr; Emīn Pasha; Rābiḥ b. Faḍl Allāh
physical geography
waters al-Nīl
population ʿAbābda; ʿAlwa; (Banū) ʿĀmir; Baḳḳāra; Barābra; Djaʿaliyyūn; Ghuzz.iii; Nūba.4; Rashāʾida
see also Fallāta
religious orders Mīrghaniyya
toponyms
ancient ʿAydhāb
present-day
provinces Baḥr al-Ghazāl.3; Berber.2; Dār Fūr; Fāshōda; Kasala
regions Fāzūghlī; Kordofān
towns Atbara; Berber.3; Dongola; al-Fāshir; Kasala; Ḳerrī; al-Khurṭūm; Omdurman

SUPERSTITION ʿAyn; Faʾl; Ghurāb; Ḥinnāʾ; Khamsa; Ṣadā
see also ʿAḳīḳ; Bāriḥ; Laḳab

SYRIA
and → LEBANON
architecture → ARCHITECTURE.REGIONS
before Islam → PRE-ISLAM.IN FERTILE CRESCENT
dynasties ʿAmmār; Ayyūbids; Būrids; Fāṭimids; Ḥamdānids; Mamlūks
see also [in Suppl.] al-Djazzār Pasha; *and* → DYNASTIES.EGYPT AND THE FERTILE CRESCENT; LEBANON
historians of al-ʿAẓīmī; Ibn Abī Ṭayyiʾ; Ibn al-ʿAdīm; Ibn ʿAsākir; Ibn al-Ḳalānisī; Ibn Kathīr; Ibn Shaddād; Kurd ʿAlī; al-Kutubī
and → DYNASTIES.EGYPT AND THE FERTILE CRESCENT
modern period Djarīda.i.A; Djāmiʿa; Dustūr.ix; Ḥizb.i; Ḥukūma.iii; Madjlis.4.A.v; Madjmaʿ ʿIlmī.i.2.a; Maḥkama.4.ii; Mandates; Maysalūn; Salafiyya.2(b)

see also Baladiyya.2; Kurd ʿAlī; Mardam.2; [in Suppl.] Demography.III

statesmen al-Khūrī; Mardam.1

physical geography

mountains Ḳāsiyūn; al-Lukkām

waters ʿAfrīn; al-ʿĀṣī; Baradā

toponyms

ancient Afāmiya; ʿArbān; al-Bakhrāʾ; al-Bāra; Barḳaʿīd; Dābiḳ; Diyār Muḍar; Diyār Rabīʿa; al-Djābiya; al-Djazīra; Djillik; Manbidj; Namāra.1; al-Raḥba; Raʾs al-ʿAyn; Rīḥā.2; al-Ruṣāfa.3

present-day

districts al-Bathaniyya; al-Djawlān

regions al-Ghāb; Ḥawrān; Ḳinnasrīn.2; Ladjāʾ; al-Ṣafā.2

see also Ghūṭa

towns Adhriʿāt; Bāniyās; Boṣrā; Buzāʿā; Dayr al-Zōr; Dimashḳ; Djabala; al-Djabbūl; Djisr al-Shughr; Ḥalab; Ḥamāt; Ḥārim; Ḥimṣ; Ḥuwwārīn; Ḳanawāt; Ḳarḳīsiyā; Khawlān.2; Ḳinnasrīn.1; al-Lādhiḳiyya; Maʿarrat Maṣrīn; Maʿarrat al-Nuʿmān; Maʿlūlā; Maskana; Maṣyād; al-Mizza; Namāra.2 and 3; al-Raḳḳa; Ṣāfītha; Salamiyya; Ṣalkhad

see also al-Marḳab

T

TANZANIA Dar-es-Salaam; Kilwa; Mikindani; Mkwaja, Mtambwe Mkuu

TAXATION Bādj; **Bayt al-Māl**; Ḍarība; Djizya; Ḳānūn.ii and iii; Kharādj; [in Suppl.] Ḍarība.7

see also Ḍabṭ; Djahbadh; Māʾ; Maʾṣir; Raʿiyya

collectors ʿĀmil; Dihḳan; Muḥaṣṣil; Mültezim; Mustakhridj

see also Amīr

taxes ʿArūs Resmi; ʿAwāriḍ; Bād-i Hawā; Badal; Bādj; Djawālī; Djizya; Filori; Furḍa; Ispendje; Ḳūbčūr; Maks; Mālikāne; Muḳāṭaʿa; Pīshkash; Resm

see also Ḥisba.ii; Ḳaṭīʿa

land taxes Bashmaḳlïḳ; Bennāk; Čift-resmi; **Kharādj**; Mīrī; Muḳāsama

see also Daftar; Daftar-i Khāḳānī; Ḳabāla; Ḳānūn.iii.1; Rawk

tithe-lands Ḍayʿa; Īghār; Iḳṭāʿ; Iltizām; Khāliṣa; Khāṣṣ; Ṣafī

see also Baʿl.2.b; Dār al-ʿAhd; Fayʾ; Filāḥa.iv

treatises on al-Makhzūmī

THAILAND Patani

THEOLOGY   'Aḳīda; Allāh; Dīn; D̲j̲anna; 'Ilm al-Kalām; Imāma; Īmān; Kalām; al-Mahdī
    see also 'Ālam.1; Hilāl.i; *and* → ISLAM
disputation   Masāʾil wa-Ad̲j̲wiba; Munāẓara; Radd; [in Suppl.] 'Ibādat K̲h̲āna
    see also Mubāhala
treatises on   al-Samarḳandī, S̲h̲ams al-Dīn
schools
    Shiite   Ismāʿīliyya; It̲h̲nā 'As̲h̲ariyya; Ḳarmaṭī; [in Suppl.] Ak̲h̲bāriyya
        see also Muʿtazila
    Sunni   As̲h̲ʿariyya; Ḥanābila; Māturīdiyya; Muʿtazila
        see also 'Ilm al-Kalām.II; Ḳadariyya; Karāmat 'Alī; Murd̲j̲iʾa; al-Nad̲j̲d̲j̲āriyya
terms   Ad̲j̲al; Ad̲j̲r; 'Adl; 'Ahd; Ahl al-ahwāʾ; Ahl al-kitāb; Āk̲h̲ira; 'Aḳīda; 'Aḳl; 'Aḳliyyāt; 'Ālam.2.; 'Amal.2; Amr; al-Aṣlaḥ; Baʿt̲h̲; Bāṭiniyya; Bidʿa; Birr; Daʿwa; Dīn; D̲j̲amāʿa; D̲j̲azāʾ; D̲j̲ism; Duʿāʾ; Fard; Fāsiḳ; Fiʿl; Fitna; Fiṭra; al-G̲h̲ayb; G̲h̲ayba; G̲h̲ufrān; Ḥadd; Ḥaḳḳ; Ḥaraka wa-Sukūn.I.2 and 3; Ḥisāb; Ḥud̲j̲d̲j̲a; Ḥudūt̲h̲ al-ʿĀlam; Ḥulūl; Iʿd̲j̲āz; Iḍṭirār; Ik̲h̲lāṣ; Ik̲h̲tiyār; 'Illa.ii.III; Imāma; Īmān; Islām; 'Iṣma; Istiṭāʿa; Ittiḥād; al-Ḳaḍāʾ wa ʾl-Ḳadar; Kaffāra; Kāfir; Kalima; Karāma; Kasb; Kas̲h̲f; K̲h̲alḳ; K̲h̲aṭīʾa; K̲h̲id̲h̲lān; Ḳidam; Kumūn; Ḳunūt; Ḳuwwa.3; Luṭf; Maʿād; al-Mahdī; al-Manzila bayn al-Manzilatayn; al-Mug̲h̲ayyabāt al-K̲h̲ams; al-Munāfiḳūn.2; Murtadd; Muṭlaḳ; Nāfila; Nafs; Nāmūs.1; Nūr Muḥammadī; Riyāʾ; Rizḳ; Rud̲j̲ūʿ; Ruʾyat Allāh; Sabīl.1; [in Suppl.] Ḥāl
    see also Abad; Allāh.ii; In S̲h̲āʾ Allāh; 'Ināya; *and* → ESCHATOLOGY
    Shiite   Badāʾ; G̲h̲ayba; Ibdāʿ; Kas̲h̲f; Lāhūt and Nāsūt.5; Maẓhar; Maẓlūm; al-Munāfiḳūn.2; Naḳd al-Mīt̲h̲āḳ; Rad̲j̲ʿa; al-Sābiḳūn; Safīr.1; al-Ṣāmit
        and → SHIITES.DOCTRINES AND INSTITUTIONS
theologians
    in early Islam   D̲j̲ahm b. Ṣafwān; al-Ḥasan al-Baṣrī; [in Suppl.] al-Aṣamm; al-Ḥasan b. Muḥammad b. al-Ḥanafiyya; Ibn Kullāb
    Ashʿarī   al-Āmidī; al-As̲h̲ʿarī, Abu ʾl-Ḥasan; al-Bag̲h̲dādī; al-Bāḳillānī; al-Bayhaḳī; al-D̲j̲uwaynī; al-Faḍālī; Fak̲h̲r al-Dīn al-Rāzī; al-G̲h̲azālī, Abū Ḥāmid; Ibn Fūrak; al-Īd̲j̲ī; al-Isfarāyīnī; al-Kiyā al-Harrāsī; al-Ḳus̲h̲ayrī
        see also Allāh.ii; 'Ilm al-Kalām.II.C; Imāma; Īmān; [in Suppl.] Ḥāl
    Ḥanbalī   'Abd al-Ḳādir al-D̲j̲īlānī; Aḥmad b. Ḥanbal; al-Anṣārī al-Harawī; al-Barbahārī; Ibn 'Abd al-Wahhāb; Ibn 'Aḳīl; Ibn Baṭṭa al-ʿUkbarī; Ibn al-D̲j̲awzī; Ibn Ḳayyim al-D̲j̲awziyya; Ibn Ḳudāma al-Maḳdisī; Ibn Taymiyya; al-K̲h̲allāl
        see also Īmān; *and* → LAW
    Māturīdī   'Abd al-Ḥayy; Bis̲h̲r b. G̲h̲iyāt̲h̲; al-Māturīdī
        see also Allāh.ii; 'Ilm al-Kalām.II.D; Imāma; Īmān
    Muʿtazilī   'Abbād b. Sulaymān; 'Abd al-D̲j̲abbār b. Aḥmad; Abu ʾl-Hud̲h̲ayl

al-ʿAllāf; Aḥmad b. Abī Duʾād; Aḥmad b. Ḥābiṭ; ʿAmr b. ʿUbayd; al-Balkhī; Bishr b. al-Muʿtamir; Djaʿfar b. Ḥarb; Djaʿfar b. Mubashshir; Djāḥiẓ; al-Djubbāʾī; Hishām b. ʿAmr al-Fuwaṭī; Ibn al-Ikhshīd; Ibn Khallād; al-Iskāfī; al-Khayyāṭ; Muʿammar b. ʿAbbād; al-Murdār; al-Nāshiʾ al-Akbar; al-Naẓẓām; [in Suppl.] Abū ʿAbd Allāh al-Baṣrī; Abu ʾl-Ḥusayn al-Baṣrī; Abū Rashīd al-Nīsābūrī; Ḍirār b. ʿAmr; al-Ḥākim al-Djushamī; Ibn Mattawayh

see also Ahl al-Naẓar; Allāh.ii; Ḥafṣ al-Fard; Ibn Abi ʾl-Ḥadīd; Ibn al-Rāwandī; ʿIlm al-Kalām.II.B; Imāma; Khalḳ.V; Lawn; Luṭf; al-Maʾmūn; al-Manzila bayn al-Manzilatayn; [in Suppl.] al-Aṣamm; Ḥāl

Shiite → SHIITES

Wahhābī Ibn ʿAbd al-Wahhāb; Ibn Ghannām

Indo-Muslim ʿAbd al-ʿAzīz al-Dihlawī; ʿAbd al-Ḳādir Dihlawī; Ashraf ʿAlī; Baḥr al-ʿUlūm; al-Dihlawī, Shāh Walī Allāh; al-ʿImrānī; ʿIwaḍ Wadjīh; [in Suppl.] ʿAbd Allāh Sulṭānpūrī; Farangī Maḥall

see also Hind.v.b; al-Maʿbarī; Mappila

Jewish Ibn Maymūn; Saʿadyā Ben Yōsēf

19th and 20th centuries Muḥammad ʿAbduh; Muḥammad Abū Zayd

TIME Abad; Dahr; Ḳidam

see also Ibn al-Sāʿātī

calendars Djalālī; Hidjra; Nasīʾ; [in Suppl.] Ilāhī Era

see also Nawrūz; Rabīʿ b. Zayd

day and night ʿAṣr; ʿAtama; Layl and Nahār

days of the week Djumʿa; Sabt

months

see also al-Ḳamar

Islamic al-Muḥarram; Rabīʿ; Radjab; Ramaḍān; Ṣafar

Syrian Nīsān

Turkish Odjaḳ

timekeeping Anwāʾ; al-Ḳamar; Mīḳāt; Mizwala; Sāʿa.1

see also Asṭurlāb; Ayyām al-ʿAdjūz; Hilāl.i; Rubʿ

TOGO Kabou; Kubafolo

TRANSPORT **Naḳl**

and → ANIMALS.CAMELS *and* EQUINES; HOSTELRY; NAVIGATION

caravans Azalay; **Kārwān**; Maḥmal; [in Suppl.] Djammāl

see also Anadolu.iii.5; Darb al-Arbaʿīn; Khān

mountain passes Bāb al-Lān; Bībān; Dār-i Āhanīn; Deve Boynu; Khaybar

see also Chitral

postal service **Barīd**; Fuyūdj; Ḥamām; Posta; Raḳḳāṣ

see also Anadolu.iii.5
stamps **Posta**
railways Ḥidjāz Railway
see also Anadolu.iii.5; al-Ḳāhira (442a); Khurramshahr
wheeled vehicles ʿAdjala; Araba

TRAVEL **Riḥla**; Safar
and → LITERATURE.TRAVEL-LITERATURE
supplies Mifrash
and → NOMADISM

TREASURY **Bayt al-Māl**; Khazīne; Makhzān
and → ADMINISTRATION.FINANCIAL

TREATIES Baḳṭ; Küčük Ḳaynardja; Mandates; Mondros; **Muʿāhada**
see also Dār al-ʿAhd; Ḥilf al-Fuḍūl; Mīthāḳ-i Millī
tributes Baḳṭ; Parias
and → TAXATION

TRIBES ʿĀʾila; ʿAshīra; Ḥayy; **Ḳabīla**
see also ʿAṣabiyya; Ḥilf; Khaṭīb; [in Suppl.] Bisāṭ.iii; *and* → NOMADISM
Afghanistan and India Abdālī; Afrīdī; Bhaṭṭi; Čahar Aymaḳ; Dāwūdpōtrās; Djāṭ; Durrānī; Gakkhaŕ; Gandāpur; Ghalzay; Güdjar; Khaṭak; Khokars; Lambadis; Mahsūd; Mēʾō; Mohmand; Mullagorī; [in Suppl.] Gurčānī
see also Afghān.i; Afghānistān.ii
Africa ʿAbābda; ʿĀmir; Antemuru; Bedja; Beleyn; Bishārīn; Danḳalī; Djaʿaliyyūn; Kunta; Makua; Māryā; Mazrūʿī
see also Diglal; Fulbe; al-Manāṣir; Mande
Arabian peninsula
ancient ʿAbd al-Ḳays; al-Abnāʾ.I; ʿĀd; ʿAkk; ʿĀmila; ʿĀmir b. Ṣaʿṣaʿa; al-Aws; Azd; Badjīla; Bāhila; Bakr b. Wāʾil; Ḍabba; Djadhīma b. ʿĀmir; Djurhum; Fazāra; Ghanī b. Aʿṣur; Ghassān; Ghaṭafān; Ghifār; Hamdān; Ḥanīfa b. Ludjaym; Ḥanẓala b. Mālik; Ḥārith b. Kaʿb; Hawāzin; Hilāl; ʿIdjl; Iram; Iyād; Kalb b. Wabara; al-Ḳayn; Khafādja; Khathʿam; al-Khazradj; Kilāb b. Rabīʿa; Kināna; Kinda; Khuzāʿa; Ḳuraysh; Ḳushayr; Laʿaḳat al-Dam; Lakhm; Liḥyān.2; Maʿadd; Maʿāfir; Māzin; Muḥārib; Murād; Murra; Naḍīr; Nawfal; Riyām; Saʿd b. Bakr; Saʿd b. Zayd Manāt al-Fizr; Salīḥ; Salūl
see also Asad (Banū); Ḥabash (Aḥābīsh); al-Ḥidjāz; Makhzūm; Mustaʿriba; Mutaʿarriba; Nizār b. Maʿadd; Numayr; Rabīʿa (and Muḍar); [in Suppl.] Aʿyāṣ
present-day ʿAbdalī; ʿAḳrabī; ʿAwāmir; ʿAwāzim; Banyar; al-Baṭāḥira;

Buḳūm; al-Dawāsir; al-Dhīʾāb; Djaʿda (ʿĀmir); al-Djanaba; al-Durūʿ; Ghāmid; Hādjir; Ḥakam b. Saʿd; Hamdān; al-Ḥarāsīs; Ḥarb; Ḥāshid wa-Bakīl; Ḥassān, Bā; Ḥawshabī; Hinā; al-Ḥubūs; Hudhayl; Ḥudjriyya; Hutaym; al-Ḥuwayṭāt; al-ʿIfār; Ḳaḥṭān; Khālid; (Banū) Kharūṣ; Khawlān; Ḳudāʿa; Madhḥidj; Mahra; al-Manāṣir; Mazrūʿī; Murra; Muṭayr; Muzayna; Nabhān; Ruwala

see also (Djazīrat) al-ʿArab.vi; Badw; al-Ḥidjāz

Central Asia and Mongolia Čāwdors; Dūghlāt; Emreli; Gagauz; Göklän; Ḳarluḳ; Ḳungrāt; Mangît; Mongols; Özbeg; Pečenegs; Salur

see also Ghuzz; Īlāt; Ḳāyî; Khaladj

Egypt and North Africa ʿAbābda; Ahaggar; al-Butr; Djazūla; Dukkāla; Ifoghas; Khulṭ; Kūmiya; al-Maʿḳil; Mandīl; Riyāḥ

see also Khumayr; *and* → BERBERS

Fertile Crescent

ancient Asad; Bahrāʾ; Djarrāḥids; Djudhām; Muhannā; al-Muntafiḳ.1

present-day ʿAnaza; Asad (Banū); Bādjalān; Bilbās; Ḍafīr; Djāf; Djubūr; Dulaym; Hamawand; al-Ḥuwayṭāt; Kurds.iv.A; Lām; al-Manāṣir; al-Muntafiḳ.2; Ṣakhr

see also al-Baṭīḥa

Iran Bāzūkiyyūn; Bilbās; Djāf; Eymir.2 and 3; (Banū) Kaʿb; Ḳarā Gözlū; Kurds.iv.A; Lak; Lām

see also Daylam; Dulafids; Fīrūzānids; Göklän; Īlāt

Turkey Afshār; Bayat; Bayîndîr; Begdili; Čepni; Döger; Eymir.1; Ḳādjār; Ḳāyî; [in Suppl.] Čawdor

TUNISIA Baladiyya.3; Djāmiʿa; Djamʿiyya.iv; Djarīda.i.B; Dustūr.i; Ḥizb.i; Ḥukūma.iv; Istiḳlāl; al-Khaldūniyya; Maʿārif.2.A; Madjlis.4.A.xix; Salafiyya.1(a); [in Suppl.] Demography.IV

see also Fallāḳ; Ḥimāya.ii; Khalīfa b. ʿAskar; Ṣafar; [in Suppl.] al-Ḥaddād, al-Ṭāhir; Inzāl; *and* → BERBERS; DYNASTIES.SPAIN AND NORTH AFRICA

historians of Ibn Abī Dīnār; Ibn Abi ʾl-Ḍiyāf; Ibn ʿIdhārī; [in Suppl.] ʿAbd al-Wahhāb

see also Ibn al-Raḳīḳ; *and* → DYNASTIES.SPAIN AND NORTH AFRICA

institutions

educational al-Ṣādiḳiyya; [in Suppl.] Institut des hautes études de Tunis

see also [in Suppl.] ʿAbd al-Wahhāb

musical al-Rashīdiyya

press al-Rāʾid al-Tūnusī

language ʿArabiyya.A.iii.3

literature Malḥūn; *and* → LITERATURE

Ottoman period (1574-1881) Aḥmad Bey; al-Ḥusayn (b. ʿAlī); Ḥusaynids; Khayr al-Dīn Pasha; Muḥammad Bayram al-Khāmis; Muḥammad Bey;

Muḥammad al-Ṣādiḳ Bey; Muṣṭafā Khaznadār; [in Suppl.] Ibn Ghidhāhum
pre-Ottoman period ʿAbd al-Raḥmān al-Fihrī; Aghlabids; Ḥafṣids; Ḥassān b. al-Nuʿmān al-Ghassānī; (Banū) Khurāsān
and → Berbers; Dynasties.spain and north africa
toponyms
ancient al-ʿAbbāsiyya; Ḥaydarān; Ḳalʿat Banī Ḥammād; Manzil Bashshū; Raḳḳāda; Ṣabra (al-Manṣūriyya)
present-day
districts Djarīd
islands Djarba; Ḳarḳana
regions Djazīrat Sharīk; Ḳasṭīliya.2; Nafzāwa; Sāḥil.1
towns Bādja; Banzart; Ḥalḳ al-Wādī; Ḳābis; al-Kāf; Ḳafsa; Ḳallala; al-Ḳayrawān; al-Mahdiyya; Monastir; Nafṭa; Safāḳus

Turkey Anadolu; Armīniya; Istanbul; Ḳarā Deniz
see also Libās.iv; *and* → Ottoman Empire
architecture → Architecture.regions
dynasties → Dynasties.anatolia and the turks; Ottoman Empire
language → Languages.turkic
literature → Literature
modern period (1920-) Baladiyya.1; Demokrat Parti; Djāmiʿa; Djarīda.iii; Djümhūriyyet Khalḳ Fîrḳasî; Dustūr.ii; Ḥizb.ii; Ishtirākiyya; Khalḳevi; Köy Enstitüleri; Kurds.iii.C; Madjlis.4.A.ii; Mīthāḳ-i Millī; [in Suppl.] Demography.III
see also Djamʿiyya.ii; Iskandarūn; Iṣlāḥ.iii; Ittiḥād we Teraḳḳī Djemʿiyyeti; Karakol Djemʿīyyetī; Ḳawmiyya.iv; Kemāl; Kirkūk; Maʿārif.1.i; Māliyye; Nurculuk; *and* → Literature
religious leaders Nursī
statesmen/women Atatürk; Çakmak; Ḥusayn Djāhid; Ileri, Djelāl Nūrī; Kāẓîm Karabekir; Khālide Edīb; Köprülü (Mehmed Fuad); Meḥmed ʿĀkif; Menderes; Okyar; Orbay, Ḥüseyin Raʾūf; [in Suppl.] Adîvar; Aghaoghlu; Atay; Esendal
see also Čerkes Edhem; Gökalp, Ziya; Hîsar; *and* → Turkey.ottoman period.young turks
mysticism → Mysticism.mystics; Sainthood
Ottoman period (1342-1924) Ḥizb.ii; Istanbul; Ittiḥād-i Muḥammedī Djemʿiyyeti; Ittiḥād we Teraḳḳī Djemʿiyyeti; Maʿārif.1.i; Madjlis.4.A.i; Madjlis al-Shūrā; Maṭbakh.2; **ʿOthmānli**
see also Aywaz.1; Derebey; Djamʿiyya.ii; Khalīfa.i.E; [in Suppl.] Demography.II; Djalālī; *and* → Ottoman Empire
Young Turks Djawīd; Djemāl Pasha; Enwer Pasha; (Tunalî) Ḥilmī; Isḥāḳ Sükutī; Kemāl, Meḥmed Nāmîḳ; Mīzāndjî Meḥmed Murād; Niyāzī Bey;

Ṣabāḥ al-Dīn

see also Djamʿiyya; Djewdet; Dustūr.ii; Fāḍil Pasha; Ḥukūma.i; Ḥurriyya.ii; Ittiḥād we Teraḳḳī Djemʿiyyeti

physical geography

mountains Aghrî Dagh; Ala Dagh; Aladja Dagh; Beshparmaḳ; Bingöl Dagh; Deve Boynu; Elma Daghî; Erdjiyas Daghî; Gāwur Daghlarî

waters Boghaz-iči; Čanaḳ-ḳalʿe Boghazî; Čoruh.I; Djayḥān; Gediz Čayî; Göksu; Ḳîzîl-irmāḳ; Lamas-ṣū; Marmara Deñizi; Menderes; al-Rass; Sakarya

population [in Suppl.] Demography.II

see also Muhādjir.2

pre-Ottoman period Mengüček

see also Kitābāt.7; *and* → DYNASTIES.ANATOLIA AND THE TURKS; TURKEY. TOPONYMS

toponyms

ancient ʿAmmūriya; Ānī; Arzan; ʿAyn Zarba; Baghrās; Bālis; Beshike; Būḳa; al-Djazīra; Dulūk; Dunaysir; Ḥarrān; Lādhiḳ.1

see also Diyār Bakr

present-day

islands Bozdja-ada; Imroz

provinces Aghrî; Čoruh; Diyar Bakr; Hakkārī; Ičil; Kars; Ḳasṭamūnī; Khanzīt; Ḳodja Eli; Mūsh; Newshehir

regions al-ʿAmḳ; Cilicia; Dersim; Diyār Muḍar; Djānīk; Menteshe-eli

towns Ada Pāzārî; Adana; Adiyaman; Afyūn Ḳara Ḥiṣār; Aḳ Ḥiṣār.1 and 2; Aḳ Shehr; Akhlāṭ; Ala Shehir; Alanya; Altîntash; Amasya; Anadolu; Anamur; Anḳara; Anṭākiya; Antalya; ʿArabkīr; Ardahān; Artvin; Aya Solūk; Āyās; Aydîn; ʿAynṭāb; Aywalîk; Babaeski; Bālā; Bālā Ḥiṣār; Balāṭ; Bālikesrı; Bālṭa Līmānī; Bandirma; Bāyazīd; Bāybūrd; Baylān; Bergama; Besni; Beyshehir; Bidlīs; Bīgha; Biledjik; Bingöl; Bīredjik; Birge; Bodrum; Bolu; Bolwadin; Bozanti; Burdur; Bursa; Čankîrî; Čatāldja; Česhme; Čölemerik; Čorlu; Čorum; Deñizli; Diwrīgī; Diyār Bakr; Edirne; Edremit; Eğin; Eğridir; Elbistan; Elmalî; Enos; Ereğli; Ergani; Ermenak; Erzindjan; Erzurum; Eskishehir; Gebze; Gelibolu; Gemlik; Giresun; Göksun; Gördes; Gümüsh-khāne; al-Hārūniyya; Ḥiṣn Kayfā; Iskandarūn; Isparta; Istanbul; Iznīḳ; Ḳarā Ḥiṣār; Ḳaradja Ḥiṣār; Kars; Ḳasṭamūnī; Ḳayṣariyya; Kemākh; Killiz; Ḳîrḳ Kilise; Kirmāstī; Ḳîrshehir; Ḳoč Ḥiṣār; Konya; Köprü Ḥiṣārî; Ḳoylu Ḥiṣār; Ḳōzān; Ḳūla; Kutāhiya; Lādhiḳ.2 and 3; Lāranda; Lüleburgaz; Maghnisa; Malaṭya; Malāzgird.1; Malkara; Maʿmūrat al-ʿAzīz; Marʿash; Mārdīn; al-Maṣṣīṣa; Mayyāfāriḳīn; Menemen; Mersin; Merzifūn; Mīlās; Mudanya; Mughla; Mūsh; Naṣībīn; Newshehir; Nīgde; Nīksār; Nizīb;

Orāmār; ʿOthmānd̲jik̊; Payās; Rize; al-Ruhā; Ṣaband̲ja; Ṣāmsūn; [in Suppl.] G̲h̲alaṭa
see also Fener; Ḳarasi̊.2; (al-)Ḳusṭanṭīniyya

U

UMAYYADS → CALIPHATE; DYNASTIES.SPAIN AND NORTH AFRICA

UNITED ARAB EMIRATES al-Ḳawāsim; Mad̲jlis.4.A.xii; Maḥkama.4.ix; [in Suppl.] **al-Imārāt al-ʿArabiyya al-Muttaḥida**
population Mazrūʿī
and → TRIBES.ARABIAN PENINSULA
toponyms Abū Ẓabī; al-D̲jiwāʾ; Dubayy; al-Fud̲jayra; Raʾs al-K̲h̲ayma; [in Suppl.] ʿAd̲jmān
see also (D̲jazīrat) al-ʿArab; al-K̲h̲aṭṭ

(former) USSR → CAUCASUS; CENTRAL ASIA.FORMER SOVIET UNION; COMMUNISM; EUROPE.EASTERN EUROPE; SIBERIA

V

VIRTUES Ḍayf; Futuwwa; Ḥasab wa-Nasab; Ḥilm; ʿIrḍ; Karāma; Murūʾa; Ṣabr
vices Buk̲h̲l

W

WEIGHTS AND MEASUREMENTS Ag̲h̲ač; Arpa; D̲h̲irāʿ; Dirham.1; Farsak̲h̲; Ḥabba; Iṣbaʿ; Istār; **Makāyil**; Marḥala; Miḳyās; **Misāḥa**; al-Mīzān; Ṣāʿ; [in Suppl.] Gaz
see also al-Ḳarasṭūn

WINE **K̲h̲amr**; Sāḳī
see also Karm
bacchic poetry **K̲h̲amriyya**
Arabic Abū Nuwās; Abū Miḥd̲jan; Abu ʾl-S̲h̲īṣ; ʿAdī b. Zayd; Ḥārit̲h̲a b. Badr al-G̲h̲udānī; (al-)Ḥusayn b. al-Ḍaḥḥāk; Ibn al-ʿAfīf al-Tilimsānī; Ibn Sayḥān
see also al-Babbag̲h̲āʾ; Ibn al-Fāriḍ; Ibn Harma; al-Nawād̲jī
Turkish Rewānī; Riyāḍī

boon companions Ibn Ḥamdūn; al-Ḳāshānī; Khālid b. Yazīd al-Kātib al-Tamīmī
see also Abu 'l-Shīṣ; ʿAlī b. al-Djahm

WOMEN ʿAbd; Ḥarīm; Ḥayḍ; Ḥidjāb.I; ʿIdda; Istibrāʾ; Khafḍ; **al-Marʾa**; Nikāḥ; [in Suppl.] Bighāʾ
see also ʿArūs Resmi; Bashmaḳlïḳ; Khayr; Khiḍr-ilyās; Lithām; *and* → CHILD; DIVORCE; MARRIAGE
and literature al-Marʾa.1
see also Ḳiṣṣa
Arabic authors al-Bāʿūni.6; Ḥafṣa bint al-Ḥādjdj; ʿInān; al-Khansāʾ; Laylā al-Akhyaliyya; Mayy Ziyāda; [in Suppl.] Faḍl al-Shāʿira
see also ʿAbbāsa; ʿĀtika; Khunātha; Ḳiṣṣa.2
Persian authors Ḳurrat al-ʿAyn; Mahsatī; Parwīn Iʿtiṣāmī
see also Gulbadan Bēgam; Makhfī
Turkish authors Fiṭnat; Khālide Edib; Laylā Khānïm (2x); Mihrī Khātūn
see also Ḳiṣṣa.3(b)
concubinage ʿAbd.3.f; Khaṣṣekī
emancipation Ḳāsim Amīn; Malak Ḥifnī Nāṣif; Saʿīd Abū Bakr; Salāma Mūsā; [in Suppl.] al-Ḥaddād, al-Ṭāhir
see also Ḥidjāb; Ileri, Djelāl Nūrī; al-Marʾa; [in Suppl.] Ashraf al-Dīn Gīlānī
influential women
Arabic ʿĀʾisha bint Ṭalḥa; Asmāʾ; Barīra; Būrān; Hind bint ʿUtba; al-Khayzurān bint ʿAṭāʾ al-Djurashiyya; Khunātha; [in Suppl.] Asmāʾ
see also al-Maʿāfirī; *and* → MUḤAMMAD, THE PROPHET.WIVES OF
Indo-Muslim Nūr Djahān; Samrū
Mongolian Baghdād Khātūn; Khān-zāda Bēgum
Ottoman ʿĀdila Khātūn; Khurrem; Kösem Wālide; Mihr-i Māh Sulṭān; Nīlūfer Khātūn; Nūr Bānū; Ṣafiyye Wālide Sulṭān
legendary women al-Basūs; Bilḳīs; Hind bint al-Khuss
see also Āsiya
musicians ʿAzza al-Maylaʾ; Djamīla; Ḥabāba; Rāʾiḳa; Sallāma al-Zarḳāʾ; [in Suppl.] Badhl al-Kubrā; al-Djarādatān[i]; Faḍl al-Shāʿira; Ḥabba Khātūn
see also ʿĀlima; Ḳayna
mystics ʿĀʾisha al-Mannūbiyya; Djahānārā Bēgam; Nafīsa; Rābiʿa al-ʿAdawiyya al-Ḳaysiyya

WRITING **Khaṭṭ**
see also Ibn Muḳla; Kitābāt; *and* → ART.CALLIGRAPHY; EPIGRAPHY
manuscripts and books Daftar; Ḥāshiya; **Kitāb**; Muḳābala.2; **Nuskha**; [in Suppl.] Abbreviations
see also Ḳaṭʿ; Maktaba
bookbinding Īlkhāns; Kitāb; Nuskha; ʿOthmānli.VII.c

materials Djild; Kāghad; Ḳalam; Khātam; Ḳirṭās; Midād; Papyrus; Raḳḳ; [in Suppl.] Dawāt
see also ʿAfṣ; Afsantīn; Diplomatic; Īlkhāns; Maʿdin.4

Y

YEMEN Djarīda.i.A; Dustūr.viii; Madjlis.4.A.xiv and xv; Maḥkama.4.viii
see also ʿAsīr; Ismāʿīliyya; Mahrī; Makramids; [in Suppl.] Abū Mismār
architecture → ARCHITECTURE.REGIONS
before Islam al-Abnāʾ.II; Abraha; Dhū Nuwās; (Djazīrat) al-ʿArab; Ḥabashat; Ḥaḍramawt; Ḳatabān; Ḳayl; Mārib; al-Mathāmina; Sabaʾ; [in Suppl.] Ḥaḍramawt
see also [in Suppl.] Bādhām
dynasties Hamdānids; Mahdids; Rasūlids
see also Rassids; *and* → DYNASTIES.ARABIAN PENINSULA
historians of al-Djanadī; al-Khazradjī; al-Mawzaʿī; al-Nahrawālī; al-Rāzī, Aḥmad b. ʿAbd Allāh
see also Ibn al-Mudjāwir
Ottoman period (1517-1635) Maḥmūd Pasha; al-Muṭahhar; Özdemir Pasha; Riḍwān Pasha
see also Baladiyya.2; Khādim Süleymān Pasha
physical geography
mountains Ḥaḍūr; Ḥarāz; Ḥiṣn al-Ghurāb
wadis Barhūt; al-Khārid; al-Saḥūl
population ʿAbdalī; ʿAḳrabī; Banyar; Hamdān; Ḥāshid wa-Bakīl; Ḥawshabī; Ḥudjriyya; Ḳaḥṭān; Khawlān; Madhḥidj; Mahra
and → TRIBES.ARABIAN PENINSULA
toponyms
ancient al-ʿĀra
see also Nadjrān
present-day
districts Abyan; ʿAlawī; ʿĀmiri; ʿAwdhalī; Dathīna; Faḍlī; Ḥarāz; Ḥarīb; al-Ḥayma; Ḥudjriyya
islands Ḳamarān; Mayyūn
regions ʿAwlaḳī; Ḥaḍramawt; Laḥdj; [in Suppl.] Ḥaḍramawt.ii
towns ʿAdan; ʿAthr; Bayt al-Faḳīh; Dhamār; Ghalāfiḳa; Ḥabbān; Hadjarayn; Ḥāmī; Ḥawra; al-Ḥawṭa; al-Ḥudayda; Ibb; ʿIrḳa; Ḳaʿṭaba; Kawkabān; Ḳishn; Laḥdj; al-Luḥayya; Mārib; al-Mukallā; al-Mukhā; Rayda; Ṣaʿda; al-Saḥūl; [in Suppl.] ʿĪnāt
see also (Djazīrat) al-ʿArab

(former) YUGOSLAVIA   Džabić; <u>Kh</u>osrew Beg; Muslimūn.1.B.6; Pomaks; Riḍwān Begović; [in Suppl.] Handžić

see also ʿÖmer Efendi

toponyms

    republics   Bosna; Ḳaradag̲h̲; Ḳoṣowa; Māḳadūnyā

       see also [in Suppl.] Dalmatia

    towns   Aḳ Ḥiṣār.3; Aladja Ḥiṣār; Banjaluka; Belgrade; Eszék; I<u>sh</u>tib; Ḳarlofča; Livno; Manāṣtīr; Mostar; Ni<u>sh</u>; O<u>kh</u>rī; Pasarofča; Pirlepe; Pri<u>sh</u>tina; Prizren; Rag̲h̲ūsa

Z

ZAIRE   Katanga; Kisangani

ZANZIBAR   Barg̲h̲a<u>sh</u>; Bū Saʿīd; Kizimkazi

ZOOLOGY   **Ḥayawān.7**

    and → ANIMALS

writers on   al-Damīrī; al-Marwazī, <u>Sh</u>araf al-Zamān

    see also al-Dj̲āḥiẓ

ZOROASTRIANS   Gabr; Iran.vi; **Madjūs**; Mōba<u>dh</u>

    see also Bihʾāfrīd b. Farwardīn; G̲h̲azal.ii; Gudj̲arāt.a; Pārsīs; Pūr-i Dāwūd

dynasties   Maṣmug̲h̲ān

gods   Bahrām

PRÉFACE À LA TROISIÈME ÉDITION

Cette édition de l'Index des Matières comprend une Liste d'Entrées additionnelle précédant l'index des matières proprement dit. La Liste des Entrées renvoie le lecteur aux articles particuliers de l'*Encyclopédie de l'Islam.* Le fait que les entrées figurent dans l'*Encyclopédie* sous un intitulé en arabe, persan ou turc, etc. plutôt qu'en français est susceptible de dérouter l'usager non familier de ces langues. Un index des matières faisant le même peut donc s'avérer moins utile qu'il ne le devrait.

Ainsi, bien qu'il existe dans l'*Encyclopédie* un article sur le calame, et que la référence à cet instrument soit disponible sous ÉCRITURE.FOURNITURES, un non-arabisant aura quelque peine à la découvrir sans consulter l'ensemble des références fournies à cet endroit. Pour simplifier cet état de choses, la Liste des Entrées renvoie le lecteur à l'article de l'*Encyclopédie* (dans le cas présent, pour 'calame', voir Ḳalam). Néanmoins, pour se faire une idée générale de ce que l'*Encyclopédie* propose sur un sujet plus développé, le lecteur peut encore consulter l'Index des Matières proprement dit. Le mode d'emploi de l'Index des Matières figure p. 155.

Comme précédemment, cette nouvelle édition de l'Index des Matières inclut les références jusqu'au dernier volume publié de l'*Encyclopédie* (vol. VIII), paru en octobre 1995.

Mai 1996 Peri Bearman

LISTE DES ENTRÉES

Les références concernent soit l'article de base de l'*Encyclopédie*, soit l'Index des Matières proprement dit, lequel rassemble tous les articles concernés par le sujet sous un seul intitulé. Une flèche renvoie le lecteur à l'entrée existant dans l'Index des Matières, qui suit la Liste des Entrées à la p. 155. Les noms de pays, de dynasties et de califats, figurant *in extenso* dans l'Index des Matières, ne sont pas donnés dans la liste qui suit.

A

Abatteur [au Suppl.] Djazzār
Abeille Naḥl
Ablution → ABLUTION
Abricot Mishmish
Abstinence Istibrā'
Académie Madjma' 'Ilmī
Accident 'Araḍ
Accouchement → ENFANT
Acquisition Kasb
Acrobate Djānbāz
Action 'Amal; Fi'l
Activisme → RÉFORME.POLITICO-RELIGIEUSE.MILITANTE
Addax Mahāt
Administration → ADMINISTRATION
Adoption → ADOPTION
Adultère → ADULTÈRE
Agriculture → AGRICULTURE
Agrumes Nārandj
Aiguière [au Suppl.] Ibrīḳ
Album Muraḳḳa'
Alchimie → ALCHIMIE
Alfa Ḥalfā'
Algèbre → MATHÉMATIQUES
Aliments → CUISINE
Allaitement → ENFANT
Aloès Ṣabr
Alphabet → ALPHABET
Ambre gris 'Anbar
Ambre jaune Kahrubā
Âme Nafs
Amende Djurm
Amérique → NOUVEAU MONDE
Ameublement → MOBILIER
Amiral Ḳapudan Pasha
Amour → AMOUR
Amusement → RÉCRÉATION
Analogie Ḳiyās
Anatomie → ANATOMIE
Anche (instrument à) Ghayṭa
Âne Ḥimār
Anecdote Nādira
Angélologie → ANGÉLOLOGIE
Animal → ANIMAUX
Anthropomorphisme → ANTHROPOMORPHISME
Antilope → ANIMAUX
Antinomianisme Ibāḥa.II
Apostasie → APOSTASIE
Appel Du'ā'; Isti'nāf
Appel à la prière Adhān
Aqueduc → ARCHITECTURE.MONUMENTS
Arabe → LANGUES.AFRO-ASIATIQUES; LINGUISTIQUE
Arachnides → ANIMAUX

Araignée ʿAnkabūt
Araire Miḥrāth
Arbitre Ḥakam
Arbres → FLORE
Arc Ḳaws
Arc-en-ciel Ḳaws Ḳuzaḥ
Archéologie → ARCHÉOLOGIE
Architecture → ARCHITECTURE
Archives → ADMINISTRATION
Argent Fiḍḍa; *et* → NUMISMATIQUE
Arithmétique → MATHÉMATIQUES
Armée → MILITAIRES
Armes → MILITAIRES
Armoise Afsantīn
Arsenal Dār al-Ṣināʿa
Art → ART
Article Maḳāla
Artisanat → ART
Artisans → PROFESSIONS
Artistes → PROFESSIONS
Ascensions al-Maṭāliʿ
Ascétisme → ASCÉTISME
Asphalte Mūmiyāʾ
Association Andjuman; Djamʿiyya
Astrolabe Asṭurlāb
Astrologie → ASTROLOGIE
Astronomie → ASTRONOMIE
Atomism Djuzʾ
l'Au-delà → ESCHATOLOGIE
Aumônes → AUMÔNES
Autruche Naʿām
Avant l'Islam → PÉRIODE PRÉISLAMIQUE
Avant-propos Muḳaddima
Avarice Bukhl

B

Bābisme → SECTES
Bachisme → VIN.POÉSIE BACHIQUE
Baguette ʿAṣā; Ḳaḍīb
Bahāʾīs → BAHĀʾĪS
Bain → ARCHITECTURE.MONUMENTS
Balance al-Mīzān
Balayeur Kannās
Banque → BANQUE
Barbier [au Suppl.] Ḥallāḳ
Barrage → ARCHITECTURE.MONUMENTS
Basques → BASQUES
Bateau Safīna
Beauté ʿIlm al-Djamāl
Bédouin → BÉDOUINS
Belette Ibn ʿIrs
Bélomancie Istiḳsām
Bénédiction Baraka
Benjoin, noisetier à Bān
Berbères → BERBÈRES
Bestiaux Baḳar
Beurre al-Samn
Bible → BIBLE
Bibliographie → BIBLIOGRAPHIE
Bibliothèque → EDUCATION
Bien-être Maṣlaḥa
Bijoux → BIJOUX
Biographie → LITTÉRATURE.BIOGRAPHIQUE
Bitume Mūmiyāʾ
Bivalve Ṣadaf
Blanchisseur [au Suppl.] Ghassāl
Blé Ḳamḥ
Bois Khashab
Boissons → CUISINE
Botanique → BOTANIQUE
Boucher [au Suppl.] Djazzār
Bouddhisme Budd
Bouquetin Ayyil
Boussole Maghnāṭīs.II

Brique Labin
Brosse à dents Miswāk
Buffle [au Suppl.] D̲j̲āmūs
Bure K̲h̲irḳa
Butin → MILITAIRES
Byzantins → BYZANTINS

C

Cadavre D̲j̲anāza
Cadeau → CADEAUX
Cadran Rubʿ
Cadran solaire Mizwala
Café Ḳahwa
Caille Salwā
Calame Ḳalam
Calendrier → TEMPS
Califat → CALIFAT
Calife K̲h̲alīfa
Calligraphie → ART
Calomnie Ḳad̲h̲f
Caméléon Ḥirbāʾ
Camomille [au Suppl.] Bābūnad̲j̲
Camphre Kāfūr
Canal Ḳanāt
Canne à sucre Ḳaṣab al-Sukkar
Cannelle [au Suppl.] Dār Ṣīnī
Capitulations Imtiyāzāt
Caprins [au Suppl.] G̲h̲anam
Caravane → TRANSPORT
Carte K̲h̲arīṭa
Cartographie → CARTOGRAPHIE
Cause ʿIlla
Cautionnement Kafāla
Cavalier Fāris
Céramique → ART.POTERIE
Cérémonies de la cour → CÉRÉMONIES DE LA COUR
Cession Ḥawāla
Chacal Ibn Āwā
Chaire Minbar
Chaise Kursī
Chalumeau Mizmār
Chambellan Ḥād̲j̲ib
Chameau → ANIMAUX
Chamelier [au Suppl.] D̲j̲ammal
Chamito-sémitique Ḥām
Chancellerie → DOCUMENTS
Chant → MUSIQUE
Chanteur → MUSIQUE
Chanvre Ḥas̲h̲īs̲h̲
Chapiteau ʿAmūd
Chariot ʿAd̲j̲ala; Araba
Charité → ALMS
Charmes → CHARMES
Charmeur de serpents Ḥāwī
Charrette ʿAd̲j̲ala; Araba
Charrue Miḥrāt̲h̲
Chasse → CHASSE
Châtiment → CHÂTIMENT (DIVIN); DROIT.DROIT PÉNAL
Chemins de fer → TRANSPORT
Chêne ʿAfṣ
Cheval Faras
Chevaux → ANIMAUX.ÉQUINES
Cheveux → ANATOMIE
Chien Kalb
Chiffre → NUMÉRO
Chiisme → CHIITES
Chirognomie al-Kaff
Chirurgien D̲j̲arrāḥ
Chrétiens → CHRISTIANISME
Christianisme → CHRISTIANISME
Ciel Samāʾ
Cimetière Maḳbara
Cinéma Cinématographe
Cinq K̲h̲amsa
Circoncision → CIRCONCISION
Circoncision des filles K̲h̲afḍ

Citadelle → ARCHITECTURE.MONUMENTS.FORTERESSES
Citerne Ḥawḍ
Citoyen Muwāṭin
Citron Nārandj
Civière Djanāza
Civilisation Medeniyyet
Clan Āl
Climat Iḳlīm
Clou de girofle Ḳaranful
Codes → CRYPTOGRAPHIE
Coeur Ḳalb
Coiffeur [au Suppl.] Ḥallāḳ
Coiffure → VÊTEMENTS
Coït Bāh
Coitus interruptus ʿAzl
Collyre Kuḥl
Colombe Ḥamām
Colonne ʿAmūd
Commensal Nadīm
Commentaire (coranique) → CORAN
Commerce → COMMERCE
Commissionnaire Dallāl
Communications → COMMUNICATIONS
Communisme → COMMUNISME
Compagnons (du Prophète) → MUḤAMMAD, LE PROPHÈTE
Comptabilité → COMPTABILITÉ
Concubinage → FEMMES
Conférence Muʾtamar
Confrérie → MYSTICISME
Congrès Muʾtamar
Conjonction Ḳirān
Connaissance ʿIlm; Maʿrifa
Constellation → ASTRONOMIE
Constitution Dustūr
Construction Bināʾ
Consul Consul
Conte Ḥikāya
Conteur Ḳāṣṣ; Maddāḥ
Contrainte [au Suppl.] Ikrāh
Contraires Aḍdād; Ḍidd
Contrat → DROIT.DROIT CONTRACTUEL
Coptes → CHRISTIANISME.CONFESSIONS
Coq Dīk
Cor Būḳ
Corail Mardjān
Coran → CORAN
Corbeau Ghurāb
Cornaline ʿAḳīḳ
Corporation → CORPORATIONS
Corps Djism
Corruption → PAIEMENTS
Cosmétique → COSMÉTIQUE
Cosmographie → COSMOGRAPHIE
Costume → VÊTEMENTS
Coton Ḳuṭn
Cotonnade (indienne) Ḳalamkārī
Coudée Dhirāʿ
Couleur → COULEUR
Cours d'eau → GÉOGRAPHIE.GÉOGRAPHIE PHYSIQUE.EAUX
Courtier Dallāl
Courtisan Nadīm
Couscous Kuskusū
Coutume → COUTUME
Couturier Khayyāṭ
Couvent → CHRISTIANISME
Couverture → ART.TAPISSERIE
Créancier Ghārim
Création → CRÉATION
Cristal Billawr
Critique, littéraire → LITTÉRATURE
Croisades → CROISADES
Croissant Hilāl
Croix al-Ṣalīb
Croyance ʿAḳīda
Crucifixion Ṣalb
Cryptographie → CRYPTOGRAPHIE
Cuir Djild
Cuisine → CUISINE

Cuivre Nuḥās; *et voir* Malachite
Culture (agriculture) → AGRICULTURE
Cumin Kammūn
Cure-dents Miswāk

D

Dactylonomie Ḥisāb al-ʿAḳd
Daim Ayyil
Danse Raḳṣ
Datte Nakhl
Débat → THÉOLOGIE
Débit d'eau → Architecture.monuments
Débiteur Ghārim
Déclinaison (grammaire) Iʿrāb
Déclinaison (astronomie) al-Mayl
Décoration → ARCHITECTURE; ART.DÉCORATIF; MILITAIRES
Décret divin al-Ḳaḍāʾ wa 'l-Ḳadar
Demeure Bayt; Dār
Démographie [au Suppl.] Démographie
Démon Djinn
Dents → MÉDECINE.DENTAIRE
Derviche → MYSTICISME
Désert → DÉSERTS
Dessin → ART
Destin → PRÉDESTINATION
Détroits → GÉOGRAPHIE.GÉOGRAPHIE PHYSIQUE.EAUX
Dette [au Suppl.] Dayn
Diable Iblīs
Dialecte → LANGUES.AFRO-ASIATIQUES.ARABE; LINGUISTIQUE.PHONÉTIQUE
Diamant Almās
Dictionnaire → DICTIONNAIRE
Dieu Allāh; Ilāh
Dieux préislamiques → PÉRIODE PRÉISLAMIQUE
Dîme → TAXATION
Diplomatie → DIPLOMATIE
Dissolution Faskh
Divination → DIVINATION
Divorce → DIVORCE
Documents → ADMINISTRATION; DOCUMENTS
Domaine Ḍayʿa
Dot → MARIAGE
Drame → LITTÉRATURE
Drapeau ʿAlam
Drogues → DROGUES
Droguiste al-ʿAṭṭār
Droit → DROIT
Droit coutumier → DROIT
Dromadaire → ANIMAUX.CHAMEAUX
Druzes → DRUZES
Duodécimains → CHIITES.BRANCHES
Dynastie → DYNASTIES

E

Eau Māʾ
Ebène Abanūs
Eclipse Kusūf
Ecliptique Minṭaḳat al-Burūdj
Ecole élémentaire Kuttāb
Economique → ECONOMIQUE
Ecriture → ECRITURE
Edit Farmān
Education → EDUCATION
Eglise Kanīsa

Elégie Marthiya
Eléphant Fīl
Elixir al-Iksīr
Eloge Madīḥ
Eloquence Balāgha; Bayān; Faṣāḥa
Emancipation → EMANCIPATION
Embaumement Ḥināṭa
Emigration → EMIGRATION
Empire byzantin → BYZANTINS
Empire ottoman → EMPIRE OTTOMAN
Encens Lubān
Encre Midād
Encrier [au Suppl.] Dawāt
Encyclopédie Mawsūʿa
Endive [au Suppl.] Hindibāʾ
Enfance → ENFANT
Enfant trouvé Laḳīṭ
Enfer → ENFER
Enigme Lughz
Enterrement Djanāza
Envoyé Rasūl
Epices → CUISINE
Epicier Baḳḳāl
Epigraphie → EPIGRAPHIE
Epique Ḥamāsa
Epistolographie → LITTÉRATURE. EPISTOLAIRE
Epithète → ONOMASTIQUE
Equateur Istiwāʾ
Equines → ANIMAUX
Equitation Furūsiyya
Erreur Khaṭaʾ
Escargot Ṣadaf
Eschatologie → ESCHATOLOGIE
Esclavage → ESCLAVAGE
Esclave ʿAbd
Espion Djāsūs
Espionnage *voir* Espion
Esthétique ʿIlm al-Djamāl
Etable Iṣṭabl
Eternité Abad; Ḳidam
Ethique → ETHIQUE
Ethnicité → ETHNICITÉ
Etiquette → ETIQUETTE
Etoile → ASTRONOMIE
Etymologie Ishtiḳāḳ
Eunuque → EUNUQUE
Evangile Indjīl
Eventail Mirwaḥa
Exorde Ibtidāʾ
Expédition → MILITAIRES
Expiation Kaffāra

F

Faculté Kulliyya
Faïence Kāshī
Famille ʿĀʾila
Fauconnerie → FAUCONNERIE
Faune → ANIMAUX
Félins → ANIMAUX
Femmes → FEMMES
Fennec Fanak
Fenouil [au Suppl.] Basbās
Fer Ḥadīd
Fête → FÊTE
Feu Nār
Feutre Lubūd
Fiançailles Khiṭba
Fief Iḳṭāʿ
Film Cinématographe
Fils Ibn
Finance → ADMINISTRATION
Fisc → TAXATION
Flamant-rose Nuḥām
Fleurs → FLORE
Flore → FLORE
Foi → FOI
Foie Kabid

Fondamentalisme → RÉFORME. POLITICO-RELIGIEUSE.MILITANTE
Forêt Ghāba
Forgeron Ḳayn
Formules → ISLAM
Forteresse → ARCHITECTURE.MONUMENTS
Fossé Khandaḳ
Fou Madjnūn
Fourmis Naml
Fourrure Farw
Fraction Kasr
Franc-maçonnerie [au Suppl.] Farāmūsh-khāna; Farmāsūniyya
Fruit *voir* Agrumes

G

Gage Rahn
Gain Kasb
Gangas Ḳaṭā
Garde (de l'enfant) Ḥaḍāna
Garde-robe → VÊTEMENTS
Gazelle Ghazāl
Gemmes → BIJOUX
Généalogie → GÉNÉALOGIE
Géographie → GÉOGRAPHIE
Géométrie → MATHÉMATIQUES
Geste Ishāra
Gitans → GITANS
Glose Hāshiya
Gomme-résine Ṣamgh
Goudron Ḳaṭrān
Gouvernement Ḥukūma
Grammaire → LINGUISTIQUE
Grenadier (fleur de) Djullanār
Grossesse → ENFANT
Guépard Fahd
Guerre Ḥarb
Gynécologie → ENFANT

H

Habillement → VÊTEMENTS
Hagiographie → HAGIOGRAPHIE
Hautbois Ghayṭa
Hémérologie Ikhtiyārāt
Henné Ḥinnā'
Héraldique → HÉRALDIQUE
Hérésie → HÉRÉSIE
Hérisson Ḳunfudh
Héritage → HÉRITAGE
Hippopotame [au Suppl.] Faras al-Mā'
Historiographie → LITTÉRATURE. HISTORIQUE
Homicide Ḳatl
Homme Insān
Homonyme Aḍdād
Homosexualité Liwāṭ
Honneur ʿIrḍ
Horloge Sāʿa
Horticulture → ARCHITECTURE. MONUMENTS.JARDINS DE PLAISANCE; FLORE
Hôtel (monnaies) Dār al-Ḍarb
Hôtellerie → HÔTELLERIE
Houris Ḥūr
Humoristes → HUMOUR
Humour → HUMOUR
Huppe Hudhud
Hydrologie → HYDROLOGIE
Hydromancie Istinzāl

Hyène [au Suppl.] Ḍabuʿ
Hymne Nas̲h̲īd
Hyperbole Mubālag̲h̲a
Hypocrisie Riyāʾ

I

Iconographie → ART
Idole → IDOLES
Impôt de capitation D̲j̲izya
Imprimerie Maṭbaʿa
Inclination → PRIÈRE
Incubation Istik̲h̲āra
Indépendance Istiḳlāl
Indigo Nīl
Industrie → INDUSTRIE
Infidèle Kāfir
Inflexion Imāla
Inimitabilité (du Ḳurʾān) Iʿd̲j̲āz
Innovation Bidʿa
Inscriptions → EPIGRAPHIE
Insectes → ANIMAUX
Insignes → MILITAIRES. DÉCORATIONS
Inspection (des troupes) Istiʿrāḍ
Instrument Āla
Instrument (de musique) → MUSIQUE
Insulte rimée Hid̲j̲āʾ
Intellect ʿAḳl
Interdiction Ḥad̲j̲r
Intérêt Ribā
Interrogation Istifhām
Introduction Ibtidāʾ; Muḳaddima
Inventions → INVENTIONS
Invocation Duʿāʾ
Ipséité Huwiyya
Irrigation → IRRIGATION
Islam → ISLAM
Ivoire ʿĀd̲j̲

J

Jardin → ARCHITECTURE. MONUMENTS.JARDINS DE PLAISANCE
Javelot D̲j̲erīd
Jeu → JEU
Jeûne → JEÛNE
Jeunes Turcs → TURQUIE.PÉRIODE OTTOMANE
Jeux → RÉCRÉATION
Jouets → RÉCRÉATION.JEUX
Jour → TEMPS
Journal D̲j̲arīda
Journalisme → PRESSE
Judaïsme → JUDAÏSME
Juge Ḳāḍī
Jurisconsulte → DROIT.JURISTE
Jurisprudence → DROIT
Juriste → DROIT
Jusquiame Band̲j̲
Justice ʿAdl

K

Kat Ḳāt
Kurdes → KURDES

L

Lacs → GÉOGRAPHIE.GÉOGRAPHIE PHYSIQUE.EAUX
Lamentation → LAMENTATION
Langue → LANGUES
Lavage → ABLUTION
Lavage (des morts) Ghusl
Laveur (des morts) [au Suppl.] Ghassāl
Lecture (Coranique) → CORAN
Légende → LÉGENDES
Lèpre [au Suppl.] Djudhām
Lettre(s) Ḥarf; Ḥurūf al-Hidjā᾽
Lévrier Salūḳī
Lexicographie → LEXICOGRAPHIE
Lézard Ḍabb
Liberté Ḥurriyya; [au Suppl.] Āzādī
Libre arbitre → PRÉDESTINATION
Lièvre [au Suppl.] Arnab
Lin Kattān
Linguistique → LINGUISTIQUE
Lion al-Asad
Literie Mafrūshāt; Mifrash
Lithographie → IMPRIMERIE
Littérature → LITTÉRATURE
Livre Kitāb
Logique → PHILOSOPHIE
Longévité Muʿammar
Louage Kirā᾽
Louage, contrat de → DROIT
Loup Dhi᾽b
Loup-garou Ḳuṭrub
Lumière Nūr
Lune Hilāl; al-Ḳamar
Lutte Pahlawān
Lyre Ḳithāra

M

Maçonnerie Binā᾽
Magie → MAGIE
Magnétite Maghnāṭīs.I
Maire Ra᾽īs
Maison *voir* Demeure; Thé, maison de
Malachite al-Dahnadj
Maladie → MALADIES
Malaria Malāryā
Mangouste Nims
Manuscrit Nuskha
Marchands → PROFESSIONS
Marée al-Madd wa-l-Djazr
Mariage → MARIAGE
Marine → MILITAIRES
Martyre → MARTYRE
Marxisme Mārk(i)siyya
Masse Dūrbāsh
Mathématiques → MATHÉMATIQUES
Matière Hayūlā
Mausolée → ARCHITECTURE.MONUMENTS.TOMBEAUX
Mécanique → MÉCANIQUE
Médecin → MÉDECINE
Médecine → MÉDECINE
Médecine dentaire → MÉDECINE
Melilot [au Suppl.] Iklīl al-Malik
Menstrues Ḥayḍ
Menthe [au Suppl.] Fūdhandj
Mer → OCÉANS ET MERS
Messie al-Masīḥ
Mesures → POIDS ET MESURES
Métal → ART
Métallurgie → MÉTALLURGIE
Métamorphose → ANIMAUX.TRANSFORMATION EN
Métaphore Istiʿāra

Métaphysique → MÉTAPHYSIQUE
Météorologie → MÉTÉOROLOGIE
Métonymie Kināya
Métrique → MÉTRIQUE
Meurtre Ḳatl
Migration → EMIGRATION
Militaires → MILITAIRES
Millet [au Suppl.] Djāwars
Minaret Manāra
Minéralogie → MINÉRALOGIE
Miniatures → ART.PEINTURE
Miracle → MIRACLES
Miroir Mirʾāt
Mise à part Istithnāʾ
Mobilier → MOBILIER
Modernisme → RÉFORME
Modes musicaux Maḳām
Moine Rāhib
Mois → TEMPS
Mollusques → ANIMAUX
Monachisme Rahbāniyya
Monarchie → MONARCHIE
Monastère → CHRISTIANISME.COUVENTS
Monde ʿĀlam
Mongols → MONGOLIE
Monnaies → NUMISMATIQUE
Montagne → MONTAGNES
Mort → MORT
Mosaïque → ART
Mosquée → ARCHITECTURE.MONUMENTS
Mouche Dhubāb
Mouchoir Mandīl
Mouillage Mīnāʾ
Mulet Baghl
Municipalité Baladiyya
Musc Misk
Musique → MUSIQUE
Myrobolan [au Suppl.] Halīladj
Myrte [au Suppl.] Ās
Mysticisme → MYSTICISME
Mystique → MYSTICISME
Mythes → LÉGENDES

N

Nacre Ṣadaf
Narcisse Nardjis
Narcotiques → DROGUES
Nationalisme → NATIONALISME
Natron [au Suppl.] Bawraḳ
Navigation → NAVIGATION
Navire → NAVIGATION
Nilomètre Miḳyās
Noix [au Suppl.] Djawz
Nom Ism
Nomadisme → NOMADISME
Noria Nāʿūra
Nourriture → CUISINE
Nouveau Monde → NOUVEAU MONDE
Nuit Layl et Nahār
Nullité Fāsid wa-Bāṭil
Numéraux → NUMÉRO
Numismatique → NUMISMATIQUE

O

Obélisque → ARCHITECTURE.MONUMENTS
Observatoire → ASTRONOMIE
Obstétrique → MÉDECINE
Océan → OCÉANS ET MERS
Octogone Muthamman

Oeil → ANATOMIE; MAUVAIS OEIL
Oiseau → ANIMAUX
Ombre, théâtre d' Ḳaragöz; Khayāl al-Ẓill
Omoplatoscopie Katif
Oncle Khāl
Onirocritique → RÊVES
Onomastique → ONOMASTIQUE
Onomatomancie Ḥurūf, ʿIlm al-
Ophtalmologie → MÉDECINE
Opium Afyūn
Optique → OPTIQUE
Or Dhahab
Orange Nārandj
Orchestre Mehter
Orfèvre Ṣāʾigh
Organes (corps) → ANATOMIE
Orientalisme Mustashriḳūn
Ornithomancie ʿIyāfa
Oryx Lamṭ; Mahāt
Ostentation Riyāʾ
Ouvriers → PROFESSIONS
Ovins [au Suppl.] Ghanam

P

Paganisme → PÉRIODE PRÉISLAMIQUE
Paiement → PAIEMENTS
Pain Khubz
Palais → ARCHITECTURE. MONUMENTS
Palanquin Maḥmal
Paléographie → ECRITURE; EPIGRAPHIE
Palmier Nakhl
Palmomancie Ikhtilādj
Paludisme Malāryā
Panarabisme → PANARABISME
Panégyrique Madīḥ
Panislamisme → PANISLAMISME
Panthéisme → RELIGION
Panthère Namir
Panturquisme → PANTURQUISME
Papier Kāghad
Papyrologie → PAPYROLOGIE
Papyrus Papyrus
Paradis → PARADIS
Parasol Miẓalla
Parchemin Raḳḳ
Parenté Ḳarāba
Parfum → PARFUM
Parlement Madjlis
Paronomase Muzāwadja
Parti politique → POLITIQUE
Passé Māḍī
Patronyme Kunya
Pâturage Marʿā
Pauvre Faḳīr; Miskīn
Pavillon → ARCHITECTURE.MONUMENTS
Pêche Samak.3
Péché Khaṭīʾa
Pédiatrie → ENFANT
Peinture → ART
Pèlerinage → PÈLERINAGE
Pensée Fikr
Périodiques → PRESSE
Perle al-Durr; Luʾluʾ
Perroquet Babbaghāʾ
Perruche Babbaghāʾ
Persan → LANGUES.INDO-EUROPÉENNES.IRANIENNES; LINGUISTIQUE
Perse → IRAN
Peste → PESTE
Pétrole → PÉTROLE
Peuple Ḳawm
Phare → ARCHITECTURE.MONUMENTS

Pharmacologie → PHARMACOLOGIE
Philatélie → PHILATÉLIE
Philologie → LINGUISTIQUE
Philosophie → PHILOSOPHIE
Phlébotomiste [au Suppl.] Faṣṣād
Phonétique → LINGUISTIQUE
Physiognomancie Ḳiyāfa
Physionomie → PHYSIONOMIE
Pierre Ḥadjar
Pierres précieuses → BIJOUX
Pigeon Ḥamām
Pilier Rukn
Pirate → PIRATERIE
Piraterie → PIRATERIE
Plan Kharīṭa
Planche Lawḥ
Planète → ASTRONOMIE
Plantes → FLORE
Plaques → ART
Plâtre Djiṣṣ
Pluie (prière de la) Istisḳāʾ
Pluriel Djamʿ
Poème → LITTÉRATURE.GENRES.POÉSIE
Poésie → LITTÉRATURE
Poids → POIDS ET MESURES
Poisson → ANIMAUX
Poitrine → ANATOMIE
Pôle Ḳuṭb
Police → MILITAIRES
Politique → POLITIQUE
Pont → ARCHITECTURE.MONUMENTS
Porc Khinzīr
Porc-épic Ḳunfudh
Port Mīnāʾ
Porte → ARCHITECTURE.MONUMENTS
Portefaix Ḥammāl
Porteur Ḥammāl
Porteur d'eau Saḳḳāʾ
Possession Milk
Poste (histoire de la) → PHILATÉLIE
Poste (services postaux) → TRANSPORT
Potasse Ḳily
Poterie → ART
Pou *voir* Poux
Poudre Bārūd
Poule Dadjādja
Poule sultane [au Suppl.] Abū Barāḳish.II
Poux Ḳaml
Pré-Islam → PÉRIODE PRÉISLAMIQUE
Prédestination → PRÉDESTINATION
Préface Muḳaddima
Présage Faʾl
Presse → PRESSE
Preuve Bayyina
Prière → PRIÈRE
Prière (direction de la) Ḳibla
Prière (niche) Miḥrāb
Prisonnier → MILITAIRES
Procédure légale → DROIT.DROIT DE LA PROCÉDURE
Processions Mawākib
Professions → PROFESSIONS
Profit Kasb
Prophétat → PROPHÉTAT
Prophète → MUḤAMMAD, LE PROPHÈTE; PROPHÉTAT
Prophétie → PROPHÉTAT
Propriété → PROPRIÉTÉ
Prose → LITTÉRATURE
Prosodie → LITTÉRATURE.POÉSIE; METRIQUE; RIME
Prostitution [au Suppl.] Bighāʾ
Protection Ḥimāya; Idjāra
Proverbe → LITTÉRATURE; PROVERBES
Puit → ARCHITECTURE.MONUMENTS
Pyramide Haram

Q

Qarmates → CHIITES.BRANCHES
Quiddité Māhiyya

R

Radiodiffusion I<u>dh</u>āʿa
Rage *voir* Chien
Raid → RAIDS
Rançon [au Suppl.] Fidāʾ
Rapports, sexuels Bāh
Récitation → CORAN.LECTURE
Récréation → RÉCRÉATION
Réflexion Fikr
Réforme → RÉFORME
Registre → ADMINISTRATION.DOCUMENTS
Religion → RELIGION
Reliure → ECRITURE
Renard Fanak
Reptiles → ANIMAUX
République <u>D</u>jumhūriyya
Résurrection Ḳiyāma
Retraite <u>Kh</u>alwa
Rêve → RÊVES
Révélation Ilhām
Rhapsodomancie Ḳurʿa
Rhétorique → RHÉTORIQUE
Rhinocéros Karkaddan
Rime → RIME
Rituel → RITUELS
Rivière → RIVIÈRES
Riz al-Ruzz
Robe d'honneur <u>Kh</u>ilʿa
Roi Malik
Roman Ḳiṣṣa
Ronde de nuit ʿAsas
Rongeurs → ANIMAUX
Rose Gul
Roseau Ḳaṣab
Rossignol Bulbul
Royaume Mamlaka

S

Sable Raml
Sagesse Ḥikma
Saignée [au Suppl.] Faṣṣād
Saint → SAINT
Sainteté Ḳadāsa
Salamandre Samandal
Sang [au Suppl.] Dam
Sang, vengeance du Ḳiṣāṣ
Sanglier <u>Kh</u>inzīr
Santé → MÉDECINE
Sappan, bois de Baḳḳam
Satire Hi<u>dj</u>āʾ
Sauterelle <u>D</u>jarād
Savon Ṣābūn
Scapulomancie Katif
Sceau <u>Kh</u>ātam; Muhr
Science → SCIENCES; SCIENCES NATURELLES
Scorpion ʿAḳrab
Scribe Kātib; [au Suppl.] Dabīr
Secrétaire Kātib; [au Suppl.] Dabīr
Sel Milḥ
Semaine → TEMPS
Sémitique (langues) Sām.2
Sens Ḥiss; Maḥsūsāt
Sept Sabʿ

Septimains → CHIITES.BRANCHES
Serment Ḳasam
Sermon Khuṭba
Sermonnaire Ḳāṣṣ
Serpent Ḥayya
Serviteur Khādim
Sexe Djins
Sexualité → SEXUALITÉ
Siège, guerre de Ḥiṣār
Siège, machinerie de Ḥiṣār; Mandjanīḳ
Singe Ḳird
Socialisme Ishtirākiyya
Société Djamʿiyya
Sodium Naṭrūn; *et voir* Natron
Sodomie Liwāṭ
Soie Ḥarīr
Sorcellerie → MAGIE
Soude Ḳily; *et voir* Natron
Soufisme → MYSTICISME
Soufre Kibrīt
Sources → GÉOGRAPHIE.GÉOGRAPHIE PHYSIQUE
Sphère Falak; Kura
Sport → ANIMAUX.SPORT; RÉCRÉATION
Substance Djawhar
Succession → HÉRITAGE
Suicide Intiḥār
Superstition → SUPERSTITION
Surnom Laḳab
Swahili → KENYA
Symbolisme Ramz.3
Syndicat Niḳāba

T

Tablette Lawḥ
Tabouret Kursī
Tailleur Khayyāṭ
Talion Ḳiṣāṣ
Talisman → CHARMES
Tambour Darabukka
Tambourin Duff
Tanneur [au Suppl.] Dabbāgh
Tapis → ART.TAPISSERIE
Tapisserie → ART
Taxation → TAXATION
Teck Sādj
Teinture → TEINTURE
Teinturier → TEINTURE
Temps → MÉTÉOROLOGIE; TEMPS
Tente Khayma
Terre → TERRE
Textiles → ART; VÊTEMENTS. MATÉRIAUX
Thé Čay
Thé, maison de [au Suppl.] Čāy-khāna
Théâtre → LITTÉRATURE.DRAME
Théâtre d'ombre Ḳaragöz; Khayāl al-Ẓill
Théologie → THÉOLOGIE
Théophanie Maẓhar
Thrène Marthiya
Tissage → ART.TEXTILES
Tisserand al-Nassādj; [au Suppl.] Ḥāʾik
Tisserin [au Suppl.] Abū Barāḳish.1
Titres → ONOMASTIQUE
Toile Kattān; Khaysh
Tombeau → ARCHITECTURE. MONUMENTS
Tour Burdj
Tradition → LITTÉRATURE.TRADITION
Traduction → LITTÉRATURE. TRADUCTIONS
Traité → TRAITÉS
Transfert Ḥawāla
Transport → TRANSPORT

Travail *voir* Syndicat
Tremblements de terre → TREMBLEMENTS DE TERRE
Trésor → TRÉSOR
Triangle Muthallath
Tribu → TRIBUS
Tribunal Maḥkama
Tribut → TRAITÉS
Trictrac, jeu de Nard
Troc Muʿāwaḍa
Trompette Būḳ
Trope Madjāz
Turquoise Fīrūzadj
Tziganes → GITANS

U

Université Djāmiʿa
Urbanisation → ARCHITECTURE; GÉOGRAPHIE
Usure Ribā
Usurpation Ghaṣb

V

Vautour Humā; Nasr
Véhicule → TRANSPORT
Vengeance (du sang) Ḳiṣāṣ
Vent → MÉTÉOROLOGIE
Vente, contrat de → DROIT
Ventilation → ARCHITECTURE. URBAINE
Ventouseur [au Suppl.] Faṣṣād
Verbe Fiʿl
Verre → Art
Verset Āya
Vêtements → VÊTEMENTS
Vétérinaire → MÉDECINE
Vices → VERTUS
Vie Ḥayāt
Vigne Karm
Vikings al-Madjūs
Village Ḳarya
Ville Ḳarya; Ḳaṣaba
Vin → VIN
Viol Rabāb
Vipère Afʿā
Voeu Nadhr
Voie Lactée al-Madjarra
Voile → VÊTEMENTS.COIFFURES
Volcans → GÉOGRAPHIE. GÉOGRAPHIE PHYSIQUE
Voleur Liṣṣ
Voyage → VOYAGE

W

Wagon *voir* Charrette

Z

Zaydites → CHIITES
Zodiaque Minṭaḳat al-Burūdj
Zoologie → ZOOLOGIE
Zoroastriens → ZOROASTRIENS

INDEX DES MATIÈRES

Le monde musulman dont il est question dans l'Index des Matières est le monde actuel. Ce qui jadis constituait le royaume de Perse est représenté ici par l'Asie centrale, le Caucase et l'Afghanistan, de même qu'une partie des territoires autrefois gouvernés par l'empire Ottoman englobe à présent des pays individuels de l'Europe de l'est et du Moyen-Orient. Des pays modernes, tels que la Jordanie et le Liban, ont la place qui leur revient. Pour les pays où l'islam est installé de longue date, on trouve une subdivision 'période moderne', tandis qu'on a réuni les articles de l'*Encyclopédie* qui traitent du 19ᵉ et du 20ᵉ siècles. Lorsqu'un poète est classé au '15ᵉ siècle', cette datation indique l'année de sa mort A.D.

Les références en caractères réguliers renvoient aux articles de l'*Encyclopédie*. Toutefois celles qui sont imprimées en caractères gras indiquent l'article principal. Les entrées en lettres capitales précédées d'une flèche renvoient à des rubriques dans l'Index des Matières. Ainsi dans le cas de

> BÉDOUINS **Badw**; Biʾr; Dawār; G͟hanīma; G͟hazw
> *voir aussi* Liṣṣ; *et* → ARABIE SÉOUDITE; NOMADISME

Badw; Biʾr; Dawār; G͟hanīma; G͟hazw renvoient à des articles de l'*Encyclopédie* qui traitent principalement des Bédouins, Badw étant l'article sur les Bédouins. Liṣṣ fait allusion à un article de l'*Encyclopédie* qui contient des informations sur les Bédouins, et ARABIE SÉOUDITE, NOMADISME renvoient le lecteur à des rubriques analogues dans l'Index des Matières.

A

ʿABBĀSIDES → CALIFAT

ABLUTION **G͟husl**; Istind͟jāʾ; Istins͟hāḳ; al-Masḥ ʿalā l-K͟huffayn
voir aussi D͟janāba; Ḥadat͟h; Ḥammām; Ḥawḍ; Ḥayḍ

ABYSSINIE → ÉTHIOPIE

ADMINISTRATION Barīd; Bayt al-Māl; Daftar; Diplomatique; **Dīwān**; D͟jizya; Kātib; [au Suppl.] Démographie.I
voir aussi al-Ḳalḳas͟handī.I
pour les califats ou dynasties spécifiques → CALIFAT; DYNASTIES; EMPIRE OTTOMAN

diplomatique → DIPLOMATIE
documents **Daftar.I**
et → DOCUMENTS; EMPIRE OTTOMAN.ADMINISTRATION
archives Dār al-Maḥfūẓāt al-ʿUmūmiyya; Geniza
et → EMPIRE OTTOMAN.ADMINISTRATION
financière ʿAṭāʾ; Bayt al-Māl; Daftar; Dār al-Ḍarb; Ḳānūn.II; Kasb; Khāzin; Khaznadār; Makhzan; Muṣādara.2; Mustawfī; Rūznāma
voir aussi Dhahab; Fiḍḍa; Ḥisba; *et* → EMPIRE OTTOMAN.ADMINISTRATION; NUMISMATIQUE
fiscale → TAXATION
fonctionnaires ʿĀmil; Amīn; Amīr; Amīr al-Ḥādjdj; ʿArīf; Dawādār; Djahbadh; Ḥisba; Īshīk-āḳāsī; Kalāntar; Kātib; Khāzin; Mushīr; Mushrif; Mustakhridj; Mustawfī; Parwānačī; Raʾīs; Ṣāḥib al-Madīna; [au Suppl.] Dabīr
voir aussi Barīd; Consul; Fatwā; Fuyūdj; Kotwāl; Malik al-Tudjdjār; Mawlā; Muwāḍaʿa; *et* → DROIT.FONCTIONS; EMPIRE OTTOMAN; MILITAIRES.FONCTIONS
géographie → GÉOGRAPHIE.ADMINISTRATIVE
juridique → DROIT
militaire → MILITAIRES
ottomane → EMPIRE OTTOMAN

ADOPTION [au Suppl.] ʿĀr
voir aussi ʿĀda.III

ADULTÈRE Ḳadhf; Liʿān
voir aussi al-Marʾa.II
sanctions Ḥadd

AFGHANISTAN Afghān; **Afghānistān**
architecture → ARCHITECTURE.RÉGIONS
dynasties Aḥmad Shāh Durrānī; Ghaznawides; Ghūrides; Kart
et → DYNASTIES.AFGHANISTAN ET INDE
géographie physique Afghānistān.I
eaux Dehās; Hāmūn; Harī Rūd; Kābul.I; Ḳunduz; Kurram; Murghāb; Pandjhīr; [au Suppl.] Gūmāl
voir aussi Afghānistān.I
montagnes Hindū Kush; Kūh-i Bābā; Safīd Kūh
voir aussi Afghānistān.I
langue → LANGUES.INDO-IRANIENNES.IRANIENNES
période moderne Djāmiʿa; Dustūr.V; Khaybar; Madjlis.IV.B; Maṭbaʿa.V
voir aussi Muhādjir.3
hommes d'état ʿAbd al-Raḥmān Khān; Ayyūb Khān; Dūst Muḥammad;

Ḥabīb Allāh Khān; Muḥammad Dāwūd Khān; [au Suppl.] Amān Allāh
voir aussi [au Suppl.] Faḳīr d'Ipi

population Abdālī; Čahār Aymaḳ; Durrānī; Ghalča; Ghalzay; Moghols; Mohmand; [au Suppl.] Démographie.III; Hazāra
voir aussi Afghān.I; Afghānistān.II; Khaladj; Özbeg.I.d; [au Suppl.] Djirga

toponymes
anciens Būshandj; Bust; Dihistān; Djuwayn.3; Farmūl; Fīrūzkūh.I; Khōst; Khudjistān; Marw al-Rūdh; al-Rukhkhadj
actuels
districts Andarāb.1; Bādghīs; Farwān; Ḳūhistān.III; Lamghānāt
régions Badakhshan; Dardistān; Djūzdjān; Ghardjistān; Ghūr; Kāfiristān; Khōst; Nangrahār; [au Suppl.] Hazāradjāt
voir aussi Pandjhīr
villes Andkhūy; Balkh; Bāmiyān; Djām; Farāh; Faryāb.I; Gardīz; Ghazna; Girishk; Harāt; Kābul.II; Ḳandahār; Karūkh; Khulm; Ḳunduz; Maymana; Mazār-i Sharīf; Rūdhbār.1; Sabzawār.2; [au Suppl.] Djalālābād

AFRIQUE Lamlam

Afrique centrale Cameroun; Congo; Gabon; [au Suppl.] Čad
voir aussi Hausa; Muḥammad Bello; al-Murdjibī; [au Suppl.] Démographie.V
pour les pays individuels → CONGO; NIGER; NIGÉRIA; TCHAD; ZAÏRE
géographie physique
déserts Sāḥil.2
population Kanuri; Kotoko

Afrique du Nord Algérie; Atlas; Ifrīḳiya; Lībiyā; Maghāriba; al-Maghrib (2x); Mashāriḳa
voir aussi al-ʿArab.V; ʿArabiyya.A.III.3; Badw.II.D; Baladiyya.III; Djamāʿa; Djarīda.I.B; Djaysh.III; Ghuzz.II; Ḥawz; Hilāl; Ḳawmiyya.II; Kharbga; Kitābāt.IV; Lamṭ; Léon l'Africain; Libās.II; Maḥalla; Mānū; Ṣaff.3; [au Suppl.] ʿĀr; *et* → DYNASTIES.ESPAGNE ET AFRIQUE DU NORD
pour les pays individuels → ALGÉRIE; LIBYE; MAROC; TUNISIE
architecture → ARCHITECTURE.RÉGIONS
géographie physique Reg; Rīf; Sabkha; al-Ṣaḥrāʾ
et → *l'entrée Géographie Physique sous pays individuels*
mysticisme → MYSTICISME
population Ahaggar; Berbères; Dukkāla; Khulṭ; al-Maʿḳil; [au Suppl.] Démographie.IV
voir aussi Khumayr; Kūmiya; al-Manāṣīr; Mandīl; Maures; *et* → BERBÈRES

Afrique méridionale Mozambique
voir aussi [au Suppl.] Djarīda.IX

pour les pays individuels → MOZAMBIQUE

Afrique occidentale Côte d'Ivoire; Dahomey; Gambie; Ghāna; Guinée; Libéria; Mali; Mūrītāniyā; Niger; Nigeria
voir aussi Fūta Djallon; Kitābāt.V; Ḳunbi Ṣāliḥ; al-Maghīlī; Malam; Mande; Muḥammad b. Abī Bakr; Murīdiyya; Oyo; Samori Ture
pour les pays individuels → BÉNIN; CÔTE D'IVOIRE; GUINÉE; MALI; MAURITANIE; NIGER; NIGERIA; SÉNÉGAL; TOGO
architecture Ḳunbi Ṣāliḥ; Masdjid.VII
géographie physique
déserts Sāḥil.2
eaux Niger
population Fulbé; Ḥarṭānī; Ifoghas; Kunta; [au Suppl.] Démographie.V
voir aussi Lamlam; Mande

Afrique orientale Adal; Dawāro; Djibūtī; Érythrée; Ḥabesh; Ḳumr; Madagascar; Mafia
voir aussi Baḥr al-Hind; Baḥr al-Zandj; Emīn Pasha; Kūsh; Mawlid.2; Muṣāḥib; Nawrūz.II; Nikāḥ.II.5; al-Nudjūm; [au Suppl.] Djarīda.VIII
pour les pays individuels → ÉTHIOPIE; KENYA; MADAGASCAR; MALAWI; SOMALIE; SOUDAN; TANZANIE; ZANZIBAR
architecture Manāra.III; Masdjid.VI; Mbweni; Minbar.IV
géographie physique
eaux Atbara; Baḥr al-Ghazāl.1
littérature Miʿrādj.III
voir aussi Kitābāt.VI; *et* → KENYA.LITTÉRATURE SWAHILIE
population ʿAbābda; ʿĀmir; Antemuru; Bedja; Beleyn; Bishārīn; Danḳalī; Djaʿaliyyūn; Galla; Māryā; Mazrūʿī; Oromo; [au Suppl.] Démographie.V
voir aussi Diglal; Lamlam; al-Manāṣīr

AGRICULTURE **Filāḥa**; Marʿā; Raʿiyya
voir aussi Mazraʿa; Mughārasa; Musāḳāt; Muzāraʿa; [au Suppl.] Akkār; *et* → BOTANIQUE; FLORE; IRRIGATION
outils Miḥrāth
produits Ḳahwa; Ḳamḥ; Karm; Ḳaṣab al-Sukkar; Khamr.II; Ḳuṭn; [au Suppl.] Djāwars; Hindibāʾ
voir aussi Ḥarīr; *et* → CUISINE
termes Āgdāl; Baʿl.2.b; Čiftlik; Ghūṭa; Maṭmūra
traités sur Abū l-Khayr al-Ishbīlī; Ibn Wāfid; Ibn Waḥshiyya

ALBANIE **Arnawutluḳ**; Iskender Beg; Ḳarā Maḥmūd Pasha
voir aussi Muslimūn.I.B.4; Sāmī; *et* → EMPIRE OTTOMAN
toponymes Aḳ Ḥiṣār.IV; Awlonya; Delvina; Drač; Elbasan; Ergiri; Korča; Krujë; Lesh

ALCHIMIE Dhahab; Fiḍḍa; al-Iksīr; Kibrīt; **al-Kīmiyā'**
voir aussi Ḳārūn; Maʿdin; al-Nūshādir; *et* → MÉTALLURGIE; MINÉRALOGIE
alchimistes Djābir b. Ḥayyān; Ibn Umayl; Ibn Waḥshiyya; al-Rāzī, Abū Bakr; [au Suppl.] Abū l-Ḥasan al-Anṣārī; al-Djildakī
voir aussi Hirmis; Khālid b. Yazīd b. Muʿāwiya; [au Suppl.] al-Djawbarī, ʿAbd al-Raḥīm; Findiriskī; Ibn Daḳīḳ al-ʿĪd
outillage al-Anbīḳ
termes Rukn.2

ALGÉRIE **Algérie**
voir aussi ʿArabiyya.A.III.3; ʿArsh; Ḥalḳa; *et* → BERBÈRES; DYNASTIES. ESPAGNE ET AFRIQUE DU NORD
architecture → ARCHITECTURE.RÉGIONS.AFRIQUE DU NORD
dynasties ʿAbd al-Wādides; Fāṭimides; Ḥammādides; Rustamides
et → DYNASTIES.ESPAGNE ET AFRIQUE DU NORD
géographie physique Algérie.I
montagnes ʿAmūr; Atlas; Awrās; Bībān; Djurdjura; Kabylie
littérature Ḥawfī
période moderne Djāmiʿa; Djarīda.I.B; Ḥizb.I; Ḥukūma.IV; Maʿārif.II; Madjlis. IV.A.20
réforme Ibn Bādīs; (al-)Ibrāhīmī; Salafiyya.1(b)
voir aussi Fallāḳ
période ottomane (1518-1830) ʿAbd al-Ḳādir b. Muḥyī l-Dīn; Algérie.II.b; ʿArūdj; Ḥasan Agha; Ḥasan Baba; Ḥasan Pasha; al-Ḥusayn; Ḥusayn Pasha, Mezzomorto; Khayr al-Dīn Pasha
population Algérie.III
voir aussi Kabylie; *et* → AFRIQUE.AFRIQUE DU NORD
religion Algérie.III
confréries religieuses ʿAmmāriyya; Raḥmāniyya
voir aussi Darḳāwa; *et* → MYSTICISME
toponymes
anciens Arshgūl; Ashīr; al-Manṣūra; Sadrāta; [au Suppl.] Hunayn
actuels
oasis Biskra; Ḳanṭara.1; al-Ḳulayʿa.II.1; Laghouat; [au Suppl.] Gourara
régions Ḥuḍna; Mzab; Sāḥil.1.b
villes Adrar.1; al-ʿAnnāba; Ārzāw; ʿAyn Temushent; Bidjāya; Biskra; Bulayda; Colomb-Béchar; al-Djazā'ir; Djidjelli; Ghardāya; Ḳalʿat Banī ʿAbbās; Ḳalʿat Huwwāra; al-Ḳulayʿa.II.2; Ḳusṭanṭīna; Laghouat; al-Madiyya; Masīla; Milyāna; al-Muʿaskar; Mustaghānim; Nadrūma; Saʿīda

ALPHABET **Abdjad**; Ḥarf; Ḥisāb; **Ḥurūf al-Hidjā'**
voir aussi Djafr; Khaṭṭ; [au Suppl.] Budūḥ
pour les lettres de l'alphabet arabe et persan, voir Ḍād; Dāl; Dhāl; Djīm; Fā'; Ghayn; Hā'; Ḥā'; Hamza; Kāf; Ḳāf; Khā'; Lām; Mīm; Nūn; Pā'; Rā'; Ṣād
secret → CRYPTOGRAPHIE

AMOUR **ʿIshḳ**
voir aussi Ishāra; Ḳalb.II; *et* → LITTÉRATURE.POÉSIE.D'AMOUR
mystique ʿĀshiḳ; ʿIshḳ
et → LITTÉRATURE.POÉSIE.MYSTIQUE; MYSTICISME
platonique Djamīl al-ʿUdhrī; Ghazal.I.3; Ibn Dāwūd; Kuthayyir b. ʿAbd al-Raḥmān; Laylā al-Akhyaliyya; Nuṣayb b. Rabāḥ; al-Ramādī
et → LITTÉRATURE.POÉSIE.D'AMOUR
traités sur al-Antāḳī, Dāwūd; Ibn Ḥazm, Abū Muḥammad; Rafīʿ al-Dīn
voir aussi Bukhtīshūʿ

ANATOMIE Djism; Katif; [au Suppl.] Aflīmūn
voir aussi Ishāra; Khiḍāb; Ḳiyāfa; [au Suppl.] Dam
cheveux ʿAfṣ; Afsantīn; Ḥinnā'; Liḥya-yi Sherīf
voir aussi [au Suppl.] Ḥallāḳ
dents → MÉDECINE.DENTAIRE
oeil **ʿAyn**; Kuḥl; Manāẓir; Ramad
et → MÉDECINE.OPHTALMOLOGISTES; OPTIQUE
organes Kabid; Ḳalb
poitrine **Ṣadr**

ANDALOUSIE **al-Andalus**; Gharb al-Andalus; Morisques; Mozárabe; Mudéjar
voir aussi Kitābāt.III; Libās.II; Mā'.VII; al-Madjūs; Maures; Muwallad; Safīr.2.b; Ṣā'ifa.2; *et* → DYNASTIES.ESPAGNE ET AFRIQUE DU NORD; ESPAGNE
administration Dīwān.III; Ḳūmis; Ṣāḥib al-Madīna
voir aussi Fatā
architecture → ARCHITECTURE.RÉGIONS
belles-lettres Aljamía; ʿArabiyya.B.Appendice; Fahrasa
et → ANDALOUSIE.HISTORIENS; LITTÉRATURE.POÉSIE
dynasties al-Murābiṭūn.IV; al-Muwaḥḥidūn; [au Suppl.] ʿAzafī
voir aussi al-Andalus.VI; (Banū) Ḳasī; *et* → DYNASTIES.ESPAGNE ET AFRIQUE DU NORD
période des "reyes de taifas" (11e siècle) ʿAbbādides; Afṭasides; ʿĀmirides; Dhū l-Nūnides; Djahwarides; Ḥammūdides; Hūdides; **Mulūk al-Ṭawā'if**.II; Razīn, Banū
voir aussi Balansiya; Dāniya; Gharnāṭa; Ibn Ghalbūn; Ibn Rashīḳ, Abū Muḥammad; Ishbīliya; Ḳurṭuba; Mudjāhid al-ʿĀmirī; Parias

gouverneurs jusqu'à la conquête umayyade ʿAbd al-Malik b. Ḳaṭan; ʿAbd al-Raḥmān al-Ghāfiḳī; Abū l-Khaṭṭār; al-Ḥurr b. ʿAbd al-Raḥmān al-Thaḳafī; al-Ḥusām b. Ḍirār
voir aussi Kalb b. Wabara; Mūsā b. Nuṣayr
historiens al-Ḍabbī, Abū Djaʿfar; Ibn al-Abbār, Abū ʿAbd Allāh; Ibn ʿAbd al-Malik al-Marrākushī; Ibn Bashkuwāl; Ibn Burd.I; Ibn al-Faraḍī; Ibn Ghālib; Ibn Ḥayyān; Ibn ʿIdhārī; Ibn al-Khaṭīb; Ibn al-Ḳūṭiyya; Ibn Saʿīd al-Maghribī; al-Maḳḳarī; al-Rushāṭī
et → DYNASTIES.ESPAGNE ET AFRIQUE DU NORD
juristes al-Bādjī; al-Dānī; al-Ḥumaydī; Ibn Abī Zamanayn; Ibn ʿĀṣim; Ibn al-Faraḍī; Ibn Ḥabīb, Abū Marwān; Ibn Ḥazm, Abū Muḥammad; Ibn Maḍāʾ; Ibn Rushayd; ʿĪsā b. Dīnār; ʿIyāḍ b. Mūsā; al-Ḳalaṣādī; al-Ḳurṭubī, Abū ʿAbd Allāh; al-Ḳurṭubī, Yaḥyā; (al-)Mundhir b. Saʿīd; Ṣāʿid al-Andalusī; [au Suppl.] Ibn Rushd
voir aussi al-Khushanī; Mālikiyya; [au Suppl.] Ibn al-Rūmiyya
mysticisme → MYSTICISME.MYSTIQUES
toponymes → ESPAGNE

ANGÉLOLOGIE **Malāʾika**
voir aussi ʿAdhāb al-Ḳabr; Dīk; Iblīs; Ḳarīn; Rūḥāniyya
anges ʿAzāzīl; Djabrāʾīl; Hārūt wa-Mārūt; Isrāfīl; ʿIzrāʿīl; **Malāʾika**; Mīkāl; Munkar wa-Nakīr

ANIMAUX Dābba; **Ḥayawān**
voir aussi Badw; (Djazīrat) al-ʿArab.V; Farw; Hind.I.l; Khāṣī; Marbaṭ; [au Suppl.] Djazzār; *et* → ZOOLOGIE
antilopes Ghazāl; Lamṭ; Mahāt
arachnides ʿAḳrab; ʿAnkabūt
canidés Dhiʾb; Fanak; Ibn Āwā; Kalb; Salūḳī; [au Suppl.] Ḍabuʿ
chameaux **Ibil**
voir aussi (Djazīrat) al-ʿArab.V; Badw.II.c et d; Kārwān; Raḥīl; [au Suppl.] Djammāl; *et* → TRANSPORT.CARAVANES
domestiqués Baḳar; Fīl; Ibil; Kalb; Khinzīr; Nims; [au Suppl.] Djāmūs; Ghanam
et → ANIMAUX.ÉQUINES
équines Badw.II; Baghl; **Faras**; Ḥimār; **Khayl**
voir aussi Fāris; Furūsiyya; Ḥazīn; Ibn Hudhayl; Ibn al-Mundhir; Iṣṭabl; Marbaṭ; Maydān; Mīr-Ākhūr
et l'art al-Asad; Fahd; Fīl; Ḥayawān.VI; Karkaddan; Maʿdin; Namir et Nimr; [au Suppl.] Arnab
et proverbes Ḥayawān.II; Mathal
voir aussi les articles sur les animaux individuels, en particulier Afʿā; Dhiʾb; Fahd; Ghurāb; Ḳaṭā; Khinzīr; Ḳird; Lamṭ; Naml

félins ʿAnāḳ; al-Asad; Fahd; Namir et Nimr
insectes Dhubāb; Djarād; Ḳaml; Naḥl; Naml; Nāmūs.2
mollusques Ṣadaf
oiseaux Babbaghāʾ; Dadjādja; Dīk; Ghurāb; Ḥamām; Hudhud; Humā; Ḳaṭā; Naʿām; Nasr; Nuḥām; al-Rukhkh; Salwā; [au Suppl.] Abū Barāḳish
voir aussi Bayzara; Bulbul; ʿIyāfa; al-Ramādī
poisson **Samak**
reptiles Afʿā; Ḍabb; Ḥayya; Ḥirbāʾ; Samandal
voir aussi Ādam; Almās
rongeurs [au Suppl.] Faʾr
sauvages *outre les articles ci-dessus, voir aussi* Ayyil; Fanak; Fīl; Ibn ʿIrs; Karkaddan; Ḳird; Ḳunfudh; [au Suppl.] Arnab; Faras al-Māʾ
sport Bayzara; Fahd; Furūsiyya; Ḥamām; Khinzīr; Mahāt; [au Suppl.] Ḍabuʿ
voir aussi Čaki̊rdji̊-bashi̊; Doghandji̊; Kurdes et Kurdistān.IV.C.5; *et* → CHASSE
transformation en Ḥayawān.III; Ḳird; **Maskh**

ANTHROPOMORPHISME Ḥashwiyya; Karrāmiyya
voir aussi Bayān b. Samʿān; Djism; Hishām b. al-Ḥakam; Ḥulmāniyya

APOSTASIE Mulḥid; Murtadd
voir aussi Ḳatl; *et* → HÉRÉSIE

ARABIE SÉOUDITE (Djazīrat) al-ʿArab; Djarīda.I.A; Djāmiʿa; Dustūr.VII; al-Hidjar; al-Ikhwān; Madjlis.IV.A.8; Maḥkama.IV.7
voir aussi Bā ʿAlawī; Badw; Baladiyya.II; Barakāt; Makka; [au Suppl.] Démographie.III; *et* → PÉRIODE PRÉISLAMIQUE.DANS LA PÉNINSULE ARABIQUE; TRIBUS.PÉNINSULE ARABIQUE
avant l'Islam → PÉRIODE PRÉISLAMIQUE.DANS LA PÉNINSULE ARABIQUE
dynasties Hāshimides (2x); Rashīd, Āl
voir aussi Muḥammad b. Suʿūd; [au Suppl.] ʿAbd al-ʿAzīz; Fayṣal b. ʿAbd al ʿAzīz; *et* → DYNASTIES.PÉNINSULE ARABIQUE
géographie physique
déserts al-Aḥḳāf; al-Dahnāʾ; Nafūd; al-Rubʿ al-Khālī
voir aussi Badw.II; Ḥarra
eaux Dawʿan
montagnes Djabala; Ḥufāsh; Raḍwā
voir aussi Adjaʾ et Salmā
plaines ʿArafa; al-Dibdiba; al-Ṣammān
wadis al-ʿAtk; al-Bāṭin; Bayḥān; Bayḥān al-Ḳaṣāb; Djayzān; Fāʾw; (Wādī l-) Ḥamḍ; Rumma, Wādī; al-Sahbāʾ
historiens al-Azraḳī; Daḥlān; al-Fāḳihī; al-Fāsī; Ibn Fahd; Ibn Manda; Ibn al-

Mudjāwir; Ibn al-Nadjdjār; al-Samhūdī
voir aussi al-Diyārbakrī
population → TRIBUS.PÉNINSULE ARABIQUE
toponymes
anciens Badr; al-Djār; Fadak; al-Ḥidjr; al-Ḥudaybiya; Ḳurḥ; Madyan Shuʿayb; al-Rabadha
voir aussi Fāʾw
actuels
districts al-Aflādj; al-Djawf; al-Ḳaṣīm; al-Khardj
îles Farasān
oasis al-Dirʿiyya; Dūmat al-Djandal; al-Ḥasā; al-Khurma
régions ʿAsīr; ʿAwlaḳī; Bayḥān; al-Ḥāḍina; Ḥaly; al-Ḥawṭa; al-Ḥidjāz; Ḳurayyāt al-Milḥ; Nadjd; Nafūd; Raʾs (al-)Tannūra; al-Rubʿ al-Khālī
villes Abhā; Abḳayḳ; Abū ʿArīsh; Burayda; al-Dammām; al-Djawf; Djayzān; al-Djubayl; al-Djubayla; Djudda; Fakhkh; Ghāmid; Ḥayil; al-Hufūf; Ḥuraymilā; Ḳarya al-Suflā; Ḳarya al-ʿUlyā; al Ḳaṣāb; al-Ḳaṭīf; Khamīs Mushayṭ; Khaybar; al-Khubar; al-Ḳunfudha; al-Madīna; Makka; Minā; al-Mubarraz; Nadjrān; Rābigh; al-Riyāḍ; [au Suppl.] Fayd
voir aussi (Djazīrat) al-ʿArab; al-ʿĀriḍ; Bīsha; Ḍariyya

ARCHÉOLOGIE
et → ARCHITECTURE.RÉGIONS; ÉPIGRAPHIE; *et l'entrée Toponymes sous les pays individuels*
archéologues turques ʿOthmān Ḥamdī

ARCHITECTURE **Architecture**; Bināʾ
voir aussi Kitābāt; *et* → MILITAIRES
architectes Ḳasim Agha; Khayr al-Dīn
décorative Fusayfisāʾ; Kāshī; Khaṭṭ; Parčīn-kārī
matériaux Djiṣṣ; Labin
voir aussi Bināʾ
monuments
aqueducs Ḳanṭara.5 et 6
voir aussi Faḳīr
bains **Ḥammām**; Ḥammām al-Ṣarakh
barrages **Band**
voir aussi Dizfūl; [au Suppl.] Abū Sinbil; *et* → HYDROLOGIE
débits d'eau **Sabīl.2**
voir aussi Ḥawḍ
forteresses Burdj; Ḥiṣār; **Ḥiṣn**; Ḳaṣaba
voir aussi Bāb.2; al-Ḳalʿa; Ribāṭ

forteresses individuelles Abū Safyān; Āgra; Alamūt.I; Alindjaḳ; ʿAmādiya; Anadolu Ḥiṣārī; Anamur; Anapa; Asīrgarh; Atak; al-ʿAwāṣim; Bāb al-Abwāb; Bālā Ḥiṣār; Balāṭunus; Barzūya; Baynūn; Bhakkar; Čandērī; Čirmen; al-Dārūm; Djaʿbar; al-Djarbāʾ; Gaban; Gāwilgaṙh; Ghumdān; Gök Tepe; Golkondā; Ḥadjar al-Nasr; Hānsī; Ḥarrān.II.a; Ḥiṣn al-Akrād; Ḥiṣn Kayfā; Iṣṭakhr; Kakhtā; Ḳalʿat Nadjm; Ḳalʿat al-Shaḳīf; Ḳalāwdhiya; Ḳalʿe-i Sefīd; Ḳandahār; Kanizsa; al-Karak; Kawkab; Kharāna; Khartpert; Khērla; Khotin; Khunāṣira; Kilāt-i Nādirī; Ḳoron; Ḳoyul Ḥiṣār; Lanbasar; Lüleburgaz; Māndū; Manōhar; al-Marḳab; Mudgal; Narnālā; Parendā; al-Rāwandān; Rōhtās; Rūm Ḳalʿesi; Rūmeli Ḥiṣārī; Ṣahyūn; [au Suppl.] Bādiya; Bubashtru; al-Dīkdān; Firrīm

voir aussi Ashīr; Bahmanides; Bīdar; Dawlatābād; Diyār Bakr; Ḥimṣ; Kawkabān.II; Khursābād; Maḥall; Māhūr

jardins de plaisance Būstān; Ḥāʾir

voir aussi Bostāndjī; Gharnāṭa.B; Ḥawḍ; Māʾ.XI

mausolées → ARCHITECTURE.MONUMENTS.TOMBEAUX

monastères → CHRISTIANISME.COUVENTS

mosquées Ḥawḍ; Külliyye; Manāra; **Masdjid**; Miḥrāb; Minbar

voir aussi ʿAnaza; Bāb.1; Bahw; Balāṭ; Dikka; Khaṭīb; Muṣallā.2

mosquées individuelles Aya Sofya; al-Azhar; Ḥarrān.II.b; Ḥusaynī Dālān; Kaʿba; al-Ḳarawiyyīn; Ḳubbat al-Ṣakhra; Ḳuṭb Mīnār; al-Masdjid al-Aḳṣā; al-Masdjid al-Ḥarām

voir aussi Anḳara; Architecture; Bahmanides; Dhār; Djām; Edirne; Ḥamāt; Ḥimṣ; Kāẓimayn; Ḳazwīn; Maʿarrat al-Nuʿmān; Makka.IV

obélisques **Misalla**

palais Čirāghān; Ḳaṣr al-Ḥayr al-Gharbī; Ḳaṣr al-Ḥayr al-Sharḳī; Kayḳubādiyya; Khirbat al-Mafdjar; Khirbat al-Minya; Ḳubādābād; Maḥall; al-Mushattā; [au Suppl.] Djabal Says

voir aussi Gharnāṭa.B; Khirbat al-Bayḍāʾ; Ḳubbat al-Hawāʾ; Lashkar-i Bāzār

pavillons Köshk

phares **Manār**; al-Nāẓūr

ponts **Djisr**; Djisr Banāt Yaʿḳūb; Djisr al-Ḥadīd; Djisr al-Shughr

voir aussi Dizfūl; Ḳanṭara

portes **Bāb**; Bāb-i Humāyūn; Ḥarrān.II.d

puits Bāʾolī; **Biʾr**; Biʾr Maymūn

tombeaux **Ḳabr**; **Ḳubba**; **Maḳbara**; Mashhad

voir aussi Muthamman

constructions individuelles Baḳīʿ al-Gharḳad; Golkondā; Ḥarrān.II.c; Maklī; Nafīsa; Rādkān; Sahsarām

voir aussi Abarḳūh; Abū Ayyūb al-Anṣārī; Abū Madyan; Āgra;

Aḥmad al-Badawī; Aḥmad Yasawī; Bahmanides; Barīd Shāhides; Djahāngīr; Ghāzī Miyān; Gunbadh-i Ḳābūs; Ḥimṣ; Imāmzāda; Karak Nūḥ; Karbalāʾ; Ḳazwīn; al-Khalīl; Ḳubbat al-Hawāʾ; Maʿarrat al-Nuʿmān; al-Madīna

régions

Afghanistan et le sous-continent indien Āgra; Bahmanides; Barīd Shāhides; Bharōč; Bīdar; Bīdjāpūr; Bihār; Čāmpānēr; Dawlatābād; Dihlī.II; Djūnāgaṙh; Ghaznawides; Ghūrides; Golkonḍā; Hampī; Hānsī; Ḥaydarābād; Hind.VII; Ḥusaynī Dālān; Ḳuṭb Mīnār; Lāhawr; Lakhnaw; Maḥall; Mahisur; Māndū.2; Mughals.VII; Multān.2; Nāgawr
voir aussi Burdj.3; Bustān.II; Imām-bārā; Lashkar-i Bāzār; Māʾ.XI; Maḳbara.V; Maklī; Manāra.II; Masdjid.II; Miḥrāb; Minbar.III; Miẓalla.5; Muthamman; Parčīn-kārī; Pīshṭāḳ

Afrique → Afrique; *pour l'architecture d'Afrique du Nord, voir ci-dessous*

Afrique du Nord Fās; Fāṭimides.L'art faṭimide; Ḥiṣn.I; Ḳalʿat Banī Ḥammād; al-Ḳarawiyyīn
voir aussi ʿAnaza; Bidjāya; Miḥrāb

Andalousie al-Andalus.IX; Burdj.II; Gharnāṭa; Ishbīliya; Ḳurṭuba; Naṣrides.B
voir aussi al-Nāẓūr

Asie centrale Bukhārā; Ḥiṣn.III; Īlkhāns; Samarḳand.2
voir aussi Miḥrāb

Asie du Sud-Est Ḥiṣn.IV; Indonésie.V; Masdjid.III-V

Croissant fertile Baghdād; Dimashḳ; Ḥarrān.II; Ḥimṣ; ʿIrāḳ.VII; Ḳubbat al-Ṣakhra; al-Ḳuds; Maʿarrat al-Nuʿmān; al-Marḳab; al-Masdjid al-Aḳṣā; al-Raḳḳa; [au Suppl.] Bādiya; Dār al-Ḥadīth.I
voir aussi Ḳaṣr al-Ḥayr al-Gharbī; Ḳaṣr al-Ḥayr al-Sharḳī; Khirbat al-Mafdjar; Miḥrāb; al-Rāwandān

Égypte Abū l-Hawl; al-Azhar; Haram; al-Ḳāhira; Mashrabiyya.1; Nafīsa
voir aussi Miḥrāb; Misalla; Miṣr; Saʿīd al-Suʿadāʾ; [au Suppl.] Abū Sinbil

Iran Ḥisn.II; Iṣfahān.II; Iṣṭakhr; Ḳazwīn; Khursābād; Mashrabiyya.2; Rādkān; al-Rayy.2; Ṣafawides.V; Saldjūḳides.VI; Sāmānides.2(b)
voir aussi Ḳaṣr-i Shīrīn; Miḥrāb; Ribāṭ-i Sharaf

Péninsule arabique al-Ḥidjr; Kaʿba; al-Masdjid al-Ḥarām
voir aussi Makka.IV

Turquie Adana; Anḳara; Aya Sofya; Diwrīgī; Diyār Bakr; Edirne; Ḥarrān.II; Ḥiṣn Kayfā; Istanbul; Konya.II; Lāranda; ʿOthmānli̊.V
voir aussi Ḳapli̊dja; Ḳāsim Agha; Khayr al-Dīn; Köshk; Miḥrāb; Rūm Ḳalʿesi

termes ʿAmūd; ʿAnaza; Bahw; Balāṭ; Īwān; Muḳarbaṣ; Muḳarnas; Muthamman; Pīshṭāḳ; Riwāḳ

urbaine Dār; Funduḳ; Ḥammām; Īwān; Ḳaysāriyya; Khān.II; Madrasa.III;

Masdjid; Muṣallā.2; Rabʿ
voir aussi Kanīsa
ventilation Mirwaḥa; [au Suppl.] Bādgīr
voir aussi Khaysh

Arménie **Armīniya**; Rewān
et → Caucase

Art Arabesque; Fann; Fusayfisāʾ; Kāshī; Khaṭṭ; Khazaf; Kitābāt; Lawn; Maʿdin.IV; Parčīn-kārī; Rasm
voir aussi Architecture; Billawr; Dhahab; Fiḍḍa; ʿIlm al-Djamāl; Khātam; Muhr; *et* → Animaux.et l'art; Architecture
artisanat Ḳalamkārī; [au Suppl.] Bisāṭ; Dawāt
voir aussi Ḥalfāʾ
calligraphie **Khaṭṭ**
voir aussi ʿAlī; Inal; Ḳum(m)ī; Muraḳḳaʿ; Nuskha; *et* → Écriture
calligraphes ʿAlī Riḍā-i ʿAbbāsī; Ḥamza al-Ḥarrānī; Ibn al-Bawwāb; Ibn Muḳla; Muḥammad Ḥusayn Tabrīzī; Müstaḳīm-zāde
céramique → Art.poterie
décoratif ʿĀdj; al-Asad; Djiṣṣ; Fahd; Ḥayawān.VI; Hilāl.II; Īlkhāns; al-Ḳamar.II; Mashrabiyya; Parčīn-kārī
voir aussi Kāshī; Maʿdin.IV
découpage de silhouettes Fakhrī
dessin **Rasm**
métal Bīdar; Īlkhāns; Maʿdin.IV; ʿOthmānli̊.VII.b; Sāmānides.2(a); [au Suppl.] Ibrīḳ
mosaïque **Fusayfisāʾ**; Kāshī
peinture
miniatures Īlkhāns; Mughals.IX; Naḳḳāsh-khāna; ʿOthmānli̊.VIII
voir aussi Fīl; Kalīla wa-Dimna.16; Mānḍū.3; Miʿrādj.V; al-Mīzān.III; Muraḳḳaʿ; Rustam.2; Sāḳī.3; [au Suppl.] Djawhar; *et* → Animaux.et l'art; Art.dessin
miniaturistes Bihzād; Manṣūr; Maṭrāḳči̊; Naḳḳāsh Ḥasan (Pasha); Riḍā ʿAbbāsī; Riḍāʾī
voir aussi ʿAlī; Luḳmān b. Sayyid Ḥusayn
peinture moderne Djabrān Khalīl Djabrān; ʿOthmān Ḥamdī; [au Suppl.] Dinet; Eyyūboghlu, Bedrī
et → Animaux.et l'art
plaques **Kāshī**
poterie Anadolu.III.6; al-Andalus.IX; **Fakhkhār**; Īlkhāns; Iznīḳ; Ḳallala; **Khazaf**; Mināʾī; ʿOthmānli̊.VII.a; Sāmānides.2(a)
régional et d'époque al-Andalus.IX; Berbères.VI; Fāṭimides.L'art fāṭimide;

Īlkhāns; ʿIrāḳ.VII; Mughals.VIII et IX; ʿOthmānli̊.VII; Saldjūḳides.VI; Sāmānides.2(a)
tapisserie ʿOthmānli̊.VI; Sadjdjāda.2; [au Suppl.] **Bisāṭ**
voir aussi Karkaddan; Mafrūshāt; Mifrash; Mīlās
textiles Anadolu.III.6; al-Andalus.IX; al-Bahnasā; Bursa; Dabīḳ; Ḥarīr; Īlkhāns; Ḳumāsh; Mughals.VII; ʿOthmānli̊.VI; al-Rayy.2; Sāmānides.2(a); [au Suppl.] Ḥāʾik
voir aussi Ḳalamkārī; Ḳaṣab; Kattān; Ḳurḳūb; Mandīl; al-Nassādj; *et* → VÊTEMENTS
verre Ḳily; ʿOthmānli̊.VII.d; Sāmānides.2(a)

ASCÉTISME Bakkāʾ; Malāmatiyya
voir aussi Khalwa; Manāḳib; [au Suppl.] Asad b. Mūsā
pour les ascètes → MYSTICISME.MYSTIQUES; SAINT

ASIE Almali̊gh; Baikal
voir aussi Baraba; Mogholistān; *et* → CHINA; MONGOLIE
Centrale → ASIE CENTRALE
du Sud Birmanie; Ceylan; Hind; Laquedives; Maldives; Maurice; Minicoy; Népal; Nicobar
voir aussi Ruhmī
pour les pays individuels → BANGLADESH; BIRMANIE; INDE; PAKISTAN; SRI LANKA
du Sud-Est Čam; Djāwī; Indochine; Indonésie; Ḳimār; (Péninsule) Malaise; Malaisie; Patani; Philippines; [au Suppl.] Brunei
voir aussi Kitābāt.VIII; [au Suppl.] Démographie.VIII; *et* → ARCHITECTURE; DROIT
pour les pays individuels → CHINE; INDONÉSIE; MALAISIE; THAÏLANDE
Eurasie → EUROPE

ASIE CENTRALE Badakhshān; Čaghāniyān; Khʷārazm; **Mā warāʾ al-Nahr**; Mogholistān
voir aussi Hayāṭila; Ismāʿīl b. Aḥmad; Ḳarā Khiṭāy; Ḳazaḳ; Nīzak, Ṭarkhān; [au Suppl.] Atali̊ḳ; Djulfā.II; *et* → DYNASTIES.MONGOLES; MONGOLIE; ONOMASTIQUE
architecture → ARCHITECTURE.RÉGIONS
belles-lettres → LITTÉRATURE.DRAME *et* POÉSIE.TURQUE.EN TURC ORIENTAL
géographie physique
déserts Ḳaraḳum; Ḳi̊zi̊l-ḳum
eaux Aḳ Ṣu; Amū Daryā; Aral; Atrek; Baḥr al-Khazar; Balkhash; Čaghān-rūd; Ču; Ili; İssi̊ḳ-kul; Ḳarā-köl; Murghāb
montagnes Ala Dagh; Altaï; Balkhān; Pamir
voir aussi Čopan-ata

historiens ʿAbd al-Karīm Bukhārī
voir aussi Ḥaydar b. ʿAlī
mysticisme → Mysticisme; Saint
population Balūč; Čāwdors (*et* [au Suppl.] Čawdor); Emreli; Gagauz; Ḳara-ḳalpaḳ; Khaladj; Ḳungrāt; Kurama; Özbeg; [au Suppl.] Démographie.VI
voir aussi Altaï; al-ʿArab.III.Appendice; Ghalča; Ghuzz; Ḳarluḳ; Ḳazaḳ; Ḳipčaḳ; Ḳi̊rgi̊z; Ḳumān; Kumīdjīs; Ḳun; [au Suppl.] Ersari̊
toponymes
anciens Abaskūn; Abīward; Akhsīkath; Ardjīsh; Balāsāghūn; Banākat; Fārāb; Firabr; Gurgandj; Kāth; Ḳayali̊ḳ; Marw al-Rūdh; Marw al-Shāhidjān; Mashhad-i Miṣriyān; Nakhshab; Pishpek; [au Suppl.] Dandānḳān; Djand; Īlāḳ
actuels
districts Atek; Ḳaratigin
voir aussi Ākhāl Tekke
régions Farghānā; Khwārazm; Khuttalān; Labāb; Mangi̊shlak; [au Suppl.] Dasht-i Ḳi̊pčaḳ
villes Aḳ Masdjid.2; Alma Ata; Āmul.2; Andidjān; ʿAshḳābād; Awliyā Ata; Bayram ʿAlī; Bukhārā; Čimkent; Djalālābād; Ghudjduwān; Hazārasp; Ḥiṣār; Kash; Khīwa; Khoḳand; Khudjand(a); Kish; Ḳubādhiyān; Marghīnān; Mayhana; Ordūbād; Özkend; Pandjdih; Samarḳand
Union Soviétique ancienne al-ʿArab.III.Appendice; Basmačis; Djarīda.IV; Fiṭrat; Ḥizb.V; Khodjaev; Ṣadr al-Dīn ʿAynī; [au Suppl.] Démographie.VI
et → l'entrée Toponymes dans cette rubrique

Assyrie Khursābād; Nimrūd; Nīnawā.1; [au Suppl.] Athūr

Astrologie Ikhtiyārāt; Ḳaws Ḳuzaḥ; al-Kayd; Ḳirān; Minṭaḳat al-Burūdj; Munadjdjim; **Nudjūm (Aḥkām al-)**
voir aussi Khaṭṭ
astrologues Abū Maʿshar al-Balkhī; al-Bīrūnī; Ibn Abī l-Ridjāl, Abū l-Ḥasan; Ibn al-Khaṣīb, Abū Bakr; al-Ḳabīṣī; al-Khayyāṭ, Abū ʿAlī; Māshāʾ Allāh
voir aussi Baṭlamiyūs; *et* → Astronomie; Divination
termes al-Djawzahar; Ḥadd; Ḳaṭʿ; Muthallath; Saʿd wa-Naḥs (*et* al-Saʿdāni); al-Sahm.1.b

Astronomie Anwāʾ; Asṭurlāb; Falak; Hayʾa; **ʿIlm al-Hayʾa**; al-Ḳamar.I; al-Kayd; Kusūf; Ḳuṭb; al-Madd wa-l-Djazr; al-Madjarra; al-Manāzil; Minṭaḳat al-Burūdj; al-Nudjūm
voir aussi Djughrāfiyā; Ḳibla.II; al-Ḳubba; Kura; Makka.IV; Mīḳāt.2; Mizwala
astronomes ʿAbd al-Raḥmān al-Ṣūfī; Abū l-Ṣalt; ʿAlī al-Ḳūshdjī; al-Badīʿ al-

Asṭurlābī; al-Battānī; al-Bīrūnī; al-Biṭrūdjī; Djābir b. Aflaḥ; al-Djaghmīnī; al-Farghānī; Ḥabash al-Ḥāsib al-Marwazī; Ibn Amādjūr; Ibn al-Bannāʾ al-Marrākushī; Ibn ʿIrāḳ; Ibn al-Ṣaffār; Ibn al-Samḥ; Ibn Yūnus; al-Kāshī; al-Khʷārazmī, Abū Djaʿfar; al-Khāzin; al-Khazīnī; al-Khudjandī; Kushiyār; Ḳuṭb al-Dīn Shīrāzī; al-Madjrīṭī; al-Mārdīnī; al-Marrākushī; Muḥammad b. ʿĪsā b. Aḥmad al-Māhānī; Muḥammad b. ʿUmar; al-Nayrīzī; [au Suppl.] ʿAbd al-Salām b. Muḥammad

voir aussi Baṭlamiyūs; al-Falakī; Falakī Shirwānī; Ibn al-Haytham; Ḳusṭā b. Lūḳā; [au Suppl.] Ibn al-Adjdābī; *et* → Astrologie

corps célestes

comètes **al-Nudjūm**.III.b

étoiles et constellations ʿAḳrab; ʿAnāḳ; al-Asad; Dadjādja; Fard; Kalb; Ḳird; Mahāt; Minṭaḳat al-Burūdj; Muthallath; Naʿām; Nasr; **al-Nudjūm**; Radīf.1; al-Sahm.1.c; Samak.9; [au Suppl.] Arnab; Ghanam

voir aussi al-Kayd; Saʿd wa-Naḥs (*et* al-Saʿdān[i]); al-Sāḳ

planètes al-Ḳamar.I; al-Mirrīkh; al-Mushtarī; **al-Nudjūm**.II

voir aussi Minṭaḳat al-Burūdj; Ruʾyat al-Hilāl; al-Saʿdān[i]

observatoire Marṣad

termes al-Djawzahar; Istiḳbāl; al-Maṭāliʿ; al-Maṭlaʿ; Mayl; Muḳābala.I; Muḳanṭarāt; Niṣf al-Nahār; Radīf.1; Rubʿ; Ruʾyat al-Hilāl; al-Sāḳ; al-Samt

Aumônes Khayr; **Ṣadaḳa**

Autriche Beč; **Nemče**

voir aussi Muslimūn.II.2

B

Bābisme → Sectes

Bahāʾīs Bāb; Bābīs; Bahāʾ Allāh; **Bahāʾīs**; Mashriḳ al-Adhkār; Naḳḍ al-Mīthāḳ

voir aussi Lawḥ; Maẓhar; [au Suppl.] Anṣārī

Bahrain **al-Baḥrayn**; āl-Khalīfa; Madjlis.IV.A.10; Maḥkama.IV.9

voir aussi Ḳarmaṭī

toponymes al-Manāma; al-Muḥarraḳ

voir aussi al-Mushaḳḳar

Balkans **Balḳan**; **Rūmeli**; al-Ṣaḳāliba

et → Europe

BANGLADESH **Bangāla**; Ma**d**jlis.IV.C
voir aussi Bengali; Na**dh**r al-Islām; [au Suppl.] Djarīda.VII
littérature → LITTÉRATURE.EN D'AUTRES LANGUES
toponymes Bāḳarganḏj; Bangāla; Bōgrā; Chittagong; Ḍhākā; Dīnāḏjpur; Ḏjassawr; Farīdpur
voir aussi Ruhmī

BANQUE Muḍāraba; Ribā.5
voir aussi Ḏjahbaḏh

BASQUES **al-Bashkunish**
voir aussi Ibn Gharsiya

BÉDOUINS **Badw**; Biʾr; Dawār; Ghanīma; Ghazw; al-Hiḏjar
voir aussi Liṣṣ; *et* → ARABIE SÉOUDITE; NOMADISME
traités sur Rzewuski

BÉNIN Kandi; Kotonou; Kouandé

BERBÈRES **Berbères**; Judéo-berbère
voir aussi Ḥimāya.II.2; Imẓad; al-Irḏjānī; Ḳallāla; Ḳiṣṣa.VIII; Leff; Libās.II; Lithām; Mafākhir al-Barbar; Ṣaff.3; *et* → ALGÉRIE; LANGUES.AFRO-ASIATIQUES
droit coutumier ʿĀda.II; Ḳānūn.IV
dynasties ʿAbd al-Wādides; ʿAmmār; Marīnides; Midrār; al-Murābiṭūn; al-Muwaḥḥidūn; Razīn, Banū
religion al-Baḏjalī; Berbères.III; Ḥā-Mīm; Ṣāliḥ b. Ṭarīf
résistance Berbères.I.c; al-Kāhina; Kusayla; Maysara
tribus al-Barānis; Barghawāṭa; Birzāl; al-Butr; Ḏjazūla; Ghāniya; Ghubrīnī; Ghumāra; Glāwā; Gudāla; Ḥāḥā; Hargha; Hawwāra; Hintāta; Ifoghas; Īfran; Iraten; Kutāma; Lamṭa; Lamtūna; Lawāta; Maghīla; Maghrāwa; Malzūza; Maṣmūda; Māssa; Maṭghara; Maṭmāṭa; Mazāta; Midyūna; Misrāta; al-Nafūsa; Nafza; Nafzāwa; [au Suppl.] Awraba

BIBLE **Inḏjīl**
et → CHRISTIANISME; JUDAÏSME
personnages bibliques Ādam; ʿAmālīḳ; Ayyūb; Āzar; ʿAzāzīl; Balʿam; Bilḳīs; Binyāmīn; Bukht-naṣ(ṣ)ar; Dāniyāl; Dāwūd; Ḏjabrāʾīl; Ḏjālūt; Firʿawn; Ḥābīl wa-Ḳābīl; Ḥām; Hāmān; Hārūn b. ʿImrān; Hārūt wa-Mārūt; Ḥawwāʾ; Ḥizḳīl; Ilyās; ʿImrān; Irmiyā; ʿĪsā; Isḥāḳ; Ismāʿīl; Kanʿān; Ḳārūn; Ḳiṭfīr; Kūsh; Lamak; Lazare; Lūṭ; Maryam; al-Masīḥ; Namrūd; Nūḥ; Rāḥīl; Sām.1; al-Sāmirī

voir aussi Dhū l-Kifl; Djūdī; al-Fayyūm; Hūd; Idrīs
traductions
en arabe Fāris al-Shidyāḳ; Saʿadyā; [au Suppl.] al-Bustānī.2
voir aussi ʿArabiyya.A.II.1; Judéo-arabe.III.B
en persan Abū l-Faḍl ʿAllāmī
voir aussi Judéo-persan.I.2

BIBLIOGRAPHIE **Bibliographie**; Fahrasa

BIJOUX [au Suppl.] **Djawhar**
voir aussi Khātam
perles et pierres précieuses ʿAḳīḳ; Durr; Kūh-i Nūr; Luʾluʾ; Mardjān
voir aussi Dhahab; Fiḍḍa; Ḥadjar; Kahrubā; Maʿdin.II

BIRMANIE Arakan; **Birmanie**; Mergui; Rangoun

BOTANIQUE Adwiya; al-ʿAshshāb; Nabāt
et → AGRICULTURE; FLORE; MÉDECINE; PHARMACOLOGIE
botanistes Abū ʿUbayd al-Bakrī; al-Dīnawarī; Abū Ḥanīfa; Ibn al-Bayṭar; [au Suppl.] al-Ghāfiḳī; Ibn al-Rūmiyya
voir aussi Abū l-Khayr al-Ishbīlī; Filāḥa; Nīḳūlāʾūs

BULGARIE **Bulgarie**; Pomáks
voir aussi Küčük Ḳaynardja; Muhādjir.2; Muslimūn.I.B.5
fleuves Merič
toponymes Burgas; Deli-Orman; Dobrudja; Filibe; Hezārghrad; Küstendil; Newrokop; Nīkbūlī; ʿOthmān Pazar; Plewna; Rusčuk

BYZANTINS Biṭrīḳ; Ḳayṣar; Rūm
voir aussi Anadolu.III.1 et 2; Hiba.I; Iznīḳ; Ḳalāwdhiya; Ḳubrus; (al-)Ḳusṭanṭīniyya; al-Maṣṣīṣa; Muʾta; Nauplion; [au Suppl.] Djabala b. al-Ḥārith;
et → PALESTINE; SYRIE; TURQUIE
alliés Djarādjima; Djarrāḥides; Ghassān; al-Ḥārith b. Djabala; Kinda.1; Salīḥ; [au Suppl.] Djabala b. al-Ḥārith
militaires Alay; Lamas-ṣū; Malāzgird.II; Nafṭ.II; [au Suppl.] Dhāt al-Ṣawārī
voir aussi al-ʿAwāṣim; Cilicie; Ṣāʾifa.1

C

CADEAUX **Hiba**
voir aussi Bakhshīsh; Nithār; Pīshkash; Rashwa

CALIFAT Ahl al-Ḥall wa-l-ʿAḳd; Bayʿa; Ḥādjib.I; Ḥarb.II; Hiba.I; Imāma; Ḳaḍīb; Kātib; **Khalīfa**; Libās.I; Madjlis.I; Marāsim.1; Mawākib.I
voir aussi Amīr al-Muʾminīn; Ghulām.I; Khilʿa.2; Laḳab.II; Māl al-Bayʿa; *et* → CÉRÉMONIES DE LA COUR

ʿAbbāsides (750-1258) **ʿAbbāsides**; Baghdād; Dīwān.I; Ḥādjib.I; Khalīfa.I.B; Marāsim.1; Mawākib.I; Muṣādara.2; Musawwida; Naḳīb.1; Naḳīb al-Ashrāf.1; Sāmarrāʾ
voir aussi al-Abnāʾ.3; ʿAlī b. ʿAbd Allāh b. al-ʿAbbās; ʿAlides; Architecture.I.3; Ḍarība; Hāshimiyya; al-Hāshimiyya; Laḳab.II; Libās.I.D; Riḍā.2; *et* → DYNASTIES.PERSE

califes Abū l-ʿAbbās al-Saffāḥ; al-Amīn; al-Hādī ilā l-Ḥaḳḳ; Hārūn al-Rashīd; al-Ḳādir bi-llāh; al-Ḳāhir bi-llāh; al-Ḳāʾim bi-Amr Allāh; al-Mahdī; al-Maʾmūn; al-Manṣūr; al-Muhtadī; al-Muḳtadī; al-Muḳtadir; al-Muktafī bi-llāh; al-Muktafī li-Amr Allāh; al-Muntaṣir; al-Mustaḍīʾ; al-Mustaʿīn (Ier); al-Mustaʿīn (II); al-Mustakfī; al-Mustandjid (Ier); al-Mustandjid (II); al-Mustanṣir (Ier); al-Mustanṣir (II); al-Mustarshid; al-Mustaʿṣim bi-llāh; al-Mustaẓhir bi-llāh; al-Muʿtaḍid bi-llāh; al-Muʿtamid ʿalā llāh; al-Muʿtaṣim bi-llāh; al-Mutawakkil ʿalā llāh; al-Muʿtazz bi-llāh; al-Muṭīʿ li-llāh; al-Muttaḳī li-llāh; al-Nāṣir li-Dīn Allāh, Abū l-ʿAbbās; al-Rāḍī bi-llāh; al-Rāshid
voir aussi ʿAbd Allāh b. ʿAlī; Būrān; al-Khayzurān; Muḥammad b. ʿAlī b. ʿAbd Allāh; al-Muwaffaḳ; al-Ruṣāfa.2

vizirs Abū ʿAbd Allāh Yaʿḳūb; Abū Salāma al-Khallāl; Abū ʿUbayd Allāh; ʿAḍud al-Dīn; ʿAlī b. ʿĪsā; al-Barāmika.3; al-Barīdī; al-Djardjarāʾī.1-3; al-Faḍl b. Marwān; al-Faḍl b. al-Rabīʿ; al-Faḍl b. Sahl; al-Fayḍ b. Abī Ṣāliḥ; Ḥamīd b. al-ʿAbbās; Hibat Allāh b. Muḥammad; Ibn al-Alḳamī; Ibn al-Baladī; Ibn al-Furāt; Ibn Hubayra; Ibn Khāḳan.II et III; Ibn Makhlad; Ibn Muḳla; Ibn al-Muslima; Ibn al-Zayyāt; al-Iskāfī, Abū l-Faḍl; al-Iskāfī, Abū Isḥāḳ; Ismāʿīl b. Bulbul; al-Khaṣībī; al-Rabīʿ b. Yūnus; Rabīb al-Dawla; al-Rūdhrāwarī
voir aussi al-Djahshiyārī; Hilāl al-Ṣābiʾ; Khātam

secrétaires Aḥmad b. Abī Khālid; Aḥmad b. Yūsuf; ʿAmr b. Masʿada; al-Ḥasan b. Sahl; Ibn al-Djarrāḥ; Ibn Khāḳan.I et IV; Ibn al-Māshiṭa; al-Mūriyānī

historiens des al-Djahshiyārī; Ibn Abī l-Dam; Ibn Abī Ṭāhir Ṭayfūr; Ibn al-Djawzī; Ibn al-Naṭṭāḥ; Ibn al-Sāʿī; Ibn al-Ṭiḳṭaḳā; al-Madāʾinī; Ṣābiʾ.3.4

autres personnages al-ʿAbbās b. ʿAmr; al-ʿAbbās b. al-Maʾmūn; al-ʿAbbās b. Muḥammad; ʿAbd Allāh b. ʿAlī; ʿAbd al-Djabbār b. ʿAbd al-Raḥmān; ʿAbd al-Malik b. Ṣāliḥ; Abū ʿAwn; ʿAlī al-Riḍā; Badjkam; Badr al-Kharshanī; Bughā al-Kabīr; Bughā al-Sharābī; Dulafides; al-Fatḥ b. Khāḳān; Harthama b. Aʿyan; al-Ḥasan b. Zayd b. al-Ḥasan; Ḥātim b. Harthama; Ḥumayd b. ʿAbd al-Ḥamīd; Ibn Abī l-Shawārib; Ibn Buhlūl;

Ibn al-Djaṣṣāṣ.II; Ibn Ḥamdūn; Ibn Māhān; Ibn al-Mudabbir; Ibn al-Muʿtazz; Ibn Rāʾiḳ; Ibn Thawāba; Ibrāhīm b. ʿAbd Allāh; ʿĪsā b. Mūsā; ʿĪsā b. al-Shaykh; Ḳaḥṭaba; al-Ḳāsim b. ʿĪsā; Maʿn b. Zāʾida; al-Mubarḳaʿ; Muhallabides; Muḥammad b. ʿAbd Allāh (al-Nafs al-Zakiyya); Muḥammad b. Ṭughdj al-Ikhshīd; Muḥammad b. Yāḳūt; Muʾnis al-Faḥl; Muʾnis al-Muẓaffar; al-Muwaffaḳ; Naṣr b. Shabath; al-Nāṭiḳ bi-l-Ḥaḳḳ; al-Nūsharī; Rāfiʿ b. Harthama; Rāfiʿ b. al-Layth b. Naṣr b. Sayyār; al-Rāwandiyya; Rawḥ b. Ḥātim; Sādjides; Ṣāliḥ b. ʿAlī; [au Suppl.] Abū Manṣūr Ibn Yūsuf; Aytākh al-Turkī; Badr al-Muʿtaḍidī; al-Dāmaghānī.1 et 2; al-Ghiṭrīf b. ʿAṭāʾ; Ibn Dirham

Fāṭimides (909-1171) Dīwan.I et II.II; **Fāṭimides**; Ḥādjib.IV, Ḥidjāb.II; al-Ḳāhira; Khalīfa.I.D; Libās.I.E; Marāsim.1; Mawākib.I

voir aussi Laḳab.II; Ṣāḥib al-Bāb

califes Abū ʿAbd Allāh al-Shīʿī; al-ʿĀḍid li-Dīni llāh; al-Āmir; al-ʿAzīz bi-llāh; al-Ḥāfiẓ; al-Ḥākim bi-Amr Allāh; al-Ḳāʾim bi-Amr Allāh; al-Mahdī ʿUbayd Allāh; al-Manṣūr bi llāh; al-Muʿizz li-Dīn Allāh; al-Mustaʿlī bi-llāh; al-Mustanṣir (Ier)

vizirs ʿAbbās b. Abī l-Futūḥ; al-ʿĀdil b. al-Salār; al-Afḍal b. Badr al-Djamālī; al-Afḍal (Kutayfāt); Badr al-Djamālī; Bahrām; al-Baṭāʾiḥī; Ḍirgham; Djabr b. al-Ḳāsim; al-Djardjarāʾī.4; Ibn Killis; Ibn Maṣāl; Ruzzīk Ibn Ṭalāʾiʿ; [au Suppl.] Ibn Khalaf.II

secrétaires Ibn Mammātī; Ibn al-Ṣayrafī; [au Suppl.] Ibn Khalaf, Abū l-Ḥasan

historiens des Ibn al-Ṭuwayr; al-Maḳrīzī; al-Musabbiḥī

voir aussi Djawdhar

autres personnages Abū Yazīd al-Nukkārī; Bardjawān; Djawdhar; Djawhar al-Ṣiḳillī; Khalaf b. Mulāʿib; al-Kirmānī; Nizār b. al-Mustanṣir; al-Nuʿmān

voir aussi al-Farghānī

les Califes orthodoxes (632-661)

califes Abū Bakr; ʿAlī b. Abī Ṭālib

voir aussi Ḥarūrāʾ; Ibn Muldjam; Khalīfa.I.A; al-Saḳīfa

autres personnages Abān b. ʿUthmān; ʿAbd Allāh b. al-ʿAbbās; ʿAbd Allāh b. ʿĀmir; ʿAbd Allāh b. Saʿd; ʿAbd Allāh b. Salām; ʿAbd Allāh b. Wahb; ʿAbd al-Raḥmān b. ʿAwf; ʿAbd al-Raḥmān b. Samura; Abū l-Aswad al-Duʾalī; Abū Ayyūb al-Anṣārī; Abū l-Dunyā; Abū ʿUbayda al-Djarrāḥ; al-Aḥnaf b. Ḳays; al-Aḳraʿ b. Ḥābis; ʿAmr b. al-ʿĀṣ; al-Ashʿarī, Abū Mūsā; al-Ashʿath; al-Ashtar; al-Bāhilī; Ḥabīb b. Maslama; al-Ḳaʿḳāʿ b. ʿAmr; Khālid b. al-Walīd; Muḥammad b. Abī Bakr; al-Muthannā b. Ḥāritha; Saʿīd b. al-ʿĀṣ

et → MUḤAMMAD, LE PROPHÈTE.COMPAGNONS DU PROPHÈTE *et* FAMILLE DU PROPHÈTE

Umayyades (661-750) Dima<u>sh</u>ḳ; Dīwān.I; Hā<u>dj</u>ib.I; <u>Kh</u>alīfa.I.A; Mawlā.II.2; [au
Suppl.] Bādiya
voir aussi Architecture.I.2; Ḳays ʿAylān; Libās.I.D; Marwānides; *et* →
DYNASTIES.ESPAGNE ET AFRIQUE DU NORD
califes ʿAbd al-Malik b. Marwān; Hi<u>sh</u>ām; Marwān Iᵉʳ b. al-Ḥakam; Marwān
II; Muʿāwiya Iᵉʳ; Muʿāwiya II
voir aussi Būṣīr; al-Ruṣāfa.3
historiens des ʿAwāna b. al-Ḥakam; al-Azdī
autres personnages ʿAbbād b. Ziyād; al-ʿAbbās b. al-Walīd; ʿAbd Allāh b.
ʿAbd al-Malik; ʿAbd Allāh b. Hammām; ʿAbd Allāh b. Ḥanẓala; ʿAbd
Allāh b. <u>Kh</u>āzim; ʿAbd Allāh b. Muṭīʿ; ʿAbd Allāh b. al-Zubayr; ʿAbd al-
ʿAzīz b. al-Ḥa<u>dj</u><u>dj</u>ā<u>dj</u>; ʿAbd al-ʿAzīz b. Marwān; ʿAbd al-ʿAzīz b. al-
Walīd; ʿAbd al-Raḥmān b. <u>Kh</u>ālid b. al-Walīd; ʿAmr b. Saʿīd; Asad b.
ʿAbd Allāh; al-Aṣamm.1; Bal<u>dj</u>; Bi<u>sh</u>r b. Marwān; Bi<u>sh</u>r b. al-Walīd;
Bukayr b. Māhān; Bukayr b. Wi<u>sh</u>āḥ; Busr b. Abī Arṭāt; al-Ḍaḥḥāk b.
Ḳays al-Fihrī; al-<u>Dj</u>arrāḥ b. ʿAbd Allāh; al-<u>Dj</u>unayd b. ʿAbd Allāh; al-
Ḥa<u>dj</u><u>dj</u>ā<u>dj</u> b. Yūsuf; Ḥanẓala b. Ṣafwān; al-Ḥāri<u>th</u> b. Suray<u>dj</u>; Ḥassān b.
Mālik; Ḥassān b. al-Nuʿmān al-<u>Gh</u>assānī; al-Ḥurr b. Yazīd; al-Ḥusayn b.
Numayr; Ibn al-A<u>sh</u>ʿath; Ibn al-Ḥaḍramī; Ibn Hubayra; <u>Kh</u>ālid al-Ḳasrī;
<u>Kh</u>ālid b. Yazīd; Kul<u>th</u>ūm b. ʿIyāḍ; Ḳurra b. <u>Sh</u>arīk; Ḳutayba b. Muslim;
Maʿn b. Zāʾida; Masāmiʿa; Maslama b. ʿAbd al-Malik b. Marwān;
Maymūn b. Mihrān; Muʿāwiya b. Hi<u>sh</u>ām; al-Mu<u>gh</u>īra b. <u>Sh</u>uʿba;
Muhallabides; Muḥammad b. al-Ḳāsim; Muslim b. ʿUḳba; Naṣr b.
Sayyār; al-Nuʿmān b. Ba<u>sh</u>īr; Rawḥ b. Zinbāʿ; Salm b. Ziyād b. Abīhi; [au
Suppl.] ʿAdī b. Arṭāt
voir aussi al-Baṭṭāl; Iyās b. Muʿāwiya
traités sur al-Ḳalḳa<u>sh</u>andī.I

CARTOGRAPHIE <u>Kh</u>arīṭa
et → GÉOGRAPHIE; NAVIGATION
cartographes al-Falakī; Ibn Sarābiyūn; Meḥmed Reʾīs; Pīrī Reʾīs

CAUCASE Ā<u>dh</u>arbay<u>dj</u>ān.II; Armīniya; Dā<u>gh</u>istān; **al-Ḳabḳ**; al-Kur<u>dj</u>
voir aussi al-Bāhilī; <u>Dj</u>arīda.IV; Ḥamza Beg; Ḥizb.IV; Ḳarā Bā<u>gh</u>; Muhā<u>dj</u>ir.2
géographie physique
eaux Alin<u>dj</u>aḳ; Gökče-tengiz; Ḳarā Deniz; Ḳîzîl-üzen; Ḳuban; Kur; al-Rass;
Safīd Rūd
montagnes al-Ḳabḳ
population Ab<u>kh</u>āz.2; Alān; Andi; Arči; Avares; Balkar; Čečens; Čerkesses;
Dar<u>gh</u>ins; Dido; Ingu<u>sh</u>; Kabard; Ḳapuča; Ḳaračay; Ḳarata; Ḳaytaḳ;
<u>Kh</u>aput; <u>Kh</u>em<u>sh</u>in; <u>Kh</u>inalug; <u>Kh</u>unzal; <u>Kh</u>var<u>sh</u>î; Ḳrîz; Ḳubači; Kwanadi;
Laḳ; Laz; Lez<u>gh</u>; No<u>gh</u>ay; Ossètes; Rūs; Rutul; [au Suppl.] Démographie.VI
voir aussi Ḳumuḳ

toponymes
anciens Alindjaḳ; Arrān; Bādjarwān.1; Balandjar; Dwin
actuels Akhiskha; Bāb al-Abwāb; Bākū; Bardhaʿa; Batumi; Derbend; Gandja; Ḳubba; Lankoran; Makhač-ḳalʿe; Nakhčiwān; [au Suppl.] Djulfā.I

CÉRÉMONIES DE LA COUR **Marāsim**; Mawākib
voir aussi Hiba; Khilʿa; Miẓalla; Naḳḳāra-khāna; Nithār

CHARMES Afsūn; Ḥidjāb.IV; Kabid.4; Māshāʾ Allāh; [au Suppl.] Budūḥ
voir aussi Kahrubā; Ḳarwasha; *et* → MAGIE

CHASSE Bayzara; Fahd; Khinzīr; Mahāt; Naʿām; Namir et Nimr; Salūḳī; [au Suppl] Ḍabuʿ
voir aussi Kurdes et Kurdistān.IVC.5
traités sur Kushādjim; [au Suppl.] Ibn Manglī

CHĀTIMENT (DIVIN) **ʿAdhāb**; ʿAdhāb al-Ḳabr; Djazāʾ; Falaḳa; Ḥadd; Maskh; Ṣalb
voir aussi ʿAbd.3.i; ʿĀd; Kaffāra; Ḳiyāma; Munkar wa-Nakīr; Murtadd; *et* → DROIT

CHIITES ʿAbd Allāh b. Sabaʾ; ʿAlides; Ghulāt; Imāma; Ismāʿīliyya; Ithnā ʿAshariyya; Sabʿiyya
voir aussi Abū l-Sarāyā al-Shaybānī; ʿAlī b. Abī Ṭālib; ʿAlī Mardān; Madjlis.III; [au Suppl.] Batriyya; *et* → CHIITES.SECTES
branches Ismāʿīliyya; Ithnā ʿAshariyya; Ḳarmaṭī
voir aussi Hind.V.D; *et* → CHIITES.SECTES
Duodécimains Imāma; **Ithnā ʿAshariyya**; Mudjtahid.II; Mutawālī; al-Rāfiḍa
et → CHIITES.IMAMS
Ismāʿīliyya ʿAbd Allāh b. Maymūn; Abū ʿAbd Allāh al-Shīʿī; Abū l-Khattāb al-Asadī; Allāh.III.1; (Djazīrat) al-ʿArab.VII; Bāb; Baṭiniyya; Bohorās; Dāʿī; Daʿwa; Fāṭimides; Ḥaḳāʾiḳ; Hind.V.D; Ibn ʿAttāsh; Ikhwān al-Ṣafāʾ; Imāma; **Ismāʿīliyya**; Lanbasar; Madjlis.II; al-Mahdī ʿUbayd Allāh; Malāʾika.II; Manṣūr al-Yaman; Maymūn-diz; Sabʿiyya; [au Suppl.] Dawr
voir aussi Ḥawwāʾ; Ikhlāṣ; Maṣyād; Sabʿ; Salamiyya; *et* → CALIFAT. FĀṬIMIDES; CHIITES.IMAMS
auteurs Abū Ḥātim al-Rāzī; Abū Yaʿḳūb al-Sidjzī; al-Kirmānī; al-Muʾayyad fī l-Dīn; Nāṣir-i Khusraw; [au Suppl.] al-Bazdawī; Djaʿfar b. Manṣūr al-Yaman; Idrīs b. al-Ḥasan
et → CHIITES.BRANCHES.ṬAYYIBITES

Nizārites Agha Khān; Alamūt.II; Buzurg-ummīd; Fidā'ī; Ḥasan-i Ṣabbāḥ; Ḥashīshiyya; Khōdja; Maḥallātī; Nizār b. al-Mustanṣir; Nizāriyya; Nūr al-Dīn Muḥammad II; Pīr Ṣadr al-Dīn; Pīr Shams; Rāshid al-Dīn Sinān; Rukn al-Dīn Khurshāh; Sabz ʿAlī

Qarmates (Djazīrat) al-ʿArab.VII; al-Djannābī, Abū Saʿīd; al-Djannābī, Abū Ṭāhir; Ḥamdān Ḳarmaṭ; al-Ḥasan al-Aʿṣam; **Ḳarmaṭī**

voir aussi ʿAbdān; al-Baḥrayn; Baḳliyya; Daʿwa

Septimains Sabʿiyya

voir aussi Sabʿ

Ṭayyibites al-Ḥāmidī; Luḳmāndjī; al-Makramī; Makramides; Muḥammad b. Ṭāhir al-Ḥārithī; [au Suppl.] ʿAlī b. Ḥanẓala; ʿAlī b. Muḥammad b. Djaʿfar; Amīndjī b. Djalāl

Zaydites al-Ḥasan b. Ṣāliḥ b. Ḥayy; Ibn Abī l-Ridjāl; al-Mahdī li-Dīn Allāh Aḥmad; Muḥammad b. Zayd; al-Nāṣir (li-Dīn Allāh); al-Rassī; [au Suppl.] Abū l-Barakāt; Abū l-Fatḥ al-Daylamī; Aḥmad b. ʿĪsā; Djaʿfar b. Abī Yaḥyā; al-Ḥākim al-Djushamī

voir aussi Imāma; Muṭarrifiyya; Rassides; *et* → DYNASTIES.PÉNINSULE ARABIQUE

doctrines et institutions Bāṭiniyya; Djafr; Ḳā'im Āl Muḥammad; Khalḳ.VII; Madjlis.II et III; al-Mahdī; Malā'ika.II; Mardjaʿ-i Taḳlīd; Maẓhar; Maẓlūm; Mudjtahid.II; Mutʿa.V; Radjʿa; Safīr.1; [au Suppl.] Āyatullāh

voir aussi Adhān; Ahl al-Bayt; ʿAḳīda; Bāb; Ghayba; Ḥudjdja; Imāma; ʿIlm al-Ridjāl; Imām-bārā; Imāmzāda; Mollā; *et* → THÉOLOGIE.TERMES. CHIITES

dynasties Buwayhides; Fāṭimides; Ṣafawides

voir aussi Mushaʿshaʿ

imams ʿAlī b. Abī Ṭālib; ʿAlī al-Riḍā; al-ʿAskarī; Djaʿfar al-Ṣādiḳ; (al-)Ḥasan b. ʿAlī b. Abī Ṭālib; (al-)Ḥusayn b. ʿAlī b. Abī Ṭālib; Muḥammad b. ʿAlī al-Riḍā; Muḥammad b. ʿAlī (al-Bāḳir); Muḥammad al-Ḳā'im; Mūsā al-Kāẓim

voir aussi Bāb; Ghayba; Imāmzāda; Malā'ika.II; Maẓlūm; Riḍā.2; Safīr.1

juristes al-ʿĀmilī; al-Ḥillī; al-Māmaḳānī; al-Mufīd; Muḥammad b. Makkī; [au Suppl.] Anṣārī; Bihbihānī

voir aussi ʿĀḳila; Madjlisī; Madjlisī-ya Awwal; Mardjaʿ-i Taḳlīd; Mudjtahid.II; Mutʿa.V

lieux de pèlerinage Karbalā'; Kāẓimayn; al-Nadjaf; [au Suppl.] ʿAtabāt

rituels Rawḍa-khwānī

sectes Ahl-i Ḥaḳḳ; ʿAlides; Baḳliyya; Bohorās; Djābir b. Ḥayyān; al-Djanāḥiyya; al-Djārūdiyya; Ghurābiyya; Ḥurūfiyya; Ibāḥa.II; Kaysāniyya; Khashabiyya; Khaṭṭābiyya; Khōdja; Khurramiyya; Kuraybiyya; Manṣūriyya; al-Mughīriyya; Muḥammadiyya; Mukhammisa; Muṭarrifiyya; al-Muʿtazila; Nāwūsiyya; al-Rāwandiyya; Salmāniyya

voir aussi ʿAbd Allāh b. Saba'; Bāṭiniyya; Bayān b. Samʿān; Bektāshiyya;

Ghulāt; Hind.V.D; Imām Shāh; Ḳaṭʿ; al-Kayyāl; Kāẓim Rashtī; Ḳïzïl-bāsh; Mushaʿshaʿ; [au Suppl.] Ibn Warsand; *et* → DRUZES; SECTES.ʿALIDES
Kaysāniyya Abū Hāshim; Kaysān; **Kaysāniyya**
Khaṭṭābiyya Abū l-Khaṭṭāb al-Asadī; Bashshār al-Shaʿīrī; Bazīgh b. Mūsā; **Khaṭṭābiyya**
voir aussi Mukhammisa; al-Ṣāmit
Khurramiyya Bābak; [au Suppl.] Bādhām
Mukhammisa **Mukhammisa**
voir aussi al-Muḥassin b. ʿAlī
Shaykhisme al-Aḥsāʾī; Rashtī, Sayyid Kāẓim
théologiens al-Dāmad; al-Ḥillī; Hishām b. al-Ḥakam; al-Ḥurr al-ʿĀmilī; Ibn Bābawayh(i); Ibn Shahrāshūb; al-Karakī; Kāshif al-Ghiṭāʾ; Khʷānsārī, Sayyid Mīrzā; al-Kulaynī; Lāhīdjī.II; Mīr Lawḥī; al-Mufīd; Mullā Ṣadrā Shīrāzī; [au Suppl.] Akhbāriyya; Anṣārī; al-Bazdawī; Fayḍ-i Kāshānī; Ibn Abī Djumhūr al-Aḥsāʾī; Ibn Mītham
voir aussi al-ʿAyyāshī; Ḥudjdja; Imāma; Khalḳ.VII; Mollā
du vingtième siècle Kāshānī; Khʷānsārī, Sayyid Muḥammad; Khiyābānī; Khurāsānī; Muṭahharī; Nāʾīnī; [au Suppl.] Āḳā Nadjafī; Burūdjirdī; Ḥāʾirī

CHINE Djarīda.V; Masdjid.V
voir aussi Bahādur; Khoḳand
dynasties Ḳarā Khiṭāy
voir aussi Faghfūr; Gūrkhān
géographie physique
eaux Aḳ Ṣu; Ili
personnages
pour les chefs de rebellions, voir ci-dessous
fonctionnaires P'u Shou-keng
littérateurs Liu Tchih; Ma Huan
rebellions Panthay
chefs Ma Hua-lung; Ma Ming-hsin; Ma Tchung-ying; Pai Yen-hu
toponymes
anciens Bishbalïḳ; Khansā
actuels Aḳ Ṣu; Alti Shahr; Kansu; Kāshghar; Khānbalïḳ; Khānfū; Khotan; Ḳuldja; Ning-hsia
traités sur ʿAlī Akbar Khiṭāʾī

CHRISTIANISME Ahl al-Kitāb; Dayr; Dayṣāniyya; ʿĪsā; Kanīsa; Maryam; **Naṣārā**; Rāhib; Ṣalīb
voir aussi Dhimma; Djizya; Ghiyār; al-Ḥākim bi-Amr Allāh; Ifrandj; Karshūnī; Ḳūmis; Lāhūt et Nāsūt.II; Maʿalthāyā; [au Suppl.] Dāwiyya et

Isbitāriyya; Fidāʾ; *et* → BIBLE; CROISADES; NUBIE

apologistes   Ibn Zurʿa; al-Kindī, ʿAbd al-Masīḥ

communautés   Anadolu.III.4; al-Andalus.IV; Istanbul.VII.2; Mozárabe
>   *voir aussi* Fener

confessions   Ḳibṭ; Nasṭūriyyūn
>   *et* → JUDAÏSME.SECTES JUIVES

> *catholiques*   Ba<u>sh</u>īr <u>Sh</u>ihāb II; Isḥāḳ, Adīb; Ṣābundjī; [au Suppl.] Buṭrus
>   Karāma

> *coptes*   Ibn al-ʿAssāl; Ibn Mammātī; Ibn al-Muḵaffaʿ; **Ḳibṭ**; al-Makīn b. al-
>   ʿAmīd; Māriya; al-Mufaḍḍal b. Abī l-Faḍāʾil; [au Suppl.] Ibn Kabar; Ibn
>   al-Rāhib
>   *et* → ÉGYPTE.TOPONYMES; NUBIE

> *jacobites*   Ibn al-ʿIbrī; Ibn Zurʿa
>   *voir aussi* al-Kindī, ʿAbd al-Masīḥ; Paṭrīk

> *maronites*   Farḥāt; Isṭifān al-Duwayhī; al-Rayḥānī; Salīm al-Naḳḳā<u>sh</u>; [au
>   Suppl.] Abū <u>Sh</u>abaka; al-Bustānī
>   *voir aussi* B<u>sh</u>arrā; Durūz.Période ottomane; Paṭrīk; *et* → LIBAN

> *melkites*   Abū Ḳurra; al-Anṭāḵī; Mī<u>kh</u>āʾīl Ṣabbā<u>gh</u>; al-Muḳawḳis; Saʿīd b. al-
>   Biṭrīḵ; [au Suppl.] Ibn al-Ḳuff
>   *voir aussi* Ma<u>sh</u>āḳa; Paṭrīk

> *monophysites*   al-A<u>kh</u>ṭal; al-Ḳuṭāmī

> *nestoriens*   Ibn Buṭlān; Ibn al-Ṭayyib; al-Kindī, ʿAbd al-Masīḥ; Mattā b.
>   Yūnus; **Nasṭūriyyūn**; Sābūr b. Sahl

> *non-spécifiés*   Baḥdal; Ibn al-Tilmī<u>dh</u>; al-Masīḥī; Petrus Alfonsi; [au Suppl.]
>   Ḥubay<u>sh</u> b. al-Ḥasan al-Dima<u>sh</u>ḳī; Ibn al-Ṣuḳāʿī

> *orthodoxes grecs*   Gagauz
>   *voir aussi* Paṭrīk

> *protestants*   Fāris al-<u>Sh</u>idyāḵ; Ma<u>sh</u>āḳa; [au Suppl.] al-Bustānī.2
>   *voir aussi* Nimr

couvents   **Dayr**; Dayr al-<u>Dj</u>ā<u>th</u>alīḵ; Dayr Kaʿb; Dayr Ḳunnā; Dayr Murrān; Dayr
>   Samʿān
>   *voir aussi* <u>Kh</u>ānḵāh; Rāhib

> *du vingtième siècle*   al-<u>Kh</u>ūrī; [au Suppl.] Abū <u>Sh</u>abaka; Abyaḍ
>   *voir aussi* al-Maʿlūf

polémiques
> *anti-juives*   Petrus Alfonsi

pré-islamique   Abraha; ʿAdī b. Zayd; ʿAmr b. ʿAdī; ʿAmr b. Hind; Baḥīrā;
>   Bahrām
>   *voir aussi* <u>Gh</u>assān; La<u>kh</u>mides

saints   <u>Dj</u>ird<u>j</u>īs; <u>Dj</u>uray<u>dj</u>

CHYPRE   **Ḳubrus**; Ma<u>dj</u>lis.IV.A.24

toponymes
villes Lefḳō<u>sh</u>a; Ma<u>gh</u>ō<u>sh</u>a

CIRCONCISION <u>Kh</u>afḍ; **<u>Kh</u>itān**
voir aussi ʿAbdī; ʿAlī; Kurdes et Kurdistān.IV.A.1; Mawākib.IV.11

COMMERCE Bayʿ; Imtiyāzāt; Kasb; Ḳirāḍ
voir aussi In<u>sh</u>āʾ; *et* → DROIT.DROIT CONTRACTUEL; INDUSTRIE
commerce Ḳahwa; Kārimī; Ḳuṭn; Lubān
voir aussi Kalah; Kārwān; Ḳaysāriyya; Kirmān; Mīnāʾ; Ṣafawides.II
fonctions Dallāl; Malik al-Tu<u>dj</u><u>dj</u>ār
termes juridico-commercials Mufāwaḍa; Mu<u>sh</u>āraka

COMMUNAUTÉ DES ÉTATS INDÉPENDANTS → ASIE CENTRALE; CAUCASE; COMMUNISME; EUROPE.ORIENTALE

COMMUNICATIONS Barīd; Ḥamām; Manār
voir aussi Anadolu.III.5; *et* → TRANSPORT

COMMUNISME Ḥizb.I
voir aussi Lahūtī

COMPTABILITÉ Muḥāsaba.II; Mustawfī
voir aussi Daftar; *et* → ADMINISTRATION.FINANCIÈRE

CONGO **Congo**; al-Mur<u>dj</u>ibī

CORAN Allāh.I; Āya; Fāṣila; Iʿ<u>dj</u>āz; Ḳirāʾa; **al-Ḳurʾān**; Muḳaṭṭaʿāt; Muṣḥaf; Nas<u>kh</u>
voir aussi ʿArabiyya.A.II; Basmala; Faḍīla; Hamza; In<u>dj</u>īl; Iṣlāḥ.I.B.1; <u>Kh</u>alḳ.II; <u>Kh</u>awāṣṣ al-Ḳurʾān
caractère créé Miḥna
voir aussi <u>Dj</u>ahmiyya
commentaires
en arabe ʿAbd al-Razzāḳ al-Ḳā<u>sh</u>ānī; Abū l-Faḍl ʿAllāmī; Abū Ḥayyān al-<u>Gh</u>arnāṭī; Abū l-Lay<u>th</u> al-Samarḳandī; Abū l-Suʿūd; Abū ʿUbayda; al-ʿAskarī.II; al-Ba<u>gh</u>awī; Baḳī b. Ma<u>kh</u>lad; al-Bayḍāwī; al-Bulḳīnī.4; al-Dāmād; al-Dārimī; <u>Dj</u>īwan; Fa<u>kh</u>r al-Dīn al-Rāzī; Fayḍī; <u>Gh</u>ulām Ḥusayn <u>Kh</u>ān Ṭabāṭabāʾī; Gīsū Darāz; Gūrānī; Ibn Abī l-Ri<u>dj</u>āl; Ibn ʿA<u>dj</u>ība; Ibn Barra<u>dj</u>ān; Ibn Ka<u>th</u>īr, ʿImād al-dīn; Ismāʿīl Ḥaḳḳī; al-Kalbī.I; Kalīm Allāh al-<u>Dj</u>ahānābādī; Kemāl Pa<u>sh</u>a-zāde; al-Ḳurṭubī, Abū ʿAbd Allāh; al-Ḳu<u>sh</u>ayrī.I; al-Maḥallī; al-Māturīdī; Mu<u>dj</u>āhid b.

D̲j̲abr al-Makkī; Mud̲j̲īr al-Dīn al-ʿUlaymī; Muḥsin-i Fayḍ-i Kās̲h̲ānī; Muḳātil b. Sulaymān; al-Nīsābūrī; al-Rāg̲h̲ib al-Iṣfahānī; al-Rummānī; Sahl al-Tustarī; [au Suppl.] ʿAbd al-Wahhāb Buk̲h̲ārī; Abū l-Fatḥ al-Daylamī; al-Aṣamm

voir aussi ʿAbd Allāh b. al-ʿAbbās; Abū Nuʿaym al-Mulāʾī; Aḥmadiyya; al-ʿAlamī; al-Dihlawī, S̲h̲āh Walī Allāh; D̲j̲afr; D̲j̲ilwatiyya; Ḥād̲j̲d̲j̲ī Pas̲h̲a; Hind.V.E; Ibn Masʿūd; Ḳuṭb al-Dīn S̲h̲īrāzī; al-Manār

19e-20e siècles al-Ālūsī.II; Aṭfiyās̲h̲; Mawdūdī; Muḥammad b. Aḥmad al-Iskandarānī; Muḥammad Abū Zayd; Muḥammad Farīd Wad̲j̲dī; [au Suppl.] D̲j̲awharī, Ṭanṭāwī

en ourdou As̲h̲raf ʿAlī

en persan Abū l-Futūḥ al-Rāzī; al-Dawlatābādī; D̲j̲āmī; Kās̲h̲ifī; al-Maybudī.I; Muṣannifak

en turque Aḳ Ḥiṣārī.b

histoires ʿĀd; Ādam; Aṣḥāb al-Kahf; Ayyūb; Bilḳīs; Dāwūd; D̲j̲ālūt; Firʿawn; Ḥābīl wa-Ḳābīl; Ḥawwāʾ; Ibrāhīm; ʿĪsā; Iskandar; al-K̲h̲aḍir; Lūṭ; Maryam; Mūsā; Nūḥ

voir aussi Ḳiṣaṣ al-Anbiyāʾ; *et* → BIBLE.PERSONNAGES BIBLIQUES

lecteurs ʿAbd Allāh b. Abī Isḥāḳ; Abūʿ Amr b. al-ʿAlāʾ; al-Aʿmas̲h̲; ʿĀṣim; al-Dānī; Ḥamza b. Ḥabīb; Ibn ʿĀmir; ʿĪsā b. ʿUmar; al-Kisāʾī; Nāfiʿ b. ʿAbd al-Raḥmān; al-Sad̲j̲āwandī, Abū ʿAbd Allāh

voir aussi Abū l-ʿĀliya al-Riyāḥī; al-Dāraḳuṭnī; Ḥafs b. Sulaymān; Ibn al-D̲j̲azarī; Ibn al-Faḥḥām; Ibn Mud̲j̲āhid; Ibn S̲h̲anabūd̲h̲; al-Ḳasṭallānī; Makkī b. Abī Ṭālib; al-Malaṭī; Mud̲j̲āhid b. D̲j̲abr al-Makkī; [au Suppl.] Ibn Miḳsam

lecture Adāʾ; Ḥarf; Ḳaṭʿ; K̲h̲atma; **Ḳirāʾa**

recensions ʿAbd Allāh b. al-Zubayr; ʿAbd al-Malik b. Marwān; Abū l-Dardāʾ; ʿĀʾis̲h̲a bint Abī Bakr; ʿĀṣim; al-Dimyāṭī; al-Ḥad̲j̲d̲j̲ād̲j̲ b. Yūsuf; Ibn Masʿūd; Nāfiʿ b. ʿAbd al-Raḥmān

voir aussi Abū l-Aswad al-Duʾalī; ʿArabiyya.II.1 et 2; al-Ḥuṣrī.II

sourates al-Aḥḳāf; Aṣḥāb al-Kahf; Fātiḥa; al-Fīl; G̲h̲ās̲h̲iya; Kawt̲h̲ar; Luḳmān; al-Muʿawwid̲h̲atān[i]; al-Muddat̲h̲t̲h̲ir et al-Muzzammil; al-Musabbiḥāt; Sad̲j̲da; al-Ṣāffāt

voir aussi Ḥayawān.III

termes Aḥkām; ʿĀlam; Amr; al-Aʿrāf; ʿAṣā; Aṣḥāb al-Kahf; Aṣḥāb al-Rass; Aṣḥāb al-Uk̲h̲dūd; Āya; Baḥīra; al-Baḥrayn; Baʿl; Barāʾa; Baraka; Barzak̲h̲; Birr; Dābba; Daʿwa; D̲h̲arra; Dīn; D̲j̲ahannam; D̲j̲āhiliyya; D̲j̲anna; D̲j̲inn; Dunyā; Faḳīr; Farāʾiḍ; Fitna; Fiṭra; Furḳān; al-G̲h̲ayb; Ḥadd; Ḥaḳḳ; Ḥanīf; Hātif; Ḥawārī; Ḥayāt; Ḥid̲j̲āb; Ḥisāb; Ḥizb; Ḥud̲j̲d̲j̲a; Ḥūr; Iblīs; Īlāf; Ilhām; ʿIlliyyūn; Kaffāra; Kāfir; Kalima; Ḳarīn; Ḳarya; Ḳawm; Ḳayyim; K̲h̲alḳ; K̲h̲aṭīʾa; Ḳiyāma; Kursī; Ḳuwwa; Lawḥ; Mad̲j̲nūn; Maḳām Ibrāhīm; Milla; Millet; Miskīn; Mīt̲h̲āḳ; al-Munāfiḳūn.1; Nad̲h̲īr; Nafs.1; Nār; Raḥma; Rizḳ;

Rudjūʿ; Rukn; Sabab.4; Ṣabr; Ṣadr; al-Ṣāffāt; Ṣaḥīfa; Sakīna; Salām; al-Ṣāliḥūn; [au Suppl.] Asāṭir al-Awwalīn
voir aussi Ḥikāya.I; Samāʾ.1
traductions al-Ḳurʾān.I
voir aussi Aljamía
en anglais Aḥmadiyya; Pickthall
en malais ʿAbd al-Raʾūf al-Sinkilī
en ourdou ʿAbd al-Ḳādir Dihlawī; Djawān; Rafīʿ al-Dīn
en persan al-Dihlawī, Shāh Walī Allāh
voir aussi Khaṭṭ.II
en swahilie Kenya (923b)

CORPORATIONS
arabes Amīn; ʿArīf; Futuwwa.2 et 3; Ḥammāl; Ḥarfūsh; Khātam; Khayyāṭ
turques Akhī; Akhī Baba; Anadolu.III.6; Ḥarīr.II; Ketkhudā.II; [au Suppl.] Ikhtiyāriyya; Inḥiṣār
voir aussi Akhī Ewrān; ʿĀlima; Čāʾūsh; Kannās; Mawākib.IV.4; Muhr.1

COSMÉTIQUE Kuḥl
voir aussi Khiḍāb

COSMOGRAPHIE ʿAdjāʾib; ʿĀlam; Falak; Ḳāf; Samāʾ.1
voir aussi Djughrāfiyā; al-Khaḍir; Kharīṭa; Kura; Makka.IV; *et* → ASTROLOGIE; ASTRONOMIE; GÉOGRAPHIE
traités sur al-Dimashḳī; al-Ḳazwīnī, Zakariyyāʾ; al-Kharaḳī
voir aussi Kitāb al-Djilwa

CÔTE D'IVOIRE **Côte d'Ivoire**; Kong

COULEUR **Lawn**; Musawwida
et → TEINTURE
couleurs Asfar

COUTUMES **ʿĀda**; Adab
voir aussi ʿAbd al-Raḥmān al-Fāsī; ʿĀshūrāʾ.II; Hiba; Ḥidjāb.I; Īdjāra; Khilʿa; Mandīl; *et* → DROIT.DROIT COUTUMIER
coutumes tribales ʿAbābda; al-Dhunūb (Dafn-); Khāwa; Muwāraba; [au Suppl.] ʿĀr
voir aussi Īdjāra

CRÉATION **Ibdāʿ**; **Khalḳ**
voir aussi Ḥudūth al-ʿĀlam; Insān

CRÉTE **Iḳriṭish**
voir aussi Abū Ḥafṣ ʿUmar al-Ballūṭī
toponymes
villes Ḳandiya

CROISADES **Croisades**; [au Suppl.] Dāwiyya et Isbitāriyya
voir aussi al-ʿĀdil.1; al-Afḍal b. Badr al-Djamālī; ʿAntar; Ayyūbides; Balak; Baybars Ier; Fāṭimides; Ifrandj; Ḳalāwūn; Ḳi̊li̊dj Arslan Ier; Nūr al-Dīn Maḥmūd b. Zankī; Ṣalāḥ al-Dīn; *et* → *l'entrée Toponymes sous* PALESTINE *et* SYRIE
batailles al-Manṣūra; Mardj al-Ṣuffar; Nīkbūlī
châteaux al-Dārūm; Ḥārim; Ḥiṣn al-Akrād; Ḳalʿat al-Shaḳīf; Ṣāfītha
conquêtes ʿAkkā; Anadolu.III.1; ʿĀsḳalān; Ayla; Ghazza; Ḥayfā; Ḳayṣariyya; al-Khalīl; Ḳubrus.II; al-ḲudsA.I.10; Ludd; Maʿarrat al-Nuʿmān
historiens des Ibn al-Ḳalānisī
voir aussi al-Nuwayrī, Muḥammad

CRYPTOGRAPHIE **Muʿammā**; Ramz.2

CUISINE **Maṭbakh**
aliments **Ghidhāʾ**; Kabid.5; Khubz; Kuskusū; Mishmish; Nārandj; al-Ruzz; al-Samn; [au Suppl.] Basbās; Djawz; Ḥays; Hindibāʾ
voir aussi Baḳḳāl; Filāḥa; Ḳamḥ; Maḍīra; Milḥ; Naḥl; [au Suppl.] Ibn Shaḳrūn
boissons Čāy; Ḳahwa; Khamr; Kumi̊s; **Mashrūbāt**; Nabīdh
voir aussi Naḥl; [au Suppl.] Čāy-khāna
épices Kammūn; Ḳaranful; [au Suppl.] **Afāwīh**; Dār Ṣīnī
voir aussi Kārimī; Ḳūṣ; Milḥ
prohibitions Ghidhāʾ.III et IV.7; Ḳahwa; Khamr; Mashrūbāt; Mayta; Nabīdh
voir aussi Dhabīḥa.1; Ḥayawān.IV; Nadjis; *et* → *articles individuels sous* ANIMAUX

D

DÉSERTS al-Aḥḳāf; Biyābānak; al-Dahnāʾ; Ḳaraḳum; Ḳi̊zi̊l-ḳum; al-Naḳb; al-Rubʿ al-Khālī; Sāḥil; al-Ṣaḥrāʾ
voir aussi (Djazīrat) al-ʿArab.II; Badw.II; Ḥarra; Khabrāʾ; Reg; Samūm

DICTIONNAIRE **Ḳāmūs**
voir aussi Fāris al-Shidyāḳ; *et* → LEXICOGRAPHIE

DIPLOMATIE Imtiyāzāt; Mübādele

voir aussi Amān; Bālyōs, Berātlî; Daftar; Hiba; Inshā'; Kātib; Ḳawwās; Mandats
diplomats Consul; Elči; Safīr.2
relations diplomatiques Aḥmad Rasmī; Ibn Faḍlān; Meḥmed Yirmisekiz; [au Suppl.] al-Ghazzāl; Ibn ʿUthmān al-Miknāsī

DIVINATION **Kihāna**
voir aussi Djafr; Ibn Barradjān; Malāḥim; Nudjūm (Aḥkām al-); *et* → ASTROLOGIE; RÊVES
devins ʿArrāf; Kāhin
pratiques Fa'l; Firāsa; Ghurāb; Ḥisāb al-Djummal; Ḥurūf; Ikhtilādj; Istiḳsām; ʿIyāfa; al-Kaff; Katif; Khaṭṭ; Khawāṣṣ al-Ḳur'ān; Ḳiyāfa; Ḳurʿa; Mā'.I; Riyāfa
voir aussi Būḳalā; Ikhtiyārāt; Mir'āt
traités sur Fāl-nāma; Ibn al-Bannā' al-Marrakushī; Malḥama; [au Suppl.] Ibn ʿAzzūz
voir aussi Djafr; Nudjūm (Aḥkām al-)

DIVORCE Barā'a; Faskh
voir aussi ʿAbd.3; ʿĀda; Ghā'ib; Ḥaḍāna; Ibn Suraydj; ʿIdda; ʿIwaḍ; Ḳasam; Liʿān; al-Mar'a.II; Rapak

DOCUMENTS ʿAlāma; **Diplomatique**; Farmān; Inshā'; Kātib; Manshūr; Papyrus; [au Suppl.] Dabīr
voir aussi Barā'a; Ḳaṭʿ; *et* → ADMINISTRATION.DOCUMENTS; ÉCRITURE
ottomans ʿArḍ Ḥāl; Berāt; **Diplomatique**.IV; Farmān.II; Irāde; Khaṭṭ-î Humāyūn et Khaṭṭ-î Sherīf
et → EMPIRE OTTOMAN.ADMINISTRATION

DROGUES **Adwiya**; [au Suppl.] Anzarūt
voir aussi Kahrubā; Kuḥl; *et* → MÉDECINE; PHARMACOLOGIE
narcotiques Afyūn; Bandj; Ḥashīsh; Ḳāt
voir aussi Filāḥa.III

DROIT ʿĀda; Dustūr; **Fiḳh**; Idjmāʿ; **Ḳānūn**.I; Ḳiyās; Maḥkama
voir aussi Aṣḥab al-Ra'y; Ḥuḳūḳ; *et* → HÉRITAGE
pour les questions légales, voir ʿAbd.3; Djāsūs; Filāḥa.I.4; Ḥarb.I; Ḥarīr; In Shā' Allāh; Intiḥār; Ḳabr; Kāfir; Khāliṣa; Khiṭba; Mā'; al-Mar'a; Murtadd; Raḍāʿ; Rāḳid; Rashwa; Safar.1
ancien droit religieux Abū Ḥanīfa; Abū Yūsuf Yaʿḳūb; al-Ashʿarī, Abū Burda; ʿAṭā' b. Abī Rabāḥ; al-Awzāʿī; Ibn Abī Laylā.2; Ibn Shubruma; al-Layth b. Saʿd; Mālik b. Anas; Maymūn b. Mihrān; al-Nakhaʿī; [au Suppl.] Fuḳahā' al-

Madīna al-Sabʿa; Ibn Abī l-Zinād
droit 'anglo-mohammedan' ʿĀda.III; Amīr ʿAlī; Munṣif
voir aussi Ḥanafiyya
droit contractuel ʿAḳd; ʿĀriyya; Bayʿ; Ḍamān; Dhimma; Fāsid wa-Bāṭil; Faskh; Hiba; Īdjāb; Īdjār; Iḳrār; Inkār; ʿIwaḍ; Kafāla; Khiyār; Ḳirāḍ; Muʿāmalāt; Muʿāwaḍa.3; Muḍāraba; Mufāwaḍa; Mughārasa; Mushāraka; Rahn; [au Suppl.] Dayn; Ghārūḳa
voir aussi ʿAmal.4; Djāʾiz; Ghaṣb; Ḳabḍ.I; Ḳasam; Maḍmūn; [au Suppl.] Ikrāh
contrat de louage Adjr; **Īdjār**; Kirāʾ; Musāḳāt; Muzāraʿa; [au Suppl.] Ḥikr; Inzāl
contrat de vente Barāʾa; **Bayʿ**; Iḳāla; ʿIwaḍ; Muʿāwaḍa.1; Muwāḍaʿa; Salam; [au Suppl.] Darak
voir aussi Ḍarūra; Ildjāʾ; Mukhāṭara; Ṣafḳa; Salaf
droit coutumier **ʿĀda**; Dakhīl; Ḳānūn.IV; [au Suppl.] Djirga
voir aussi Baranta; Berbères.IV; al-Māmī; al-Marʾa.II; Mushāʿ
droit de la procédure ʿAdl; Amīn; Bayyina; Daʿwā; Ghāʾib; Ḥakam; Ḳaḍāʾ; Maẓālim
droit ibāḍite ʿAbd al-ʿAzīz b. al-Ḥādjdj Ibrāhīm; Abū Ghānim; Abū Muḥammad al-ʿUmānī (*et* Ibn Baraka); Abū Zakariyyāʾ al-Djanāwunī; Ibn Djaʿfar
voir aussi al-Djayṭālī; Maḥkama.IV.9 (Oman)
droit pénal ʿĀḳila; Diya; Ḥadd; Ḳadhf; Ḳatl; Khaṭaʾ; Ḳiṣāṣ.5; Ṣalb
voir aussi Muḥṣan; Ṣalīb; [au Suppl.] Ikrāh
écoles Ḥanābila; Ḥanafiyya; Mālikiyya
voir aussi Ibn Abī Laylā.2
en Asie du Sud-est Penghulu; Rapak
fonctions Faḳīh; Ḥakam; Ḳāḍī; Ḳāḍī ʿAskar; Ḳassām; Mardjaʿ-i Taḳlīd; Nāʾib.1
voir aussi Amīn; Fatwā; Khalīfa.II; Maḥkama
jurisprudence Fatwā; **Fiḳh**; Īdjāb; Idjmāʿ; Idjtihād; Ikhtilāf; Istiḥsān; Ḳiyās; Maṣlaḥa; Nāzila
voir aussi Sadd al-Dharāʾiʿ
juristes Faḳīh; Mardjaʿ-i Taḳlīd; Mudjtahid
ḥanafites Abū Ḥanīfa; Abū l-Layth al-Samarḳandī; Abū l-Suʿūd; al-ʿAmīdī; al-Bihārī; al-Djaṣṣāṣ; al-Ḥalabī; Ḥamza al-Ḥarrānī; Ibn ʿĀbidīn; Ibn Buhlūl; Ibn Ghānim; Ibn Ḳuṭlūbugha; Ibn Nudjaym; Ibn al-Shiḥna; Ḳāḍī Khān; al-Kāsānī; Ḳasṭallānī; al-Ḳudūrī; al-Marghīnānī; al-Nasafī.IV; al-Sadjāwandī, Sirādj al-dīn; [au Suppl.] Abū ʿAbd Allāh al-Baṣrī; Abū l-Barakāt; al-Dāmaghānī.1 et 2
voir aussi ʿAbd al-Ḳādir al-Ḳurashī; al-Fatāwā al-ʿĀlamgīriyya; Ibn Duḳmāḳ
ḥanbalites Aḥmad b. Ḥanbal; al-Bahūtī; al-Barbahārī; Ghulām al-Khallāl; Ibn ʿAḳīl; Ibn al-Bannāʾ; Ibn Baṭṭa al-ʿUkbarī; Ibn al-Djawzī; Ibn al-

Farrāʾ; Ibn Ḥāmid; Ibn Ḳayyim al-Djawziyya; Ibn Ḳudāma al-Maḳdisī; Ibn Mufliḥ; Ibn Radjab; Ibn Taymiyya; al-Kalwadhānī; al-Khallāl; al-Khiraḳī; al-Marwazī

et → THÉOLOGIE

chiites → CHIITES

mālikites Aḥmad Bābā; Asad b. al-Furāt; al-Bādjī; al-Bāḳillānī; Bannānī; al-Burzulī; al-Dānī; al-Fāsī; Ibn ʿAbd al-Ḥakam; Ibn Abī Zamanayn; Ibn Abī Zayd al-Ḳayrawānī; Ibn ʿAmmār, Abū l-ʿAbbās; Ibn ʿArafa; Ibn ʿĀṣim; Ibn al-Faraḍī; Ibn Farḥūn; Ibn Ḥabīb, Abū Marwān; Ibn al-Ḥādjdj; Ibn al-Ḥādjib; Ibn al-Ḳāsim; Ibn Maḍāʾ; Ibn Rushayd; Ibn Sūda; al-Ibshīhī; ʿĪsā b. Dīnār; ʿIyāḍ b. Mūsā, al-Ḳābisī; al-Ḳalaṣādī; al-Kardūdī; Ḳaṣṣāra; Khalīl b. Isḥāḳ; al-Khushanī; al-Ḳurṭubī, Abū ʿAbd Allāh; al-Ḳurṭubī, Yaḥyā; Mālik b. Anas; al-Manūfī.IV et V; al-Māzarī; Muḥammad b. Saḥnūn; Saḥnūn; Sālim b. Muḥammad; [au Suppl.] Abū ʿImrān al-Fāsī; al-Azdī; Ibn Daḳīḳ al-ʿĪd; Ibn Dirham; Ibn Rushd

voir aussi Ibn ʿAbd al-Barr; al-Ḳaṣṣār; Laḳīṭ

shāfiʿites al-ʿAbbādī; Abū Shudjāʿ; Bādjūrī; al-Baghawī; al-Bulḳīnī; Daḥlān; al-Djanadī; al-Djīzī; al-Djuwaynī; Ibn Abī ʿAṣrūn; Ibn Abī l-Dam; Ibn ʿAḳīl; Ibn ʿAsākir; Ibn Djamāʿa; Ibn Ḥabīb, Badr al-dīn; Ibn Ḥadjar al-Haytamī; Ibn Ḳāḍī Shuhba.1; Ibn Ḳāsim al-Ghazzī; Ibn al-Ṣalāḥ; Ibn Suraydj; al-Ḳalḳashandī; al-Ḳalyūbī; al-Ḳazwīnī, Abū Ḥātim; al-Ḳazwīnī, Djalāl al-dīn; al-Ḳazwīnī, Nadjm al-dīn; al-Kiyā al-Harrāsī; Makhrama; al-Māwardī; al-Mutawallī; al-Muzanī; al-Nawawī; al-Rāfiʿī; al-Ramlī; [au Suppl.] Abū Zurʿa; Ibn Daḳīḳ al-ʿĪd

voir aussi Abū Thawr; Dāwud b. Khalaf; al-Isfarāyīnī

Ẓāhirites Dāwūd b. Khalaf; al-Ḥumaydī; Ibn Dāwūd; Ibn Ḥazm, Abū Muḥammad; (al-)Mundhir b. Saʿīd

voir aussi [au Suppl.] Ibn al-Rūmiyya

ottoman Bāb-i Mashīkhat, Djazāʾ, Djurm; Fatwā; ʿIlmiyye; Ḳānūnnāme; Ḳassām; Maḥkama.II; Makhredj; Medjelle; Medjlis-i Wālā; Mewlewiyyet; Narkh

voir aussi Ḥanafiyya; al-Ḥaramayn; *et* → DYNASTIES.ANATOLIE ET LES TURCS.OTTOMANS.GRANDS-MUFTIS

réforme du droit → RÉFORME

termes Adāʾ; Adjr; ʿAdl; Aḥkām; Ahl al-Ḥall wa-l-ʿAḳd; ʿAḳd; Akdariyya; ʿAḳīḳa; ʿĀḳila; ʿAmal.3 et 4; Amān; ʿĀmil; Amīn; ʿĀriyya; ʿArsh; ʿAwl; ʿAzīma.1; Baʿl.2.b; Bāligh; Barāʾa; Bayʿ; Bayʿa; Bayyina; Burhān; Ḍamān; Dār al-ʿAhd; Dār al-Ḥarb; Dār al-Islām; Dār al-Ṣulḥ; Ḍarūra; Daʿwā; Dhabīḥa; Dhimma; Diya; Djāʾiz; Djanāba; Djazāʾ; Djihād; Djizya; Djurm; Faḳīh; Farāʾiḍ; Farḍ; Fāsid wa-Bāṭil; Fāsiḳ; Faskh; Fatwā; Fayʾ; Fiḳh; Ghāʾib; Ghanīma; Ghārim; Ghaṣb; Ghusl; Ḥaḍāna; Ḥadath; Ḥadd; Ḥadjr; Hady; Ḥakam; Ḥaḳḳ; Ḥawāla; Ḥayḍ; Hiba; Ḥiyal; Ḥuḳūḳ; Ḥulūl; ʿIbādāt;

Ibāḥa.I; ʿIdda; Idhn; Īdjāb; Īdjār; Idjmāʿ; Idjtihād; Iḥrām; Iḥyāʾ; Iḳāla; Ikhtilāf; Iḳrār; Ildjāʾ; Inkār; Inṣāf; Istibrāʾ; Istiḥsān; Istiʾnāf; Istiṣḥāb; ʿIwaḍ; Ḳabāla; Ḳabḍ.I; Ḳaḍāʾ; Ḳadhf; Kafāʾa; Kafāla; Ḳānūn; Ḳānūnnāme; Ḳasam; Ḳatl; Khaṭaʾ; Khiyār; Kirāʾ; Ḳirāḍ; Ḳiṣāṣ; Ḳiyās; Liʿān; Liṣṣ; Luḳaṭa; Maḍmūn; Mafṣūl; Mahr; Maṣlaḥa; Mawāt; Mawlā.E; Maẓālim; Milk; Muʿāmalāt; Muʿāwaḍa; Muḍāraba; Mudjtahid; Mufāwaḍa; Mughārasa; Muḥṣan; Mukhāṭara; Munāṣafa; Musāḳāt; Mushāraka; Mutʿa; Muṭlaḳ; Muwāḍaʿa; Muzāraʿa; Nadjis; Nāfila; Naṣṣ; Nāzila; Niyya; Rahn; Ribā; Rukhṣa.1; Sabab.5; Ṣadaḳa; Sadd al-Dharāʾiʿ; Ṣafḳa; Ṣaḥīḥ.2; al-Sahm.2; Salaf; Salam; [au Suppl.] ʿAḳār; Darak; Dayn; Djabr; Ghārūḳa; Ḥikr; Ikrāh; Inzāl

voir aussi Bayt al-Māl; Hudna; Ṣaghīr

DRUZES al-Darazī; **Durūz**; Ḥamza b. ʿAlī b. Aḥmad; al-Muḳtanā; [au Suppl.] Binn

voir aussi Ḥadd; Maḥkama.IV.2, 3 et 5; Maʿn; [au Suppl.] Dawr; Ḥinn; *et* → LIBAN

historiens des Ṣāliḥ b. Yaḥyā

DYNASTIES **Dawla**; Ḥādjib; Mushīr

voir aussi Čashna-gīr; Khādim al-Ḥaramayn; Laḳab; Libās.I; Malik; Marāsim; Mashwara; Mawākib; Pādishāh; Parda-dār; *et* → ADMINISTRATION; ONOMASTIQUE.TITRES

Afghanistan et Inde ʿĀdil-Shāhs; Arghūn; Bahmanides; Barīd Shāhides; Dihlī (Sultanat de); Fārūḳides; Ghaznawides; Ghūrides; Hindū-shāhides; ʿImād Shāhides; Kart; Khaldjis; Ḳuṭb-Shāhides; Lōdīs; Mughals; Niẓām Shāhides; [au Suppl.] Bānīdjūrides

voir aussi Afghānistān.V.2 et 3; Burhān al-Mulk; Dāwūdpōtrās; Dīwān.V; Hind.IV; Kh^{w}ādja-i Djahān; Kōtwāl; Lashkar; Marāsim.5; Mawākib.V; Nithār.2; Rānā Sāngā; Sammā; [au Suppl.] Fakhr-i Mudabbir; *et* → ARCHITECTURE.RÉGIONS; MILITAIRES.INDO-MUSULMANS

ʿĀdil-Shāhides (1490-1686) **ʿĀdil-Shāhs**; Bīdjāpūr; Hind.VII.IX

souverains Muḥammad b. Ibrāhīm II

Awadh (1722-1856) **Awadh**

souverains Ghāzī l-Dīn Ḥaydar; Saʿādat ʿAlī Khān; Ṣafdar Djang

vizirs Mahdī ʿAlī Khān

Bahmanides (1347-1527) **Bahmanides**; Hind.VII.VII

voir aussi Bīdar; Gulbargā; Pēshwā

sultans Humāyūn Shāh Bahmanī; Maḥmūd Shihāb al-Dīn; Muḥammad Ier; Muḥammad II; Muḥammad III

autres personnages Khalīl Allāh; Maḥmūd Gāwān

Bārakzays (1819-1973) **Afghānistān**.V.3.b

rois ʿAbd al-Raḥmān Khān; Ḥabīb Allāh Khān; [au Suppl.] Amān Allāh

Durrānīs (1747-1842)

rois Aḥmad Shāh Durrānī

historiens des ʿAbd al-Karīm Munshī

autres personnages Kāmrān Shāh Durrānī

Fārūḳides (1370-1601)

souverains Mīrān Muḥammad Shāh Ier

Ghaznawides (977-1186) ʿAmīd; Dīwān.V; **Ghaznawides**

voir aussi Ḥiṣār.III

sultans Alp Takīn; Bahrām Shah; Ismaʿīl b. Sebüktigin; Maḥmūd b. Sebüktigin; Masʿūd b. Maḥmūd; Mawdūd b. Masʿūd; Muḥammad b. Maḥmūd b. Sebüktigin

vizirs Aḥmad b. Muḥammad; Altūntāsh; al-Faḍl b. Aḥmad al-Isfarāʾinī; Ḥasanak; Maymandī

historiens des Bayhaḳī

voir aussi al-Ḳāshānī; [au Suppl.] Fakhr-i Mudabbir

autres personnages Muḥammad Bakhtiyār Khaldjī

Ghūrides (circa 1000-1215)

sultans Djahān-sūz; Muḥammad b. Sām

Langāh de Multān

sultans Ḥusayn Shāh Langāh Ier; Ḥusayn Shāh Langāh II

Mughals (1526-1858) Ḍarība.VI.b et c; Dīwān.V; Manṣab; **Mughals**; [au Suppl.] Ilāhī

voir aussi Fawdjdār; Kōtwāl; Maṭbakh.IV; Nithār.2; Ṣadr al-Ṣudūr.3; [au Suppl.] Dāgh u taṣḥīḥa; ʿIbādat Khāna

empereurs Aḥmad Shāh.1; Akbar; Awrangzīb; Bābur; Bahādur Shāh Ier; Bahādur Shāh II; Djahāndār Shāh; Djahāngīr; Farrukh-siyar; Humāyūn; Muḥammad Shāh

voir aussi Darshan; Mumtāz Maḥall; Nūr Djahān

vizirs Iʿtimād al-Dawla

secrétaires Abū l-Faḍl ʿAllāmī; Muḥammad Kāẓim

historiens des ʿAbd al-Ḥamīd Lāhawrī; Abū l-Faḍl ʿAllāmī; Bakhtāwar Khān; Djawhar; Ghulām Ḥusayn Khān Ṭabāṭabāʾī; ʿInāyat Allāh Khān; Īsar-dās; Khʷāfī Khān; Muḥammad Kāẓim; Muḥammad Sharīf; Mustaʿidd Khān; Muʿtamad Khān; Niʿmat Allāh b. Ḥabīb Allāh Harawī; Nūr al-Ḥaḳḳ al-Dihlawī; [au Suppl.] ʿĀḳil Khān Rāzī

voir aussi Aẓfarī; Badāʾūnī; Maʾāthir al-Umarāʾ

autres personnages ʿAbd al-Raḥīm Khān; ʿAlī Werdī Khān; Āṣaf Khān; Bakhtāwar Khān; Bayram Khān; Burhān al-Mulk; Dāniyāl; Ghulām Ḳādir Rohilla; Hindāl; Iʿtibār Khān; Iʿtiḳād Khān; ʿIwaḍ Wadjīh; Kāmrān; Khān Djahān Lōdī; Khusraw Sulṭān; Mahābat

Khān; Makhdūm al-Mulk (*et* [au Suppl.] ʿAbd Allāh Sulṭānpūrī); Mān Singh; Mīr Djumla; Mīrzā ʿAskarī; Mīrzā ʿAzīz "Kōka"; Murād; Murād Bakhsh; Murshid Ḳulī Khān; Niẓām al-Mulk; [au Suppl.] Akbar b. Awrangzīb; ʿĀḳil Khān Rāzī; Ghāzī Khān; Gūran; ʿInāyat Khān (2x)

voir aussi Bāra Sayyids (*et* [au Suppl.] Bārha Sayyids); Marāṭhās

Niẓām Shāhides (1491-1633) **Niẓām Shāhides**

sultans Ḥusayn Niẓām Shāh; Malik Aḥmad Baḥrī

autres personnages Malik ʿAmbar

Sultans de Bengale (1336-1576)

sultans Dāwūd Khān Kararānī; Fakhr al-Dīn Mubārakshāh; Ḥusayn Shāh; Maḥmūd; Rādjā Ganesh; Rukn al-Dīn Bārbak Shāh

historiens des [au Suppl.] ʿAbbās Sarwānī

Sultans de Dihlī (1206-1555) Ḍarība.VI.a; **Dihlī** (Sultanat de); Dīwān.V; Nāʾib.1; Naḳīb.2

voir aussi Burdj.III.2

sultans Fīrūz Shāh Tughluḳ; Ghiyāth al-Dīn Tughluḳ Iᵉʳ; Ghiyāth al-Dīn Tughluḳ Shāh II; Iltutmish; Kayḳubād; Khiḍr Khān; Ḳuṭb al-Dīn Aybak; Maḥmūd; Ibrāhīm Lōdī; Mubārak Shāh; Muḥammad b. Tughluḳ; Muḥammad Shāh Iᵉʳ Khaldjī; Raḍiyya; [au Suppl.] Balban; Dawlat Khān Lōdī

vizirs Kāfūr (*et* Malik Kāfūr); Khān-i Djahān Maḳbūl; Miʾān Bhuʾā

historiens des Baranī; al-Djuzdjānī; Niẓāmī (*et* [au Suppl.] Ḥasan Niẓāmī)

autres personnages Mallū Iḳbāl Khān; [au Suppl.] ʿAbd al-Wahhāb Bukhārī; ʿAyn al-Mulk Multānī; Daryā Khān Noḥānī; Ikhtisān

voir aussi ʿAlī Mardān; Hūlāgū; Khaldjīs; Sammā

Sultans du Gudjarāt (1391-1583)

sultans Bahādur Shāh Gudjarātī; Maḥmūd

historiens des [au Suppl.] Ḥādjdjī al-Dabīr

autres personnages Malik Ayāz

Sultans de Kālpī

sultans Maḥmūd Khān

Sultans de Kashmīr (1346-1589)

sultans [au Suppl.] Čaks

voir aussi [au Suppl.] Gul Khātūn

historiens des [au Suppl.] Ḥaydar Malik

autres personnages [au Suppl.] Bayhaḳis

Sultans de Madura

sultans Djalāl al-Dīn Aḥsan

Sultans de Mālwā (1401-1531)

sultans Dilāwar Khān; Hūshang Shāh Ghūrī; Maḥmūd

voir aussi Bāz Bahādur

vizirs Mēdinī Rā'ī
autres personnages Malik Mug͟hīt͟h
Sultans s͟hark̲ides de D̲jawnpur (1394-1479)
sultans Ḥusayn S͟hāh; Ibrāhīm S͟hāh S͟hark̲ī; Maḥmūd S͟hāh S͟hark̲ī; Malik Sarwar
Afrique Fund̲j; Gwandu
voir aussi Bū Saʿīd; Dār Fūr
Anatolie et les Turcs Artuk̲ides; Aydi̊n-og͟hlu; Dānis͟hmendides; D͟hū l-K̲adr; Eretna; Germiyān-og͟hullari̊; Ḥamīd Og͟hullari̊; Īnāl; Isfendiyār Og͟hlu; K̲arāmān-og͟hullari̊; K̲arasi̊; Mentes͟he-og͟hullari̊; ʿOt͟hmānli̊; Saltuk̲ Og͟hullari̊
voir aussi Būrides; Derebey; Mangi̊ts; Mengüček; Ramaḍān Og͟hullari̊; *et* › ONOMASTIQUE.TITRES
Artuk̲ides (1102-1408)
souverains Īlg͟hāzī; Nūr al-Dīn Muḥammad
Aydi̊n-og͟hlu (1308-1425)
amīrs D̲junayd
Ottomans (1281-1924) **ʿOt͟hmānli̊**
voir aussi ʿOt͟hmān Ier; *et* → EMPIRE OTTOMAN; TURQUIE.PÉRIODE OTTOMANE
sultans ʿAbd al-ʿAzīz; ʿAbd al-Ḥamīd Ier; ʿAbd al-Ḥamīd II; ʿAbd al-Mad̲jīd Ier; ʿAbd al-Mad̲jīd II; Aḥmad Ier; Aḥmad II; Aḥmad III; Bāyazīd Ier; Bāyazīd II; Ibrāhīm; Maḥmūd; Meḥemmed Ier; Meḥemmed II; Meḥemmed III; Meḥemmed IV; Meḥemmed V Res͟hād; Meḥemmed VI Waḥīd al-Dīn; Murād Ier; Murād II; Murād III; Murād IV; Murād V; Muṣṭafā Ier; Muṣṭafā II; Muṣṭafā III; Muṣṭafā IV; Ork͟han; ʿOt͟hmān Ier; ʿOt͟hmān II; ʿOt͟hmān III
voir aussi Bāb-i Humāyūn; D̲jem; Ertog͟hrul; K͟hādim al-Ḥaramayn; K͟halīfa.I.E; K͟hurrem; Kösem Wālide; Mas͟hwara; Muhr.1; Muṣṭafā.I et II; Müteferrik̲a; Nīlūfer K͟hātūn; Nūr Bānū; Rikāb; Ṣafiyye Wālide Sulṭān
grands-vizirs **Ṣadr-ı Aʿẓam**
14e siècle ʿAlī Pas͟ha Čandārli̊zāde; D̲jandarli̊.I
15e siècle Aḥmad Pas͟ha Gedik; Dāwūd Pas͟ha, Kod̲ja; D̲jandarli̊; K͟halīl Pas͟ha D̲jandarli̊; Maḥmūd Pas͟ha; Meḥmed Pas͟ha, K̲aramānī; Meḥmed Pas͟ha, Rūm
16e siècle Aḥmad Pas͟ha K̲ara; ʿAlī Pas͟ha K͟hādim; ʿAlī Pas͟ha Semiz; Ayās Pas͟ha; Čig͟hāla-zāde Sinān Pas͟ha; Derwīs͟h Pas͟ha; Ferhād Pas͟ha; Hersek-zāde; Ibrāhīm Pas͟ha; Ibrāhīm Pas͟ha, Dāmād; K͟hādi̊m Ḥasan Pas͟ha Ṣok̲olli̊; K͟hādi̊m Süleymān Pas͟ha; Lala Meḥmed Pas͟ha (*et* Meḥmed Pas͟ha, Lālā, S͟hāhīnog͟hlu); Luṭfī Pas͟ha; Meḥmed Pas͟ha, Lālā, Melek-Nihād; Mesīḥ Meḥmed Pas͟ha; Mesīḥ Pas͟ha; ʿOt͟hmān Pas͟ha; Pīrī Meḥmed Pas͟ha; Rüstem Pas͟ha

17ᵉ siècle ʿAlī Pasha ʿArabadjī; ʿAlī Pasha Güzeldje; ʿAlī Pasha Sürmeli; Dāwūd Pasha, Ḳara; Derwīsh Meḥmed Pasha; Dilāwar Pasha; Ḥāfiẓ Aḥmed Pasha; Ḥusayn Pasha; Ibrāhīm Pasha, Kara; Ipshir Muṣṭafā Pasha; Ismāʿīl Pasha, Nishāndjî; Ḳarā Muṣṭafā Pasha; Kemānkesh; Khalīl Pasha Ḳayṣariyyeli; Khosrew Pasha, Bosniak; Köprülü.I-III; Meḥmed Pasha, Čerkes; Meḥmed Pasha, Elmās; Meḥmed Pasha, Gürdjü (I); Meḥmed Pasha, Gürdjü (II); Meḥmed Pasha, Öküz; Meḥmed Pasha, Sulṭān-zāde; Meḥmed Pasha, Tabanîyassî; Murād Pasha, Kuyudju; Naṣūḥ Pasha; Redjeb Pasha

18ᵉ siècle ʿAbd Allāh Pasha; ʿAlī Pasha Čorlulu; ʿAlī Pasha Dāmād; ʿAlī Pasha Ḥakīm-oghlu; Derwīsh Meḥmed Pasha; Ḥamza Ḥāmid Pasha; Ḥamza Pasha; (Dāmād) Ḥasan Pasha; (Seyyid) Ḥasan Pasha; (Sherīf) Ḥasan Pasha; Ibrāhīm Pasha, Nevshehirli; Kaḥyā Ḥasan Pasha; Khalīl Pasha; Köprülü.V; Meḥmed Pasha, Balṭadjî; Meḥmed Pasha, ʿIwaḍ; Meḥmed Pasha, Melek; Meḥmed Pasha, Muḥsin-zāde; Meḥmed Pasha Rāmī; Meḥmed Pasha, Tiryāḳī; Meḥmed Pasha, Yegen, Gümrükčü; Meḥmed Pasha, Yegen, Ḥādjdjī; Rāghib Pasha; Saʿīd Efendi

à partir du 19ᵉ siècle Aḥmad Wafīḳ Pasha; ʿAlī Pasha Muḥammad Amīn; Dāmād Ferīd Pasha; Derwīsh Meḥmed Pasha; Djawād Pasha; Fuʾād Pasha; Ḥusayn ʿAwnī Pasha; Ḥusayn Ḥilmī Pasha; Ibrāhīm Edhem Pasha; Ibrāhīm Ḥaḳḳī Pasha; ʿIzzet Pasha; Kečiboynuzu; Khayr al-Dīn Pasha; Khosrew Pasha, Meḥmed; Küčük Saʿīd Pasha; Maḥmūd Nedīm Pasha; Maḥmūd Shewḳat Pasha; Meḥmed Saʿīd Ghālib Pasha; Midḥat Pasha; Muṣṭafā Pasha, Bayraḳdār; Reshīd Pasha, Muṣṭafā; [au Suppl.] Esʿad Pasha

voir aussi Bāb-i ʿĀlī; Başvekil; Ḳapî; ʿOthmān-zāde

grands-muftis Abū l-Suʿūd; ʿĀrif Ḥikmet Bey; Bahāʾī Meḥmed Efendi; Bostānzāde.2; Čelebi-zāde; Čiwi-zāde; Djamāl al-Dīn Efendi; Dürrizāde.I-V; Dürrizāde, ʿAbd Allāh; Esʿad Efendi, Aḥmed; Esʿad Efendi, Meḥmed (3x); Fenārī-zāde; Gūrānī; Ḥasan Fehmī; Ḥayātī-zāde.2; Ḳarā-Čelebi-zāde.4; Kemāl Pasha-zāde; Khōdja Efendi; Khosrew; Meḥmed Ṣāliḥ Efendi; Muṣṭafā Khayrī Efendi; Pīrī-zāde

voir aussi Bāb-i Mashīkhat; Fatwā

grands-amiraux ʿAlī Pasha Güzeldje; Čighāla-zāde Sinān Pasha; Djaʿfar Beg; Djezāʾirli Ghāzī Ḥasan Pasha; Ḥasan Pasha; Ḥusayn Pasha; Kenʿān Pasha; Khalīl Pasha Ḳayṣariyyeli; Khayr al-Dīn Pasha; Piyāle Pasha

voir aussi Raʾīs.3

historiens des ʿAbdī; ʿAbdī Efendi; ʿAbdī Pasha; Aḥmad Djewdet Pasha; Aḥmad Rasmī; ʿAlī; ʿAlī Amīrī; ʿĀshîḳ-Pasha-Zāde; ʿĀṣim; ʿAṭāʾ Bey; al-Bakrī.I; Bidlīsī; Bihishtī; Čelebi-zāde; Česhmīzāde;

Djalālzāde Muṣṭafā Čelebi; Djalālzāde Ṣāliḥ Čelebi; Enwerī; Esʿad Efendi, Meḥmed; Ḥasan Bey-zāde; ʿIzzī; Ḳarā-čelebi-zāde.4; Kātib Čelebi; Kemāl, Meḥmed Nāmiḳ; Kemāl Pasha-zāde; Khayr Allāh Efendi; Luḳmān b. Sayyid Ḥusayn; Luṭfī Efendi; Maṭrāḳčī; Meḥmed Ḥākim Efendi; Meḥmed Khalīfe b. Ḥüseyn; Meḥmed Pasha, Ḳaramānī; Meḥmed Zaʿīm; Muḥyī l-Dīn Meḥmed; Naʿīmā; ʿOthmān-zāde; Pečewī; Ramaḍān-zāde; Rāshid, Meḥmed; Rūḥī

voir aussi Ḥadīdī

autres personnages

14e siècle ʿAlāʾ al-Dīn Beg; Badr al-Dīn Ibn Ḳāḍī Samāwnā; Ḳāsim.I

15e siècle Aḥmad Pasha Khāʾin; Ewrenos; Ewrenos Oghullari; Fenārī-zāde; Ḳāsim.II et III; Ḳāsim Pasha; Mūsā Čelebi; Muṣṭafā.I et II

16e siècle Bostānzāde; Čiwi-zāde; Derwīsh Pasha; Djaʿfar Čelebi; Djalālzāde Muṣṭafa Čelebi; Ferīdūn Beg; Ḳāsim.IV; Ḳāsim Agha; Ḳāsim Pasha; Kemāl Reʾīs; Khosrew Pasha; Ḳorḳud b. Bāyazīd; Maḥmūd Pasha; Maḥmūd Tardjumān; Meḥmed Pasha, Bïyïḳlï; Muṣṭafā.III; Muṣṭafā Pasha, Ḳara Shāhīn; Muṣṭafā Pasha, Lala; Muṣṭafā Pasha al Nashshār; Özdemir Pasha; Pertew Pasha.I; Ramaḍān-zāde; Riḍwān Pasha

17e siècle Ābāza; Ḥaydar-oghlu, Meḥmed; Ḥusayn Pasha; Ḳāsim. V; Ḳāṭïrdjï-oghlï; Maʿn-zada; Meḥmed Khalīfe b. Ḥüseyn; ʿOthmān Pasha, Yegen; [au Suppl.] Aḥmad Pasha Küčük; Cōbān-oghullari

18e siècle Ābāza; Aḥmad Pasha; Aḥmad Pasha Bonneval; Aḥmad Rasmī; Djānïkli Ḥādjdji ʿAlī Pasha; Meḥmed Ḥākim Efendi; Meḥmed Yirmisekiz; Paswan-oghlu; Patrona Khalīl

à partir du 19e siècle ʿAbd al-Ḥaḳḳ Ḥāmid; Aḥmad Djewdet Pasha; ʿAlī Pasha Tepedelenli; Ayyūb Ṣabrī Pasha; Bahdjat Muṣṭafā Efendi; Dāwūd Pasha (2x); Djawād Pasha; Djāwīd; Djemāl Pasha; Enwer Pasha; Fāḍil Pasha; Fehīm Pasha; Ḥālet Efendi; Hāmōn; Ḥasan Fehmī; Ḥusayn Pasha; Ibn ʿArabshāh; Ibrāhīm Derwīsh Pasha; ʿIzzet Pasha; Kabakčïoghlu Muṣṭafā; Kāẓïm Ḳadrī; Kāẓïm Karabekir; Ḳōzān-oghullari; Mukhtār Pasha; Münīf Pasha; Muṣṭafā Pasha, Bushatlï; Pertew Pasha.II; Riḍwān Begovic; Ṣādïḳ Rifʿat Pasha; [au Suppl.] Camondo

Saldjūḳides de Rūm (1077-1307) **Saldjūḳides**

sultans Kaykāʾūs; Kaykhusraw; Kayḳubād; Ḳïlïdj Arslan Ier; Ḳïlïdj Arslan II; Ḳïlïdj Arslan III; Ḳïlïdj Arslan IV; Malik-Shāh.IV

historiens des Ibn Bībī

autres personnages Ashraf Oghullari; Muʿīn al-Dīn Sulaymān Parwāna; Saʿd al-Dīn Köpek

Égypte et le Croissant fertile ʿAbbāsides; ʿAnnāzides; Ayyūbides; Bābān; Būrides; Fāṭimides; Ḥamdānides; Ḥasanwayh; Mamlūks; Marwānides; Mazyad; Mirdās
voir aussi ʿAmmār; Begteginides; Djalīlī; Ṣadaḳa, Banū; *et* → ÉGYPTE. PÉRIODE MODERNE.LIGNE DE MUḤAMMAD ʿALĪ
ʿAbbāsides (749-1258) → CALIFAT
Ayyūbides (1169-fin du 15e siècle) **Ayyūbides**
voir aussi Rank
souverains al-ʿĀdil; al-Afḍal; Bahrām Shāh; al-Kāmil; (al-Malik) al-Muʿaẓẓam; al-Nāṣir; Ṣalāḥ al-Dīn; (al-Malik) al-Ṣāliḥ ʿImād al-Dīn; (al-Malik) al-Ṣāliḥ Nadjm al-Dīn Ayyūb
voir aussi Dīwān.II.III
vizirs Ibn al-ʿAdīm; Ibn al-Athīr.III; Ibn Maṭrūḥ
secrétaires ʿImād al-Dīn; al-Ḳāḍī al-Fāḍil
historiens des Abū l-Fidā; Abū Shāma; Ibn Shaddād; ʿImād al-Dīn; al-Maḳrīzī; al-Manṣūr, al-Malik
autres personnages Abū l-Fidā; Aybak; Ibn al-ʿAssāl; (Bahāʾ al-dīn) Ḳarāḳūsh; (Sharaf al-dīn) Ḳarāḳūsh; (al-Malik) al-Muẓaffar
Fāṭimides (909-1171) → CALIFAT
Ḥamdānides (905-1004)
souverains Nāṣir al-Dawla; [au Suppl.] Abū Taghlib
autres personnages Ḥusayn b. Ḥamdān; Luʾluʾ
Ikhshīdides (935-969)
souverains Kāfūr
vizirs Ibn al-Furāt.V
Mamlūks (1250-1517) Dhū l-Faḳāriyya; Dīwān.II.IV; Ḥādjib.IV; Hiba.II; Khādim al-Ḥaramayn; Khaznadār; **Mamlūks**; Mashwara; Nāʾib.1
voir aussi Ḥarfūsh; Ḳumāsh; Mamlūk; Manshūr; Rank; *et* → MILITAIRES.MAMELUKS
sultans Barḳūḳ; Barsbāy; Baybars Ier; Baybars II; Čaḳmaḳ; Faradj; Ḥasan; Īnāl al-Adjrūd; Ḳāʾit Bāy; Ḳalāwūn; Ḳānṣawh al-Ghawrī; Khalīl; Khushḳadam; Ḳuṭuz; Lādjīn; al-Muʾayyad Shaykh; al-Nāṣir; (al-Malik) al-Ṣāliḥ
administrateurs Faḍl Allāh; Ibn ʿAbd al-Ẓāhir; Ibn Faḍl al-ʿUmarī; Ibn Ghurāb; Ibn Ḥidjdja; Ibn al-Sadīd (Ibn al-Muzawwiḳ); Ibn al-Sadīd, Karīm al-dīn; al-Ḳalḳashandī.I; [au Suppl.] Ibn al-Ṣuḳāʿ
historiens des Abū l-Maḥāsin Ibn Taghrībirdī; Baybars al-Manṣūrī; Ibn ʿAbd al-Ẓāhir; Ibn Duḳmāḳ; Ibn Ḥabīb, Badr al-dīn; Ibn Iyās; Ibn Shāhin al-Ẓāhirī; al-Maḳrīzī; al-Mufaḍḍal b. Abī l-Fadāʾil; al-Nuwayrī, Shihāb al-dīn; al-Ṣafadī, al-Ḥasan
autres personnages Abū l-Fidā; al-ʿAynī; Ibn Djamāʿa; Ibn al-Mundhir
Marwānides (983-1085)

souverains Naṣr al-Dawla
Mazyadides (circa 961-1150) **Mazyad**; Ṣadaḳa, Banū
souverains Ṣadaḳa b. Manṣūr
Mirdāsides (1023-1079) **Mirdās**
voir aussi Asad al-Dawla
Ṭūlūnides (868-905)
souverains Aḥmad b. Ṭūlūn; Khumārawayh
voir aussi Ibn al-Mudabbir.I
historiens des al-Balawī; Ibn al-Dāya
autres personnages [au Suppl.] al-ʿAbbās b. Aḥmad b. Tūlūn
ʿUḳaylides (circa 990-1096)
souverains Muslim b. Ḳuraysh
Espagne et Afrique du Nord ʿAbbādides; ʿAbd al-Wādides; Afṭasides; Aghlabides; ʿAlawīs; ʿĀmirides; ʿAmmār; Dhū l-Nūnides; Djahwarides; Ḥafṣides; Ḥammādides; Ḥammūdides; Hūdides; Ḥusaynides; Idrīsides; Khurāsān, Banū; Marīnides; Midrār; al-Murābiṭūn; al-Muwaḥḥidūn; Naṣrides; Razīn, Banū; Rustamides; Saʿdides
voir aussi ʿAlāma; Dīwān.III; Ḥādjib.II et V; Hiba.III; Ḥiṣār.II; al-Ḥulal al-Mawshiyya; Ḳaramānlı; Khalīfa.I.C et D; Laḳab.III; Marāsim.2; Mawākib.II; Parias; *et* → CALIFAT.FĀṬIMIDES
ʿAbbādides (1023-1091) **ʿAbbādides**; Ishbīliya
souverains al-Muʿtaḍid bi-llāh; al-Muʿtamid ibn ʿAbbād
voir aussi al-Rundī
vizirs Ibn ʿAmmār, Abū Bakr
ʿAbd al-Wādides (1236-1550)
souverains Abū Ḥammū Ier; Abū Ḥammū II; Abū Tāshufīn Ier; Abū Tāshufīn II; Abū Zayyān Ier; Abū Zayyān II; Abū Zayyān III
historiens des Ibn Khaldūn, Abū Zakariyyāʾ
Afṭasides (1022-1094)
souverains al-Mutawakkil ʿalā llāh, Ibn al-Afṭas
vizirs Ibn Ḳuzmān.II
secrétaires Ibn ʿAbdūn; Ibn Ḳabṭūrnu
Aghlabides (800-909) al-ʿAbbāsiyya; **Aghlabides**; Raḳḳāda
souverains Ibrāhīm Ier; Ibrāhīm II
ʿAlawides (1631-) **ʿAlawīs**; Ḳāʾid; Mawlāy
souverains ʿAbd Allāh b. Ismāʿīl; ʿAbd al-ʿAzīz b. al-Ḥasan; ʿAbd al-Raḥmān b. Hishām; Ḥafīẓ (ʿAbd al-); (Mawlāy) al-Ḥasan; Mawlāy Ismāʿīl; Muḥammad [III] b. ʿAbd Allāh; Muḥammad IV b. ʿAbd al-Raḥmān; Muḥammad [V] b. Yūsuf; al-Rashīd (Mawlāy)
vizirs Akanṣūs; Ibn Idrīs [I]; [au Suppl.] Bā Ḥmād; Ibn ʿUthmān al-Miknāsī
historiens des Akanṣūs; Ibn Zaydān; al-Kardūdī

autres personnages Aḥmad al-Nāṣirī (*et* al-Nāṣirī al-Salāwī); Ibn Idrīs [II]; Khunātha
Almohades (1130-1269) Hargha; al-ʿIḳāb; Mizwār; **al-Muwaḥḥidūn**
souverains ʿAbd al-Muʾmin b. ʿAlī; Abū Yaʿḳūb Yūsuf; Abū Yūsuf Yaʿḳūb al-Manṣūr; Ibn Tūmart; al-Maʾmūn; al-Nāṣir
historiens des ʿAbd al-Wāḥid al-Marrākushī; al-Baydhaḳ; Ibn Ṣāḥib al-Ṣalāt
voir aussi al-Ḥulal al-Mawshiyya
autres personnages [au Suppl.] Ibn al-Ḳaṭṭān
voir aussi Abū Ḥafṣ ʿUmar al-Hintātī; Ibn Mardanīsh
Almoravides (1056-1147) Amīr al-Muslimīn; **al-Murābiṭūn**
souverains ʿAlī b. Yūsuf; al-Lamtūnī
secrétaires Ibn ʿAbdūn
historiens des Ibn al-Ṣayrafī
voir aussi al-Ḥulal al-Mawshiyya
autres personnages Ibn Bādjdja; Ibn Ḳasī
ʿĀmirides (1021-1096)
souverains ʿAbd al-Malik b. Abī ʿĀmir; al-Muẓaffar
vizirs Ibn al-Ḳaṭṭāʿ
autres personnages ʿAbd al-Raḥmān b. Abī ʿĀmir
Djahwarides (1030-1070)
autres personnages (al-)Ḥakam ibn ʿUk(k)āsha; Ibn ʿAbdūs
Ḥafṣides (1228-1574)
secrétaires Ḥāzim
historiens des al-Ḥādjdj Ḥammūda
autres personnages Ibn ʿArafa
Ḥammādides (972-1152)
souverains Bādīs; al-Manṣūr; al-Nāṣir
voir aussi Ḳalʿat Banī Ḥammād
Ḥammūdides (1010-1057)
vizirs Ibn Dhakwān
Hūdides (1039-1142)
souverains al-Muʾtamin ibn Hūd
Ḥusaynides (1705-1957)
souverains Aḥmad Bey; al-Ḥusayn (b. ʿAlī); Muḥammad Bey; Muḥammad al-Ṣādiḳ Bey
ministres Khayr al-Dīn Pasha; Muṣṭafā Khaznadār
Idrīsides (789-926)
souverains Idrīs Ier; Idrīs II
Marīnides (1196-1465)
souverains Abū l-Ḥasan; Abū ʿInān
Naṣrides (1230-1492) **Naṣrids**

vizirs Ibn al-Khaṭīb
autres personnages [au Suppl.] Ibn al-Sarrādj
Rustamides (777-909) **Rustamides**
historiens des Ibn al-Ṣaghīr
Saʿdides (1511-1659) **Saʿdides**
sultans ʿAbd Allāh al-Ghālib billāh; Aḥmad al-Manṣūr; Mawlāy Maḥammad al-Shaykh
voir aussi Mawlāy
vizirs Ibn ʿĪsā
historiens des ʿAbd al-ʿAzīz b. Muḥammad; al-Ifrānī
autres personnages [au Suppl.] Abū Maḥallī
Tudjībides (1019-1039)
souverains Maʿn b. Muḥammad; al-Muʿtaṣim
ʿUbaydides
historiens des Ibn Ḥamādu
Umayyades (756-1031)
émirs et califes ʿAbd Allāh b. Muḥammad; ʿAbd al-Raḥmān; al-Ḥakam Ier; al-Ḥakam II; Hishām Ier; Hishām II; Hishām III; al-Mahdī; al-Mundhir b. Muḥammad
voir aussi Madīnat al-Zahrāʾ; Muʿāwiya b. Hishām; Rabaḍ; al-Ruṣāfa.4; [au Suppl.] Bubashtru
vizirs Ibn ʿAlḳama.II; Ibn Shuhayd
secrétaires ʿArīb b. Saʿd; Ibn Burd.I
autres personnages ʿAbd al-Raḥmān b. Marwān; Ghālib b. ʿAbd al-Raḥmān; Ḥabīb b. ʿAbd al-Malik; Ḥasdāy b. Shaprūṭ; Ibn ʿAlḳama.I; Ibn Dhakwān; Ibn al-Ḥannāṭ; Ibn Ḳasī; Ibn al-Ḳiṭṭ; al-Manṣūr; Rabīʿ b. Zayd
Zīrides (972-1152)
souverains Buluggīn b. Zīrī; al-Muʿizz b. Bādīs
autres personnages Ibn Abī l-Ridjāl
voir aussi Ḳurhub
Zīrides de Granade (1012-1090)
souverains ʿAbd Allāh b. Buluggīn
Mongols Bātūʾides; Čaghatay; Čingizides; Djalāyir; Djānides; Girāy; Īlkhāns; Ḳarā Khiṭāy; **Mongols**
voir aussi Čūbānides; Ḳāzān; [au Suppl.] Āgahī; Dīwān-begi; Djamāl Ḳarshī; Ordu.2; *et* → ONOMASTIQUE.TITRES
Bātūʾides (1236-1502)
souverains Bātū; Berke Khān; Mangū-tīmūr
autres personnages Masʿūd Beg
Djānides (1598-1785)
souverains Nadhr Muḥammad
voir aussi Bukhārā

Grands-Khāns (1206-1634)
khāns Činghiz Khān; Ḳubilay; Möngke; Ögedey
autres personnages Ḳaydu; Maḥmūd Yalawač
Īlkhāns (1256-1353)
voir aussi Ṣadr.1
khāns Baydu; Gaykhātū; Ghāzān; Hūlāgū; Öldjeytü
historiens des Ḥamd Allāh al-Mustawfī al-Ḳazwinī; Rashīd al-Dīn Ṭabīb
autres personnages Djuwaynī, ʿAlāʾ al-dīn; Ḳutlugh-Shāh Noyan
Khānat de Čaghatay (1227-1370)
souverains Burāḳ Khān; Čaghatay Khān
historiens des Ḥaydar Mīrzā
Khānat de Girāy (circa 1426-1792)
souverains Dawlat Giray; Ghāzī Girāy Ier; Ghāzī Girāy II; Ghāzī Girāy III; Ḥādjdjī Girāy; Islām Girāy; Ḳaplan Girāy Ier; Ḳaplan Girāy II; Meḥmed Girāy Ier; Mengli Girāy Ier; Ṣāḥib Girāy Khān I
voir aussi Ḳalghay; Meḥmed Baghčesarāyī; Meḥmed Girāy
Shaybānides (1500-1598)
souverains ʿAbd Allāh b. Iskandar; Abū l-Khayr
historiens des Abū l-Ghāzī; [au Suppl.] Ḥāfiẓ Tanïsh
Péninsule arabique Bū Saʿīd; Hamdānides; Hāshimides (2x); āl Khalīfa; Mahdides; Nadjāḥides; Rashīd, Āl; Rasūlides; Ṣabaḥ, Āl; [au Suppl.] Djabrides
Āl Saʿūd (1746-)
souverains [au Suppl.] ʿAbd al-ʿAzīz; Fayṣal b. ʿAbd al-ʿAzīz
voir aussi Muḥammad b. Suʿūd
Bū Saʿīd (1741-) **Bū Saʿīd**
sultans Barghash; Saʿīd b. Sulṭān
Hāshimides (1908-1925)
souverains Ḥusayn (b. ʿAlī)
voir aussi ʿAbd Allāh b. al Ḥusayn; Fayṣal Ier; Fayṣal II
Ḳarmaṭes (894-fin du 11e siècle)
souverains al-Djannābī, Abū Saʿīd; al-Djannābī, Abū Ṭāhir
Rasūlides (1229-1454) **Rasūlides**
historiens des al-Khazradjī
autres personnages [au Suppl.] Ibn Ḥātim
Ṭāhirides (1454-1517)
souverains ʿĀmir Ier; ʿĀmir II
Zaydīs (860-) Rassides
imāms Ḥasan al-Uṭrūsh; al-Mahdī li-Dīn Allāh Aḥmad; al-Manṣūr bi-llāh, ʿAbd Allāh; al-Manṣūr bi-llāh, al-Ḳāsim b. ʿAlī; al-Manṣūr bi-llāh al-Ḳāsim b. Muḥammad; al-Muʾayyad bi-llāh Muḥammad;

Muḥammad al-Murtaḍā li-Dīn Allāh; al-Mutawakkil ʿalā llāh, Ismāʿīl;
al-Mutawakkil ʿalā llāh, S̲h̲araf al-dīn; al-Nāṣir li-Dīn Allāh, Abū l-
Ḥasan; al-Rassī; [au Suppl.] al-Hādī ilā l-Ḥaḳḳ
   voir aussi Imāma
   autres personnages   al-Muṭahhar; al-Nāṣir (li-dīn Allāh)
Zurayʿides (1138-1174)
   vizirs   Bilāl b. D̲j̲arīr al-Muḥammadī
Perse   Afrāsiyābides; Aḥmadīlīs; Aḳ Ḳoyunlu; Bādūsbānides; Bāwand; Buwayhides; Dulafides; Faḍlawayh; Farīg̲h̲ūnides; Ḥasanwayh; Hazāraspides;
Ildeñizides; Ilek-K̲h̲āns; Ilyāsides; Īnd̲j̲ū; Ḳād̲j̲ār; Kākūyides; Ḳarā-ḳoyunlu;
Kārinides; Kāwūs; K̲h̲ʷārazm-s̲h̲āhs; Ḳutlug̲h̲-k̲h̲ānides; Lur-i Buzurg; Lur-
i Kūčik; Mangîts; Marʿas̲h̲īs; Muhtād̲j̲ides; Musāfirides; Mus̲h̲aʿs̲h̲aʿ;
Muẓaffarides; Rawwādides; Ṣafawides; Ṣaffārides; Sald̲j̲ūḳides; Salg̲h̲u-
rides; Sāmānides
   voir aussi Ardalān; Atabak; ʿAwfī; Čās̲h̲na-gīr; Daylam; Dīwān.IV;
D̲j̲alāyir; G̲h̲ulām.II; Ḥād̲j̲ib.III; Ḥarb.V; al-Ḥasan b. Zayd b. Muḥammad;
Hiba.IV; Ḥiṣār.III; Īlk̲h̲āns; Īrān.V; Kayānides; Marāsim.3; Mawākib.III
Afs̲h̲ārides (1736-1795)
   souverains   Nādir S̲h̲āh Afs̲h̲ār
   historiens des   ʿAbd al-Karīm Kas̲h̲mīrī; Mahdī K̲h̲ān Astarābādī
Buwayhides (932-1062)   **Buwayhides**
   souverains   Abū Kālīd̲j̲ār; ʿAḍud al-Dawla; Bak̲h̲tiyār; D̲j̲alāl al-Dawla;
Fak̲h̲r al-Dawla; ʿImād al-Dawla; K̲h̲usraw Fīrūz (*et* al-Malik al-
Raḥīm); Mad̲j̲d al-Dawla; Muʾayyid al-Dawla; Muʿizz al-Dawla;
Rukn al-Dawla; Ṣamṣām al-Dawla; [au Suppl.] Bahāʾ al-Dawla wa-
Ḍiyāʾ al-Milla
   vizirs   al-ʿAbbās b. al-Ḥusayn; Ibn ʿAbbād; Ibn al-ʿAmīd; Ibn Baḳiyya;
Ibn Mākūlā.I et II; al-Muhallabī, Abū Muḥammad; Sābūr b. Ardas̲h̲īr;
[au Suppl.] ʿAbd al-ʿAzīz b. Yūsuf; Ibn K̲h̲alaf.I; Ibn Saʿdān
   secrétaires   Hilāl al-Ṣābiʾ (*et* Ṣābiʾ.(3).9); Ibn Hindū; Ṣābiʾ.(3).7
   historiens des   Ṣābiʾ.(3).7
   autres personnages   al-Basāsīrī; Fasand̲j̲us; Ḥasan b. Ustād̲h̲-hurmuz;
Ibn Ḥād̲j̲ib al-Nuʿmān; ʿImrān b. S̲h̲āhīn; al-Malik al-ʿAzīz; [au
Suppl.] Ibrāhīm S̲h̲īrāzī
Dābūyides (660-760)
   souverains   Dābūya
Ildeñizides (1137-1225)
   souverains   Ildeñiz; Özbeg b. Muḥammad Pahlawān; Pahlawān
Ḳād̲j̲ārs (1779-1924)   **Ḳād̲j̲ār**; Mus̲h̲īr al-Dawla
   voir aussi   Ḳāʾim-maḳām-i Farāhānī; Mad̲j̲lis al-S̲h̲ūrā; *et* → IRAN.
PÉRIODE MODERNE
   souverains   Āg̲h̲ā Muḥammad S̲h̲āh; Fatḥ ʿAlī S̲h̲āh; Muḥammad ʿAlī

Shāh Ḳādjār; Muḥammad Shāh; Muẓaffar al-Dīn Shāh Ḳādjār; Nāṣir al-Dīn Shāh
autres personnages ʿAbbās Mīrzā; [au Suppl.] Amīr Niẓām; Ḥādjdjī Ibrāhīm
Khānat de Khīwa
souverains Abū l-Ghāzī
Khwārazm-Shāhs (circa 995-1231)
souverains Atsïz b. Anūshtigin; Djalāl al-Dīn Khʷārizm-shāh; Maʾmūn b. Muḥammad
historiens des Djuwaynī; al-Nasawī
autres personnages Burāḳ Ḥādjib
Muẓaffarides (1314-1393)
historiens des Muʿīn al-Dīn Yazdī
Pahlawīs (1926-1979) **Pahlawī**
et → IRAN.PÉRIODE MODERNE
souverains Muḥammad Riḍā Shāh Pahlawī; Riḍā Shāh
Sādjides (circa 856-circa 930) **Sādjides**
souverains Abū l-Sādj; Muḥammad b. Abī l-Sādj
Ṣafawides (1501-1732) Bārūd.V; Īshīk-āḳāsī; Iʿtimād al-Dawla; Ḳūrčī; Libās.III; **Ṣafawides**
voir aussi Ḥaydar; Ḳïzïl-bāsh; Nuḳṭawiyya; Ṣadr.3; Ṣadr al-Dīn Ardabīlī; Ṣadr al-Dīn Mūsā; Ṣafī al-Dīn Ardabīlī
souverains ʿAbbās Iᵉʳ; Ḥusayn; Ismāʿīl Iᵉʳ; Ismāʿīl II
historiens des Ḥasan-i Rūmlū; Iskandar Beg; Ḳummī
voir aussi [au Suppl.] Ibn al-Bazzāz al-Ardabīlī
autres personnages Alḳāṣ Mīrzā; Ḥamza Mīrzā; al-Karakī; Madjlisī
Ṣaffārides (867-circa 1495) **Ṣaffārides**
souverains ʿAmr b. al-Layth
Saldjūḳides (1038-1194) Amīr Dād; Arslan b. Saldjūḳ; Atabak; **Saldjūḳides**
et → DYNASTIES.ANATOLIE ET LES TURCS.SALDJŪḲIDES DE RŪM
souverains Alp Arslan; Bahrām Shāh; Barkyārūḳ; Maḥmūd b. Muḥammad b. Malik-shāh; Malik-Shāh.I-III; Masʿūd b. Muḥammad b. Malik-Shāh; Muḥammad b. Maḥmūd b. Muḥammad b. Malik-shāh; Muḥammad b. Malik-shāh; Riḍwān
voir aussi Čaghrï-beg
vizirs Anūshirwān b. Khālid; Djahīr; al-Kundurī; Madjd al-Mulk al-Balāsānī; al-Maybudī.III; Niẓām al-Mulk; Rabīb al-Dawla; [au Suppl.] Ibn Dārust
historiens des al-Bundārī; ʿImād al-Dīn; Nīshāpūrī; Rāwandī; [au Suppl.] al-Ḥusaynī
autres personnages Āḳ Sunḳur al-Bursuḳī; Arslan-Arghūn; Ayāz; al-Basāsīrī; Būrī-bars; Bursuḳ; Būz-abeh; Ḳāwurd; Khalaf b. Mulāʿib;

Kh̲āṣṣ Beg; Kurbuḳa; Niẓāmiyya; [au Suppl.] Ekinči

Salgh̲urides (1148-1270) **Salgh̲urides**
  souverains Saʿd b. Zangī
Sāmānides (819-1005) **Sāmānides**
  souverains Ismāʿīl b. Aḥmad; Ismāʿīl b. Nūḥ; Manṣūr b. Nūḥ; Naṣr b.
    Aḥmad b. Ismāʿīl; Nūḥ (Iᵉʳ); Nūḥ (II)
  vizirs Balʿamī; al-Muṣʿabī; [au Suppl.] al-Dj̲ayhānī
  historiens des Narshakh̲ī
    voir aussi al-Sallāmī
  autres personnages Arslan b. Saldj̲ūḳ; [au Suppl.] al-Dj̲ayhānī
Ṭāhirides (821-873)
  souverains ʿAbd Allāh b. Ṭāhir; Muḥammad b. Ṭāhir
  historiens des Ibn al-Daybaʿ
  autres personnages Muḥammad b. ʿAbd Allāh (b. Ṭāhir)
Tīmūrides (1370-1506)
  voir aussi Ṣadr.2
  souverains Abū Saʿīd b. Tīmūr; Bāyḳarā; Baysongh̲or; Ḥusayn
    voir aussi Kh̲ān-zāda Bēgum
  historiens des Ibn ʿArabsh̲āh; Kh̲ʷāfī Kh̲ān
  autres personnages Mīr ʿAlī Sh̲īr Nawāʾī; Mīrānsh̲āh b. Tīmūr
Zands (1750-1794)
  souverains Karīm Kh̲ān; Luṭf ʿAlī Kh̲ān
    voir aussi Lak
Zangides (1127-1222)
  souverains Masʿūd b. Mawdūd b. Zangī; Mawdūd b. ʿImād al-Dīn
    Zankī; Nūr al-Dīn Arslān Sh̲āh; Nur al-Dīn Maḥmūd b. Zankī
  vizirs al-Dj̲awād al-Iṣfahānī
    voir aussi Begteginides; Karīm Kh̲ān; Luʾluʾ
  historiens des Ibn al-Ath̲īr.II
Ziyārides (927- circa 1090)
  souverains Ḳābūs b. Wush̲magīr; Kay Kāʾūs b. Iskandar; Mardāwīdj

E

ÉCONOMIQUE Bayʿ; Kasb; Māl
  voir aussi Muḍāraba

ÉCRITURE **Kh̲aṭṭ**
  voir aussi Ibn Muḳla; Kitābāt; *et* → ART.CALLIGRAPHIE. ÉPIGRAPHIE
  fournitures Dj̲ild; Kāgh̲ad; Ḳalam; Kh̲ātam; Ḳirṭās; Kitāb; Midād; Papyrus;
    Raḳḳ; [au Suppl.] Dawāt

voir aussi ʿAfṣ; Afsantīn; Diplomatique; Īlkhāns; Maʿdin.IV
manuscrits et livres Daftar; Ḥāshiya; **Kitāb**; Muḳābala.II; **Nuskha**; [au Suppl.] Abréviations
voir aussi Ḳaṭʿ; Maktaba
reliure Īlkhāns; Kitāb; Nuskha; ʿOthmānli̊.VII.c

ÉDUCATION **Maʿārif**
voir aussi ʿArabiyya.B.IV; Idjāza
bibliothèques Dār al-ʿIlm; **Maktaba**
voir aussi ʿAlī Pasha Mubārak; Khāzin; al-Madīna.I.5
bibliothécaires Ibn al-Fuwaṭī; Ibn Ḥadjar al-ʿAsḳalānī; Ibn al-Sāʿī; al-Kattānī
collections ʿAlī Amīrī (*et* [au Suppl.] ʿAlī Emīrī); Esʿad Efendi, Meḥmed; Khudā Bakhsh; [au Suppl.] ʿAbd al-Wahhāb
voir aussi Geniza
établissements d'éducation Dār al-Ḥadīth; Djāmiʿa; Köy Enstitüleri; Kuttāb; Madrasa; Maktab; Pesantren
voir aussi Kulliyya; Ṣadr.c; Samāʿ.2; *et* → ÉDUCATION.BIBLIOTHÈQUES
établissements individuels al-Azhar; Bayt al-Ḥikma; Dār al-Ḥikma; Dār al-ʿUlūm; Ghalaṭa-sarāyi̊; Ḥarbiye; al-Ḳarawiyyīn.II; al-Khaldūniyya; Makhredj; Mulkiyya; al-Ṣādiḳiyya; [au Suppl.] Institut des hautes études marocaines; Institut des hautes études de Tunis
voir aussi Aligarh; Deoband; Filāḥa.III; al-Ḳāhira; Lakhnaw; al-Madīna.I.5; Makka.III; Muṣṭafā ʿAbd al-Rāziḳ; al-Mustanṣir (I); Nadwat al-ʿUlamāʾ; [au Suppl.] ʿAbd al-Bārī; ʿAbd al-Wahhāb; Farangī Maḥall
sociétés savantes et académies Andjuman; Djamʿiyya; Djemʿiyyet-i ʿIlmiyye-i ʿOthmāniyye; Institut d'Égypte; Khalḳevi; Madjmaʿ ʿIlmī
réforme → RÉFORME
traités sur Ergin, Osman

ÉGYPTE al-Azhar; al-Ḳāhira; Ḳibṭ; **Miṣr**; Nūba; al-Ṣaʿīd
voir aussi al-ʿArab.IV; al-Fusṭāṭ; *et* → DYNASTIES.ÉGYPTE ET LE CROISSANT FERTILE; NUBIE
administration Dār al-Maḥfūẓāt al-ʿUmūmiyya; Dīwān.II; Ḳabāla; Kharādj.I; Rawk
voir aussi Miṣr.D.1.b; *et* → CALIFAT.ʿABBĀSIDES *et* FĀṬIMIDES; DYNASTIES.ÉGYPTE ET LE CROISSANT FERTILE.MAMLŪKS; EMPIRE OTTOMAN.ADMINISTRATION
architecture → ARCHITECTURE.RÉGIONS
avant l'Islam Firʿawn; Manf; Miṣr.D.1; Nūba.II; Saḳḳāra; [au Suppl.] Abū Sinbil
dynasties ʿAbbāsides; Ayyūbides; Fāṭimides; Mamlūks; Muḥammad ʿAlī Pasha *et* → DYNASTIES.ÉGYPTE ET LE CROISSANT FERTILE
géographie physique
eaux Burullus; al-Nīl

historiens Abū l-Maḥāsin Ibn Taghrībirdī; ʿAlī Pasha Mubārak; al-Bakrī.II; al-Balawī; al-Damurdāshī; al-Djabartī; Ibn ʿAbd al-Ḥakam.IV; Ibn Duḳmāḳ; Ibn Iyās; Ibn Muyassar; al-Kindī, Abū ʿUmar Muḥammad; al-Maḳrīzī; al-Nuwayrī, Muḥammad; Rifāʿa Bey; al-Ṣafadī, al-Ḥasan; Salīm al-Naḳḳāsh
et → DYNASTIES.ÉGYPTE ET LE CROISSANT FERTILE

période moderne Ḍarība.IV; Djarīda.I.A; Djāmiʿa; Dustūr.III; Ḥizb.I; Ḥukūma.III; al-Ikhwān al-Muslimūn; Iltizām; Imtiyāzāt.IV; Institut d'Égypte; Maʿārif.I.2; Madjlis.IV.A.16; Madjmaʿ ʿIlmī.I.2; Maḥkama.IV.1; Miṣr.D.7; Salafiyya.2a
voir aussi Baladiyya.II; al-Bannāʾ; Madjlis al-Shūrā

hommes d'état ʿAlī Pasha Mubārak; al-Bārūdī; Fikrī; Ismāʿīl Ṣidḳī; Luṭfī al-Sayyid; Muḥammad Farīd Bey; Muḥammad Nadjīb; al-Naḥḥās; Nūbār Pasha; Saʿd Zaghlūl; al-Sādāt; [au Suppl.] ʿAbd al-Nāṣir
voir aussi Muṣṭafā Kāmil Pasha

ligne de Muḥammad ʿAlī ʿAbbās Ḥilmī Ier; ʿAbbās Ḥilmī II; Fuʾād al-Awwal; Ḥusayn Kāmil; Ibrāhīm Pasha; Ismāʿīl Pasha; Muḥammad ʿAlī Pasha; Saʿīd Pasha; [au Suppl.] Bakhīt al-Muṭīʿī; Fārūḳ
voir aussi ʿAzīz Miṣr; Khidīw; [au Suppl.] Dāʾira Saniyya; Ibʿādiyya

personnes influentes Djamāl al-Dīn al-Afghānī; al-Marṣafī; Muḥammad ʿAbduh; Muṣṭafā Kāmil Pasha; al-Muwayliḥī.I; Rifāʿa Bey; Salāma Mūsā; [au Suppl.] Abū l-ʿAzāʾim; al-ʿAdawī; al-Bakrī; al-Biblāwī; Djawharī, Ṭanṭāwī; al-ʿIdwī al-Ḥamzāwī; ʿIllaysh

période ottomane (1517-1798) Dhū l-Faḳāriyya; Ḳāsimiyya; Ḳāzdughliyya; Miṣr.D.6; Muḥammad ʿAlī Pasha
voir aussi Ḥurriyya.Époque moderne

beys ʿAlī Bey; Muḥammad Abū l-Dhahab (*et* [au Suppl.] Abū l-Dhahab)

population ʿAbābda; Ḳibṭ
voir aussi [au Suppl.] Démographie.IV; *et* → CHRISTIANISME.CONFESSIONS.COPTES

toponymes

anciens Adfū; Bābalyūn; al-Bahnasā; Burullus; Dabīḳ; al-Ḳulzum; Manf

actuels

régions Buḥayra; al-Fayyūm; al-Gharbiyya; Girgā
voir aussi al-Ṣaʿīd

villes ʿAbbāsa; Abūḳīr; Akhmīm; al-ʿAllāḳī; al-ʿArīsh; Asyūṭ; Aṭfīḥ; ʿAyn Shams; Banhā; Banī Suwayf; Bilbays; Būlāḳ; Būṣīr; Dahshūr; Daḳahliyya; Damanhūr; Dimyāṭ; al-Farāfra; al-Fusṭāṭ; Girgā; Ḥulwān; al-Iskandariyya; Ismāʿīliyya; Isna; al-Ḳāhira; Ḳalyūb; Ḳanṭara.3; Ḳifṭ; Ḳunā; Ḳūṣ; Ḳuṣayr; al-Maḥalla al-Kubra; al-Manṣūra; Manūf; Port-Saïd; Rafaḥ; Rashīd; Saḳḳāra; Samannūd; [au Suppl.] Abū Zaʿbal
voir aussi al-Muḳaṭṭam; Rawḍa

ÉMANCIPATION   Ḥurriyya
pour l'affranchissement, voir ʿAbd; *et pour l'émancipation des femmes* → FEM-
MES

ÉMIGRATION   Ḏjāliya; **Hidjra**
voir aussi al-Mahḏjar; Muhāḏjir; al-Muhāḏjirūn; Pārsīs; *et* → NOUVEAU
MONDE

ÉMIRATS ARABES UNIS   al-Ḳawāsim; Maḏjlis.IV.A.12; Maḥkama.IV.9; [au
Suppl.] **al-Imārāt al-ʿArabiyya al-Muttaḥida**
population   Mazrūʿī
    et → TRIBUS.PÉNINSULE ARABIQUE
toponymes   Abū Ẓabī; al-Ḏjiwāʾ; Dubayy; al-Fuḏjayra; Raʾs al-Khayma; [au
Suppl.] ʿAḏjmān
    voir aussi (Ḏjazīrat) al-ʿArab; al-Khaṭṭ

EMPIRE OTTOMAN   Anadolu.III.2 et 3; Ertoghrul.I; Istanbul; Lāle Devri;
ʿOthmānli
voir aussi Bāb-i ʿĀlī; Ḥidjāz; Maṭbakh.II; Pasha Ḳapusu; *et* → DROIT.OTTOMAN;
DYNASTIES.ANATOLIE ET LES TURCS; EUROPE.EUROPE ORIENTALE; MILITAIRES.
OTTOMANS; *et l'entrée Période Ottomane sous pays individuels*
administration   Beratlı̊; Ḍabṭiyya; Dīwān-i Humāyūn; Eyālet; Imtiyāzāt.II;
    Khāṣṣ; Khazīne; Mashwara; Millet.3; Mukhtār; Mülāzemet; Mulāzim;
    Mulkiyya; Nāḥiye; Nishāndjı̊; Reʾīs ül-Küttāb; [au Suppl.] Dāʾira Saniyya
    voir aussi Ḳaḍāʾ; Maʾmūr; Oḏjaḳ; *et* → DOCUMENTS.OTTOMANS;
    DROIT.OTTOMAN; MILITAIRES.OTTOMANS
  archives et registres   Başvekalet Arşivi; Daftar-i Khāḳānī; Maṣraf Defteri;
      Mühimme Defterleri; Sāl-nāme
      voir aussi Daftar.III; Ferīdūn Beg; Maḥlūl
  financière   Arpalı̊ḳ; Ashām; Bayt al-Māl.II; Daftardār; Dār al-Ḍarb; Dirlik;
      Ḏjayb-i Humāyūn; Duyūn-i ʿUmūmiyye; Irsāliyye; Ḳāʾime; Khazīne;
      Māliyye; Muḥāsaba.II; Mukhallefāt; Muṣādara.3; Rūznāmeḏji; Sāliyāne
      voir aussi Bakhshīsh
  fiscale   Ḍarība.III; Ḏjizya.II; Ḥisba.II; Kharādj.III; Muḥaṣṣil; Mültezim;
      ʿOthmānli̊.II; Resm
      voir aussi Mutaṣarrı̊f
agriculture   Filāḥa.IV; Māʾ.VIII; Raʿiyya.2
    et → AGRICULTURE
cérémonies de la cour   Čāʾūsh; Khı̊rḳa-i Sherīf; Marāsim.4; Mawākib.IV; Mehter
diplomatie   Balyos; Consul; Elči; Hiba.V; Penče
    voir aussi Beratlı̊; Imtiyāzāt.II; Ḳawwās; *et* → DIPLOMATIE
éducation   Ghalaṭa-sarāyı̊; Külliyye; Maʿārif.I.1; Makhredj; Mulkiyya; Ṣaḥn-i

<u>Th</u>amān
voir aussi Ḥarbiye; *et* → ÉDUCATION; RÉFORME.D'ÉDUCATION
fonctionnaires   Āmed<u>dj</u>i; A'yān; Bazîrgan; Bostān<u>dj</u>i; Bostāndji-ba<u>sh</u>î; Čakîrdji-ba<u>sh</u>î; Čā<u>sh</u>nagīr-ba<u>sh</u>î; Ḍābiṭ; Ḍabṭiyya; Daftardār; Dilsiz; Do<u>gh</u>andji; Elči; Emīn; <u>Gh</u>ulām.IV; Ḥekīm-ba<u>sh</u>î; Ič-o<u>gh</u>lanî; 'Ilmiyye; Ḳā'im-maḳām; Ḳapu A<u>gh</u>asî; Ḳawwās; Ket<u>kh</u>udā; <u>Kh</u>aznadār; <u>Kh</u>ʷādjegān-i Dīwān-i Humāyūn; Ma'mūr; Mewḳūfātči; Mīr-Ā<u>kh</u>ūr; Mu<u>sh</u>īr; Musta<u>sh</u>ār; Mutaṣarrîf; Ni<u>sh</u>āndji; Re'is ül-Küttāb; Rūznāme<u>dj</u>i; Ṣadr-ı A'ẓam
   voir aussi 'Ad<u>jam</u>ī o<u>gh</u>lān; 'Asas; Bālā; Balṭadji; Balyos; Bīrūn; Enderun; al-Ḥaramayn; <u>Kh</u>aṣī; <u>Kh</u>āṣṣ Oda; <u>Kh</u>āṣṣekī; Mābeyn; *et* → DROIT.OTTOMAN; MILITARES.OTTOMANS
histoire   'O<u>th</u>mānlî.I
   et › DYNASTIES.ANATOLIE ET LES TURCS; LITTÉRATURE.HISTORIQUE.TURQUE; TURQUIE.PÉRIODE OTTOMANE
industrie et commerce   Ḥarīr.II; Kārwān; Ḳuṭn.II; Milḥ.3; 'O<u>th</u>mānlî.II
   voir aussi Ma'din.III
littérature   → LITTÉRATURE
modernisation   Baladiyya.I; Ḥukūma.I; Ḥurriyya; Iṣlāḥ.III; Ittiḥād we Teraḳḳī Djem'iyyeti; Ma<u>dj</u>lis.IV.A.1; Ma<u>dj</u>lis al-<u>Sh</u>ūrā
   et → TURQUIE.PÉRIODE OTTOMANE

ENFANT   Ṣa<u>gh</u>īr
   et › CIRCONCISION; ÉDUCATION
accouchement   'Aḳīḳa; Āl; Li'ān; al-Mar'a.II.3; Mawākib.IV.2
   voir aussi Raḍā'
   traités sur   'Arīb b. Sa'd
allaitement   Raḍā'
enfance   Ṣa<u>gh</u>īr
   voir aussi Ḥaḍāna
grossesse   Rāḳid

ENFER   Aṣḥāb al-U<u>kh</u>dūd; **Djahannam**; Sa'īr; Saḳar
   voir aussi al-A'rāf

ÉPIGRAPHIE   **Kitābāt**
   voir aussi Eldem, <u>Kh</u>alīl Edhem; Ḥisāb al-<u>Dj</u>ummal; <u>Kh</u>aṭṭ; Musnad.1
lieux des inscriptions   Lībiyā.II; Liḥyān; Or<u>kh</u>on
   voir aussi Ḥaḍramawt; Saba'; Ṣafaïtique

ESCHATOLOGIE   'A<u>dh</u>āb al-Ḳabr; Ā<u>kh</u>ira; al-A'rāf; Barza<u>kh</u>; Ba'<u>th</u>; Djahannam; Djanna; Djazā'; Dunyā; Ḥawḍ; Ḥisāb; Isrāfīl; 'Izrā'īl; Ḳiyāma; Ma'ād; al-Mahdī; Mawḳif.2; Munkar wa-Nakīr; Sā'a.3

voir aussi Ḳayyim; et → MORT; PARADIS
l'au-delà   Adjr.1; **Āk̲h̲ira**
    voir aussi Dunyā
signes   ʿAṣā; Dābba; al-Dad̲j̲d̲j̲āl
    voir aussi Baʿt̲h̲

ESCLAVAGE   **ʿAbd**; G̲h̲ulām; ʿItḳnāme; Ḳayna; K̲h̲āṣī; Mamlūk; Mawlā; al-Ṣaḳāliba
    voir aussi Ḥabas̲h̲.I; Ḥabs̲h̲ī; Hausa; ʿIdda.V; Istibrāʾ; K̲h̲ādim; Ḳul; Maṭmūra; et → MUSIQUE.CHANT.CHANTEURS

ESPAGNE   Aljamía; Almogávares; al-Burt; al-Bus̲h̲ārrāt; Morisques
    voir aussi Ibn al-Ḳiṭṭ; Ifni; al-ʿIḳāb; et → ANDALOUSIE; DYNASTIES.ESPAGNE ET AFRIQUE DU NORD
géographie physique
    eaux   al-Ḥamma; Ibruh; al-Mudawwar; [au Suppl.] Arag̲h̲ūn
toponymes
    anciens   Barbas̲h̲turu; Bulāy; Ḳasṭīliya; Labla; al-Madīna al-Zāhira; [au Suppl.] Āfrāg; Balyūnas̲h̲
        voir aussi Rayya
    actuels
        îles   al-D̲j̲azāʾir al-K̲h̲ālidāt; Mayūrḳa; Minūrḳa
        régions   Ālaba wa-l-Ḳilāʿ; D̲j̲illīḳiyya; Faḥṣ al-Ballūṭ; Firrīs̲h̲; Ḳanbāniya; Ḳas̲h̲tāla; Navarra; [au Suppl.] Arag̲h̲ūn
        villes   Als̲h̲; Arkus̲h̲; Arnīṭ; Bad̲j̲d̲j̲āna; Balansiya; Bālis̲h̲; Banbalūna; Bars̲h̲alūna; al-Basīt; Basta; Baṭalyaws; Bayyāna; Bayyāsa; Biṭraws̲h̲; al-Bunt; Burg̲h̲us̲h̲; Dāniya; D̲j̲arunda; D̲j̲ayyān; al-D̲j̲azīra al-K̲h̲aḍrāʾ; D̲j̲azīrat S̲h̲uḳr; Finyāna; G̲h̲arnāṭa; Ifrāg̲h̲a; Ilbīra; Is̲h̲bīliya; Istid̲j̲a; Ḳabra; Ḳādis; Ḳalʿat Ayyūb; Ḳalʿat Rabāḥ; Ḳanṭara.2; Ḳarmūna; Ḳarṭād̲j̲anna; al-Ḳulayʿa; Ḳūnka; Ḳūriya; Ḳurṭuba; Laḳant; Lārida; Laws̲h̲a; Liyūn; Lūrḳa; al-Maʿdin; Madīnat Sālim; Madīnat al-Zahrāʾ; Mad̲j̲rīṭ; Mālaḳa; Mārida; al-Mariyya; Mawrūr; al-Munakkab; Mursiya; Runda; [au Suppl.] As̲h̲turḳa
        voir aussi al-Andalus.III.3; Balāṭ; D̲j̲abal Ṭāriḳ; al-Ḳalʿa; et → PORTUGAL

ÉTERNITÉ   **Abad**; Ḳidam

ÉTHIOPIE   Adal; Aḥmad Grāñ; Awfāt; Bāli; D̲j̲abart; D̲j̲immā; **Ḥabas̲h̲**; Ḥabas̲h̲at; al-Nad̲j̲ās̲h̲ī
    voir aussi Ḥabes̲h̲; Kūs̲h̲; et → LANGUES.AFRO-ASIATIQUES
historiens   ʿArabfaḳīh

population ʿĀmir; Diglal; D̲jabart; Galla; Māryā; Oromo; Ras̲h̲āʾida
toponymes Assab; Dahlak; Dire Dawa; Érythrée; Harar; Maṣawwaʿ; Ogādēn

ÉTHIQUE Adab; **Ak̲h̲lāḳ**; Ḥisba
voir aussi Ḥurriyya; al-Maḥāsin wa-l-Masāwī; Miskawayh; *et* → VERTUS

ETHNICITÉ Mag̲h̲āriba; Mas̲h̲āriḳa
voir aussi Fatā; Ibn G̲h̲arsiya; Ismāʿīl b. Yasār; Mawlā

ÉTIQUETTE **Adab**
voir aussi Āʾīn; Hiba; *et* → LITTÉRATURE

EUNUQUE **K̲h̲aṣī**
voir aussi K̲h̲ādim; Mamlūk.3

EUROPE
Europe occidentale al-Bas̲h̲kunis̲h̲; Ifrand̲j; Iḳrīṭis̲h̲; Īṭaliya; Ḳubrus; Malta; Nemče
voir aussi Ibn Idrīs [II]; Ibrāhīm b. Yaʿḳūb; al-Mad̲j̲ūs; Muslimūn.II
pour les pays individuels → AUTRICHE; CHYPRE; CRÈTE; ESPAGNE; FRANCE; GRÈCE; ITALIE; PORTUGAL
Europe orientale Arnawutluḳ; Balḳan; Bulgarie; Itil; Leh; [au Suppl.] Čeh
voir aussi Bulg̲h̲ar; Ḥizb.V; Ibrāhīm b. Yaʿḳūb; Muhād̲j̲ir.2; Muslimūn.I; Rūmeli; al-Ṣaḳāliba
pour les pays individuels → ALBANIE; BULGARIE; HONGRIE; POLOGNE; (ex-) TCHÉCOSLOVAQUIE; (ex-)YOUGOSLAVIE
Union Soviétique ancienne Ḳiri̊m
voir aussi Bulg̲h̲ār; D̲j̲adīd; Ḥizb.V; Ḳayyūm Nāṣirī
dynasties Girāy
population Bas̲h̲d̲j̲irt; Besermyans; Beskesek-abaza; Buk̲h̲ārli̊k; Burṭās; Čeremisses; Čuli̊m; Čuwas̲h̲es; Gagauz; Ḳarapapak̲h̲; Lipḳa; Rūs
voir aussi Ḳang̲h̲li; K̲h̲azar; Kimäk; Pečenegs; al-Ṣaḳāliba
toponymes
anciens Atil; Saḳsīn
actuels Aḳ Kirmān; Aḳ Masd̲j̲id.1; Astrak̲h̲ān; Azaḳ; Bāg̲h̲če Sarāy; Ismāʿīl; Ḳamāniča; Ḳaraṣū-bāzār; Ḳāsimov; Ḳāzān; Kefe; Kerč; Khotin; Ḳi̊lburun

F

FĀṬIMIDES → CALIFAT

FAUCONNERIE **Bayzara**; Čakîrdjî-ba<u>sh</u>î; Dog<u>h</u>and<u>j</u>ĭ

FEMMES ʿAbd; Ḥarīm; Ḥayḍ; Ḥidjāb.I; ʿIdda; Istibrāʾ; <u>Kh</u>afḍ; **al-Marʾa**; Nikāḥ; [au Suppl.] Big<u>h</u>āʾ
voir aussi ʿArūs Resmi; Ba<u>sh</u>maklîk̊; <u>Kh</u>ayr; <u>Kh</u>iḍr-ilyās; Li<u>th</u>ām; et → DI-VORCE; ENFANT; MARIAGE
concubinage ʿAbd.3.f; <u>Kh</u>aṣṣekī
émancipation des Ḳāsim Amīn; Malak Ḥifnī Nāṣif; Saʿīd Abū Bakr; Salāma Mūsā; [au Suppl.] al-Ḥaddād, al-Ṭāhir
voir aussi Ḥidjāb; Ileri, <u>Dj</u>elāl Nūrī; al-Marʾa; [au Suppl.] A<u>sh</u>raf al-Dīn Gīlānī
et littérature al-Marʾa.I
voir aussi Ḳiṣṣa
auteurs arabes al-Bāʿūnī.6; Ḥafṣa bint al-Ḥādjdj; ʿInān; al-<u>Kh</u>ansāʾ; Laylā al-A<u>kh</u>yaliyya; Mayy Ziyāda; [au Suppl.] Faḍl al-<u>Sh</u>āʿira
voir aussi ʿAbbāsa; ʿĀtika; <u>Kh</u>unā<u>th</u>a; Ḳiṣṣa.II
auteurs persanes Ḳurrat al-ʿAyn; Mahsatī; Parwīn Iʿtiṣāmī
voir aussi Gulbadan Bēgam; Ma<u>kh</u>fī
auteurs turques Fiṭnat; <u>Kh</u>ālide Edīb; Laylā <u>Kh</u>ānĭm (2x); Mihrī <u>Kh</u>atun
voir aussi Ḳiṣṣa.III.B
femmes influentes
arabes ʿĀʾi<u>sh</u>a bint Ṭalḥa; Asmāʾ; Barīra; Būrān; Hind bint ʿUtba; al-<u>Kh</u>ayzurān; <u>Kh</u>unā<u>th</u>a; [au Suppl.] Asmāʾ
voir aussi al-Maʿāfirī; et → MUḤAMMAD, LE PROPHÈTE.FEMMES DU PRO-PHÈTE
indo-musulmanes Nūr <u>Dj</u>ahān; Samrū
mongoles Bag<u>h</u>dād <u>Kh</u>ātūn; <u>Kh</u>ān-zāda Bēgam
ottomanes ʿĀdila <u>Kh</u>ātūn; <u>Kh</u>urrem; Kösem Wālide; Mihr-i Māh Sulṭān; Nīlūfer <u>Kh</u>ātūn; Nūr Bānū; Ṣafiyye Wālide Sulṭān
femmes légendaires al-Basūs; Bilḳīs; Hind bint al-<u>Kh</u>uss
voir aussi Āsiya
musiciennes ʿAzza al-Maylāʾ; <u>Dj</u>amīla; Ḥabāba; Rāʾiḳa; Sallāma al-Zarḳāʾ; [au Suppl.] Bad<u>h</u>l al-Kubrā; al-<u>Dj</u>arādatānⁱ; Faḍl al-<u>Sh</u>āʿira; Ḥabba <u>Kh</u>ātūn
mystiques ʿĀʾi<u>sh</u>a al-Mannūbiyya; <u>Dj</u>ahānārā Bēgam; Nafīsa; Rābiʿa al-ʿAdawiyya al-Ḳaysiyya

FÊTE ʿĪd; Kandūrī; Mawlid; Mawsim
voir aussi Maṭba<u>kh</u>.II

fêtes ʿAnṣāra; ʿĀs̲h̲ūrāʾ.II; Bārā Wafāt; ʿĪd al-Aḍhā; ʿĪd al-Fiṭr; K̲h̲iḍr-ilyās; Mihragān; Nawrūz
voir aussi G̲h̲adīr K̲h̲umm; Kurdes et Kurdistān.IV.C.3; Lālis̲h̲; Lĕbaran; Raʾs al-ʿĀm

FLORE (D̲j̲azīrat) al-ʿArab.V; Būstān; Filāḥa; Hind.I.k
et → BOTANIQUE
arbres Abanūs; ʿAfṣ; Argan; Bak̲k̲am; Bān; K̲h̲as̲h̲ab; Nak̲h̲l; Sād̲j̲; [au Suppl.] D̲j̲awz; D̲j̲ullanār
voir aussi ʿAyn S̲h̲ams; G̲h̲āba; Kāfūr; Kahrubā; Ḳaṭrān; Lubān; Ṣamg̲h̲; [au Suppl.] Halīlad̲j̲
fleurs Nard̲j̲is; [au Suppl.] Bābūnad̲j̲; D̲j̲ullanār
voir aussi Filāḥa.IV; Lāle Devri; Lālezarī; Nawriyya; *et* → ARCHITECTURE.
MONUMENTS.JARDINS DE PLAISANCE
plantes Ad̲h̲argūn; Afsantīn; Afyūn; Ḥalfāʾ; Ḥinnāʾ; Kammūn; Ḳaranful; Karm; Ḳaṣab; Naʿām; **Nabāt**; Namir et Nimr; Nasr; Ṣabr; [au Suppl.] Aḳūnīṭun; Ās; Bābūnad̲j̲; D̲j̲āwars; Fūd̲h̲and̲j̲; Hindibāʾ; Iklīl al-Malik
voir aussi Maryam; Naḥl; Ṣamg̲h̲; *et* → DROGUES.NARCOTIQUES

FOI ʿAḳīda; **Īmān**
et → ISLAM; RELIGION

FRANCE Arbūna; Fraxinetum
voir aussi Balāṭ al-S̲h̲uhadāʾ; Muslimūn.II; Rifāʿa Bey

FRANCS **Ifrand̲j̲**
et → CROISADES

G

GÉNÉALOGIE **Ḥasab wa-Nasab**; **Nasab**
voir aussi Naḳīb al-As̲h̲rāf; *et* → LITTÉRATURE.GÉNÉALOGIQUE; ONOMASTIQUE

GÉOGRAPHIE **D̲j̲ug̲h̲rāfiyā**; Iḳlīm; Istiwāʾ; K̲h̲arīṭa; al-Ḳubba
voir aussi Mag̲h̲rib; Makka.IV; Mas̲h̲riḳ
pour la géographie détaillée des régions, voir Adamawa; Ād̲h̲arbaydjān.I; Afg̲h̲ānistān.I; Aḳ Ṣu; Algérie.I; Anadolu.II; al-Andalus.II et III.2; (D̲j̲azīrat) al-ʿArab.II; Armīniya; Arnawutluḳ.III; ʿAsīr; Baḥr; D̲j̲azīra; Filāḥa; Ḥammāda; Indonésie; ʿIrāḳ; Īrān; Lībiyā; al-Mag̲h̲rib
administrative Kūra; Mamlaka; Mik̲h̲lāf; Rustāḳ.1
voir aussi D̲j̲und; Iḳlīm

géographes   Abū l-Fidā; Abū ʿUbayd al-Bakrī; ʿĀs̲h̲īḳ; al-Bal̲k̲h̲ī, Abū Zayd; al-
Dimas̲h̲ḳī; Ibn ʿAbd al-Munʿim al-Ḥimyarī; Ibn al-Faḳīh; Ibn G̲h̲ālib; Ibn
Ḥawḳal; Ibn K̲h̲urradād̲h̲bih; Ibn Mād̲j̲id; Ibn Rusta; Ibn Sarābiyūn; al-
Idrīsī; al-Iṣṭak̲h̲rī; al-Ḳazwīnī; al-Masʿūdī; al-Muhallabī, Abū l-Ḥusayn; al-
Muḳaddasī
    voir aussi Baṭlamiyūs; Istibṣār; Ḳāsim b. Aṣbag̲h̲; al-Masālik wa-l-
Mamālik; [au Suppl.] al-D̲j̲ayhānī; Ḥudūd al-ʿĀlam
géographie physique
    déserts   → Déserts
    eaux
        détroits   Bāb al-Mandab; Bog̲h̲az-iči; Čanaḳ-ḳalʿe Bog̲h̲azi̊
        lacs   Baikal; Bak̲h̲tigān; Balk̲h̲as̲h̲; Burullus; Gökče-tengiz; Hāmūn; al-
        Ḥūla; İssi̊k-kul; Ḳarā-köl
            voir aussi Buḥayra; al-Ḳulzum; *et* → Océans et Mers
        rivières   → Rivières
    montagnes   → Montagnes
    sources   ʿAyn Dilfa; ʿAyn Mūsā; al-Ḥamma; Ḥasan Abdāl
        voir aussi Ḳapli̊d̲j̲a
    volcans   *voir* ʿAdan; Ag̲h̲ri̊ Dag̲h̲; Damāwand; Ḥarra; Lad̲j̲āʾ; al-Ṣafā.2; [au
        Suppl.] D̲j̲abal Says
littérature   D̲j̲ug̲h̲rāfiyā.IV.C et V
        et → Littérature.voyages, relations de
termes   Ḥarra; K̲h̲abrāʾ; Nahr; Reg; Rīf; Sabk̲h̲a
urbaine   Ḳarya; Ḳaṣaba; K̲h̲iṭṭa; Maḥalle; Medina; Rabaḍ
        voir aussi Fener; Ḥayy; K̲h̲iṭaṭ; Mallāḥ; *et* → Architecture.urbaine

Gitans   **Čingāne**; **Lūlī**; Nūrī

Grèce
    voir aussi Muhād̲j̲ir.2; Muslimūn.I.B.3; Pomáks
toponymes
    districts   Karli̊-īli
    îles   Čoka Adasi̊; Eğriboz; Körfüz; Levkas; Limni; Midilli; Naks̲h̲e; On Iki
        Ada; Para; Rodos; Ṣaḳi̊z
        voir aussi D̲j̲azāʾir-i Baḥr-i Safīd
    régions   Mora
    villes   Atīna; Aynabak̲h̲ti̊; Baliabadra; Dede Ag̲h̲ač; Dimetoḳa; Karaferye;
        Ḳawāla; Kerbenes̲h̲; Kesriye; Ḳordos; Ḳoron; Livadya; Meneks̲h̲e;
        Modon; Nauplion; Navarin; Olendirek; Preveze
        voir aussi [au Suppl.] Gümüld̲j̲ine

Guinée   Fūta D̲j̲allon; **Guinée**; Konakry

H

HADITH → LITTÉRATURE.TRADITION

HAGIOGRAPHIE **Manāḳib**
et → SAINT
hagiographes Aflākī; ʿAṭāʾī; al-Bādisī.2; Djamālī; Ḥasan Dihlawī; Ibn ʿAskar; Ibn Maryam; al-Ifrānī; al-Ḳādirī al-Ḥasanī, Abū ʿAbd Allāh
voir aussi Aḥmad Bābā; Bāḳiḳhānli; al-Kattānī

HEPHTALITES Hayāṭila; Nīzak, Ṭarkhān

HÉRALDIQUE al-Asad

HÉRÉSIE Bidʿa; Dahriyya; Dīn-i Ilāhī; Ghulāt; Ḳabiḍ; Kāfir; Khūbmesīḥī; Mulḥid
voir aussi Ṣalīb
hérétiques Abū ʿĪsā al-Warrāḳ; Abū l-Khaṭṭāb al-Asadī; Bashshār b. Burd; Bishr b. Ghiyāth al-Marīsī; Ibn Dirham; Ibn al-Rāwandī; Mollā Ḳābiḍ; Muḥammad b. ʿAlī al-Shalmaghānī
et → SECTES
réfutations Ibn al-Djawzī, ʿAbd al-Raḥmān; [au Suppl.] Afḍal al-Dīn Turka

HÉRITAGE ʿĀda.III; Akdariyya; ʿAwl; **Farāʾiḍ**; **Mīrāth**; al-Sahm.2
voir aussi Ḳassām; Khāl; Makhredj; Mukhallefāt
traités sur al-Sadjāwandī; Sirādj al-dīn

HONGRIE Budīn; Eğri; Esztergom; Istolnī (Istōnī) Belghrād; **Madjar**; Mohács; Pécs; Pest
voir aussi Bashdjirt; Kanisza; Maḥmūd Tardjumān; Mezőkeresztes; Muslimūn.I.B.1; Ofen

HÔTELLERIE **Funduḳ**; **Khān**; Manzil
voir aussi Ribāṭ.1.II

HUMOUR al-Djidd wa-l-Hazl; Nādira
voir aussi Hidjāʾ.II; Mudjūn
bouffons Djuḥā; Ibn al-Djaṣṣāṣ.II; Naṣr al-Dīn Khodja
humoristes Ashʿab; al-Ghāḍirī; Ibn Abī ʿAtīḳ; Ibn Dāniyāl; Ḳaṣāb; [au Suppl.] Abū l-ʿAnbas al-Ṣaymarī

HYDROLOGIE Biʾr; Ḳanāt; Māʾ; Maʾṣir

voir aussi Filāḥa; Ḳanṭara.5 et 6; Madjrīṭ; al-Mīzān.II; Sāʿa.1; *et* → GÉOGRAPHIE.EAUX

I

IDOLES Nuṣub
et → PÉRIODE PRÉISLAMIQUE.DANS LA PÉNINSULE ARABIQUE

INDE **Hind**; Hindī
voir aussi ʿĀda.III; Balharā; Imām-bārā; Maṭbaʿa.IV; *et* → LITTÉRATURE; MILITAIRES; MUSIQUE
administration Baladiyya.V; Ḍarība.VI; Dīwān.V; Djizya.III; Ḥisba.IV; Kātib; Kharādj.IV; Pargana; Safīr.2.c
voir aussi Kitābāt.X; Māʾ.IX; *et* → MILITAIRES.INDO-MUSULMANES
agriculture Filāḥa.V
architecture → ARCHITECTURE.RÉGIONS
belles-lettres → LITTÉRATURE.EN D'AUTRES LANGUES.AUTEURS HINDIS *et* POÉSIE.INDO-PERSANE
dynasties ʿĀdil-Shāhs; Bahminides; Barīd Shāhides; Dihlī (Sultanat de); Farūḳides; Ghaznawides; Ghūrides; Hindū-Shāhides; ʿImād Shāhides; Khaldjis; Ḳuṭb-Shāhides; Lōdīs; Mughals; Niẓām Shāhides
voir aussi Awadh; Dār al-Ḍarb; Rānā Sāngā; *et* → DYNASTIES.AFGHANISTAN ET INDE
éducation Dār al-ʿUlūm.c et d.; Djāmiʿa; Madjmaʿ ʿIlmī.IV; Madrasa.II; Nadwat al-ʿUlamāʾ; [au Suppl.] Farangī Maḥall
voir aussi Aḥmad Khān; Deoband; Maḥmūdābād
géographie physique
eaux Djamnā; Gangā
voir aussi Nahr
historiens Ghulām Ḥusayn Khān Ṭabāṭabāʾī; Niẓām al-Dīn, Aḥmad
voir aussi Djaʿfar Sharīf; al-Maʿbarī; Mīr Muḥammad Maʿṣūm; *et* → DYNASTIES.AFGHANISTAN ET INDE; LITTÉRATURE.HISTORIQUE
langues Gudjarātī; Hindī; Hindustānī.1 et 2; Lahndā; Marāṭhī; Pandjābī.1
voir aussi Kitābāt.X; *et* → LANGUES.INDO-IRANIENNES
mysticisme → MYSTICISME.MYSTIQUES; SAINT
période moderne Djamʿiyya; Hindustānī.3; Ḥizb.VI; Indian National Congress; Iṣlāḥ.IV; Kashmīr; Ḳawmiyya.VI; Khāksār; Khilāfa; Madjlis.IV.C; al-Marʾa.V; Nikāḥ.II.3; [au Suppl.] Djarīda.VII
voir aussi Mahsūd; Mappila; [au Suppl.] Faḳīr d'Ipi; *et* → INDE.ÉDUCATION
hommes d'état Nawwāb Sayyid Ṣiddīḳ Ḥasan Khān; Sālār Djang; [au Suppl.] Āzād, Abū l-Kalām
voir aussi Maḥmūdābād

le 'Mutiny' Aẓim Allāh Khān; Bakht Khān; Imdād Allāh; Kānpur
mouvement 'Khilāfat' **Khilāfa**; Muḥammad ʿAlī; Mushīr Ḥusayn Ḳidwāʾī; [au Suppl.] ʿAbd al-Bārī; Ḥasrat Mohānī
voir aussi Amīr ʿAlī
population Bhaṭṭi; Bohorās; Dāwūdpōtrās; Djāṭ; Gakkhaṛ; Gandāpur; Güdjar; Ḥabshī; Hind.II; Khaṭak; Khokars; Lambadi; Mappila; Mēd; Memon; Mēʾō; Naitias; Pārsīs; Rādjpūts; Rohillas; [au Suppl.] Démographie.VII
voir aussi Khōdja; Marāṭhā
Tamils Ceylan; Labbai; Marakkayar; Rawther
religion Ahl-i Ḥadīth; Barāhima; Djayn; Hindū; Ibāḥatiya; Mahdawī; Pandj Pīr
voir aussi Khʷādja Khiḍr; Pārsīs; [au Suppl.] Andjuman-i Khuddām-i Kaʿba; *et* → MYSTICISME; SAINT; THÉOLOGIE
réforme Aḥmad Brēlwī; al-Dihlawī, Shāh Walī Allāh; Ismāʿīl Shahīd; Karāmat ʿAlī; Nānak
toponymes
anciens Arūr; Čāmpānēr; Čhat; Djāba; Djandjīra; Fatḥpūr-sikrī; Hampī; Ḥusaynābād; Kūlam; Lakhnawtī; al-Manṣūra; Mēwāṛ; Nandurbār; Nārnawl; Pāndʾa
actuels
régions Assam; Bihār; Bombay; Dakhan; Djaypur; Doʾāb; Gudjarāt; Hariyānā; Ḥaydarābād.II; Kāmrūp; Kashmīr; Khāndēsh; Ḳūhistān.IV; Ladākh; Lūdhiāna; Maʿbar; Mahisur; Malabar; Mēwāt; Muẓaffarpur; Nāgpur; Palamāw; Pālānpur; Pandjāb; Rādhanpūr; Rāmpur; Rohilkhand; [au Suppl.] Djammū
voir aussi Alwār; Banganapalle; Bāonī; Berār; Djōdhpur; Hunza et Nagir
villes Adjmēr; Āgra; Aḥmadābād; Aḥmadnagar; Aligarh; Allāhābād; Ambāla; Amritsar; Anhalwāra; Arcot; Awadh; Awrangābād; Awrangābād Sayyid; Aʿẓamgarh; Badāʾūn; Bālā-ghāt; Bāndā; Bānkīpūr; Banūr; Bareilly; Barōda; Bénarès; Bharatpūr; Bharoč; Bhattinda; Bhōpāl; Bīdar; Bīdjāpūr; Bidjnawr; Bilgrām; Bombay; Bulandshahr; Burhānpūr; Buxar; Calcutta; Čandērī; Dawlatābād; Deoband; Dhār; Dhārwār; Dihlī; Diū; Djālor; Djawnpur; Djūnāgaṛh; Djunnar; Dwārkā; Farīdkōṭ; Farrukhābād; Fayḍābād; Fīrūzpūr; Gulbargā; Gwāliyār; Hānsī; Ḥaydarābād.I; Ḥiṣār Fīrūza; Īdar; Islāmābād; Iṭāwā; Kalpī; Kalyāni; Kanawdj; Kāṅgṛā; Kannanūr; Kānpur; Karnāl; Karnāṭak; Katahr; Khambāyat; Khayrābād; Khuldābād; Kōṛā; Koyl; Lakhnaw; Lalitpūr; Lūdhiāna; Madras; Mahīm; Māhīm; Māhūr; Mālda; Mālwā; Māndū; Manēr; Mangrōl; Mathurā; Mīraṭh; Mīrzāpur; Multān; Mungīr; Murādābād; Murshidābād; Muẓaffarpur; Nadjībabad; Nagar; Nāgawr; Nāgpur; Naldrug; Nāndeṛ; Pānīpat; Parendā; Pāṭan; Paṭnā; Pūna; Rādjmahāl; Rāyčūr; Sahāranpūr;

Sahsarām; [au Suppl.] Amrōhā; Eličpur; Ghāzīpūr
et → ASIE.DU SUD

INDONÉSIE Baladiyya.VII; Djāmiʿa; Dustūr.XI; Ḥizb.VII; Ḥukūma.VI; **Indonésie**; Maḥkama.VI; Malais; Masjumi; [au Suppl.] Ḍarība.VII; Hoesein Djajadiningrat
voir aussi ʿĀda.IV; Nikāḥ.II.4; Pasisir; Prang Sabil
architecture → ARCHITECTURE.RÉGIONS
éducation Pesantren
littérature Indonésie.VI; Ḳiṣṣa.VI; Miʿrādj.IV
voir aussi Kitābāt.VIII; Malais; *et* → LITTÉRATURE.POÉSIE.MYSTIQUE
mouvement revivaliste Padri
population Malais; Minangkabau; [au Suppl.] Démographie.VIII
religion → MYSTICISME.MYSTIQUES
fêtes Kandūrī; Lĕbaran
toponymes Ambon; Atjèh; Banda; Bandjarmasin; Bangka; Batjan; Billiton; Bornéo (*et* [au Suppl.]); Célèbes; Djakarta; Kubu; Kutai; Lombok; Madura; Makassar; Palembang; Pasè; Pasir; Pontianak; Riau; Sambas

INDUSTRIE Ḥarīr; Kattān; Ḳuṭn; Lubūd; Milḥ
voir aussi Bursa; al-Iskandariyya; Ḳayṣariyya

INVENTIONS ʿAbbās b. Firnās; Ibn Mādjid; Mūsā (Banū); Sāʿa.1

IRAK **ʿIrāḳ**; Kurdes et Kurdistān
voir aussi al-ʿArabiyya; Djalīlī; Lakhmides; *et* → CALIFAT.ʿABBĀSIDES; DYNASTIES.ÉGYPTE ET LE CROISSANT FERTILE
architecture → ARCHITECTURE.RÉGIONS
avant l'Islam → PÉRIODE PRÉISLAMIQUE.DANS LE CROISSANT FERTILE
géographie physique
eaux Abū l-Khaṣīb; al-ʿAḍaym; Didjla; Diyālā; al-Furāt; Khābūr; al-Khāzir
historiens al-Azdī; Baḥshal; Ibn Abī Ṭāhir Ṭayfūr; Ibn al-Bannāʾ; Ibn al-Dubaythī; al-Khaṭīb al-Baghdādī
voir aussi Ibn al-Nadjdjār; *et* → CALIFAT.ʿABBĀSIDES; DYNASTIES.ÉGYPTE ET LE CROISSANT FERTILE
période moderne Djarīda.I.A; Djāmiʿa; Dustūr.VI; Ḥizb.I; Ḥukūma.III; Kurdes et Kurdistān.III.C; Madjlis.IV.A.4; Madjmaʿ ʿIlmī.I.II.3; Maḥkama.IV.4; Mandats
voir aussi Bābān; Kūt al-ʿAmāra; al-Mawṣil.2
leaders d'opposition Ḳāsim, ʿAbd al-Karīm; Muṣṭafā Barzānī
monarchie Fayṣal Ier; Fayṣal II; Ghāzī
voir aussi Hāshimides

premiers ministres Nūrī al-Saʿīd; Rashīd ʿAlī al-Gaylānī
population Bādjalān; Bilbās; Djubūr; Dulaym; Lām; al-Manāṣir
voir aussi [au Suppl.] Démographie.III; *et* → KURDES
toponymes
anciens Abarḳubādh; ʿAḳarḳūf; ʿAlth; al-Anbār; Bābil; Badjimzā; Bādjisrā; Bādūrayā; Bākhamrā; Baradān; Barāthā; Bawāzīdj; Bihḳubādh; Birs; Dayr ʿAbd al-Raḥmān; Dayr al-ʿĀḳūl; Dayr al-Aʿwar; Dayr al-Djamādjim; Diyār Rabīʿa; Djabbul; al-Djazīra; Fallūdja; Ḥadītha.I; Ḥarbāʾ; Ḥarūrāʾ; Ḥawīza; al-Ḳādisiyya; Kalwādhā; Kaskar; Ḳaṣr Ibn Hubayra; Khāniḳīn; al-Khawarnaḳ; Kūthā; Ḳuṭrabbul; al-Madāʾin; Niffar; Nimrūd; Nīnawā; al-Nukhayla; al-Ruṣāfa.1; Sāmarrāʾ
voir aussi al-Karkh; Nuṣratābād
actuels
régions Bahdīnān; al-Baṭīḥa; Maysān
voir aussi Lālish
villes Altin Köprü; ʿAmādiya; ʿAmāra; ʿĀna; ʿAyn al-Tamr; Badrā; Baghdād; Baʿḳūba; Balāwāt; Bārzān; al-Baṣra; Daḳūḳāʾ; Daltāwa; Dīwāniyya; al-Fallūdja; Ḥadītha.II; al-Ḥilla; Hīt; Irbil; Karbalāʾ; Kāẓimayn; Kirkūk; al-Kūfa; Kūt al-ʿAmāra; Maʿalthāyā; al-Mawṣil; al-Nadjaf; al-Nāṣiriyya; Nuṣratābād; Rawāndīz; Sāmarrāʾ; al-Samāwa.2; [au Suppl.] Athūr
voir aussi Djalūlāʾ; *et* → KURDES.TOPONYMES

IRAN al-Furs; **Īrān**; Kurdes et Kurdistān; Lur
voir aussi al-ʿArab.III; Ḥarb.V; Kitābāt.IX; Libās.III; *et* → CHIITES; DYNASTIES.PERSE; ZOROASTRIENS
administration Ḍarība.V; Diplomatique.III; Dīwān.IV; Ghulām.II; Imtiyāzāt.III; Kātib; Khāliṣa; Kharādj.II; Maḥkama.III; Parwānačī
voir aussi Kalāntar; *et* → IRAN.PÉRIODE MODERNE
agriculture Filāḥa.III
architecture → ARCHITECTURE.RÉGIONS
avant l'Islam Anūshirwān; Ardashīr; Bahrām; Dārā; Dārābdjird; Dihḳān; Djamshīd; Farīdūn; al-Ḥaḍr; Hayāṭila; Hurmuz; al-Hurmuzān; Ḳārinides; Kayānides; Kay Kāʾūs; Kay-Khusraw; Khurshīd; Kisrā; Marzpān; Mazdak; Mulūk al-Ṭawāʾif.I; Parwīz, Khusraw (II); Pīshdādides; [au Suppl.] Farrukhān
voir aussi Afrāsiyāb; Buzurgmihr; Hamadhān; Ikhshīd; Īrān.IV; Ispahbadh; Ḳaṣr-i Shīrīn; Ḳūmis; al-Madāʾin; al-Rayy; Rustam b. Farrukh Hurmuzd; [au Suppl.] Dabīr; *et* → ZOROASTRIENS
géographie physique
déserts Biyābānak
eaux Bakhtigān; Hāmūn; Karkha; Kārūn; Mānd; Ruknābād; Safīd Rūd

voir aussi Baḥr Fāris

montagnes Ala Dagh; Alburz; Alwand Kūh; Bīsutūn; Damāwand; Hamrīn; Hawrāmān

historiens Ḥamza al-Iṣfahānī; Ibn Manda; al-Māfarrukhī; al-Rāfiʿī
et → DYNASTIES.PERSE

langue → LANGUES.INDO-IRANIENNES

littérature → LITTÉRATURE

période moderne Baladiyya.IV; Djāmiʿa; Djamʿiyya; Djarīda.II; Dustūr.IV; Ḥizb.III; Ḥukūma.II; Īrān.V.B; Iṣlāḥ.II; Ḳawmiyya.III; Maʿārif.III; Madjlis.IV.A.3; Madjmaʿ ʿIlmī.II; al-Marʾa.III; [au Suppl.] Démographie.III
voir aussi Khazʿal Khān; Madjlis al-Shūrā; Maḥkama.III; [au Suppl.] Amīr Niẓām; *et* → CHIITES; DYNASTIES.PERSE.ḲĀDJĀRS *et* PAHLAWĪS

activistes Fidāʾiyyān-i Islām; Kāshānī, Āyat Allāh; Kasrawī Tabrīzī; Khwānsārī, Sayyid Muḥammad; Khiyābānī; Khurāsānī; Kūčak Khān Djangalī; Lāhūtī; Maḥallātī; Malkom Khān; Muṣaddiḳ; Muṭahharī; Nāʾīnī; Nūrī, Shaykh Faḍl Allāh; Ṣamṣām al-Salṭana; [au Suppl.] Āḳā Khān Kirmānī; Āḳā Nadjafī; Amīr Kabīr; Ḥaydar Khān ʿAmū Ughlī
voir aussi Djangalī; Kurdes et Kurdistān.III.C; [au Suppl.] Āzādī; Farāmūsh-khāna

population Bakhtiyārī; Bāzūkiyyūn; Bilbās; Djāf; Eymir.III; Göklän; Gūrān; (Banū) Kaʿb; Ḳarā Gözlu; Ḳāshḳāy; Kurdes et Kurdistān; Lām; Lur
voir aussi Daylam; Dulafides; Eymir.II; Fīrūzānides; Īrān.II; Ḳufṣ; [au Suppl.] Démographie.III

religion Īrān.VI; Ṣafawides.IV
et → MYSTICISME.MYSTIQUES; SAINT

toponymes

anciens Abarshahr; Ardalān; Arradjān; ʿAskar Mukram; Bādj; Bākusāyā; Bayhaḳ; Dārābdjird; Daskara; Dawraḳ; Dihistān; Dīnawar; al-Djazīra; Djibāl; Djīruft; Gurgān; Ḥafrak; Ḥulwān; Īdhadj; Iṣṭakhr; (al-)Karadj; Khargird.II; Ḳūmis; Ḳurḳūb; Mihragān.IV.1; Narmāshīr; Nasā; Nawbandadjān; al-Rayy; Rūdhbār.2; Rūdhrāwar; [au Suppl.] Arghiyān; Ghubayrā

actuels

îles al-Fārisiyya

provinces Ādharbaydjān; Balūčistān; Fārs; Gīlān; Hamadhān; Iṣfahān; Khurāsān; Khūzistān; Kirmān; Kirmānshāh; Kurdistān; Māzandarān
voir aussi Astarābādh.2; Rūyān

régions Bākharz; Hawrāmān; Ḳūhistān.I; Makrān; [au Suppl.] Bashkard
voir aussi Gulistān

villes Ābādah; Abarḳūh; ʿAbbādān; ʿAbbāsābād; Abhar; al-Ahwāz; Āmul.1; Ardakān; Ardistān; Asadābādh; Ashraf; Astarābādh.1; Āwa;

Bam; Bampūr; Bandar ʿAbbās; Bandar Pahlawī; Bārfurūsh; Barūdjird; Barzand; Bīrdjand; Bisṭām; Būshahr; Dāmghān; Dizfūl; Djannāba; Djuwayn.1 et 2; Faraḥābād; Faryāb; Fasā; Fīrūzābād; Fūman; Gulpāyagān; Gunbadh-i Ḳābūs; Hurmuz; Iṣfahān; Isfarāyīn; Kāshān; Ḳaṣr-i Shīrīn; Kāzarūn; Ḳazwīn; Khʷāf; Khalkhāl; Khʷār; Khārag; Khargird.I; Khōī; Khurramābād; Khurramshahr; Kinkiwar; Ḳishm; Ḳūčān; Ḳūhistān.II; Ḳuhrūd; Ḳum; Lāhīdjān; Lār (2x); Linga; Luristān; Mahābād; Mākū; Marāgha; Marand; Mashhad; Miyāna; Narāḳ; Naṭanz; Nayrīz; Nihāwand; Nīshāpūr; Rafsandjān; Rām-hurmuz; Rasht; Rūdhbār.3; Sabzawār.1; Ṣaḥna; Ṣāʾīn Ḳalʿa; Saḳḳiz; Salmās; [au Suppl.] Bashkard; Biyār; Djārdjarm; Djulfa.II; Ḥawsam; *et* → Kurdes.toponymes

Irrigation Band; Ḳanāt; Māʾ; Nāʿūra
voir aussi Filāḥa; Kārūn; al-Nahrawān; *et* → Rivières
eau **Māʾ**
voir aussi Ḥawḍ; Sabīl.2; Saḳḳāʾ; *et* → Architecture.monuments.débits d'eau; Navigation; Océans et Mers; Rivières

Islam ʿAḳīda; Dīn; Djamāʿa; **Islām**; Masdjid; Muḥammad; Murtadd; Muslim; Rukn.1; Ṣadaḳa
voir aussi Iṣlāḥ; Iʿtikāf; Nubuwwa; Rahbāniyya; *et* → Aumônes; Coran; Jeûne; Pèlerinage; Prière
cinq piliers de l'Islam Ḥadjdj; Ṣalāt
voir aussi al-Ḳurṭubī, Yaḥyā; Rukn.1
conversion à l'Islam Islām.II
convertis européens Pickthall
croyances populaires ʿAyn; Dīw; Djinn; Ghūl; Muḥammad.II; [au Suppl.] ʿĀʾisha Ḳandīsha; Ḥinn
voir aussi ʿAnḳāʾ; *et* → Droit.droit coutumier
formules Allāhumma; Basmala; Ḥamdala; In Shāʾ Allāh; Māshāʾ Allāh; Salām
voir aussi [au Suppl.] Abréviations

Israël → Palestine

Italie **Īṭaliya**; Ḳawṣara; Ḳillawriya; Rūmiya
et → Sicile

J

Jacobites → Christianisme.confessions

JEU **Ḳimār**; al-Maysir
et → ANIMAUX.SPORT; RÉCRÉATION.JEUX

JEÛNE ʿĀshūrāʾ; Ramaḍān
voir aussi ʿĪd al-Fiṭr

JORDANIE Dustūr.X; Ḥukūma.III; Madjlis.IV.A.7; Maḥkama.IV.6; Mandats
géographie physique
montagnes al-Djibāl
hommes d'état ʿAbd Allāh b. al-Ḥusayn
voir aussi Hāshimides
population al-Ḥuwayṭāt; al-Manāṣīr
voir aussi [au Suppl.] Démographie.III
toponymes
anciens Adhruḥ; Ayla; al-Balḳāʾ; Djarash; al-Djarbāʾ; al-Djibāl; Faḥl; al-Ḥumayma; al-Muwaḳḳar
actuels ʿAdjlūn; al-ʿAḳaba; ʿAmmān; Bayt Rās; al-Ghawr.1; Irbid.I; Maʿān; al-Salṭ

JUDAÏSME Ahl al-Kitāb; Banū Isrāʾīl
voir aussi Filasṭīn; Hūd; Nasīʾ; al-Sāmira; *et* → BIBLE; PALESTINE
communautés al-Andalus.IV; al-Fāsiyyūn; Īrān.II et VI; Iṣfahān.I; al-Iskandariyya; Istanbul.VII.2; al-Ḳuds; Lār et Lāristān.II; Mallāḥ; Marrākush
influences sur l'Islam ʿĀshūrāʾ.I
voir aussi Ḳibla; Muḥammad.I.1.C.2
langue et littérature Judéo-arabe; Judéo-berbère; Judéo-persan; Ḳiṣṣa.VIII; Risāla.VII
voir aussi Geniza; Musammaṭ; Muwashshaḥ; *et* → LEXICOGRAPHIE; LITTÉRATURE.EN D'AUTRES LANGUES
personnages juifs en Islam ʿAbd Allāh b. Salām; Abū ʿĪsā al-Iṣfahānī; Abū Naḍḍāra; Dhū Nuwās; Hāmōn; Ḥasdāy b. Shaprūṭ; Ibn Abī l-Bayān; Ibn Djāmiʿ; Ibn Djanāḥ; Ibn Gabirol; Ibn Kammūna; Ibn Maymūn; Ibn Yaʿīsh; Ibrāhīm b. Yaʿḳūb; Isḥāḳ al-Isrāʾīlī; Kaʿb b. al-Ashraf; al-Kōhēn al-ʿAṭṭār; Māsardjawayh; Māshāʾ Allāh; Mūsā b. ʿAzra; al-Rādhāniyya; Saʿadyā; Saʿd al-Dawla; al-Samawʾal b. ʿĀdiyā; [au Suppl.] Ibn Biklārish
voir aussi Abū l-Barakāt; Kaʿb al-Aḥbār; Ḳaynuḳāʿ; Ḳurayẓa
rapports juives-musulmanes
avec Muḥammad Fadak; Ḳaynuḳāʿ; Khaybar; Ḳurayẓa; al-Madīna.I.1; Naḍīr
voir aussi Muḥammad.I.1.C
persécution Dhimma; Djizya; Ghiyār; al-Ḥākim bi-Amr Allāh; al-Maghīlī
polémique Abū Isḥāḳ al-Ilbīrī; Ibn Ḥazm, Abū Muḥammad
voir aussi Ahl al-Kitāb

sectes juives ʿĀnāniyya; al-ʿĪsāwiyya; Karaïtes
sectes judéo-chrétiennes Ṣābiʾa.I
voir aussi Naṣārā

K

KENYA Gedi; **Kenya**; Kilifi; Lamu; Malindi; Manda; Mazrūʿī; Mombasa; Pate
voir aussi Nabhān; [au Suppl.] Djarīda.VIII
littérature swahilie Ḳiṣṣa.VII; Madīḥ.V; Marthiya.V; Mathal.V; [au Suppl.] Ḥamāsa.VI
voir aussi Miʿrādj.III

KOWEIT Djarīda.I.A; Dustūr.XVI; **al-Kuwayt**; Madjlis.IV.A.9; Maḥkama.IV.9; Ṣabāḥ, Āl
voir aussi (Djazīrat) al-ʿArab; al-ʿArabiyya; Djāmiʿa
toponymes al-Dibdiba; [au Suppl.] Aḥmadī
voir aussi Ḳarya al-ʿUlyā

KURDES **Kurdes et Kurdistān**
voir aussi Kitāb al-Djilwa; *et* → IRAK; IRAN; TURQUIE
dynasties ʿAnnāzides; Bābān; Faḍlawayh; Ḥasanwayh; Marwānides; Rawwādides
voir aussi Kurdes et Kurdistān.III.B
mouvement nationale kurde Badrkhānī; Ḳāḍī Muḥammad; Kurdes et Kurdistān.III.C; Muṣṭafā Barzānī
voir aussi Bārzān; Mahābād
toponymes Ardalān; Barādūst; Bahdīnān; Bārzān; Djawānrūd; Hakkārī; Rawāndīz; Saḳḳiz
voir aussi Kirkūk; Kurdes et Kurdistān.II; Orāmār
tribus Djāf; Hakkārī; Hamawand; Kurdes et Kurdistān.III.B et IV.A.2; Lak.I

L

LAMENTATION Bakkāʾ; **Niyāḥa**; Rawḍa-khwānī

LANGUES **Lugha**
et → LINGUISTIQUE
afro-asiatiques Ḥām; Sām.2
voir aussi Karshūnī; Maʿlūlā.II
arabe Algérie.V; Aljamía; al-Andalus.X; **ʿArabiyya**.A; ʿIrāḳ.IV; Judéo-

arabe.I et II; Lībiyā.II; al-Maghrib.VII; Malta.2; Mūrītāniyā.6
voir aussi Ibn Makkī; Ḳarwasha; Khaṭṭ; Madjma‘ ‘Ilmī.I; [au Suppl.] Ḥaḍramawt.III
dialectes ‘Arabiyya.A.III; al-Ṣa‘īd (Ṣa‘īd Miṣr).2
et → LINGUISTIQUE.PHONÉTIQUE; LITTÉRATURE.POÉSIE.DIALECTALE
berbère **Berbères**.V; Judéo-berbère; Mūrītāniyā.6
voir aussi Mzab
mots berbères en arabe Āfrāg; Agadir, Āgdāl; Aménokal; Amghar; Argan; Ayt; Imẓad
voir aussi Ḳallala; Rīf.I.2.a
éthiopien Érythrée; Ḥabash.IV; Kūsh
hébreu Ibn Djanāḥ
(nigéro-)kordofanien Nūba.III
nilo-saharien Nūba.III
nordarabique Ṣafaïtique
voir aussi Liḥyān; *et* → ÉPIGRAPHIE
sud-arabique Saba’
voir aussi Ḥaḍramawt (*et* [au Suppl.] Ḥaḍramawt.III); al-Ḥarāsīs; *et* → ÉPIGRAPHIE
sud-arabique moderne Mahrī
voir aussi al-Ḥarāsīs; [au Suppl.] Ḥaḍramawt.III
tchadique Hausa.II
teda-daza Kanuri
austronésiennes Atjèh; Indonésie.III; Malais
ibéro-caucasiennes Andi; Beskesek-abaza; Čerkes; Dāghistān; Darghin; al-Ḳabḳ; Ḳayyūm Nāṣirī
indo-européennes Arnawutluḳ.I
voir aussi al-Ḳabḳ
indo-iraniennes
indiennes Afghānistān.III; Bengali.I; Ceylan; Chitral.II; Dardiques et Kāfires; Gudjarātī; Hind.III; Hindī; Hindustānī; Kashmīrī; Lahndā; Maldives.II; Marāṭhī; Pandjābī.1
voir aussi Madjma‘ ‘Ilmī.IV; [au Suppl.] Burushaski
iraniennes Afghān.II; Afghānistān.III; Balūčistān.II; Darī; Gūrān; Hind.III; ‘Irāḳ.IV; Judéo-persan.II; Kurdes et Kurdistān.V; Lur
voir aussi Dāghistān; al-Ḳabḳ; Khwārazm; Madjma‘ ‘Ilmī.II; Ossètes
turciques Ādharī; Balkar; Bulghār; Gagauz; Khaladj.II
voir aussi Afghānistān.III; Dāghistān; al-Ḳabḳ; Khazar; Madjma‘ ‘Ilmī.III

LÉGENDES Ḥikāya
et → BIBLE.PERSONNAGES BIBLIQUES; CORAN.HISTOIRES; ESCHATOLOGIE
endroits légendaires Damāwand; Djūdī; Ergenekon; Ḥūsh; Ḳi̊zi̊l-elma

êtres légendaires ʿAnḳāʾ; al-Burāḳ; Dīw; al-Djassāsa; Djinn; Ghūl; Hātif; ʿIfrīt; Ḳuṭrub; Parī
voir aussi al-Rukhkh
gens légendaires Abū Righāl; Abū Safyān; Abū Zayd; ʿAdnān; Afrāsiyāb; Ahl al-Ṣuffa; Amīna; Āṣāf b. Barakhyā; Asḥāb al-Kahf; Barṣīṣā; al-Basūs; Bilḳīs; al-Dadjdjāl; Djamshīd; Ḥabīb al-Nadjdjār; Ḥanẓala b. Ṣafwān; Hind bint al-Khuss; Hirmis; Hūshang; Ibn Buḳayla; al-Kāhina; Ḳaḥṭān; Kāwah; al-Khaḍir; Luḳmān; Masʿūd; Naṣr al-Dīn Khodja; Sām
voir aussi Akhī Ewrān; Amr b. ʿAdī; ʿAmr b. Luḥayy; Aṣḥāb al-Rass; Ḳuss b. Sāʿida; Muʿammar; *et* → CORAN.HISTOIRES
histoires légendaires ʿAbd Allāh b. Djudʿān; Aktham b. Ṣayfī; Almās; al-Baṭṭāl; Buhlūl; Damāwand; Djirdjīs; Djūdī; Durr; Fāṭima; al-Ghazāl; al-Ḥaḍr; Ḥāʾiṭ al-ʿAdjūz; Haram; Hārūt wa-Mārūt; Hudhud; Isrāʾīliyyāt; Khālid b. Yazīd; Ḳiṣaṣ al-Anbiyāʾ; Nūḥ

LEXICOGRAPHIE **Ḳāmūs**; Laḥn al-ʿĀmma
et → LINGUISTIQUE
lexicographes
arabes Abū Zayd al-Anṣārī; al-Azharī; al-Djawālīḳī; al-Djawharī; Farḥāt; al-Fīrūzābādī; Ibn al-Birr; Ibn Durayd; Ibn Fāris; Ibn Makkī; Ibn Manẓūr; Ibn Sīda; Ibn al-Sikkīt; al-Ḳazzāz; al-Khalīl b. Aḥmad; Muḥammad Murtaḍā; Nashwān b. Saʿīd; al-Ṣaghānī, Raḍī al-dīn; [au Suppl.] Abū ʿAmr al-Shaybānī; Abū Isḥāḳ al-Fārisī; al-Bustānī.1 et 2; al-Fārābī
voir aussi Abū Ḥātim al-Rāzī; Akhtarī; al-Rāghib al-Iṣfahānī; [au Suppl.] Ibn Kabar
hébraïques Ibn Djanāḥ
voir aussi Judéo-arabe.III.B
persans ʿAbd al-Rashīd b. ʿAbd al-Ghafūr; Aḥmad Wafīḳ Pasha; Burhān; [au Suppl.] Dehkhudā
voir aussi Ārzū Khān; Mahdī Khān Astarābādī; Riḍā Ḳulī Khān
turcs Akhtarī; al-Kāshgharī; Kāẓim Ḳadrī; Niʿmat Allāh b. Aḥmad; Sāmī
voir aussi Esʿad Efendi, Meḥmed; Luṭfī Efendi; Riyāḍī
termes Fard.2

LIBAN Djarīda.I.A; Djāmiʿa; Dustūr.IX; Ḥizb.I; Ḥukūma.III; **Lubnān**; Madjlis.IV.A.6; Maḥkama.IV.3; Mandats; Mutawālī
voir aussi Baladiyya.II; Djāliya; Ḳays ʿAylān; al-Maʿlūf; [au Suppl.] Aḥmad Pasha Küčük; al-Bustānī; Démographie.III
gouverneurs Bashīr Shihāb II; Dāwūd Pasha; Djānbulāt; Fakhr al-Dīn; Ḥarfūsh
voir aussi Maʿn; Maʿn-zāde
historiens Iskandar Agha
toponymes
anciens ʿAyn al-Djarr

actuels
régions al-Biḳāʿ
villes Baʿlabakk; Batrūn; Bayrūt; Bsharrā; Bteddīn; Djubayl; Karak Nūḥ

LIBYE Djāmiʿa; Djarīda.I.B; Dustūr.XII; **Lībiyā**; Madjlis.IV.A.18
voir aussi ʿArabiyya.A.III.3; al-Bārūnī; Ḳarāmānlı̊; Khalīfa b. ʿAskar; *et* → DYNASTIES.ESPAGNE ET AFRIQUE DU NORD
population → AFRIQUE.AFRIQUE DU NORD; BERBÈRES
toponymes
anciens Ṣabra
actuels
oasis Awdjila; Baḥriyya; al-Djaghbūb; Djawf Kufra; al-Djufra; Ghadamès; Kufra
régions Barḳa; al-Djufra; Fazzān
voir aussi Nafūsa
villes Adjdābiya; Benghāzī; Darna; Djādū; Murzuḳ
voir aussi Ghāt

LIEUX SACRÉS Abū Ḳubays; al-Ḥaram al-Sharīf; Ḥudjra; Kaʿba; Karbalāʾ; Kāẓimayn; al-Khalīl; al-Ḳuds.II; al-Madīna; Makka; al-Muḳaṭṭam; al-Nadjaf
voir aussi Ḥawṭa; Ḥimā; Ḳāsiyūn; Mawlāy Idrīs; Mudjāwir; *et* → ARCHITECTURE.MONUMENTS; SAINT

LINGUISTIQUE **Lugha**; Naḥw
voir aussi Balāgha; Bayān; Laḥn al-ʿĀmma; *et* → LANGUES; LEXICOGRAPHIE
grammairiens
8e-9e siècles ʿAbd Allāh b. Abī Isḥāḳ; Abū ʿAmr al-ʿAlāʾ; Abū Ḥātim al-Sidjistānī; Abū ʿUbayd al-Ḳāsim b. Sallām; Abū ʿUbayda; Abū Zayd al-Anṣārī; al-Akhfash.I et II; al-Aṣmaʿī; al-Bāhilī; Djūdī al-Mawrūrī; al-Farrāʾ; Ibn al-Aʿrābī; Ibn Sallām al-Djumaḥī; Ibn al-Sikkīt; ʿĪsā b. ʿUmar; al-Khalīl b. Aḥmad; al-Kisāʾī; Ḳuṭrub; al-Layth b. al-Muẓaffar; al-Māzinī; al-Mubarrad; al-Mufaḍḍal al-Ḍabbī; Muḥammad b. Ḥabīb; al-Ruʾāsī; [au Suppl.] Abū l-ʿAmaythal; Abū ʿAmr al-Shaybānī
voir aussi [au Suppl.] Abū l-Baydāʾ al-Riyāḥī
10e-11e siècles Abū ʿUbayd al-Bakrī; al-Adjdābī; al-Akhfash.III; al-Anbārī, Abū Bakr; al-Anbārī, Abū Muḥammad; al-ʿAskarī; Djaḥẓa; al-Fārisī; Ghulām Thaʿlab; Ḥamza al-Iṣfahānī; Ibn al-ʿArīf; Ibn al-Birr; Ibn Djinnī; Ibn Durayd; Ibn Durustawayh; Ibn Fāris; Ibn al-Ḥādjdj; Ibn al-Iflīlī; Ibn Kaysān; Ibn Khālawayh; Ibn al-Khayyāṭ; Ibn al-Ḳūṭiyya; Ibn Makkī; Ibn al-Naḥḥās; Ibn al-Sarrādj; Ibn Sīda; al-Ḳālī; al-Ḳazzāz; Ḳudāma b. Djaʿfar; al-Marzūḳī; Nifṭawayh; al-Rabāḥī; al-Rabaʿī; al-Rummānī; [au

Suppl.] Abū Isḥāḳ al-Fārisī; Abū Riyāsh al-Ḳaysī; Abū l-Ṭayyib al-Lughawī; Abū Usāma al-Harawī; al-Djurdjānī; al-Ḥātimī; Ibn Kaysān; Ibn Miḳsam

12ᵉ-18ᵉ siècles ʿAbd al-Ḳādir al-Baghdādī; Abū Ḥayyān al-Gharnāṭī; al-Anbārī, Abū l-Barakāt; al-Astarābādhī; al-Azharī; al-Baṭalyawsī, Ibn al-Sīd; al-Djawālīḳī; al-Djazūlī; Fakhrī; Farḥāt; al-Ḥarīrī; Ibn al-Adjdābī; Ibn Ādjurrūm; Ibn ʿAḳīl; Ibn ʿĀṣim; Ibn al-Athīr.I; Ibn Barrī, Abū l-Ḥasan; Ibn Barrī, Abū Muḥammad; Ibn al-Ḥādjdj; Ibn al-Ḥādjib; Ibn Hishām; Ibn Khātima; Ibn Maḍāʾ; Ibn Malik; Ibn Muʿṭī; Ibn al-Sāʾigh; Ibn al-Shadjarī al-Baghdādī; al-Maydānī; al-Muṭarrizī; [au Suppl.] Abū l-Barakāt; al-Balaṭī; Ibn al-Adjdābī; Ibn Hishām al-Lakhmī

19ᵉ-20ᵉ siècles Fāris al-Shidyāḳ; Ibn al-Ḥādjdj; al-Nabarāwī; [au Suppl.] Arat

voir aussi Fuʾād Pasha

phonétique Ḥurūf al-Hidjāʾ.II; Makhāridj al-Ḥurūf; Mushtarik

voir aussi Ḍād; Dāl; Dhāl; Djīm; Fāʾ; Ghayn; Hāʾ; Ḥāʾ; Hamza; Hāwī; Ḥurūf al-Hidjāʾ; Imāla; Kāf; Ḳāf; Khāʾ; Lām; Mīm; Nūn; Pāʾ; Rāʾ; Ṣād

pour les dialectes arabes, voir Algérie.V; al-Andalus.X; ʿIrāḳ.IV; Lībīya.II; al-Maghrib.VII; Mahrī; Malta.2

termes Aḍdād; Ala.I.; ʿĀmil; ʿAṭf; Dakhīl; Djāmʿ; Fard; Fiʿl; Gharīb; Ḥaraka wa-Sukūn.II; Ḥarf; Hāwī; Ḥikāya.I; Ḥukm.II; Ḥulūl; Ibdāl; Iḍāfa; Idghām; Iḍmār; ʿIlla.I; Imāla; Iʿrāb; Ishtiḳāḳ; Ism; Istifhām; Istithnāʾ; Kasra; Ḳaṭʿ; Khabar; Ḳiyās; Māḍī; Maʿnā.I; Muʿarrab; Mubālagha; Mubtadaʾ.I; Muḍāriʿ; Mudhakkar; Muḍmar; Musnad.2; Muṭlaḳ; Muwallad; Muzdawidj; Nafy; Naṣb; Naʿt; Nisba.1; Rafʿ; Sabab.6; Ṣaḥīḥ.3; Sālim.2; [au Suppl.] Ḥāl

voir aussi Basīṭ wa-Murakkab; Ghalaṭāt-i Meshhūre; Ḥurūf al-Hidjāʾ

LITTÉRATURE **Adab**; ʿArabiyya.B; ʿIrāḳ.V; Īrān.VII; ʿOthmānlï.III

autobiographique Nuʿayma, Mikhāʾīl; Sālim

biographique Faḍīla; **Manāḳib**; Mathālib

voir aussi ʿIlm al-Ridjāl; Maʾāthir al-Umarāʾ; Mughals.X; *et* → HAGIOGRAPHIE; LITTÉRATURE.HISTORIQUE *et* POÉSIE; MÉDECINE.MÉDECINS.BIOGRAPHIES DES; MUḤAMMAD, LE PROPHÈTE

critique Ibn al-Athīr.III; Ibn Rashīḳ; Ḳudāma b. Djaʿfar; [au Suppl.] al-Djurdjānī; al-Ḥātimī

moderne Kemāl, Meḥmed Nāmïḳ; Köprülü; Kurd ʿAlī; al-Māzinī; Olghun, Meḥmed Ṭāhir; [au Suppl.] Alangu; Atač

termes Mubālagha

drame **Masraḥ**

arabe Khayāl al-Ẓill; Masraḥ.I et II

voir aussi ʿArabiyya.B.V

dramaturges Abū Naḍḍāra; Faraḥ Anṭūn; Ibn Dāniyāl; al-Ḳusanṭīnī; al-

Maʿlūf; Nadjīb b. Sulaymān al-Ḥaddād; Nadjīb Muḥammad Surūr; al-Naḳḳāsh; Ṣalāḥ ʿAbd al-Ṣabūr; Salīm al-Naḳḳāsh; [au Suppl.] al-Bustānī.1

voir aussi Isḥāḳ, Adīb; Ismāʿīl Ṣabrī; Khalīl Muṭrān

en Asie centrale Masraḥ.V

ourdo Masraḥ.VI

dramaturges Amānat; [au Suppl.] Āghā Ḥashar Kashmīrī

persan Masraḥ.IV

dramaturges Muḥammad Djaʿfar Ḳaradja-dāghī; [au Suppl.] Amīrī

turc Ḳaragöz; Ḳawuḳlu; Masraḥ.III; Orta Oyunu

dramaturges ʿAbd al-Ḥaḳḳ Ḥāmid; Aḥmad Wafīḳ Pasha; Ākhundzāda; Djewdet; Karay, Refīḳ Khālid; Ḳaṣāb; Kemāl, Meḥmed Nāmiḳ; Khayr Allāh Efendi; Manāṣtirli Meḥmed Rifʿat; Meḥmed Raʾūf; Mīzāndji Meḥmed Murād; Muḥibb Aḥmed “Diranas”; Muṣāhib-zāde Djelāl; Oktay Rifat; [au Suppl.] Alus; Bashḳut; Čamlibel; Ḥasan Bedr al-Dīn

voir aussi Djanāb Shihāb al-Dīn; Ebüzziya Tevfik; Ekrem Bey; Kaygili; Khālide Edīb; Muʿallim Nādjī

en d'autres langues Afghān.III; Aljamía; Bengali.II; Berbères.VI; Beskesek-abaza; Bosna.III; Hausa.III; Hindī; Indonésie.VI; Judéo-arabe.III; Judéo-persan.I; Kano; Ḳiṣṣa.VIII; Lahndā.II; Laḳ; Masraḥ.VI; Pandjābī.2

pour la littérature swahilienne → KENYA; *pour la littérature malaise* → MALAISIE; *et* → LITTÉRATURE.POÉSIE.MYSTIQUE

auteurs bengalis Nadhr al-Islām; Nūr Ḳuṭb al-ʿĀlam

auteurs hindis Malik Muḥammad Djāyasī; Nihāl Čand Lāhawrī; Prēm Čand

voir aussi ʿAbd al-Raḥīm Khān; Inshāʾ; Lallūdjī Lāl

auteurs judéo-arabes Mūsā b. ʿAzra; al-Samawʾal b. ʿĀdiyā

et → JUDAÏSME.LANGUE ET LITTÉRATURE

auteurs pashtōs Khushḥāl Khān Khaṭak

auteurs tatars Ghafūrī, Medjīd

épistolaire **Inshāʾ**; Kātib **Risāla**

voir aussi Ṣadr.(b)

recueils épistolaires ʿAbd al-Ḥamīd b. Yaḥyā; Aḥmad Sirhindī; ʿAmr b. Masʿada; al-Babbaghāʾ; Ghālib; Ḥāletī; al-Hamadhānī; Harkarn; Ibn ʿAmīra; Ibn al-Athīr.III; Ibn Idrīs [I]; Ibn Ḳalāḳis; Ibn al-Khaṣīb; Ibn al-Ṣayrafī; al-Ḳabtawrī; Kānī; Khalīfa Shāh Muḥammad; Khʷāndamīr; al-Khʷārazmī; al-Maʿarrī; Makhdūm al-Mulk; Meḥmed Pasha Rāmī; Muḥammad b. Hindū-Shāh; Oḳču-zāde; Rashīd al-Dīn (al-Waṭwaṭ); Saʿīd b. Ḥumayd; [au Suppl.] ʿAbd al-ʿAzīz b. Yūsuf; Amīr Niẓām; Ibn Khalaf

voir aussi Aljamía; al-Djunayd; Ibn al-ʿAmīd.I; Ibn al-Khaṭīb; Mughals.X

étiquette, littérature de l' **Adab**; al-Maḥāsin wa-l-Masāwī
voir aussi al-Djidd wa-l-Hazl; Djins; Ḥiyal; Iyās b. Muʿāwiya; Kalīla wa-Dimna; Kātib; Marzban-nāma; Nadīm
auteurs Abū Ḥayyān al-Tawḥīdī; al-Bayhaḳī; Djāḥiẓ; al-Ghuzūlī; Hilāl al-Ṣābiʾ; al-Ḥuṣrī.I; Ibn ʿAbd Rabbih; Ibn Abī l-Dunyā; Ibn al-Muḳaffaʿ; al-Ḳalyūbī; al-Ḳāshānī; al-Kisrawī; al-Marzubānī; Merdjümek; al-Nīsābūrī; al-Rāghib al-Iṣfahānī
voir aussi al-Djahshiyārī; al-Ḳalḳashandī.I
généalogique Mathālib
généalogistes al-Abīwardī; al-Djawwānī; al-Hamdānī; al-Kalbī.II; al-Ḳalḳashandī.I; Ḳāsim b. Aṣbagh; al-Marwazī; Muṣʿab; al-Rushāṭī; [au Suppl.] Fakhr-i Mudabbir
voir aussi Ibn Daʾb; al-Ḳādirī al-Ḥasanī; al-Khʷārazmī; Mihmindār
genres
poésie Ghazal; Hidjāʾ; Ḳaṣīda; Khamriyya; Madīḥ; Marthiya; Mathnawī; Mufākhara; Munṣifa; Musammaṭ; Muwashshaḥ; Nawriyya
voir aussi ʿArabiyya.B; Īrān.VII; Rabīʿiyyāt; Sāḳī.2
prose Adab; Adjāʾib; Awāʾil; Badīʿ; Bilmedje; Djafr; Faḍīla; Fahrasa; Ḥikāya; Ilāhī; Inshāʾ; Isrāʾīliyyat; Kan wa-Kān; Khiṭaṭ; Ḳiṣṣa; al-Ḳūmā; Laḥn al-ʿĀmma; Lughz; al-Maghāzī; al-Maḥāsin wa-l-Masāwī; Maḳāla; Maḳāma; Malḥūn; Manāḳib; Masāʾil wa-Adjwiba; al-Masālik wa-l-Mamālik; Mathālib; Mawsūʿa; Muḳaddima; Mukhtaṣar; Munāẓara; Nādira; Naḳāʾiḍ; Naṣīḥat al-Mulūk; Risāla; [au Suppl.] Arbaʿūn Ḥadīth; Ḥabsiyya
voir aussi Alf layla wa-Layla (374b); ʿArabiyya.B; Bibliographie; Djughrāfiyā; Fatḥnāme; Ḥayawān; Ḥiyal; Īrān.VII; Malāḥim; Mathal
historique Isrāʾīliyyāt; al-Maghāzī
voir aussi Fatḥnāme; Ṣaḥāba; *et → les entrées* BIOGRAPHIQUE, MAGHĀZĪ *et* TRADITION, LITTÉRATURE DE LA *sous cette rubrique*
arabe
sur les pays/villes → *pays individuels*
sur les dynasties/califes → *dynasties individuelles sous* DYNASTIES
histoires universelles Abū l-Fidā; Abū Mikhnaf; Akanṣūs; al-Antāḳī; ʿArīb b. Saʿd; al-ʿAynī; al-Bakrī; al-Balādhurī; Baybars al-Manṣūrī; al-Birzālī; Daḥlān; al-Dhahabī; al-Diyārbakrī; al-Djannābī; al-Djazarī; al-Farghānī; Ḥamza al-Iṣfahānī; Ḥasan-i Rūmlū; al-Haytham b. ʿAdī; Ibn Abī Shayba; Ibn Abī Ṭayyiʾ; Ibn Aʿtham al-Kūfī; Ibn al-Athīr.II; Ibn al-Dawādārī; Ibn al-Djawzī (Sibṭ); Ibn al-Furāt; Ibn Kathīr; Ibn Khaldūn; Ibn Khayyāṭ al-ʿUṣfurī; Ibn al-Sāʿī; al-Kalbī.II; Kātib Čelebi; al-Kutubī; al-Makīn b. al-Amīd; al-Masʿūdī; Miskawayh; Münedjdjm Bāshî; al-Muṭahhar b. Ṭāhir al-Maḳdisī; al-Nuwayrī, Shihāb al-dīn; Saʿīd b. al-Biṭrīḳ

voir aussi Akhbār Madjmūʿa

8e siècle Abū Mikhnaf; ʿAwāna b. al-Ḥakam

9e siècle al-Balādhurī; al-Fāḳihī; al-Farghānī; al-Haytham b. ʿAdī; Ibn ʿAbd al-Ḥakam.IV; Ibn Abī Shayba; Ibn Abī Ṭāhir Ṭayfūr; Ibn Aʿtham al-Kūfī; Ibn Khayyāṭ al-ʿUṣfurī; Ibn al-Naṭṭāḥ; al-Kalbī.II; al-Madāʾinī; Naṣr b. Muzāḥim

10e siècle ʿArīb b. Saʿd; al-Azdī; Baḥshal; al-Balawī; al-Djahshiyārī; Ḥamza al-Iṣfahānī; Ibn al-Dāya; Ibn al-Ḳūṭiyya; Ibn Manda; Ibn al-Ṣaghīr; al-Kindī; Abū ʿUmar Muḥammad; al-Masʿūdī

11e siècle al-Antāḳī, Abū l-Faradj; Ibn al-Bannāʾ; Ibn Burd.I; Ibn Ḥayyān; Ibn al-Raḳīḳ; al-Māfarrūkhī

12e siècle al-ʿAẓīmī; Ibn al-Djawzī; Ibn Ghālib; Ibn al-Ḳalānisī; Ibn Ṣāḥib al-Ṣalāt; Ibn al-Ṣayrafī, Abū Bakr; Ibn Shaddād, Abū Muḥammad; ʿImād al-Dīn al-Iṣfahānī

voir aussi al-Baydhaḳ; Ibn Manda

13e siècle ʿAbd al-Wāḥid al-Marrākushī; Abū Shāma; al-Bundārī; al-Djanadī; Ibn Abī l-Dam; Ibn Abī Ṭayyiʾ; Ibn al-ʿAdīm; Ibn al-Athīr.II; Ibn al-Djawzī (Sibṭ); Ibn Ḥamādu; Ibn al-Mudjāwir; Ibn Muyassar; Ibn al-Nadjdjār; Ibn al-Sāʿī; Ibn Saʿīd al-Maghribī; Ibn Shaddād, ʿIzz al-dīn; Ibn Shaddād, Bahāʾ al-dīn; Ibn al-Ṭuwayr; al-Makīn b. al-Amīd; al-Manṣūr; al-Rāfiʿī; [au Suppl.] Ibn ʿAskar; Ibn Ḥātim

14e siècle Abū l-Fidā; Baybars al-Manṣūrī; al-Birzālī; al-Dhahabī; al-Djazarī; Ibn Abī Zarʿ; Ibn al-Dawādārī; Ibn Duḳmāḳ; Ibn al-Furāt, Nāṣir al-dīn; Ibn Ḥabīb, Badr al-dīn; Ibn ʿIdhārī; Ibn Kathīr, ʿImād al-dīn; Ibn Khaldūn; Ibn al-Khaṭīb; Ibn al-Ṭiḳṭaḳā; al-Khazradjī, Muwaffaḳ al-dīn; al-Kutubī; al-Mufaḍḍal b. Abī l-Faḍāʾil; al-Ṣafadī, Ṣalāḥ al-dīn

15e siècle Abū l-Maḥāsin Ibn Taghrābirdī; ʿArabfaḳih; al-ʿAynī; al-Fāsī; Ibn ʿArabshāh; Ibn Shāhīn al-Ẓāhirī; al-Maḳrīzī; al-Sakhāwī

16e siècle al-Diyārbakrī; al-Djannābī, Abū Muḥammad; Ḥasan-i Rūmlū; Ibn al-Daybaʿ; Ibn Iyās; Mudjīr al-Dīn al-ʿUlaymī

17e siècle ʿAbd al-ʿAzīz b. Muḥammad; al-Bakrī.I et II; Ibn Abī Dīnār; Kātib Čelebi; al-Maḳḳarī; al-Mawzaʿī

18e siècle al-Damurdāshī; al-Ḥādjdj Ḥammūda; al-Ifrānī; Münedjdjim Bashî

19e siècle Aḥmad al-Nāṣirī (*et* al-Nāṣirī al-Salāwī); Akanṣūs; ʿAlī Pasha Mubārak; Daḥlān; al-Djabartī; Ghulām Ḥusayn Khān Ṭabāṭabāʾī; Ibn Abī l-Ḍiyāf

voir aussi al-Kardūdī

20e siècle Ibn Zaydān; Kurd ʿAlī

indo-persane Mughals.X

13e-14e siècles Baranī; al-Djūzdjānī

15ᵉ-16ᵉ siècles   Abū l-Faḍl ʿAllāmī; D̲j̲awhar; Gulbadan Bēgam; Niẓām al-Dīn, Aḥmad; [au Suppl.] ʿAbbās Sarwānī

17ᵉ-18ᵉ siècles   ʿAbd al-Ḥamīd Lāhawrī; ʿAbd al-Karīm Kas̲h̲mīrī; Bak̲h̲tāwar K̲h̲ān; Firis̲h̲ta; G̲h̲ulām Ḥusayn K̲h̲ān Ṭabāṭabāʾī; G̲h̲ulām Ḥusayn "Salīm"; ʿInāyat Allāh Kawbū; Ḳāniʿ; K̲h̲ʷāfī K̲h̲ān; Mīr Muḥammad Maʿṣūm; Niʿmat Allāh b. Ḥabīb Allāh Harawī; Niʿmat K̲h̲ān; Nūr al-Ḥaḳḳ al-Dihlawī; [au Suppl.] ʿĀḳil K̲h̲ān Rāzī; Ḥād̲j̲d̲j̲ī al-Dabīr; Ḥaydar Malik
    voir aussi Badāʾūnī

19ᵉ siècle   ʿAbd al-Karīm Muns̲h̲ī
    voir aussi Aẓfarī

persane   [au Suppl.] Čač-nāma
histoires universelles   Mīrk̲h̲wānd; Niẓām S̲h̲āhī

10ᵉ siècle   Balʿamī

11ᵉ-12ᵉ siècles   Anūs̲h̲irwān b. K̲h̲ālid; Bayhaḳī; al Bayhaḳī, Ẓahīr al-dīn; Gardīzī; [au Suppl.] Ibn al-Balk̲h̲ī

13ᵉ-14ᵉ siècles   Banākitī; D̲j̲uwaynī; Ḥamd Allāh al-Mustawfī al-Ḳazwīnī; Ibn Bībī; Ibn Isfandiyār; [au Suppl.] al-Aḳsarāyī; Ḥasan Niẓāmī; al-Ḥusaynī

15ᵉ-16ᵉ siècles   ʿAbd al-Razzāḳ al-Samarḳandī; Bidlīsī; D̲j̲amāl al-Ḥusaynī; G̲h̲affārī; Ḥāfiẓ-i Abrū; Ḥaydar Mīrzā; K̲h̲ʷandamīr; Ḳum(m)ī; al-Lārī; Rāzī, Amīn Aḥmad; [au Suppl.] Ḥāfiẓ Tanīs̲h̲

17ᵉ-18ᵉ siècles   ʿAbd al-Fattāḥ Fūmanī; Ḥaydar b. ʿAlī; Iskandar Beg; Mahdī K̲h̲ān Astarābādī
    voir aussi Īsar-dās

19ᵉ-20ᵉ siècles   ʿAbd al-Karīm Buk̲h̲ārī; [au Suppl.] Fasāʾī
    voir aussi ʿAlī b. S̲h̲ams al-Dīn

turque
    et → Dynasties.Anatolie et les turcs.ottomans.historiens des
    histoires universelles
        voir aussi Nes̲h̲rī

15ᵉ-16ᵉ siècles   ʿAlī; ʿĀs̲h̲iḳ-pas̲h̲a-zāde; Bihis̲h̲tī; D̲j̲alālzāde Muṣṭafā Čelebi; D̲j̲alālzāde Ṣāliḥ Čelebi; Kemāl Pas̲h̲a-zāde; Luḳmān b. Sayyid Ḥusayn; Maṭrāḳči; Meḥmed Pas̲h̲a, Ḳaramānī; Meḥmed Zaʿīm; Nes̲h̲rī; Riḍā
    voir aussi Ḥadīdī; Med̲j̲dī

17ᵉ-18ᵉ siècles   ʿAbdī; ʿAbdī Efendi; ʿAbdī Pas̲h̲a; Aḥmad Rasmī; Čelebi-zāde; Čes̲h̲mīzāde; Enwerī; Ḥasan Bey-zāde; Ḥibrī; ʿIzzī; Ḳarā-čelebi-zāde.4; Kātib Čelebi; Kemāl, Meḥmed Namîḳ; Meḥmed K̲h̲alīfe b. Ḥüseyn; Müned̲j̲d̲j̲im Bas̲h̲î; ʿOt̲h̲mān-zāde

19ᵉ-20ᵉ siècles   Aḥmad D̲j̲ewdet Pas̲h̲a; Aḥmad Rafīḳ; ʿAlī Amīrī; ʿĀṣim; ʿAṭāʾ Bey, Ṭayyārzāde; (Meḥmed) ʿAṭāʾ Bey; Esʿad Efendi,

Meḥmed; Khayr Allāh Efendi; Luṭfī Efendi; Mīzāndjï Meḥmed Murād
voir aussi Ḥilmī
en turc oriental Abū l-Ghāzī; Bāḳïkhānlï; Mu'nis
maghāzī Abū Ma'shar al Sindī; Ibn 'Ā'idh; al-Kalā'ī; **al-Maghāzī**; Mūsā b. 'Uḳba
voir aussi al-Baṭṭāl
merveilles, collections des Abū Ḥāmid al-Gharnāṭī; **'Adjā'ib**; Buzurg b. Shahriyār; al-Ḳazwīnī
voir aussi Ibn Sarābiyūn; Ḳiṣaṣ al-Anbiyā'
personnages dans la littérature Abū Ḍamḍam; Abū l-Ḳāsim; Abū Zayd; Ali Baba; Ayāz; Aywaz.2; al-Basūs; al-Baṭṭāl; Bekrī Muṣṭafā Agha; Buzurgmihr; Dhū l-Himma; Djamshīd; Djuḥā; al-Ghāḍirī; Ḥamza b. 'Abd al-Muṭṭalib; Ḥātim al-Ṭā'ī; Ḥayy b. Yaḳẓān; Köroghlu; Manas; Naṣr al-Dīn Khodja; Rustam; Sām
picaresque Maḳāma; Mukaddī
poésie 'Arūḍ; Ghazal; Ḥamāsa; Hidjā'; Ḳāfiya; Ḳaṣīda; Khamriyya; Lughz; Madīḥ; Ma'nā.III; Marthiya; Mufākhara; Mukhtārāt; Munṣifa; Musammaṭ; Muwashshaḥ; Muzdawidj; Nawriyya
voir aussi Rāwī; *et* → MÉTRIQUE
andalouse 'Arabiyya.B.Appendice; Khamriyya.VI; Muwashshaḥ; Nawriyya
anthologies al-Fatḥ b. Khāḳān; al-Fihrī; Ibn Bassām; Ibn Diḥya; Ibn Faradj al-Djayyānī
8e siècle Ghirbīb b. 'Abd Allāh
9e siécle 'Abbās b. Firnās; 'Abbās b. Nāṣih; al-Ghazāl
voir aussi Ibn 'Alḳama.II
10e siècle Ibn 'Abd Rabbih; Ibn Abī Zamanayn; Ibn Faradj al-Djayyānī; Ibn Ḳuzmān.I; Muḳaddam b. Mu'āfā; al-Ramādī
11e siècle Abū Isḥāḳ al-Ilbīrī; Ibn al-Abbār; Ibn 'Abd al-Ṣamad; Ibn 'Ammār; Ibn Burd.II; Ibn Darrādj al-Ḳasṭallī; Ibn Gharsiya; Ibn al-Ḥaddād; Ibn al-Ḥannāṭ; Ibn al-Labbāna; Ibn Mā' al-Samā'; Ibn al-Shahīd; Ibn Shuhayd; Ibn Zaydūn; al-Mu'tamid Ibn 'Abbād
voir aussi Ṣā'id al-Baghdādī
12e siècle al-A'mā al-Tuṭīlī; Ḥafṣa bint al-Ḥādjdj; Ibn 'Abdūn; Ibn Baḳī; Ibn Ḳabṭūrnu; Ibn Khafādja; Ibn Ḳuzmān.II et V; Ibn al-Ṣayrafī; al-Ḳurṭubī; al-Ruṣāfī; Ṣafwān b. Idrīs
voir aussi Mūsā b. 'Azra
13e siècle Ḥāzim; Ibn al-Abbār; Ibn 'Amīra; Ibn Sahl; Ibn Sa'id al-Maghribī; al-Ḳabtawrī
14e siècle Ibn al-Ḥādjdj; Ibn Khātima; Ibn Luyūn; Ibn al-Murābi'
arabe 'Atāba; Ghazal.I; Ḥamāsa.I; Hidjā'; Kān wa-Kān; Ḳaṣīda.I; al-Ḳūmā; Madīḥ.I; Maḳṣūra; Malḥūn; Marthiya.I; Mawāliyā; Mawlidiyya; Mukh-

tārāt.I; Musammaṭ.1; Muwa<u>sh</u><u>sh</u>aḥ; Naḳā'iḍ; Nasīb; Rubā'ī.3
voir aussi 'Antar; 'Arabiyya.B.II; Bānat Su'ād; Burda.2; 'Ilm al-<u>Dj</u>amāl; Ḳalb.II; Kalīla wa-Dimna; Ma<u>dj</u>nūn Laylā.I; Mawlid; al-Mu'allaḳāt; Muwallad; *et* → LITTÉRATURE.POÉSIE.ANDALOUSE *et* POÉSIE.MYSTIQUE

anthologies al-Mu'allaḳāt; al-Mufaḍḍaliyyāt; **Mu<u>kh</u>tārāt**.I

anthologistes Abū l-Fara<u>dj</u> al-Iṣbahānī; Abū Tammām; al-'Alamī; al-Bā<u>kh</u>arzī; al-Buḥturī; Di'bil; al-Hamdānī; Ḥammād al-Rāwiya; Ibn Abī Ṭāhir Ṭayfūr; Ibn Dāwūd; Ibn al-Ḳutayba; Ibn al-Mu'tazz; Ibn al-Ṣayrafī; 'Imād al-Dīn al-Iṣfahānī; al-Nawā<u>dj</u>ī; [au Suppl.] Abū Zayd al-Ḳura<u>sh</u>ī; al-Bustānī.3

préislamique 'Abīd b. al-Abraṣ; Abū <u>Dh</u>u'ayb al-Hu<u>dh</u>alī; Abū Du'ād al-Iyādī; Abū Kabīr al-Hu<u>dh</u>alī; 'Adī b. Zayd; al-Afwah al-Awdī; al-A<u>gh</u>lab al-'I<u>dj</u>lī; 'Alḳama b. 'Abada; 'Āmir b. al-Ṭufayl; 'Amr b. al-Ahtam; 'Amr b. Ḳamī'a; 'Amr b. Kul<u>th</u>ūm; 'Antara; al-A'<u>sh</u>ā; al-Aswad b. Ya'fur; Aws b. Ḥa<u>dj</u>ar; Bi<u>sh</u>r b. Abī <u>Kh</u>āzim; Bisṭām b. Ḳays; Durayd b. al-Ṣimma; al-Ḥadira; al-Ḥāri<u>th</u> b. Ḥilliza; Ḥassān b. <u>Th</u>ābit; Ḥātim al-Ṭā'ī; Ibn al-Iṭnāba al-<u>Kh</u>azra<u>dj</u>ī; Imru' al-Ḳays b. Ḥu<u>dj</u>r; Ḳays b. al-<u>Kh</u>aṭīm; al-<u>Kh</u>ansā'; Laḳīṭ al-Iyādī; Laḳīṭ b. Zurāra; al-Munakhkhal al-Yashkurī; Muraḳḳish; al-Mutalammis; al-Nābigha al-<u>Dh</u>ubyānī; Salāma b. <u>Dj</u>andal; al-Samaw'al b. 'Ādiyā
voir aussi 'Arabiyya.B.I; <u>Gh</u>azal; Hu<u>dh</u>ayl; al-Mu'allaḳāt; al-Mufaḍḍaliyyāt; Mufā<u>kh</u>ara2; Nasīb.2.A

mu<u>kh</u>aḍramūn (6e-7e siècles) al-'Abbās b. Mirdās; 'Abd Allāh b. Rawāḥa; Abū <u>Kh</u>irā<u>sh</u> al-Hu<u>dh</u>alī; Abū Miḥ<u>dj</u>ān; 'Amr b. Ma'dīkarib; Ḍirār b. al-<u>Kh</u>aṭṭāb; Ḥassān b. <u>Th</u>ābit; al-Ḥuṭay'a; Ibn (al-)Aḥmar; Ka'b b. Mālik; Ka'b b. Zuhayr; <u>Kh</u>idā<u>sh</u> b. Zuhayr; Labīd b. Rabī'a; Ma'n b. Aws al-Muzanī; **Mu<u>kh</u>aḍram**; Mutammim b. Nuwayra; al-Nābi<u>gh</u>a al-<u>Dj</u>a'dī; al-Namir b. Tawlab al-'Uklī; [au Suppl.] Abū l-Ṭamaḥān al-Ḳaynī; Ibn Muḳbil
voir aussi Hu<u>dh</u>ayl; Nasīb.2.B

7e-8e siècles al-'Abbās b. al-Aḥnaf; 'Abd Allāh b. Hammān; Abū 'Aṭā' al-Sindī; Abū Dahbal al-<u>Dj</u>umaḥī; Abū Dulāma; Abū l-Na<u>dj</u>m al-'I<u>dj</u>lī; Abū Ṣa<u>kh</u>r al-Hu<u>dh</u>alī; Abū l-<u>Sh</u>amaḳmaḳ; Adī b. al-Riḳā'; al-'A<u>dj</u><u>dj</u>ā<u>dj</u>; al-Aḥwaṣ al-Anṣārī; al-A<u>kh</u>ṭal; al-'Ar<u>dj</u>ī; A'<u>sh</u>ā Hamdān; al-A<u>sh</u><u>dj</u>a' b. 'Amr al-Sulamī; Ayman b. <u>Kh</u>uraym; al-Ba'ī<u>th</u>; Ba<u>sh</u><u>sh</u>ār b. Burd; <u>Dh</u>ū l-Rumma; <u>Dj</u>amīl al-'U<u>dh</u>rī; <u>Dj</u>arīr; Dukayn al-Rā<u>dj</u>iz; al-Farazdaḳ; al-Ḥakam b. 'Abdal; al-Ḥakam b. Ḳanbar; Ḥammād 'A<u>dj</u>rad; Ḥamza b. Bīḍ; Ḥāri<u>th</u>a b. Badr al-<u>Gh</u>udānī; al-Ḥuḍayn; Ḥumayd b. <u>Th</u>awr; Ḥumayd al-Arḳaṭ; Ibn Abī 'Uyayna; Ibn al-Dumayna; Ibn Harma; Ibn Ḳays al-Ruḳayyāt; Ibn La<u>dj</u>a'; Ibn al-Mawlā; Ibn Mayyāda; Ibn Mufarri<u>gh</u>; Ibn Muṭayr; Ibn Sayḥān; 'Imrān b. Ḥiṭṭān; 'Inān; Ismā'īl b. Yasār; Ka'b b. <u>Dj</u>u'ayl al-Ta<u>gh</u>labī; Ḳaṭarī

b. al-Fudjāʾa; al-Kumayt b. Zayd al-Asadī; al-Ḳuṭāmī; Kuthayyir b. ʿAbd al-Raḥmān; Laylā al-Akhyaliyya; Manṣūr al-Namarī; Marwān; Miskīn al-Dārimī; Mūsā Shahawātin; Musāwir al-Warrāḳ; Muṭīʿ b. Iyās; Nubāta b. ʿAbd Allāh; Nuṣayb; Nuṣayb b. Rabāḥ; al-Rāʿī; Ruʾba b. al-ʿAdjdjādj; Ṣafī al-Dīn al-Ḥillī; Ṣafwān al-Anṣārī; Saḥbān Wāʾil; Ṣāliḥ b. ʿAbd al-Ḳuddūs; Salm al-Khāsir; [au Suppl.] ʿAbd al-Raḥmān b. Ḥassān; Abū ʿAmr al-Shaybānī; Abū Ḥayyā al-Numayrī; Abū Ḥuzāba; Abū Nukhayla; Bakr b. al-Naṭṭāḥ
voir aussi Nasīb.2.C et D

9e-10e siècles Abān b. ʿAbd al-Ḥamīd; ʿAbd Allāh b. Ṭāhir; Abū l-ʿAtāhiya; Abū Dulaf; Abū l-Faradj al-Iṣbahānī; Abū Firās al Ḥamdānī; Abū Nuwās; Abū l-Shīṣ; Abū Tammām; Abū Yaʿḳūb al-Khuraymī; al-ʿAkawwak; ʿAlī b. al-Djahm; al-ʿAttābī; al-Babbaghāʾ; al-Baṣīr; al-Buḥturī; al-Bustī; Diʿbil; Dīk al-Djinn al-Ḥimṣī; al-Djammāz; al-Hamdānī; (al-)Ḥusayn b. al-Ḍaḥḥāk; Ibn al-ʿAllāf; Ibn Bassām; Ibn al-Ḥadjdjādj; Ibn Kunāsa; Ibn Lankak; Ibn al-Muʿadhdhal; Ibn Munādhir; Ibn al-Muʿtazz; Ibn al-Rūmī; al-Ḳāsim b. ʿĪsā; Khālid b. Yazīd; al-Khālidiyyāni; al-Khaṭṭābī; al-Khubzaʾaruzzī; al-Kisrawī; Kushādjim; al-Maʾmūnī; Muḥammad b. ʿAbd al-Raḥmān al-ʿAṭawī; Muḥammad b. Ḥāzim al-Bāhilī; Muḥammad b. Umayya; Muḥammad b. Yasīr al-Riyāshī; al-Muṣʿabī; Muslim b. al-Walīd; al-Mutanabbī; Naṣr b. Nuṣayr; Sahl b. Hārūn; Saʿīd b. Ḥumayd; [au Suppl.] Abū l-ʿAmaythal; Abū l-Asad al-Ḥimmānī; Abū l-Ḥasan al-Maghribī; Abū Hiffān; Abū l-ʿIbar; Abū Riyāsh al-Ḳaysī; Abū Saʿd al-Makhzūmī; Abū Shurāʿa; ʿAlī b. Muḥammad; Faḍl al-Shāʿira; al-Fazārī; al-Ḥamdawī
voir aussi al-Hamadhānī; Ibn Abī Zamanayn; Nasīb.2.D

11e-13e siècles al-Abīwardī; ʿAmīd al-Dīn al-Abzārī; al-Arradjānī; al-Badīʿ al-Asṭurlābī; Bahāʾ al-Dīn Zuhayr; al-Bākharzī; Ḥayṣa Bayṣa; al-Ḥuṣrī.II; Ibn Abī l-Ḥadīd; Ibn Abī Ḥaṣīna; Ibn al-ʿAfīf al-Tilimsānī; Ibn al-Habbāriyya; Ibn al-Ḥamdīs; Ibn Ḥayyūs; Ibn Hindū; Ibn al-Ḳaṭṭān; Ibn al-Ḳaysarānī.II; Ibn Khamīs; Ibn Maṭrūḥ; Ibn al-Nabīh; Ibn Rashīḳ; Ibn Sanāʾ al-Mulk; Ibn al-Shadjarī al-Baghdādī; Ibn Sharaf al-Ḳayrawānī; Ibn Shibl; Ibn al-Taʿāwīdhī; al-Kammūnī; Ḳurhub b. Djābir; al-Maʿarrī; al-Marwazī; Mihyār; Muḥammad b. ʿAlī b. ʿUmar; al-Rūdhrāwarī; al-Ṣaghānī, ʿAbd al-Muʾmin; Ṣāʿid al-Baghdādī; [au Suppl.] Abū l-Ḥasan al-Anṣārī; al-Balaṭī; al-Būṣīrī; al-Ghazzī
voir aussi al-Khazradjī; Nasīb.2.D

14e-18e siècles ʿAbd al-ʿAzīz b. Muḥammad; ʿAbd al-Ghanī b. Ismāʿīl; al-Bakrī; al-Būrīnī; Farḥāt; Ibn Abī Ḥadjala; Ibn ʿAmmār; Ibn Ḥidjdja; Ibn Nubāta; Ibn al-Ṣāʾigh; Ibn al-Wannān
voir aussi Khiḍr Beg

19e-20e siècles al-Akhras; al-Bārūdī; Fāris al-Shidyāḳ; al-Fārūḳī; Fikrī; Ḥāfiẓ Ibrāhīm; Ibn Idrīs [I]; Ismāʿīl Ṣabrī; Ismāʿīl Ṣabrī Pasha; Ḳaddūr al-ʿAlamī; al-Kāẓimī; Khalīl Muṭrān; al-Khūrī; al-Maʿlūf; al-Manfalūṭī; Mardam.II; Maʿrūf al-Ruṣāfī; al-Māzinī; Nādjī; Nadjīb b. Sulaymān al-Ḥaddād; Nadjīb Muḥammad Surūr; Saʿīd Abū Bakr; Ṣalāḥ ʿAbd al-Ṣabūr; [au Suppl.] Abū Māḍī; Abū Shādī; al-ʿAḳḳād; al-Bustānī; Buṭrus Karāma; Ibn ʿAmr al-Ribāṭī; Ibn al-Ḥādjdj

transmetteurs Ḥammād al-Rāwiya; Ibn Daʾb; Ibn Kunāsa; Khalaf al-Aḥmar; Khālid b. Ṣafwān; al-Kisrawī; Muḥammad b. al-Ḥasan b. Dīnār; [au Suppl.] Abū ʿAmr al-Shaybānī

et → LINGUISTIQUE.GRAMMAIRIENS.8E-9E SIÈCLES

transmission de **Rāwī**

d'amour **Ghazal**; **Nasīb**; Raḳīb

voir aussi Ibn Sahl; al-Marzubānī; *et* → AMOUR.PLATONIQUE

dialectale Nabaṭī

indo-persane Mughals.X; Sabk-i Hindī

voir aussi Pandjābī.2; *et* → LITTÉRATURE.POÉSIE.MYSTIQUE

11e siècle Masʿūd-i Saʿd-i Salmān; [au Suppl.] Abū l-Faradj Ibn Masʿūd Rūnī

14e siècle Amīr Khusraw Dihlawī; Ḥasan Dihlawī; [au Suppl.] Ḥamīd Ḳalandar

16e siècle Fayḍī

voir aussi ʿAbd al-Raḥīm Khān

17e-18e siècles Ārzū Khān; Ashraf ʿAlī Khān; Bīdil; Dard; Ghanī; Ghanīmaṭ Ḥazīn; Idrākī Bēglārī; Ḳāniʿ; Ḳudsī; Makhfī; Malik Ḳummī; Munīr Lāhawrī; Nāṣir ʿAlī Sirhindī; Naẓīrī; Salīm, Muḥammad Ḳulī; [au Suppl.] Ghanīmat Kundjāhī

19e siècle Aẓfarī; Ghālib; Rangīn; [au Suppl.] Adīb Pīshāwarī

voir aussi Afsūs

mystique

arabe ʿAbd al-Ghanī b. Ismāʿīl; al-Bakrī, Muḥammad; al-Bakrī, Muṣṭafā; al-Dimyāṭī; al-Ḥallādj; Ibn ʿAdjība; Ibn ʿAlīwa; Ibn al-ʿArabī; al-Madjdhūb; Makhrama.III

voir aussi ʿAbd al-Ḳādir al-Djīlānī; Abū Madyan; al-Ḳādirī al-Ḥasanī; [au Suppl.] al-Hilālī

en Asie centrale Aḥmad Yasawī

indienne Bāḳī bi-llāh; Bīdil; Dard; Djamālī; Ḥānsawī; Ḥusaynī Sādāt Amīr; Imdād Allāh; Malik Muḥammad Djāyasī; [au Suppl.] Ḥamīd Ḳalandar

voir aussi Bhitāʾī; Pandjābī.2

indonésienne Ḥamza Fanṣūrī

persane Aḥmad-i Djām; ʿAṭṭār; Bābā-Ṭāhir; Djalāl al-Dīn Rūmī; Faḍl

Allāh Ḥurūfī; Ghudjduwānī; Humām al-Dīn b. ʿAlāʾ Tabrīzī; ʿIrāḳī; Kamāl Khudjandī; Ḳāsim-i Anwār; al-Kirmānī; Lāhīdjī.I; Maḥmūd Shabistarī; [au Suppl.] ʿĀrif Čelebī; ʿImād al-Dīn ʿAlī, Faḳīh-i Kirmānī
voir aussi Abū Saʿīd b. Abī l-Khayr; Kharaḳānī; [au Suppl.] Aḥmad-i Rūmī
turque ʿĀshiḳ Pasha; Faṣīḥ Dede; Gulshanī; Gülshehrī; Hüdāʾī; Münedjdjim Bashi; Nefes; Nesīmī; Refīʿī; [au Suppl.] Eshrefoghlu ʿAbd Allāh; Esrār Dede
voir aussi Ḥusām al-Dīn Čelebi; Ismāʿīl al-Anḳarawī; Ismāʿīl Ḥaḳḳī; Ḳayghusuz Abdāl; Khalīlī
ourdou Ghazal.IV; Ḥamāsa.V; Hidjāʾ.IV; Ḳaṣīda.IV; Madīḥ.IV; Madjnūn Laylā.IV; Marthiya.IV; Mathnawī.IV; Mukhtārāt.IV; Musammaṭ.2; Mushāʿara
17ᵉ siècle Nuṣratī
18ᵉ siècle Ashraf ʿAlī Khān; Dard; Djurʾat; Maẓhar; [au Suppl.] Ḥasan
voir aussi Ārzū Khān
19ᵉ siècle Amānat; Anīs; Aẓfarī; Dabīr, Salāmat ʿAlī; Dāgh; Dhawḳ; Ghālib; Faḳīr Muḥammad Khān; Ḥālī; Ilāhī Bakhsh; Inshāʾ; Mīr Muḥammad Taḳi; Muḥsin ʿAlī Muḥsin; Muʾmin; Muṣḥafī; Nāsikh; Nasīm; Rangīn; [au Suppl.] Ātish
voir aussi [au Suppl.] Āzād
20ᵉ siècle Akbar, Ḥusayn Allāhābādī; Āzād; Djawān; Iḳbāl; Muḥammad ʿAlī; Rāshid, N.M.; Ruswā; [au Suppl.] Ḥasrat Mohānī
voir aussi Āzurda
persane Ghazal.II; Ḥamāsa.II; Hidjāʾ.II; Ḳaṣīda.II; Khamsa; Madīḥ.II; Malik al-Shuʿarāʾ; Marthiya.II; Mathnawī.II; Mukhtārāt.II; Musammaṭ; Mustazād; Rubāʿī; [au Suppl.] Ḥabsiyya
voir aussi Barzū-nāma; Farhād wa-Shirīn; Iskandar Nāma.II; Kalīla wa-Dimna; Madjnūn Laylā.II; Radīf.2; Ṣafawides.III; Sāḳī.2; *et* → LITTÉRATURE.POÉSIE.INDO-PERSANE *et* POÉSIE.MYSTIQUE
anthologies **Mukhtārāt**.II
anthologistes ʿAwfī; Dawlat-Shāh; Luṭf ʿAlī Beg; [au Suppl.] Djādjarmī.II
biographies des poètes Sām Mīrzā
9ᵉ siècle Muḥammad b. Waṣīf
voir aussi Sahl b. Hārūn
10ᵉ siècle Bābā-Ṭāhir; Daḳīḳī; Kisāʾī; al-Muṣʿabī; Rūdakī; [au Suppl.] Abū Shakūr Balkhī
11ᵉ-13ᵉ siècles ʿAbd al-Wāsiʿ Djabalī; Anwarī; Asadī; ʿAṭṭār; Azraḳī; Bābā Afḍal; Djalāl al-Dīn Rūmī; Falakī Shirwānī; Farrukhī; Firdawsī; Gurgānī; Humām al-Dīn b. ʿAlāʾ Tabrīzī; ʿImādī (*et* [au Suppl.]);

ʿIrāḳī; Kamāl al-Dīn Ismāʿīl; Ḳaṭrān; Khʷādjū; Khāḳānī; Labībī; Lāmiʿī; Mahsatī; Manūčihrī; Muʿizzī; Mukhtārī; Niẓāmī Gandjawī; Pūr-i Bahāʾ; Ṣābir; Saʿdī; [au Suppl.] ʿAmʿaḳ; Djādjarmī; Djamāl al-Dīn Iṣfahānī

14ᵉ-15ᵉ siècles ʿAṣṣār; Awḥadī; Banākitī; Busḥāḳ; Djāmī; Faḍl Allāh Ḥurūfī; Fattāḥī; Ḥāfiẓ; Ḥāmidī; Ibn-i Yamīn; ʿIṣāmī; Kātibī; Nizārī Ḳuhistānī; Rāmī Tabrīzī; Salmān-i Sāwadjī; [au Suppl.] ʿĀrifī; Badr-i Čāčī; ʿImād al-Dīn ʿAlī, Faḳīh-i Kirmānī

voir aussi Djem; Ḥamd Allāh al-Mustawfī al-Ḳazwīnī

16ᵉ siècle Bannāʾī; Baṣīrī; Fayḍī; Fighānī; Hātifī; Hilālī; Muḥtasham-i Kāshānī; Mushtiḳī; Nawʿı; Saḥabı Astarābādī; Sām Mīrzā

voir aussi Luḳmān b. Sayyid Ḥusayn

17ᵉ siècle Asīr; al-Dāmād; Ḳadrī; Ḳalīm Abū Ṭālib; Kāshif; Lāhīdjī.II; Nāẓim Farrukh Ḥusayn; Ṣāʾib; Saʿīdā Gīlānī

voir aussi al-ʿĀmilī; Ghanīmat; Khushḥāl Khān Khaṭak; [au Suppl.] Findiriskī; *et* › LITTÉRATURE.POÉSIE.INDO-PERSANE

18ᵉ siècle Hātif; Ḥazīn; Luṭf ʿAlī Beg; Nadjāt

voir aussi Āzād Bilgrāmī

19ᵉ-20ᵉ siècles Bahār; Furūgh; Furūghī; Ḳāʾānī; Ḳurrat al-ʿAyn; Lāhūtī; Nafīsī; Nashāṭ; Nīmā Yūshīdj; Parwīn Iʿtiṣāmī; Pūr-i Dāwūd; Rashīd Yāsimī; Riḍā Ḳulī Khān; Ṣabā; Sabzawārī, Ḥādjdj Mullā Hādī; [au Suppl.] ʿĀrif, Mīrzā; Ashraf al-Dīn Gīlānī; Dehkhudā

voir aussi Ghālib; Iḳbāl; Ḳāʾim-maḳām-i Farāhānī

turque Ḥamāsa.III; Hidjāʾ.III; Ḳaṣīda.III; Khamsa; Ḳoshma; Madīḥ.III; Mani; Marthiya.III; Mathnawī.III; Mukhtārāt.III; Musammaṭ.1; Rabīʿiyyāt; Rubāʿī.2; [au Suppl.] Ghazal.III

voir aussi Alpamïsh; ʿĀshiḳ; Farhād wa-Shīrīn; Ilāhī; Iskandar Nāma. III; Karadja Oghlan; Madjnūn Laylā.III; Ozan; *et* › LITTÉRATURE. POÉSIE.MYSTIQUE

anthologies **Mukhtārāt**.III

biographies des poètes Riḍā; Riyāḍī; Sālim

11ᵉ-12ᵉ siècles Aḥmad Yuknakī; Ḥakīm Ata; Ḳutadghu Bilig

13ᵉ-14ᵉ siècles Aḥmadī; ʿĀshïḳ Pasha; Burhān al-Dīn; Dehhānī, Khodja; Gülshehrī

15ᵉ siècle Āhī; Aḥmad Pasha Bursalï; Dāʿī; Firdewsī; Gulshanī; Ḥamdī, Ḥamd Allāh; Ḳāsïm Pasha; Ḳayghusuz Abdāl; Khalīlī; Khiḍr Beg

voir aussi Djem; Ḥāmidī

16ᵉ siècle Āgehī; ʿAzīzī; Bāḳī; Baṣīrī; Bihishtī; Dhātī; Djaʿfar Čelebi; Djalāl Ḥusayn Čelebi; Djalālzāde Muṣṭafā Čelebi; Djalālzāde Ṣāliḥ Čelebi; Faḍlī; Faḳīrī; Fawrī; Ferdī; Fighānī; Fuḍūlī; Ghazālī; Gulshanī; Ḥadīdī; Ḳarā-čelebi-zāde; Kemāl Pasha-zāde; Khāḳānī;

Khayālī; Ḳorḳud b. Bāyazīd; Lāmiʿī; Laṭīfī; Luḳmān b. Sayyid Ḥusayn; Meʾalī; Medjdī; Mesīḥī; Mihrī Khatun; Naẓmī, Edirneli; Nedjātī; Newʿī; Rewānī

17ᵉ siècle ʿAṭāʾī; ʿAzmī-zāde; Bahāʾī Meḥmed Efendi; Faṣīḥ Dede; Fehīm, Undjuzāde Muṣṭafā; Ḥāletī; Ḳarā-čelebi-zāde; Ḳul Muṣṭafā; Ḳuloghlu; Naʾilī; Nāẓim; Naẓmī; Nefʿī; Niyāzī; ʿÖmer ʿĀshiḳ; Riyāḍī

18ᵉ siècle Belīgh, Ismāʿīl; Belīgh, Meḥmed Emīn; Čelebi-zāde; Česhmīzāde; Fiṭnat; Gevherī; Ghālib; Ḥāmī-i Āmidī; Ḥashmet; Kānī; Meḥmed Pasha Rāmī; Nābī; Naḥīfī; Naẓīm; Nedīm; Neshʾet; Newres.I; ʿOthmān-zāde; Rāghib Pasha

19ᵉ siècle *ʿĀrif Hi*kmet Bey; ʿAynī; Dadaloghlu; Derdli, Ibrāhīm; Dhihnī; Fāḍil Bey; Faṭīn; Fehīm, Süleymān; Ismāʿīl Ṣafā; ʿIzzet Molla; Kemāl, Meḥmed Nāmiḳ; Laylā Khānim; Menemenli-zāde Meḥmed Ṭāhir; Muʿallim Nādjī; Newres.II; Pertew Pasha.II; Redjāʾī-zāde

20ᵉ siècle ʿAbd al-Ḥaḳḳ Ḥāmid; Djanāb Shihāb al-Dīn; Djewdet; Ekrem Bey; Hāshim; Kanık; Köprülü (Meḥmed Fuad); Ḳoryürek; Laylā Khānim; Meḥmed ʿĀkif; Meḥmed Emīn; Muḥibb Aḥmed "Diranas"; Nāẓim Ḥikmet; Oktay Rifat; Orkhan Seyfī; Ortač, Yūsuf Ḍiyā; Sāhir, Djelal; [au Suppl.] ʿĀshiḳ Weysel; Bölükbashi Riḍā Tewfīḳ; Čamlibel; Eshref; Eyyūboghlu; Gövsa

voir aussi [au Suppl.] Ergun; Findiḳoghlu

en turc oriental Ādharī.II; Bābur; Bāḳikhānli; Dhākir; Djambul Djabaev; Ghafūrī, Medjīd; Ghāzī Girāy II; Ḥamāsa.IV; Hidjāʾ.III; Iskandar Nāma.III; Ismāʿīl Iᵉʳ; Ḳayyūm Nāṣirī; Ḳutadghu Bilig; Luṭfī; Mīr ʿAlī Shīr Nawāʾī; Muʾnis; Sakkākī

traductions de langues européennes Ismāʿīl Ḥaḳḳi ʿĀlīshān; Kanık

prose Adab; Ḥikāya; Ḳiṣṣa; Maḳāma; Muḳaddima; Naṣīḥat al-Mulūk; Risāla

et → LITTÉRATURE.ÉTIQUETTE *et* HISTORIQUE; PRESSE

arabe ʿArabiyya.B.V; Ḥikāya; Ḳiṣṣa.II; Maḳāla.1; Maḳāma; Nahḍa; Naṣīḥat al-Mulūk.I; Risāla; Sadjʿ.3

et → LITTÉRATURE.DRAME; PRESSE

ouvrages Alf layla wa-Layla; Baybars; Bilawhar wa-Yūdāsaf; Dhū l-Himma; Kalīla wa-Dimna; Luḳmān.3

9ᵉ-10ᵉ siècles al-Djāḥiẓ; al-Hamadhānī; Ibn al-Muḳaffaʿ; [au Suppl.] Abū l-ʿAnbas al-Ṣaymarī

11ᵉ-13ᵉ siècles al-Ḥarīrī; Ibn Nāḳiyā; [au Suppl.] Abū l-Muṭahhar al-Azdī; al-Djazarī

14ᵉ-18ᵉ siècles Ibn Abī Ḥadjala

voir aussi al-Ibshīhī

19ᵉ-20ᵉ siècles Aḥmad Amīn; Faraḥ Anṭūn; Ḥāfiẓ Ibrāhīm; Maḥmūd Taymūr; al-Maʿlūf; al-Manfalūṭī; Mayy Ziyāda; al-Māzinī;

Muḥammad Ḥusayn Haykal; al-Muwayliḥī.II; Nuʿayma, Mik͟hāʾīl; al-Rayḥānī; Salāma Mūsā; [au Suppl.] Abū S͟hādī; al-ʿAḳḳād; al-Bustānī.6
voir aussi D̲jamīl al-Mudawwar; al-K͟hālidī; Kurd ʿAlī

ourdou Ḥikāya.IV; Ḳiṣṣa.V
et → LITTÉRATURE.DRAME; PRESSE
19e-20e siècles Amān, Mīr; D̲jawān; Faḳīr Muḥammad K͟hān; Iḳbāl; Nad͟hīr Aḥmad Dihlawī; Prēm Čand; Ruswā; [au Suppl.] Āzād

persane Ḥikāya.II; Īrān.VII; Ḳiṣṣa.IV; Maḳāla.II; Naṣīḥat al-Mulūk.II; Risāla.2
voir aussi Ṣafawides.III; *et* → LITTÉRATURE.DRAME; PRESSE
ouvrages Bak͟htiyār-nāma; Dabistān al-Mad͟hāhib; Ḳahramān-nāma; Kalīla wa-Dimna; Mad̲jnūn Laylā.II; Marzbān-nāma
voir aussi Niẓām al-Mulk; Niẓāmī ʿArūḍī Samarḳandī
11e-12e siècles Ḥamīdī; al-Ḳās͟hānī; Kay Kāʾūs (b. Iskandar); Nāṣir-i K͟husraw; Naṣr Allāh b. Muḥammad; Niẓāmī ʿArūḍī Samarḳandī; Ras͟hīd al-Dīn (al-Waṭwāṭ); al-Samʿānī, Abū l-Ḳāsim
13e siècle Saʿdī
14e siècle Nak͟hs͟habī
15e siècle Kās͟hifī
17e-18e siècles ʿInāyat Allāh Kańbū; Mumtāz
19e-20e siècles Bahār; Hidāyat, Ṣādiḳ; Nafīsī; [au Suppl.] Āl-i Aḥmad; Bihrangī; Dehk͟hudā
voir aussi Furūg͟h.2

turque Ḥikāya.III; Ḳiṣṣa.III; Maddāḥ; Maḳāla.III; Risāla.3
voir aussi Bilmed̲je; *et* → LITTÉRATURE.DRAME; PRESSE
ouvrages Alpamîs͟h; Billūr Kös͟hk; Dede Ḳorḳut; Ḳahramān-nāma; Og͟huz-nāma
voir aussi Merd̲jümek
17e siècle Nergisī
18e siècle ʿAlī ʿAzīz, Giridli; Nābī
19e-20e siècles Aḥmad Ḥikmet; Aḥmad Midḥat; Aḥmad Rāsim; D̲janāb S͟hihāb al-Dīn; Ebüzziya Tevfik; Ekrem Bey; Fiṭrat; Hîsar; Ḥusayn D̲jāhid; Ḥusayn Raḥmī; Karay, Refīḳ K͟hālid; Ḳaṣāb; Kaygîlî; Kemāl; Kemāl, Meḥmed Nāmîḳ; Kemal Tahir; K͟hālid Ḍiyāʾ; K͟hālide Edīb; Laylā K͟hānîm; Meḥmed Raʾūf; Oktay Rifat; ʿÖmer Seyf ül-Dīn; Ork͟han Kemāl; Res͟hād Nūrī; Sabahattin Ali; Sāmī; [au Suppl.] Atač; Atay; Čaylaḳ Tewfīḳ; Esendal; Haliḳarnas Balîḳčîsî
voir aussi Aḥmad Iḥsān; Ileri, D̲jelāl Nūrī; İnal; Ismāʿīl Ḥaḳḳi ʿĀlīs͟hān; Ḳiṣṣa.III.B; [au Suppl.] Eyyūbog͟hlu
en turc oriental Rabg͟hūzī

proverbes dans la littérature Mat͟hal.IV

voir aussi Ḥamza al-Iṣfahānī; Rashīd al-Dīn (al-Waṭwāṭ)

sagesse, littérature de al-Aḥnaf b. Ḳays; ʿAlī b. Abī Ṭālib; Buzurgmihr; Hūshang; Luḳmān; Sahl b. Hārūn; [au Suppl.] Djāwīdhān Khirad

voir aussi Aktham b. Ṣayfī; Buhlūl; al-Ibshīhī

termes littéraires ʿArūḍ; ʿAtāba; Badīʿ; Balāgha; Bayān; Dakhīl; Fard; Faṣāḥa; Fāṣila; Ibtidāʾ; Idjāza; Iḍmār; Iḳtibās; Intihāʾ; Irtidjāl; Istiʿāra; Ḳabḍ.III; Ḳāfiya; Ḳaṭʿ; Kināya; Luzūm mā lā yalzam; al-Maʿānī wa-l-Bayān; Madjāz; Maʿnā.III; Muʿāraḍa; Muzāwadja; Radīf.2; Radjaz.4

et → LITTÉRATURE.GENRES; MÉTRIQUE

topoi Bukhl; Bulbul; Ghurāb; Gul; Ḥamām; Ḥayawān.V; Inṣāf; al-Ḳamar.II; Ḳaṭā; Nardjis; Raḥīl; Sāḳī

voir aussi Ghazal.II; ʿIshḳ; Khamriyya; Rabīʿiyyāt

Tradition, littérature de la Athar; **Ḥadīth**; Ḥadīth Ḳudsī; Hind.V.E; [au Suppl.] Arbaʿūn Ḥadīth

voir aussi Ahl al-Ḥadīth; Ḥashwiyya; Khabar; Mustamlī; Naskh; Riwāya

collections canoniques Abū Dāʾūd al-Sidjistānī; Aḥmad b. Ḥanbal; Anas b. Mālik; al-Bayhaḳī; al-Bukhārī; al-Dāraḳuṭnī; al-Dārimī; Ibn Ḥibbān; Ibn Mādja; Muslim b. al-Ḥadjdjādj; al-Nasāʾī

voir aussi al-ʿAynī; Ibn Hubayra

termes al-Djarḥ wa-l-Taʿdīl; Fard; Gharīb; Ḥikāya.I; Idjāza; Isnād; Khabar al-Wāḥid; Mashhūr; Matn; Muʿanʿan; Munkar; Mursal; Muṣannaf; Musnad.3; Mustamlī; Mutawātir.a; Rafʿ; Ridjāl; Ṣaḥīḥ.1; Ṣāliḥ

voir aussi Ḥadīth

traditionnistes Rāwī; Ridjāl

voir aussi al-Rāmahurmuzī

7e siècle ʿAbd Allāh b. ʿUmar b. al-Khaṭṭāb; Abū Bakra; Abū Hurayra; al-Aʿmash; Ibn Abī Laylā.1; Ibn Masʿūd; Kaʿb al-Aḥbār; al-Khawlānī, Abū Idrīs; al-Khawlānī, Abū Muslim; [au Suppl.] Djābir b. ʿAbd Allāh

8e siècle Abū l-ʿĀliya al-Riyāḥī; Abū Mikhnaf; al-Ashʿarī, Abū Burda; Djābir b. Zayd; al-Fuḍayl b. ʿIyāḍ; Ghundjār; al-Ḥasan b. Ṣāliḥ b. Ḥayy; al-Ḥasan al-Baṣrī; Ibn Abī Laylā.2; Ibn Daʾb; Ibn Isḥāḳ; Ibn al-Naṭṭāḥ; Ibn Shubruma; Ibn Sīrīn; ʿIkrima; al-Layth b. Saʿd; Maymūn b. Mihrān; Muḳātil b. Sulaymān; Nāfiʿ; al-Nakhaʿī; Saʿīd b. Abī Arūba; [au Suppl.] Abū ʿAmr al-Shaybānī; Ibn Djuraydj

9e siècle Abū Nuʿaym al-Mulāʾī; Baḳī b. Makhlad; Ibn Abī Khaythama; Ibn Abī l-Shawārib; Ibn Abī Shayba; Ibn ʿĀʾisha.IV; Ibn Rāhwayh; Ibn Saʿd; Ibn Sallām al-Djumaḥī; Ibrāhīm al-Ḥarbī; al-Karābīsī.2; al-Marwazī; Muslim b. al-Ḥadjdjādj; Nuʿaym b. Ḥammād; [au Suppl.] Abū ʿĀṣim al-Nabīl; Asad b. Mūsā

voir aussi Ibn Khayyāṭ al-ʿUṣfurī; Ibn Ḳuṭlūbughā

10e siècle Abū ʿArūba; al-Anbārī, Abū Bakr; al-Anbārī, Abū

Muḥammad; G̱ẖulām Thaʿlab; Ibn al-ʿAllāf; Ḳāsim b. Aṣbag̱ẖ; al-Ḵẖaṭṭābī; [au Suppl.] Ibn ʿUḳda

11ᵉ siècle   al-Ḥākim al-Naysābūrī; Ibn ʿAbd al-Barr; Ibn al-Bannāʾ; Ibn Fūrak; Ibn Mākūlā.III; al-Ḳābisī; al-Ḵẖaṭīb al-Bag̱ẖdādī; al-Sahmī

12ᵉ siècle   al-Bag̱ẖawī; Ibn al-ʿArabī; Ibn ʿAsākir; Ibn Ḥubays̱ẖ; Ibn al-Ḳaysarānī.1; Ibn al-Nadjdjār; al-Lawātī; Razīn b. Muʿāwiya; al-Rus̱ẖāṭī; al-Ṣadafī
      voir aussi al-Samʿānī, Abū Saʿd

13ᵉ siècle   al-Dimyāṭī; Ibn al-Ath̲īr.I; Ibn Diḥya; Ibn Faraḥ al-Is̱ẖbīlī; al-Ṣag̱ẖānī, Raḍī al-dīn; [au Suppl.] Ibn Daḳīḳ al-ʿĪd

14ᵉ siècle   al-D̲h̲ahabī; Ibn Kath̲īr; al-Mizzī

15ᵉ siècle   Ibn Ḥadjar al-ʿAsḳalānī; al-Ibs̱ẖīhī; al-Ḳasṭallānī; Muʿīn al-Miskīn
      voir aussi Ibn Ḳuṭlūbug̱ẖā

chiites   ʿAbd Allāh b. Maymūn; Dindān; Djaʿfar al-Ṣādiḳ; Ibn Bābawayh(i); al-Kas̱ẖs̱ẖī; al-Kāẓimī; al-Kulaynī; Madjlisī; Muḥammad b. Makkī; [au Suppl.] Akh̲bāriyya; al-Barḳī; Djābir al-Djuʿfī
      voir aussi Asmāʾ

traductions de langues européennes
   en arabe   Muḥammad Bey ʿUth̲mān Djalāl
   en persan   Muḥammad Ḥasan Ḵẖān; Nafīsī
   en turc   Ismāʿīl Ḥaḳḳī ʿĀlīs̱ẖān; Kanık

voyages, relations de   Djug̱ẖrāfiyā.V.E; **Riḥla**
   auteurs   ʿAbd al-G̱ẖanī b. Ismāʿīl; al-ʿAbdarī; Abū Dulaf; Abū Ṭālib Ḵẖān; Aḥmad Iḥsan; ʿAlı Bey al-ʿAbbāsī; ʿAlī Ḵẖān; al-ʿAyyās̱ẖī; Ewlīyā Čelebi; Fāris al-S̱ẖidyāḳ; al-G̱ẖassānī; G̱ẖiyāth̲ al-Dīn Naḳḳās̱ẖ; Ibn Baṭṭūṭa; Ibn Djubayr; Ibn Idrīs [II]; Kurd ʿAlī; Ma Huan; Meḥmed Yirmisekiz; Nāṣir-i Ḵẖusraw; [au Suppl.] al-G̱ẖazzāl; Ibn Nāṣir.III
      voir aussi Hārūn b. Yaḥyā; Ibn Djuzayy; Ibn Rus̱ẖayd; Ibn Saʿīd al-Mag̱ẖribī; Ibrāhīm b. Yaʿḳūb; Ḵẖayr Allāh Efendi; Léon l'Africain
   récits   [au Suppl.] Akh̲bār al-Ṣīn wa-l-Hind

M

MADAGASCAR   **Madagascar**; Massalajem

MAGIE   ʿAzīma.2; Djadwal; Istinzāl; Ḵẖāṣṣa; Nīrandj; Ruḳya; [au Suppl.] Budūḥ
   voir aussi ʿAbd Allāh b. Hilāl; Antemuru; Djinn; Ḥadjar; Ḥurūf; Istik̲ẖāra; Istiḳsām; Istisḳāʾ; Kabid.4; al-Ḳamar.II; Ḳatl.II.2; Ḵẖawāṣṣ al-Ḳurʾān; Kihāna; Kitābāt.V; Rūḥāniyya
   traités sur   al-Maḳḳarī; [au Suppl.] Ibn ʿAzzūz; al-Būnī

MALADIES Madjnūn; Malāryā; Ramad; [au Suppl.] Djudhām
 voir aussi Kalb; Ḳuṭrub
traités sur Ḥayātī-zāde; Ibn Buṭlān; Ibn Djazla
 et → MÉDECINE

MALAISIE Malacca; Malais; **(Péninsule) Malaise**; **Malaisie**
 voir aussi Baladiyya.VI; Djāmiʿa; Indonésie; Kandūrī; Kitābāt.VIII; Partai Islam se Malaysia (Pas); Rembau
architecture → ARCHITECTURE.RÉGIONS
belles-lettres ʿAbd Allāh b. ʿAbd al-Ḳādir; Dāwūd al-Faṭānī; Ḥikāya.V; Ḳiṣṣa.VI; Malais
 voir aussi Indonésie.VI
états Penang; Pérak; Sabah

MALAWI Kota Kota

MALI Adrar.2; Aḥmad al-Shaykh; Aḥmadu Lobbo; Ḥamāliyya; Kaʿti; **Mali**; Mansa Mūsā
 voir aussi Mande
historiens al-Saʿdī
toponymes
 régions Kaarta
 villes Bamako; Dienné; Gao

MAMELUKS **Mamlūks**
 voir aussi Ḥarfūsh; Manshūr; Mihmindār; Rank; *et* → DYNASTIES.ÉGYPTE ET LE CROISSANT FERTILE; MILITAIRES.MAMELUKS

MARIAGE Djilwa; Khiṭba; Mutʿa; **Nikāḥ**; [au Suppl.] Djabr
 voir aussi ʿAbd.3.e; ʿĀda.III et IV.4; ʿArūs Resmi; Fāsid wa-Bāṭil.III; Ghāʾib; Ḥaḍāna; Kafāʾa; Kurdes et Kurdistān.IV.A.1; al-Marʾa.II; Mawākib.IV.3 et 5; Raḍāʿ
douaire **Mahr**; Ṣadāḳ

MAROC **al-Maghrib**
 voir aussi ʿArabiyya.A.III.3; Ḥimāya.II; Mallāḥ; Rīf.II
architecture → ARCHITECTURE.RÉGIONS.AFRIQUE DU NORD
dynasties ʿAlawīs; Idrīsides; Marīnides; Saʿdides
 voir aussi Bū Ḥmāra; Ḥasanī; [au Suppl.] Aḥmad al-Hiba; *et* → DYNASTIES.ESPAGNE ET AFRIQUE DU NORD
historiens Aḥmad al-Nāṣirī (*et* al-Nāṣirī al-Salāwī); Akanṣūs; Ibn Abī Zarʿ; Ibn al-Ḳāḍī

voir aussi Ibn al-Raḳīḳ; al-Kattānī; [au Suppl.] ʿAllāl al-Fāsī; *et* → DYNASTIES.ESPAGNE ET AFRIQUE DU NORD

période moderne Baladiyya.III; Dj̲āmiʿa; Dj̲arīda.I.B; Dj̲aysh̲.III.2; Dustūr. XVII; Ḥizb.I; Ḥukūma.IV; Maʿārif.II; Mad̲j̲lis.IV.A.21; Mad̲j̲maʿ ʿIlmī.I.II. 4; Maḥkama.IV.10; Mak̲h̲zan; [au Suppl.] Institut des hautes études marocaines

hommes d'état [au Suppl.] ʿAllāl al-Fāsī

réforme Salafiyya.1(c)

population Glāwā; Dukkāla; Ḥarṭānī; K̲h̲ulṭ; [au Suppl.] Awraba

voir aussi al-Fāsiyyūn; *et* → BERBÈRES

religion al-Mag̲h̲rib.VI

confréries mystiques Darḳāwa; Hansaliyya; Hazmīriyyūn; ʿĪsāwā; al-Nāṣiriyya; [au Suppl.] Ḥamādis̲h̲a

pour Dj̲azūliyya, *voir* al-Dj̲azūlī, Abū ʿAbd Allāh

voir aussi [au Suppl.] ʿĀʾis̲h̲a Ḳandīs̲h̲a; *et* → MYSTICISME; SAINT

toponymes

anciens Anfā; Bādis; al-Baṣra; Fāzāz; al-Ḳaṣr al-Ṣag̲h̲īr; Nakūr

actuels

îles [au Suppl.] al-Ḥusayma

régions Darʿa; Figuig; G̲h̲arb; Ḥawz; Ifni; Rīf.I.2

villes Agadir-ighir; Āg̲h̲māt; al-ʿArāʾis̲h̲; Aṣfī; Aṣīla; Azammūr; Damnāt; (al-)Dār al-Bayḍāʾ; al-Dj̲adīda; Dubdū; Faḍāla; Fās; Garsīf; al-Ḳaṣr al-Kabīr; al-Mahdiyya; Marrākus̲h̲; Mawlāy Idrīs; Melilla; Miknās; Ribāṭ al-Fatḥ; Sabta; Salā; [au Suppl.] Azrū; Benī Mellāl

voir aussi al-Ḥamrāʾ

MARONITES → CHRISTIANISME.CONFESSIONS; LIBAN

MARTYRE Fidāʾī; Maẓlūm

voir aussi Ḥabīb al-Nad̲j̲d̲j̲ār; (al-)Ḥusayn b. ʿAlī b. Abī Ṭālib; K̲h̲ubayb; Mad̲j̲lis.III; Mas̲h̲had; Masʿūd, Sayyid Sālār; [au Suppl.] ʿAbd Allāh b. Abī Bakr al-Miyanad̲j̲ı

MATHÉMATIQUES Algorithme; al-Dj̲abr wa-l-Muḳābala; Fard; Ḥisāb al-ʿAḳd; Ḥisāb al-G̲h̲ubār; **ʿIlm al-Ḥisāb**; Kasr; Ḳaṭʿ; Ḳuṭr; Māl; Mans̲h̲ūr; Misāḥā; Muḳaddam; Muṣādara.1; Mut̲h̲allat̲h̲; **al-Riyāḍiyyāt**; al-Sahm.1.a; [au Suppl.] ʿIlm al-Handasa

voir aussi al-Mīzān; [au Suppl.] Halīlad̲j̲

algèbre **al-Dj̲abr wa-l-Muḳābala**

géométrie **Misāḥā**; [au Suppl.] **ʿIlm al-Handasa**

mathématiciens Abū Kāmil; Abū l-Wafāʾ al-Būzad̲j̲ānī; ʿAlī al-Ḳūs̲h̲d̲j̲ī; al-Bīrūnī; Ibn al-Bannāʾ al-Marrākus̲h̲ī; Ibn al-Hayt̲h̲am; Ibn ʿIrāḳ; Isḥāḳ

Efendi; al-Ḳalaṣādī; al-Karābīsī.1; al-Karad̲j̲ī; al-Kās̲h̲ī; al-K̲h̲ʷārazmī; al-K̲h̲āzin; al-K̲h̲ud̲j̲andī; Kus̲h̲iyār; al-Mad̲j̲rīṭī; al-Mārdīnī; Muḥammad b. ʿĪsā b. Aḥmad al-Māhānī; Muḥammad b. ʿUmar

voir aussi Balīnūs; Ḳusṭā b. Lūḳā

MAURITANIE Adrar.3; Atar; Ḥawḍ; Māʾ al-ʿAynayn; Mad̲j̲lis.IV.A.22; **Mūrītāniyā**

voir aussi Dustūr.XV; Lamtūna; al-Māmī

toponymes

anciens Awdag̲h̲ost; G̲h̲āna; Ḳunbi Ṣāliḥ

actuels Nouakchott

MAUVAIS OEIL **ʿAyn**

voir aussi Karkaddan; *et* → CHARMES; ISLAM.CROYANCES POPULAIRES

MÉCANIQUE Ḥiyal.II; al-Ḳarasṭūn; [au Suppl.] al-D̲j̲azarī; **Ḥiyal**

voir aussi Ibn al-Sāʿātī; *et* → HYDROLOGIE

MÉDECINE

et → ANATOMIE; DROGUES; MALADIES; PHARMACOLOGIE

centres de Bīmāristān; Gondēs̲h̲āpūr; Ḳalāwūn; [au Suppl.] Abū Zaʿbal

voir aussi Bag̲h̲dād; Dimas̲h̲ḳ; al-Madīna

dentaire Miswāk

voir aussi ʿAḳīḳ; Mard̲j̲ān

traités sur Hāmōn

voir aussi Ibn Abī l-Bayān

manuels/encyclopédies de médecine ʿAlī b. al-ʿAbbās; al-D̲j̲urd̲j̲ānī, Ismāʿīl b. al-Ḥusayn; Ibn al-Nafīs; Ibn Sīnā; al-Masīḥī

médecins D̲j̲arrāḥ; Ḥāwī; [au Suppl.] Faṣṣād

voir aussi ʿAyn; Constantin l'Africain; Ḥikma; Kabid.3; Masāʾil wa-Ad̲j̲wiba; *et* → MÉDICINE.OPHTALMOLOGISTES; PHARMACOLOGIE

biographies des Ibn Abī Uṣaybiʿa; Ibn D̲j̲uld̲j̲ul; Ibn al-Ḳāḍī; Isḥāḳ b. Ḥunayn

voir aussi Ibn al-Ḳifṭī

7e siècle [au Suppl.] al-Ḥārit̲h̲ b. Kalada

9e siècle Buk̲h̲tīs̲h̲ūʿ; Ḥunayn b. Isḥāḳ al-ʿIbādī; Ibn Māsawayh; Sābūr b. Sahl

voir aussi Māsard̲j̲awayh

10e siècle ʿAlī b. al-ʿAbbās; ʿArīb b. Saʿd; Ibn D̲j̲uld̲j̲ul; Isḥāḳ b. Ḥunayn; Isḥāḳ al-Isrāʾīlī; Ḳusṭā b. Lūḳā; al-Rāzī, Abū Bakr; Ṣābiʾ.(3); Saʿīd b. Yaʿḳūb al-Dimas̲h̲ḳī; [au Suppl.] Ibn Abī l-As̲h̲ʿat̲h̲

11e siècle al-Anṭākī, Abū l-Farad̲j̲; Ibn Buṭlān; Ibn D̲j̲anāḥ; Ibn D̲j̲azla; Ibn al-D̲j̲azzār; Ibn Riḍwān; Ibn Sīnā; Ibn al-Ṭayyib; Ibn Wāfid; Ibn Zuhr.II; al-Masīḥī

12e siècle Abū l-Barakāt; al-Djurdjānī, Ismāʿīl b. al-Ḥusayn; Ibn Djāmiʿ; Ibn al-Tilmīdh; Ibn Zuhr.III et IV; al-Marwazī, Sharaf al-Zamān; [au Suppl.] Ibn Biklārish
voir aussi Ibn Rushd
13e siècle Ibn Abī l-Bayān; Ibn Abī Uṣaybiʿa; Ibn Hubal; Ibn al-Nafīs; Ibn Ṭumlūs; Saʿd al-Dawla; [au Suppl.] Ibn al-Ḳuff
14e siècle Ḥādjdjī Pasha; Ibn al-Khaṭīb; Isḥāḳ b. Murād; Ḳuṭb al-Dīn Shīrāzī
15e siècle Bashīr Čelebi
16e siècle al-Anṭākī, Dāwūd; Hāmōn
17e siècle Ḥayātī-zāde
18e siècle [au Suppl.] Ādarrāḳ; Ibn Shaḳrūn
à partir du 19e siècle Bahdjat Muṣṭafā Efendi; Muḥammad b. Aḥmad al-Iskandarānī; [au Suppl.] ʿAbd al-Salām b. Muḥammad
grecs Diyusḳuridīs; Djālīnūs; Rūfus al-Afsīsī; [au Suppl.] Ahrun; Buḳrāṭ
voir aussi Ḥunayn b. Isḥaḳ al-ʿIbādī; Ibn Riḍwān; Ibn al-Ṭayyib; Isḥāḳ b. Ḥunayn; Iṣṭifan b. Basīl; [au Suppl.] Ḥubaysh b. al-Ḥasan al-Dimashḳī; Ibn Abī l-Ashʿath
juifs Hāmōn; Ibn Abī l-Bayān; Ibn Djāmiʿ; Ibn Djanāḥ; Isḥāḳ al-Isrāʾīlī; Māsardjawayh; Saʿd al-Dawla; [in Suppl.] Ibn Biklarish
voir aussi Abū l-Barakāt; Ḥayātī-zāde.1
ottomans Bahdjat Muṣṭafā Efendi; Bashīr Čelebi; Ḥādjdjī Pasha; Hāmōn; Ḥayātī-zāde; Isḥāḳ b. Murād
voir aussi Ḥekīm-bashï
médicaments Abanūs; Adhargūn; ʿAfṣ; Afsantīn; Almās; ʿAnbar; Baḳḳam; Bān; al-Dahnadj; Dhahab; Durr; Fiḍḍa; Ḥinnāʾ; Kāfūr; Ḳaranful; Ḳaṭrān; Ḳily; Kuḥl; Lubān; Maghnāṭīs; Mardjān; Milḥ.2; Misk; Mūmiyāʾ; Ṣabr; Ṣābūn; Sādj; Ṣamgh; [au Suppl.] Ās; Bawraḳ; Djawz; Halīladj; Hindibāʾ; Iklīl al-Malik
voir aussi Bāzahr; al-Iksīr; Kabid.3, [au Suppl.] Afāwīh; Dam; *pour l'usage médicinal des parties anatomiques des animaux, voir les articles sur les animaux individuels*
obstétrique ʿArīb b. Saʿd
et → ENFANT.ACCOUCHEMENT
ophtalmologistes ʿAlī b. ʿĪsā (al-Kaḥḥāl); ʿAmmār al-Mawṣilī; al-Ghāfiḳī; Ibn Dāniyāl; Khalīfa b. Abī l-Maḥāsin
voir aussi ʿAyn; Ḥunayn b. Isḥāḳ al-ʿIbādī; Ibn al-Nafīs; Ibn Zuhr.V; *et* → ANATOMIE.OEIL
termes Bīmāristān; Djarrāḥ; Ḥidjāb; Ḳuwwa.5; Sabab.2
voir aussi Ḥāl
vétérinaire Bayṭār; Ibn Hudhayl; Ibn al-Mundhir

MELKITES → CHRISTIANISME.CONFESSIONS

Mésopotamie → Irak

Métallurgie Ḳalʿī; Khārṣīnī; **Maʿdin**
voir aussi Kalah; al-Mīzān.I; *et* → Minéralogie.mines
métaux Dhahab; Fiḍḍa; Ḥadīd; Nuḥās
et → Minéralogie.minéraux; Professions.artisans

Métaphysique **Mā baʿd al-Ṭabīʿa**
voir aussi ʿAbd al-Laṭīf al-Baghdādī; Māhiyya; Muṭlaḳ

Météorologie al-Āthār al-ʿUlwiyya
voir aussi Anwāʾ; Sadjʿ.2; [au Suppl.] Ibn al-Adjdābī
vent **Rīḥ**; Samūm

Métrique **ʿArūḍ**
voir aussi al-Djawharī; al-Khalīl b. Aḥmad; al-Khazradjī; *et* → Littérature.poésie
mètres Mudjtathth; Mutadārik; Mutaḳārib; Mutawātir.b; Radjaz; Ramal.1
termes Dakhīl; Fard; Ḳaṭʿ; Sabab.3; Ṣadr.(a); Sālim.3

Militaires Baḥriyya; Djaysh; **Ḥarb**; [au Suppl.] Baḥriyya
voir aussi Dār al-Ḥarb; Djihād; Fatḥnāme; Ghazw; Naḳḳāra-khāna
architecture Ribāṭ
et → Architecture.monuments.forteresses
armée **Djaysh**; Istiʿrāḍ (Arḍ); **Lashkar**; Radīf.3
voir aussi Djāsūs; Ṣaff.2; *et* → Militaires.mameluks *et* ottomans
contingents Bāzinḳir; Djāndār; Djaysh.III.2; Djund; Ghulām; Gūm; Ḳūrčī; Maḥalla; Mamlūk; Mutaṭawwiʿa
voir aussi Almogávares; Fāris
armes ʿAnaza; ʿArrāda; Balyemez; Bārūd; Dūrbāsh; Ḳaws; Mandjanīḳ; Nafṭ.II
voir aussi ʿAlam; Asad Allāh Iṣfahānī; Hilāl.II; Ḥiṣār; Ḳalʿī; Lamṭ; Marātib
batailles
et → Militaires.expéditions
avant 622 Buʿāth; Dhū Ḳār; Djabala; Fidjār; Ḥalīma; [au Suppl.] Dāḥis
voir aussi Ayyām al-ʿArab; Ḥanẓala
622-632 Badr; Biʾr Maʿūna; Buzākha; Ḥunayn; Khandaḳ; Khaybar; Muʾta
voir aussi Mālik b. ʿAwf
633-660 Adjnādayn; ʿAḳrabāʾ; al-Djamal; Djisr; Faḥl; Ḥarūrāʾ; al-Ḳādisiyya.II; Mardj al-Ṣuffar; [au Suppl.] Dhāt al-Ṣawārī
voir aussi ʿAbd Allāh b. Saʿd; ʿĀʾisha bint Abī Bakr; ʿAlī b. Abī Ṭālib; al-Hurmuzān; al-Nahrawān; Rustam b. Farrukh Hurmuzd
661-750 ʿAyn al-Warda; Balāṭ al-Shuhadāʾ; Baldj; al-Bishr; Dayr al-

Djamādjim; Dayr al-Djāthalīḳ; al-Ḥarra; al-Khāzir; Mardj Rāhiṭ
voir aussi (al-)Ḥusayn b. ʿAlī b. Abī Ṭālib; Kulthūm b. ʿIyāḍ; (al-) Ḳusṭanṭīniyya

751-1258 al-Arak; Bākhamrā; Dayr al-ʿĀḳūl; Fakhkh; Ḥaydarān; Hazārasp; al-ʿIḳāb; Köse-Dagh; Malāzgird.II; [au Suppl.] Dandānḳān
voir aussi Ḥadjar al-Nasr; al-Madjūs; al-Manṣūr bi-llāh, Ismāʿīl; Mardj Dābiḳ

1258-18e siècle ʿAyn Djālūt; Čāldirān; Dābiḳ; Djarba; Ḥimṣ; Ḳoṣowa; Mardj Dābiḳ; Mardj Rāhiṭ; Mardj al-Ṣuffar; Mezőkeresztes; Mohács.1 et 2; Nīkbūlī; Pānīpat
voir aussi Baḥriyya.III; Fatḥnāme; Ḥarb; Nahr Abī Fuṭrus; ʿOthmān Pasha

après le 18e siècle Abuklea; Atjèh; Česhme; Farwān; Gök Tepe; Isly; Kūt al-ʿAmāra; Maysalūn; Nizīb; Rīf.II
voir aussi al-ʿAḳaba; Gulistān

butin Fayʾ; **Ghanīma**
voir aussi Baranta; Ghazw; Khāliṣa; Pendjik; *et* → MILITAIRES.PRISONNIERS

corps ʿAyyār; Dawāʾir; Djaysh.III.1; Futuwwa; Ghāzī
voir aussi ʿAlī b. Muḥammad al-Zandjī; al-Ikhwān; Khashabiyya

décorations **Nishān**

expéditions Ghāzī; **Ṣāʾifa**
voir aussi Ghazw

fonctions Amīr; ʿArīf; Atābak al-ʿAsākir; Fawdjdār; Ispahbadh; Ispahsālār; Istiʿrāḍ (Arḍ); Ḳāʾid; Manṣab; Sālār
voir aussi Amīr al-Umarāʾ; Dārūgha; Ḳāḍī ʿAskar; Ḳūrčī; *et* → MILITAIRES.OTTOMANS

indo-musulmans Bārūd.VI; Ghulām.III; Ḥarb.VI; Ḥiṣār.VI; Lashkar
voir aussi Istiʿrāḍ (Arḍ)

mameluks al-Baḥriyya, Baḥriyya.II; Bārūd.III; Burdjiyya; Ḥalḳa; Ḥarb.III; Ḥiṣār.IV; **Mamlūk**
voir aussi Amīr Ākhūr; al-Amīr al-Kabīr; Atābak al-ʿAsākir; ʿAyn Djālūt; Čerkesses; Ḥimṣ; ʿĪsā b. Muhannā; Khāṣṣakiyya; Ḳumāsh; Rikābdār

marine **Baḥriyya**; Dār al-Ṣināʿa; Daryā-begi; Ḳapudan Pasha; Lewend; Nassades; Raʾīs.3; Riyāla; [au Suppl.] **Baḥriyya**
voir aussi ʿAzab; Gelibolu; Kātib Čelebi; [au Suppl.] Dhāt al-Ṣawārī; *et* → DYNASTIES.ANATOLIE ET LES TURCS.OTTOMANS.GRANDS-AMIRAUX; NAVIGATION.NAVIRES; PIRATERIE

ottomans Bāb-i Serʿaskerī; Baḥriyya.III; Balyemez; Bārūd.IV; Devshirme; Djebeli; Ghulām.IV; Ḥarb.IV; Ḥarbiye; Ḥiṣār.V; Müsellem; Radīf.3; [au Suppl.] Djebedji
voir aussi ʿAskarī; Ḍabṭiyya; Gelibolu; Gūm; Ḥareket Ordusu; Istiʿrāḍ (Arḍ); Ḳapîdjî; Karakol; Martolos; Mensūkhāt; Mondros; Nefīr; Ordu;

Pendjik; *et* → MILITAIRES.MARINE

contingents de l'armée al-Abnāʾ.5; ʿAdjamī Oghlān; Akïndjï; Alay; ʿAzab; Bashï-bozuḳ; Bölük; Deli; Devedji; Djānbāzān; Eshkindji; Ghurabāʾ; Gönüllü; Khāṣṣekī; Khumbaradjï; Lewend; Niẓām-ï Djedīd; Odjaḳ; Orta; [au Suppl.] Djebedji

voir aussi Akhī; Nefīr

officiers Bayraḳdār; Biñbashï; Bölük-bashï; Čāʾūsh; Čorbadjï.I; Ḍābiṭ; Daryā-begi; Ḳapudan Pasha; Mushīr; Rikābdār; Riyāla

police Aḥdāth; ʿAsas; Ḍabṭiyya; Karakol

voir aussi Dawāʾir; Futuwwa; Kotwāl; Martolos; Naḳīb.2

prisonniers Lamas-ṣū; Mübādele.2; [au Suppl.] Fidāʾ

et → MILITAIRES.BUTIN

réforme → RÉFORME.MILITAIRES

soldes ʿAṭāʾ; Inʿām; Māl al-Bayʿa; Rizḳ.3

tactique Ḥarb; Ḥiṣār; Ḥiyal.I

voir aussi Fīl; *et* → ARCHITECTURE.MONUMENTS.FORTERESSES

traités sur Ibn Hudhayl; [au Suppl.] Fakhr-i Mudabbir

voir aussi Ḥarb.II; Ḥiyal.I

MINÉRALOGIE **Maʿdin**

voir aussi al-Mīzān.I

minéraux Abū Ḳalamūn; ʿAḳīḳ; Almās; Bārūd; Billawr; al-Dahnadj; Fīrūzadj; Kibrīt; Kuḥl; Maghnāṭīs.I; Milḥ; Mūmiyāʾ; Naṭrūn; [au Suppl.] Bawraḳ

voir aussi al-Andalus.V; Damāwand; Golkonḍā; Ḥadjar; Kirmān; Maʿdin; Malindi; *et* → BIJOUX; MÉTALLURGIE

mines al-ʿAllāḳī; Anadolu.III.6; al-Andalus.V.2; ʿAraba; Armīniya.III; Azalay; Badakhshān; Billiton; Bilma; Čankïrï; al-Djabbūl; Djayzān; al-Durūʿ; Farghānā; Firrīsh; Gümüsh-khāne; Kalah; Ḳarā Ḥiṣār.2 et 3; Ḳayṣariyya; Ḳily; Ḳishm; Maʿdin.II; al-Maʿdin

voir aussi Fāzūghlī; Filasṭīn; Milḥ

MIRACLES **Karāma; Muʿdjiza**

voir aussi Āya; Dawsa; Māʾ al-ʿAynayn; Miʿrādj; *et* → SAINT

MOBILIER Mafrūshāt; [au Suppl.] **Athāth**

MONACHISME **Rahbāniyya**

et → CHRISTIANISME.COUVENTS

MONARCHIE Malik; Mamlaka

voir aussi Darshan

MONGOLIE Ḳaraḳorum; Khalkha; **Mongolie**; Mongols
géographie physique
eaux Orkhon
Mongols Batu'ides; Čaghatay; Čūbānides; Djalāyir; Djānides; Giray; Hayāṭila; Ilkhāns; Kalmuk; Ḳarā Khiṭāy; Ḳūrīltāy; Mangit; **Mongols**
voir aussi ʿAyn Djālūt; Dūghlāt; Ergenekon; Ḥimṣ; Khānbaliḳ; Ḳūbčūr; Ḳungrāt; Libās.III; Ötüken; *et* → DYNASTIES.MONGOLS
historiens Rashīd al-Dīn Ṭabīb
et → DYNASTIES.MONGOLS *et l'entrée Historiens sous dynasties individuelles*

MONOPHYSITES → CHRISTIANISME.CONFESSIONS

MONTAGNES Adja' et Salmā; Adrar.2; Aghri Dagh; Aïr; Ala Dagh; Aladja Dagh; Alburz; Altai; Alwand Kūh; ʿAmūr; Atlas; Awrās; Balkhan; Beshparmaḳ; Bībān; Bingöl Dagh; Bīsutūn; Čopan-ata; Damāwand; Deve Boynu; Djabala; al-Djibāl; Djūdī; Djurdjura; Elma Daghi; Erdjiyas Daghi; Fūta Djallon; Gāwur Daghlari; Ḥaḍūr; Ḥamrīn; Ḥarāz; Hawrāmān; Hindū Kush; Ḥiṣn al-Ghurāb; Ḥufāsh; al-Ḳabḳ; Kabylie; Ḳaraḳorum; Ḳāsiyūn; Khumayr; Kūh-i Bāba; al-Lukkām; Nafūsa, Djabal; Pamirs; Safīd Kūh
voir aussi Hind.I.i; Ḳarā Bāgh; *et* → *l'entrée Géographie Physique sous pays individuels*

MORT Djanāza; Ḥināṭa; Intiḥār; Ḳabr; Maḳbara; **Mawt**; Niyāḥa; [au Suppl.] Ghassāl
voir aussi Ghā'ib; Ghusl; Ḳatl; Marthiya; *et* → ARCHITECTURE.MONUMENTS.TOMBEAUX; ESCHATOLOGIE

MOZAMBIQUE Kerimba; Makua; **Mozambique**; Pemba

MUḤAMMAD, LE PROPHÈTE Hidjra; Ḥirā'; al-Ḥudaybiya; Khaybar; Khuzāʿa; Ḳudāʿa; Ḳuraysh; al-Madīna.I.2; Mawlid; Miʿrādj; **Muḥammad**; Ṣaḥāba
voir aussi al-Ḳur'ān; Mu'ākhāt; al-Mu'allafa Ḳulūbuhum; Nubuwwa; Nūr Muḥammadī; [au Suppl.] Bayʿat al-Riḍwān
biographies du Prophète ʿAbd al-Ḥaḳḳ b. Sayf al-Dīn; al-Bakrī, Abū l-Ḥasan; Daḥlān; al-Diyārbakrī; al-Djawwānī; al-Ḥalabī, Nūr al-dīn; Ibn Hishām; Ibn Isḥāḳ; Ibn Sayyid al-Nās; ʿIyāḍ b. Mūsā; Ḳarā-čelebi-zāde.4; al-Ḳasṭallānī; Liu Tchih; al-Maghāzī; Mughulṭāy; Muḥammad Ḥusayn Haykal; Muʿīn al-Miskīn
voir aussi Hind.V.e; Ibn Saʿd; al-Khargūshī; [au Suppl.] Dinet
compagnons du Prophète Abū Ayyūb al-Anṣārī; Abū Bakra; Abū l-Dardā'; Abū Dharr al-Ghifārī; Abū Hurayra; ʿAdī b. Ḥātim; ʿAmmār b. Yāsir; Anas b.

Mālik; al-Arḳam; al-Ashʿarī, Abū Mūsā; ʿAttāb b. Asīd; al-Barāʾ b. ʿĀzib; al-Barāʾ b. Maʿrūr; Bashīr b. Saʿd; Bilāl b. Rabāḥ; Bishr b. al-Barāʾ; Burayda b. al-Ḥuṣayb; Diḥya; Djāriya b. Ḳudāma; Ghasīl al-Malāʾika; Hāshim b. ʿUtba; Ḥurḳūṣ b. Zuhayr al-Saʿdī; Ibn Masʿūd; Kaʿb b. Mālik; Khabbāb b. al-Aratt; Khālid b. Saʿīd; Ḳutham b. al-ʿAbbās; Maslama b. Mukhallad; al-Miḳdād b. ʿAmr; Muʿāwiya b. Ḥudaydj; al-Mughīra b. Shuʿba; Muḥammad b. Abī Ḥudhayfa; Muṣʿab b. ʿUmayr; al-Nābigha al-Djaʿdī; al-Nuʿmān b. Bashīr; Saʿd b. Abī Waḳḳāṣ; Ṣafwān b. al-Muʿaṭṭal; Saʿīd b. Zayd; [au Suppl.] Djābir b. ʿAbd Allāh; Ibn Mītham

voir aussi Ahl al-Ṣuffa; al-Ḳaʿḳāʿ; Khawlān; Ḳuss b. Sāʿida; Rawḥ b. Zinbāʿ; al-Salaf wa-l-Khalaf

effets du Prophète Athar; al-Burāḳ; Burda.1; Dhū l-Faḳār; Duldul; Emānet-i Muḳaddese; Ḳadam Sharīf; Khirḳa-i Sherīf; Liḥya-yi Sherīf

famille du Prophète al-ʿAbbās b. ʿAbd al-Muṭṭalib; ʿAbd Allāh b. ʿAbd al-Muṭṭalib; ʿAbd al-Muṭṭalib b. Hāshim; Abū Lahab; Abū Ṭālib; ʿAḳīl b. Abī Ṭālib; ʿAlī b. Abī Ṭālib; Āmina; Djaʿfar b. Abī Ṭālib; Fāṭima; Ḥalīma bint Abī Dhuʾayb; Ḥamza b. ʿAbd al-Muṭṭalib; (al-)Ḥasan b. ʿAlī b. Abī Ṭālib; al-Ḥasan b. Zayd b. al-Ḥasan; Hāshim b. ʿAbd Manāf; (al-)Ḥusayn b. ʿAlī b. Abī Ṭālib; Ruḳayya

voir aussi Ahl al-Bayt

femmes du Prophète ʿĀʾisha bint Abī Bakr; Ḥafṣa; Khadīdja; Māriya; Maymūna bint al-Ḥārith; Ṣafiyya

MUSIQUE Ghināʾ; Ḳayna; Maḳām; Malāhī; **Mūsīḳī**; Ramal.2; [au Suppl.] Īḳāʿ

voir aussi Kurdes et Kurdistān.IV.C.4; Lamak; Naḳḳāra-khāna; al-Rashīdiyya; Samāʿ.1

andalouse al-Ḥāʾik

chant **Ghināʾ**; Ḳayna; Khayāl; Nashīd; Nawba

voir aussi Abū l-Faradj al-Iṣbahānī; Ḥawfī; Ilāhī; Mawāliyā.3

chanteurs/chanteuses ʿĀlima; ʿAzza al-Maylāʾ; Djamīla; al-Gharīḍ; Ḥabāba; Ibn ʿĀʾisha.I; Ibn Bāna; Ibn Djāmiʿ; Ibn Misdjaḥ; Ibn Muḥriz; Ibn Suraydj; Ibrāhīm al-Mawṣilī; Ḳayna; Maʿbad b. Wahb; Mālik b. Abī l-Samḥ; Mukhāriḳ; Nashīṭ; Rāʾiḳa; Sāʾib Khāthir; Sallāma al-Zarḳāʾ; [au Suppl.] Badhl al-Kubrā; al-Dalāl; al-Djarādatāni; Faḍl al-Shāʿira; Ḥabba Khātūn

voir aussi ʿĀshiḳ; al-Barāmika.5

compositeurs Ibrāhīm al-Mawṣilī; Ismāʿīl Ḥaḳḳi; al-Ḳusanṭīnī; Lāhūtī; Laylā Khānim; Maʿbad b. Wahb; Ṣafī al-Dīn al-Urmawī; [au Suppl.] ʿAllawayh al-Aʿsar; al-Dalāl; Ḥabba Khātūn

indienne **Hind.VIII**; Khayāl

voir aussi Bāyazīd Anṣārī; [au Suppl.] Ḥabba Khātūn

instruments Būḳ; Darabukka; Duff; Ghayṭa; Imẓad; Ḳithāra; Miʿzaf; Mizmār; Nefīr; Rabāb

voir aussi Mehter; Mūristus; Naḳḳāra-khāna
musiciens ʿAzza al-Maylāʾ; Djahẓa; Ibn Djāmiʿ; Ibn Muḥriz; Ibrāhīm al-Mawṣilī; Isḥāḳ b. Ibrāhīm al-Mawṣilī; Ṣafī al-Dīn al-Urmawī; [au Suppl.] ʿAllawayh al-Aʿsar; Barṣawma al-Zamīr; al-Dalāl; Faḍl al-Shāʿira
voir aussi al-Ḳāsim b. ʿĪsā
persane Mihragān.IV.3
voir aussi Lāhūtī; Naḳḳāra-khāna
traités sur ʿAbd al-Ḳādir b. Ghaybī; Abū l-Faradj al-Iṣbahānī; al-Ḥāʾik; Ibn Bāna; Ibn Khurradādhbih; Mashāḳa; al-Munadjdjim.IV; Mūristus; Mushāḳa; Ṣafī al-Dīn al-Urmawī
voir aussi Abū l-Maḥāsin Ibn Taghrībirdī; Inal; Malāhī
turque Ilāhī; Ḳoshma; Mehter
voir aussi Laylā Khānïm; Māni; Nefīr

MYSTICISME Allāh.III.4; Darwīsh; Dhikr; Ibāḥa.II; Karāma; Murīd; Murshid; Pīr; Samāʿ.1
voir aussi Sadjdjāda.3; Saʿīd al-Suʿadāʾ; *et* → DYNASTIES.PERSE.ṢAFAWIDES
ascètes primitifs ʿĀmir b. ʿAbd al-Ḳays; al-Ḥasan al-Baṣrī; al-Fuḍayl b. ʿIyāḍ; Ibrāhīm b. Adham
voir aussi Bakkāʾ
concepts Baḳāʾ wa-Fanāʾ; al-Insān al-Kāmil; Ishrāḳ; Lāhūt et Nāsūt
voir aussi Allāh.III.4; al-Ḥallādj.IV; Ibn al-ʿArabī; al-Niffarī
confréries ʿAmmāriyya; ʿArūsiyya; Ashrafiyya; Bakriyya; Bayrāmiyya; Bayyūmiyya; Bektāshiyya; Čishtiyya; Darḳāwa; Djilwatiyya; Hansaliyya; Hazmīriyyūn; ʿĪsāwā; Ḳādiriyya; Ḳalandariyya; Khalwatiyya; Madaniyya; Marwāniyya; Mawlawiyya; Mīrghaniyya; Murīdiyya; Naḳshbandiyya; al-Nāṣiriyya; Niʿmat-Allāhiyya; Pārsāʾiyya; Raḥmāniyya; Rifāʿiyya; Saʿdiyya; Ṣāliḥiyya; [au Suppl.] Demirdāshiyya; Ḥamādisha
pour ʿAdawiyya, *voir* ʿAdī b. Musāfir; *pour* ʿAfīfiyya, *voir* [au Suppl.] al-ʿAfīfī; *pour* Dasūḳiyya (Burhāmiyya), *voir* al-Dasūḳī, Ibrāhīm b. ʿAbd al-ʿAzīz; *pour* al-Djazūliyya, *voir* al-Djazūlī; *pour* Gulshaniyya, *voir* Gulshanī; *pour* Idrīsiyya, *voir* Aḥmad b. Idrīs; *pour* Kāzarūniyya (Murshidiyya, Isḥāḳiyya), *voir* Kāzarūnī; *pour* Kubrawiyya, *voir* Kubrā; *pour* Suhrawardiyya, *voir* Bahāʾ al-Dīn Zakariyyā
voir aussi Nūrbakhshiyya; Ṣafawides.I.B
costume Khirḳa; Pālāhang
derviches **Darwīsh**; Raḳṣ
voir aussi [au Suppl.] Buḳʿa; *et* → MYSTICISME.CONFRÉRIES
mystiques Darwīsh
voir aussi Pist; *et* → HAGIOGRAPHIE
africains (à l'exception d'Afrique du Nord) [au Suppl.] al-Duwayḥī
voir aussi Ṣāliḥiyya

andalous Abū Madyan; Ibn al-ʿArabī; Ibn al-ʿArīf; Ibn ʿĀshir; Ibn Barradjān; Ibn Ḳasī; Ibn Masarra

arabes (à l'exception d'Afrique du Nord et Andalousie) ʿAbd al-Ghanī b. Ismāʿīl; ʿAbd al-Ḳādir al-Djīlānī; ʿAbd al-Karīm al-Djīlī; ʿAdī b. Musāfir; Aḥmad al-Badawī; ʿAydarūs; al-Bakrī, Muḥammad; al-Bakrī, Muṣṭafā; Bishr al-Ḥāfī; al-Bisṭāmī; al-Damīrī; al-Dasūḳī, Ibrāhīm b. ʿAbd al-ʿAzīz; al-Dasūḳī, Ibrāhīm b. Muḥammad; Dhū l-Nūn, Abū l-Fayḍ; al-Dimyāṭī, al-Bannāʾ; al-Dimyāṭī, Nūr al-dīn; al-Djunayd; al-Ghazālī, Abū Ḥāmid; al-Ghazālī, Aḥmad; al-Ḥallādj; al-Harawī al-Mawṣilī; Ibn ʿAṭāʾ Allāh; al-Ḳazwīnī, Nadjm al-dīn; al-Kharrāz; al-Kurdī; al-Ḳushashī; Makhrama; al-Manūfī; al-Muḥāsibī; al-Munāwī; al-Niffarī; al-Nūrī; Rābiʿa al-ʿAdawiyya al-Ḳaysiyya; al-Rifāʿī; Sahl al-Tustarī; [au Suppl.] Abū l-ʿAzāʾim; al-ʿAdawī; al-ʿAfīfī; al-Ḥiṣāfī

voir aussi Abū Nuʿaym al-Iṣfahānī; Abū Ṭālib al-Makkī; Bā ʿAlawī; Baḥraḳ; Bakriyya; Bayyūmiyya; Faḍl, Bā; Faḳīh, Bā; Faḳīh, Bal; Hurmuz, Bā; Ḳādiriyya; Marwāniyya; Saʿdiyya; [au Suppl.] al-Bakrī; Demirdāshiyya

d'Asie centrale Aḥmad Yasawī; Ḥakīm Ata; Naḳshband; [au Suppl.] Aḥrār

voir aussi Ḳalandariyya; Pārsāʾiyya

indiens Abū ʿAlī Ḳalandar; Aḥmad Sirhindī; Ashraf ʿAlī; Bahāʾ al-Dīn Zakariyyāʾ; Bāḳī bi-llāh (*et* [au Suppl.]); al-Banūrī; Budhan; Burhān al-Dīn Gharīb; Burhān al-Dīn Ḳuṭb-i ʿĀlam; Čirāgh-i Dihlī; Čishtī; Djahānārā Bēgam; Djalāl al-Dīn Ḥusayn al-Bukhārī; Djamālī; Farīd al-Dīn Masʿūd "Gandj-i-Shakar"; Gīsū Darāz; Hānsawī; Ḥusaynī Sādāt Amīr; Imdād Allāh; Kalīm Allāh al-Djahānābādī; Ḳuṭb al-Dīn Bakhtiyār; Malik Muḥammad Djāyasī; Miyān Mīr, Miyāndjī; Mubārak Ghāzī; Muḥammad Ghawth Gwāliyārī; al-Muttaḳī al-Hindī; Muẓaffar Shams Balkhī; Niẓām al-Dīn Awliyāʾ; Niẓām al-Dīn, Mullā Muḥammad; Nūr Ḳuṭb al-ʿĀlam; [au Suppl.] ʿAbd al-Bārī; ʿAbd al-Wahhāb Bukhārī; Bulbul Shāh; Farangī Maḥall; Gadāʾī Kambō; Ḥamīd Ḳalandar; Ḥamīd al-Dīn Ḳāḍī Nāgawrī; Ḥamīd al-Dīn Ṣūfī Nāgawrī Siwālī; Ḥamza Makhdūm

voir aussi ʿAydarūs; Čishtiyya; Dārā Shukōh; Dard; Djīwan; Hind.V; Khalīl Allāh (*et* Khalīl Allāh But-shikan); Malang; Mughals.VI; Naḳshbandiyya.III

indonésiens ʿAbd al-Raʾūf al-Sinkilī; ʿAbd al-Ṣamad al-Palimbānī; Ḥamza Fanṣūrī

nord-africains ʿAbd al-Ḳādir al-Fāsī; ʿAbd al-Salām b. Mashīsh; Abū l-Maḥāsin al-Fāsī; Abū Muḥammad Ṣāliḥ; Aḥmad b. Idrīs; ʿAlī b. Maymūn; al-ʿAyyāshī; al-Daḳḳāḳ; al-Djazūlī; al-Hāshimī; Ḥmād u-Mūsā; Ibn ʿAbbād; Ibn ʿAdjība; Ibn ʿAlīwa; Ibn ʿArūs; Ibn Ḥirzihim; al-Ḳādirī al-Ḥasanī; al-Kūhin; al-Lamaṭī; Māʾ al-ʿAynayn; al-Madjdhūb;

[au Suppl.] al-Asmar; al-Dilāʾ; al-Fāsī; Ibn ʿAzzūz

voir aussi ʿAmmāriyya; ʿArūsiyya; Darkāwa; Hansaliyya; Hazmīriyyūn; al-Ifrānī; ʿĪsāwā; Madaniyya; al-Nāṣiriyya; Raḥmāniyya; [au Suppl.] Ḥamādisha

persans ʿAbd al-Razzāk al-Kāshānī; Abū Saʿīd b. Abī l-Khayr; Abū Yazīd al-Bisṭāmī; Aḥmad-i Djām; ʿAlāʾ al-Dawla al-Simnānī; ʿAlī al-Hamadhānī; al-Anṣārī al-Harawī; Ashraf Djahāngīr; Bābā-Ṭāhir; Djalāl al-Dīn Rūmī; Faḍl Allāh Ḥurūfī; Ghudjduwānī; Ḥamdūn al-Kaṣṣār; Hudjwīrī; Ibn Khafīf; ʿIrākī; al-Kalābādhī; Kamāl Khudjandī; Kāsim-i Anwār; Kāzarūnī; Khalīl Allāh (*et* Khalīl Allāh But-shikan); Kharakānī; al-Khargūshī; Kirmānī; Kubrā; al-Kushayrī.I; Lāhīdjī.I; Maḥmūd Shabistarī; Nadjm al-Dīn Rāzī Dāya; Nakshband; Rūzbihān; Saʿd al-Dīn al-Ḥammūʾī; Saʿd al-Dīn (Kāshgharī); Ṣadr al-Dīn Ardabīlī; Ṣadr al-Dīn Mūsā; Ṣafī; Saʿīd al-Dīn Farghānī; [au Suppl.] ʿAbd Allāh b. Abī Bakr al-Miyānadjī; Abū ʿAlī al-Farmadī; Aḥmad-i Rūmī; ʿAyn al-Kuḍāt al-Hamadhānī; Ibn al-Bazzāz al-Ardabīlı

voir aussi Djāmī; Madjlisī-yi Awwal; Nakshbandiyya.I; Niʿmat-Allāhiyya; Ṣafawids.I.B

turcs Ak Shams al-Dīn; Altı̊ Parmak; ʿĀshı̊k Pasha; Badr al-Dīn Ibn Kāḍī Samāwnā; Barak Baba; Bīdjān; Emīr Sulṭān; Faṣīḥ Dede; Fehmī; Gulshanī; Gülshehrī; Ḥādjdjī Bayrām Walī; Hüdāʾī; Ḥusām al-Dīn Čelebi; Ismāʿīl al-Ankarawī; Ismāʿīl Ḥakki; Kayghusuz Abdāl; Khalīlī; Kuṭb al-Dīn-zāde; Merkez; Niyāzī; [au Suppl.] ʿĀrif Čelebi; Eshrefoghlu ʿAbd Allāh; Esrār Dede

voir aussi Ashrafiyya; Bakriyya; Bayrāmiyya; Bektāshıyya; Djilwatiyya; Gülbaba; Ilāhī; Khalwatiyya; Mawlawiyya; Nakshbandiyya.II

poésie mystique → LITTÉRATURE.POÉSIE

termes Abdāl; ʿĀshik; Awtād; Bakāʾ wa-Fanāʾ; Basṭ; Bīsharʿ; Čāʾush; Darwīsh; Dawsa; Dede; Dhawk; Dhikr; Djilwa; Fakīr; Fikr; al-Ghayb; Ghayba; Ghufrān; Ḥaḍra; Ḥakīka.3; Ḥakk; Ḥāl; Ḥidjāb.III; Ḥukūk; Ḥulūl; Ḥurriyya; Huwa huwa; Ikhlāṣ; Ilhām; ʿInāya; al-Insān al-Kāmil; Ishān; Ishāra; ʿIshk; Ishrāk; Ithbāt; Ittiḥād; Kabḍ.II; Kāfir; Kalb.I; Kalima; Karāma; Kashf; Khalīfa.III; Khalwa; Khānkāh; Khirka; Kuṭb; Lāhūt et Nāsūt; Madjdhūb; Manzil; Maʿrifa; Muḥāsaba.I; Munādjāt; Murīd; Murshid; Nafs; Odjak; Pālāhang; Pīr; Pūst; Pūst-neshīn; Rābiṭa; Ramz.3; Rātib; Ribāṭ; Riḍā.1; Rind; Rūḥāniyya; Rukhṣa.2; Ṣabr; Ṣadr; [au Suppl.] Bukʿa; Ghawth

voir aussi Čelebī; Futuwwa; Gülbaba; Lawḥ; Lawn

N

NATIONALISME Istiḳlāl; **Ḳawmiyya**
  voir aussi D̲jangalī; K̲h̲ilāfa; Pās̲h̲tūnistān; *et* → POLITIQUE.MOUVEMENTS

NAVIGATION D̲jug̲h̲rāfiyā; Ibn Mād̲jid; Iṣbaʿ; K̲h̲arīṭa; Mag̲h̲nāṭīs.II; Manār;
  Meḥmed Reʾīs; **Milāḥa**; Mīnāʾ
  voir aussi al-K̲h̲as̲h̲abāt; Rīḥ
chantiers Dār al-Ṣināʿa
navires Milāḥa; Nassades; **Safīna**
  voir aussi Baḥriyya.II; Kelek; *et* → MILITAIRES.MARINE

NÉPAL **Népal**

NESTORIENS → CHRISTIANISME.CONFESSIONS

NIGER **Niger**
toponymes Bilma; D̲jādū; Kawār

NIGÉRIA Hausa; **Nigeria**
  voir aussi D̲jarīda.VI; Fulbé; al-Kānemī; Kanuri; Nikāḥ.II.6
leaders Muḥammad Bello
  voir aussi Gwandu
toponymes
  provinces Adamawa; Bornū
  villes Ibadan; Kano; Katsina; Kūkawa

NOMADISME **Badw**; Horde; Īlāt; K̲h̲āwa; K̲h̲ayma; Marʿā
  voir aussi Baḳḳāra; Baranta; Dak̲h̲īl; Dawār; Ḥayy; Ḳayn; *et* → BÉDOUINS; GI-
  TANS; TRIBUS
effets nomades K̲h̲ayma; Mifras̲h̲
  voir aussi K̲h̲ayl

NOUVEAU MONDE D̲jāliya; D̲jarīda.I.C.; **al-Mahd̲jar**
émigrants D̲jabrān K̲h̲alīl D̲jabrān; al-Maʿlūf; Nuʿayma, Mik̲h̲āʾīl; al-Rayḥānī;
  [au Suppl.] Abū Māḍī; Abū S̲h̲ādī
  voir aussi Pārsīs

NUBIE ʿAlwa; Barābra; Dongola; al-Marīs; **Nūba**
  voir aussi Baḳt; Dār al-Ṣulḥ; Ibn Sulaym al-Aswānī; al-Muḳurra; *et* →
  ÉGYPTE.TOPONYMES; SOUDAN.TOPONYMES
langues Nūba.III

peuples Nūba.IV

NUMÉRO Abdjad; Ḥisāb al-ʿAḳd; Ḥisāb al-Djummal; Ḥurūf; ʿIlm al-Ḥisāb
et → MATHÉMATIQUES
chiffres Khamsa; Sabʿ

NUMISMATIQUE Dār al-Ḍarb
voir aussi ʿAlī Pasha Mubārak; Andarāb.1; Ismāʿīl Ghālib; Makāyil; Mawlāy Idrīs; Nithār
monnaies Akče; Bālish; Čao; Čeyrek; Dīnār; Dirham.II; Fals; Ḥasanī; Larin; Mohur; Pāʾī; Pāra; Pawlā; Paysā; Riyāl; Rūpiyya; Ṣadīḳī
voir aussi Abarshahr; al-ʿAbbāsiyya; ʿAbd al-Malik b. Marwān; al-Afḍal Kutayfāt; ʿAlī Bey; Ānī; Bāghče Sarāy; Dhahab; Fidda; Filori; Ghāzī l-Dīn Ḥaydar; Hilāl.II; Islāmābād; Iṣṭakhr; Ḳaṭarī b. al-Fudjāʾa; Khurshīd; al-Kurdj; Māh al-Baṣra; al-Manṣūr; Māzandarān.7; Muṣṭafā.I; Ṣāḥib Ḳirān; [au Suppl.] Biyār; Farrukhān.II; Firrīm; al-Ghiṭrīf b. ʿAṭāʾ; *et* → DYNASTIES
pour les monnaies sous les dynasties, voir en particulier Artuḳides; Barīd Shāhides; Khwārazm-shāhs; Lōdīs.V; Mughals.X; al-Muwaḥḥidūn; ʿOthmānli.IX; Rasūlids.2; Ṣafawids.VI; Saldjūḳids.VIII
termes ʿAdl.2; Salām (*et* Sālim.1)

O

OCÉANS ET MERS **Baḥr;** al-Madd wa-l-Djazr
voir aussi Kharīṭa; *et* → CARTOGRAPHIE; NAVIGATION
eaux Aral; Baḥr Adriyas; Baḥr Bunṭus; Baḥr Fāris; Baḥr al-Hind; Baḥr al-Khazar; Baḥr al-Ḳulzum; Baḥr Lūṭ; Baḥr Māyuṭis; al-Baḥr al-Muḥīṭ; Baḥr al-Rūm; Baḥr al-Zandj; Marmara Deñizi

OMAN Bū Saʿīd; Madjlis.IV.A.13; Maḥkama.IV.9; Nabhān
voir aussi [au Suppl.] al-Ḥārithī
population ʿAwāmir; al-Baṭāḥira; al-Djanaba; al-Durūʿ; Hinā; al-Ḥubūs; al-ʿIfār; Kharūṣ; Mahra; Mazrūʿī; Nabhān
et → TRIBUS.PÉNINSULE ARABIQUE
toponymes
îles Khūryān-mūryān; Maṣīra
régions al-Bāṭina; Raʾs Musandam; al-Rustāḳ
villes al-Buraymī; Ḥāsik; ʿIbrī; Ḳalhāt; Masḳaṭ; Maṭraḥ; Mirbāṭ; Nizwa; al-Rustāḳ; Ṣalāla
voir aussi (Djazīrat) al-ʿArab; [au Suppl.] Gwādar

ONOMASTIQUE Bā; Ibn; Ism; Kisrā; Kunya; Laḳab; Nisba.2
voir aussi al-Asmāʾ al-Ḥusnā; Og͟hul
comme forme d'adresse Ag͟ha; Āk͟hūnd; Beg; Begum; Čelebī; Efendi; K͟hʷād͟ja; K͟hātūn; K͟hudāwand
voir aussi Ak͟hī
épithètes Ata; Baba; G͟hufrān; Humāyūn
noms propres Aḥmad; D͟hū l-Faḳār; Humā; Marzpān; Meḥemmed; Mihragān.IV.2
voir aussi al-Asad; Payg͟hū
titres
africains Diglal
arabes ʿAmīd; Amīr al-Muʾminīn; Amīr al-Muslimīn; Asad al-Dawla; ʿAzīz Miṣr; ʿIzz al-Dawla; ʿIzz al-Dīn; K͟hādim al-Ḥaramayn; K͟hidīw; Malik; Mihmindār; Mus͟hīr
voir aussi Dawla
d'Asie centrale Afs͟hīn; Ik͟hs͟hīd; Ḳos͟h-begi; [au Suppl.] Atalïḳ; Dīwān-begi; İnaḳ
d'Asie du Sud-est Pengg͟hulu
indo-musulmans Āṣāf-D͟jāh; K͟hʷād͟ja-i D͟jahān; K͟hān K͟hānān; Nawwāb; Niẓām; Pēs͟hwā; Ṣāḥib Ḳirān
mongols Noyan; Ṣāḥib Ḳirān
persans Ag͟ha K͟hān; Ispahbad͟h; Ispahsālār; Iʿtimād al-Dawla; K͟hʷād͟ja; Marzpān; Mīr; Mīrzā; Mollā; Pādis͟hāh; Ṣadr; Sālār
turcs Alp; Beglerbegi; Dāmād; Daryā-begi; Dayï; Gülbaba; K͟hʷād͟jegān-i Dīwān-i Humāyūn; K͟hāḳān; K͟hān; K͟hudāwendigār; Mīr-i Mīrān; Mus͟hīr; Pas͟ha; Payg͟hū; Ṣadr-i Aʿẓam
voir aussi Čorbad͟jï

OPTIQUE Ḳaws Ḳuzaḥ; Manāẓir
voir aussi Mirʾāt
traités sur Ibn al-Hayt͟ham; Kamāl al-Dīn al-Fārisī
voir aussi Ḳuṭb al-Dīn S͟hīrāzī

P

PAIEMENTS ʿAṭāʾ; D͟jāmakiyya; Ḥawāla; Inʿām; Māl al-Bayʿa; Maʿūna
corruption Marāfiḳ; **Ras͟hwa**

PAKISTAN D͟jināḥ; Dustūr.XIV; Ḥizb.VI; Ḥukūma.V; Mad͟jlis.IV.C; al-Marʾa.V; **Pākistān**; [au Suppl.] D͟jarīda.VII
voir aussi Ahl-i Ḥadīt͟h; Dār al-ʿUlūm.c; D͟jamʿiyya; D͟jūnāgaṛh; Hind.II et IV;

Kashmīr; Ḳawmiyya.VI; Khaybar; Muhādjir.3; Pashtūnistān; *et* → INDE
architecture → ARCHITECTURE.RÉGIONS
éducation Djāmiʿa
géographie physique
eaux Kurram; Mihrān
hommes d'état Djināḥ; Liyāḳat ʿAlī Khān
voir aussi Mawdūdī
population Afrīdī; Dāwūdpōtrās; Mahsūd; Mohmand; Mullagorī; [au Suppl.] Démographie.VII; Gurčānī
voir aussi Djirga
toponymes
anciens Čīnīōt; Daybul; Ḳandābīl; Khayrābād
actuels
districts Chitral; Ḥāfiẓābād; Hazāra; Khārān; Khayrpūr; Kilāt.II; Kōhāt; Kwaťťa; Mastūdj
régions Balūčistān; Dardistān; Deradjāt; Dīr; Djahlāwān; Kaččhī; Las Bēla; Makrān; Pandjāb
villes Amarkot; Bādjawr; Bahāwalpūr; Bakkār; Bannū; Bhakkar; Gūdjrāṅwāla; Gudjrāt; Ḥasan Abdāl; Ḥaydarābād; Islāmābād; Karāčī; Kilāt.I; Ḳuṣdār; Kwaťťa; Lāhawr; Mastūdj; Peshāwar; Rāwalpindi; [au Suppl.] Gilgit; Gwādar

PALESTINE Djarīda.I.A; **Filasṭīn**; Ḥizb.I; Madjlis.IV.A.23; Maḥkama.IV.5; Mandats
voir aussi Djarrāḥides; Ḳays ʿAylān; al Khālidī; [au Suppl.] Démographie.III; *et* → CROISADES
architecture Ḳubbat al-Ṣakhra; al-Ḳuds; al-Masdjid al-Aḳṣā
voir aussi Kawkab
géographie physique
eaux Baḥr Lūṭ; al-Ḥūla; Nahr Abī Fuṭrus
historiens Mudjīr al-Dīn al-ʿUlaymī
sous le mandat britannique Filasṭīn.II; Muḥammad ʿIzzat Darwaza; [au Suppl.] Amīn al-Ḥusaynī
voir aussi Mandats
toponymes
anciens Arsūf; ʿAthlīth; ʿAyn Djālūt; Bayt Djibrīn; al-Darūm; Irbid.II; Sabasṭiyya.1
actuels
régions al-Ghawr.1; Mardj Banī ʿĀmir; al-Naḳb
villes ʿAkkā; ʿAmwās; ʿĀsḳalān; Baysān; Bayt Laḥm; Bīr al-Sabʿ; Ghazza; Ḥayfā; Ḥiṭṭīn; al-Khalīl; al-Ḳuds; Ladjdjūn; Ludd; Nābulus; al-Nāṣira; Rafaḥ; al-Ramla; Rīḥā.1; Ṣafad
voir aussi Ḳayṣariyya

PANARABISME Ḳawmiyya; **Panarabisme**; [au Suppl.] ʿAbd al-Nāṣir; al-Djāmiʿa al-ʿArabiyya
partisans de al-Kawākibī; Nūrī al-Saʿīd; Rashīd Riḍā; [au Suppl.] ʿAbd al-Nāṣir
voir aussi al-Kāẓimī, ʿAbd al-Muḥsin

PANISLAMISME Ḳawmiyya; **Panislamisme**; **al-Rābiṭa al-Islāmiyya**
voir aussi Dustūr.XVIII; Iṣlāḥ.II; Khilāfa, Khilāfat Movement; Muʾtamar
partisans de ʿAbd al-Ḥamīd II; Djamāl al-Dīn al-Afghānī; Fiṭrat; Gasprali̊ (Gasprinski), Ismāʿīl; Ḥālī; Kūčak Khān Djangalī; Māʾ al-ʿAynayn; Meḥmed ʿĀkif; Rashīd Riḍā; Ṣafar; [au Suppl.] Andjuman-i Khuddām-i Kaʿba; al-Bakrī
voir aussi Djadīd

PANTURKISME Ḳawmiyya; **Panturquisme**
partisans de Gasprali̊ (Gasprinski), Ismāʿīl; Gökalp, Ziya; Ri̊ḍā Nūr

PAPYROLOGIE Ḳirṭās; Papyrus
voir aussi Diplomatique.I.15; *et* → DOCUMENTS

PARADIS al-ʿAshara al-Mubashshara; Dār al-Salām; **Djanna**; Ḥūr; Kawthar; Riḍwān; Salsabīl
voir aussi al-Aʿrāf

PARFUM Bān; Ḥinnāʾ; Kāfūr; Misk
voir aussi al-Aṭṭār; Maʿdin.IV.B.b

PÈLERINAGE ʿArafa; al-Djamra; **Ḥadjdj**; Hady; Iḥrām; Kaʿba; Minā; Muṭawwif; al-Muzdalifa; Radjm; al-Ṣafā.1
voir aussi Amīr al-Ḥādjdj; Ḥidjāz; Kārwān; Kāẓimayn; Makka; [au Suppl.] ʿAtabāt; Darb Zubayda; Fayd; *et* → ISLAM

PÉRIODE PRÉISLAMIQUE al-ʿArab.I; (Djazīrat) al-ʿArab.VII; Armīniya.II.1; Badw.III; Djāhiliyya; Ghassān; Kinda.1 et Appendice; Lakhmides; Liḥyān; Maʿin; Makka.I; Nabaṭ; Rūm
voir aussi Ḥayawān.II; Ilāh; al-Kalbī.II; Lībiyā.II; *et* → ASSYRIE; BYZANTINS; MILITAIRES.BATAILLES; ZOROASTRIENS
coutumes/institutions ʿAtīra; Baliyya; Ghidhāʾ.I et II; Ḥadjdj.I; Ḥilf; Ḥimā; Ḥimāya; Istisḳāʾ; Kāhin; Khafāra; Mawlā; Nuṣub; Raḍāʿ.2; Sādin
voir aussi Fayʾ; Ghanīma; Īlāf; Karkūr; Nār; Ṣadā
dans la péninsule arabique Abraha; (Djazīrat) al-ʿArab.I et VI; Bakr b. Wāʾil; Djadhīma al-Abrash; Ghumdān; Ḥabashat; Ḥādjib b. Zurāra; Ḥaḍramawt; Hāshim b. ʿAbd Manāf; Hind bint al-Khuss; Ḥums; Ḳatabān; Ḳayl; Ḳuṣayy;

Ḳuss b. Sāʿida; Mārib; Nuṣub; Sabaʾ; Sadjʿ.1; Salḥīn; [au Suppl.] Ḥaḍramawt.I
voir aussi Badw.III; Dār al-Nadwa; Ḥanīf.4; Ḥarrān; Kinda.Appendice; *et* → Arabie Séoudite.toponymes; Littérature.poésie.arabe; Oman.toponymes; Tribus.péninsule arabique; Yémen.toponymes
dans le Croissant fertile Khursābād; Manbidj; Maysān; Nabaṭ; [au Suppl.] Athūr
voir aussi Biṭrīḳ.I; Ḥarrān
Ghassānides Djabala b. al-Ayham; Djilliḳ; **Ghassān**; al-Ḥārith b. Djabala; [au Suppl.] Djabala b. al-Ḥārith
Lakhmides ʿAmr b. ʿAdī; ʿAmr b. Hind; al-Ḥīra; **Lakhmides**; al-Mundhir IV; al-Nuʿmān [III] b. al-Mundhir
dieux Dhū l-Khalaṣa; Hubal; Isāf wa-Nāʾila; Ḳaws Ḳuzaḥ; al-Lāt; Manāf; Manāt; Nasr
voir aussi ʿAmr b. Luḥayy; Djāhiliyya; Ilāh; Kaʿba.V; al-Ḳamar.II; Mawḳif.3; Rabb
en Égypte → Égypte.avant l'islam
en Iran → Iran.avant l'islam

Perse → Iran

Peste ʿAmwās
voir aussi Ibn Khaldūn, Walī al-dīn
traités sur Ibn Khātima; Ibn Riḍwān; al-Masīḥī

Pétrole **Nafṭ**.III
champs pétrolifères ʿAbbādān; Abḳayḳ; Altîn Köprü; al-Baḥrayn; al-Dahnāʾ; al-Ghawār; al-Ḥasā; al-Ḳaṭīf; Khārag; Khūzistān; Kirkūk; Kirmānshāh; al-Kuwayt; Lībiyā; Nadjd.3; Rām-hurmuz; Raʾs (al-)Tannūra; [au Suppl.] Aḥmadī
voir aussi Djannābā; Fārs; al-Khubar

Pharmacologie Adwiya; Aḳrābādhīn
voir aussi Diyusḳuridīs; Djālīnūs; Nabāt; *et* → Botanique; Drogues; Médecine
pharmacologues Ibn al-Bayṭār; Ibn Samadjūn; Ibn al-Tilmīdh; Ibn Wāfid; al-Kōhēn al-ʿAṭṭār; Sābūr b. Sahl; [au Suppl.] al-Ghāfiḳī; Ibn Biklārish; Ibn al-Rūmiyya
voir aussi al-ʿAshshāb; al-ʿAṭṭār

Philatelie **Posta**
et → Transport.postale

PHILOSOPHIE Falāsifa; **Falsafa**; Ḥikma; Mā baʿd al-Ṭabīʿa; Manṭiḳ; Naẓar
voir aussi ʿĀlam.1; Allāh.III.2; al-Maḳūlāt
logique **Manṭiḳ**
termes Āla.III; ʿAraḍ; Dalīl; Faṣl; Fiʿl; Ḥadd; Ḥaḳīḳa.2; Ḥudjdja; Ḥukm.I; Huwa huwa.A; Muḳaddam; Natīdja
voir aussi Ḳaṭʿ
philosophes **Falāsifa**
chrétiens Ibn al-Ṭayyib; Ibn Zurʿa; Mattā b. Yūnus
grecs Aflāṭūn; Anbaduḳlīs; Arisṭūṭālīs; Balīnūs; Baṭlamiyūs; Buruḳlus; Djālīnūs; Fīthāghūras; Furfūriyūs; al-Iskandar al-Afrūdīsī
voir aussi Ḥunayn b. Isḥāḳ al-ʿIbādī; Īsāghūdjī; Isḥāḳ b. Ḥunayn; Lawn; al-Maḳūlāt; Mattā b. Yūnus; Nīḳūlāʾūs
juifs Ibn Gabirol; Ibn Kammūna; Isḥāḳ al-Isrāʾīlī; Judéo-arabe.III; Saʿadyā
voir aussi Abū l- Barakāt
musulmans
9e siècle Abū l-Hudhayl al-ʿAllāf; al-Kindī, Abū Yūsuf
voir aussi Dahriyya; Falāsifa; Lawn
10e siècle Abū Sulaymān al-Manṭiḳī; al-Fārābī; Ibn Masarra; al-Mawṣilī; al-Rāzī, Abū Bakr; [au Suppl.] al-ʿĀmirī
11e siècle Abū Ḥayyān al-Tawḥīdī; Bahmanyār; Ibn Ḥazm; Ibn Sīnā; Miskawayh
12e siècle Abū l-Barakāt; al-Baṭalyawsī; Ibn Bādjdja; Ibn Rushd; Ibn Ṭufayl
voir aussi al-Ghazālī; Ḥayy b. Yaḳẓān; Ishrāḳiyyūn
13e siècle al-Abharī; Ibn Sabʿīn; al-Kātibī; Ṣadr al-Dīn al-Ḳūnawī
voir aussi Fakhr al-Dīn al-Rāzī
14e siècle Djamāl al-Dīn Aḳsarayī
16e siècle al-Maybudī.II
17e siècle al-Dāmād; Lāhīdjī.II; [au Suppl.] Findiriskī
19e siècle al-Fārūḳī; Sabzawarī, Ḥādjdj Mullā Hādī; [au Suppl.] Abū l-Ḥasan Djilwa
termes Abad; ʿAdam; ʿAḳl; ʿAmal.1; Anniyya; Awwal; Basīṭ wa-Murakkab; Dhāt; Dhawḳ; Ḍidd; Djawhar; Djins; Djism; Djuzʾ; Fard; Ḥadd; Ḥaraka wa-Sukūn.I.1; Hayʾa; Ḥayāt; Hayūlā; Ḥiss; Ḥudūth al-ʿĀlam; Ḥulūl; Huwiyya; Ibdāʿ; Idrāk; Iḥdāth; Ikhtiyār; ʿIlla.II; ʿInāya; Inṣāf; ʿIshḳ; Ishrāḳ; al-Ḳaḍāʾ wa-l-Ḳadar.A.3; Kawn wa-Fasād; Ḳidam; Ḳuwwa.4, 6 et 7; Maʿād; Māhiyya; Maḥsūsāt; Malaka; Maʿnā.II; Nafs; Nihāya; Nūr.II; Saʿāda; Sabab.1
voir aussi Athar.III; ʿAyn; Dahriyya; Insān; Ḳaṭʿ; Ḳiyāma

PHYSIONOMIE Firāsa; Ḳiyāfa; [au Suppl.] Aflīmūn
et → ANATOMIE

PIRATERIE **Ḳurṣān**
voir aussi al-ʿAnnāba; ʿArūdj; Ḥasan Baba; Ḥusayn Pasha, Mezzomorto; Kemāl Reʾīs; Khayr al-Dīn Pasha; Lewend

POIDS ET MESURES Aghač; Arpa; Dhirāʿ; Dirham.I; Farsakh; Ḥabba; Iṣbaʿ; Istār; **Makāyil**; Marḥala; Miḳyās; **Misāḥa**; al-Mīzān; Ṣāʿ; [au Suppl.] Gaz
voir aussi al-Ḳarasṭūn

POLITIQUE Baladiyya; Dawla; Djumhūriyya; Dustūr; Ḥimāya.II; Ḥizb; Ḥukūma; Ḥurriyya; Istiḳlāl; Ḳawmiyya; Madjlis; Makhzan; Mandats; Mashyakha; Medeniyyet; Musāwāt; Muwāṭin; Nāʾib.2; [au Suppl.] Āzādī; al-Djāmiʿa al-ʿArabiyya
voir aussi Ahl al-Ḥall wa-l-ʿAḳd; Imtiyāzāt; Mashwara; Salṭana; *et* → ADMINISTRATION; DIPLOMATIE; EMPIRE OTTOMAN
doctrines Ḥizb.I; Ishtirākiyya; Mārk(i)siyya; [au Suppl.] Hidjra
voir aussi Musāwāt; Muslimūn.IV; Radjʿiyya; *et* → PANARABISME; PANISLAMISME; PANTURQUISME
mouvements Djadīd; Djangalī; Istiḳlāl; Ittiḥād we Teraḳḳī Djemʿiyyeti; Khāksār; Khilāfa; al-Rābiṭa al-Islāmiyya
voir aussi Fiṭrat; Ḥamza Beg; Ḥizb; Ḥurriyya; Kūčak Khān Djangalī; [au Suppl.] ʿAbd al-Bārī; *et* → PANARABISME; PANISLAMISME; PANTURQUISME
partis Demokrat Parti; **Ḥizb**; Ḥürriyyet we Iʾtilāf Fïrḳasï; Partai Islam se Malaysia (Pas)
voir aussi Andjuman; Djamʿiyya; (Tunalï) Ḥilmī; Ḥizb.I; Ishtirākiyya; Khīyābānī; Leff; Luṭfī al-Sayyid; Mārk(i)siyya; Muṣṭafā Kāmil Pasha; [au Suppl.] ʿAbd al-Nāṣir; *et* → RÉFORME
réforme → RÉFORME

POLOGNE **Leh**
voir aussi Islām Girāy; Ḳamāniča; Köprülü; Lipḳa; Muslimūn.I.A.1; *et* → EMPIRE OTTOMAN

PORTUGAL **Burtuḳāl**; Gharb al-Andalus
voir aussi Ḥabesh; *et* → ESPAGNE
toponymes Bādja; Ḳulumriya; al-Maʿdin; Mīrtula

PRÉDESTINATION Adjal; Allāh.II.B; Iḍṭirār; Ikhtiyār; Istiṭāʿa; **al-Ḳaḍāʾ wa-l-Ḳadar**; Ḳadariyya; Kasb; Ḳisma
voir aussi ʿAbd al-Razzāḳ al-Ḳāshānī; Badāʾ; Dahr; Duʿāʾ.II.b; Ḳaḍāʾ
adversaires Ghaylān b. Muslim; **Ḳadariyya**; Ḳatāda b. Diʿāma; Maʿbad al-Djuhanī
avocats Djabriyya; Djahmiyya; al-Karābīsī.2

PRESSE **Djarīda**; Maḳāla; **Maṭbaʿa**
arabe ʿArabiyya.B.V.a; Baghdād (934a); Būlāḳ; **Djarīda**.I; Ḳiṣṣa.II; Maḳāla.1; al-Manār; **Maṭbaʿa**.I; al-Rāʾid al-Tūnusī
voir aussi Nahḍa
journalisme Abū Naḍḍāra; al-Bārūnī; Djabrān Khalīl Djabrān; Djamāl al-Dīn al-Afghānī; Djamīl al-Mudawwar; Fāris al-Shidyāḳ; Ibn Bādīs; Isḥāḳ, Adīb; al-Kawākibī; al-Khaḍir; Khalīl Ghānim; Khalīl Muṭrān; Kurd ʿAlī; Luṭfī al-Sayyid; al-Maʿlūf; Mandūr; al-Manūfī.VII; al-Māzinī; Muṣṭafā ʿAbd al-Rāziḳ; al-Muwayliḥī; al-Nadīm, ʿAbd Allāh; Nadjīb b. Sulaymān al-Ḥaddād; Nimr; Rashīd Riḍā; Ṣafar; Saʿīd Abū Bakr; Salāma Mūsā; Salīm al-Naḳḳāsh; [au Suppl.] Abū Shādī; al-Bustānī
voir aussi al-Mahdjar
indienne **Maṭbaʿa**.IV; [au Suppl.] **Djarīda**.VII
journalisme Muḥammad ʿAlī; Ruswā; [au Suppl.] Āzād; Ḥasrat Mohānī
voir aussi Nadwat al-ʿUlamāʾ
persane **Djarīda**.II; Maḳāla; **Maṭbaʿa**.III
journalisme Furūghī.III; Lāhūtī; Malkom Khān; Rashīd Yāsimī; [au Suppl.] Amīrī
turque **Djarīda**.III; Djemʿiyyet-i ʿIlmiyye-i ʿOthmāniyye; Ibrāhīm Müteferriḳa; Maḳāla; **Maṭbaʿa**.II; Meshʿale; Mīzān
voir aussi Ādharī.II
journalisme Aḥmad Iḥsān; Aḥmad Midḥat; Djewdet; Ebüzziya Tevfik; Gasprali̊ (Gasprinski), Ismāʿīl; Ḥasan Fehmī; (Aḥmed) Ḥilmī; Hisar; Ḥusayn Djāhid; Ileri, Djelāl Nūrī; Inal; Ḳaṣāb; al-Kāẓimī, Meḥmed Sālim; Kemāl; Kemāl, Meḥmed Nāmi̊ḳ; Khālid Ḍiyāʾ; Köprülü (Meḥmed Fuad); Manāsti̊rli̊ Meḥmed Rifʿat; Meḥmed ʿĀkif; Mīzāndji̊ Meḥmed Murād; Örik, Nahīd Ṣi̊rrī; Orkhan Seyfī; Ortač, Yūsuf Ḍiyā; Ri̊ḍā Nūr; Sāhir, Djelal; Sāmī; [au Suppl.] Aghaoghlu; Atay; Čaylaḳ Tewfīḳ; Eshref
voir aussi Badrkhānī; Fedjr-i Ātī; Khalīl Ghānim; Saʿīd Efendi

PRIÈRE Adhān; Djumʿa; Dhikr; **Duʿāʾ**; Fātiḥa; Iḳāma; Khaṭīb; Khuṭba; Ḳibla; Ḳunūt; Ḳuʿūd; Maḥyā; Masdjid; Miḥrāb; Mīḳāt; Muṣallā; Rakʿa; Rātib; **Ṣalāt**; Ṣalāt al-Khawf
voir aussi Amīn; Dikka; Ghāʾib; Gulbāng; Istiʾnāf; Maḳām Ibrāhīm; al-Masḥ ʿalā l-Khuffayn; Namāzgāh; *et* → ABLUTION; ARCHITECTURE.MOSQUÉES; ISLAM
de demande Istisḳāʾ; Munāshada
inclination Sadjda
tapis Sadjdjāda

PROFESSIONS al-ʿAṭṭār; Baḳḳāl; Bayṭār; Dallāl; Djānbāz; Djarrāḥ; Ḥammāl; Kannās; Kātib; Ḳayn; Ḳayna; Khayyāṭ; Mukārī; Munādī; Munadjdjim; al-

Nassādj; Ṣabbāgh; Ṣā'igh; Saḳḳā'; [au Suppl.] Dabbāgh; Djammāl; Djazzār; Faṣṣād; Ghassāl; Ḥā'ik; Ḥallāḳ
voir aussi Asad Allāh Iṣfahānī; Aywaz.I; Khādim; *et* → DROIT.FONCTIONS; MILITAIRES.FONCTIONS
artisans Ṣabbāgh; Ṣā'igh; [au Suppl.] Ḥā'ik
artistes Djānbāz; Ḳayna
marchands al-ʿAṭṭār; Baḳḳāl; Mukārī; [au Suppl.] Djammāl
ouvriers Ḥammāl; Kannās; Ḳayn; Khayyāṭ; [au Suppl.] Dabbāgh; Djazzār; Ghassāl; Ḥallāḳ

PROPHÉTAT **Nubuwwa**; Rasūl
et → MUḤAMMAD, LE PROPHÈTE
prophètes Ādam; Alīsaʿ; Ḥā-Mīm; Hārūn b. ʿImrān; Hūd; Ibrāhīm; Idrīs; Lūṭ; Muḥammad; Mūsā; Nūḥ; Sadjāḥ; Ṣāliḥ
voir aussi Fatra; ʿIṣma; Khālid b. Sinān; al-Kisā'ī; Ḳiṣaṣ al-Anbiyā'; Luḳmān; *et* → MUḤAMMAD, LE PROPHÈTE

PROPRIÉTÉ **Māl**; Milk; [au Suppl.] ʿAḳār
voir aussi Munāṣafa; *et* → TAXATION.IMPÔTS

PROVERBES **Mathal**; al-Maydānī
voir aussi Iyās b. Muʿāwiya; Nār; *et* → ANIMAUX.ET PROVERBES; LITTÉRATURE

Q

QATAR al-Dawḥa; Hādjir; **Ḳaṭar**; Madjlis.IV.A.11; Maḥkama.IV.9

R

RAIDS Baranta; Ghanīma; **Ghazw**
et → BÉDOUINS; MILITAIRES.EXPÉDITIONS

RÉCRÉATION Cinématographe; Ḳaragöz; Khayāl al-Ẓill; Masraḥ; Orta Oyunu
jeux Djerīd; Kharbga; Ḳimār; **Laʿib**; al-Maysir; Mukhāradja; Nard
voir aussi Ishāra; Kurdes et Kurdistān.IV.C.5; Maydān; *et* → ANIMAUX.SPORT
sport Čawgān; Pahlawān

RÉFORME Djamʿiyya; **Iṣlāḥ**
voir aussi Baladiyya; Ḥukūma; al-Manār; *et* → FEMMES.ÉMANCIPATION DES

d'éducation Aḥmad Djewdet Pasha; Aḥmad Khān; al-Azhar.IV; Ḥabīb Allāh Khān; Maʿārif; Münīf Pasha; Nadwat al-ʿUlamāʾ; [au Suppl.] al-ʿAdawī
voir aussi al-Marṣafī
financière Muḥaṣṣil
judiciaire Abū l-Suʿūd; Aḥmad Djewdet Pasha; Küčük Saʿīd Pasha; Medjelle; Mīrāth.II; Nikāḥ.II
voir aussi Djazāʾ; Ileri, Djelāl Nūrī; Imtiyāzāt.IV; Khayr al-Dīn Pasha; Maḥkama
militaire Niẓām-i Djedīd
politico-religieuse Atatürk; Djamāl al-Dīn al-Afghānī; Ileri, Djelāl Nūrī; Ibn Bādīs; (al-)Ibrāhīmī; Ismāʿīl Ṣidḳī; Ḳāsim Amīn; Khayr al-Dīn Pasha; Midḥat Pasha; Muḥammad ʿAbduh; Muḥammad Bayram al-Khāmis; Nurculuk; Padri; Rashīd Riḍā; [au Suppl.] ʿAbd al-Nāṣir
voir aussi Baladiyya; Bast; Djamʿiyya; Dustūr; Ḥarbiye; Ibrāhīm Müteferriḳa; al-Ikhwān al-Muslimūn; Iṣlāḥ; Mappila.5.b; Salafiyya; [au Suppl.] Abu l-ʿAzāʾim; *et* → POLITIQUE
militante al-Bannāʾ; Fidāʾiyyān-i Islām; Ḥamāliyya; Ibn Bādīs; al-Ikhwān al-Muslimūn; Mawdūdī
voir aussi Ibn al-Muwaḳḳit; Mudjāhid; [au Suppl.] al-Djanbīhī

RELIGION ʿAḳīda; **Dīn**; al-Milal wa-l-Niḥal; Milla; Millet.1
voir aussi Ḥanīf; *et* → CHRISTIANISME; ISLAM; JUDAÏSME
autres que les trois principales Bābīs; Bahāʾīs; Barāhima; Budd; Dhū l-Sharā; Djayn; Gabr; Hindū; Ibāḥatiya; Ṣābiʾ; Ṣābiʾa; al-Sāmira
voir aussi Aghāthūdhīmūn; Bakhshī; al-Barāmika.1; Hirmis; Hurmuz; Khʷādja Khiḍr; Kitāb al-Djilwa; Mānī; al-Milal wa-l-Niḥal; Millet; Nānak; *et* → BAHĀʾĪS; DRUZES; ZOROASTRIENS
panthéisme ʿAmr b. Luḥayy; Djāhiliyya; Kaʿba.V
voir aussi Ḥarīriyya; Ḥadjdj.I; Ibn al-ʿArabī; Ibn al-ʿArīf; Kāfiristān; Kamāl Khudjandī; *et* → PÉRIODE PRÉISLAMIQUE.DIEUX
populaire → ISLAM.CROYANCES POPULAIRES

RÊVES **Ruʾyā**
voir aussi Istikhāra; *et les articles individuels sur les animaux, en particulier* Ayyil; Baghl; Ḍabb; Fīl; Ghurāb
traités sur al-Dīnawarī, Abū Saʿīd; Ibn Ghannām; Ibn Shāhīn al-Ẓāhirī; Ibn Sīrīn

RHÉTORIQUE Badīʿ; Balāgha; Bayān; Faṣāḥa; Ḥaḳīḳa.1; Ibtidāʾ; Idjāza; Iḳtibās; Intihāʾ; Istiʿāra; Kināya; al-Maʿānī wa-l-Bayān; Madjāz; Mubālagha; Muḳābala.3; Muwāraba; Muzāwadja; Muzdawidj; Ramz.1
voir aussi Ishāra

traités sur al-ʿAskarī.II; Ḥāzim; Ibn al-Muʿtazz; al-Ḳazwīnī (Khaṭīb Dimashḳ); al-Rādūyānī; al-Sakkākī; [au Suppl.] al-Djurdjānī; Ibn Wahb

RIME **Kāfiya**; Luzūm mā lā yalzam
et → LITTÉRATURE.POÉSIE; MÉTRIQUE

RITUELS ʿAḳīḳa; ʿAnṣāra; ʿĀshūrāʾ; Khitān; Rawḍa-khʷānī
voir aussi Bakkāʾ; Ḥammām; ʿIbādāt; al-Maghrib.VI; [au Suppl.] Dam; *et* → COUTUMES

RIVIÈRES **Nahr**
voir aussi Maʾṣir; *et* → NAVIGATION
eaux al-ʿAḍaym; ʿAfrīn; Alindjaḳ; al-ʿAlḳamī; Āmū Daryā; al-ʿĀṣī; Atbara; Atrek; Baḥr al-Ghazāl.1; Baradā; Čaghān-rūd; Congo; Čoruh; Ču; Darʿa; Dawʿan; Dehās; Didjla; Diyālā; Djamnā; Djayḥān; al-Furāt; Ganga; Gediz Čayi̊; Göksu; al-Ḥamma; Harī Rūd; Ibruh; Ili; Isly; Itil; Kābul.I; Karkha; Kārūn; Khābūr; Khalkha; al-Khāzir; Ḳi̊zi̊l İrmāḳ; Ḳi̊zi̊l-üzen; Ḳuban; Ḳunduz; Kur; Kurram; Lamas-ṣū; Mānd; Menderes; Merič; Mihrān; al-Mudawwar; Nahr Abī Fuṭrus; Niger; al-Nīl; Ob; Orkhon; Özi; al-Rass; Safīd Rūd; Saḳarya; [au Suppl.] Gūmāl
voir aussi Hind.I.j; ʿĪsā, Nahr; *et l'entrée Géographie Physique sous les pays individuels*

ROUMANIE Ada Ḳalʿe; Babadaghi̊; Bender; Boghdān; Budjāḳ; Bükresh; Deli-Orman; Dobrudja; Eflaḳ; Erdel; Ibrail; Isakča; Köstendje; Medjīdiyye; Nagyvárad
voir aussi Muslimūn.I.B.2

RUSSIE → COMMUNAUTÉ DES ÉTATS INDÉPENDANTS

S

SACRIFICES ʿAḳīḳa; ʿAtīra; Baliyya; Dhabīḥa; Fidya; Hady; Ḳurbān
voir aussi Ibil; ʿĪd al-Aḍḥā; Kaffāra; Nadhr; [au Suppl.] Dam

SAINT Mawlid
voir aussi ʿAbābda; Mawlā.I; *et* → CHRISTIANISME; HAGIOGRAPHIE; MYSTICISME
saints
arabes Aḥmad b. ʿĪsā; Aḥmad al-Badawī; Nafīsa
voir aussi Ḳunā; *et* → MYSTICISME

d'Afrique du Nord Abū Muḥammad Ṣāliḥ; Abū Yaʿazzā; ʿĀʾisha al-Mannūbiyya; al-Bādisī.1; al-Daḳḳāḳ; al-Djazūlī, Abū ʿAbd Allāh; Ḥmād u-Mūsā; Ibn ʿArūs; al-Ḳabbāb; Ḳaddūr al-ʿAlamī; al-Khaṣāṣī; Muḥriz b. Khalaf; [au Suppl.] Ḥamādisha
voir aussi al-Maghrib.VI; Sabʿatu Ridjāl; *et* → Mysticisme

d'Asie centrale Aḥmad Yasawī

indiens Abū ʿAlī Ḳalandar; Ashraf Djahāngīr; Badīʿ al-Dīn; Badr; Bahāʾ al-Dīn Zakariyyā; Čishtī; Farīd al-Dīn Masʿūd "Gandj-i Shakar"; Ghāzī Miyān; Gīsū Darāz; Imām Shāh; Khʷādja Khiḍr; Maghribī; Makhdūm al-Mulk; Masʿūd, Sayyid Sālār; Niẓām al-Dīn Awliyāʾ; Nūr Ḳuṭb al-ʿĀlam; Ratan; [au Suppl.] Bābā Nūr al-Dīn Rishī; Gadāʾī Kambō; Gangōhī; Ḥamīd al-Dīn Ḳāḍī Nāgawrī; Ḥamīd al-Dīn Ṣūfī Nāgawrī Siwālī
voir aussi Ḥasan Abdāl; Pāk Pāṭan

persans ʿAlī al-Hamadhānī; Bābā-Ṭāhir

turcs Akhī Ewrān; Emīr Sulṭān; Ḥādjdjī Bayrām Walī; Ḥakīm Ata; Ḳoyun Baba; Merkez

termes Abdāl; Ilhām

Sciences **ʿIlm**; Mawṣūʿa
voir aussi Ibn Abī Uṣaybīʿa; [au Suppl.] al-Bustānī; Ibn al-Akfānī.III; Ibn Farīghūn; *et* → Alchimie; Astrologie; Astronomie; Botanique; Mathématiques; Mécanique; Médecine; Optique; Pharmacologie; Zoologie

Sciences Naturelles **al-Āthār al-ʿUlwiyya**; **Ḥikma**; Masāʾil wa-Adjwiba
voir aussi Nūr.1

scientifiques al-Bīrūnī; al-Dimashḳī; Ibn Bādjdja; Ibn al-Haytham; Ibn Rushd; Ibn Sīnā; Ikhwān al-Ṣafāʾ; al-Ḳazwīnī; al-Marwazī, Sharaf al-zamān
et → Alchimie; Astronomie; Botanique; Métaphysique; Zoologie

Sectes ʿAdjārida; Ahl-i Ḥadīth; Ahl-i Ḥaḳḳ; Aḥmadiyya; ʿAlides; Azāriḳa; al-Badjalī; Baḳliyya; Bihʾāfrīd b. Farwardīn; Bohorās; Burghūthiyya; Djabriyya; Djahmiyya; al-Djanāḥiyya; Durūz; Farāʾiḍiyya; Ghurābiyya; Ḥarīriyya; Ḥashīshiyya; Ḥulmāniyya; Ḥurūfiyya; al-Ibāḍiyya; Ḳarmaṭī; Karrāmiyya; Kaysāniyya; al-Khalafiyya; Khāridjites; Khashabiyya; Khaṭṭābiyya; Khōdja; Khūbmesīḥī; Khurramiyya; Kuraybiyya; Mahdawī; Manṣūriyya; al-Mughīriyya; Muḥammadiyya; Mukhammisa; Muṭarrifiyya; al-Muʿtazila; Nadjadāt; Nāwūsiyya; al-Nukkār; Nuḳṭawiyya; Nūrbakhshiyya; Nuṣayriyya; Rawshaniyya; [au Suppl.] Dhikris
voir aussi Abū l-Maʿālī; al-Aḥsāʾī; ʿAlī Ilāhī; Bābāʾī; Bābīs; Bāyazīd Anṣārī; Bīsharʿ; Dahriyya; al-Dhammiyya; Dīn-i Ilāhī; Ghassāniyya; Ghulāt; Ḥā-Mīm; Imām Shāh; ʿIrāḳ.VI; Kasrawī Tabrīzī; al-Kayyāl; Kāẓim Rashtī; Ḳīzīl-bāsh;

al-Malaṭī; Mazdak; Mudjtahid.III; Sālimiyya; *et* → MYSTICISME.CONFRÉRIES
ʿAlides ʿAbd Allāh b. Muʿāwiya; Abū ʿAbd Allāh Yaʿḳūb; Abū l-Aswad al-Duʾalī; Abū Hāshim; Abū Nuʿaym al-Mulāʾī; Abū Salama al-Khallāl; Abū l-Sarāyā al-Shaybānī; ʿAlī b. Muḥammad al-Zandjī; **ʿAlides**; al-Djawwānī; Hāniʾ b. ʿUrwa al-Murādī; al-Ḥasan b. Zayd b. Muḥammad; Ḥasan al-Uṭrūsh; Ḥudjr b. ʿAdī; al-Ḥusayn b. ʿAlī, Ṣāḥib Fakhkh; Ibrāhīm b. al-Ashtar; Khidāsh; Muḥammad b. ʿAbd Allāh (al-Nafs al-Zakiyya); al-Mukhtār b. Abī ʿUbayd; Muslim b. ʿAḳīl b. Abī Ṭālib
voir aussi Dhū l-Faḳār; al-Djanāḥiyya; al-Djārūdiyya; Ghadīr Khumm; al-Maʾmūn; *et* → CHIITES
Bābisme Bāb; **Bābīs**; Kāshānī; Ḳurrat al-ʿAyn; Maẓhar; Muḥammad ʿAlī Bārfurūshī; Muḥammad ʿAlī Zandjānī; Muḥammad Ḥusayn Bushrūʾī
voir aussi al-Aḥsāʾī; Mudjtahid.III; Nuḳṭat al-Kāf; Sābiḳūn
Chiites → CHIITES
Druzes → DRUZES
Ibāḍites ʿAbd al-ʿAzīz b. al-Ḥādjdj Ibrahīm; Abū Ghānim; Abū Ḥafṣ ʿUmar b. Djamīʿ; Abū Ḥātim al-Malzūzī (*et* al-Malzūzī); Abū l-Khaṭṭāb al-Maʿāfirī; Abū Muḥammad al-ʿUmānī; Abū l-Muʾthir; Abū Zakariyyāʾ al-Djanāwunī; Abū Zakariyyāʾ al-Wardjilānī; Aṭfiyāsh; al-Barrādī; al-Bārūnī; al-Bughṭūrī; al-Dardjīnī; Djābir b. Zayd; al-Djayṭālī; al-Djulandā; **al-Ibāḍiyya**; Ibn Baraka; Ibn Djaʿfar; al-Irdjānī; al-Lawātī; Maḥbūb b. al-Raḥīl; al-Mazātī; al-Nafūsī; [au Suppl.] Abū ʿAmmār; al-Ḥārithī
voir aussi al-ʿAwāmir; Azd; Ḥalḳa; al-Khalafiyya; Kharūṣ; *et* → DROIT; DYNASTIES.ESPAGNE ET AFRIQUE DU NORD.RUSTAMIDES; SECTES.KHĀRIDJITES
historiens Abū l-Muʾthir; Abū Zakariyyāʾ al-Wardjilānī; al-Barrādī; al-Bughṭūrī; al-Dardjīnī; Ibn al-Ṣaghīr; Ibn Salām; al-Lawātī; Maḥbūb b. al-Raḥīl; al-Mazātī; al-Sālimī
voir aussi al-Nafūsī
juives → JUDAÏSME
Khāridjites Abū Bayhas; Abū Fudayk; Abū Yazīd al-Nukkārī; al-Ḍaḥḥāk b. Ḳays al-Shaybānī; Ḥurḳūṣ b. Zuhayr al-Saʿdī; ʿImrān b. Ḥiṭṭān; Ḳaṭarī b. al-Fudjāʾa; **Khāridjites**; Ḳurrāʾ; Ḳuʿūd; Mirdās b. Udayya; Nāfiʿ b. al-Azraḳ; al-Nukkār
voir aussi ʿAdjārida; Azāriḳa; Ḥarūrāʾ; al-Ibāḍiyya; Ibn Muldjam; Imāma; Istiʿrāḍ; al-Manṣūr bi-llāh; Nadjadāt
Uṣūlīs Mudjtahid.III

SÉNÉGAL Djolof; [au Suppl.] Dakar
voir aussi Murīdiyya

SEXUALITÉ ʿAzl; Bāh; Djins; Khitān; Liwāṭ; [au Suppl.] Bighāʾ
voir aussi Djanāba; Khāṣī

SHIITES → CHIITES

SIBÉRIE
géographie physique
eaux Ob
population Bukhārlïk

SICILE Benavert; Ibn al-Ḥawwās; Ibn al-Khayyāṭ; Ibn al-Thumna; Kalbides
voir aussi Aghlabides.III; Asad b. al-Furāt; Fāṭimides; Ibn Ḥamdīs; Ibn al-Ḳaṭṭāʿ; Ibn Makkī
toponymes Balarm; Benavent; Djirdjent; Ḳaṣryānnih
voir aussi al-Khāliṣa

SOMALIE
voir aussi Ḥabesh; Muḥammad b. ʿAbd Allāh Ḥassān; Ogādēn
confréries Ṣāliḥiyya
toponymes
régions Guardafui
voir aussi Ogādēn
villes Barawa; Berberā; Hargeisa; Maḳdishū; Merka

SOUDAN Dār Fūr; Dustūr.XIII; Ḥizb.I; Madjlis.IV.A.17; al-Mahdiyya
voir aussi Baladiyya.II; Fundj; Ḥabesh; Nūba
confréries Mīrghaniyya
géographie physique
eaux al-Nīl
période mahdiste ʿAbd Allāh b. Muḥammad al-Taʿāʾishī; Khalīfa.IV; **al-Mahdiyya**
voir aussi Awlād al-Balad; Dār Fūr; Emīn Pasha; Rābiḥ b. Faḍl Allāh
population ʿAbābda; ʿAlwa; (Banū) ʿĀmir; Baḳḳāra; Barābra; Djaʿaliyyūn; Ghuzz.III; Nūba.IV; Rashāʾida
voir aussi Fallāta
toponymes
anciens ʿAydhāb
actuels
provinces Baḥr al-Ghazāl.3; Berber.2; Dār Fūr; Fāshōda; Kasala
régions Fāzūghlī; Kordofān
villes Atbara; Berber.3; Dongola; al-Fāshir; Kasala; Ḳerrī; al-Khurṭūm; Omdurman

SRI LANKA **Ceylan**

Superstition ʿAyn; Faʾl; Ghurāb; Ḥinnāʾ; Khamsa; Ṣadā
voir aussi ʿAḳīḳ; Bāriḥ; Laḳab

Syrie
et → Liban
architecture → Architecture.régions
avant l'Islam → Période préislamique.dans le croissant fertile
dynasties ʿAmmār; Ayyūbides; Būrides; Fāṭimides; Ḥamdānides; Mamlūks
voir aussi [au Suppl.] al-Djazzār Pasha; *et* → Dynasties.Égypte et le croissant fertile; Liban
géographie physique
eaux ʿAfrīn; al-ʿĀṣī; Baradā
montagnes Ḳāsiyūn; al-Lukkām
historiens al-ʿAẓīmī; Ibn Abī Ṭayyiʾ; Ibn al-ʿAdīm; Ibn ʿAsākir; Ibn al-Ḳalānisī; Ibn Kathīr; Ibn Shaddad; Kurd ʿAlī; al-Kutubī
et → Dynasties.Égypte et le croissant fertile
période moderne Djarīda.I.A; Djāmiʿa; Dustūr.IX; Ḥizb.I; Ḥukūma.III; Madjlis.IV.A.5; Madjmaʿ ʿIlmī.I.II.1; Maḥkama.IV.2; Mandats; Maysalūn; Salafiyya.2.b
voir aussi Baladiyya.II; Kurd ʿAlī; Mardam.II; [au Suppl.] Démographie.III
hommes d'état al-Khūrī; Mardam.I
toponymes
anciens Afamiya; ʿArbān; al-Bakhrāʾ; al-Bāra; Barḳaʿīd; Dābiḳ; Diyār Muḍar; Diyār Rabīʿa; al-Djābiya; al-Djazīra; Djilliḳ; Manbidj; Namāra.I; al-Raḥba; Raʾs al-ʿAyn; Rīḥā.2; al-Ruṣāfa.3
actuels
districts al-Bathaniyya; al-Djawlān
régions al-Ghāb; Ḥawrān; Ḳinnasrīn; Ladjāʾ; al-Ṣafā.2
voir aussi Ghūṭa
villes Adhriʿāt; Bāniyās; Boṣrā; Buzāʿā; Dayr al-Zōr; Dimashḳ; Djabala; al-Djabbūl; Djisr al-Shughr; Ḥalab; Ḥamāt; Ḥārim; Ḥimṣ; Ḥuwwārīn; Ḳanawāt; Ḳarḳīsiyā; Khawlān; Ḳinnasrīn; al-Lādhiḳiyya; Maʿarrat Maṣrīn; Maʿarrat al-Nuʿmān; Maʿlūlā; Maskana; Maṣyād; al-Mizza; Namāra.II et III; al-Raḳḳa; Ṣāfītha; Salamiyya; Ṣalkhad
voir aussi al-Marḳab

T

Tanzanie Dar-es-Salaam; Kilwa; Mikindani; Mkwaja; Mtambwe Mkuu

Taxation Bādj; **Bayt al-Māl**; Ḍarība; Djizya; Ḳānūn.II; Kharādj; [au Suppl.] Ḍarība.VII

voir aussi Ḍabṭ; Ḏjahbad̲h̲; Māʾ; Maʾṣir; Raʿiyya

impôts   ʿArūs Resmi; ʿAwāriḍ; Bād-i Hawā; Badal; Bād̲j̲; Ḏjawālī; Ḏjizya; Filori;
     Furḍa; Ispend̲je; Ḳūbčūr; Maks; Mālikāne; Muḳāṭaʿa; Pīs̲h̲kas̲h̲; Resm
     voir aussi Ḥisba.II; Ḳaṭīʿa

impôts fonciers   Bas̲h̲maḳlîḳ; Bennāk; Čift-resmi; **Kharādj**; Mīrī; Muḳāsama
          voir aussi Daftar; Daftar-i K̲h̲āḳānī; Ḳabāla; Rawk

percepteurs   ʿĀmil; Dihḳan; Muḥaṣṣil; Mültezim; Mustak̲h̲rid̲j
     voir aussi Amīr

terres de dîme   Ḍayʿa; Īg̲h̲ār; Iḳṭāʿ; Iltizām; K̲h̲āliṣa; K̲h̲āṣṣ; Ṣafī
     voir aussi Baʿl.2.b; Dār al-ʿAhd; Fayʾ; Filāḥa.IV

traités fiscaux   al-Mak̲h̲zūmī

TCHAD   Abes̲h̲r; Bagirmi; Borkou; Kanem; Kanuri; [au Suppl.] **Čad**

(ex-)TCHÉCOSLOVAQUIE   [au Suppl.] **Čeh**

TEINTURE   ʿAfṣ; Ḥinnāʾ; Ḳalamkārī; K̲h̲iḍāb; Nīl
teinturier   Ṣabbāg̲h̲

TEMPS   Abad; Dahr; Ḳidam
     voir aussi Ibn al-Sāʿātī

calcul   Anwāʾ; al-Ḳamar; Mīḳāt; Mizwala; Sāʿa.1
          voir aussi Asṭurlāb; Ayyām al-ʿAd̲j̲ūz; Hilāl.I; Rubʿ

calendriers   Ḏjalālī; Hid̲jra; Nasīʾ; [au Suppl.] Ilāhī
     voir aussi Nawrūz; Rabīʿ b. Zayd

jour et nuit   ʿAṣr; ʿAtama; Layl et Nahār

jours de la semaine   Ḏjumʿa; Sabt

mois
     voir aussi al-Ḳamar

     islamiques   al-Muḥarram; Rabīʿ; Rad̲jab; Ramaḍān; Ṣafar

     syriaques   Nīsān

     turques   Od̲jaḳ

TERRE   → TAXATION
     pour l'agriculture, voir Filāḥa
     pour le métrage, voir Misāḥa; Rawk

THAÏLANDE   Patani

THÉOLOGIE   ʿAḳīda; Allāh; Dīn; Ḏjanna; **ʿIlm al-Kalām**; Imāma; Īmān; Kalām;
     al-Mahdī
     voir aussi ʿĀlam.1; Hilāl.I; *et* → ISLAM

débats Masāʾil wa-Adjwiba; Munāẓara; Radd; [au Suppl.] ʿIbādat Khāna
voir aussi Mubāhala
traités sur al-Samarḳandī, Shams al-dīn
écoles
chiites Ismāʿīliyya; Ithnā ʿAshariyya; Ḳarmaṭī; [au Suppl.] Akhbāriyya
voir aussi Muʿtazila
sunnites Ashʿariyya; Ḥanābila; Māturīdiyya; Muʿtazila
voir aussi ʿIlm al-Kalām.II; Ḳadariyya; Karāmat ʿAlī; Murdjiʾa; al-Nadjdjāriyya
termes Adjal; Adjr; ʿAdl; ʿAhd; Ahl al-ahwāʾ; Ahl al-Kitāb; Ākhira; ʿAḳīda; ʿAḳl; ʿAḳliyyāt; ʿĀlam.2.; ʿAmal.2; Amr; al-Aṣlaḥ; Baʿth; Bāṭiniyya; Bidʿa; Birr; Daʿwa; Dīn; Djamāʿa; Djazāʾ; Djism; Duʿāʾ; Farḍ; Fāsiḳ; Fiʿl; Fitna; Fiṭra; al-Ghayb; Ghayba; Ghufrān; Ḥadd; Ḥaḳḳ; Ḥaraka wa-Sukūn.I.2 et 3; Ḥisāb; Ḥudjdja; Ḥudūth al-ʿĀlam; Ḥulūl; Iʿdjāz; Iḍṭirār; Ikhlāṣ; Ikhtiyār; ʿIlla.II.III; Imāma; Īmān; Islām; ʿIṣma; Istiṭāʿa; Ittiḥād; al-Ḳaḍāʾ wa-l-Ḳadar; Kaffāra; Kāfir; Kalima; Karāma; Kasb; Kashf; Khalḳ; Khaṭīʾa; Khidhlān; Ḳidam; Kumūn; Ḳunūt; Ḳuwwa; Luṭf; Maʿād; al-Mahdī; al-Manzila bayn al-Manzilatayn; al-Munāfiḳūn.2; Murtadd; Muṭlaḳ; Nāfila; Nafs; Nāmūs.1; Nūr Muḥammadī; Riyāʾ; Rizḳ; Rudjuʿ; Ruʾyat Allāh; Sabīl.1; [au Suppl.] Ḥāl
voir aussi Abad; Allāh.II; In Shāʾ Allāh; ʿInāya; *et* → ESCHATOLOGIE
chiites Badāʾ; Ibdāʿ; Kashf; Lāhūt et Nāsūt.V; al-Munāfiḳūn.2; Naḳḍ al-Mīthāḳ; Radjʿa; al-Sābiḳūn; Safīr.1; al-Ṣāmit
et → CHIITES.DOCTRINES ET INSTITUTIONS
théologiens
théologiens primitifs Djahm b. Ṣafwān; al-Ḥasan al-Baṣrī; [au Suppl.] al-Aṣamm; (al-)Ḥasan b. Muḥammad Ibn al-Ḥanafiyya; Ibn Kullāb
ashʿarites al-Āmidī; al-Ashʿarī, Abū l-Ḥasan; al-Baghdādī, ʿAbd al-Ḳāhir; al-Bāḳillānī; al-Bayhaḳī; al-Djuwaynī; al-Faḍālī; Fakhr al-Dīn al-Rāzī; al-Ghazālī, Abū Ḥāmid; Ibn Fūrak; al-Īdjī; al-Isfarāyīnī; al-Kiyā al-Harrāsī; al-Ḳushayrī
voir aussi Allāh.II; ʿIlm al-Kalām.II.C; Imāma; Īmān; [au Suppl.] Ḥāl
chiites → CHIITES
ḥanbalites ʿAbd al-Ḳādir al-Djīlānī; Aḥmad b. Ḥanbal; al-Anṣārī al-Harawī; al-Barbahārī; Ibn ʿAbd al-Wahhāb; Ibn ʿAḳīl; Ibn Baṭṭa al-ʿUkbarī; Ibn al-Djawzī; Ibn Ḳayyim al-Djawziyya; Ibn Ḳudāma al-Maḳdisī; Ibn Taymiyya; al-Khallāl
voir aussi Īmān; *et* → DROIT
māturīdites ʿAbd al-Ḥayy; Bishr b. Ghiyāth al-Marīsī; al-Māturīdī
voir aussi Allāh.II; ʿIlm al-Kalām.II.D; Imāma; Īmān
muʿtazilites ʿAbbād b. Sulaymān; ʿAbd al-Djabbār b. Aḥmad; Abū l-Hudhayl al-ʿAllāf; Aḥmad b. Abī Duʾād; Aḥmad b. Ḥābiṭ; ʿAmr b. ʿUbayd; al-

Balkhī; Bishr b. al-Muʿtamir; Djaʿfar b. Ḥarb; Djaʿfar b. Mubashshir; al-Djāḥiẓ; al-Djubbāʾī; Hishām b. ʿAmr al-Fuwaṭī; Ibn al-Ikhshīd; Ibn Khallād; al-Iskāfī; al-Khayyāṭ; Muʿammar b. ʿAbbād; al-Murdār; al-Nāshiʾ al-Akbar; al-Naẓẓām; [au Suppl.] Abū ʿAbd Allāh al-Baṣrī; Abū l-Ḥusayn al-Baṣrī; Abū Rashīd al-Nīsābūrī; Ḍirār b. ʿAmr; al-Ḥākim al-Djushamī; Ibn Mattawayh
voir aussi Ahl al-Naẓar; Allāh.II; Ḥafṣ al-Fard; Ibn Abī l-Ḥadīd; Ibn al-Rāwandī; ʿIlm al-Kalām.II.B; Imāma; Khalḳ.V; Lawn; Luṭf; al-Maʾmūn; al-Manzila bayn al-Manzilatayn; [au Suppl.] al-Aṣamm; Ḥāl
wahhābites Ibn ʿAbd al-Wahhāb; Ibn Ghannām
indo-musulmans ʿAbd al-ʿAzīz al-Dihlawī; ʿAbd al-Ḳādir Dihlawī; Ashraf ʿAlī; Baḥr al-ʿUlūm; al-Dihlawī, Shāh Walī Allāh; al-ʿImrānī; ʿIwaḍ Wadjīh; [au Suppl.] ʿAbd Allāh Sulṭānpūrī; Farangī Maḥall
voir aussi Hind.v.b; al-Maʿbarī; Mappila
juifs Ibn Maymūn; Saʿadyā
du 19ᵉ et 20ᵉ siècles Muḥammad ʿAbduh; Muḥammad Abū Zayd

Togo Kabou; Kubafolo

Traités Baḳṭ; Küčük Ḳaynardja; Mandats; Mondros; **Muʿāhada**
voir aussi Dār al-ʿAhd; Ḥilf al-Fuḍūl; Mīthāḳ-i Millī
tributs Baḳṭ; Parias
et → Taxation

Transport **Naḳl**
et → Animaux.chameaux *et* équines; Hôtellerie; Navigation
caravanes Azalay; **Kārwān**; Maḥmal; [au Suppl.] Djammāl
voir aussi Anadolu.III.5; Darb al-Arbaʿīn; Khān
chemins de fer Ḥidjāz
voir aussi Anadolu.III.5; al-Ḳāhira (462a); Khurramshahr
défilés Bāb al-Lān; Bībān; Dar-i Āhanīn; Deve Boynu; Khaybar
voir aussi Chitral
postal **Barīd**; Fuyūdj; Ḥamām; Posta; Raḳḳāṣ
voir aussi Anadolu.III.5
timbres **Posta**
véhicules à roues ʿAdjala; ʿAraba

Tremblements de terre *voir* Aghri̊ Dagh; Amasya; Anṭākiya; ʿAshḳābād; Čanki̊ri̊; Cilicia; Daybul; Djidjelli; Erzindjan; Ḥarra; Ḥulwān; Istanbul.VI.6; Ḳalhāt; Kāṅgṛā; Ḳazwīn; Kilāt; Nīshāpūr; al-Ramla

Trésor **Bayt al-Māl**; Khazīne; Makhzān
et → Administration.financière

TRIBUS ʿĀʾila; ʿAshīra; Ḥayy; **Ḳabīla**
voir aussi ʿAṣabiyya; Ḥilf; Khaṭīb; [au Suppl.] Bisāṭ.III; *et* → NOMADISME

Afghanistan et Inde Abdālī; Afrīdī; Bhaṭṭi; Čahār Aymaḳ; Dāwūdpōtrās; Djāṭ; Durrānī; Gakkhaŕ; Gandāpur; Ghalzay; Güdjar; Khaṭak; Khokars; Lambadi; Mahsūd; Mēʾō; Mohmand; Mullagori; [au Suppl.] Gurčānī
voir aussi Afghān.I; Afghānistān.II

Afrique ʿAbābda; ʿĀmir; Antemuru; Bedja; Beleyn; Bishārīn; Danḳalī; Djaʿaliyyūn; Kunta; Makua; Māryā; Mazrūʿī
voir aussi Diglal; Fulbe; al-Manāṣīr; Mande

Asie centrale et Mongolie Čāwdors; Dūghlāt; Emreli; Gagauz; Göklän; Ḳarluḳ; Ḳungrāt; Mangït; Mongols; Özbeg; Pečenegs; Salur
voir aussi Ghuzz; Īlāt; Ḳāyï; Khaladj

Croissant fertile
anciens Asad; Bahrāʾ; Djarrāḥides; Djudhām; Muhannā; al-Muntafiḳ.1
actuels ʿAnaza; Asad (Banū); Bādjalan; Bilbās; Ḍafīr; Djāf; Djubūr; Dulaym; Hamawand; al-Ḥuwayṭāt; Kurdes et Kurdistan.IV.A; Lām; al-Manāṣīr; al-Muntafiḳ.2; Ṣakhr
voir aussi al-Baṭīḥa

Égypte et Afrique du Nord ʿAbābda; Ahaggar; al-Butr; Djazūla; Dukkāla; Ifoghas; Khulṭ; Kūmiya; al-Maʿḳil; Mandīl; Riyāḥ
voir aussi Khumayr; *et* → BERBÈRES

Iran Bāzukiyyūn; Bilbās; Djāf; Eymir.II et III; (Banū) Kaʿb; Ḳarā Gözlu; Kurdes et Kurdistān.IV.A; Lak; Lām
voir aussi Daylam; Dulafides; Fīrūzānides; Göklän; Īlāt

Péninsule arabique
anciens ʿAbd al-Ḳays; al-Abnāʾ; ʿĀd; ʿAkk; ʿĀmila; ʿĀmir b. Ṣaʿṣaʿa; al-Aws; Azd; Badjīla; Bāhila; Bakr b. Wāʾil; Ḍabba; Djadhīma b. ʿĀmir; Djurhum; Fazāra; Ghanī b. Aʿṣur; Ghassān; Ghaṭafān; Ghifār; Hamdān; Ḥanīfa b. Ludjaym; Ḥanẓala; Ḥārith b. Kaʿb; Hawāzin; Hilāl; ʿIdjl; Iram; Iyād; Kalb b. Wabara; al-Ḳayn; Khafādja; Khathʿam; al-Khazradj; Kilāb b. Rabīʿa; Kināna; Kinda; Khuzāʿa; Ḳuraysh; Ḳushayr; Laʿaḳat al-Dam; Lakhm; Liḥyān.II; Maʿadd; Maʿāfir; Māzin; Muḥārib; Murād; Murra; Naḍīr; Nawfal; Riyām; Saʿd b. Bakr; Saʿd al-Fizr; Salīḥ; Salūl
voir aussi Asad (Banū); Ḥabash (Aḥābīsh); al-Ḥidjāz; Makhzūm; Mustaʿriba; Mutaʿarriba; Nizār b. Maʿadd b. ʿAdnān; Numayr; Rabīʿa (et Muḍar); [au Suppl.] Aʿyāṣ
actuels ʿAbdalī; ʿAḳrabī; ʿAwāmir; ʿAwāzim; Banyar; al-Baṭāḥira; Buḳūm; al-Dawāsir; al-Dhiʾāb; Djaʿda; al-Djanaba; al-Durūʿ; Ghāmid; Hādjir; Ḥakam b. Saʿd; Hamdān; al-Ḥarāsīs; Ḥarb; Ḥāshid wa-Bakīl; Ḥassān, Bā; Ḥawshabī; Hinā; al-Hubūs; Hudhayl; Ḥudjriyya; Hutaym; al-Ḥuwayṭāt; al-ʿIfār; Ḳaḥṭān; Khālid; Kharūṣ; Khawlān; Ḳudāʿa; Madhḥidj; Mahra; al-Manāṣīr; Mazrūʿī; Murra; Muṭayr; Muzayna;

Nabhān; Ruwala
voir aussi (Djazīrat) al-ʿArab.VI; Badw; al-Ḥidjāz
Turquie Afshār; Bayat; Bayîndîr; Begdili; Čepni; Döger; Eymir.I; Ḳādjār; Ḳāyî; [au Suppl.] Čawdor

TUNISIE Baladiyya.III; Djāmiʿa; Djamʿiyya; Djarīda.I.B; Dustūr.I; Ḥizb.I; Ḥukūma.IV; Istiḳlāl; al-Khaldūniyya; Maʿārif.II; Madjlis.IV.A.19; Salafiyya.1.a; [au Suppl.] Démographie.IV
voir aussi Fallāḳ; Ḥimāya.II; Khalīfa b. ʿAskar; Ṣafar; [au Suppl.] al-Ḥaddād; Inzāl; *et* → BERBÈRES; DYNASTIES.ESPAGNE ET AFRIQUE DU NORD
historiens Ibn Abī Dīnār al-Ḳayrawānī; Ibn Abī l-Ḍiyāf; Ibn ʿIdhārī; [au Suppl.] ʿAbd al-Wahhāb
voir aussi Ibn al-Raḳīḳ; *et* → DYNASTIES.ESPAGNE ET AFRIQUE DU NORD
institutions
d'éducation al-Ṣādiḳiyya; [au Suppl.] Institut des hautes études de Tunis
voir aussi [au Suppl.] ʿAbd al-Wahhāb
de musique al-Rashīdiyya
de la presse al-Rāʾid al-Tūnusī
langue ʿArabiyya.A.III.3
littérature Malḥūn; *et* → LITTÉRATURE
période ottomane (1574-1881) Aḥmad Bey; al-Ḥusayn (b. ʿAlī); Ḥusaynides; Khayr al-Dīn Pasha; Muḥammad Bayram al-Khāmis; Muḥammad Bey; Muḥammad al-Ṣādiḳ Bey; Muṣṭafā Khaznadār; [au Suppl.] Ibn Ghidhāhum
période pré-ottomane ʿAbd al-Raḥmān al-Fihrī; Aghlabides; Ḥafṣides; Ḥassān b. al-Nuʿmān al-Ghassānī; Khurāsān (Banū)
et → BERBÈRES; DYNASTIES.ESPAGNE ET AFRIQUE DU NORD
toponymes
anciens al-ʿAbbāsiyya; Ḥaydarān; Ḳalʿat Banī Ḥammād; Manzil Bashshū; Raḳḳāda; Ṣabra Manṣūriyya
actuels
districts Djarīd
îles Djarba; Ḳarḳana
régions Djazīrat Sharīk; Ḳasṭīliya; Nafzāwa; Sāḥil.1
villes Bādja; Banzart; Ḥalḳ al-Wādī; Ḳābis; al-Kāf; Ḳafsa; Ḳallala; al-Ḳayrawān; al-Mahdiyya; Monastir; Nafṭa; Safāḳus

TURQUIE Anadolu; Armīniya; Istanbul; Ḳarā Deniz
voir aussi Libās.IV; *et* → EMPIRE OTTOMAN
architecture → ARCHITECTURE.RÉGIONS
belles-lettres → LITTÉRATURE
dynasties → DYNASTIES.ANATOLIE ET LES TURCS; EMPIRE OTTOMAN

géographie physique
eaux Boghaz-iči; Čanaḳ-ḳalʿe Boghazi̊; Čoruh.I; Djayḥān; Gediz Čayi̊; Göksu; Ḳi̊zi̊l-i̊rmāḳ; Lamas-ṣū; Marmara Deñizi; Menderes; al-Rass; Saḳārya
montagnes Aghri̊ Dagh; Ala Dagh; Aladja Dagh; Beshparmaḳ; Bingöl Dagh; Deve Boynu; Elma Daghi̊; Erdjiyas Daghi̊; Gāwur Daghlari̊
langue → LANGUES.TURCIQUES
mysticisme → MYSTICISME.MYSTIQUES; SAINT
période moderne (1920-) Baladiyya.I; Demokrat Parti; Djāmiʿa; Djarīda.III; Djümhūriyyet Khalḳ Fi̊rḳasi̊; Dustūr.II; Ḥizb.II; Ishtirākiyya; Khalḳevi; Köy Enstitüleri; Kurdes et Kurdistān.III.C; Madjlis.IV.A.2; Mīthāḳ-i Millī; [au Suppl.] Démographie.III
voir aussi Djamʿiyya; Iskandarūn; Iṣlāḥ.III; Ittiḥād we Teraḳḳī Djemʿiyyeti; Karakol Djemʿiyyeti; Ḳawmiyya.IV; Kemāl; Kirkūk; Maʿarif.I.1; Māliyye; Nurculuk; *et* → LITTÉRATURE
chefs religieux Nursī
hommes/femmes d'état Atatürk; Çakmak; Ḥusayn Djāhid; Ileri, Djelāl Nūrī; Kāẓi̊m Karābekir; Khālide Edīb; Köprülü (Meḥmed Fuad); Meḥmed ʿĀkif; Menderes; Okyar; Orbay, Ḥüseyin Raʾūf; [au Suppl.] Adi̊var; Aghaoghlu; Atay; Esendal
voir aussi Čerkes Edhem; Gökalp, Ziya; Hi̊sar; *et* → TURQUIE.PÉRIODE OTTOMANE.JEUNES TURCS
période ottomane (1342-1924) Ḥizb.II; Istanbul; Ittiḥād-i Muḥammedī Djemʿiyyeti; Ittiḥād we Teraḳḳī Djemʿiyyeti; Maʿārif.I.1; Madjlis.IV.A.1; Madjlis al-Shūrā; Maṭbakh.II; **ʿOthmānli̊**
voir aussi Aywaz.1; Derebey; Djamʿiyya; Khalīfa.I.E; [au Suppl.] Démographie.II; Djalālī; *et* → EMPIRE OTTOMAN
Jeunes Turcs Djāwīd; Djemāl Pasha; Enwer Pasha; Ḥilmī; Isḥāḳ Sükūtī; Kemāl, Meḥmed Nāmi̊ḳ; Mīzāndji̊ Meḥmed Murād; Niyazı; Ṣabāḥ al-Dīn
voir aussi Djamʿiyya; Djewdet; Dustūr.II; Fāḍil Pasha; Ḥukūma.I; Ḥurriyya; Ittiḥād we Teraḳḳī Djemʿiyyeti
période pré-ottomane Mengüček
voir aussi Kitābāt.VII; *et* → DYNASTIES.ANATOLIE ET LES TURCS; TURQUIE.TOPONYMES
population [au Suppl.] Démographie.II
voir aussi Muhādjir.2
toponymes
anciens ʿAmmūriya; Ānī; Arzan; ʿAyn Zarba; Baghrās; Bālis; Beshike; Būḳa; al-Djazīra; Dulūk; Dunaysir; Ḥarrān; Lādhiḳ.I
voir aussi Diyār Bakr

actuels

îles Bozdja-ada; Imroz

provinces Aghri; Čoruh; Diyār Bakr; Hakkārī; Ičil; Kars; Ḳasṭamūnī; Khanzīt; Ḳodja Eli; Mūsh; Newshehir

régions al-ʿAmḳ; Cilicia; Dersim; Diyār Muḍar; Djānīk; Menteshe-eli

villes Ada Pazari; Adana; Adiyaman; Afyūn Ḳara Ḥiṣār; Aḳ Ḥiṣār.I et II; Aḳ Shehr; Akhlāṭ; Ala Shehr; Alanya; Altintash; Amasya; Anadolu; Anamur; Anḳara; Anṭākiya; Antalya; ʿArabkīr; Ardahān; Artvin; Aya Solūḳ; Āyās; Aydin; ʿAynṭāb; Aywalik; Babaeski; Bālā; Bālā Ḥiṣār; Balāṭ; Bālikesrī; Bālṭa Līmānī; Bandirma; Bāyazīd; Bāybūrd; Baylān; Bergama; Besni; Beyshehir; Bidlīs; Bīgha; Biledjik; Bingöl; Bīredjik; Birge; Bodrum; Bolu; Bolwadin; Bozanti; Burdur; Bursa; Čankiri; Čatāldja; Česhme; Čölemerik; Čorlu; Čorum; Deñizli; Diwrīgī; Diyār Bakr; Edirne; Edremit; Eğin; Eğridir; Elbistan; Elmali; Enos; Ereğli; Ergani; Ermenak; Erzindjan; Erzurum; Eskishehir; Gebze; Gelibolu; Gemlik; Giresun; Göksun; Gördes; Gümüsh-khāne; al-Hārūniyya; Ḥiṣn Kayfā; Iskandarūn; Isparta; Istanbul; Iznīḳ; Ḳarā Ḥiṣār; Ḳaradja Ḥiṣār; Kars; Ḳasṭamūnī; Ḳayṣariyya; Kemākh; Killiz; Ḳirḳ Kilise; Kirmāstī; Ḳirshehir; Ḳoč Ḥiṣār; Konya; Köprü Ḥiṣāri; Ḳoylu Ḥiṣār; Ḳōzān; Ḳūla; Kutāhiya; Lādhiḳ.II et III; Lāranda; Lüleburgaz; Maghnisa; Malaṭya; Malāzgird.I; Malkara; Maʿmūrat al-ʿAzīz; Marʿash; Mārdīn; al-Maṣṣīṣa; Mayyāfāriḳīn; Menemen; Mersin; Merzifūn; Mīlās; Mudanya; Mughla; Mūsh; Naṣībīn; Newshehir; Nīgde; Nīksār; Nizīb; Orāmār; ʿOthmāndjiḳ; Payās; Rize; al-Ruhā; Ṣabandja; Ṣāmsūn;[au Suppl.] Ghalaṭa

voir aussi Fener; Ḳarasi; (al-)Ḳusṭanṭīniyya

U

UMAYYADES → CALIFAT; DYNASTIES.ESPAGNE ET AFRIQUE DU NORD

(ex-)URSS → ASIE CENTRALE.UNION SOVIÉTIQUE ANCIENNE; CAUCASE; COMMUNISME; EUROPE.EUROPE ORIENTALE; SIBÉRIE

V

VERTUS Ḍayf; Futuwwa; Ḥasab wa-Nasab; Ḥilm; ʿIrḍ; Karāma; Murūʾa; Ṣabr

vices Bukhl

VÊTEMENTS Banīḳa; Djallāb; Farw; Ḳumāsh; **Libās**

voir aussi Ghiyār; Iḥrām; Khayyāṭ; Khilʿa; Kurdes et Kurdistān.IV.C.1; *et* → MYSTICISME.COSTUME

accessoires Mandīl; Mirwaḥa
coiffures Ḳawuḳlu
voiles Ḥidjāb.I; Lithām
matériaux Farw; Ḥarīr; Kattān; Khaysh; Ḳuṭn
voir aussi Fanak; Ḳalamkārī; Ḳumāsh; Lubūd; Mukhattam

VIN **Khamr**; Sāḳī
voir aussi Karm
commensaux Ibn Ḥamdūn; al-Ḳāshānī; Khālid b. Yazīd
voir aussi Abū l-Shīṣ; ʿAlī b. al-Djahm
poésie bachique **Khamriyya**
arabe Abū Nuwās; Abū Miḥdjan; Abū l-Shīṣ; ʿAdī b. Zayd; Ḥāritha b. Badr al-Ghudānī; (al-)Ḥusayn b. al-Ḍaḥḥāk; Ibn al-ʿAfīf al-Tilimsānī; Ibn Sayḥān
voir aussi al-Babbaghā'; Ibn al-Fāriḍ; Ibn Harma; al-Nawadjī
turque Rewānī; Riyāḍī

VOYAGES **Riḥla**; Safar
et → LITTÉRATURE.VOYAGES, RELATIONS DE
fournitures Mifrāsh
et → NOMADISME

Y

YÉMEN Djarīda.I.A; Dustūr.VIII; Madjlis.IV.A.14 et 15; Maḥkama.IV.8
voir aussi ʿAsīr; Ismāʿīliyya; Mahrī; Makramides; [au Suppl.] Abū Mismār
architecture → ARCHITECTURE.RÉGIONS
avant l'Islam al-Abnā'.2; Abraha; Dhū Nuwās; (Djazīrat) al-ʿArab; Ḥabashat; Ḥaḍramawt; Ḳatabān; Ḳayl; Mārib; al-Mathāmina; Saba'; [au Suppl.] Ḥaḍramawt
voir aussi [au Suppl.] Bādhām
dynasties Hamdānides; Mahdides; Rasūlides
voir aussi Rassides; *et* → DYNASTIES.PÉNINSULE ARABIQUE
géographie physique
montagnes Ḥaḍūr; Ḥarāz; Ḥiṣn al-Ghurab
wadis Barhūt; al-Kharid; al-Saḥūl
historiens al-Djanadī; al-Khazradjī; al-Mawzaʿī; al-Nahrawālī; al-Rāzī, Aḥmad
voir aussi Ibn al-Mudjāwir
période ottomane (1517-1635) Maḥmūd Pasha; al-Muṭahhar; Özdemir Pasha; Riḍwān Pasha
voir aussi Baladiyya.II; Khādim Süleymān Pasha
population ʿAbdalī; ʿAḳrabī; Banyar; Hamdān; Ḥāshid wa-Bakīl; Ḥawshabī; Ḥudjriyya; Ḳaḥṭān; Khawlān; Madhḥidj; Mahra

et → TRIBUS.PÉNINSULE ARABIQUE

toponymes

anciens al-ʿĀra

voir aussi Nadjrān

actuels

districts Abyan; ʿAlawī; ʿĀmirī; ʿAwdhalī; Dathīna; Faḍlī; Ḥarāz; Ḥarīb; al-Ḥayma; Ḥudjriyya

îles Ḳamarān; Mayyūn

régions ʿAwlaḳī; Ḥaḍramawt; Laḥdj; [au Suppl.] Ḥaḍramawt.II

villes ʿAdan; ʿAthr; Bayt al-Faḳīh; Dhamār; Ghalāfiḳa; Ḥabbān; Hadjarayn; Ḥāmī; Ḥawra; al-Ḥawṭa; al-Ḥudayda; Ibb; ʿIrḳa; Ḳaʿṭaba; Kawkabān; Ḳishn; Laḥdj; al-Luḥayya; Mārib; al-Mukallā; al-Mukhā; Rayda; Ṣaʿda; al-Saḥūl; [au Suppl.] ʿĪnāt

voir aussi (Djazīrat) al-ʿArab

(ex-)YOUGOSLAVIE Džabić; Khosrew Beg; Muslimūn.I.B.6; Pomáks; Riḍwān Begović; [au Suppl.] Handžić

voir aussi ʿÖmer Efendi

toponymes

républiques Bosna; Ḳarā Dāgh; Ḳoṣowa; Māḳadūnyā

voir aussi [au Suppl.] Dalmatie

villes Aḳ Ḥiṣār.III; Aladja Ḥiṣār; Banjaluka; Belgrade; Eszék; Ishtib; Ḳarlofča; Livno; Manāṣṭi̊r; Mostar; Nish; Okhrī; Pasarofča; Pirlepe; Prishtina; Prizren; Raghūsa

Z

ZAÏRE Katanga; Kisangani

ZANZIBAR Barghash b. Saʿīd b. Sulṭān; Bū Saʿīd; Kizimkazi

ZOOLOGIE **Ḥayawān.VII**

et → ANIMAUX

écrivains sur al-Damīrī; al-Marwazī, Sharaf al-zamān

voir aussi al-Djāḥiẓ

ZOROASTRIENS Gabr; Iran.VI; **Madjūs**; Mōbadh

voir aussi Bihʾāfrīd b. Farwardīn; Ghazal.II; Gudjarāt; Pārsīs; Pūr-i Dāwūd

dieux Bahrām

dynasties Maṣmughān